Robert

MALTING AND BREWING SCIENCE

Volume II   Hopped Wort and Beer

MALTING AND BREWING SCIENCE

Volume II Hopped Wort and Beer

J. S. HOUGH, D. E. BRIGGS

Department of Biochemistry
The University of Birmingham

R. STEVENS

School of Pharmacy
Sunderland Polytechnic

and

T. W. YOUNG

Department of Biochemistry
The University of Birmingham

SECOND EDITION

LONDON NEW YORK

CHAPMAN AND HALL

First published 1971
by Chapman and Hall Ltd
11 New Fetter Lane, London EC4P 4EE
Second edition 1982

Published in the USA by
Chapman and Hall
in association with
Methuen, Inc.
733 Third Avenue, New York NY 10017

© *1982 J. S. Hough, D. E. Briggs, R. Stevens, T. W. Young*

ISBN 0 412 16590 2

Printed in Great Britain at the University Press, Cambridge

British Library Cataloguing in Publication Data

Malting and brewing science.—2nd ed.

Vol. 2: Hopped wort and beer
1. Brewing industry
I. Hough, J. S.
663'.3   TP570

ISBN 0-412-16590-2

CONTENTS

PREFACE

Some ten years have passed since the publication of the first edition of *Malting and Brewing Science*, a period of many changes. As before, this edition is an aid to teaching, particularly the MSc course in Brewing Science at Birmingham University, but it is also aimed at the requirements of other students of the science of malting and brewing throughout the world. In general, technological aspects are covered more fully in this new edition, although not malting and brewing practices that are exclusive to Britain. Nevertheless, the amount of technological information available is too great to be comprehensively covered in one book. Scientific principles and information receive more attention, but for details of analytical procedures reference should be made to the most recently published material of the American Society of Brewing Chemists, the European Brewery Convention and the Institute of Brewing.

The new edition appears as two volumes because a single one would be inconveniently bulky. The first volume outlines the entire process and leads from barley, malting and water to the production of sweet wort. In the second volume there are chapters on hops and hop products, production of hopped wort, fermentation, yeast biology and all aspects of beer qualities and treatment.

Decisions about the units of measurement proved difficult; metric units commonly used in the Industry are given and in parentheses are equivalents in degrees Fahrenheit, Imperial measures and UK barrels. Considerable information on equivalents is given in a special section in each volume.

References given with each chapter are aimed at offering the reader an entry into the appropriate literature. This restriction offers an economy of space but often fails to mark the special contribution of particular authors. Only for historical reasons or where a method bears the name of its developer or where a diagram or table is acknowledged have authors' names been included in the text.

The authors of the second volume wish to thank all those who have helped in its production, particularly the constructive critics. We wish to thank Miss J. Gainham and Mrs L. C. Winter for typing and secretarial work, Mrs P. Hill for art work, Mrs D. Clarke and Mr J. Redfern for photography. Specialized advice has been received from the following: R. J. Anderson, A. J. Barker, P. A. D. Davies, D. Flesher Clarke, D. Harding, G. A. Howard, C. Lowe, R. A. Neave, R. J. Rench, E. Rowbotham, G. Sharpe and J. H. Wilson.

Chapter 12

HOPS

12.1 Introduction [1, 2]

From medieval times, herbs have been used to flavour and preserve fermented malt liquors but only the hop (*Humulus lupulus* L.) is used on a commercial scale today. It is grown throughout the temperate regions of the world solely to meet the demands of the brewing industry (Table 12.1). Hops of commerce are the dried cones of the female plant but much of the crop is processed into powder, pellets or extract. In Western Europe the yield of hops is now expressed in zentners (1 zentner = 50 kg = 110 lb). Earlier, centals (100 lb) and hundredweight (112 lb) were used in Britain.

TABLE 12.1

World hop production 1978

{s. h. STEINER, Hopfen GmbH Laupheim}

Countries producing more than 1000 Zentner	Acreage (Hectare)	Yield (Ztr/Hectare)	Production (Zentner)
England	5 897	31·8	187 374
Germany (W)	17 622	34·4	606 602
Germany (E)	2 200	21·7	47 730
Czechoslovakia	10 400	19·4	201 757
France	864	34·8	30 029
Belgium	850	32·3	27 482
Yugoslavia	3 240	26·7	86 632
Spain	1 803	23·2	41 796
Poland	2 400	16·2	38 850
Roumania	800	18·8	15 000
Bulgaria	1 200	13·3	16 000
USSR	13 000	16·9	220 000
Europe	61 277	25·2	1 544 052
USA	12 546	39·7	498 269
Australia	1 060	34·2	36 260
Japan	1 167	37·1	43 340
World	77 868	27·7	2 160 533

The brewing value of the hop is found in its resins and essential oils. In the traditional brewing process hops are boiled with wort in a copper for 1–2 hr, during which time the resins go into solution and are isomerized to produce the bitter principles of beer. The majority of essential oil constituents will be lost during 2 hr of boiling, so, to increase the hop aroma of their beers, brewers either add a portion of choice aroma hops late in the boil or add them to the beer during conditioning, either in tank or cask – a process known as dry hopping.

The resins are also responsible for the preservative value of the hop although the current view is that hops contribute little to the biological stability of beer. In the past the results of both microbiological and chemical assays were expressed in terms of preservative value (PV) and this term is still sometimes used as though it was synonymous with the resin content. The fractionation of the resins and their chemical constitutions is discussed fully in Chapter 13, but it should be noted here that the majority of the brewing value is found in the α-acid fraction of the resins and that hops can contain 2–12% of α-acid.

12.2 Botany

Only two species of *Humulus* are recognized: *Humulus lupupus* L. (*H. americanus*, *H. neomexicanus*, and *H. cordifolius*) and *H. japonicus* Sieb. et Zucc. (*H. scandens* (Lour.) Merr). The latter is an annual ornamental climbing plant from Japan devoid of resin and therefore of brewing value. The genus *Humulus* is included in the natural family *Cannabinaceae* together with *Cannabis*, which is only represented by *C. sativa* (Indian hemp, marihuana, or hashish). Chemical similarities are seen between *H. lupulus* and *C. sativa* but the resins of the two species are completely distinct. Those of the hop provide the bitter principles of beer whilst those of *Cannabis* include the psychotomimetic principles of the drug. *Cannabis* and *Humulus* spp. have been grafted on to each other but the characteristic resins do not cross the grafts [3].

The hop cone (Fig. 12.1) consists of (*i*) valueless stipular bracts and (*ii*) seed-bearing bracteoles attached to a central axis or strig. At the base of the bracteoles the lupulin glands and seeds develop as the hop ripens. The lupulin glands contain the brewing principles, both the resins and the essential oils. They can contain as much as 57% of α-acids and the sum of the ($\alpha + \beta$)-acids is equal to $73 \pm 6\%$. The ratio of α/β acids can range from 0 to about 4·0. It is predicted that the maximum lupulin content that could be obtained by breeding is about 32% w/w of the cone which corresponds to a ($\alpha + \beta$) content of the cone equal to 23% [4.]

The amount of seed in the hop cone will depend on the method of culti-vation practised. On the Continent of Europe, the planting of male hops is

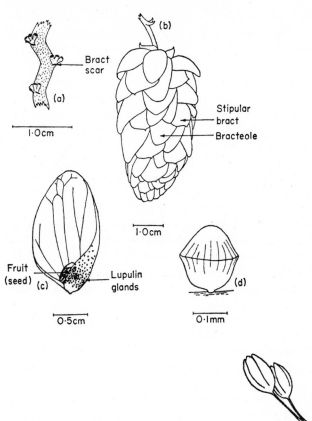

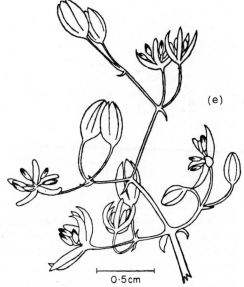

Fig. 12.1 Hop (*Humulus Lupulus* L.). (a) Part of axis ('strig') of cone; (b) Single mature hop cone; (c) Bracteole with seed and lupulin glands; (d) Lupulin gland; (e) Male hop flowers. (After BURGESS [1].)

restricted by law to breeding stations and so hops are grown seedless, i.e. with less than 2% w/w of seed. In England until 1976 male plants were deliberately planted in hop gardens and many grow wild in the hedgerows so that the hops were fertilized and contained up to 25% w/w seed. Lager brewers will not use seeded hops so there was limited demand for English hops in export markets. The English Hops Marketing Board therefore decided to pursue the production of seedless hops and the isolated hop-growing area of Hampshire went seedless in 1976. With the high α-acid varieties, Wye Northdown, Wye Challenger, and Northern Brewer, the seedless hops were richer in α-acid than those with seeds but the reverse was often true with low α-acid varieties. Even with the high α-acid varieties, the overall yield of α-acid/hectare was lower without pollination [5].

Seedless hops command a higher price than those with seeds but it will no doubt be some time before all other English hop-growing areas only produce seedless hops. An alternative approach to the production of seedless hops is the breeding of triploid varieties which are sterile and thus do not produce seed even in the presence of male hops. In America most hops are grown seedless but in Oregon they are fertilized.

12.3 *Cultivation* [1, 2]

The hop is a hardy, climbing, herbaceous, perennial plant. The rootstock therefore stays in the ground from year to year and the plant must be provided with some support on which to grow. Originally hops grew up pea-sticks but today they are trained up strings to overhead wirework.

The construction of the wirework is the largest capital cost in setting up a hop garden, or yard as it is called in the West Midlands. Before the advent of mechanical picking in the fifties, the wirework in English gardens was 3·75–4·25 m (12·5–14 ft) high but the modern trend is to higher wirework as in America (4·0–5·5 m; 13–18 ft) and on the Continent (6·0–7·0 m; 20–23 ft). In height-of-wirework and spacing trials carried out at Wye College, Kent, the maximum yield of most varieties, occurred at 5 m (16 ft) but some, e.g. Bullion, Saaz and Wye Target, showed an increased yield at 5·5 m (18 ft) [6].

The wirework must be sufficiently robust to support the full weight of the crop in adverse (windy and wet) weather. The corner posts should be at least 15 cm (6 in) in diameter and 1·25–1·40 m (4–4·5 ft) longer than the height of the wirework. The other outside poles and the inside poles, which are placed at every third hill in alternate rows, need not be quite as strong. Anchor and anchor wire failures are the most common sources of damaged wirework. With 5·5 m (18 ft) wirework the tension in the anchor wires increases from about 410 kg (900 lb) in March to 680 kg (1500 lb) just before harvest [7]. When wirework is set up lewing (coarse netting) is usually attached to the poles along the exposed edges of the garden to protect the crop from wind damage and to reduce the fluctuating tensions on the wirework. The garden is also often surrounded by a tall thick hedge.

Apart from breeding, new varieties of hops are propagated vegetatively from 'setts'. These are produced (*i*) from hardwood cuttings taken from the base of the bine, (*ii*) by mist propagation or (*iii*) by layering. For layering, a bine of a young plant is allowed to grow until it is about 0·6 m (2 ft) taller than the distance to the next plant ('hill' in South-East England or 'stock' in the West Midlands). One string is then cut down, the bine laid along the ground, covered with soil and trained up the next hill. In the autumn the hardwood bine is uncovered and cut up, each piece retaining a node, and planted out in nursery beds. With mist propagation, growing shoots are cut up, each piece with two nodes and each node with two leaves, and the cuttings planted in sterilized peat, usually in pots. The cuttings are then placed in glass-houses where the soil temperature is maintained at 21°C (70°F) and they are watered automatically with a fine spray. The watering is controlled by an 'electronic leaf' which turns the water on whenever its surface is dry. Under these conditions the plants remain turgid and rooting takes place in 10–14 days, depending on the light intensity. The rooted cuttings are planted out in late June. It should be emphasized that whatever the method of propagation selected, only healthy plant material should be used. In order to reduce the risk of infection, many commercial hop propagators have their nurseries away from the main growing areas. For example, in England they are in East Anglia away from the main hop-growing areas in the South-East and the West Midlands.

One-year-old plants are used to lay out a new garden or yard. The rows are usually about 2 m (6·5 ft) apart to allow tractors to pass for cultural operations. With the Butcher and Umbrella systems of stringing, the plants are also put about 2 m (6·5 ft) apart but with the Worcester system they are put closer together, about 1 m (3–4 ft). A firm hook is fixed in the ground next to each hill and, in the early spring, strings are arranged from the hook to the overhead wirework. The Umbrella system, with four strings to a hill, is the most common and is the typical system of the Weald of Kent (Fig. 12.2a). The Butcher system (Fig. 12.2b) which is popular in East Kent, uses three strings while the Worcester method only utilizes two (Fig. 12.2c). In a series of angle-of-growth trials it was found that growth was most rapid in plants trained at 85° to the horizontal but the maximum yield was obtained from plants grown at 65°.

In April or early May suitable bines are selected for training up the strings and the remainder are sacrificed. Usually two bines are twined up each string in a clockwise direction but for very vigorous varieties only one is necessary. Bullion is a very vigorous variety, but in view of its susceptibility to downy mildew, many growers train two bines originally and remove the surplus one in June. Additional training will be necessary until the end of June by which time the bine will have reached the top of the string. As the bine grows, leaves are stripped from the lower part of the plant, up to about 1 m (3 ft) to reduce the risk of infection from soil-borne organisms and spores.

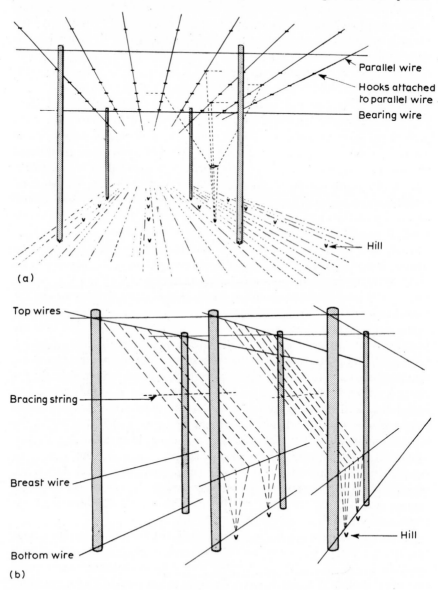

(a)

(b)

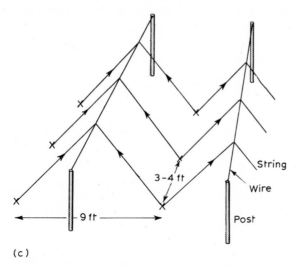

(c)

Fig. 12.2 Wirework and stringing systems used to support hops. (a) Umbrella system; (b) Butcher system; (c) Worcester system.

Traditional hop-growing practice makes heavy demands on labour. In addition to stripping and training it was thought necessary to cultivate between the plants and to earth up each hill. The modern trend is to reduce labour requirements to the minimum and soil cultivation is being replaced by applications of herbicides such as Simazine and Paraquat. Stripping is being replaced by the use of chemical defoliants such as tar oil and complete or partial self-training is also being carried out.

The rapid luxurious growth of the hop plant makes heavy demands on soil nutrients. A normal crop may take up to 89–100 kg/hectare (80–90 lb/acre) of nitrogen, 11–16 kg/hectare (10–15 lb/acre) of phosphorus, 67–78 kg/hectare (60–70 lb/acre) of potassium, and 78–89 kg/hectare (70–80 lb/acre) of calcium [1]. All these must be replaced with manures and fertilizers. The amount of nitrogen added is critical; too little causes a marked reduction in yield but too much results in vigorous growth with fewer cones on the shaded part of the bine. Traditionally, half the required nitrogen was applied as bulky organic matter such as dung or shoddy but these are generally in short supply. Straw, together with inorganic fertilizers, is therefore used as an alternative.

The development of the resins (α- and β-acids) and the essential oils during ripening of the hop has been studied [8, 9]. In the Northern Hemisphere the first traces of resin can be detected early in August, the β-acids appearing a few days before the α-acids, and synthesis is almost complete by the end of the month. Essential oil synthesis starts later and in some varieties resin synthesis may be complete before essential oil synthesis starts. Oxygenated components and sesquiterpenes are developed first but as the hop ripens the synthesis of myrcene becomes quantitatively the most important process [10]. Different varieties mature at different rates and as a rule some early and some late varieties are grown to spread picking over three to four weeks in September.

The characteristics by which a grower assesses that a hop is fit for picking are [1]:

1. The bracts and bracteoles close towards the axis of the cone, giving it a compact form.
2. The full growth of the terminal bracteole, when seeded, causes it to protrude from the top of the cone.
3. The bracts and bracteoles become firm and slightly resilient. They rustle when squeezed in the hand and are rather easily detached from the axis.
4. The colour of the bracteoles and, to a less extent, of the bracts, changes to a yellowish-green.
5. The contents of the seed become firm. The fruit coat (pericarp) becomes brittle and of purplish colour.
6. The lupulin glands are completely filled with resins.
7. The aroma of the hop is fully developed.

Hops should be picked as soon as possible after they become ripe; overripe cones tend to open and become more fragile, and thus may be easily shattered by the wind, birds, or during picking. In all cases the hops should be picked within ten days of ripening.

Before 1950 the English hop crop was entirely picked by hand using casual labour from near-by cities; today more than 95% of the crop is picked by machine. The hand-pickers worked in the gardens and picked the hops directly into baskets or bins. After being measured the hops were transported to the kiln for drying in coarse-woven sacks called pokes. With hand-picking the bine is not detached and as it slowly withers some nutrients return to the rootstock. This is not possible with machine-picking when the whole bine on its string is cut off at the top of the wirework and 1·20–1·50 m (4–5 ft) from the ground and carefully transported to the picking machine. In the USA a few mobile harvesters are in use, in conjunction with stationary cleaning equipment [11]. With stationary picking machines (Fig. 12.3), the bine is attached to a trackway and enters the machine, depending on the design, either horizontally or vertically. The hops and leaves are stripped from the bine by numerous moving wire hooks and then passed over various screens to separate the hop cones from the unwanted debris. According to EEC regulations certified hops must not contain more than 6% of leaf and stem and more than 3% waste. The waste from the picking machine is composted, or burnt if there is any possibility of disease.

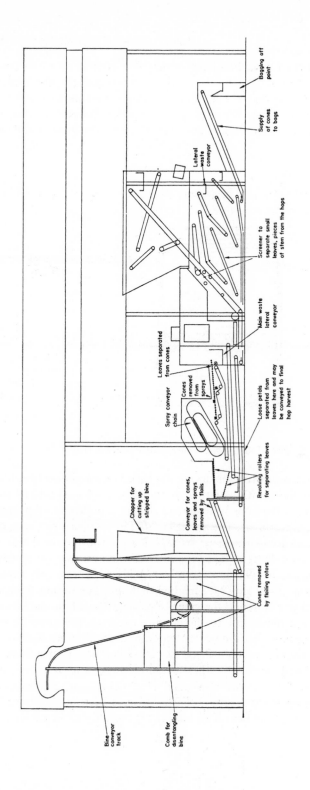

Fig. 12.3 Hop picking machine. (Courtesy of Bruff Mfg. Co. Ltd.)

Green hops, whether picked by hand or machine, contain about 80% w/w moisture and it is necessary to dry the hops as soon as possible after picking. While waiting to be put on the kiln the hops must not be allowed to 'sweat' as this will seriously reduce the quality of the crop. To prevent this, the coarse-woven pokes are stored on racks raised above the ground and well ventilated.

12.4 *Drying* [1, 2, 12]

The principles involved in hop drying are similar to those involved in barley drying and the kilning of malt (see Vol. I, Chapter 6).

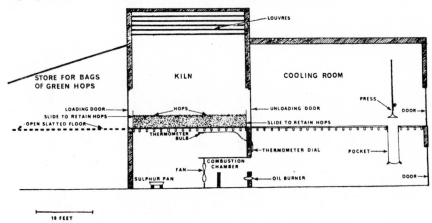

Fig. 12.4 Modern Oast House. (After BURGESS [1].)

The traditional structure for hop drying was called an oast-house (Fig. 12.4). It was a round building with a slatted wooden floor 4–5 m (12–16 ft) from the ground on which the hops were spread out on a horse-hair cloth to be dried in a current of warm air. The air was heated by an open anthracite coal fire and the natural draught assisted by tapering the roof above the drying floor and fixing a cowl. Depending on the external wind velocity, air speeds of between 0–5·75 m/min (0–19 ft/min) were achieved which were only capable of drying a shallow 20–27 cm (8–12 in) bed of hops. The drying floor was provided with two sets of doors; the green hops were loaded on one side and and the dried cones removed into the cooling room on the opposite side.

In view of the cheaper building costs, modern kilns are more likely to be rectangular than round, the air will be heated either by an open-flame oil burner or by a closed stove and either forced or drawn through the bed of hops with a powerful fan. Air speeds of about 15 m/min (50 ft/min) are normal, although up to 30 m/min (100 ft/min) have been used. Above this speed dried bracts may be blown off the kiln. Using these higher air speeds much deeper beds of hops (up to 60 cm; 2 ft) can be dried. The higher the air speed, the higher the initial temperature can be (up to 55°C (130°F) at 12 m/min (40 ft/min)). The temperature is then raised about 5°C (10°F)/hr until the maximum temperature required 60–65°C (149–150°F) is reached. The maximum temperature required is usually determined by the need to complete the drying within 10 hr so that the kiln can be loaded twice a day. The lower the temperature used however, the better the valuation the hops receive and in no case should the temperature exceed 71°C (160°F). α-Acids are increasingly destroyed at higher temperatures.

In normal English practice, hops are treated with sulphur dioxide as soon as drying commences, by burning rock sulphur in the kiln. The value of this procedure has been the subject of much debate. It causes the hops to lose their green colour and to assume a more uniform bright yellowish tinge which is rated highly in hand evaluation. Indeed, merchants often have difficulty in evaluating hops which have not been sulphured. Sulphuring is also said to prevent the formation of 'raw' aromas in the hops. On the other hand, sulphuring causes a loss of α-acid and reduces the bittering potential of the hop [13] which makes the process economically questionable. Indeed, some brewer-growers, whose hops do not have to be valued by merchants, do not sulphur their hops. In trials conducted by the Institute of Brewing, beers produced from sulphured and unsulphured hops were judged of generally equal merit although the latter were more bitter [14]. In some parts of America such as Idaho, hops are not usually sulphured and on the continent of Europe practice is also variable. In some cases merchants may sulphur unsulphured hops themselves. On the kiln, sulphur is burnt in the first 30–45 min to give a concentration of 1·4–1·5 g of sulphur dioxide/m³ of air (1·4–1·5 oz/1000 ft³). Under-ripe hops require about 10% more sulphur, while hops wet with dew or rain need about 10% less.

Hops are dried on the kiln to a moisture level of about 6% but it is quite difficult in practice to determine when this is reached, and the experience of the oast man is important. The moisture remaining in the bed of hops is unevenly distributed; within the load it is concentrated in the top layer and within the hop cone it is largely in the strig. Hops from the kiln are also very hygroscopic and all these factors make sampling for conventional moisture analysis difficult.

When the hops are judged dry, they are unloaded by removing them on the 'lifter' cloths on to the conditioning room floor. Here they are left in heaps covered with cloths to cool and to allow the remaining moisture to equilibrate throughout the cone before packing. The final moisture level is about 10%. In the EEC certified hops must not contain more than 12% moisture.

In traditional oasts the heated air is only passed through the bed of hops once. Two- and even three-tiered kilns have been built which use the heat more efficiently [15]. The green hops are loaded on to the upper floor, which consists of movable slats. Half-way through the drying period the floor is tilted and the hops dropped to the lower level. The upper floor is then reloaded. When the hops at the lower level are dry, they are removed and the process is repeated. The lower deck may be fitted with trays to facilitate the unloading. Oasts have also been developed [15] in which hops are collected from the picking machine into bins which have open-mesh bottoms and are mounted on rails. The hops remain in these bins during sulphuring, kilning, and conditioning. Sulphuring is usually carried out first for about 30 min. Several bins may then be loaded on to the kiln and dried in the traditional manner or they may pass progressively over separate fan-heaters at different temperatures. Continuous driers have been used on the Continent but not extensively in Britain. Chemical methods for detecting the sulphuring of hops have been described [48].

Most English hops are packed in strong jute and/or polypropylene sacks about 2·1 m (7 ft) long and 0·6 m (2 ft) in diameter, called pockets. These hold about 76 kg (1·5 cwt) of dried hops packed at a density of 137–145 kg/m^3 (8·5–9 lb/ft^3). The empty pocket is suspended through a hole in the cooling room floor beneath a press equipped with a circular foot and usually operated by an electric motor. The base of the suspended pocket is supported further by a strong canvas webbing belt. The cooled hops are pushed into the pocket with a canvas shovel called a scuppet. When the pocket is full the press is operated and then more hops are added. The process is repeated until the pocket is tightly filled. The pocket is then supported on the webbing belt while it is sewn up. The webbing belt is then released and the pocket falls to the oast-house floor where it is stored until transported to the merchant's warehouse or coldstore.

In America, hops are packed in rectangular bales measuring 137 × 51 × 76 cm (4 ft 6 in × 1 ft 8 in × 2 ft 6 in) containing about 90·7 kg (200 lb) of hops so that the density is about 108 kg/m^3 (13 lb/ft^3). The baling press is essentially a tall box with detachable steel sides in which a ram operates. The box is lined with hessian and before the final filling a hessian cloth is placed over the hops. While the hops are still compressed by the ram, the sides of the box are removed and the two hessian cloths are sewn together. Bales are more expensive to produce than pockets but occupy less space for transport and storage. On the other hand, brewery workers prefer pockets which can be rolled whereas bales have to be lifted. Also, tightly compressed hops disperse less easily in the copper.

For export or when space is at a premium, bales (and sometimes pockets) are compressed to half their original size and densities up to 577 kg/m^3 (36 lb/ft^3) are achieved. Such compression causes no detectable effect on the α-acid content of the hops but encourages a significant loss in essential oils, noticeably myrcene [16]. Microscopical examination shows that the majority of the lupulin glands are ruptured in the highly compressed hops. Since myrcene catalyses the oxidation of α-acid [17], it has been suggested that extra compression could stabilize the α-acid content by allowing myrcene to escape. A similar explanation can be advanced for the Weiner process for stabilizing hops [18]. Here, the pocket or bale of hops is placed in a pressure cylinder and subjected to a vacuum which causes the most volatile constituents of the essential oil and considerable quantities of myrcene to be removed. The vacuum is released by allowing carbon dioxide to enter the cylinder. The pockets may then be stored normally or wrapped in polythene sheeting.

Hops deteriorate on storage, in some cases significantly, before the next season's crop makes up 100% of the hop grist (70–100 weeks). The chemical changes undergone by both the resins and the essential oil are discussed in Chapter 13, but one obvious feature is the development of a cheesy aroma in old hops, due to the formation of volatile acids by oxidative cleavage of the acyl side chains of the hop resins. The rate of deterioration appears to be a varietal characteristic; some varieties, such as Bullion and Wye Target, deteriorate much faster than others. The rate of deterioration also depends upon temperature and is reduced by cold storage at $0.20°C$ ($33°F$). Aroma hops, intended for late addition to the copper or dry hopping, must be cold stored but it has been argued [19], without convincing most brewers, that this is not necessary for copper hops added at the beginning of the boil (see [20]).

The acids responsible for the cheesy aroma are expelled during vigorous wort boiling and some oxidation products of the hop resins are still capable of bittering beer. In high α-acid varieties the ratio of α- to β-acids is usually high (3:1). When oxidation occurs, the amount of bitter β-acid oxidation products produced is not sufficient to compensate for the loss of α-acids, and the bittering potential decreases. Low α-acid varieties, such as Hallertau, Tettnanger, or Cascade, have a higher proportion of β-acids ($α:β = 1:1$). Therefore the loss of α-acids is compensated for by β-acid oxidation products, and the bittering potential is virtually unchanged [21]. Until recently there has been no accepted method for the analysis of these bitter oxidation products of the hop resins and they are not included in estimates of the α-acids. It follows therefore that α-acid analysis of partially deteriorated hops will only give an imperfect guide to hopping rate and that this can be determined more accurately from the α-acid content at harvest. Accordingly, the English hop crop has been analysed for α-acid soon after harvest each year since 1970. A sampling rate of 1 in 10 or 1 in 20 pockets is used. The hop storage index (HSI) [21] is calculated from absorbance measurements made in the spectroscopic method for the analysis of the α- and β-acids in hops (see p. 433) which is commonly used in America. From the hop storage index, estimates of the losses of α- and β-acids that have occurred during storage can be made, and the initial level of α- and β-acids in the hop computed. The hop storage index cannot be obtained from the conductometric method of analysis of α-acids commonly used in Europe.

12.5 *Hop Products*

Natural hop cones, normally dried and pressed, are a bulky product which only contains 5–15% of active principles. Thus, any process of concentration will reduce handling, transport, and storage costs. Mechanical concentration is used to produce hop powders and pellets while solvent extraction is used to manufacture hop extracts. In addition, the essential oil may be separated by steam distillation.

12.5.1 HOP POWDERS

Three types of hop powder have been defined [22]:

Hop Powder. Any preparation made by grinding hops, without any mechanical concentration.
Enriched Hop Powder. Any preparation made by grinding hops, with some mechanical concentration.
Lupulin. A technically pure preparation of lupulin glands.

In order to produce hop powders the hops may be first dried at 65°C to reduce the moisture content to between 6% and 7%. On account of their inherent stickiness the hops are then cooled to between −35°C and −40°C before being ground in a hammer mill. The hop powder produced will occupy about one sixth of the volume of the hops used to produce it. Enriched or concentrated hop powders [23, 24] are obtained by sieving hop powder at −35°C when the fine particles contain the lupulin and brewing principles are retained and the coarse particles, say 50% may be discarded. Further sieving can give a powder that is essentially pure lupulin glands but with increasing losses of α-acid and this is not normally necessary for brewing purposes. Hop powders are not very convenient to handle and so they are usually pressed, in the presence of liquid carbon dioxide, into pellets. The pellets are then sealed into aluminium-PVC sachets in an atmosphere of nitrogen or carbon dioxide.

Hop powders and pellets deteriorate on storage in the same manner as hop cones [20]. Comminution increases the surface area and the risk of aerial oxidation but the reduced volume allows packaging under an inert atmosphere and/or a partial vacuum. Deterioration in cold store (0–4°C) is less than at ambient temperature (10–30°C) but the loss of α-acid at ambient temperature is considerably less than that experienced by baled hops of the same variety [25, 26]. The replacement of whole hops in the copper by powder and/or pellets will only result in a small improvement in utilization but it simplifies the separation of wort when a whirlpool separator can replace the conventional hop back (see Chapter 15). Enriched hop pellets will be more expensive to produce than normal pellets but if the capacity of the whirlpool is limiting this may be justified. Enriched hop pellets are more convenient than whole hops for dry hopping. Hop pellets containing bentonite are commercially available and in pilot scale brewing trials resulted in a 20% increase in utilization [27]. Stabilized hop pellets [28] are prepared by mixing about 1% w/w of magnesium (or calcium) hydroxide with the hop powder before pressing into pellets. In the die the α-acids are converted into their more stable salts. During the storage of stabilized hop pellets there is little loss of bittering potential but some of the α-acids may isomerize into salts of iso-α-acids. Stabilized pellets readily go into solution and are rapidly isomerized during wort boiling. Stabilized pellets may be completely isomerized by heating at 80°C for 2 hr with only small losses of β-acids and hop oil. Such isomerized pellets give good utilization in the copper or may be used for dry hopping [28].

12.5.2 HOP EXTRACTS [30]
Two types have been defined [22]:

Hop extracts. Any preparation prepared by solvent extraction of hops.
Isomerized hop extracts. Any preparation prepared by solvent extraction of hops in which the α-acids have been isomerized.

Hops may be replaced partially or wholly in the copper by an equivalent amount of straight hop extract but isomerized hop extract is usually added later in the process. The preparation of isomerized hop extracts is discussed later in Chapter 14 after consideration of the isomerization reaction. Many solvents have been used to extract the brewing principles of hops; amongst others hexane (b.p. 69°C), methanol (b.p. 64°C), methylene chloride (b.p. 40°C), and trichloroethylene (b.p. 87°C) have been used commercially. The solution of resins and essential oils obtained is concentrated in a cyclone evaporator, which minimizes heating time, and the final traces of solvent and the more volatile essential oils are removed by heating the residue in a vacuum. The extract is obtained as a viscous green syrup. One manufacturer combines the solvent extract of hops with an aqueous extract of the spent hops as it is claimed that the pectins, polyphenols, etc. in this fraction, provide a natural base for the dispersion of the less soluble resins. Other manufacturers dilute the solvent extract of hops with glucose syrup to a given α-acid content. Solvent extracts of hops can contain up to 50% of α-acid dependent on the variety of hops extracted. It is only economic to prepare extract from hops rich in α-acid (i.e. > 8%). Since much of the essential oil is separated during extract manufacture it is possible to use hops with a high resin content but an unacceptable 'American' aroma to prepare high quality extract with no trace of the undesirable aroma.

Hop extracts are usually marketed in tins which only occupy 7% of the space occupied by pockets, which makes them very suitable for export. Pure resin extracts are stable when stored in sealed containers, either at 0°C or 25°C for at least six years. They are thus more stable than hops and, in years when hops are plentiful and cheap on the open market, it may pay brewers to lay down stocks of resin extract. Extracts which contain water-soluble material are much less stable on storage.

The major question over the use of hop extracts is the problem of solvent residues which, if present, introduce foreign substances into the beer. Not only may they give an unacceptable taint to the beer but many commercial solvents are toxic. In practice, traces of solvent in hop extract will be lost by evaporation from a vigorous boil in a well-ventilated copper but probably not completely from pressure coppers. Nevertheless the risk of solvent residues make hop extracts unacceptable to many brewers. An important development, therefore, is the use of carbon dioxide to extract hops. Carbon dioxide is a gas at atmospheric pressure but at higher pressures it is liquified. Below the critical temperature (31·1°C) a mixture of saturated liquid and vapour exist together – liquid CO_2. Above the critical temperature it is not possible to liquify the gas no matter what pressure is applied. When hops are extracted with supercritical carbon dioxide at 45–50°C and up to 400 atmospheres pressure, most of the resins, essential oils and pigments are extracted. In contrast, extraction with liquid CO_2 at 5–15°C and about 50 atmospheres pressure selectively removes the important brewing principles. After evaporation of the carbon dioxide a pale yellow extract is obtained which contains 40–44% of α-acids together with β-acids and essential oils but which is free of hard resins, polyphenols, fats, waxes and chlorophyll [31]. This high quality extract with no possibility of organic solvent residue is finding wide acceptance both for use in the copper and as the raw material for isomerized extract manufacture [32, 33].

When a column of finely milled hops is extracted with liquid CO_2 at about 50 atm. pressure, chromatographic separation occurs. The early fractions are rich in essential oil, the β-acids are concentrated in the middle fractions, and the acids are found in the final fractions [34]. The early fractions (ca. 0·5 hr) obtained at −20°C contains the bulk of the essential oil and is a suitable material either for late addition to the copper or for dry hopping [35]. The maximum solubility of the α-acids in liquid CO_2 occurs at 7°C and at this temperature fractions can be obtained that are rich (66–70%) in α-acid. These fractions, because of the low level of β-acids, are suitable for direct conversion to isomerized extracts. The middle fractions, rich in β-acids but still containing α-acids can be used as copper extracts. Attempts are being made to chemically convert the β-acid fraction into more valuable bittering materials.

Granular hop extract, which is commercially available, is prepared by mixing hop powder with hop extract and pressing the mixture into pellets. Such preparations have a similar level of α-acids to enriched hop powders but lower levels of essential oil.

12.5.3 HOP OIL [36]

The essential oil of hops may be separated by steam distillation and is commercially available. The industrial plant is fundamentally the same as the analytical apparatus [37]: after condensation the oil separates from the aqueous phase and is collected in a trap which allows the aqueous phase to return to the boiler – a process known as cohobation. It follows that most essential oil components will be lost during wort boiling from an open copper. To overcome this, a few brewers add hop oil during conditioning. However, some of the constituents of the essential oil are decomposed at 100°C so that the aroma of hop oil can usually be distinguished from that of the hops that produced it. Further, beers that have been dry-hopped are usually preferred to those which have been treated with hop oil. A recent development is the separation of the essential oil by steam distillation at 25°C under reduced pressure (0·02 mm) which minimizes chemical changes [38]. This gives rise to a stable emulsion containing 1000 to 2000 ppm of hop oil which may be added directly to bright beer or beer at racking to produce beers with a pleasant hop aroma similar to those obtained by dry hopping. Alternatively, liquid CO_2 extracts of hops contain the essential oil in its natural form, unmodified by steam distillation, and can be used for imparting a good hop aroma to beer. Liquid CO_2 solutions of the essential oil can be injected directly into a beer main to give immediately beers with a good hop aroma whereas traditional dry hopping requires 2–3 weeks. This method of addition obviates the use of organic solvents or emulsifiers [39].

12.6 *Varieties* [40]

Until hop breeding started early in this century there had been little change in the varieties or cultivars grown in the traditional regions. English Goldings and Continental varieties such as Saaz and Hallertau Mittelfruh have been grown for at least 250 years. Later, selections were made by individual growers. For example, that made by Richard Fuggle of Brenchley, Kent, in 1875 was widely adopted and accounted for 77·8 % of the English crop by 1950.

Hop breeding aims to satisfy both the brewer, who wants hops rich in resin and essential oil that do not deteriorate rapidly, and the grower, who wants varieties resistant to disease. In addition the grower wants hops that will ripen at different times during the harvest season and which will not shatter during machine picking. In Britain, hop breeding started at Wye College, Kent, where many new varieties were raised by E. S. Salmon between 1907 and 1954. In particular he aimed to produce hops with high resin contents and for this purpose he introduced American hops into his breeding programme. Of his varieties Brewers Gold (C9A), Bullion (Q43) and Northern Brewer (WFB135) are the most important commercially today and together occupy 45% of the West German, 65% of the Belgian, 6% of the American, and 13% of the English hop growing area. These varieties are considerably richer in resin (6–10% α-acid) than Fuggles or Goldings (3–6% α-acid) but were not immediately accepted. Many American hops have a very strong aroma and this feature was found in many of Salmon's varieties. Thus, although many British brewers accepted Northern Brewer, they rejected Bullion and Brewers Gold on account of their 'American' aroma. Nevertheless, perfectly acceptable beers can be brewed from these hops if care is taken to adjust the hop rate on the basis of the α-acid content at harvest and ensure that the copper is well ventilated to allow the escape of unwanted volatile substances. Alternatively the hops may be processed into extract in which the undesirable constituents of the essential oil are removed.

The spread of *Verticillium* wilt disease in the Weald of Kent in the 1930s and later in the Hallertauer district of Germany placed new demands on hop breeding programmes. All English commercial varieties were susceptible to the disease for which there is no chemical control. W. G. Keyworth at East Malling found that three of Salmon's seedlings were resistant to the disease. Keyworth's Midseason (OR55) was intensively propagated and distributed to wilt-infested farms but, on account of its 'American' aroma, it was not popular with brewers. Another wilt-tolerant selection, Bramling Cross (OT 48) was more acceptable. At that time the requirement was for a wilt-tolerant Fuggle replacement and this was partly met by the introduction of Janus (J2), Density (D1), and Defender (D3) in 1957 and by Whitbread's Golding Variety (1147). This last hop was originally raised by E. A. White in 1911 but it was only maintained on one farm until, in the thirties, it was observed to be wilt-tolerant. Two further wilt-tolerant Fuggle replacements, Progress (WE 1008) and Alliance (WE 1778), which were bred from Whitbread's Golding Variety, were released in 1966 but by that time economic pressures and technological advance dictated that the brewing industry required high α-acid hops. Here Wye had anticipated the brewers' requirements and a series of new varieties were released in the 1970s (Table 12.2) of which Wye Target and Wye Saxon are resistant to wilt. The three varieties: Wye Northdown, Wye Challenger and Wye Target, together now comprise 45% of the Engish hop area. The price of these high α-acid hops is partly determined by their α-acid content and is adjusted for each 1% above or below the standard values given in Table 12.2

Breeding programmes are also being carried out to develop varieties

TABLE 12.2

Wye varieties of hops

	Introduced	Ripens	Pocket code	Standard α-acid content (%)		Disease resistance		
				Seeded	Seedless	*Verticillium* wilt	Powdery mildew	Downy mildew
Bullion	1938	Late	B	7·0	9·0	S		S
Northern Brewer	1944	Mid	N	7·0	9·0	S		S
Keyworth Midseason	1949	Mid	K	6·5	—	R		S
Wye Northdown	1970	Mid	D	8·0	10·0	S	S	R
Wye Challenger	1972	Late	C	7·0	8·8	S	R	R
Wye Target	1973	Late	R	9·5	10·5	R	R	S
Wye Saxon	1974	Early		7·0	8·5	R		S
Wye Viking	1974	Early		7·0	8·5	S		R
Wye Yeoman		Mid				R	S	R
Wye Zenith						S	R	R

R, Resistant.
S, Susceptible.

resistant to other diseases, in particular downy mildew. Plant breeders aiming to produce resistance to one disease must also try to ensure that their selections are not sensitive to another disease but this is not always easy as Table 12.2 indicates. Most of the wilt-tolerant varieties are susceptible to downy mildew but, in contrast to wilt, this can be partly controlled by chemical treatment. Of the new varieties, Wye Northdown and Wye Challenger are resistant to downy mildew. The relationships of many of the new English varieties are illustrated in Fig. 12.5.

The most important hop growing areas of West Germany are Hallertau (15 012 ha), Tettnang (1109 ha), Spalt (797 ha), Jura (512 ha), and Hersbrucker Gebirge (169 ha), where traditional varieties, prized for their aromas, have been grown for many years [41]. Following outbreaks of *Verticillium* wilt in Hallertau, wilt-resistant varieties were planted so that more than one variety is now grown in many areas. Somewhat surprisingly, Northern Brewer and Brewer's Gold, which are susceptible to English strains of *Verticillium* wilt, were resistant to the German strain of the disease. Accordingly they were widely planted in Germany together with Record, a Northern Brewer seedling originally developed in Belgium. These hops are richer in resin but lack the characteristic aroma of the traditional German varieties. This led to a classification of hops into "high-alpha" acid and 'aroma' varieties. The 'alpha' hops are added to the copper at the beginning of the boil and the 'aroma' hops are added later, e.g. 15 min before strike-off. However, such distinctions are artificial as some of the new varieties combine high alpha with a good aroma. Hop breeding started at Hüll in Germany in 1962 in order to produce aroma varieties resistant to downy mildew but the appearance of *Verticillium* wilt necessitated new breeding programmes. From these Hüller Bitterer was produced from Northern Brewer and a German male hop. It is a medium-alpha aroma hop resistant to downy mildew and *Verticillium* wilt which now occupies 9% of the West German hop growing area. Perle, another Northern Brewer seedling with up to 9% α-acid and a good aroma, was released in 1978 and has been accepted by the German brewing industry as being equivalent to Hallertau mittelfruh.

The second most important continental hop-growing country is Czechoslovakia where 75% of the crop is grown in the Saaz area around Zatec, fifty miles north-west of Prague. Hops are grown in two areas of Yugoslavia – in the Savinja Valley of Slovenia (2135 ha) and in the Bačka region of Serbia (1002 ha). In Slovenia the major variety is the Savinski or Styrian Golding, a direct descendent of Fuggle. Breeding has resulted in the so-called Super Styrians: Aurora, Atlas, Apolon, and Ahil. The first of these is related to Northern Brewer, the others to Brewer's Gold. The majority of French hops are grown in Alsace although some are grown in Flanders adjacent to the Belgium growing area around Poperinghe. In both these countries Brewer's

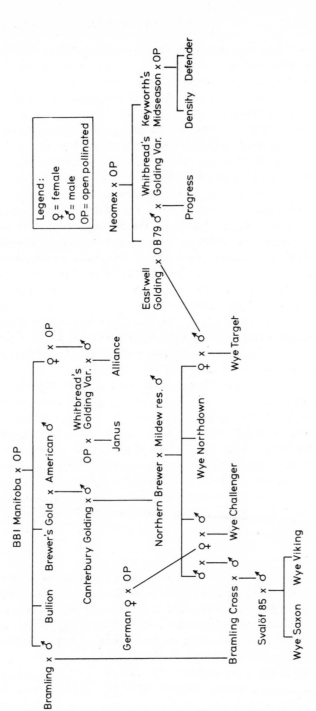

Fig. 12.5 English hop breeding activities (after Neve, via [40]).

Gold and Northern Brewer are grown; in France an old variety Strisselspalt is also grown while in Belgium Hallertau, Record, and Saaz make up the crop. A considerable number of hops are grown in Poland, East Germany, and Bulgaria but these, like those grown in the Soviet Union, do not normally find their way into Western European markets.

In the United States hops are now grown along the western seaboard in the states of Washington (8637 ha), Oregon (2215 ha), Idaho (1081 ha), and California (593 ha) [40, 42]. The major varieties are Early, Late, and California Clusters. These are medium-alpha varieties with characteristically strong aromas which are sensitive to downy mildew. Yakima Cluster (L–1) is a high yielding early maturing selection and L–8 is a Late Cluster selection; these are now the major strains grown in Washington State. Talisman resulted from a open pollenated seedling of Late Cluster. It is a medium-alpha hop grown in Oregon and Idaho. High-alpha hops grown in the United States include English (a collective trade term for Bullion and Brewer's Gold) and Comet, a selection from a cross between Sunshine (bred at Wye) and an American male hop. Low-alpha aroma hops grown in the United States include Fuggle, Hallertau, and Tettnang but the major hop in this class is Cascade, an open pollenated seedling with Fuggle and the Russian Serebrianka in its pedigree. Also in this class are the triploids Columbia and Willamette which were bred from the tetraploid Fuggle-T.

In Australia, Pride of Ringwood was bred from a cross between the English variety Pride of Kent and a Tasmanian male hop. This high-yielding, high-alpha selection now occupies most of the Australian hop growing area in both Victoria and Tasmania. In Japan also, one variety, Shinshuwase, occupies 95% of the hop growing area. In New Zealand varieties resistant to Phytophthora root rot were developed in the 1960s namely First Choice, Smooth Cone and CaliCross. From these, naturally seedless triploid varieties, Sticklebract, Harley's Fulbright, and Green Bullet have been developed. Another new variety Super Alpha is a tetraploid hop reported to produce high yields with up to 15% of α-acids.

12.7 Marketing

Hops are only grown to meet the requirements of the brewing industry (Table 12.1) so it is in both the growers' and the brewers' interest that supply equals demand. Both West Germany and the United States of America export over 50% of their production and Czechoslovakia, Yugoslavia, and Australia are significant exporters. Other countries produce hops essentially for their own consumption.

In West Germany there is a completely free market with no regulation of production and no control of price. Growers make forward contracts for most of their crop with merchants who collect hops from the farm, grade them in their own warehouses, then sulphur, dry and pack them. All hops are sealed and given a certificate as to origin and weight by a local official. Prices are set by free negotiation for forward contracts or for spot purchases at or after harvest time. There are thus large fluctuations in price from year to year. Encouraged by EEC subsidies the area of hops grown in West Germany doubled so that in the mid-70s there was a serious over-production of hops, the price fell to a twenty-year low, and many brewers laid in stocks of either hops or extract. Although the price paid did not cover production costs few farmers went out of hops. Most German hop farms only grow a few hectares, largely with family labour, and the capital costs involved in wirework, driers, etc., are not readily redeemable. However, EEC grubbing grants have helped to reduce the West German hop growing area towards a more economic level. Another factor has been the replacement of the tradi-tional aroma varieties with high-alpha varieties, thus increasing the production of α-acids even more than the production of hops.

In the United States, the Hops Administrative Committee controls production but not price. Each grower has a basic quota and an annual quota based on the prospect of total sales. Most prices are negotiated as forward contracts between the grower and the dealer on one hand and between the dealer and the brewer on the other. American hop farms are much larger than their European counterparts and their production costs are undoubtedly lower.

In Britain between 1932 and 1972 the Hops Marketing Board controlled the supply of hops to meet the brewers' requirements and regulated the price on a cost-accounting basis. The grower had a guaranteed price for the bulk of his crop – the annual quota. On the other hand, in years of shortage when all their requirements could not be met, brewers got a large percentage of their needs at a stabilized price. Such tight control was only applicable to a self-contained domestic market and was contrary to the requirements of EEC membership. It inhibited both the import and export of hops. Since 1977 the Board has offered Primary Indexed forward contracts to brewers, which contain inflation clauses and, for high-alpha hops, adjustment for deviation from the standard α-acid content (Table 12.2). These controls are for specific growths of hops. Under British practice the brewer who bought hops from a particular garden or yard in one year has the first offer or 'call' on the hops from the same garden in the following year. After the Primary contracts have been settled the Board will offer the brewers Secondary Indexed contracts for a named variety but not for a specific growth. Alternatively the brewer may make spot purchases at or after harvest of uncommitted English or foreign hops.

All hops consigned to the Board are graded both on the basis of hand evaluation and α-acid analysis. High-alpha hops will be placed in one of two grades on the basis of hand evaluation and the price will also be adjusted on the basis of the α-acid content. For other (aroma) varieties three grades are determined by hand evaluation: choicest, grade I and grade II.

Merchants show great skill in the hand evaluation of hops. Usually three samples are cut from a pocket using a sharp knife. From the nature of the cutting action an experienced examiner can tell whether or not the hops are under-dried. He then inspects the sample visually taking note of the colour and brightness of the sample, the uniformity and wholeness of the cones, the amount of extraneous matter such as leaves, strig and seeds, and any damage due to pests or diseases. EEC regulations require that commercial hops shall not contain more than 6% w/w of leaf and stem. Finally the merchant rubs a sample of the hops in his hand and sniffs the aroma. From the stickiness of the rub he can make a rough estimate of the amount of resin in the sample. This part of the evaluation has been superceded by chemical analysis of the α-acid, but no instrument can replace the human nose in assessing aroma.

12.8 *Hop diseases* [1, 2]
Growing hops are liable to attack by both fungi and viruses. Severe attacks can result in the partial or complete loss of a crop and those hops which are salvaged will probably receive a low valuation. Accordingly, most growers take control measures against diseases which are prevalent in their locality. In Britain, the most important diseases are downy mildew, powdery mildew, and *Verticillium* wilt of fungal origin, and the virus diseases: nettle-head, mosaic, and split-leaf blotch.

12.8.1 DOWNY MILDEW
Downy mildew is caused by the fungus *Pseudoperonospora humuli* (Miyabe and Tak.), G. W. Wilson. It was first observed in Japan in 1905 and in the United States in 1909. At that time hops were grown in the United States along the east coast and the incidence of downy mildew was one of the major factors which determined the transfer of the hop-growing industry to the west coast. In Britain the disease was unknown before 1920 but since then it has spread to all the hop-growing areas and some infection can be found in most gardens. Epidemics can readily occur under suitable weather conditions if control measures are not carried out. As discussed above, new varieties resistant to downy mildew are now available.

The fungus is an obligate parasite for hops that overwinters as mycelium in an infected rootstock. In spring when the buds on the crown start to lengthen, those infected with the mycelium produce thick stunted primary basal spikes which are the most characteristic symptom of the disease (Fig. 12.6). On the undersides of the leaves of these spikes are thick black patches of sporangiophores which release the sporangia (Fig. 12.7) which infect the whole of the growing plant. Near-by healthy shoots may become

Fig. 12.6 Hop plant infected with downy mildew.
Left: Healthy shoot. Right: Basal spike.

Fig. 12.7 Downy mildew (*Pseudoperonospora humuli*).
Sporangiophore with sporangia.

infected and form secondary basal spikes. Infection of the growing tip of the bine will cause extension to cease and a terminal spike will be formed. Infection will also be rapidly transmitted to the leaves, the flowers, and the cones. If sporangia land on a flower or 'burr' no cone will develop. If they infect the cone later, a proportion of the bracts and bracteoles will become brown giving the hop a variegated appearance which will receive a low valuation.

Control involves the regular inspection of all the plants in the garden from early spring when the first shoots appear. All infected basal spikes should be removed together with the lower leaves, which would be the first to be infected. All infected material should be burnt.

Traditional treatment of downy mildew involved the use of Bordeaux mixture or other forms of copper but this is being replaced by systemic fungicides such as Metalaxyl (Ridomil ®) [43]. Application of Ridomil as a soil drench when the hop plants were 10–15 cm high followed by a foliar spray after 10–12 weeks has resulted in a crop free of all symptoms of downy mildew in a year when climatic conditions favoured the disease. Alternatively, fungicides may only be applied when climatic conditions favour infection [44].

Once the rootstock has been infected the mycelia may persist in it for at least four years, even if no further infection occurs, so control measures must be carried out each year. A very severe infection may kill the rootstock and badly infected hills should then be grubbed and replaced by healthy material.

12.8.2 POWDERY MILDEW

Mould, white mould, red mould or powdery mildew are synonyms for the disease produced by the fungus *Sphaerotheca macularis* (Wallr. ex Fries) Jaczewski. The spores overwinter in the soil and usually mature in May when they are ejected forcibly from their cases into the air and land on young shoots or leaves. Here myriads of spores develop which are readily dispersed through the garden. The spores landing on a leaf germinate under humid conditions and cover the surface with hyphae. The damage to the leaves is rarely serious but becomes so if the fungus alights on a burr or immature cone. In late summer the fungus forms red spots or patches on leaves or mature cones. Within these red patches minute black spore cases form which fall to the ground when the cones shatter and so repeat the cycle.

For powdery mildew the systemic fungicide Triadimefon (Bayleton) is replacing traditional treatments with sulphur or dinocap. Spraying should start in April when the plants are about 0·3 m high.

12.8.3 VERTICILLIUM WILT

Two strains of *Verticillium albo-atrum* Reinke and Berth, are recognized: (*i*) the mild strain ('fluctuating'), non-lethal with symptoms *fluctuating* in extent and intensity in the field, and (*ii*) the virulent strain ('progressive'), lethal to Fuggle and other sensitive varieties in which there is a *progressive* spread in the field; in tolerant varieties this strain is not lethal and causes symptoms resembling those induced by the mild strain [45]. The two strains can only be distinguished by the reaction of a sensitive host, such as Fuggles. They cannot be distinguished in artificial culture. The mild strain was first recognized in a garden at Penshurst, Kent in 1923 but it appears to be quite common in some soil types and is found in most hop-growing countries. The severity of the disease it produces is dependent on drainage and other environmental conditions and so varies, or fluctuates, from year to year.

In 1930 a new virulent strain arose in a Fuggle garden near Paddock Wood, Kent, which rapidly killed infected plants. By 1962 over half the farms in the Weald of Kent and in Sussex had been infected, but fortunately the disease has been largely contained within this area and only isolated outbreaks have occurred in other hop-growing areas of Britain.

If a hill, killed by progressive *Verticillium* wilt, is allowed to disintegrate, the dead infected plant material will rapidly transfer the disease to the adjacent hills and so through the garden. Wind-blown fragments and infected soil on boots and wheels may well be responsible for introducing the disease to other gardens.

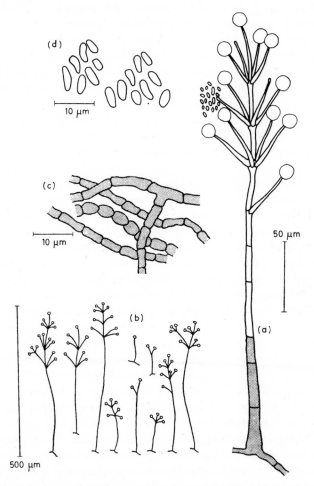

Fig. 12.8 Verticillium wilt (*Verticillium albo-atrum*). (a) Conidiophore; conidial heads, and conidia; (b) Groups of conidiophore; (c) 'Dark mycelium'; (d) Conidia.

The infecting organism (Fig. 12.8) enters the roots of the host from the soil where it occurs either as spores called conidia, or as mycelium in infected debris. The dark coffee-brown mycelia then spread through the vascular system of the bine to the leaves which develop a characteristic 'tiger stripe', become progressively yellow, then brown, and gradually wither and drop off. The base of the bine may thicken and it becomes easily detached from the rootstock. It is very difficult to distinguish between fluctuating and progressive wilt and if either form is suspected expert advice should be sought without delay. The *Progressive* Verticillium *Wilt Disease of Hops Order 1965* requires the immediate notification by the grower of a suspected outbreak. With progressive wilt the symptoms may appear any time from May onwards and the bines infected usually die within a few days or weeks. With fluctuating wilt the symptoms seldom appear before July and only a proportion of the bines in any hill become infected. The mycelia enter the roots of both wilt-sensitive and wilt-tolerant varieties but in the latter they do not usually penetrate the endodermis, the layer of cells surrounding the vascular system [46]. If the mycelia do enter the vascular system, balloon-shaped intrusions called tyloses may develop to obstruct the passage of the mycelia up the bine. These two defence systems are not absolutely efficient and so fluctuating wilt develops.

Control of fluctuating wilt may be achieved by cutting out and burning the infected bines but it is not usually necessary to dig up and burn the rootstock which may not show any symptoms the following season. For progressive wilt, the Order in Council referred to above requires (*i*) that the grower shall burn on his premises all dead and dying bines and leaves from infected plants, (*ii*) that the infected rootstocks and those of adjoining hills shall be lifted and burnt, (*iii*) that land so grubbed must not be replanted except under licence, and (*iv*) that the movement, for planting elsewhere, of any hop material from a farm known to have carried wilt is prohibited. It is common for hop farmers to restrict entry of people on foot, animals, and vehicles into hop gardens as far as possible in order to prevent conidia and mycelia of the organism being carried in from affected gardens on feet or tyres.

The virulent strain of *V. albo-atrum* will remain in the soil for 3–4 years after an initial infection and chemical disinfection of the soil has had only limited success. The disease can be eradicated from the soil by growing non-susceptible plants such as grasses but it is essential that certain weeds are eliminated. Groundsel, for example, is a symptomless carrier of the disease. In the Weald, where there is a higher chance of reinfection, most gardens that have been attacked by progressive wilt have been replanted with wilt-tolerant varieties. This is not the practice elsewhere because the tolerant varieties could become symptomless carriers of the disease.

Other fungal diseases which infect hops from time to time are canker (*Gibberella pulicaris* (Fr.) Sacc.), armillaria root rot (*Armillaria mellea*

(Fr.) Quel.), phytophthora root rot (*Phytophthora citricola* (Sawaba), and sclerotinia canker (*Sclerotinia sclerotiorum* (Lib.) de Bary).

12.8.4 VIRUS DISEASES

Nettlehead, first described in 1894, is economically the most serious of the virus diseases. At least two viruses are involved: Arabis mosaic virus and Prunus necrotic ringspot virus. Both are sap-transmissible and the former is carried by the eelworm *Xiphinema* in the soil. The same two viruses are also responsible for another virus disease, split-leaf blotch.

Plants showing symptoms of nettlehead should be grubbed and the land left fallow for two years (or eighteen months if treated with dichloropropene) before being replanted with stocks certified as being free of the disease.

Before 1950 mosaic was regarded as being a lethal disease but since then a mild strain of the virus has appeared. Hops infected with the latter usually survive but with loss of vigour and yield. It is thought that all hops can become infected with the virus, but while Goldings show the symptoms of the disease others, including Fuggles, WGV, Bullion and Northern Brewer, are symptomless carriers. For this reason Fuggles and Goldings should never be planted in the same or even in adjacent gardens. The disease is spread by the winged form of the damson-hop aphid which sucks sap containing the virus from infected plants and transmits it to those which are healthy. Infected plants should be grubbed immediately and replaced by clean stock. Aphids should be controlled.

12.9 *Pests* [1, 2]

At least forty different insect species have been recorded as living on the hop, but only a few of these are of economic importance and the control methods necessary to combat these usually keep the others in check. The most serious pest on the hop is the damson-hop aphid or hop-fly (*Phorodon humuli*

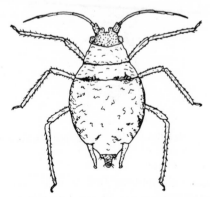

Fig. 12.9 Damson-hop aphid (*Phorodon humuli* Schr.).

Schrank) (Fig. 12.9). As its name implies this insect has a complex life-cycle infesting two host plants. It spends the winter as shiny black eggs in the bark of *Prunus* spp., notably damson or sloe (blackthorn), but occasionally plum. In early April, wingless female insects hatch out and give birth to live young which rapidly multiply. After several generations winged females arise which then migrate to the hop, infesting the undersides of the leaves and the growing points. Once on the hop the insects continue to reproduce as wingless females (plant lice or nits) and, if control measures are not taken, will rapidly infest the whole plant including the cones. Infested cones will receive a low valuation and may be unsaleable. The American Society of Brewing Chemists give methods for estimating the number of aphids in a sample of hops [47].

The migration on to the hop usually starts in mid-May and continues until mid-July with maximum activity in early June but in some years migration has continued well into August. This makes control difficult because once aphids enter the cones insecticidal sprays cannot reach them. Normally, spraying with systemic organophosphorus insecticides starts as soon as the insects appear on the hop plant and is repeated as necessary. Every effort is made to eliminate the pest before burr formation in late July. The organophosphorus insecticides are extremely toxic and residues must not remain on the hop at harvest. Aphids develop resistance to systemic organophosphorus insecticides and new agents are required every few years. At the time of writing mephosfolan as a soil drench in May is a popular treatment.

Those aphids which survive the summer on the hop produce winged forms, both male and female, in early September which migrate back to the damson. Here wingless females are born which lay the eggs that survive the winter. It is obviously desirable to eliminate *Prunus* spp., which can act as host to aphids and the prunus necrotic ringspot virus, from the vicinity of the hop garden.

Fig. 12.10 Hop flea beetle (*Psylliodes attenuata*, Koch).

The red spider (*Tetranchus urticae*, Koch) was a major pest on the hop but with the use of organophosphorus insecticides it virtually disappeared. However, resistant strains appeared in the late 1960s which responded to dicofol but it now seems that strains resistant to this acaricide are developing. The hop flea beetle (*Psylliodes attenuata*, Koch) (Fig. 12.10) which emerges in late April and early May and can eat holes in young leaves, can usually be controlled by dusting with DDT.

Other pests which may infect hops include the clay-coloured weevil (*Otiorrhynchus singularis* L.), the hop root weevil (*Epipolaeus caliginosus* F.), wireworms (*Agriotes* spp.), leather-jackets (*Tipula* spp.), slugs, and eelworms.

Herbicides

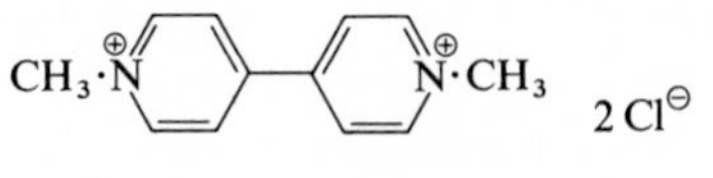

Paraquat

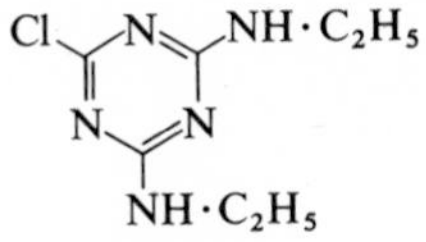

Simazine

Fungicides

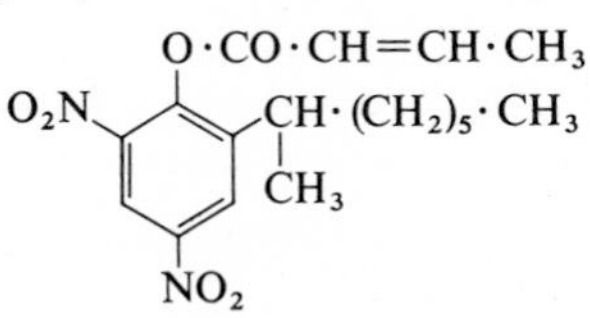

Dinocap

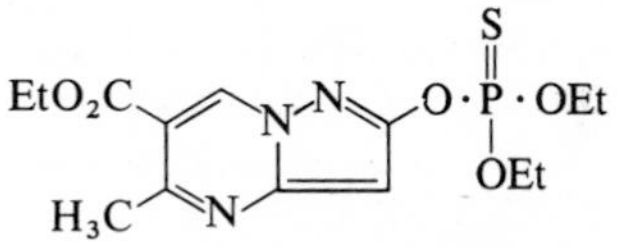

Pyrazophos (Afugan)

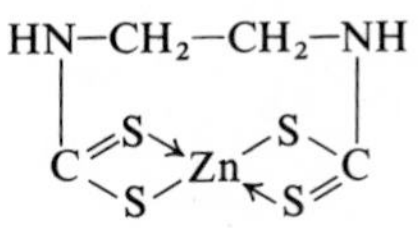

Zineb

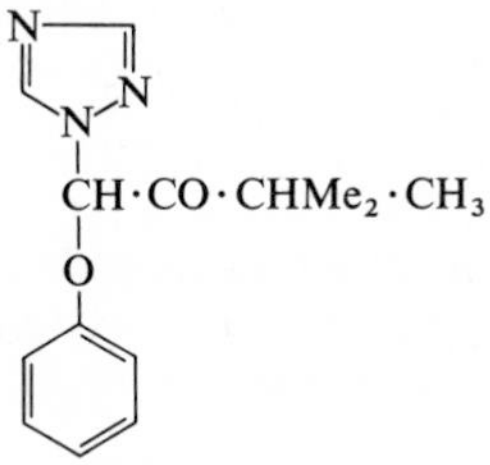

Triadimefon (Bayleton)

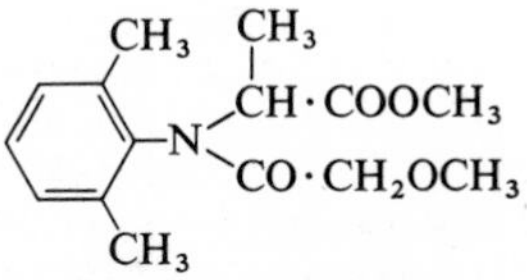

Metalaxyl (Ridomil)

Elemental sulphur
Copper preparations

Insecticides

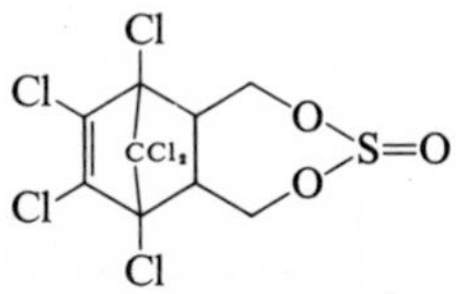

Endosulfan (Thiodan)

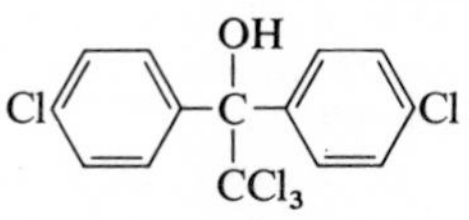

Dicofol

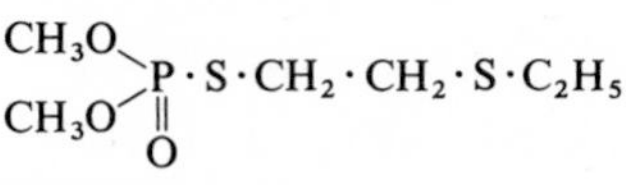

Demeton-S-methyl

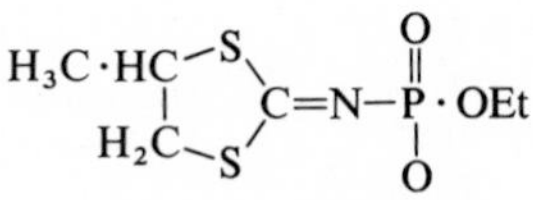

Mephosfolan (Cytrolane)

Fig. 12.11 Some agricultural chemicals used in hop production.

It will be seen from the foregoing that farmers have to use a wide range of powerful agents (Fig. 12.11) to produce high yields of good quality, undamaged hops. Brewers are worried that residues from these chemicals may persist on the hops at harvest and so find their way into the beer. (The detection of such residues is a difficult analytical problem.) Hop varieties selected for resistance to disease, which require minimal chemical treatment, would be preferred but the breeding of a variety resistant to all the pests and diseases which can attack hops is unlikely.

REFERENCES

[1] BURGESS, A. H. (1964). *Hops, Botany, Cultivation and Utilization*, Leonard Hill, London, 300 pp.
[2] Ministry of Agriculture, Fisheries and Food. (1968). *Hop Growing and Drying*, Bulletin no. 164, 2nd edition, HMSO, London, pp. iv + 90.
[3] CROMBIE, L. and CROMBIE, W. M. L. (1975). *Phytochemistry*, **14**, 409.
[4] LIKENS, S. T., NICKERSON, G. B., HAVNOLD, A. and ZIMMERMAN, C. E. (1978). *Crop Sciences*, **18**, 380.
[5] THOMAS, G. G. and NEVE, R. A. (1976). *J. Inst. Brewing*, **82**, 41.
[6] THOMAS, G. G. (1979). *A.R. Wye College*, p. 43.
[7] BAILEY, P. H. (1962). *A.R. Wye College*, pp. 64 and 70.
[8] ROBERTS, J. B. and STEVENS, R. (1962). *J. Inst. Brewing*, **68**, 247 and references there cited.
[9] BULLIS, C. E. and LIKENS, S. T. (1962). *Brewers' Digest*, 37, 54.
[10] HOWARD, G. A. and SLATER, C. A. (1958). *J. Inst. Brewing*, **64**, 234.
[11] SHEA, M. W. (1980). *A.R. Wye College*, p. 44.
[12] BAILEY, P. H. (1959). *A.R. Wye College*, p. 120.
[13] HALL, R. D. (1957), *Proc. Eur. Brewery Conv. Congr., Copenhagen*, p. 314.
[14] Institute of Brewing, Hops Advisory Committee (1970), *J. Inst. Brewing*, **76**, 295.
[15] ASTON, P. (1967). *Report on Co-operative Hop Drying Project*, Rother Valley Farmers Ltd, Rye, 68 pp.
[16] LIKENS, S. T. and NICKERSON, G. B. (Jan. 1963). *Am. Brewer*, 50.
[17] BURGESS, A. H. and TATCHELL, A. R. (1950). *A.R. Wye College*, p. 21.
[18] DE CLERCK, J., (1959). *Brewers Guild J.*, **47**, 239.
[19] BIRTWHISTLE, S. E., HUDSON, J. R. and WHITEAR, A. L. (1963). *J. Inst. Brewing*, **69**, 239.
[20] WAIN, J., BAKER, C. D. and LAWS, D. R. J. (1977). *J. Inst. Brewing*, **83**, 235.
[21] NICKERSON, G. B. and LIKENS, S. T. (1979), *J. Am. Soc. Brewing Chemists*, **37**, 184.
[22] Hop Liaison Committee (1967). *J. Inst. Brewing*, **73**, 421.
[23] LEMMEN, G. W. C. (1975). *The Brewer*, 435.
[24] GRANT, H. L. (1979). *J. Am. Soc. Brewing Chemists*, **37**, 55.
[25] SKINNER, R. N., KAVANAGH, T. E. and CLARKE, B. J. (1979). *J. Inst. Brewing*, **85**, 7.
[26] BROWN, R. G., ENGLISH, A. E., LAWS, D. J. R., GILL, R. and GOLDFINCH, P. (1980). *J. Inst. Brewing*, **86**, 65.

[27] NARZISS, L., REICHENEVER, E. and NGO,-DA, P. (1979). *Brauwelt*, **119**, 1366.

[28] GRANT, H. L. (1979). *Master Brewers Am. Assoc. Techn. Quart.*, **16**, 79.

[29] GRANT, H. L. (1979). *Proc. Eur. Brewery Conv. Congr.*, *Berlin*, p. 441.

[30] LAWS, D. R. J. (1981). *J. Inst. Brewing*, **87**, 24

[31] LAWS, D. R. J., BATH, N. A., PICKETT, J. A., ENNIS, C. S. and WELDON, A. G. (1977). *J. Inst. Brewing*, **83**, 39.

[32] HAROLD, F. V. and CLARKE, B. J. (1979). *Brewers Digest*, Sept. p. 45.

[33] LAWS, D. J. R., BAKER, C. D. and WAIN, J. (1979). *Proc. Eur. Brewery Conv. Congr.*, *Berlin*, p. 393.

[34] SHARPE, F. R., GRIMMETT, C. M., LAWS, D. R. J. and BETT, G. (1980). *J. Inst. Brewing*, **86**, 234.

[35] SCOTT, R. W., THEAKER, P. D., MARSH, A. S., GRIMMETT, C. M., LAWS, D. R. J. and SHARPE, F. R. (1981). *J. Inst. Brewing*, **87**, 252.

[36] SHARPE, F. R. and LAWS, D. R. J. (1981). *J. Inst. Brewing*, **87**, 96.

[37] Institute of Brewing (1977) *Recommended Methods of Analysis*, p. 25.

[38] PICKETT, J. A., COATES, J. and SHARPE, F. R. (1977). *Proc. Eur. Brewery Conv. Congr.*, *Amsterdam*, p. 123; *J. Inst. Brewing*, 1977, **83**, 302.

[39] BETT, G., GRIMMETT, C. M. and LAWS, D. R. J. (1980). *J. Inst. Brewing*, **86**, 175.

[40] HAUNOLD, A. (1981). *J. Am. Soc. Brewing Chemists*, **39**, 27.

[41] CMA-Centrale Marketinggesellschaft der deutschen Agrarwirtschaft mbH (1974). *Hops from Germany CMA, Bonn-Bad Godesberg*, 144 pp.

[42] Steiners Guide to American Hops (1973).

[43] URECH, P. A., SCHWINN, F. and STAUB, T. (1977). Proc. British Crop Protection Conference, 623.

[44] ROYLE, D. J. (1979). *A.R. Wye College*, 1978, p. 49.

[45] POSNETT, A. F. (1969). *J. Inst. Brewing*, **75**, 334.

[46] TALLBOYS, P. W. (1958). *Trans. Brit. Mycol.*, *Soc.*, **41**, 227; 299.

[47] American Society of Brewing Chemists (1976). Methods of Analysis 7th edn. Hops (3).

[48] BUCKEE, G. K. (1981). *J. Inst. Brewing*, **87**, 360.

Chapter 13

THE CHEMISTRY OF HOP CONSTITUENTS

Commercial hops have approximately the following percentage composition:

1.	Water	10·0
2.	Total resins	15·0
3.	Essential oil	0·5
4.	Tannins	4·0
5.	Monosaccharides	2·0
6.	Pectin	2·0
7.	Amino acids	0·1
8.	Proteins (N × 6·25)	15·0
9.	Lipids and wax	3·0
10.	Ash	8·0
11.	Cellulose, lignin, etc.	40·4
		100·0

Of these constituents, the resins and essential oil are peculiar to the hop and are responsible for its brewing value. In wort boiling tannins, sugars, amino acids, and proteins derived from the hop will go into solution and react as discussed in Chapter 14 but in general the larger proportion of these constituents in beer will be derived from malt. The chemistry of the resins and essential oil will be discussed in this chapter. During wort boiling, the α-acids are isomerized into iso-α-acids but discussion of this most important reaction is deferred until Chapter 14.

13.1 *Hop resins* [1, 2, 3]
Authoritative recommendations concerning the nomenclature of hop resin components, published in 1969 [4], defined *inter alia:*

(a) *Non-specific fractions*
Total resins. The part of the hop constituents which is characterized by solubility both in cold methanol and diethyl ether (mainly hard resins, uncharacterized soft resins, α-acids, and β-acids).

Total soft resins. The fraction of the total resins which is characterized by solubility in hexane (mainly α-acids, β-acids, and uncharacterized soft resins).
Hard resins. The fraction of the total resins which is characterized by insolubility in hexane. It is calculated as the difference between total resins and total soft resins.
β-fraction. The total soft resins minus α-acids.
Uncharacterized soft resins. That portion of the total soft resins which has not been characterized as specific compounds.

(b) *Specific compounds and mixtures of specific compounds*

The α-acids. These are mainly humulone, cohumulone, and adhumulone.
The β-acids. These are mainly lupulone, colupulone, and adlupulone.

The physical properties and structures of the individual α-acids and β-acids, as given in the recommendations [4], are presented in Table 13.1, together with some data on minor constituents. Other specific compounds defined are discussed in Chapter 14.

The total resins and the total soft resins are to be determined by methods recommended by the German Commission for Brewing Analysis [5]. Agreed procedures are necessary because differences based on solvent solubility are not absolutely clear cut and some constituents may distribute between the two fractions. The provision that the total resins should be soluble in cold methanol is included to distinguish between the resins and wax. Hop wax, a mixture of long chain alcohols, acids, esters, and hydrocarbons, together with β-sitosterol [6], will slowly crystallize from a cold methanolic solution but the process is not quantitative [7].

In the older literature, the hard resins are sometimes described as the γ-fraction while the δ-resin is that part of the hard resin which is soluble in water.

The α-acids can be separated from other soft resins by their ability to form a lead salt which is insoluble in methanol. Thus, when a methanolic solution of lead acetate is added to a methanolic solution of the soft resins, a bright yellow precipitate forms which can be recovered by filtration or centrifugation. For quantitative recovery of the lead salt of the α-acid, it is necessary to avoid an excess of the lead acetate reagent. Free Pb^{2+} ions can be detected by the use of sodium sulphide as an external indicator or by observing the increased electrical conductivity of the solution. The α-acids may be recovered from the lead salts by treating a suspension of the powdered salt in methanol either with an equivalent quantity of sulphuric acid or by passing a stream of hydrogen sulphide when the α-acids go into solution leaving an insoluble inorganic residue. The latter technique is probably quicker but should be avoided if the α-acids are to be introduced into beer at a later stage. Concentration of the

TABLE 13.1

Analogues of the α- and β-acids

Structure 1 (α-acids) and structure 2 (β-acids)

Acyl side chain (R)	α-acids Name	Formula	m.p.	$[\alpha]_D^{26}$	pk_a	β-acids Name	Formula	m.p.
—CO·CH₂·CH(CH₃)₂ isovaleryl	Humulone	$C_{21}H_{30}O_5$	64·5°	−211°	5·5	Lupulone	$C_{26}H_{38}O_4$	92°
—CO·CH(CH₃)₂ isobutyryl	Cohumulone	$C_{20}H_{28}O_5$	Oil	−208·5°	4·7	Colupulone	$C_{25}H_{36}O_4$	93–94°
—CO·CH(CH₃)·CH₂·CH₃ 2-methylbutyryl	Adhumulone	$C_{21}H_{30}O_5$	Oil	−187°	5·7	Adhumulone	$C_{26}H_{38}O_4$	82–83°[c]
—CO·CH₂·CH₃ propionyl	Posthumulone[a]	$C_{19}H_{26}O_5$					$C_{24}H_{34}O_4$	101°[c]
—CO·CH₂·CH₂·CH(CH₃)₂	Prehumulone[b]	$C_{22}H_{32}O_5$	Oil	−172°				
—CO·CH₂·CH₂·CH₂·CH₃ 4-methylpentanoyl						—	$C_{27}H_{40}O_4$	91°[c]
—CO·CH₂·CH₂·CH(CH₃)·CH₂·CH₃	—					—	$C_{28}H_{43}O_4$	91°[c]
—CO·CH₂·CH₂·CH₂·CH₃ 4-methylhexanoyl								

(a) VERZELE (1958) [62].
(b) RILLAERS and VERZELE (1962) [63].
(c) By synthesis [1].

filtrate affords the α-acids as a pale yellow oil from which humulone may slowly crystallize on storage.

Concentration of the filtrate after precipitation of the lead salts of the α-acids affords a crystalline β-acid, but in practice it is often more convenient to dilute the residue with brine and extract the soft resin constituents into light petroleum. Lupulone was first isolated by Lermer in 1863 when it crystallized directly from an extract of continental hops. Humulone (1) and lupulone (2) were the only hop resins characterized before 1950. Their structures, except in minor detail, were worked out by Wollmer and Wieland. The main reactions are set out in Fig. 13.1. A more detailed account with an extensive bibliography is given elsewhere [1, 2, 3]. In 1952 the heterogeneous nature of the α-acids was shown by counter-current distribution and partition chromatography when two further analogues, cohumulone, and adhumulone, were isolated. Their chemistry closely paralleled that of humulone and it was found that the individual α-acids only differed in the nature of the acyl side-chain (R) (Table 13.1). Trace amounts of further analogues, pre- and post-humulone also occur.

The β-acids were found to be a similar mixture of analogues. Although they are too sensitive to oxidation to be resolved by counter-current distribution, they could be converted to tetrahydro-humulones (9) (Fig.13.1) which can be separated by this technique. It was thus found that although the β-acid which crystallized from continental varieties of hops was indeed the isovaleryl analogue, lupulone, that from English and American varieties was the isobutyryl analogue, colupulone. In addition, adlupulone and an analogue with a 4-methylhexanoyl side-chain are found (Table 13.1).

Separation of individual analogues by counter-current distribution, partition, or reversed-phase chromatography is a lengthy process. A mixture of α-acids and β-acids can be resolved into the individual analogues by gas chromatography of the trimethylsilyl derivatives, by high pressure liquid chromatography [8], or analysed by proton magnetic resonance spectroscopy [9]. Alternatively, the acyl side-chains of α- and β-acids can be oxidized with alkaline hydrogen peroxide and the mixture of isovaleric, isobutyric, and 2-methylbutyric acids formed analysed by gas chromatography. The same mixture of acids can be obtained by pyrolysis of the lead salts of the α-acids. Using these and similar techniques it has been established that the proportion of adhumulone in the α-acids is fairly constantly 10–15% of the mixture but that the proportion of humulone and cohumulone varies with the variety of the hop examined (Table 13.2). Thus Hallertau hops contain approximately 20% of cohumulone in their α-acids, whereas Bullion may have 40–50% of the co-compound. With regard to the β-acids it is found that this fraction is always richer in the isobutyryl analogue than the α-acid fraction and a regression equation has been calculated to relate the two proportions [10].

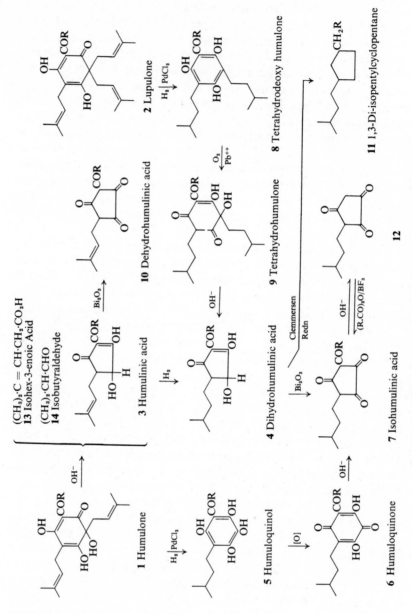

Fig. 13.1 Reactions of humulone and lupulone (R=CH₂·CH(CH₃)₂).

TABLE 13.2

The dependence of α-acid composition upon variety

Variety	Cohumulone in α-acids (%)
Hallertau	19·5
Wye Saxon	21
Saaz	22
Wye Challenger	26
Bramling	27
Wye Northdown	29
Fuggles	30
Eastwell Golding	30
Whitbread Golding Variety (1147)	32
Cascade	33
Bramling Cross (OT 48)	32·5
Northern Brewer	31
Wye Target	36
US Cluster	39
Keyworth's Midseason (OR 55)	43
Brewer's Gold	43
Bullion	46
Humulus neomexicanus	65

The percentage of colupulone in β-acid is:

$$0 \cdot 943 \, (\% \text{ cohumulone in } \alpha\text{-acid}) + 20 \cdot 2$$

The α-acids form crystalline adducts with 1,2-diaminobenzene (*o*-phenylene diamine) and repeated recrystallization of the adduct of the mixed α-acids from benzene or cyclohexane affords the humulone complex, m.p. 118°, free of that of cohumulone. Decomposition of the adduct with hydrochloric acid gives pure humulone.

It is difficult to write a single structure for the majority of hop resins because they exhibit keto-enol tautomerism whereby ketones exist in equilibrium with the related enol:

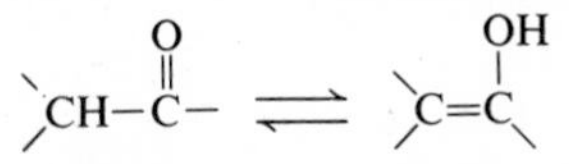

With an isolated carbonyl group, as in acetone (**15**), the equilibrium lies well on the ketone side:

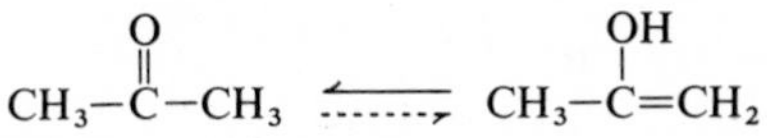

15

but β-dicarbonyl compounds, such as acetylacetone (16), exist largely in the enol form which is stabilized by hydrogen bonding:

16

Most of the hop resins contain β-di- and β-tri-carbonyl functions which are enolized. It is seldom possible to isolate the individual tautomers but estimates of the relative proportions can be obtained by proton magnetic resonance (PMR) spectroscopy and other physical methods. Irrespective of the major component a tautomeric mixture can react in any form; if, for example, a minor tautomer is consumed in a reaction it will be regenerated from the major tautomers, according to the equilibrium, until the reaction is complete. Thus phloroglucinol, the parent of the hop resin, exists almost entirely in the trienol form (17) but can react as cyclohexone-1,3,5 trione (18) to form a tri-oxime (19).

17   18   19

PMR measurements show that humulone exists principally as a dienol. Of the possible tautomer structures (1a–d), structure 1a is thought to represent the major tautomer; structures 1b and 1d are excluded on the basis of optical rotatory dispersion measurements and 1a was preferred over 1c by comparison with model compounds [11].

1a   1b   1c   1d

$$R = CH_2 \cdot CH(CH_3)_2$$
$$R^1 = CH_2 \cdot CH = C(CH_3)_2$$

Similarly by PMR measurements the β-acids were found to exist as a mixture of two tautomers (2a) and (2b) in the proportions 7: 3 [12].

2a   2b

All the natural α- and β-acids have been synthesized. Phloroglucinol is first acylated to give the desired phloracylphenone (20), which is then alkylated

17   20

with 1-bromo-3-methylbut-2-ene (isoprene hydrobromide) (22). Isoprene hydrobromide is made by 1, 4-addition of hydrogen bromide to isoprene (21).

21   22

Alkylation can give a mixture of mono- (23), di- (24) and (25), tri- (26) and tetra- (27) isoprenylated derivatives. Using one molecule of alkylating agent and base the mono-substituted derivative (23) can be obtained in good yield and by reaction in liquid ammonia the tri-isoprenylated derivatives (26) or β-acids can be obtained in up to 70% yield [13, 14]. It is more difficult to stop the alkylation after di-substitution and the deoxyhumulones (24) can only be obtained in 10–20% yield [15, 16, 17]. The di-substituted derivative (25) and the tetra-substituted derivative (27) (lupones) [16] have been synthesized but neither have been detected in hops. The mono-isoprenylated derivatives (23) have been found in hops [18] and the mono-isoprenylated chalcone xantho-humol (28) is the major constituent of the hard resin. Deoxyhumulones (24) are present in mature hops but the concentration is only about 0·3% [19]. The

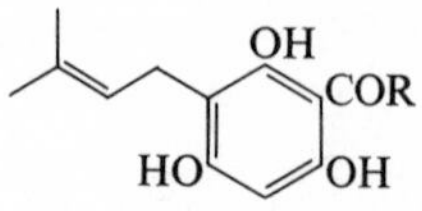

23

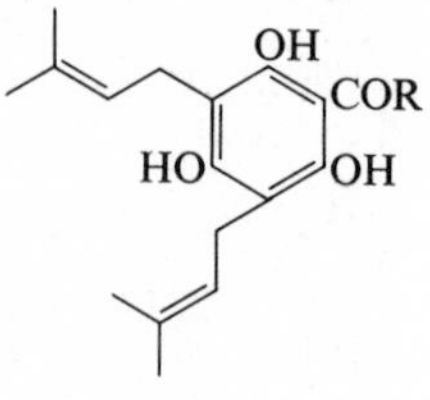

24

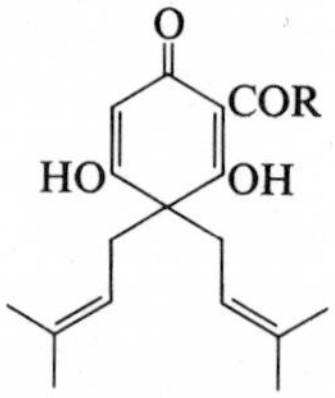

25

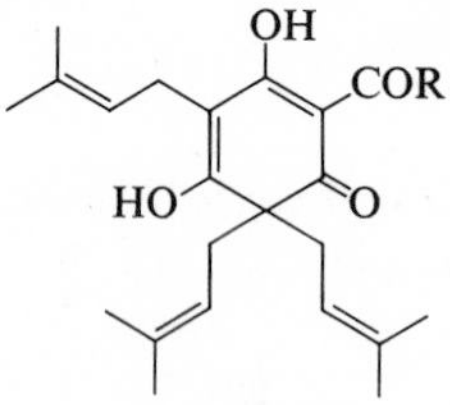

26

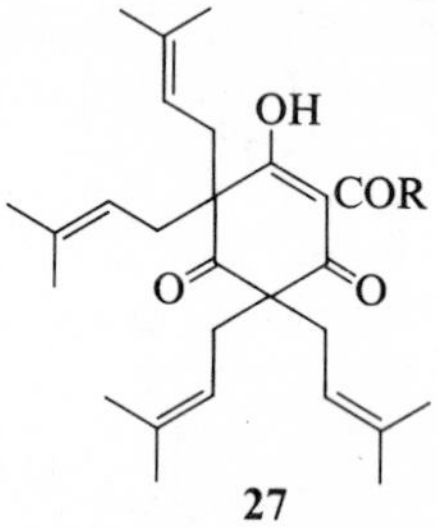

27

oxidation of deoxyhumulone (24) to humulone in the hop plant is stereo-specific, probably enzymatic, giving rise to (R)(—)-humulone (1) [11]. *In vitro* when deoxyhumulones are dissolved in a methanolic solution of lead acetate and shaken in an atmosphere of oxygen they are converted, in low yield, into the lead salts of racemic α-acids. Racemic (±)- humulone has not been resolved into its optically active forms. With improved yields these processes are the basis of a commercial process to produce synthetic α-acids and iso-α-acids [20].

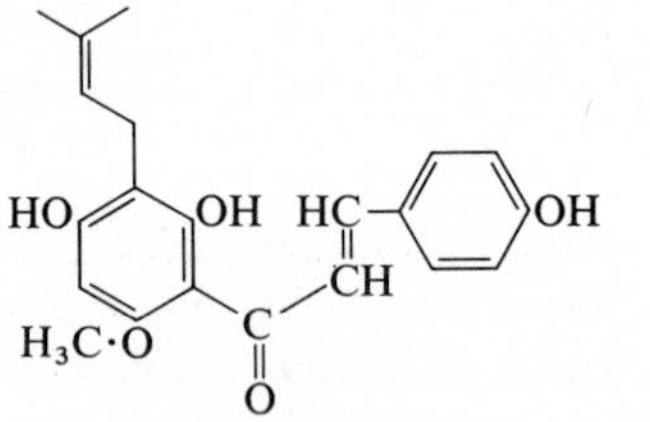

28 Xanthohumol

The biosynthesis of the hop resins occurs by similar routes. Experiments with radioactively labelled substrates have established that the phloroglucinol nucleus is formed from three molecules of acetic acid and not from sugars or shikimate. The acyl side-chains are formed from amino acids or intermediates in their biosynthesis. Thus, in humulone and lupulone they arise from leucine, in the co-analogues from valine, and in the ad-analogues from isoleucine. The amino acids themselves undergo transamination and decarboxylation to give the coenzyme A esters of isovaleric acid, isobutyric acid, and 2-methylbutyric acid respectively. It is proposed [18] that these residues combine with malonyl-CoA to give the polyketide (29) which is isoprenylated to (30) before cyclization to the mono-isoprenylated acylphloroglucinol (23). This is then isoprenylated further to deoxyhumulone (24) and the β-acids (26). However, phloro-isobutyrophenone glucoside has been isolated from hops which suggests that cyclization of the polyketide (29: R = Pr^i) can also occur before isoprenyl-ation. The biological isoprenylating agent is either isopentenyl pyrophosphate (32) or γγ-dimethylallyl pyrophosphate (33). These intermediates are also built up from acetic acid via mevalonic acid (31) as shown in Fig. 13.2. The degradation of the humulone produced in a hop plant after injection with (CH$_3$^{14}COONa) gave fragments labelled in agreement with the proposed scheme [21]. The same intermediates are probably responsible for the bio-synthesis of the essential oil constituents (see p. 447).

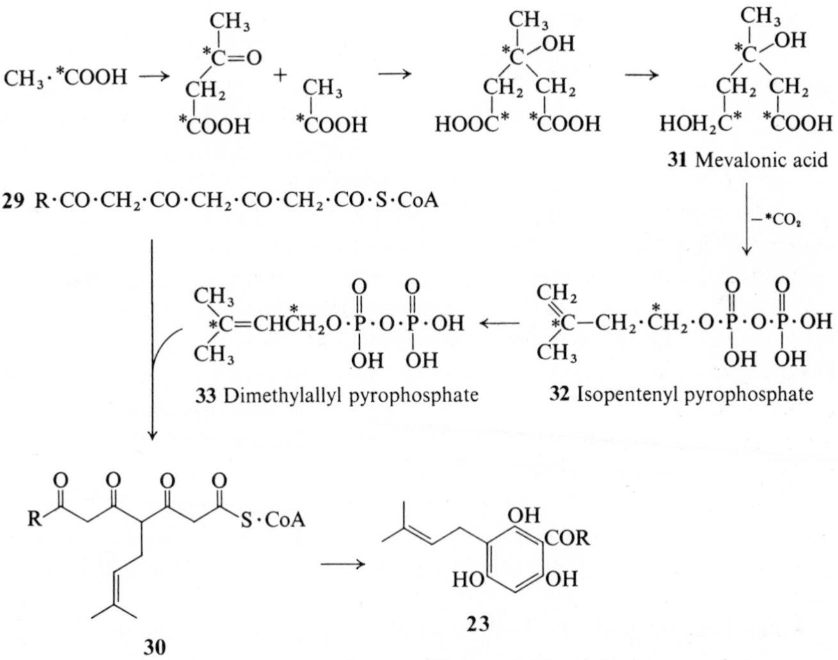

Fig. 13.2 Biosynthesis of hop resin intermediates.

In the fresh hop the α- and β-acids make up the bulk of the soft resin; the deoxyhumulones contribute to the uncharacterized soft resins. Only the α-acids have brewing value. The major constituent of the hard resin is xanthohumol (28). During storage of hops, powder, pellets, and, to a lesser extent, extracts, the α- and β-acids undergo oxidation. Some of these oxidation products are capable of bittering beer and thus compensate, to some extent, for the loss of α-acids.

Some of these oxidation products are soluble in hexane and are thus uncharacterized soft resins. Others are more polar, insoluble in hexane but soluble in ether; these are hard resins. However, even for those oxidation products which have been characterized (see later) the relative solubilities are often not reported, so it is impossible to classify them according to the above scheme.

13.2 Analysis of hops and hop products [22, 23]

There is little international agreement about the methods used for the analysis of hop resins. In Central Europe the classical Wollmer fractionation is often required. Elsewhere in Europe and in Britain the lead conductometric analysis for α-acids is the basis for commercial transactions. In the United States the spectrophotometric method for the estimation of α- and β-acids is commonly employed. Modified methods are often required for extracts. The special methods required for isomerized extracts are discussed in Chapter 14.

Sampling of hops is extremely difficult due to their heterogeneous nature and to the fact that mechanical treatment will dislodge the lupulin glands from the cones [24, 25, 26]. At least five or ten samples should be taken from a pile of uncompressed hops (approx. 200 g) and with pressed hops 10% of the number of pockets which make up a purchase should be sampled using a suitable tool. Samples should be tightly pressed in sealed tins for despatch and and storage. Such tins should be allowed to attemperate for two hours before being opened and samples should be weighed as quickly as possible as hops rapidly gain or lose weight if not in equilibrium with their surroundings. Hop extracts, especially those with water soluble materials, readily separate into layers. Accordingly, hop extracts should be heated in their tins in a water bath at 40°C for 30 min and then well mixed before sampling.

The moisture content of hops may be determined by (i) drying in an oven at 102–107°C for 1–1·5 hr [24, 25, 26] (ii) by drying in a vacuum at 60°C and 175–200 mm of Hg [26] and (iii) by azeotropic (Dean and Stark) distillation [26].

A modified method for Wollmer analysis of hop extracts is given by the EBC [25]. This method gives values for total resins and soft resins (and hard resins by difference). The α-acid content can be determined by conductometric lead titration of the soft resin which, when deducted from the soft resin figure, gives a value for the β-fraction.

The α-acid content of hops can estimated by (a) titration with lead acetate, (b) ultraviolet spectrophotometry, or (c) polarimetry:

(a) *Lead salt formation*

Originally α-acids were estimated gravimetrically as their lead salts (see [22]) but this lengthy procedure has been superceded by conductometric estimation of the end point in the titration of α-acids against lead acetate. Typically [24, 25, 26] a toluene extract of hops is diluted with methanol and the conductivity measured. Small aliquots (0·2 ml) of a methanolic solution of lead acetate (2 or 4 %) are added and the conductivity measured after each addition. A graph is plotted of conductivity against volume of lead acetate solution added and the end point determined from the intersection of two straight lines (Fig. 13.3). The curves may show different shapes in other solvents [27].

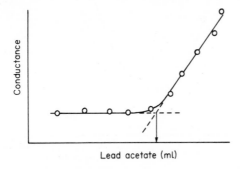

Fig. 13.3 Conductometric titration of α-acids.

The absolute value of the conductivity is not required. The EBC Analysis committee recommend that only this method should be used for commercial transactions and since the method is not specific for α-acids results should be expressed as the Lead Conductance Value (LCV) [28]. With fresh hops the lead conductance value and the α-acid content are very similar. With older hops oxidation products will be included in the LCV. Hop extracts, especially those which contain water, may give abnormal titration curves. It is therefore necessary to partition the extract between toluene and either sodium chloride solution [24] or 0·1 M sodium phosphate buffer solution pH 7·0 [25, 27] and dilute an aliquot of the toluene layer for titration. The addition of 20% dimethyl sulphoxide [25, 27] or pyridine [26, 27] to the conductometric titration sharpens the curves obtained. The procedure has been critically examined and modifications proposed [29] including automation [81].

(b) *Spectrophotometric method* [26]

The light absorption of the hop resins depends on the pH of the solution and is accordingly measured under defined acidic or basic conditions. The absorption curves of humulone and lupulone are given in Fig. 13.4. From these curves regression equations were devised [30]. Optical density measure-

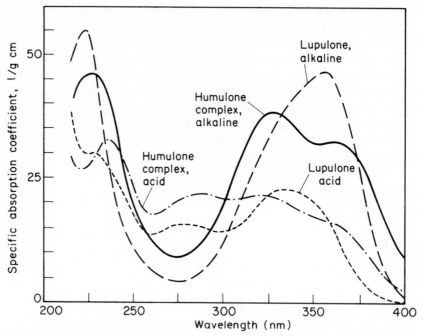

Fig. 13.4 Absorption spectra of lupulone and humulone complex in acidic (0·002 N) and alkaline (0·002 N) methanol [30].

ments were made in basic solution at 325 nm (λ_{max} for α-acids), 355 nm (λ_{max} for β-acids), and 275 nm (λ_{min} for both α- and β-acids background absorption), then:

$$\text{Concentration of } \alpha\text{-acids} = 73\cdot79A_{325} - 51\cdot56A_{355} - 19\cdot07A_{275} \text{ mg/l}$$

$$\text{Concentration of } \beta\text{-acids} = 55\cdot57A_{355} - 47\cdot59A_{325} + 5\cdot10A_{275} \text{ mg/l}$$

where A = absorbance or optical density at the specified wavelength. These equations have large multiplying factors so that small errors in the measurement of the optical density will be multiplied. The assumption that the solution of resins is a binary mixture of α- and β-acids with constant background absorption is probably true with fresh hops but will not hold with deteriorated samples. Based on this method of analysis the ratio of the OD at 275 nm/OD at 325 nm has been proposed as a hop storage index (HSI) [31]. The ratio increases from 0·24 in fresh hops to 2·5 in completely oxidized lupulin. Over several seasons the regression equation:

$$\% (\alpha + \beta) \text{ lost} = 110 \log (\text{HSI}/0\cdot25)$$

was arrived at and used to compare the storage characteristics of commercial varieties of hops. There was a linear relationship between the $\%$ ($\alpha + \beta$) lost, determined from the HSI, and the formation of hard resin [32].

(c) *Polarimetric analysis*

The α-acids are the only important resin constituents which show optical activity ($[\alpha]_D^{20} - 237°$ in hexane, $-206·24°$ in methanol, $-212·53°$ in ethanol, and $-190·4°$ in ether). The major difficulty is the preparation of a solution of resins sufficiently transparent to light. Special grades of silica gel and activated charcoal which retain chlorophyll degradation products but not the resins have been prepared and a satisfactory grade of charcoal can be made by saturating a suspension of charcoal in ether with sulphur dioxide.

The polarimetric estimation is regarded as being the most specific method for α-acids and gives accurate results with fresh hops. However, the naturally occurring laevorotatory ($-$)-α-acids are racemized on heating or during storage. Racemic ($\pm$)-α-acids are not included in polarimetric estimates but racemic ($\pm$)-iso-α-acids are as bitter as optically active iso-α-acids [27]. Polarimetric methods will thus give low results with old hops and with hop extracts. The lead conductance value is regarded as giving a better indication of brewing value.

More detailed analysis of hop resins, extracts, and isomerized extracts requires resolution of the complex mixture before estimation. Counter-current distribution was originally the method of choice but this has been superseded by column chromatography on ion-exchange resins. The ASBC [26] describe two such reference methods for the analysis of hops and/or extract. In both the various classes of resin (e.g. α-acids, β-acids, etc.] are eluted together without resolution of the individual analogues. HPLC (High pressure or high precision liquid chromatography) will probably become the method of choice. In some methods [29] the isobutyryl (co-) analogues are well resolved from the parent isovaleryl analogue but this analogue is not resolved from the isomeric 2-methylbutyryl (ad-) component. Complete resolution of the individual analogues has also been achieved but the optimum conditions have probably not been found.

13.3 *Chemical changes on storage*

The enzymatic activity of the green hop will be terminated during kilning but the composition of the hop will not remain constant and deterioration will start to take place. At first there is a lag period, the length of which appears to be a varietal characteristic, but thereafter the rate of loss of both α- and β-acids can be fitted to either zero order or first order equations [33].

In a series of storage trials at 0 and 25°C in which conventional analyses were augmented by brewing trials, it was found that the bittering power of stored hops did not decrease at such a rapid rate as their analysis indicated (Fig. 13.5) [34]. In these experiments the recoveries of the α-acids from stored hops by thin layer chromatography (TLC) was in good agreement with polarimetric estimates, so undoubtedly some of the oxidation products of the hop resins are capable of bittering beer. The oxidation products are more polar than the α- and β-acids themselves and therefore more soluble in water and chloroform than in hydrocarbon solvents such as toluene. On the basis of these experiments the economics of cold storage for copper hops was questioned [34] and some breweries examined storage at ambient temperatures. However, on a commercial scale over two years the loss of α-acids in terms of brewing value was as high as 15–20% of the original α-acids at harvest [35]. As mentioned earlier, the brewing value of hops with a low α/β ratio (1 : 1) will decrease less on storage than those with a high α/β ratio (3 : 1).

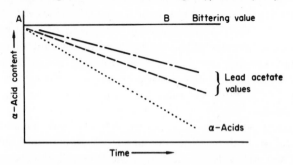

Fig. 13.5 Schematic diagram of changes in resin content and bittering value of hops during storage. .-.-.-, Conductometric analysis using chloroform as extractant; --- Conductometric analysis using toluene as extractant; ..., Polarimetric analysis.

Many oxidation products of the hop resins have now been characterized but it is not known which of these are the most important bittering principles in beer brewed from old hops. The development of cheesy aromas in old hops is due to volatile fatty acids, principally isobutyric, isovaleric, and 2-methylbutyric acids, thought to be produced by oxidative cleavage of the acyl side chains of the hop resins. The essential oil of fresh hops contains 1–3% of free acids. After a storage period of three years the acids amounted to 20% [36]. The isoprenyl side chains of the hop resins can also be removed. Photolysis of colupulone (**2**:R = Pr^i) affords deoxycohumulone (**24**:R = Pr^i) which can be subsequently oxidized to cohumulone (**1**: R = Pr^i). These reactions are the basis for a scheme to improve the utilization of the β-acids into bittering principles [37]. Mild acid hydrolysis, wort boiling, or atmospheric degradation of β-acids causes loss of the isoprenyl side chains as either 2-methylbut-3-en-2-ol (**34**) or 3-methylbut-2-en-1-ol (**35**) giving eventually the phloracylphenone (**20**) [38].

$$\begin{array}{cc}
\underset{H_3C}{\overset{H_3C}{>}}\!\!\underset{OH}{\overset{|}{C}}\!\cdot CH=CH_2 & \underset{H_3C}{\overset{H_3C}{>}}\!C=CH\cdot CH_2OH \\
34 & 35
\end{array}$$

2-Methylbut-3-en-2-ol (**34**) is the principal volatile water soluble constituent of hops [39] and is responsible for the soporific effect of hops [82]. Although not present in the head-space vapour of green hops, it is present after kilning and its concentration increases during storage [40]. Other substances in the head-space vapour include 2-methylbut-2-ene, isoprene (**21**), acetone, methyl isopropyl ketone, and methyl isobutyl ketone. The last two compounds arise by degradation of the acyl side chains of the α- and β-acids [40].

13.4 *Oxidation products of hop resins*

Aerial oxidation of most hop resins can occur by attack of oxygen either in the ring or on the isoprenyl (dimethylallyl) side chains. Oxidation in the ring can often be studied in hydrogenated derivatives with saturated side chains.

(a) *Deoxyhumulone* (*24*) [41] (Fig. 13.6)

Autoxidation of deoxyhumulones (**24**) occurs in the ring to give (±)-humulones (**1**) or in the side chains to give products such as (**36**) and (**37**). The α-acids if not removed from the mixture, by, for example, precipitation as their lead salts, will be oxidized further. Racemic (±)-α-acids will be included in conductometric but not in polarimetric estimations of α-acids.

(b) *Humulone* (*1*) [41] (Fig. 13.6)

Oxidation of humulone with *m*-chloroperbenzoic acid occurs only in the side chain to give (**35**) but with most other reagents oxidation is accompanied by a ring contraction analogous to the isomerization of humulone that occurs in wort boiling (see Chapter 14). Thus, treatment of humulone with monoperphthalic acid gives the glycol (**39**). This may be an intermediate in the formation of (**40**) which is obtained by autoxidation of humulone in light petroleum. This latter compound (**40**) has a bitter taste and was reported to account for 20% of the hard resin but its isolation could not be repeated. Probably more important is the bitter tricyclo-dehydroisohumulone (**41**) which accounts for 0·3% of stored hops and can occur in beer (up to 4 ppm) (see also [83]). It is formed when humulone is boiled in water or, in better yield, by oxidation with lead tetra-acetate. Oxidation of humulone with organic peroxides in the presence of base gives humulinone (**42**) which is intensely bitter. However there is conflicting evidence regarding its occurence in stored hops.

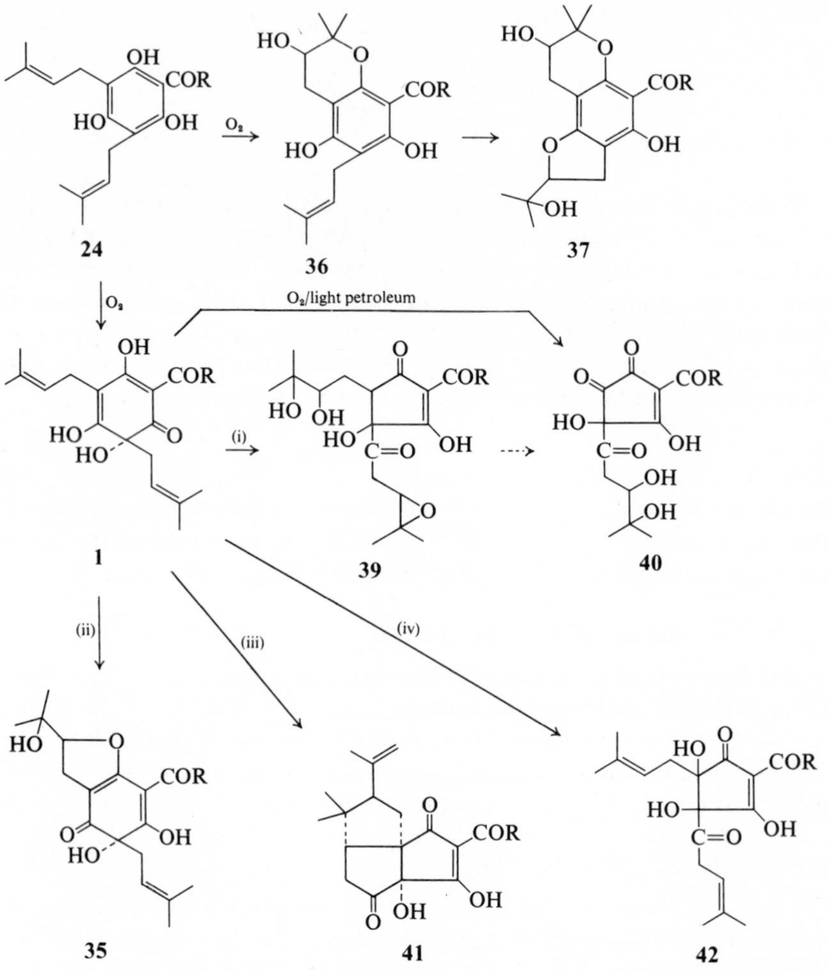

Fig. 13.6 Oxidation products of deoxyhumulone (**24**) and humulone (**1**) (R=Bu^i). (*i*) Monoperphthalic acid; (*ii*) *m*-Chlorobenzoic acid; (*iii*) Lead tetra-acetate; (*iv*) Peroxide/base.

(c) *Lupulone* (**2**) (Fig. 13.7)

The first oxidation products of the β-acids to be characterized were the hulupones (**44**). Autoxidation of hexahydrocolupulone gives a hydroperoxide which is readily converted into tetra-hydrocohulupone so the β-acids are probably converted into hulupones (**44**) via the hydroperoxide (**43**). Hulupones were not found in green hops but accumulate during storage (up to 1 %). They can be formed when hops are macerated with a solvent in a blender in the presence of air so the original estimates of the amount of hulupones in hops

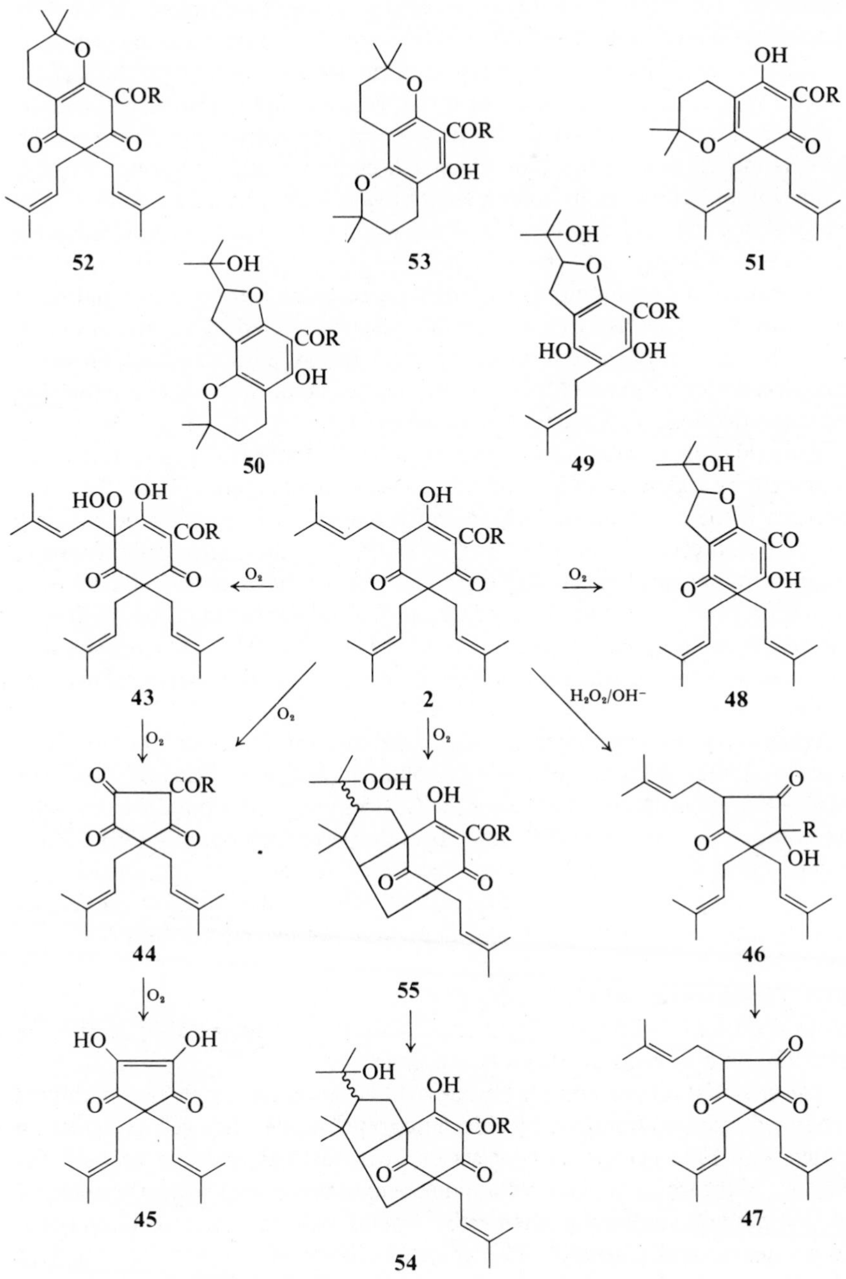

Fig. 13.7 Oxidation products of lupulone (R=Bu^i).

were high. These bitter tasting oils are also produced to a limited extent when β-acids are boiled in wort and account for about 5 % of the bittering principles present in beer. They can be prepared in the laboratory by oxidation of the β-acids with sodium persulphate or by oxygenation in the presence of sodium sulphite. Many patents describe procedures for converting the insoluble β-acids into bittering principles which will be principally hulupones. Further oxidation of hulupones in boiling ethanol gave hulupinic acid (45) by loss of the acyl side chain. Hulupinic acid, which is not bitter, has been detected in the hard resin of hops.

Oxidation of (co)-lupulone with alkaline peroxide gives rise to lupuloxinic acid (46: R = COOH) which is readily decarboxylated to lupulenol (46: R = H) but neither of these products has been found in hops or beer. However the related trione, dehydrolupulenol (47) has been reported to account for 15 % of the autoxidation products of the β-acids [42].

Autoxidation of colupulone gives a similar mixture of products to that obtained by oxidation with sodium or ammonium persulphate. A major product is the dihydrofuran (48) in which one of the isoprenyl side chains is oxidized and cyclized. In other products (49)–(53) alternative cyclizations to furan or pyran rings occur [43]. Japanese workers have described a series of oxidation products of lupulone of which the lupoxes contain one additional oxygen atom ($C_{26}H_{33}O_5$) and the lupdoxes two ($C_{26}H_{38}O_6$). Colupox a is identical with the dihydrofuran (48) but the identity of the other products has not been confirmed.

When oxygen was bubbled through a boiling solution of colupulone in an aqueous buffer solution (pH 5·5) cohulupone (44: R = Pr^i) and four new products were isolated. These were the C_3 -exo and -endo epimers of tricyclo-oxycolupulone (TCOC) (54) and tricyclo-peroxycolupulone (55). These compounds, which are not bitter, accounted for 80 % of the β-acid. The peroxy compounds (55) were formed first and the alcohols (54) on further heating but neither is very soluble. They were not detected in beer [44].

13.5 The essential oil [1, 45, 46, 61]
Hops produce 0·1–1·5 % of essential oil mainly in the later stages of ripening after the bulk of resin synthesis is complete.

The essential oil is a complex mixture of compounds which can readily be separated into two fractions by chromatography upon silica gel. The fraction eluted with light petroleum consists of hydrocarbons and can account for 50–80 % of the whole oil. The remaining constituents, eluted with ether, consist of compounds containing chemically bound oxygen, i.e. esters, carbonyl components, and alcohols. The major constituents of the hydrocarbon fraction were isolated and characterized by classical methods and include myrcene (57) farnesene (63), humulene (64), and caryophyllene (65). The

TABLE 13.3

Hydrocarbons present in the Essential Oil of hops (a)

(% in whole oil)

Component	Reference to first isolation	Gebrig (Germany)	Tettnang (Germany)	Styrian (Yugoslavia)	Hallertau (Germany)	Spalt (Germany)	Brewer's Gold	Threshold conc (ppb)	Odour units ($\times 10^{-6}$)	% Total odour units
n-Pentane/2-pentene	a	0·04	0·06	0·02	0·05	—	—			
Isoprene (21)	a	0·07	0·09	0·06	0·1	—	—			
Octane	a	0·07	0·02	0·09	0·04	0·07	—			
α-Pinene (59)	a	0·09	0·2	0·2	0·3	0·2	0·09	6	0·15	0·2
β-Pinene (60)	a	0·6	1·1	1·0	0·7	0·8	0·7	140	0·06	0·1
Myrcene (57)	b	16	28	19	20	23	63	13	48·50	58
Ocimene (58)	c						—			
	a	0·2	0·3	0·4	0·2	0·2	—			
	a	0·06	0·05	0·06	0·05	0·05				
Caryophyllene (65)	b, d	14	8·7	15	12	11	8·1	64	1·30	1·6
Farnesene (63)	d	—	16	12	—	19	—			
Humulene (64)	b, d	25	22	25	33	22	15	120	1·25	1·5
α-and β-Selinene (67, 68)	e, f	3·0	—	2·3	2·4	1·4	—			
Germacratriene (66)	g									
Selina-3, 7 (11)-diene (69)										
Selina-4 (14), 7 (11)-diene (70)										
γ-Cadinene (71)	f									
δ-Cadinene (72)	f									
Copaene (73)	f									
							86·89	—	51·26	61·4

(a) BUTTERY et al. (1964) [64].
(b) CHAPMAN (1895) [65].
(c) GOEDKOOP (1961) [66].
(d) ŠORM et al. (1949) [67].
(e) STEVENS (1964) [68].
(f) BUTTERY et al. (1966) [69].
(g) HARTLEY and FAWCETT (1969) [70].

TABLE 13.4
Oxygenated components of hop oil [a, b, c]
(% in whole oil)

Peak no. (a, b)		Fuggle	Hallertau	Idaho Cluster	Brewer's Gold	Brewer's Gold	Threshold conc. (ppb)	Odour units ($\times 10^{-6}$)	% Total odour units
4	2-Methylpropyl isobutyrate	0·8	0·05	1·1	0·6	0·39	30	0·13	0·2
5	Methyl hexanoate	0·05	—	0·1	—				
6	(Methyl thio-2-methylbutyrate)	—	—	0·1	0·04				
7	Butyl isobutyrate								
8	2-Methylbutyl propionate	0·5	0·1	1·4	0·3	0·30	28	0·11	0·1
9	Methyl 5-methylhexanoate	0·1	—	0·4	0·2				
10	—	0·05	—	0·1	0·03				
11	2-Methylpropyl 2-methylbutyrate	0·1	—	0·1	0·1				
12	3-Methylbutyl isobutyrate	0·5	0·05	0·8	0·3				
13	2-Methylbutyl isobutyrate[d]	2·1	0·3	4·1	2·6	1·40	14	1·00	1·2
14	Methyl heptanoate and	1·2	0·5	1·0	0·5	0·25	4	0·63	0·8
	Methyl 4-methylhex-2-enoate	0·2	0·01	—	—				
15	Pentyl isobutyrate	—	—		0·1				
16	(2-Methylpropyl branched pentenoate and		0·01	0·06	0·05				
	methyl thiohexanoate (branched))								
17	(Pentenyl isobutyrate)	0·1	—	—	0·2				
18	Methyl 2, 5-dimethylhexanoate	—	0·1	0·1					
19	Methyl thiohexanoate and	0·7	0·2	1·0	0·4	0·12	0·3	4·00	4·8
	Methyl 6-methylheptanoate								
20	Ethyl heptanoate	0·3	—	—					
20a	2-Nonanone and 2-methyl-5-pentenyl furan	—	—	0·1	0·04				
21	Hexyl propionate	0·7	0·08	0·6	0·6	0·11	8	0·14	0·2
22	2-Methylbutyl isovalerate			0·3	0·5				
23	2-Methylbutyl 2-methylbutyrate and	1·2	0·05			0·10	24	0·04	—
	linalool					0·17	6	0·28	0·3
24	Methyl octanoate	0·6	0·3	1·3	0·3				
25	Hexyl isobutyrate	0·2	0·02	0·1	0·1	0·06	6	0·10	0·1
26	(Methyl thioisoheptanoate)	—	—	—		0·01	2	0·05	0·01
26c	(Oxygenated terpene)	—	—	0·2	0·04				
28	Methyl thioheptanoate and 2-decanone	0·4	0·2						

TABLE 13.4 (continued)

Peak no. (a, b)	Fuggle	Hallertau	Idaho Cluster	Brewer's Gold	Brewer's Gold	Threshold conc. (ppb)	Odour units (×10⁻⁶)	% Total odour units
29 (Methyl nonanoate (branched))	0·1	—	0·2	0·1				—
30 Heptyl propionate	0·1	—	0·03	0·03	0·01	4	0·02	—
31 Octyl acetate and methyl nonanoate	0·2 / 0·2	0·08 / 0·2	0·2 / 0·4	0·1 / 0·3	0·01	12	0·01	—
32 Methyl nonanoate	0·2	0·2	—	0·04				
33 Heptyl isobutyrate	0·2	—	0·03	0·03	0·02	13	0·02	
34 2-Methyl hexanoate	0·03	0·1	0·09	0·05				
35 (Branched 2-undecanone)	0·3	—	0·1	—				
35a (Methyl 2-methylnonanoate)	—	0·3	0·02	0·04				
36 MW 204	0·3	0·3	—	0·01				
37 —	0·1	—	—	0·07				
38 (Methyl 8-methylnonanoate)	0·1	0·03	0·7	0·2	0·01	7	0·01	—
39 2-Undecanone (luparone)	0·8	1·8	1·0	0·02				
40 —	0·06		—	—				
41 Methyl dec-4-enoate	2·0	1·5	2·5	0·9	0·75	3	2·50	3·0
42 Methyl dec-4, 8-dienoate	1·9	0·9	1·9	0·6	0·43	10	0·43	0·5
43 Methyl geranate	0·6	0·04	0·1	0·4				
44 Methyl decanoate	0·4	0·07	1·3	0·4				
45 (Methyl decenoate)	—	—	0·1	0·03				
46 Octyl isobutyrate	0·2	0·02	0·07	0·02	0·01	6	0·02	—
47 2-Methylbutyl heptanoate	—	—	0·1	—				
48 (2-Tridecanone branched)		—	0·1	0·03				
48a Neryl acetate	—		0·07					
48b (Branched nonanyl isobutyrate)								
48c (Methyl undecenoate-branched)								
49 Geranyl acetate	—	0·02	0·07	1·6	0·78	9	0·87	1·0
50 (Methyl 9-methyl decanoate)	0·2	0·2	0·3	0·05				
51 —	—	—	0·2	0·09				
52 (Methyl undecenoate)	0·05	—	0·07	0·03				
53 (Methyl undecadienoate)	0·05	—	0·06	0·05				
54 (Methyl undecenoate)	0·06	—	0·03	0·04				
55 Methyl undecanoate	—	—	0·1	0·03				
56 (Methyl undecenoate)	—	—	—	0·02				
57 Neryl propionate	—	—	0·03	0·05				
58 (2-Tridecanone-branched)	0·05	0·03	0·1	0·04				

TABLE 13.4 (continued)

Peak no. (a, b)		Fuggle	Hallertau	Idaho Cluster	Brewer's Gold	Brewer's Gold	Threshold conc. (ppb)	Odour units ($\times 10^{-6}$)	% Total odour units
59	—								
60	Geranyl propionate	0·02	0·1	0·04	1·2	0·66	10	0·66	0·8
61	—	0·01	—	0·06	—				
62	Neryl isobutyrate (and methyl dodecenoate-branched)								
63	2-Tridecanone	0·1	—	0·1	0·08				
64	(Methyl dodec-8-enoate	0·8	1·0	0·9	0·1				
65	and methyl dodecadienoate)	0·1	—	1·1	0·09				
66	(Linalyl propionate)								
67	Geranyl isobutyrate[h, j]	0·5	0·4	0·8	1·9	1·00	13	0·77	0·9
68	—	—	—	0·06	0·04				
69	Methyl dodecanoate			0·08	—				
70	(Methyl dodecenoate)	0·09	0·05	—	0·05				
71	(Branched 2-tetradecanone)	0·07	0·2	0·2	0·09				
72	(Tetradec-9-en-2-one)								
73	(MW 204)								
74	(MW 204)	0·2	—	0·07	0·07				
75	Caryophyllene[k]	0·04	—	0·07	—				
76	—								
77	2-Tetradecanone								
78	(Methyl tridecenoate)								
79	(Methyl tridecenoate)	—		—	0·08				
80	(Humulene epoxide)	2·2	0·5	0·4	0·4				
81	(MW 222)	0·1	—	0·08	0·06				
82	—								
83	—								
84	(Pentadeca-6, 9-dien-2-one)	0·9	0·8	1·0	0·6				
85	(MW 220)	0·4	0·4	0·2	0·2				
86	(MW 222)	0·2	0·07	0·1	—				
87	2-Pentadecanone								
	Totals	29	17	31	19	6·59		11·69	14·0

(a) BUTTERY et al. (1965) [71].
(b) BUTTERY et al. (1965) [72].
(c) LIKENS et al. (1970) [31].
(d) HOWARD and STEVENS (1959) [73].
(e) ŠORM et al. (1949) [74].
(f) CHAPMAN (1928) [75].
(g) BUTTERY et al. (1963) [76].
(h) ROBERTS and STEVENS (1965) [77].
(i) BUTTERY et al. (1966) [78].
(j) SHIGEMATSU and KITAGAWA (1962) [79].
(k) ROBERTS (1963) [80].

complexity of the essential oil was revealed by gas chromatography and advances in this technique have led to the identification of an increasing number of components which are listed in Tables 13.3, 13.4, 13.5 and 13.6. Most have been identified by the refined technique of using a capillary column capable of high resolution in conjunction with a time-of-flight mass spectrometer.

TABLE 13.5

Volatile acids in fresh and stored Spalter hops [36]

Fraction number	Acid	Concentration (ppm)	
		At harvest 1974	Stored 1977
1	2-Methylpropionic acid	16	220
2	2-Methylbutyric acid	165	690
3	3-Methylbutyric acid	165	690
4	Pentanoic acid	0·5	20
5	4-Methylpentanoic acid	20	40
6	Pent-2-enoic acid	0·2	13
7	Hexanoic acid	15	140
8	4-Methylpent-3-enoic acid	1	40
9	Hex-3-enoic acid	—	25
10	Hex-2-enoic acid	—	40
11	Heptanoic acid	22	95
12	4-Methylhex-2-enoic acid	5	15
13	Methylhexenoic acid	5	17
14	6-Methylheptanoic acid	5	78
15	Octanoic acid	4	46
16	Nonanoic acid	10	46
17	Nonenoic acid	1	15
18	8-Methylnonanoic acid	—	5
19	Decanoic acid	3	15
20	Dec-4-enoic acid	10	65
21	Deca-4, 8-dienoic acid	3	22
22	Undecenoic acid	—	2
23	Geranic acid	—	2
24	Benzoic acid	—	5
25	4-Hydroxy-4-methylpent-2-enoic acid	1·5	70

By means of the biogenetic scheme set out in Fig.13.8 the interrelationships of the hydrocarbons present in the essential oil can be seen. This scheme is produced by analogy with work with other plants and had not been confirmed for the hop. The biological isoprenylating agents isopentenyl pyrophosphate (32) and dimethylallyl pyrophosphate (33) can condense together to form geranyl pyrophosphate (56) which by transesterification can give rise to geranyl acetate, propionate, and isobutyrate which are found in the oxygenated fraction.

TABLE 13.6

Terpenoids and sesquiterpenoids in fresh and stored Spalter hops and in beer

Fraction number	Compound	Concentration					Flavour threshold	
		Fresh hops 1974 [49] (ppm)	Stored hops 1977 [48] (ppm)	Bavarian beer [58] (ppb)	American beer A* [60] (ppb)	American beer B* [60] (ppb)	in beer (ppb)	in water (ppb)
69	4,4-Dimethylbutan-4-olide			160				
70	4,4-Dimethylbut-2-en-4-olide (80)	1·5	70	1750	50	100	>40 000	
86	2,2,7,7-Tetramethyl-1, 6-dioxaspiro [4,4] non-3-ene (81)	—	15	5				
87	2,2,7,7-Tetramethyl-1, 6-dioxaspiro [4,4] nona-3, 8-diene (82)	—						
88	7,7-Dimethyl-6,8-dioxabicyclo [3,2,1] octane (83)	1	25	10				
89	Hop ether (85)	1·5	27	50				
90	Karahana ether (84)	0·5	13	35				
91	trans-Linalool oxide	1	5	60				
92	Humuladienone (79)		20	20				
93	Caryophyllene epoxide (74)	5	60	10				
94	Humulene epoxide I (75)	23	80	18		100		10
95	Humulene epoxide II (76)	33	250	125				
96	Linalool (61)	25	45	40	200	200	80	6
97	β-Fenchyl Alcohol	—	7	470				
98	Terpinen-4-ol	1	5	40				
99	α-Terpineol	3	20	15	75	—	2000	4
100	Citronellol	—	—	40				
101	Geraniol	0·5	8	10				
102	Caryolan-1-ol	6	18	5	—	25	—	—
103	Nerolidol	3	10	25	—	75	—	—
104	Junenol	—	—	25				
105	Epicubenol	16	20	5				
106	Caryophyllenol	—	—	20				
107	T-Cadinol	13	15	5	100	200	—	—
108	Humulol (77)	111	88	45	—	—	—	—
109	δ-Cadinol	16	20	220	—	100	—	—
110	Humulenol II (78)	2	290	35	250	250	—	—
111	β-Ionone (94)	—	++	1150				
112	Damascenone (93)	—	—	1	2000	200	—	—
113	cis-Jasmone	—	—	trace				
	Carvacrol	—	—	10	—	100	—	—
	α-Eudesmol	—	—	—	—	—	—	—

* American beer A was brewed with Cascade hops. American beer B was brewed with a mixture of Hallertauer mittelfruh, Tettnanger and Styrian hops.

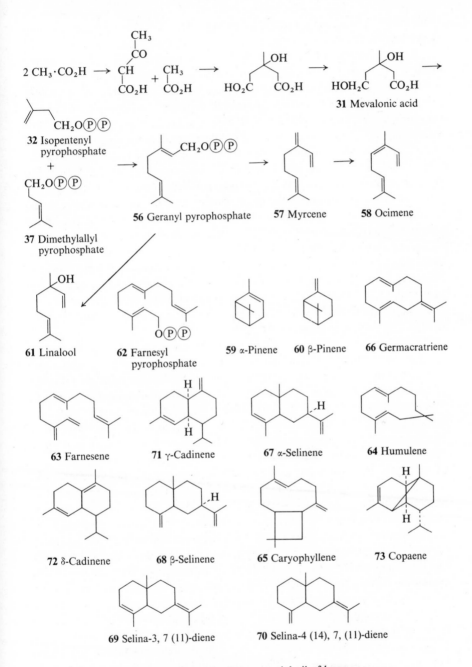

Fig. 13.8 Biogenesis of the essential oil of hops.

Elimination of phosphoric acid from geranyl pyrophosphate can give rise to myrcene (**57**), the major constituent of the essential oil, and by rearrangement the other monoterpenes ocimene (**58**), and α-(**59**) and β-(**60**)-pinene. Condensation of geranyl pyrophosphate (**56**) with a further mole of isopentenyl pyrophosphate (**32**) affords farnesyl pyrophosphate (**62**), which by a similar mechanism to that involved in formation of myrcene from (**56**) can produce the sesquiterpene farnesene (**63**). One cyclization of the farnesyl cation can afford humulene (**64**) and caryophyllene (**65**) while alternative routes can give rise to germacratriene (**66**) α-(**67**) and β-(**68**) selinene, selina-3, 7 (11)-diene (**69**), selina-4 (14), 7(11) -diene, (**70**), γ-cadinene (**71**), δ-cadinene (**72**), and copaene (**73**). Biogenetic relationships among the oxygenated components are not so obvious. Some, for example, the geranyl esters and the autoxidation products of humulene and caryophyllene, are produced by extensions of the above scheme. Others can be produced by variations of the polyketide (acetogenin) pathways and as by-products of schemes of amino acid biosynthesis. For example, intermediates associated with the biosynthesis of isoleucine are probably responsible for the side-chains of the ad-components of the hop resins, and for 2-methylbutanol present in the essential oil as the isobutyryl, propionyl, and 2-methylbutyryl esters. Geraniol and linalool contribute to the floral note in hop aroma [84].

Like the resins, the essential oil constituents undergo oxidation during storage. In particular, the autoxidation of myrcene [47] and humulene [48] have been studied. In another investigation [36, 49] Spalter hops grown in the Hallertau in 1974 were analysed at harvest and after three years' storage at 0°C. The fresh hops contained 1·63 g oil/100 g (88% hydrocarbons) which fell during storage to 0·88 g oil/100 g (7% hydrocarbons). In the stored hops, aldehydes and alcohols were detected and the level of ketones and, in particular, carboxylic acids (Table 13.5) increased. The ratio of the concentrations of isovaleric acid/isobutyric acid appears to be a varietal characteristic and may be of use in identification [36]. Some of these products will be formed by oxidation of the resins and lipids in the hop cone rather than the original essential oil constituents. Nevertheless the level of oxygenated terpenes and sesquiterpenes increases significantly during storage (Table 13.6). For example, caryophyllene epoxide (**74**), humulene epoxide I (**75**) and II (**76**), humulol (**77**), and humulenol II (**78**) were formed during storage. In addition, the level of the cyclic ethers (**80**)–(**86**), first found in Japanese hops, also increased on storage. Many of these compounds survive into beer.

Sulphur-containing constituents of hop oil [85], although only present in trace amounts, are potent flavouring agents (Table 13.7). They can be distinguished by gas chromatography using a flame photometric detector. Many hops are treated in the field with elemental sulphur to control mildew and the level of such treatment can affect the level of sulphur compounds in the oil

[50, 51]. The sesquiterpenes caryophyllene and humulene react with elemental sulphur under mild conditions to produce the episulphides (87), (88), and (89) [52]. The level of these compounds is higher in oil prepared by steam distillation at 100°C than in oil obtained by vacuum distillation at 25°C. Thus, higher levels of these compounds are likely to be introduced into beer by late addition of hops to the copper than by dry hopping. Myrcene reacts with sulphur less readily, but with a suitable activator a mixture of at least 10 products is obtained of which (90) is the major constituent present in hop oil.

TABLE 13.7
Sulphur compounds in the Essential Oil of hops

Name	Structure	Flavour threshold (ppb)
Methanethiol	CH_3SH	
Dimethyl sulphide	$CH_3S·CH_3$	7·5
Dimethyl disulphide	$CH_3S·S·CH_3$	7·5
Dimethyl trisulphide	$CH_3S·S·S·CH_3$	0·1
(2,3,4-Trithiapentane)		
2,3,5-Trithiahexane	$CH_3S·S·CH_2S·CH_3$	
Dimethyl tetrasulphide	$CH_3S·S·S·S·CH_3$	0·2
(2,3,4,5-Tetrathiahexane)		
S-Methyl 2-methylpropanethioate	$(CH_3)_2 CH·CO·SCH_3$	40 (5)
S-Methyl 2-methylbutanethioate	$CH_3CH_2CH(CH_3)CO·S·CH_3$	1
S-Methyl 3-methylbutanethioate	$(CH_3)_2CH·CH_2CO·S·CH_3$	50
S-Methyl pentanethioate	$CH_3·(CH_2)_3CO·S·CH_3$	10
S-Methyl 4-methylpentanethioate	$(CH_3)_2CH·CH_2CH_2CO·SCH_3$	15
S-Methyl hexanethioate	$CH_3(CH_2)_4CO·S·CH_3$	1
S-Methyl heptanethioate	$CH_3(CH_2)_5CO·S·CH_3$	
S-Methylthiomethyl 2-methylbutanethioate	$CH_3CH_2CH(CH_3)CO·S·CH_2S·CH_3$	1
S-Methylthiomethyl 3-methylbutanethioate	$(CH_3)_2CH·CH_2CO·S·CH_2S·CH_3$	
3-Methylthiophene	(91)	500
3-(4-Methylpent-3-enyl) thiophene	(92)	
4-(4-Methylpent-3-enyl)-3,6-dihydro-1, 2-dithiine	(90)	10
4,5-Epithiocaryophyllene	(87)	200
1,2-Epithiohumulene	(88)	1800
4,5-Epithiohumulene	(89)	1500
2-Methyl-5-thiahex-2-ene	$(CH_3)_2C=CH·CH_2·S·CH_3$	0·2
Methylthiohumulene	$C_{15}H_{23}S·CH_3$	

Several polysulphides occur in hop oil. Dimethyl trisulphide (2,3,4-trithiapentane) occurs only in oil prepared from hops which have not been treated with sulphur (dioxide) on the kiln. It is absent from oil prepared by vacuum distillation at 25°C but is formed at 100°C from the precursor S-methylcysteine sulphoxide ($CH_3SO·CH_2CH(NH_2)COOH$). This precursor is destroyed by sulphur dioxide when sulphur is burnt in the oast but is slowly regenerated on storage. Dimethyl tetrasulphide and 2,3,5-trithiahexane are also present in hop oil. These polysulphides have cooked vegetable, onion-like, rubbery, sulphury flavours with low thresholds.

Hop oil contains a series of thioesters (Table 13.7); the combined amount of which in steam-distilled hop oil usually exceeds 1000 ppm. The level of thioesters in the oil does not appear to be affected either by treatment of hops with elemental sulphur on the bine or by sulphur dioxide kilning [50]. Thioesters are formed in hops largely by the action of heat, so low levels will be introduced into beer by dry hopping. Few sulphur volatiles survive 60 min of wort boiling but after late addition of hops to the copper most of the sulphur compounds discussed above are present in the wort including the thioesters. During fermentation dimethyl trisulphide and some of the thioesters disappear but some sulphur volatiles survive into the finished beer: S-methyl 2-methylbutanethiolate is the principal thioester to survive. This last ester and S-methyl hexanethiolate, the thioester with the lowest taste threshold, are the major thioesters introduced into beer by dry hopping [50].

The essential oil and the volatile degradation products of the resins together are responsible for the characteristic aroma of hops and for the part this plays in the aroma and flavour of beer. No one constituent has been found to have the characteristic hop aroma which is probably made up by the synergistic action of many components. Tasting trials established that 1 ppm of whole hop oil was detected in water but that 3 ppm were necessary for detection in beer. The oxygenated components are more potent flavouring agents than the hydrocarbons; 0·3 ppm of the oxygenated fraction being detected in beer. Of the hydrocarbons, myrcene has a stronger aroma than the sesquiterpenes [53].

The results of a more detailed survey of the odour intensities of individual components of hop oil [54] are incorporated into Tables 13.3 and 13.4. By means of a panel the threshold concentration (T_c) in parts per 10^9 (ppb) at which a component in distilled water could be detected by smell was measured. This was arbitrarily defined as one odour unit. If the fraction or component concentration (F_c) in the whole oil is also expressed in ppb then the ratio $F_c/T_c = U_o$, the number of odour units attributable to any fraction or component. If the sum of the odour units from individual fractions equals that for the whole oil, the relative contributions by each fraction may be estimated. As shown in Table 13.8 the sum of the odour units found in the hydrocarbon and oxygenated fractions of a sample of oil from Brewer's Gold was equal to that of the whole oil.

The threshold values of twenty-five of the components found in the sample of oil from Brewer's Gold were estimated and are included in Tables 13.3 and 13.4. In this sample, the hydrocarbons accounted for 87% of the oil but only 61% of the odour units. Myrcene, which comprised 63% of the oil, was responsible for 58% of the odour units. The twenty oxygenated components studied accounted for 6·6% of the oil and provided 14% of the odour units leaving the balance of the oxygenated components (6·8 %) responsible for 25 % of odour units. It is noteworthy that of the oxygenated components, methyl thiohexanoate and methyl dec-4-enoate were the most potent constituents. With threshold values of 0·3 and 3 ppb respectively they accounted for 4·8 and 3·0 % of the odour units of the whole oil.

TABLE 13.8
Aroma of the Essential Oil from Brewer's Gold [54]

	Whole oil (%)	Threshold conc. (T_o) (ppb)	Odour units $U_o \times 10^{-6}$	Total odour units (%)
Whole oil	100	12	83·3	100
Hydrocarbons	86	15	57·3	69
Oxygenated fraction	14	5	28·0	34

In considering these results attention should also be drawn to the fact that most components can be detected by smell at a tenth of the concentration at which they can be detected by taste in water and only higher concentrations can be differentiated against the more complex background of beer.

It is generally accepted that when hops are added at the start of wort boiling, few essential-oil constituents survive into the beer. To improve the hop bouquet of beer brewers may add a portion of choice 'aroma' hops towards the end of the boil or, in Britain, the beers may be dry hopped. In the practice of dry hopping, hops, a sonic extract of hops, hop pellets and enriched hop powder or lupulin are added to the finished beer, either in cask or conditioning tank, and left in contact for a period up to three or four weeks with or without periodic agitation. The major effect is due to essential-oil constituents, notably myrcene, going into solution so that some brewers add hop oil directly to the finished beer. But, as pointed out earlier, the aroma of hop oil obtained by steam distillation at 100°C differs from that of the hop itself. Thus, emulsions of hop oil obtained by vacuum steam distillation are being used to impart a true hop aroma to finished beers [55].

Only small amounts of hop-oil constituents go into solution at wort boiling and much of this material is lost or transformed during fermentation. In many samples of American beer it was concluded there were insufficient hop-oil constituents to affect the flavour, but one commercial beer with a pronounced hop aroma contained 1079 ppb hydrocarbons (970 ppb myrcene) and over 42 ppb oxygenated components [56]. Transesterification of hop oil esters occurs during fermentation, thus methyl dec-4-enoate and methyl-deca-4, 8-dienoate present in hopped wort were converted into ethyl dec-4-enoate and ethyl deca-4, 8-dienoate in beer [57].

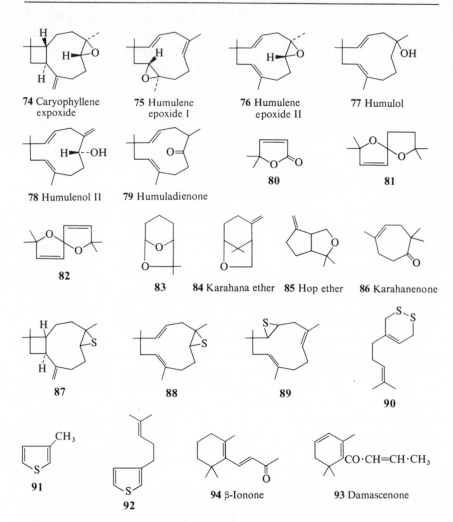

74 Caryophyllene expoxide

75 Humulene epoxide I

76 Humulene epoxide II

77 Humulol

78 Humulenol II

79 Humuladienone

80

81

82

83

84 Karahana ether

85 Hop ether

86 Karahanenone

87

88

89

90

91

92

94 β-Ionone

93 Damascenone

In a later study, the aroma constituents of a Bavarian (Pilsener) beer brewed in Hallertau, near Munich, which possessed a desirable fine hop aroma, was examined [58]. Neither the terpenes and sesquiterpenes nor the methyl esters characterized in hop oil were detected but fraction IV (Table 13.6), which contained terpenoids and sesquiterpenoids, possessed an intensive pleasant hoppy odour. Noteworthy amongst the identified constituents are the cyclic ethers (80)–(86) first found in Japanese hops, the flowery notes of which contribute to hop aroma, and the sesquiterpenoids derived from humulene such as humulene epoxide I, humulene epoxide II, humulol, and humulenol II. Similar results were found with American beers [60, 86]. Humuladienone (79) was present but not at the concentrations (30–70 ppb) found in Japanese beers where it was thought to be responsible for the hoppy aroma associated with beer: its threshold is reported as 100 ppb. Trace amounts of damascenone (93) and β-ionone (94) are present in hops and beer. These degradation products of β-carotene have very low threshold values of 0·009 and 0·008 ppb respectively. In addition to the thioesters discussed above, dimethyl trisulphide and the dithiine (90) have been detected in beer.

REFERENCES

[1] STEVENS, R. (1967). *Chem. Rev.*, **67**, 19–71.

[2] ASHURST, P. R. (1967). *Fortsch. der Chemie organische Naturstoffe*, **25**, 63–89 (in English).

[3] VERZELE, M. (1979). in *Brewing Science*, Vol. 1 (ed. POLLOCK, J. R. A.) Academic Press, London, p. 280.

[4] Hops Liaison Committee: Nomenclature Sub-Committee (1969). *J. Inst. Brewing*, **75**, 340.

[5] European Brewery Convention, Analysis Committee (1973). *J. Inst. Brewing*, **79**, 310.

[6] DELANGHE, L., STRUBBE, H. and VERZELE, M. (1969). *J. Inst. Brewing*, **75**, 445.

[7] CLARKE, B. J., HAROLD, F. V., HILDEBRAND, R. P. and MURRAY, P. J. (1961). *J. Inst. Brewing*, **67**, 529.

[8] LANCE, D. G., KAVANAGH, T. E. and CLARKE, B. J. (1981). *J. Inst. Brewing*, **87**, 225.

[9] LAWS, D. R. J., SHANNON, P. V. R. and JOHN, G. D. (1976). *J. Am. Soc. Brewing Chemists*, **34**, 166.

[10] HOWARD, G. A. and TATCHELL, A. R. (1957). *J. Inst. Brewing*, **63**, 138.

[11] DE KEUKELEIRE, D. and VERZELE, M. (1970). *Tetrahedron*, **26**, 385.

[12] COLLINS, M., LAWS, D. J. R., MCGUINESS, J. D. and ELVIDGE, J. A. (1971). *J. Chem. Soc.* (*C*), 3814.

[13] DREWETT, K. G. and LAWS, D. R. J. (1970). *J. Inst. Brewing*, **76**, 181.

[14] COLLINS, M., LAWS, D. R. J., MCGUINESS, J. D. and ELVIDGE, J. A. (1971). *J. Chem. Soc.* (*C*), 3814.

[15] COLLINS, E., DONNELLY, W. J. C. and SHANNON, P. V. R. (1972). *Chem. and Ind.*, 120.

[16] COLLINS, M. and LAWS, P. R. J. (1973). *J. Chem. Soc. Perkin, I*, 2013.

[17] COLLINS, E. and SHANNON, P. V. R. (1973). *J. Chem. Soc. Perkin, I*, 419

[18] DRAWERT, F. and BEIER, J. (1976). *Phytochemistry*, **15**, 1695.

[19] LLOYD, R. O. V., SHANNON, P. V. R. and SHAW, S. J. (1969). *J. Inst. Brewing*, **75**, 32.

[20] PFENNINGER, H. B., SCHUR, F., VATERLAUS, B. P., SIGG, T. and WILD, J. (1975). *Proc. Eur. Brewery Conv. Congr.*, Nice, p. 159.

[21] WRIGHT, D. and HOWARD, G. A. (1961). *J. Inst. Brewing*, **67**, 236.

[22] HUDSON, J. R. (1960). *Development of Brewing Analysis. A Historical Review*, The Institute of Brewing, London, p. 102.

[23] PFENNINGER, H. B., SCHUR, F. and ANDEREGG, P. (1979). in *Brewing Science*, Vol. 1 (ed. POLLOCK, J. R. A.), Academic Press, London, p. 451.

[24] Institute of Brewing (1973). Recommended Methods of Analysis.
[25] European Brewery Convention (1975). *Analytica-EBC*, 3rd Edition.
[26] American Society of Brewing Chemists (1976). *Methods of Analysis*, 7th Edition.
[27] VERZELE, M. and VAN DYCK, J. (1971). *J. Inst. Brewing*, **77**, 529.
[28] European Brewery Convention, Analysis Committee (1968). *J. Inst. Brewing*, **74**, 254.
[29] VERZELE, M., VAN DYCK, J. and CLAUS, H. (1980). *J. Inst. Brewing*, **86**, 9.
[30] ALDERTON, G., BAILEY, G. E., LEWIS, J. C. and STITT, F. (1954). *Analyt. Chem.*, **26**, 983.
[31] LIKENS, S. T., NICKERSON, G. B. and ZIMMERMANN, C. E. (1970). *Proc. Am. Soc. Brewing. Chemists*, p. 68.
[32] NICKERSON, G. B. and LIKENS, S. T. (1979). *J. Am. Soc. Brewing Chemists*, **37**, 184.
[33] GREEN, C. P. (1978). *J. Inst. Brewing*, **84**, 312.
[34] WHITEAR, A. L. (1965). *Proc. Eur. Brewery Conv. Congr.*, Stockholm, p. 405. (1966). *J. Inst. Brewing*, **72**, 177.
[35] WAIN, J. (1977). *J. Inst. Brewing*, **83**, 239.
[36] TRESSL, R., FRIESE, L., FENDESACK, F. and KRUGER, E. (1978). *Monats. fur Brauerei*, 83,
[37] BAZARD, D., FLAYEUX, R., MOLL, M., VIRIOT, M. L., ANDRE, J. C. and NICLAUSE, M. (1979). *Brauwissenschaft*, **32**, 283.
[38] REGAN, J. P. and ELVIDGE, J. A. (1969). *J. Inst. Brewing*, **75**, 10.
[39] HARTLEY, R. D. (1968). *Phytochem.*, **7**, 1641.
[40] DE METS, M. and VERZELE, M. (1968). *J. Inst. Brewing*, **74**, 74.
[41] SHANNON, P. V. R., JOHN, G. D. and DAVIS, A. M. (1978). *Brewers Digest*, Sept., p. 58.
[42] Brewing Industry Research Foundation, Annual Report (1968). *J. Inst. Brewing*, **74**, 130.
[43] BRYNE, E., CAHILL, D. M. and SHANNON, P. V. R. (1969). *Chem. and Ind.*, p. 875; (1970). *J. Chem. Soc. (C)*, p. 1637.
[44] DE POTTER, M., DE KEUKELEIRE, D., DE BRUYN, A. and VERZELE, M. (1978). *Bull. Soc. Chim., Belg.*, **87**, 459.
[45] ROBERTS, J. B. and STEVENS, R. (1962). *J. Inst. Brewing*, **68**, 420.
[46] BUTTERY, R. G. and LING, L. C. (1966). *Brewers' Digest*, Aug. 71
[47] DIECKMANN, R. H. and PALAMAND, S. R. (1974). *J. Agric. Food Chem.*, **22**, 498.
[48] PICKETT, J. A., SHARPE, F. R. and PEPPARD, T. L. (1977). *Chem. and Ind.*, p. 30.
[49] TRESSL, R., FRIESE, L., FENDESACK, F. and KOPPLER, H. (1978). *J. Agric. Food Chem.*, **26**, 1426.
[50] SUGGETT, A., MOIR, M. and SEATON, J. C. (1979). *Proc. Eur. Brewery Conv. Congr. Berlin*, p. 79.
[51] PEPPARD, T. L. and LAWS, D. R. J. (1979), *Proc. Eur. Brewery Conv. Congr., Berlin*, p. 91.
[52] PEPPARD, T. L., SHARPE, F. R. and ELVIDGE, J. A. (1980). *J. Chem. Soc. Perkin Trans I.*, p. 311.
[53] HOWARD, G. A. and STEVENS, R. (1959). *J. Inst. Brewing*, **65**, 494.
[54] GUADAGNI, D. G., BUTTERY, R. G. and HARRIS, J. (1966). *J. Sci. Food Agric.*, **17**, 142.

[55] PICKETT, J. A., COATES, J. and SHARPE, E. R. (1975). *Proc. Eur. Brewery Conv. Congr., Nice*, p. 123.

[56] LIKENS, S. T. and NICKERSON, G. B. (1964). *Proc. Annu. Meet. Am. Soc. Brewing Chemists*, 5.

[57] LIKENS, S. T. and NICKERSON, G. B. (1966). *J. Chromatog.*, **21**, 1.

[58] TRESSL, R., FRIESE, L., FENDESACK, F. and KOPPLER, H. (1978). *J. Agric. Food Chem.*, **26**, 1422.

[59] SHIMAZU, T., HASHIMOTO, N. and KUROIWA, Y. (1974). *Proc. Annu. Meet. Am. Soc. Brewing Chemists*, **9**, 7.

[60] PEACOCK, V. E., DEINZER, M. L., MCGILL, L. A. and WROLSTAD, R. E. (1980). *J. Agric. Food Chem.*, **28**, 774.

[61] SHARPE, F. R. and LAWS, D. R. J. (1981). *J. Inst. Brewing*, **87**, 96.

[62] VERZELE, M. (1958). *Bull. Soc. Chim. Belg.*, **67**, 278.

[63] RILLAERS, G. and VERZELE, M. (1962). *Bull. Soc. Chim. Belg.*, **71**, 438.

[64] BUTTERY, R. G., MCFADDEN, W. H., LUNDIN, R. E. and KEALY, M. P. (1964). *J. Inst. Brewing*, **70**, 396.

[65] CHAPMAN, A. C. (1895). *J. Chem. Soc.*, **67**, 54; (1903). **83**, 505.

[66] GOEDKOOP, W. (1961). *Int. Tijds. Brouw. Mout.*, **21**, 80.

[67] ŠORM, F., MLEZIVA, J., ARNOLD, Z. and PLIVA, J. (1949). *Coll. Czech. Chem. Commun.*, **14**, 699.

[68] STEVENS, R. (1964). *J. Chem. Soc.*, 956.

[69] BUTTERY, R. G., LUNDIN, R. E. and LING, L. (1966). *Chem. and Ind.*, 1225.

[70] HARTLEY, R. D. and FAWCETT, C. H. (1969). *Phytochem*, **8**, 1793.

[71] BUTTERY, R. G., BLACK, D. R. and KEALY, M. P. (1965). *J. Chromatog.*, **18**, 399.

[72] BUTTERY, R. G., BLACK, D. R., GUADAGNI, D. C. and KEALY, M. P. (1965). *Proc. Annu. Meet. Am. Soc. Brewing Chemists*, 103

[73] HOWARD, G. A. and STEVENS, R. (1959). *Chem. and Ind.*, 1518.

[74] ŠORM, F., MLEZIVA, J. and ARNOLD, Z. (1949). *Coll. Czech. Chem. Commun.*, **14**, 693.

[75] CHAPMAN, A. C. (1928). *J. Chem. Soc.*, 1303.

[76] BUTTERY, R. G., LUNDIN, R. E., MCFADDEN, W. H., JAHNSEN, V. J. and KEALY, M. P. (1963). *Chem. and Ind.*, 1981.

[77] ROBERTS, J. B. and STEVENS, R. (1965). *J. Inst. Brewing*, **71**, 45.

[78] BUTTERY, R. G., BLACK, D. R. and LING, L. (1966). *J. Inst. Brewing*, **72**, 202.

[79] SHIGEMATSU, N. and KITAGAWA, Y. (1962). *Bull Brew. Sci.*, Tokyo, **8**, 23.

[80] ROBERTS, J. B. (1963). *J. Inst. Brewing*, **69**, 343.

[81] SIEBERT, K. J. (1980). *J. Am. Soc. Brewing Chemists*, **38**, 119; (1981) 39, 124.

[82] HANSEL, R., WOHLFART, R. and COPER, H. (1980). *Z. fur Naturforsch.* **35C**, 1096.

[83] VERZELE, M. and DEWEALE, C. (1981). *J. Inst. Brewing*, **87**, 232.

[84] PEACOCK, V. E., DEINZER, M. L., LIKENS, S. T., NICKERSON, G. B. and MCGILL, L. A. (1981). *J. Agric. Food Chem.* **29**, 1265.

[85] PEPPARD, T. L. (1981). *J. Inst. Brewing*, **87**, 376.

[86] PEACOCK, V. L. and DEINZER, M. L. (1981). *J. Am. Soc. Brewing Chemists*, **39**, 136.

Chapter 14

CHEMISTRY OF WORT BOILING
AND HOP EXTRACTION

14.1 *Introduction*

Wort boiling may be regarded as the turning-point in the brewing of beers; it is omitted in distilling and vinegar brewing. At its simplest, in Bavarian practice, the all malt wort is boiled with hops for 1–2 hr, no other additions being permitted by aw. Elsewhere the sweet-wort may be produced from a mixed cereal grist (see Chapters 10 and 11) and additional carbohydrate may be included in the boil either as brewing sugars or wort syrups (Chapter 8). Further, part or all of the hop grist may be replaced by a suitable hop extract. Indeed, it will be shown in the sequel that hops can be utilized more efficiently if the hop principles are extracted and isomerized independently of the boiling process. The pre-isomerized extract is then added to the beer after fermentation.

Many complex reactions take place during wort boiling. As the wort is heated the residual amylases and other enzymes are inactivated which terminates the mashing process and fixes the carbohydrate composition of the wort. At the boiling-point the wort is sterilized and the microflora of the malt, hops, and other adjuncts used are destroyed. As the boil continues some proteins are coagulated and some, together with simpler nitrogenous constituents, interact with carbohydrates and/or polyphenolic constituents (tannins). The insoluble precipitate resulting from these interactions is the 'break' or 'trub'. Part of the break separates from the boiling wort (the hot break) but a further amount precipitates as the wort is cooled (cold break). At the same time the hop principles are extracted into solution and undergo transformation or interact with other wort constituents. In open coppers about 10% of the volume is evaporated during one hour's boil so that some of the dilution caused by sparging is compensated. At the same time, most of the steam-volatile essential oil of hops is lost. It is necessary that the bulk of the essential oil is eliminated in this way or the flavour of hop oil would be too pronounced. If green malt is employed in the cereal grist the 'vegetable' off-flavour which develops is lost during the boiling process.

TABLE 14.1

Carbohydrate composition of worts (results expressed as g/100 ml. wort) [1]

Origin (and ref.) Type of wort OG	Danish[a,b] Lager 1043·0	Canadian[c] Lager 1054·0	Canadian[d] Lager 1048·0	Canadian[d] Grain lager 1046·5	German[e] Lager 1048·5	British[f] Pale ale 1040	British[g] Pale ale 1040
Sugar							
Fructose	0·21	0·15	0·13	0·10	0·39	0·33	0·97
Glucose	0·91	1·03	0·87	0·50	1·47	1·00	
Sucrose	0·23	0·42	0·35	0·10	0·46	0·53	0·60
Maltose	5·24	6·04	5·57	5·50	5·78	3·89	3·91
Maltotriose	1·28	1·77	1·66	1·30	1·46	1·14	1·30
Total ferm. sugar	7·87	9·41	8·58	7·50	9·56	6·89	6·78
Maltotetraose	0·26	0·72	0·54	1·27		0·20	0·53
Higher sugars	2·13*	2·68	2·52	2·94		2·32	1·95
Total dextrins	2·39	3·40	3·06	4·21		2·52	2·48
Total sugars	10·26	12·81	11·64	11·71		9·41	9·26
Sugars (% total extract)	91·1						
Fermentability	76·7	73·7	73·7	64·1		73·3	73·2

* The contents of maltopentaose, maltohexaose and maltoheptaose in this wort were 0·13, 0·19 and 0·18 g/100 ml respectively.

(*a*) GJERTSEN (1953) [128].
(*b*) GJERTSEN (1955) [129].
(*c*) MCFARLANE and HELD (1953) [130].
(*d*) LATIMER *et al.* (1966) [131].
(*e*) KLEBER *et al.* (1963) [132]
(*f*) HARRIS *et al.* (1951) [133].
(*g*) HARRIS *et al.* (1954) [134].

14.2 *Carbohydrates*

Typical analyses of the carbohydrates present in brewery worts are given in
Table 14.1, from which it can be seen that the carbohydrates account for
91–92% of the extract, of which 68–75% is normally fermentable by yeast.
Although hops may contain up to 2% of sugars, when used at the rate of
0·28 kg/hl (1 lb/barrel) of 10° Plato wort (SG 1040) they only add 0·15% to
the total carbohydrates. Of the wort carbohydrates maltotetraose, more complex polysaccharides, and dextrins, which together account for 23–28% of the
extract, will not normally be fermented and will persist into the finished beer.
If, as in vinegar brewing and whisky distilling, the boiling process is omitted,
enzymes will survive longer and the majority of the dextrins will be broken
down to fermentable sugars [2].

14.3 *Nitrogenous constituents*

The nitrogenous constituents of wort, which account for 3–5% of the extract,
are extremely diverse in molecular size and include amino acids, peptides,
polypeptides, proteins, nucleic acids, and their degradation products. Some
of these nitrogenous constituents are essential factors for yeast growth during
fermentation and the wort must contain an adequate supply of these nutrients.
It is generally believed, however, that the yeast is only capable of assimilating
simple amino acids and peptides. Indeed, most of the amino acids in the
wort, with the exception of proline, are assimilated during fermentation.
On the other hand, the majority of the proteins are not assimilated during
fermentation, and those which persist into the beer will slowly react with
polyphenolic constituents to form non-biological haze. Part of the more
sensitive proteins are eliminated as 'break' during wort boiling and a further
portion as chill haze during conditioning. Proteins, however, must not
be eliminated entirely as they are associated with important beer characters
such as the head-forming properties and the development of a full palate.

It is not surprising, in view of the complex nature of the nitrogenous
constituents of wort, that it has been difficult to find meaningful methods of
fractionation and analysis. The total soluble nitrogen (TSN) can conveniently
be measured by Kjeldahl estimation on an aliquot of the hot-water extract and
this is probably more reliable than measurement of the permanently soluble
nitrogen (PSN), i.e. that remaining after removal of the coagulable nitrogen
by boiling. The amount of protein coagulated during wort boiling depends
inter alia on the pH and the duration and vigour of boiling. The latter is
particularly difficult to control, so that the Institute of Brewing Analysis Committee recommended evaporation of the sample to half volume and dilution
back to the original volume when estimating PSN [3]. Above pH 5 the amount
of protein coagulated is constant, but at lower pHs it is substantially reduced
(Table 14.2). Further, the cold break is only 10–20% of the hot break, and

the presence of hops does not significantly alter the amount of nitrogen coagulated. Similar results were obtained using decoction mashing (Table 14.3).

TABLE 14.2

Loss of nitrogen during wort boiling [4]

pH before wort boiling	N precipitated in 2 hr boiling (mg/l)	N precipitated during boiling and subsequent cooling (mg/l)
6·65	251	298
6·18	262	294
5·21	259	287
4·01	206	248
2·48	129	167

The wort used contained about 24% wort solids.

TABLE 14.3

Change in pH during wort boiling [5]

	pH of wort		Nitrogen precipitated (mg/l)	
Before boiling	After boiling			
	3 hr	6 hr	3 hr boil	6 hr boil
6·06	5·69	5·46	72	80
5·63	5·39	5·22	69	79
5 09	4·99	4·86	67	76

Adjusting the last results to allow for the fact that the wort only contained 12% of wort solids, the amount of nitrogen precipitated is still considerably less than that for infusion mashing. Furthermore, the pH level has little influence in the range studied but the fall in pH during boiling is noteworthy and is associated with the precipitation of calcium phosphate and phytate (see Chapter 9). It will also be seen that even after three hours' boil, more nitrogen is precipitated if the boil is continued for a further three hours. This illustrates the difficulties in removing all the potential haze-forming proteins by boiling.

The changes involved in the coagulation of proteins are not completely understood. In addition to their linear structure formed by peptide linkage between the constituent α-amino acids, proteins possess secondary and tertiary structure produced by folding and rotating peptide chains into conformations held in place by hydrogen bonding and disulphide bridges and this structure may be destroyed at denaturation. Proteins are amphoteric; although the α-amino group and the carboxylic acid of the neutral amino acids are involved in peptide linkage; aspartic and glutamic acids provide negatively charged centres and the basic amino acids, lysine, arginine, and histidine provide positively charged centres in the macromolecule. It seems likely that these charged centres are also hydrated. The acidic groups may be blocked by formation of the corresponding amides, but these are hydrolysed much more readily than the peptide links. Proteins are most readily coagulated at the isoelectric point, the pH at which the numbers of positive and negative charges are equal. The neutral molecules rapidly lose their hydrophilic nature and become hydrophobic and insoluble. In vigorously boiling wort such ultra-microscopic particles cling together and form large flocs which separate, leaving clear wort. Worts held at 98–100°C (208–212°F) without boiling or agitation sometimes remain turbid.

Several methods have been described for fractionating the nitrogenous constituents of wort. In the scheme of Lundin and Schroderheim [6] the wort is acidified with sulphuric acid and fraction A is precipitated by tannin. The nitrogen in this fraction is estimated by difference between the original wort nitrogen and that remaining in solution and usually amounts to 20–30% of the total. This fraction is regarded as containing the high molecular weight proteins which, if not removed during wort boiling and cooling, are liable to lead to haze formation in finished beer. Fractions A and B are precipitated from another aliquot of acidified wort with sodium molybdate. The material remaining in solution (fraction C) represents principally amino acids and simple peptides while fraction B, estimated by difference, is assumed to comprise polypeptides of intermediate molecular weight. Results obtained by Lundin's procedure were compared [7] with those obtained using the method of Myrbäck and Myrbäck [8], which employs magnesium sulphate to precipitate the protein fraction and uranyl acetate to remove the intermediate fraction, and were generally similar. Again, the effect of other precipitants on wort were investigated [7] and the method developed by Cohn [9] for blood-serum proteins applied to the fractionation of wort and beer [10]. All the fractions precipitated were undialysable and the bulk of the foam stabilizing activity was in particular fractions derived from the malt used. The simpler nitrogenous constituents are not precipitated in the above schemes. Some information about the proportions of high molecular weight proteins in wort have thus been obtained but the precise significance of the results remains in doubt. More precise information about the distribution of the high molecular weight nitrogen is provided by gel filtration. Using a range of gels which retard the passage of increasingly larger molecules, the results shown in Table 14.4 were obtained for Congress worts. It will be seen that much of the high molecular weight protein is lost on boiling. A method for determining high molecular weight nitrogen by gel filtration has been developed [12], and this method, or some modification thereof, is likely to become standard practice.

TABLE 14.4

Effect of boiling on the MW distribution of wort proteins [11]

Mol. wt.	< 5000	5–10 000	10–50 000	50–100 000	> 1 000 000
Boiled for 95 min	0·0175	0·0125	0·0040	0·0010	0
Not boiled	0·0336	0·0185	0·0101	0·0023	0·0028

The simpler nitrogenous constituents of wort consist principally of α-amino acids which can be estimated by the colour reaction either with indane-1,2, 3-trione hydrate (ninhydrin) or 2,4,6-trinitrobenzenesulphonic acid. With ninhydrin, α-amino acids develop a violet colour which can be measured at 570 nm while proline, an important imino acid in wort and beer, gives a yellow colour measured at 440 nm. 2,4,6-Trinitrobenzenesulphonic acid is more specific for amino acids and does not react with proline or ammonia. It forms yellow derivatives which can be estimated colorimetrically at 340 nm.

TABLE 14.5

Free amino acids in wort and beer [15] (mg/100 cm³)

Nitrogen and amino acids	Wort	Wort hopped	Beer	Beer refermented
Total nitrogen	88·0	84·8	62·6	47·0
Low molecular nitrogen alcohol-soluble	63·4	69·5	50·7	35·1
Total α-amino nitrogen	42·7	38·0	21·0	13·0
Alcohol-soluble α-amino nitrogen	37·6	30.8	18·2	2·5
Alanine	9·8	10·2	7·7	1·8
γ-Amino-butyric acid	8·3	7·9	9·6	2·5
Arginine	13·8	5·9	3·0	0·6
Aspartic acid	7·0	9·8	1·6	1·0
Glutamic acid	6·4	3·3	0·8	0·7
Glycine	2·3	2·6	2·1	1·3
Histidine	5·7	3·8	2·8	0·2
Isoleucine	6·2	6·5	2·1	0·3
Leucine	18·1	17·5	4·7	0·7
Lysine	14·9	10·7	2·2	0·5
Phenylalanine	13·7	14·0	4·4	0·6
Proline (imino acid)	45·7	48·3	31·8	33·3
Threonine	5·9	7·3	0·3	0·3
Tyrosine	10·6	9·3	5·9	1·1
Valine	11·9	16·0	6·8	0·4
Serine + Asparagine mm in 100 cm³	168·6	171·8	7·9	5·6
Ammonia	2·4	2·4	1·7	1·0

Earlier methods of estimating the α-amino nitrogen, due to Van Slyke, consisted of gasometric analysis of the nitrogen evolved when amino compounds were treated with nitrous acid or, alternatively of the carbon dioxide evolved on treatment with ninhydrin. The amino acids are readily absorbed on ion-exchange resins from which they can be eluted quantitatively either as a group or individually with a gradient of buffer solutions of increasing pH. The original method of a gradient elution, due to Moore and Stein [13], took the best part of a week for a complete amino acid analysis but later developments [14] allow measurements to be made automatically during two hours. Using the original method the results given in Table 14.5 were obtained [15]. It will be seen that, in general, there are only small changes in the concentration of the individual amino acids during wort boiling. In this experiment there was an increase in the concentration of aspartic acid, valine, and threonine, probably due to contributions from the hops, but more noteworthy is the appreciable loss of the basic amino acids, arginine, histidine, and lysine. The summarized results in Table 14.6 show that both total and α-amino nitrogen are lost when wort is boiled without hops but this is compensated to some extent by the nitrogenous constituents of the hops which go into solution.

An automatic method of amino acid analysis has been applied to many brewing problems and, in particular, much data have been accumulated on the fate of amino acids during wort boiling in a commercial brewery [16]. Under these conditions there was no increase in the amount of threonine and valine in the wort after hop boiling but similar losses of the basic amino acids were observed.

TABLE 14.6

Loss of nitrogen by boiling of wort [15]

	Wort before boiling	Wort boiled with hops	Wort boiled without hops
Total nitrogen, (mg/100 cm³)	86·0	81·9	81·5
α-Amino nitrogen (mg/100 cm³)	36·0	35·0	33·0
pH	5·6	5·7	5·7
Colour	5·0	11·0	12·0

14.4 *Carbohydrate–nitrogenous constituent interactions* [17]

It will be noticed in Table 14.6 that the loss of α-amino nitrogen during wort boiling is accompanied by an increase in the colour of the wort. This so-called browning reaction is due to complex series of interactions between primary amines and reducing sugars which take place in many biological systems. In the brewing process, the browning reaction occurs when malt is kilned (Chapter 4) and continues during wort boiling. It is estimated for American beer that about one third of the final wort colour is produced during malt kilning, the other two thirds during wort boiling. Browning reactions are also the basis for the production of caramel. The structure of the brown

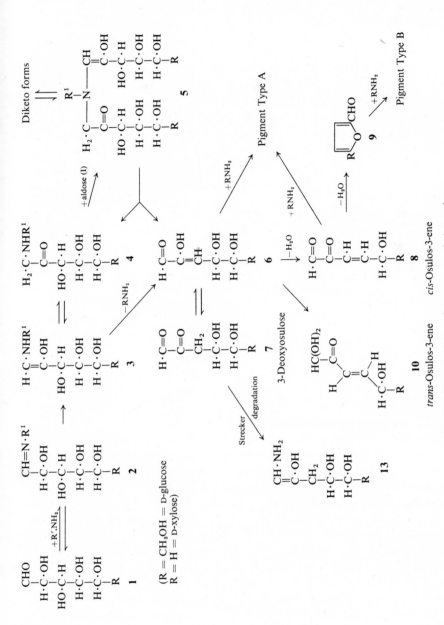

Fig. 14.1 The chemistry of non-enzymatic browning.

pigments formed is unknown; they are polymers of fairly high molecular weight soluble in water but insoluble in most organic solvents. Brown and black pigments (melanins) are formed in some biological systems by the action of polyphenol oxidase on a suitable substrate (e.g. tyrosine) but the browning reactions discussed here are not catalysed by enzymes, and, in general, do not require the presence of oxygen. The reaction is sometimes named after the French chemist Maillard and the products known as melanoidins.

Non-enzymatic browning has been reviewed extensively [17] and only the more significant reactions will be discussed here. The various intermediates involved in browning that have been characterized, and the reactions proposed, are summarized in Fig. 14.1. Aldose sugars such as glucose or xylose (1) condense with primary amines to give aldosylamines (2). The aldosylamines formed when the primary amine in the system is an amino acid have only been isolated as salts, metal complexes, or esters. They are comparatively unstable and may be either hydrolysed back to their original components or undergo an Amadori rearrangement to a ketosamine (4). For example, writing the sugars in the pyranose form, D-glucosylglycine (11), rearranges to D-fructosylglycine (12).

11   12

Ketosamines are comparatively stable especially in the absence of water. Crystalline ketosamines have been isolated from the reaction of glucose with amino acids; glycine, alanine, valine, aspartic acid, phenylalanine, tryptophan, and proline and the first three have been isolated from malt [18]. Some ketosamines are stable in dilute aqueous solution but all rapidly decompose in dilute alkali and rather slowly in hot acid. They readily condense with a further molecule of an aldose (1) to give diketosamines (5) of which difructoseglycine (5 : R = CH_2OH; R' = $CH_2 \cdot COOH$) has been obtained crystalline. The diketosamines are much more labile than the monoketosamines. Difructoseglycine is 66% decomposed in 3 min at 100°C and pH 5·5 and difructosealanine decomposes rather more rapidly [19]. The degradation products of difructoseglycine (5 : R = CH_2OH; R' = $CH_2 \cdot COOH$) have been characterized as 3-deoxyosulose (7), cis-osulos-3-ene (8) and hydroxymethylfurfural (9 : R = CH_2OH). 3-Deoxyosulose reacting as the enol (6) is probably the most important precursor of the brown pigment at pH 5·5 [19]. Only a negligible amount of hydroxymethylfurfural (9 : R = CH_2OH) are formed at this pH. Similarly at pH 3·6 less than 20% of brown pigments are formed via hydroxymethylfurfural. *cis*-Osulos-3-ene is readily converted to hydroxymethylfurfural; and half conversion in 0·03-N acetic acid at 100°C takes 12 min. On the other hand, *trans*-osulos-3-ene (as the hydrate **10**), which is also formed by decomposition of difructoseglycine, is converted forty times more slowly. Under stronger acid conditions hydroxymethylfurfural is converted to laevulic (levulinic) acid.

The scheme presented in Fig. 14.1 is based on the aldose sugars and a similar series of reactions can be envisaged starting with a ketose sugar as fructose (see [17(b)]). Examination of the scheme also reveals that the amino compound may be regarded as being a catalyst for the degradation of the sugars before it is itself incorporated into the brown pigment. The implication that the amino compound is not decomposed itself is true with simple amines but α-amino acids undergo the Strecker reaction [20] with α-dicarbonyl compounds:

$$\begin{matrix} \diagdown\text{C=O} \\ | \\ \diagup\text{C=O} \end{matrix} + \text{R} \cdot \text{CH(NH}_2) \cdot \text{COOH} \longrightarrow \begin{matrix} \diagdown\text{C} \cdot \text{NH}_2 \\ \| \\ \diagup\text{C} \cdot \text{OH} \end{matrix} + \text{R} \cdot \text{CHO} + \text{CO}_2$$

The amino acid is degraded to an aldehyde with one less carbon atom and carbon dioxide, while the nitrogen combines with the dicarbonyl compound.

The classical example of the Strecker reaction is that of the amino acids with ninhydrin (indane-1, 2, 3-trione) while in the browning reaction 3-deoxyosulone (**7**) is probably the dicarbonyl precursor. It can be speculated that the resultant amino compound (**13**) could condense with another molecule of 3-deoxyosulose (**7**) to form the brown pigment. On the other hand formaldehyde, acetaldehyde, propionaldehyde, (iso)butyraldehyde, (iso) valeraldehyde, and furfural have been isolated from boiling wort [21]. With the exception of the last compound the aldehydes originate from the amino acids, glycine, alanine, α-aminobutyric acid (or glutamic acid), valine and leucine by Strecker degradation. Although most of these aldehydes will be lost in the condensate or reduced during fermentation they are powerful flavouring agents. For example, isobutyraldehyde can be detected by smell at 0·9 ppb [22]. During the storage of beer the melanoidins present can oxidize the higher alcohols, produced by fermentation, to similar aldehydes, which give rise to stale flavours in beer [23].

The properties of the melanoidin complexes depend upon the nature of the amino compound and sugar from which they are prepared. They have characteristic flavours no doubt due, in part, to the relevant aldehydes. For example, the melanoidin from ammonia has been described as bitter [24], that from glycine reminiscent of bread crust [24] or beers [25] and that from

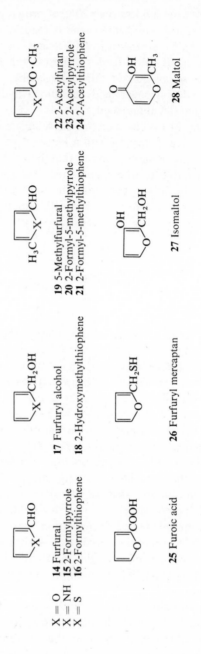

X = O   **14** Furfural
X = NH   **15** 2-Formylpyrrole
X = S   **16** 2-Formylthiophene

17 Furfuryl alcohol
18 2-Hydroxymethylthiophene

19 5-Methylfurfural
20 2-Formyl-5-methylpyrrole
21 2-Formyl-5-methylthiophene

22 2-Acetylfuran
23 2-Acetylpyrrole
24 2-Acetylthiophene

25 Furoic acid

26 Furfuryl mercaptan

27 Isomaltol

28 Maltol

Fig. 14.2 Heterocyclic compounds in roasted barley [30], malt [31] and beer [31, 32].

alanine as bread crust [24], while the valine complex is described as fine malt [24]. The leucine melanoidin has been described as malty [24] or as fresh bread [25] and that for phenylalanine as dead roses, which is the odour of phenylacetaldehyde [25].

TABLE 14.7

Derivatives of pyrrole, thiazole and pyridine in roasted barley [30], *malt* [31], *and beer* [31, 32]

29 Pyrrole	30 Thiazole	31 Pyridine
Unsubstituted	Unsubstituted	Unsubstituted
2-Methyl	4-Methyl	Methyl
	5-Methyl	
	Dimethyl	
1-Acetyl		
2-Acetyl (23)	2-Acetyl	2-Acetyl
		3-Acetyl
2-Formyl-1-methyl		
2-Formyl-5-methyl		
1-Ethyl-2-formyl		
1-Furfuryl		
	5-Hydroxyethyl-4-methyl	

As mentioned above browning reactions occur when malt is kilned and the amount of melanoidins formed depends upon the kilning temperature. Thus crystal malt and roasted barley are richer in melanoidins than lager or pale ale malts. In addition to 5-hydroxymethylfurfural (Fig 14.1; **9**, R = CH_2OH) other heterocyclic compounds resulting from browning have been found in beers (Fig 14.2). The level of 2-acetylfuran (**23**), 2-acetylthiophene (**24**), furfuryl alcohol (**17**), 5-methylfurfural (**19**), and 5-methylthiophene-carboxaldehyde (**21**) is higher in ales than lagers [26] which is probably due to the kilning temperature of the malt used. Compared with pale ale malt, crystal malt contains enhanced levels of most of the compounds shown in Fig. 14.2 but the level of these compounds in beers brewed therefrom is, with the exception of maltol (**28**) and furfuryl mercaptan (**26**), below the taste threshold level [27]. Maltol (3-hydroxy-2-methylpyran-4-one) (**28**) and isomaltol (**27**) are reported to have similar but distinguishable caramel flavours with isomaltol more fruity than maltol [28]. These compounds are obtained from the reaction of sugars with secondary amines [29]. One such secondary amine in wort and beer is pyrrolidine formed by the decarboxylation of proline. Smaller amounts of other heterocyclic bases have been detected in roasted barley [30], malt [31], and beer [31, 32] (Tables 14.7 and 14.8). The pyrazines (Table 14.8) are potent flavouring agents in many foods [33]. They are formed by condensation of the aminoketones formed in the Strecker reaction between α-amino acids and α-dicarbonyl compounds:

$$2 \begin{matrix} R^1 \\ \quad CH-NH_2 \\ \quad | \\ R^2 \quad C=O \end{matrix} \xrightarrow{-H_2O} \xrightarrow{-2H} $$

$$(32; \; R^1 = R^2 = H)$$

TABLE 14.8

Pyrazines in roasted barley [30], malt [31] and beer [31, 32]

32 Pyrazine   33 5H-Cyclopentapyrazine

Pyrazine		Concentration (ppb)	
		Malt	Beer
1	Methylpyrazine	280	70
2	2,5-Dimethylpyrazine	130	110
3	2,6-Dimethylpyrazine	120	35
4	2,3-Dimethylpyrazine	200	15
5	Ethylpyrazine	140	10
6	2-Ethyl-6-methylpyrazine	80	
7	2-Ethyl-5-methylpyrazine	40	35
8	2-Ethyl-3-methylpyrazine	80	+
9	Trimethylpyrazine	320	20
10	2-Ethyl-3,6-dimethylpyrazine	10	20
11	2-Ethyl-3,5-dimethylpyrazine	30	10
12	2-Ethyl-5,6-dimethylpyrazine	10	+
13	Tetramethylpyrazine	110	+
14	6,7-Dihydro-5H-cyclopentapyrazine	+	10
15	5-Methyl-6,7-dihydro-5H-cyclopentapyrazine	20	15
16	2-Methyl-6,7-dihydro-5H-cyclopentapyrazine	20	10
17	5-Methylcyclopentapyrazine	10	+
18	2-Furylpyrazine	+	25
19	2-(2'-Furyl)methylpyrazine	−	10
20	2-(2'-Furyl)dimethylpyrazine	−	+

+ Detected but not quantified.   − Not detected.

The level of the various pyrazines has been monitored throughout the brewing process [34]. As well as the expected rise in the level of pyrazines during wort boiling, further increases occurred during fermentation.

Hexose sugars such as glucose, galactose, mannose, fructose, and sorbose also react with secondary amines (24 hr in basic ethanol at 70–80°C) to give aminohexose reductones (34), which behave as true reductones [29, 35]. Reductones contain the grouping -C(OH) =C(OH)·C = O and the best

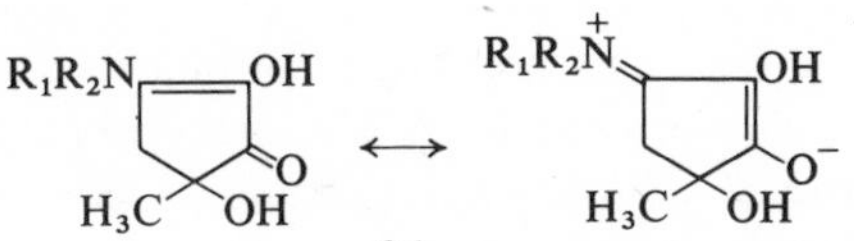

34

characterized reductone is undoubtedly ascorbic acid (vitamin C) (35) which has been detected in green malt and in the leaves of green hops but is destroyed during kilning.

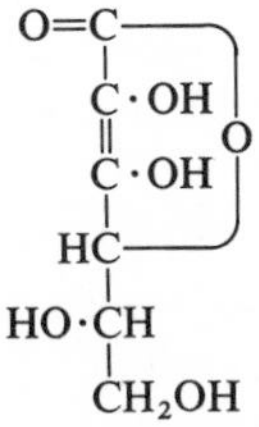

35 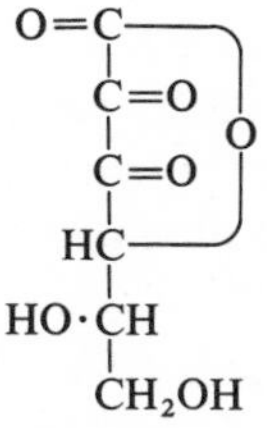   36

Ascorbic acid, and other reductones, readily combine with oxygen and accordingly ascorbic acid finds use as a chill-proofing agent in beer (see Chapter 22). Ascorbic acid (35) is reversibly oxidized to dehydroascorbic acid (36) but more extensive decomposition occurs under quite mild conditions. In model experiments designed to assess the efficiency of various substances to degrade valine to isobutyraldehyde by the Strecker mechanism, dehydro-ascorbic acid (36) was 5–10 times as active as fructose which, in turn, was 2–3 times more active than glucose or sucrose, or ascorbic, pyruvic, or chlorogenic (41) acids [36]. Ascorbic acid is usually estimated colorimetrically with the oxidation–reduction indicator, 2,6-dichlorophenolindophenol, but other reductones including aminohexose reductones (34) will interfere.

Under optimum conditions, as in caramel formation, most of the reactions discussed in this section will occur in reasonable yield. However, in wort boiling the yields of the various reactions are low and by far the majority of the sugars and amino compounds survive wort boiling unchanged. In one series of experiments [37] 8·6% of the total amino acids and 3·8% of the sugars (maltose, glucose, and fructose) were lost during wort boiling. This implies that about 1 mmol of amino acids and 10 mmol of sugars per litre were involved in melanoidin formation. Of the amino acids 82% of the threonine present was utilized but hardly any of the proline. However, in other experiments the basic amino acids were found to react most readily during wort boiling [15, 16].

Thus, the browning reactions are largely responsible for the colour and characteristic flavour of wort and beer. The measurement of the colour of worts, beers, and caramel is discussed in Chapter 22. Browning reactions can be inhibited by sulphur dioxide which reacts either with 3-deoxyosulose (7) or osulos-3-ene (8) and thus prevents pigment formation [38]. Alternatively, the colour of worts can be reduced by shorter periods of heating but at higher temperatures [39]. Satisfactory coagulation of protein and isomerization of α-acids was obtained by heating under pressure for 300 s at 130°C, 180 s at 140°C or 100 s at 150°C.

14.4.1 CARAMEL

The ultimate product of the browning reaction is caramel. Caramel is a permitted colouring matter and, in Britain, its use, sale and purity criteria are regulated by the Colouring Matter in Food Regulations 1973 [40]. Three types of caramel are manufactured: (*i*) electropositive caramel (approx. 50 000 EBC colour units) which is prepared using ammonia; (*ii*) electro-negative caramel (26 000 EBC colour units), which is prepared using ammonium metabisulphite; and (*iii*) spirit caramel (20 000–25 000 EBC colour units) which, in order to be soluble in alcoholic and acetic acid solutions, is prepared without the use of ammonia.

The electropositive caramel used by the brewing industry is prepared from glucose syrups with high dextrose equivalents and 0.880 ammonia. They are allowed to react together at ambient temperature for at least one week, then at 90°C overnight, and finally at 120°C for about 3 hr. Heating must be carefully controlled to maintain a balance between colour and viscosity. At the appropriate time the mixture is cooled to 80°C, softened water added, and the product blended as required [41]. The product contains 28 lb extract/112 lb, 65% of solids, 2·5–5·0% nitrogen. The isoelectric point lies between 5·0 and 7·0 but gel electrophoresis shows the heterogeneous nature of the product. The level of copper (< 5 ppm), iron (< 20 ppm), and arsenic (< 3 ppm) is controlled.

37

Electronegative caramels cannot be used in beer as they coprecipitate with the electropositive finings. Certain caramels have been found to contain

4-methylimidazole (37) which is toxic to rabbits, mice, and chickens. The World Health Organization has proposed a limit of 200 mg 4-methylimidazole/200 kg caramel having a colour intensity of 20 000 EBC units. None of the commercial samples examined exceeded this limit [42].

Caramel may be used either in the copper or in primings to make minor adjustments to the colour of beer but the fundamental colour of the beer will be determined by the choice of malt grist and the grade of adjuncts added to the copper.

14.5 *Protein–polyphenol (tannin) interactions*

Fundamentally, tannins are extractives of various plants which react with the proteins in animal hides to produce leather [43]. Such extractives are polyphenolic in nature so that unfortunately the term tannin is also used to cover all polyphenolic materials in a plant extract whether or not they have the ability to tan leather. In the brewing process polyphenolic constituents from both malt and hops react with proteins; (*i*) during wort boiling to form the hot break, (*ii*) during cooling to form the cold break, and (*iii*) during conditioning and storage when chill haze and permanent haze slowly develop. Tannins may be divided into hydrolysable tannins and non-hydrolysable or condensed tannins, and commercial tanning materials consist largely of hydrolysable polymers of gallic acid (38 : R = R′ = OH) (see [44] for a review). Gallic acid was found to occur in hop polyphenols as long ago as 1820 but has not been detected in malt polyphenolics so that the polyphenolic constituents extracted at wort boiling are largely condensed tannins. Both simple and polymerized phenols are extracted at wort boiling and the simple constituents may conveniently be divided into three classes:

(a) *Derivatives of hydroxybenzoic and hydroxycinnamic acids*

As well as gallic acid (38 : R = R′ = OH), whose occurrence in hops was mentioned above, *p*-hydroxybenzoic acid (38 : R = R′ = H), vanillic acid (39 : R = O·CH₃; R′ = H), syringic acid (38 : R = R′ = O·CH₃), *p*-coumaric acid (39 : R = R′ = H), and ferulic acid (39 : R = O·CH₃, R′ = H) have been detected in barley, malt and beer (see [45] and references there cited). Protocatechuic acid (38 : R = OH, R′ = H) and caffeic acid (39 : R = OH, R′ = H) have also been detected in hops. These acids, as well as occurring in free state, are also found as esters and glycosides. For example, in hydrolysates of beer polyphenols in addition to the acids listed above, sinapic acid (39 : R = R′ = O·CH₃) and gentisic acid (40) have been found. Caffeic acid (39 : R = OH; R′ = H) is found bound as chlorogenic acid (41) and neochlorogenic acid (42) in hops. Chlorogenic acid has also been found in certain malts. The level of many of these compounds has been monitored throughout the brewing process [34].

38   39   40

41   42

(b) *Flavanols*

The flavanols, which are extracted principally from hops, consist of quercetin (**43** : R = H, R′ = H) and kaempferol (**44** : R = H) and their glycosides. Fourteen glycosides have been characterized in hops including quercitrin (**43** : R = rhamnosyl, R′ = H), isoquercitrin (**43** : R = β-D-glucosyl, R′ = H), rutin (**43** : R = β-L-rhamnosido-6-β-D-glucosyl, R′ = H), and astragalin (**44** : R = β-D-glucosyl). Much smaller amounts of myricetin (**43** : R = H, R′ = OCH$_3$) have been detected in English hops.

43   44

(c) *Proanthocyanidins, anthocyanogens and catechins* [46]

The red and blue pigments found in flowers are due to anthocyanidins or their glycosides, anthocyanins. Also widely distributed in the plant kingdom are a group of compounds originally called leucoanthocyanins which liberate anthocyanidins on acid hydrolysis. For example, substances which liberate the anthocyanidins, cyanidin (**57**) and delphinidin (**58**) on acid hydrolysis are found both in hops and malt. These compounds are not leuco-compounds within the classical meaning of organic chemistry, i.e. the colour-forming reaction is not reversible, and it was suggested that the precursors should be known as anthocyanogens. This term has been widely accepted in the brewing literature. However it has been shown that there are two classes of anthocyanogens and Weinges [47] has proposed that monomeric derivatives of flavan-3, 4-diol, e.g. (54), should be called leucoanthocyanidins and that compounds with two or more linked flavan-3-ol units should be called condensed proanthocyanidins. The related flavan-3-ol (+)-catechin (49) is present in barley, hops and beer (0·5–7·0 ppm) together with smaller amounts of (−)-epicatechin (51), (+)-gallocatechin (50), and (−)-epigallocatechin (52). Many workers have detected anthocyanogens in brewing materials but were unable to isolate them due to their extreme sensitivity to acids and aerial oxidation. By chromatography on a dextran gel Gramshaw [48] was able to isolate six anthocyanogens from a beer polyamide absorbate. One of these compounds was assigned the 3,3′, 4,4′, 5,7-hexahydroxyflavan structure (54) but this identification has been questioned [49].

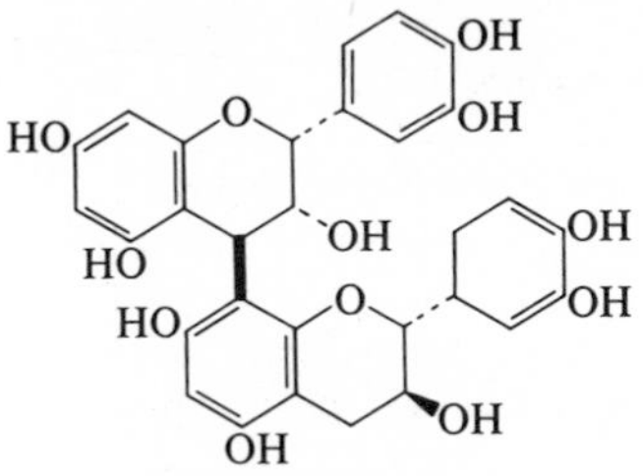

45 Procyanidin B-1
⎡epicatechin⎤
⎢ | ⎥
⎣ catechin ⎦

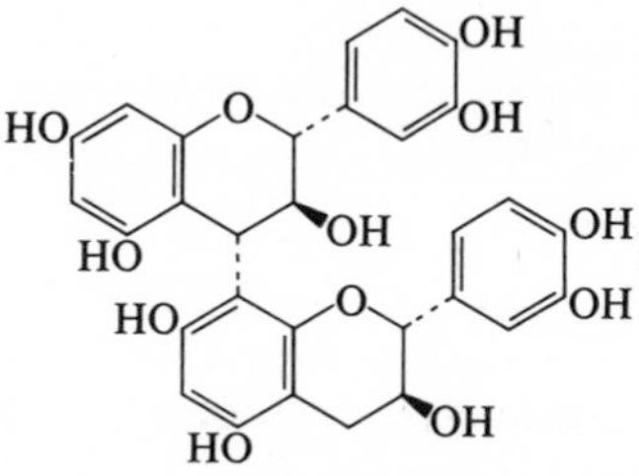

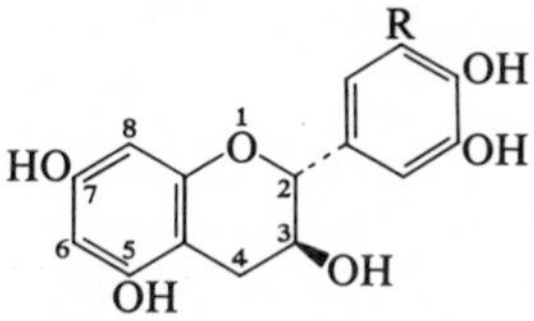

49 Catechin (R = H)
50 Gallocatechin (R = OH)

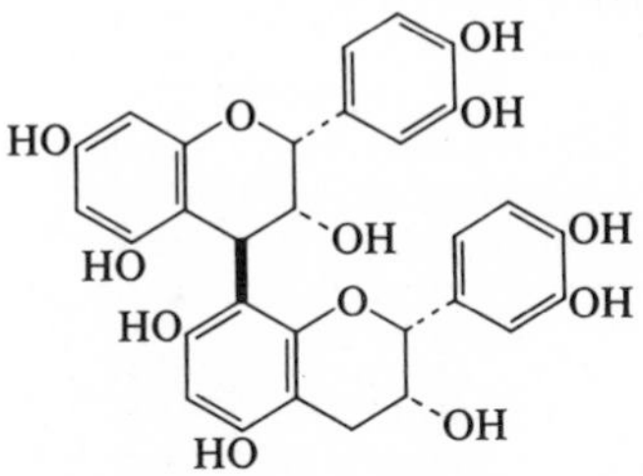

47 Procyanidin B-3
⎡ catechin ⎤
⎢ | ⎥
⎣ catechin ⎦

46 Procyanidin B-2
⎡epicatechin⎤
⎢ | ⎥
⎣epicatechin⎦

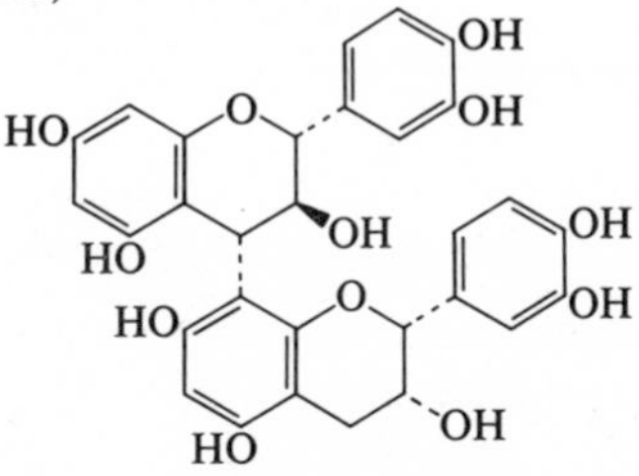

48 Procyanidin B-4
⎡ catechin ⎤
⎢ | ⎥
⎣epicatechin⎦

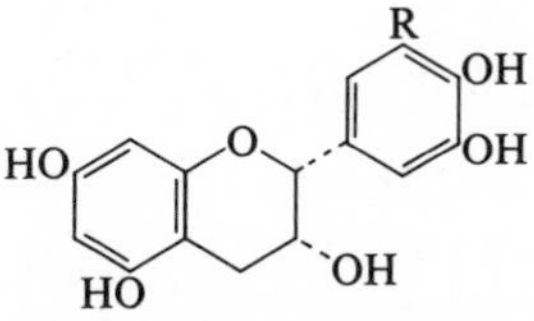

51 epiCatechin (R = H)
52 epiGallocatechin (R = OH)

Flavan-3,4-diols are now thought to be of limited natural occurrence whereas dimeric proanthocyanidins are widely distributed in nature. Weinges has characterized four dimeric procyanidins B-1 to B-4 (45)–(48). Of these procyanidins B-3 (dimeric catechin) is present in barley and malt [50] and procyanidins B-1, B-2, B-3, and B-4 are present in hops [51].

Malt contains 90–400 ppm of procyanidin B-3 of which half is extracted during infusion mashing but considerable losses occur during wort boiling and fermentation (Table 14.9) [52]. Increasing the length of the boil reduces the level of dimeric polyphenols in beer (Table 14.10). Nevertheless commercial beers contain 0·5–4·0 mg/l and one experimental beer contained 22·0 mg/l of procyanidin B-3 [53].

TABLE 14.9

Losses of dimeric polyphenols during brewing [52]

Barley cultivar	Malt		Dimeric polyphenols found (mg/l)		
	In grain (mg/kg)	Potential contribution to beer (mg/l)	Sweet wort	Boiled wort	Beer
Maris Otter	250	38	18·3	9·5	7·9
Maris Otter	230	35	15·5	7·0	6·3
Julia	155	23	11·4	6·0	4·9
Maris Mink	210	32	–	–	6·0

TABLE 14.10

Effect of wort boiling on the loss of dimeric polyphenols [52]

Malt	Length of boil (hr)	Dimeric polyphenols in beer (mg/l)	Shelf-life of beer (days)	Air in headspace (ml)
Maris Otter (A)	1·0	15·0	45	1·0
Maris Otter (A)	1·5	9·2	66	1·1
Maris Otter (A)	2·0	8·1	70	1·1
Julia (B)	1·0	7·8	77	0·9
Julia (B)	1·5	3·3	98	1·1

With acid procyanidin B-1 and B-3 yield catechin and cyanidin while procyanidin B-2 and B-4 give epicatechin and cyanidin. The formation of cyanidin (Fig. 14.3) proceeds via the carbonium ion (55) and the same intermediate is involved in the conversion of the flavan-3,4-diol (54) into cyanidin. If the carbonium ion (55) is generated, from (54), in the presence of catechin a dimeric procyanidin B is formed. Similarly, if the carbonium ion is generated in the presence of procyanidin B this will lead to a trimer (59) similar to that isolated by Gramshaw (Compound 58). It can easily be envisaged that further condensation of the triflavan (59) with a carbonium ion, as (55), will lead to polymeric anthocyanogens. These materials are involved in the development of non-biological hazes in beer as will be discussed in Chapter 22.

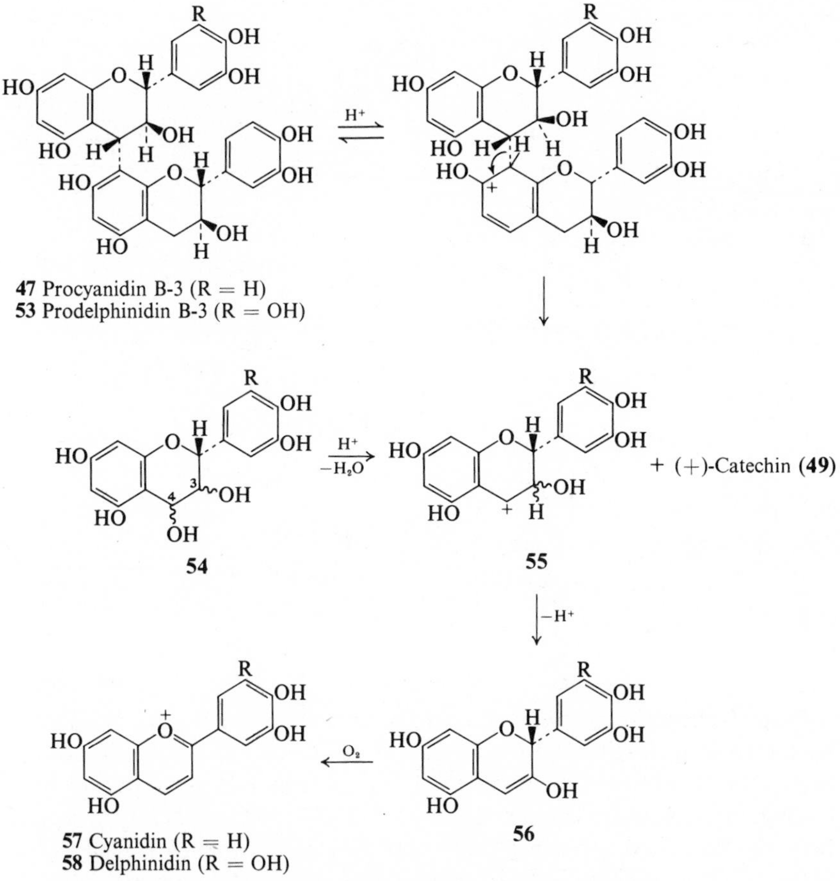

47 Procyanidin B-3 (R = H)
53 Prodelphinidin B-3 (R = OH)

54

55

+ (+)-Catechin **(49)**

57 Cyanidin (R = H)
58 Delphinidin (R = OH)

56

Fig. 14.3 Acid degradation of anthocyanogens.

The prodelphinidins are less well characterized. Barley and beer contain a biflavan which gives catechin and delphinidin (58) on treatment with acid in agreement with structure (53) with either procyanidin B-1 or B-3 stereochemistry [51, 54]. Evidence for the occurrence of a [catechin–gallocatechin] biflavan in beer has been presented [54] but [gallocatechin–gallocatechin] biflavans have not been reported.

Procyanidin B-3, [catechin–catechin] should not be confused with dicatechin (60), formed by acid treatment of catechin, which also may be present in beer [54].

Polymeric proanthocyanidins in several plant species have a homogeneous polyflavan-3-ol structure (61) with mol. wt. in the regions 1800–6400 which corresponds to 6–22 flavan-3-ol units [55].

59   60

61

Protein–phenol interactions [56] in the brewing process have principally been studied with regard to the formation of non-biological haze in bottled beer (Chapter 22) but similar reactions undoubtedly take place during wort boiling. Proteins and phenolic compounds initially react together by hydrogen bonding. The bond between phenols and N-substituted amides, such as the peptide links in proteins, is the strongest type of hydrogen bond. Accordingly, urea, $NH_2 \cdot CO \cdot NH_2$, is used to displace weaker hydrogen bonds and to destroy tertiary structure in proteins. Similarly, polyphenols are adsorbed on synthetic polyamides such as nylon or polyvinylpyrrolidone but such reactions are usually reversible and the polyphenols can be displaced. On storage, oxidation may occur with the formation of covalent bonds between proteins and polyphenols. The mechanism of these reactions is not completely understood but one suggestion (Fig. 14.4) is that catechol residues (62), as in, for example, chlorogenic acid (41), catechin (49), and procyanidins (45)–(48), are oxidized to o-quinones (63). Such quinones readily react with amino acids and free amino and thiol groups in proteins to give substituted catechols (64)–(66). These, in turn, may be oxidized again to give substituted o-quinones, such as (68), which react further to give cross-linked products, such as (69). In addition, the o-quinones may react with amino acids by a Strecker reaction (p. 465).

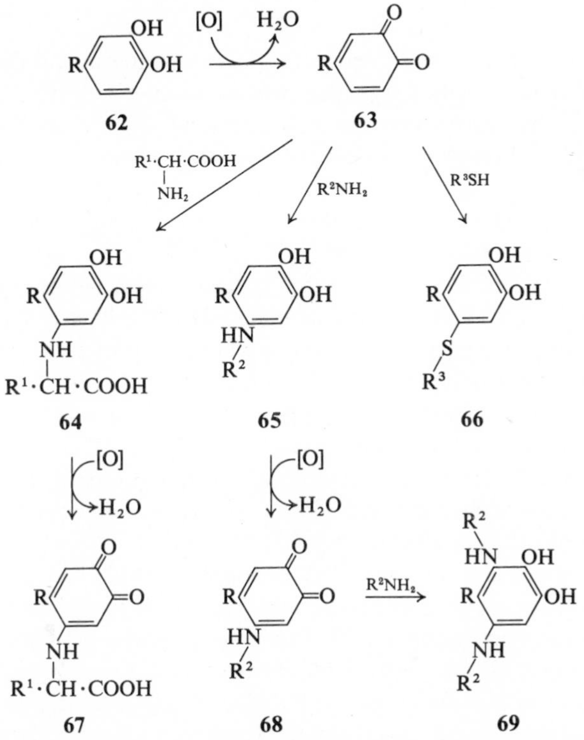

Fig. 14.4 Proposed reactions of polyphenols with reactive groups in proteins (after Pierpoint [57]).

A general colorimetric method for estimating phenols by coupling with diazotized p-aminobenzoic acid has been developed and used to investigate the changes in phenolic constituents during mashing and wort boiling [58]. Dialysable and non-dialysable compounds and the level of anthocyanogens were measured. The pattern of extraction of phenolic constituents is shown in Fig. 9.6 and the changes during wort boiling in Table 14.11. These latter

TABLE 14.11

Phenolic constituents of worts at beginning and end of copper boil [58]

Wort	Specific gravity	Beginning of boil		Hopped worts		% change	
		Total	Dialysable	Total	Dialysable	Total	Dialysable
1	1·0798	815	615	990	625	+21·0	+1·6
2	1·0750	770	585	810	595	+5·0	+1·3
3	1·0414	340	400	360	480	+5·9	+20·0
4	1·0140	190	145	160	160	−15·5	+10·0
5	1·0066	180	135	140	135	−22.0	0

results are the net effect of the extraction of hop material and the removal of phenols on the break with coagulated protein. Boiling with strong wort causes an increase in the total content of phenolic material, little of which is dialysable. Protein–flavanoid reactions have been regarded as reversible [58].

Protein + flavanoid ⇌ Soluble Complex → Complex precipitate

With each species of flavanoid the free phenol is regarded as being in equilibrium with the flavanoid–protein complex. Much evidence has been cited, however, that simple polyphenols do not react with protein to form insoluble haze and that only polymerized polyphenols are immediate haze precursors [59]. The addition of polymeric polyphenols, from various sources, to beer resulted in immediate haze formation.

The fate of the dimeric polyphenols in brewing is illustrated in Table 14.9 and it seems probable that even less of the higher oligomeric polyphenols will remain in solution after wort boiling. However, following aeration and the change of pH during fermentation, simple phenols will polymerize and then react with protein to form chill and permanent haze. Different types of polyphenol can copolymerize and permanent bonding between polyphenols and proteins may also occur by copolymerization of the polyphenols with the phenolic residues of proteins such as tyrosine, phenylalanine, and tryptophan.

The role of protein–polyphenol interactions with regard to the development of non-biological haze is discussed further in Chapter 22 together with the methods employed to inhibit these reactions and prolong the shelf-life of bottled beer.

14.6 *Hop resin interactions* [60, 61, 62]

The hop resins, discussed in Chapter 13, may be regarded as a further class of polyphenolic compounds and as such will react with protein and nitrogenous compounds by hydrogen bonding and may well copolymerize with the compounds discussed above. In addition they undergo a series of reactions leading to the bittering principles of beer.

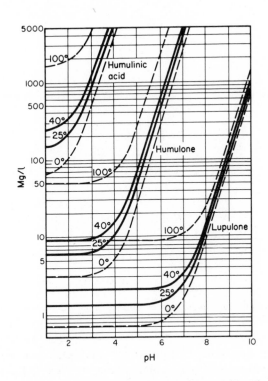

Fig. 14.5 Solubilities of humulinic acid, humulone, and lupulone [63].

The hop resins are not very soluble in wort; the solubility of humulone and lupulone is dependent on temperature as illustrated in Fig. 14.5. [63]. Thus at the pH of wort (5·0) only 40 mg of humulone is soluble in one litre of water at 25°C and 60 mg/l at 100°C. The solubility of lupulone is much less: 1·2 and 9·0 mg/l at 25°C and 100°C respectively. If, therefore, hops containing, say, 5% of α-acid are used at a rate of 0·28 kg/hl (1 lb/barrel), all the α-acid could go into solution at 100°C to produce a wort containing 56·6 mg of α-acid/l. However, on cooling such a wort, humulone would be precipitated on to the break from the supersaturated solution. After fermentation, when the pH drops to 4·0, and the wort is conditioned at about 0°C any humulone in excess of 5 mg/l (Fig. 14.5) will be precipitated, and in practice only small amounts of humulone are detected in finished beer. The most important bittering principles found in beer are the iso-α-acids formed from α-acids during wort boiling.

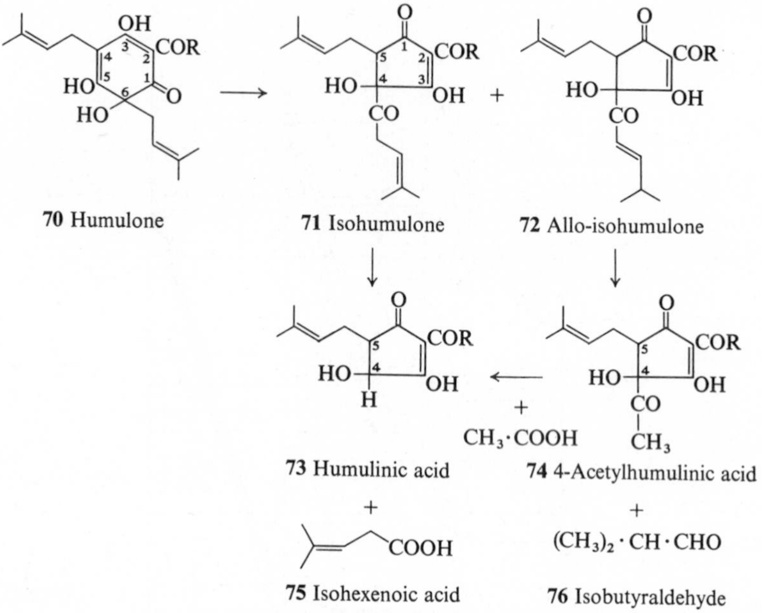

Fig. 14.6 Isomerization and hydrolysis of humulone ($R = CH_2CHMe_2$) (without stereo-chemistry).

Hydrolysis of humulone (**70**) gives humulinic acid, m.p. 95°C (**73**), now known as *trans*-humulinic acid, isobutyraldehyde (**76**), and isohexenoic acid (**75**) (Fig. 14.6). The five-membered ring structure of humulinic acid was established by the reactions set out in Fig. 13.1. In 1925 it was suggested that the hydrolysis proceeded through an intermediate which was formulated as (**71**) but not isolated at that time [64]. Later, structure (**71**) was assigned to the bitter-tasting resinous oil obtained by boiling humulone with N/15 sodium hydroxide for 3 min [65]. It was originally called 'Resin A' [65] but later the term isohumulone was adopted [66]. It was also envisaged that isohumulone could be hydrolysed to isobutyraldehyde (**76**) and 'Resin B' (4-acetylhumulinic acid) (**74**) and that the latter would break down to humulinic and acetic acids. The existence of 'Resin B' was not substantiated until 1968 when it was suggested that this mode of hydrolysis proceeded via *allo*-isohumulone (**72**).

The structures assigned to isohumulone (**71**), humulinic acid (**73**), and 4-acetylhumulinic acid (**74**) each contain two chiral centres and should exist as two pairs of enantiomers. Since natural (*R*) (—)-humulone is a single enantiomer only two diastereoisomeric forms are found; these are the *cis* and *trans* isomers (the enantiomers of these forms would be obtained from unnatural (*S*) (+)-humulone).

The following definitions have been given [67]:

The iso-α-acids. These are mainly isohumulone, isocohumulone, and iso-adhumulone.

Isohumulone. The mixture of *cis*- and *trans*-isohumulone. Similarly iso-cohumulone refers to the mixture of *cis*- and *trans*-isocohumulone and isoadhumulone refers to the mixture of *cis*- and *trans*- isoadhumulone.

cis-*Isohumulone.* The iso-α-acid with empirical formula $C_{21}H_{30}O_5$. It is an oil with the higher partition coefficient in a phase system of a hydrocarbon and a buffer, and contains an isovaleryl side-chain. *Cis* means that the 3-methyl-2-butenyl side-chain and the tertiary hydroxyl group are on the same side of the ring.

trans-*Isohumulone.* The iso-α-acid with the empirical formula $C_{21}H_{30}O_5$, with m.p. 72°C and the lower partition coefficient in a phase system of a hydrocarbon and a buffer and contains an isovaleryl side-chain. *Trans* means that the 3-methyl-2-butenyl side-chain and the tertiary hydroxyl group are on opposite sides of the ring.

cis-*Isocohumulone.* As in cis-*Isohumulone*, but with reference to $C_{20}H_{28}O_5$ and an isobutyryl side-chain.

trans-*Isocohumulone.* As in *trans-Isohumulone*, but with reference to $C_{20}H_{28}O_5$ and an isobutyryl side-chain.

cis-*Isoadhumulone.* As in cis-*isohumulone*, but with reference to a 2-methyl-butyryl side-chain.

trans-*Isoadhumulone.* As in *trans-isohumulone*, but with reference to a 2-methylbutyryl side-chain.

Allo-iso-α-acids. These are the isomers of the iso-α-acids having a shifted double bond in the isohexenoyl side-chain. Of each allo-iso-α-acid there is a *cis* and a *trans* form.

Humulinic acids. These consist of *cis* and *trans* forms of humulinic, co-humulinic, and adhumulinic acids.

cis-*Humulinic acid.* Has empirical formula $C_{15}H_{22}O_4$ with m.p. 68°C and the higher partition coefficient in a phase system of a hydrocarbon and a buffer. *Cis* means the 3-methyl-2-butenyl side-chain and the alcoholic ring hydroxyl group are on the same side of the ring.

trans-*Humulinic acid.* Has empirical formula $C_{15}H_{22}O_4$ with m.p. 95°C and the lower partition coefficent in a phase system of a hydrocarbon and a buffer. *Trans* means the 3-methyl-2-butenyl side-chain and the alcoholic ring hydroxyl group are on opposite sides of the ring.

Examination of the bittering principles of beer by counter-current distribution resolved them into three products, later shown to correspond to the isomerization products of the three α-acids present in hops [68]. It was noted, however, that the distribution curves for each product, isohumulone, iso-cohumulone, and isoadhumulone were about 15% broader than those calculated for a pure substance and two distribution curves could be accommodated under the broadened pattern [69]. The same broadened pattern was given by isohumulone prepared by boiling humulone with N/15 sodium hydroxide for 3 min [65] or with 0·1 N sodium carbonate solution for 20 min [70]. Further evidence for the heterogeneous nature of isohumulone was provided by reversed-phase chromatography [71]. The product of boiling humulone in a buffer solution at pH 5·0 gave rise to two peaks while the bittering substances of beer gave rise to six peaks, two for each isohumulone. Eventually, in 1964–5, the two isomers of isohumulone were separated on a preparative scale; (*i*) by reversed-phase chromatography [72], (*ii*) by counter-current distribution after 2000 transfers [73], and (*iii*) by partition chromatography on silica gel using a solvent mixture of iso-octane (2, 2, 4-trimethyl-pentane) and ethyl acetate [74]. It was also found that humulone can also be isomerized into *trans*-isohumulone by irradiation with visible light [74]. The properties of the two isomers of isohumulone are given in Table 14.12. With regard to bitterness, one group reports that (+)-*cis*-isohumulone, (−)-*trans*-isohumulone, and racemic (±)-*trans*-isohumulone do not show significant differences in bitter taste or bittering power [73, 75] but others think that *cis*-isohumulone is slightly more bitter than the *trans*-isomer [74, 76].

TABLE 14.12

Properties of cis- *and* trans-*isohumulone*

	cis-	*trans-*
Structure (R = CO·CH$_2$·CH = C(CH$_3$)$_2$)	**81**	**80**
Melting point	Oil	72°
[α]$_D$ (methanol) [73]	+47·6°	−7·8°
Partition coefficient in iso-octane phosphate–citrate buffer solution (pH 5·5)	0·784	0·61
pH at which eluted from reversed phase column [72]	6·0	5·8
Light absorption [73] λ$_{max}$(nm)		
in acidic methanol	227 (ε 10 740)	233 (ε 11 860)
	280 (ε 11 270)	272 (ε 10 160)
in alkaline methanol	255 (ε 18 810)	255 (ε 18 280)
	270*(ε 14 690)	270*(ε 10 160)

* Value at shoulder of curve.

The structures assigned to the two forms of isohumulone followed from earlier studies on humulinic acid. A second isomer of humulinic acid, m.p. 68°C, *cis*-humulinic acid, was isolated by countercurrent distribution of the mother liquors remaining after crystallization of the known *trans*-humulinic acid [77, 78]. It was also prepared by a chemical route: oxidation of *trans*-humulinic acid with bismuth oxide gave dehydrohumulinic acid (**78**) and reduction of this product with sodium borohydride afforded the *cis*-isomer.

Treatment of *cis*-humulinic acid with alkali caused it to revert to the *trans* form; the equilibrium mixture consists of over 90% of *trans*-humulinic acid. Oxidation of *cis*-humulinic acid with bismuth oxide also gave dehydro-humulinic acid [79]. This result suggested that the two humulinic acids were epimeric at C-4 and this was confirmed by proton magnetic resonance spectroscopy [79]. Thus in *trans*-humulinic acid (**77** or **80** : R = H) the C-4 hydroxy group and the C-5 isopentenyl chain have the *trans* configuration and lie on opposite sides of the planar cyclopentenone ring. In *cis*-humulinic acid (**79** or **81** : R = H) both bulky substituents lie on the same side of the ring. All these compounds exist as mixtures of tautomers.

These observations were readily extended to explain the occurrence of two isomeric isohumulones (**80** and **81**; R = CO·CH$_2$·CH = C (CH$_3$)$_2$). In the proton magnetic resonance spectrum of isohumulone, the signal given by the proton at C-5 was split. This indicates that it was a mixture of 60% of the isomer (**81**; R = CO·CH$_2$·CH = C(CH$_3$)$_2$) with *cis*-humulinic acid stereo-chemistry and 40% of the isomer (**80**; R = CO·CH$_2$·CH = C(CH$_3$)$_2$) with *trans*-humulinic acid stereochemistry [80]. In isohumulone there are two bulky substituents at C-4 so the two isomers will have similar stabilities. The proportions of the two isomers found by proton magnetic resonance spectroscopy were in good agreement with the estimates obtained from countercurrent distribution and reversed-phase chromatography [69, 71].

When the two stereoisomers were separated the structural assignments made on the mixture were confirmed.

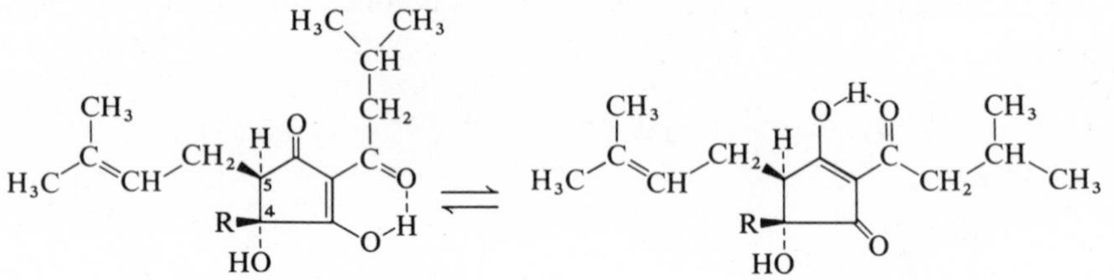

80

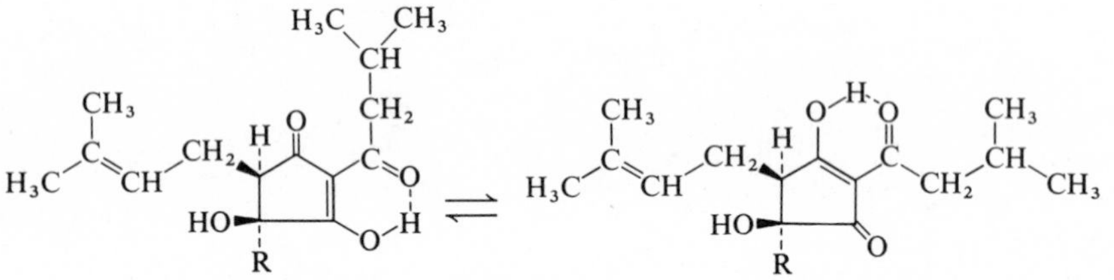

81

The gross structure of the iso-α-acids has been substantiated by an elegant synthesis of (±)-isohumulone [81]. The product was an oil which gave an infrared spectrum identical with that of isohumulone and which on hydrolysis afforded *trans*-humulinic acid. (±)-Isocohumulone and (±)-isoadhumulone were later synthesized by the same route [82]. The overall yields in these syntheses are low so that synthetic iso-α-acids are more readily available by isomerization of synthetic α-acids [83] (see Chapter 13).

The isomerization of humulone is chemically a type of benzilic acid or acyloin rearrangement and the mechanism is illustrated in Fig. 14.7. The isomerization follows first-order kinetics in buffer solutions of constant pH but in wort the rate falls off probably on account of the lowering of pH.

Further study of the isomerization of humulone into isohumulone has shown that both in 0·1 N sodium carbonate solutions (pH 10·0) and in a phosphate buffer solution (pH 9·0) some hydrolysis to humulinic acid occurs · [72, 85]. In the pH range 6·5–8·0, the isomerization is catalysed by bivalent metals as Ca^{2+}, Mg^{2+}, Cd^{2+} and Mn^{2+} in particular, the Mg^{2+} catalysed isomerization of humulone affords isohumulone free of humulinic acids [86].

The two isomers of isohumulone are not readily converted into one another but this is possible *via* humulone since the humulone–isohumulone isomerization is reversible [87, 88]. For example, when isohumulone is heated alone in a sealed tube, in a buffer solution (pH 4·5), in wort, or in 0·1 N sodium carbonate it yields 10–15% of humulone. This yield is not improved on prolonged heating when increasing amounts of decomposition products are formed so that after 35–40 hr no α-acid or iso-α-acid remain [88]. Isohumulone is also isomerized into humulone in 10–15% yield when it is shaken in a two-phase system of iso-octane and a buffer solution (pH 5.0) [87]. It follows that isohumulone of 100% purity cannot be obtained directly using 0·1 N sodium carbonate solution and that some reversion back into humulone may occur during counter-current distribution of isohumulone.

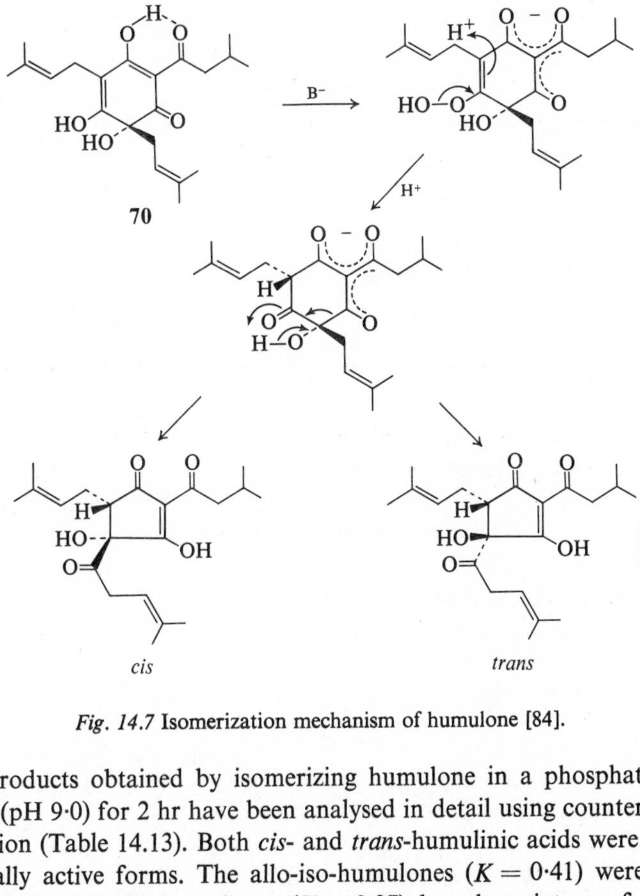

Fig. 14.7 Isomerization mechanism of humulone [84].

The products obtained by isomerizing humulone in a phosphate buffer solution (pH 9·0) for 2 hr have been analysed in detail using counter-current distribution (Table 14.13). Both *cis*- and *trans*-humulinic acids were isolated in optically active forms. The allo-iso-humulones ($K = 0·41$) were readily separated from the isohumulones ($K = 0·87$) but the mixture of allo-iso-humulone isomers was not resolved even after 1000 transfers. The proton magnetic resonance spectrum of the mixture, however, established the presence of (**80 and 81**) (R = CO·CH = CH·CH(CH$_3$)$_2$) [73, 89]. Later

cis- and trans-allo-isohumulone were resolved: trans-allo-isohumulone
(**80**; R = CO·CH = CH·CH (CH₃)₂) is a crystalline solid, m.p. 40°C,
$[\alpha]_D$ + 14° [85]. The yield of allo-isohumulone when humulone was boiled in
wort for 4 hr was 4·5% [89]. The hydrated isohumulones are oils with the
structures (**80** and **81**) (R = CO·CH₂CH (OH)·CH (CH₃)₂). It is very
probable that they are also formed during wort boiling and occur in beer [85].
A further product of the isomerization is cis-4-acetylhumulinic acid (**81**;
R = CO·CH₃), the product postulated earlier as 'Resin B' [65]. Both cis-
and trans-4-acetylhumulinic acids have now been isolated from the hydrolysis
of humulone and isohumulone. It is thought that the reaction proceeds via
allo-isohumulone [90].

TABLE 14.13

Products obtained by heating humulone in a buffer solution (pH 9.0) for 2 hr [85]

	%
Isohumulones	57
Allo-isohumulones	8
Hydrated isohumulones	5
Humulinic acids	2
Front fraction	1·5
Unaccounted (oxidation products)	(±) 26

The isomerization of tetrahydrohumulone (**82**) at pH 9·0 has also been
studied to avoid complications due to the reactivity of the unsaturated side-
chains of humulone. In addition to recovered tetrahydrohumulone (36%),
cis- and trans-tetrahydroisohumulone (51%), and cis and trans-dihydro-
humulinic acid (2·6%), cis-tetrahydrohumulinone (**83**: with side-chain double
bonds saturated) is isolated in 3% yield [91].

82   **83**

It thus appears possible that some humulone is oxidized to cis-humulinone
(**83**) during wort boiling. cis-Humulinone was previously unknown, but has
now been prepared [91] by isomerization of the trans isomer which is readily

available by oxidation of humulone using a hydroperoxide in the presence of sodium hydrogen carbonate (see Chapter 13).

In another investigation [135] (—)-humulone was kept in boiling water, open to the air, for 2·5 hr. In addition to *cis*- and *trans*-isohumulone four products were characterized. One was tricyclodehydroisohumulone (structure (**41**) p. 438), the others (**85**), (**86**), and (**86**a) were isomeric with humulone. The compound tentatively assigned structure (**86**a) was unstable and readily took up another atom of oxygen to give a product probably related to the *abeo*-iso-α-acids. Three *abeo*-iso-α-acids [92] have been isolated, two of which contained one more oxygen atom than isohumulone while the third contained two extra oxygen atoms ($C_{21}H_{30}O_7$) (see p. 790).

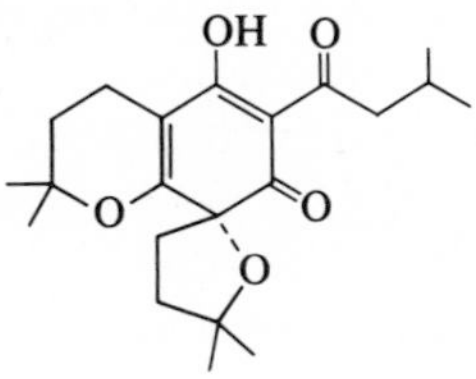

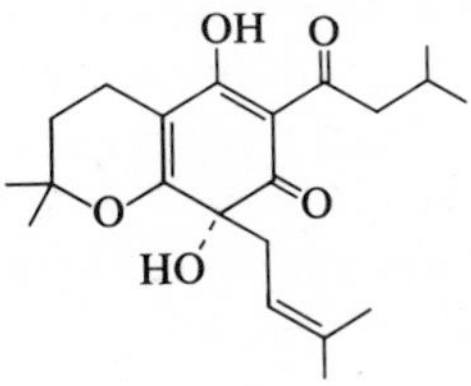

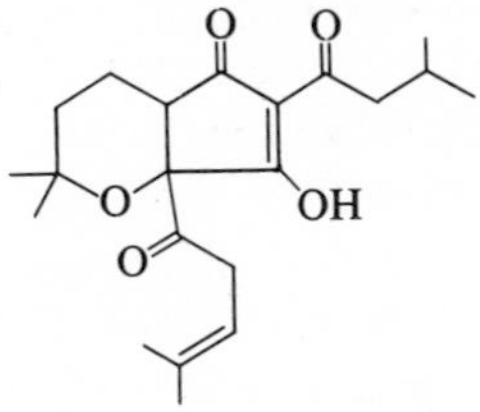

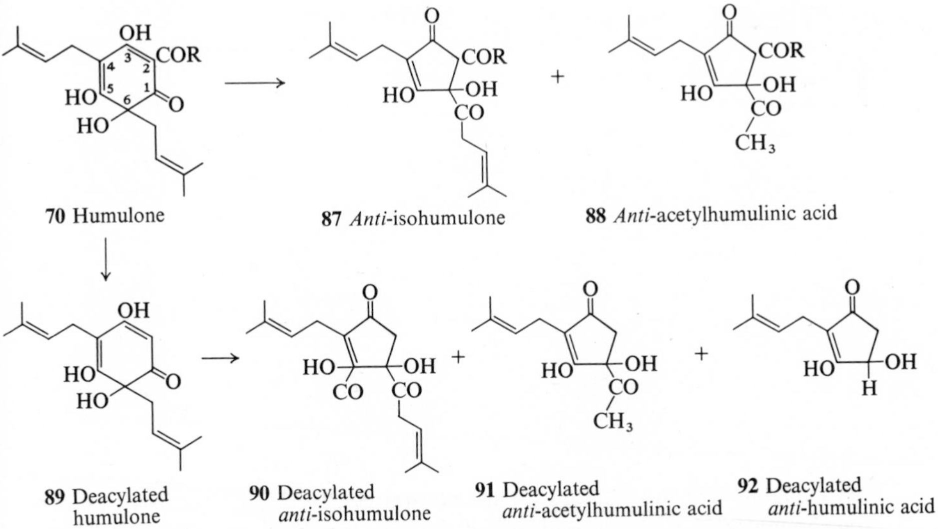

Fig. 14.8 Products of the 'reversed' isomerization of humulone.

In the normal isomerization of humulone (**70**) the bond between C-1 and C-6 is broken and a new bond is formed between C-1 and the carbonyl group at C-5 (Fig. 14.6). The 'reversed' isomerization of humulone (Fig. 14.8), in which the bond between C-5 and C-6 is broken and the new bond formed between C-5 and the carbonyl on C-1, has now been found to occur and the *anti*-products account for about 10% of the isomerization mixture [93]. By boiling humulone in a buffer solution at pH 11·0 the *cis*- and *trans*-isomers of both *anti*-isohumulone (**87**) and *anti*-acetylhumulinic acid (**88**) are formed. The *anti*-isohumulones (**87**) are twice as bitter as the normal isohumulones (**71**) and are the most bitter tasting hop acids known [94]. In the mixture of *anti*-isohumulones the *cis* isomer predominates (*cis/trans* ratio 20: 1). Also present in the isomerization mixture are deacylated *anti*-derivatives: deacylated *anti*-isohumulone (**90**), deacylated *anti*-acetylhumulinic acid (**91**), and deacylated *anti*-humulinic acid (**92**) [93]. Deacylated humulone (**89**) is readily isomerized to these products whereas the deacylation of *anti*-isohumulone only occurs to a limited extent (< 2%) so it has been proposed [95] that (**90**), (**91**) and (**92**) are formed *via* deacylated humulone (**89**). However, the relative ease of deacylation of humulone and *anti*-isohumulone has not been reported. Deacylated derivatives of isohumulone have not been characterized in isomerization mixtures.

To a small extent the β-acids (**93**) are isomerized in a similar manner to the α-acids to give (**95**), which is readily deacylated to (**96**) [96]. Both (**95**) and (**96**) are unstable in acid and give a complex mixture of pyrans. When colupulone is heated under reflux in unhopped wort for 2 hr, a similar mixture was obtained in 1% yield and 90% of the colupulone is recovered. Both (95) and (96) have been found in isomerized hop extracts. They are reported as having a harsh bitterness with a marked after-bitterness [96].

Thus, the reactions that the α-acids of hops can undergo during wort boiling are extremely complex. It is probable that new products and reaction pathways will be elucidated but the most important reaction remains, at least in fresh hops, the isomerization of the α-acids into the *cis* and *trans* isomers of the iso-α-acids. In this respect the efficiency of hop utilization can be defined by the expression:

$$\% \text{ utilization} = \frac{(\text{amount of iso-}\alpha\text{-acids present})}{(\text{amount of }\alpha\text{-acids used})} \times 100\%$$

In conventional brewing practice only about 50% of the α-acids available in the hops go into solution during wort boiling and, with most strains of yeast, further losses occur during fermentation so that the overall utilization will seldom exceed 40% and may be as low as 10%. In wort boiling higher utilization is obtained from weak worts than from strong worts and, as may be anticipated from the solubility of humulone (Fig. 14.5), hops are utilized more efficiently at low rates than at high ones. Indeed, it was concluded that the solubility of humulone was the limiting factor in its utilization [97]. When pure humulone is added to boiling wort it remains as an oily layer on the surface or as droplets of minimal surface area in suspension for the first 1·5 hr of boiling. Only after this period is the majority of the resin (humulone + isohumulone) in solution and on the break (approx. 95% recovery). Only about 7% of the humulone added was lost on the break irrespective of the amount of break formed [97]. In trials using pure humulone, only 50–60% of the resin added was isomerized during 1·5 hr boil. In contrast, 65–75% of the α-acids present in hops are isomerized in the same period, which supports the view that the isomerization of humulone is catalysed by the presence of hop cones, break, or even an inert surface such as Celite [98]. The efficiency of the utilization increases at high pH values and falls with low ones, but only small variations are possible in conventional practice. If hops are extracted and the resins isomerized away from the copper in dilute alkaline solutions, the iso-α-acids can be obtained in almost quantitative yield. When such isomerized hop extracts are used to bitter fermented wort, greatly superior utilization can be achieved [99] (see Section 14.7).

The level of α-acid in hops falls during storage but the bittering potential of the hops does not fall to the same extent (Fig. 13.5). This is because many of the oxidation products of both α- and β-acids discussed in Chapter 13 are capable of bittering beer. However, at the present time, the nature of the major bittering principles in beer brewed from old hops is not known.

Mention should be made of the alleged superior utilization of cohumulone. Analysis of the proportions of the isobutyryl, isovaleryl, and 2-methylbutyryl analogues in the bittering substances of beer indicated that the proportion of isocohumulones in beer was greater than the proportion of cohumulone in the hops used. This suggested that cohumulone was utilized more efficiently than the other α-acids and the average efficiencies were given as: cohumulone, 36%; humulone 20%; and adhumulone, 26% [100]. However, further study revealed that the bittering principles of beer also contained material derived from the β-acids (93) which was not resolved from the iso-α-acids in the systems then used [101]. As was mentioned in Chapter 13, β-acids are always richer in the isobutyryl analogue than the α-acids according to the regression equation:

$$\% \text{ colupulone in } \beta\text{-acids} = 0\cdot943 \ (\% \text{ cohumulone in } \alpha\text{-acid}) + 20\cdot2 \ [102].$$

It follows that any contamination of the isohumulones with material derived from β-acids will lead to a higher proportion of isobutyryl analogues. At least two groups of principles derived from the β-acids are present in beer in approximately equal proportions [101]. One of these was identified as the hulupones (94). Hulupones are known oxidation products of the β-acids (see Chapter 13) and are formed to a limited extent during wort boiling, although one estimate is that only 1% of the available β-acid is converted to hulupone [103].

The contamination of the iso-α-acids with material derived from the β-acids provides a satisfactory explanation for some of the reported superior utilization of cohumulone. But the levels of hulupones and other products derived from the β-acids found so far cannot account for all the superior utilization claimed. In brewing trials using mixed α-acids, and thus excluding interference from β-acids, cohumulone was utilized slightly better than the other analogues [104]. Support is given by the pK_a values quoted in Table 13.1 which indicate that cohumulone is appreciably more dissociated in wort than the other two analogues. However, more recent work has established that isohumulone is concentrated more than isocohumulone into the head and foam fractions of beer [105]. The results of one trial brew indicate that humulone and cohumulone are utilized to the same extent into wort but that isohumulone is preferentially removed with fermenter skimmings, yeast, and trub so that there is a superior utilization of cohumulone into beer [106].

It is known that increasing the pH of beer produces a coarser bitter flavour so it follows that the undissociated iso-α-acids have a finer bitter flavour than the dissociated anion. Thus, Rigby [106] has proposed that there is a similar difference between the dissociation constants of the iso-α-acids as there is between the α-acids (Table 13.1). (Accurate measurements of the pK_a of iso-α-acids is difficult : values quoted vary from 3·2–5·2.) Accordingly iso-cohumulone is appreciably more dissociated in beer than isohumulone and beers brewed from hops rich in humulone will have a finer bitter flavour. In practice traditional continental and US breweries have preferred hop varieties with low proportions of cohumulone in their α-acids and this feature is now sought in US hop breeding programmes.

14.7 *Analysis of bitter principles*

The estimation of iso-α-acids in wort, beer, and isomerized hop extracts is usually based on their light-absorption properties (Table 14.12). Measurements are made at 275 nm in acid solution or 255 nm in alkaline solution. Humulinic acids, which possess no bitterness, show similar light absorption to the iso-α-acids. Both α- and β-acids show appreciable absorption at the wavelengths mentioned so all these must be absent from the extract analysed. Hulupones exhibit 80–90% of the absorption of the iso-α-acids at these wavelengths but, since they are also bitter, it is often not regarded as so important to exclude them from the analysis. Beer produced by conventional wort boiling will contain only trace amounts of α-acids and humulinic acids, and iso-α-acids may be estimated directly on an isooctane extract of the beer. Worts, on the other hand, may also contain appreciable amounts of α-acids and isomerized hop extracts may contain α-acids, iso-α-acids, and humulinic acids.

In the internationally agreed method [107, 108] degassed, acidified beer (10·0 ml) is extracted with isooctane (2,2,4-trimethylpentane) (20 ml) and, after centrifugation, the absorbance of the isooctane layer is read at 275 nm in a 1 cm cell against a blank of pure isooctane when

$$\text{Bitterness Units (BU)} = 50 \times \text{Absorbance.}$$

This is a modification of the method of Moltke and Meilgaard [109] who used 20 ml of acidified beer and 20 ml of isooctane and gave the regression equation as:

$$\text{isohumulones (mg/l)} = (28\cdot6 \times \text{OD}) - 5\cdot9$$

This method gave a better correlation with tasting trials than the second method of Rigby and Bethune [110]. In order to avoid assumptions about the chemical nature of the bittering principles in beer the EBC Analysis Committee simplified the regression equation and expressed the results as Bitterness Units [111].

The ASBC [108] retain the second method of Ribgy and Bethune [110] as it provides a more accurate estimate of the iso-α-acids in beer. In this method acidified beer (15 ml) is extracted with isooctane (15 ml) for 30 min. An aliquot (10 ml) of the isooctane layer is then washed with a mixture of methanol and 4N hydrochloric acid (68:32 v/v) (10 ml). After separation of the phases a portion of the isooctane layer (5 ml) is diluted with alkaline methanol (to 25 ml) and the absorbance read at 255 nm. The regression equation is:

$$\text{Iso-}\alpha\text{-acids (IAA) (mg/l)} = (\text{Absorbance} \times 96\cdot15) + 0\cdot4$$

This method gave a better correlation with the iso-α-acid content found by countercurrent distribution than the first method which omits the acid washing stage. It was subsequently found that the acid washing stage removed three unknown bitter principles from beer brewed with old hops [112].

For accurate analyses of individual components, or groups of components, in wort, beer, or hop extracts, they must be separated from all interfering matter. Countercurrent distribution is a convenient way of achieving this and for a long time was the reference method to which other analytical methods were related. Modified CCD methods for estimating the iso-α-acids [113, 114] and the α-acids [114] have been described. However, the finding [87] that isohumulone can revert back to humulone under the conditions of CCD meant that it could no longer be regarded as the absolute method. Ion-exchange chromatography has been adopted as a reference method by the ASBC [108]. High pressure liquid chromatography is being developed and will probably become the method of choice. Groups of resins have been resolved [115, 116, 117] and it has been used to estimate isohumulone and isocohumulone in beer [105].

The bittering substances in beer have also been resolved by thin layer chromatography. Using a 0·025 cm layer of Kieselgel G nach Stahl and benzene–ether (16: 1) as solvent, they have been separated into nine main fractions. *cis*-Isohumulones (R_f 0·65), *trans*-isohumulones (R_f 0·47), hulupones (R_f 0·82), and α-acids (R_f 0·36) are the major components accounting for 80% of the light petroleum extract [118]. Applying the method to commercial beers it was found that 88–100% of values found in the Brenner estimations are due to *cis*- and *trans*-isohumulone but there are real differences in the ratio of *cis*-/*trans*-isohumulone (1·9–3·1) between samples [119]. The beers examined also contained hulupones (1·1–4·8 ppm) and α-acids (< 5·0 ppm). These results may be compared with earlier estimates of hop resin derivatives obtained by isomerizing humulone at pH 9·0 (Table 14.13).

14.8 *Isomerized hop extracts* [127]
As mentioned above the α-acids can be isomerized into iso-α-acids in almost quantitative yield using dilute alkaline solutions. Such isomerized extracts

can be used to bitter bright beer with a high (approx. 85%) overall utilization of α-acid. The isomerized extract must be free of α- and β-acids and other hop resins which would not dissolve in the bright beer and thus necessitate a further filtration with the concomitant loss of iso-α-acid. α-Acids are stronger acids than β-acids and are usually separated from a solvent or liquid carbon dioxide extract of hops by partition with aqueous solution of either sodium or potassium carbonate or sodium or potassium hydroxide. The aqueous solutions are then boiled to effect the isomerization and the solution of iso-α-acids obtained metered either into conditioning tanks or bright beer [120]. Care must be taken, especially if using alkali hydroxides, that no hydrolysis of the iso-α-acids to humulinic acids occurs during the isomerization. The resins remaining after the removal of the α-acids may be added to the copper either with or without deliberate oxidation of the β-acids to hulupones.

The isomerization of α-acids is catalysed by calcium or magnesium ions, either in methanol solution or the solid state, without the formation of humulinic acid [86]. In the latter case the calcium and/or magnesium salts of the α-acids are heated at 70°C for 20 min to effect the isomerization. The iso-α-acid salts are usually ground to a fine powder (particles < 10 μm) which is added to conditioning tanks where a contact time of at least 24 hr is necessary to achieve 85% utilization [121]. A modification of this process involves heating stabilized hop pellets, in which the α-acids are in the form of their calcium or magnesium salts, at 80°C for 2 hr to form isomerized pellets which contain the calcium and/or magnesium salts of iso-α-acids [122].

The analysis of isomerized hop extracts is difficult as they may contain unreacted α-acids, β-acids, and humulinic acids, in addition to the required iso-α-acids. A preliminary qualitative analysis by thin layer chromatography

[118] should be carried out. For quantitative work ion-exchange chromatography is recommended [123]. Some of the beers produced using early isomerized hop extracts showed a strong tendency to gush as is discussed in Chapter 22.

Another type of commercial hop extract is made by borohydride reduction of an isomerized extract of α-acids and is claimed to be less sensitive to light than a normal isomerized extract [124]. When beer, particularly lager beer, is exposed to sunlight in clear bottles it develops an unpleasant 'sun-struck' flavour due to the formation of isopentenyl mercaptan (98). It is envisaged that photolysis of isohumulone cleaves the isohexenoyl side-chain to form a 3-methylbut-2-enyl radical which reacts with hydrogen sulphide, or any available thiol, in the beer to produce (98) [125].

In the reduction of isohumulone with sodium borohydride the carbonyl group in the isohexenoyl side-chain is reduced to a secondary alcohol to give the so-called ρ-isohumulones [126]. Since a new asymmetric centre is produced each isomer of isohumulone affords two ρ-isohumulones (97). The principal isomer from *trans*-isohumulone (ρ-isohumulone A_1, m.p. 80°C) is reported to be 50% as bitter as isohumulone and that from *cis*-isohumulone (ρ-isohumulone B_1, m.p. 78–80°C) 80% as bitter as isohumulone [126]. ρ-Isohumulones are claimed to be less sensitive to photolysis, but in view of their reduced bittering power, extracts containing them are unlikely to be widely accepted. ρ-Isohumulones have not been characterized as normal constituents of beer but may be formed, in small amounts, from iso-α-acids during the fermentation.

REFERENCES

[1] MACWILLIAM, I. C. (1968). *J. Inst. Brewing*, **74**, 38.

[2] PYKE, M. (1965). *J. Inst. Brewing*, **71**, 209.

[3] Institute of Brewing Analysis Committee (1948). *J. Inst. Brewing*, **54**, 179.

[4] HAGUES, G. (1927). *J. Inst. Brewing*, **33**, 262.

[5] WINDISCH, W., KOLBACH, P. and VÖGL, C. (1931). *Woch. Brau.*, **48**, 139.

[6] LUNDIN, H. and SCHRÖDERHEIM, J. (1931). *Woch. Brau*, **48**, 347.

[7] DAVIES, J. W., HARRIS, G. and PARSONS, R. (1956). *J. Inst. Brewing*, **62**, 31.

[8] MYRBÄCK, K. and MYRBÄCK, S. (1931). *Woch. Brau.*, **48**, 43.

[9] COHN, E. J. *et al.* (1946). *J. Am. Chem. Soc.*, **68**, 459; (1950), **72**, 465.

[10] DAVIES, J. W., HARRIS, G., JACKSON, S. and PARSONS, R. (1956). *J. Inst. Brewing*, **62**, 239.

[11] GUENTHER, K. R. and STUTLER, J. R. (1965). *Proc. Annu. Meet. Am. Soc. Brewing Chemists*, 30.

[12] JONES, M. O. and RAINBOW, C. (1966). *Proc. Annu. Meet. Am. Soc. Brewing Chemists*, 66.

[13] MOORE, S. and STEIN, W. H. (1954). *J. Biol. Chem.*, **211**, 893.

[14] MOORE, S., SPACKMAN, D. H. and STEIN, W. H. (1958). *Analyt. Chem.*, **30**, 1185.

[15] SANDEGREN, E., ENEBO, L., GUTHENBERG, H. and LJUNGDAHL, L. (1954). *Proc. Annu. Meet. Am. Soc. Brewing Chemists*, 63.

[16] JONES, M. and PIERCE, J. S. (1967). *J. Inst. Brewing*, **73**, 342.

[17] REYNOLDS, T. M. (1963). *Adv. Food Research* (a), **12**, 1–52; (b) (1965), **14**, 167–283.

[18] YOSHIDA, T., HORIE, Y. and KUROIWA, Y. (1972). *Report Research Labs, Kirin Brew. Co.*, **15**, 45.

[19] ANET, E. L. F. J. (1959). *Australian J. Chem.*, **12**, 280; 491.

[20] SCHÖNBERG, A. and MOUBACHER, R. (1952). *Chem. Rev.*, **50**, 261.

[21] SIEFKLER, J. A. and POLLOCK, G. E. (1956). *Proc. Annu. Meet. Am. Soc. Brewing Chemists*, 5.

[22] GUADAGNI, D. G., BUTTERY, R. G. and OKANO, S. (1963). *J. Sci. Food Agric.*, **14**, 761.

[23] HASHIMOTO, N. (1972). *J. Inst. Brewing*, **78**, 43.

[24] LAUFER, S. (May 1941). *Am. Brewer*, p. 20.

[25] BARNES, H. M. and KAUFMANN, C. W. (1947). *Indust. Eng. Chem.*, **39**, 37.

[26] PICKETT, J. A., COATES, J., PEPPARD, T. L. and SHARPE, F. R. (1976). *J. Inst. Brewing*, **82**, 233.

[27] JACKSON, S. W. and HUDSON, J. R. (1978). *J. Inst. Brewing*, **84**, 34.

[28] HODGE, J. E. and MOSER, H. A. (1961). *Cereal Chem.*, **38**, 221.

[29] HODGE, J. E., FISHER, B. E. and BELSON, C. C. (1963). *Proc. Annu. Meet. Am. Soc. Brewing Chemists*, 84.

[30] HARDING, R. J., WREN, J. J. and NURSTEN, H. E. (1978). *J. Inst. Brewing*, **84**, 41.

[31] TRESSL, R., RENNER, R., KOSSA, T. and KOPPLER, H. (1977). *Proc. Eur. Brewery Conv. Congr., Amsterdam*, p. 693.

[32] HARDING, R. J., NURSTEN, H. E. and WREN, J. J. (1977). *J. Sci. Food Agric.*, **28**, 225.

[33] MAGA, J. A. and SIZER, C. E. (1973). *J. Agric. Food Chem.*, **21**, 22.

[34] QURESHI, A. A., BURGER, W. C. and PRENTICE, N. (1979). *J. Am. Soc. Brewing Chemists*, **37**, 153.

[35] SIMON, H. (1962). *Chem. Ber.*, **95**, 1003.

[36] SWAIN, T. and CASEY, J. C., unpublished, quoted in [17].

[37] HASIMOTO, N. (1973). *Report Research Labs, Kirin Brew. Co.*, **16**, 1.

[38] MCWEENY, D. J., KNOWLES, M. E. and HEARNE, J. F. (1974). *J. Sci. Food Agric.*, **25**, 735.

[39] SOMMER, G. and SCHILFARTH, H. (1975). *Proc. Eur. Brewery Conv., Congr. Nice*, p. 233.

[40] Statutory Instrument (1973). 1340. Ministry of Agriculture, Fisheries and Food. Food Additives and Contaminants Committee (1979). *Interim Report on the Review of Colouring Matter in Food Regulations*, 1973. FAC/REP/29 HMSO, London.

[41] GREENSHIELDS, R. N. (1973). *Process Biochem.*, April, p. 17.

[42] BUCKEE, G. K. and BAILEY, T. P. (1978). *J. Inst. Brewing*, **84**, 158.

[43] GUSTAVSON, K. H. (1956). *The Chemistry of Tannin Processes*, Academic Press, New York.

[44] HASLAM, E. (1966). *The Chemistry of Vegetable Tannins*, Academic Press, New York.

[45] GRAMSHAW, J. W. (1967). *J. Inst. Brewing*, **73**, 258.

[46] HASLAM, E. (1975). *The Flavonoids* (ed. HARBOURNE, J. B., MABRY, T. J. and MABRY, H.) Chapman and Hall Ltd., London, p. 505.

[47] WEINGES, K., BAHR, W., EBERT, W., GORITZ, K. and MARX, H. D. (1969) *Fortsch. der Chemie organishe Naturstoffe*, **27**, 158.

[48] GRAMSHAW, J. W. (1968). *J. Inst. Brewing*, **74**, 20.

[49] GARDNER, R. J. and MCGUINNESS, J. D. (1977). *Tech. Q. Master Brewers Assoc. Am.*, **14**, 250.

[50] EASTMOND, R. (1974). *J. Inst. Brewing*, **80**, 188.

[51] VANCRAENENBROECK, R., GORISSEN, H. and LONTIE, R. (1977). *Proc. Eur. Brewery Conv. Congr.*, *Amsterdam*, p. 429.

[52] LAWS, D. R. J., MCGUINNESS, J. D. and BATH, N. A. (1976). *J. Am. Soc. Brewing Chemists*, **34**, 170.

[53] MCGUINNESS, J. D., LAWS, D. R. J., EASTMOND, R. and GARDNER, R. J. (1975). *J. Inst. Brewing*, **81**, 237.

[54] GRACEY, D. E. F. and BARKER, R. L. (1976). *J. Inst. Brewing*, **82**, 78.

[55] CZOCHANSKA, Z., LAI YEAP FOO, NEWMAN, R. H., PORTER, L. J., THOMAS, W. A. and JONES, W. T. (1979). *Chem. Commun.*, 375.

[56] VAN SUMERE, C. F., ALBRECHT, J., DEDONDER, A., DE POOTER, H. and PÉ, I. (1975), *The Chemistry and Biochemistry of Plant Proteins* (eds. HARBOURNE, J. B. and VAN SUMERE, C. F.), Academic Press, London, p. 211.

[57] PIERPOINT, W. S. (1970). *Report of Rothamsted Experimental Station*, Part 2, p. 199.

[58] WOOF, J. and PIERCE, J. S. (1966). *J. Inst. Brewing*, **72**, 40.

[59] GRAMSHAW, J. W. (1969). *J. Inst. Brewing*, **75**, 61.

[60] STEVENS, R. (1967). *Chem. Rev.*, **67**, 19–71.

[61] ASHURST, P. R. (1967). *Fortsch. der Chemie organishe Naturstoffe*, **25**, 63–89 (in English).

[62] VERZELE, M. (1979). Brewing Science, Vol. 1 (ed. POLLOCK, J. R. A.), Academic Press, London, p. 279.

[63] SPETSIG, L. O. (1955). *Acta Chem. Scand.*, **9**, 1421.

[64] WIELAND, H. (1925). *Ber.*, **58**, 102; 2012.

[65] WINDISCH, W., KOLBACH, P. and SCHLEICHER, R. (1927). *Woch. Brau.*, **44**, 453.

[66] VERZELE, M. and GOVAERT, F. (1947). *Cong. Intein. Ind. Ferment conf. Commun.*, p. 297.

[67] Hops Liaison Committee: Nomenclature Sub-Committee (1969). *J. Inst. Brewing*, **75**, 340.

[68] RIGBY, F. L. and BETHUNE, J. L. (1952). *Proc. Annu. Meet. Am. Soc. Brewing Chemists*, 98; (1953). 119.

[69] WHITEAR, A. L. and HUDSON, J. R. (1964). *J. Inst. Brewing*, **70**, 24.

[70] HOWARD, G. A. (1959). *J. Inst. Brewing*, **65**, 417.

[71] SPETSIG, L. O. (1958). *Acta Chem. Scand.*, **12**, 592.

[72] SPETSIG, L. O. (1964). *J. Inst. Brewing*, **70**, 440.

[73] ALDERWEIRELDT, F., ANTEUNIS, M., DIERCKENS, J. and VERZELE, M. (1965). *Bull. Soc. Chim. Belg.*, **74**, 29.

[74] CLARKE, B. J. and HILDEBRAND, R. P. (1965). *J. Inst. Brewing*, **71**, 26.

[75] VERZELE, M., JANSEN, H. E. and FERDINANDUS, A. (1970). *J. Inst. Brewing*, **76**, 25.

[76] AITKEN, R. A., BRUCE, A., HARRIS, J. O. and SEATON, J. C. (1970). *J. Inst. Brewing*, **76**, 29.

[77] ANTEUNIS, M. and VERZELE, M. (1959). *Bull. Soc. Chim. Belg.*, **68**, 102.

[78] ANTEUNIS, M., BRACKE, M., VERZELE, M. and ALDERWEIRELDT, F. (196?). *Bull. Soc. Chim. Belg.*, **71**, 623.

[79] BURTON, J. S., ELVIDGE, J. A. and STEVENS, R. (1964). *J. Chem. Soc.* p. 3816.

[80] BURTON, J. S., STEVENS, R. and ELVIDGE, J. A. (1964). *J. Inst. Brewing*, **70**, 345.

[81] ASHURST, P. R. and LAWS, D. R. J. (1966). *J. Chem. Soc., C. Org.*, p. 1615.

[82] ASHURST, P. R. and LAWS, D. R. J. (1967). *J. Inst. Brewing*, **73**, 535.

[83] PFENNINGER, H. B., SCHUR, F., VATERLAUS, B. P., SIGG, T. and WILD, J. (1975), *Proc. Eur. Brewery Conv., Congr. Nice*, p. 159.

[84] DE KEUKELEIRE, D. and VERZELE, M. (1971). *Tetrahedron*, **27**, 4939.

[85] VERZELE, M. and DIERCKENS, J. (1969). *J. Inst. Brewing*, **75**, 449.

[86] KÖLLER, H. (1969). *J. Inst. Brewing*, **75**, 175.

[87] AITKEN, R. A., BRUCE, A., HARRIS, J. O. and SEATON, J. C. (1969). *J. Inst. Brewing*, **75**, 180.

[88] CONNETT, B. E. (1969). *J. Inst. Brewing*, **75**, 364.

[89] VERZELE, M., ANTEUNIS, M. and ALDERWEIRELDT, F. (1965). *J. Inst. Brewing*, **71**, 232.

[90] VAN BOVEN, M. and VERZELE, M. (1968). *J. Inst. Brewing*, **74**, 81.

[91] DIERCKENS, J. and VERZELE, M. (1969). *J. Inst. Brewing*, **75**, 453.

[92] VERZELE, M. and VANHOEY, M. (1967). *J. Inst. Brewing*, **73**, 451.

[93] DE TAEYE, L., DE KEUKELEIRE, D. and VERZELE, M. (1977). *Tetrahedron*, **33**, 573.

[94] DE TAEYE, L., DE KEUKELEIRE, D. and VERZELE, M. (1979). *Tetrahedron*, **35**, 989.

[95] DE TAEYE, L., DE KEUKELEIRE, D. and VERZELE, M. (1979). *Chem. and Ind.*, 127.

[96] REGAN, J. P. and ELVIDGE, J. A. (1969). *J. Inst. Brewing*, **75**, 10.

[97] MAULE, D. R. (1966). *J. Inst. Brewing*, **72**, 285.

[98] VERZELE, M. (1965). *Proc. Eur. Brewery Conv. Congr., Stockholm*, p. 400.

[99] HALL, R. D. (1957). *Proc. Eur. Brewery Conv. Congr., Copenhagen*, p. 314.

[100] MEILGAARD, M. (1960). *J. Inst. Brewing*, **66**, 35.

[101] LLOYD, R. O. V. (1961). *Proc. Eur. Brewery. Conv. Congr., Vienna*, p. 112.

[102] HOWARD, G. A. and TATCHELL, A. R. (1957). *J. Inst. Brewing*, **63**, 139.

[103] STEVENS, R. and WRIGHT, D. (1961). *J. Inst. Brewing*, **67**, 496.

[104] HOWARD, G. A. and SLATER, C. A. (1957). *J. Inst. Brewing*, **63**, 478.

[105] WHITT, J. T. and CUZNER, J. (1979). *J. Am. Soc. Brew. Chem.*, **37**, 41.

[106] RIGBY, F. L. (1972). *Proc. Annu. Meet. Am. Soc. Brewing Chemists* 46.

[107] European Brewery Convention (1975). *Analytica*, 3rd Ed.

[108] American Society of Brewing Chemists (1976). *Methods of Analysis*, 7th ed.

[109] MOLTKE, A. B. and MEILGAARD, M. (1955). *Brygmesteren*, **12**, 65.

[110] RIGBY, F. L. and BETHUNE, J. L. (1955). *J. Inst. Brewing*, **61**, 325.

[111] BISHOP, L. R. (1967). *J. Inst. Brewing*, **73**, 525.

[112] BISHOP, L. R. (1964). *J. Inst. Brewing*, **70**, 489.

[113] WOOD, S. A., LLOYD, R. O. V. and WHITEAR, A. L. (1968). *J. Inst. Brewing*, **74**, 510.

[114] VERZELE, M., CLAUS, H. and VAN DYCK, J. (1967). *J. Inst. Brewing*, **73**, 39.

[115] OTTER, G. E. and TAYLOR, L. (1978). *J. Inst. Brewing*, **84**, 160.

[116] GILL, R. (1979). *J. Inst. Brewing*, **85**, 15.

[117] SCHWARZENBACH, R. (1979). *J. Am. Soc. Brewing Chemists*, **37**, 180.

[118] AITKEN, R. A., BRUCE, A., HARRIS, J. O. and SEATON, J. C. (1967). *J. Inst. Brewing*, **73**, 528.

[119] AITKEN, R. A., BRUCE, A., HARRIS J. O. and SEATON, J. C. (1968). *J. Inst. Brewing*, **74**, 436.

[120] LAWS, D. R. J., BAKER, C. D. and WAIN, J. (1979). *Proc. Eur. Brewery Conv. Congr., Berlin*, p. 393.

[121] HILDEBRAND, R. P., CLARKE, B. J., LANCE, D. C. and WHITE, A. (1973). *Proc. Eur. Brewery Conv. Congr. Salzberg.* p. 125.

[122] GRANT, H. L. (1979). *Proc. Eur. Brewery Conv. Congr., Berlin*, p. 441.

[123] WHITEAR, A. L. (1977). *J. Inst. Brewing*, **83**, 85.

[124] HOUGEN, O. A. (1963). US Patent 3 079 262. *Chem. Abs.*, **58**, 10 696.

[125] GUNST, F. and VERZELE, M. (1978). *J. Inst. Brewing*, **84**, 291.

[126] VERZELE, M. and KHOKER, A. (1967). *J. Inst. Brewing*, **73**, 255.

[127] LAWS, D. J. R. (1981). *J. Inst. Brewing*, **87**, 24.

[128] GJERTSEN, P. (1953). *J. Inst. Brewing*, **59**, 296.

[129] GJERTSEN, P. (1955). *Proc. Eur. Brewery Conv. Congr., Baden-Baden*, p. 37.

[130] MCFARLANE, W. D. and HELD, H. R. (1953). *Proc. Eur. Brewery Conv. Congr., Nice*, p. 110.

[131] LATIMER, R. A., LAKSHMINARAYANAN, K., QUITTENTON, R. C. and DENNIS, G. E. (1966). *Proc. Inst. Brew., Aust. Section*, 111.

[132] KLEBER, W., SCHMID, P. and SEYFARTH, I. (1963). *Brauwissenschaft*, **16**, 1.

[133] HARRIS, G., BARTON-WRIGHT, E. C. and CURTIS, N. (1951). *J. Inst. Brewing*, **57**, 264.

[134] HARRIS, G., HALL, R. D. and MACWILLIAM, I. C. (1954). *J. Inst. Brewing*, **60**, 464.

[135] CANN, M. R., DAVIS, A.-M. and SHANNON, P. V. R. (1982). *J. Chem. Soc. Perkin Trans I*, 375.

Chapter 15

METHODS OF WORT BOILING
AND HOP EXTRACTION

The previous chapter was concerned with the many complex chemical processes and physical changes taking place during wort boiling. Under no set of practical conditions can all of these be fully optimized. It is understandable therefore that various breweries select different conditions of wort boiling and that these differences are reflected to some degree in the character of the beers produced. Illustrating the complexity of the situation, the various unit operations involved in wort boiling, hop separation, and wort cooling are set out below [1].

(a) *Wort boiling*

1. Heat transfer and evaporation.
2. Sterilization and enzyme denaturation.
3. Coagulation of protein and tannin material (trub formation).
4. Reaction of hop constituents.
5. Reaction of other materials in the wort, e.g. colour production.
6. Extraction of hop constituents.
7. Distillation of volatile materials (miscible and immiscible wort and hop volatiles).

(b) *Hop and trub separation*

1. Filtration.
2. Separation of spent hop material and of hot trub.
3. Leaching or extraction of solid material by sparging.

(c) *Wort cooling*

1. Heat transfer.
2. Production of cold trub.
3. Gas absorption (aeration or oxygenation).

15.1 *Choice of materials* [3]

In mediaeval times, wort was boiled in iron cauldrons over open fires but as the scale of production increased, the vessels were covered over and fitted with a chimney or stack to carry steam out of the building. To construct these more complex vessels, copper, rather than cast iron, became the material of choice because of its malleability, superior conductivity and better resistance to corrosion. Accordingly, vessels in which wort boiling is carried out are often called 'coppers', even if the metal of construction is not copper. Other terms used are 'kettles' or 'wort boilers.'

TABLE 15.1

Comparison between copper and stainless steel

Property	Copper	Stainless steel
Density (kg/m³)	8930	7930
Specific heat (J/kg K)	385	510
Thermal conductivity (W/m K)	385	150
Yield stress (MN/m²)	75	230
Heat flux (kW/m²)	80*	60†

* For conventional jacketted kettle.   † For flat stainless steel panels.

In the last twenty years, stainless steel has become popular as a material of construction of brewery vessels, especially vessels that are of relatively simple shape and constructed of cold-rolled stainless steel sheet. Copper is extremely attractive but is more expensive to purchase and maintain than stainless steel. It has a much higher thermal conductivity but for construction of vessels has to be of greater thickness than stainless steel sheet (Table 15.1). Copper sheet is more suitable however for complex shapes of vessels and can be joined by rivetting and brazing whereas stainless steel is welded.

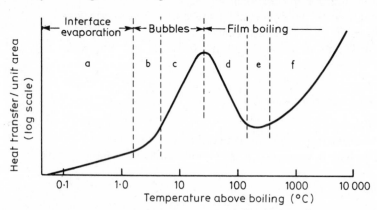

Fig. 15.1 Heat flux data from an electrically heated platinum wire in water [2]. (a) Pure convection heat transferred to water/air interface where evaporation occurs; (b) Nucleate boiling: bubbles condense in super-heated liquid; (c) Nucleate boiling: bubbles rise to surface; (d) Partial nucleate boiling and unstable nucleate film; (e) Stable film boiling; (f) Radiation coming into play.

Cold-rolled stainless steel surfaces (typically 316 [EN58J] austenitic grade) are very easily cleaned by hot 2–4% caustic soda solutions while copper is more slowly cleaned and tends to corrode unless corrosion inhibitors are present. Copper surfaces (because of their submicroscopic pitting and their effect of lowering wetting angles) are much more easily wetted than those of stainless steel. This property of 'wettability' can be extremely important in the formation and release of steam bubbles at the interface between the vessel and the wort (Fig. 15.1). Thus, under the conditions prevailing in a wort kettle, copper allows nucleated boiling while stainless steel tends to give film boiling. Circumstances can arise with stainless steel heating surfaces where the steam bubbles accumulate and provide a stable insulating blanket between hot metal surface and the wort. Unless this blanket is swept away by strong convection currents, the heat flux (the amount of heat imparted to the wort) will have little relationship to the amount of heat energy available. Indeed, increasing the steam pressure may make matters worse by increasing the thickness of the insulating steam blanket. Thus heat transfer coefficients begin to fall when a steam gauge pressure of 3 bar is exceeded in a stainless steel heater; for copper the maximum heat transfer coefficient is achieved when the steam pressure is about 5 bar. Another factor is that, at and above the air-wort interface, the hot stainless steel tends to bake wort solids onto its surface. Increasing steam pressure tends to increase the degree of baking and therefore insulation. Strong agitation of the wort aided by mechanical impellors plus relatively low heat fluxes will therefore improve heat transfer and reduce the accumulation of baked wort solids on the vessel surface.

Finally, copper is not entirely inert during wort boiling and appears to catalyse oxidation reactions involving polyphenols, giving rise to greater colour in boiled worts than is the case with stainless steel. While this may not be desirable, the oxidation of some compounds with sulphydryl groupings in copper vessels is said to reduce undesirable sulphurous aromas from the final beer.

15.2 *Heating the copper* [3, 4]

Coppers were originally heated over open coal fires housed in iron furnaces. The fire could not be made up until some wort had been transferred to the copper, otherwise the wort would char on the hot plates and also there would be a possibility that the copper would deform and leak at the seams. When boiling was complete, the fire would have to be drawn, even though a fresh charge of sweet wort was available. Direct fired coppers are still in use but they are rare and instead of coal (calorific efficiency was 40–50%), oil or natural gas are used (calorific efficiency 68–70%). When direct fired vessels were in vogue, large breweries tended to have many small coppers in order to give greater flexibility and reduce the time sweet wort had to be held before boiling. With the advent of steam heating, some breweries continued using many small coppers to even out the steam demand and maintain flexibility. Other breweries have recognized the lower cost of installing and maintaining one or two large coppers. The calorific efficiency of well-lagged steam-heated coppers can be as high as 90–95% but the steam generator will not be as efficient as this and the overall efficiency will be 65–70%.

In the last 20 years, some breweries have installed coppers heated by high-pressure hot water. Typically the water would be in the range 145–170°C (293–338°F) and to maintain the water as a liquid the gauge pressure would be about 17 bar. In contrast, a typical steam heated copper would use low pressure dry saturated steam at 148°C (298°F) and 3·5-bar gauge pressure. High pressure hot water systems involve circulation of the liquid from the heater to the copper and back to the heater. A considerable amount of heat energy is held in the volume of water circulated so that sudden large demands on the heating system are met more easily. The high pressure hot water system needs careful lagging, is normally held at its operating temperature except at periods of maintenance shut-down, and is relatively expensive. However, certain complications associated with steam heating are absent, such as the need for condensate traps, strainers and pressure-reducing valves. For large, flat-sided stainless steel wort kettles that deal with several brews per day, and operate seven days in the week, the high pressure hot water system is often preferred: There is less trouble with achieving satisfactory heat flux and with baking of wort solids, and the large heat panels do not accumulate condensate and gas.

There are several objectives to be achieved in the design of a copper. Thus the wort must be thoroughly mixed by either strong ebullition or by vigorous agitation. There must be a high and localized heat transfer rate and to attain this there should be high heat transfer coefficients. Heat energy must be used efficiently. There must be easy, inexpensive and effective cleaning in-place, and finally low capital and operating costs.

Coppers may be heated either by jackets or by heat exchangers in a loop outside the vessel. The external heating jacket may be symmetrically arranged around the vessel or, in order to encourage a rolling boil, the jacket may be placed asymmetrically. Internal exchangers which often operate at up to 5-bar (gauge) steam pressure include coils, panels radiating from a common supply pipe (star heaters), or a series of vertical hollow pipes. Such exchangers are often surmounted by a vertical hollow pipe which leads rising wort up to a splash plate like a fountain. (The effect is something like a coffee percolator.) External heaters may take the form of plates, spiral coils, or shell and tubes. The last type is normally called an external calandria.

It is desirable to heat wort in the copper as soon as possible and therefore there is usually provision for low pressure (say up to 3-bar gauge pressure) heaters in the base of the vessel to operate independently from those higher in the vessel (which may be at 5-bar gauge pressure). Therefore as soon as wort is run into the copper it can be heated, without wasting heat from the upper heaters and without baking the wort as it rises to these upper heaters. With external heaters, this requirement for independent heaters is not necessary providing that the wort circulates through the loop either by being impelled with an axial flow pump or in some instances rather more slowly by thermo-syphonic action.

15.3 *Types of copper*

Modern coppers tend to be of four general types. There are the slab-sided stainless steel ones with asymmetric heating surfaces, often heated by high pressure hot water (Fig. 15.2). A second type is the symmetrical copper with jackets or internal heating element(s) or both (Fig. 15.3). There is the symmetrical copper with a dimple in the base, jacket heaters and an agitator (Fig. 15.4). Finally, there is the external calandria copper as shown in Fig. 15.5. The advantages of the external calandria are (*i*) the heating can commence when only 10% of the charge of wort is in the copper, (*ii*) the wort is boiled very vigorously, (*iii*) there is less foaming of wort than with other coppers so that the head-space can be less than the usual 25% of total volume, (*iv*) the copper is easily cleaned by circulating detergent rather than wort through the loop, and (*v*) the volumes of wort in the copper can be very varied. As has already been mentioned, other types of copper have to receive a minimum volume of wort so that the heater is covered. Furthermore any coils or other internal heaters are not easy to clean.

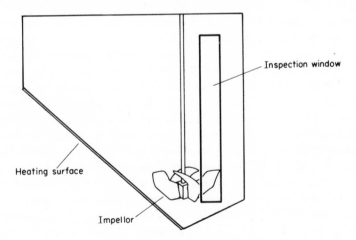

Fig. 15.2 Asymmetric copper design. The end wall shown is manufactured in uniform size but the design capacity of the copper may be varied by different lengths of side wall.

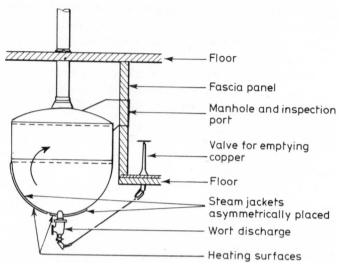

- Floor
- Fascia panel
- Manhole and inspection port
- Valve for emptying copper
- Floor
- Steam jackets asymmetrically placed
- Wort discharge
- Heating surfaces

Fig. 15.3 A symmetric copper with asymmetrically disposed steam jackets.

A stainless steel vessel suitable for boiling 1000 hl (611 brl) of wort using an external calandria might have the following characteristics. The diameter is 5·8 m (19 ft) and the height of the straight sides is 4 m (13 ft); a conical base has an included angle of 150° (Fig. 15.5). This provides for a surface area of 125 m² (1345 ft²). The thickness of the vessel is 3–5 mm (0·12–0·20 inches or 8 gauge) and is lagged with phenolic foam to a thickness of 50 mm. (Smaller coppers may be constructed from lighter gauge stainless steel, say 2–2·5 mm, especially if they are strengthened by a framework.) From this, it can be calculated that the empty copper would be approximately 17–20 tonne (or ton) and the full copper would be 120 tonne (or ton). Because of this substantial weight, the vessel needs supporting on a ring or webbing around the periphery of the vessel – usually at the top of the cone. In its turn the ring is supported by three or four legs; alternatively it can be integral with the floor supports so that the lower part of the vessel is suspended into the room below. The circulating loop tube should be about 0·3 m (1 ft) diameter and some 1·5–2·5 mm (0·05–0·10 in) thickness, leading to an axial flow pump (which is used to initiate circulation) and thence to the heat-exchanger, and finally into the vessel. Sometimes two or more circulating loops and exchangers are used in conjunction with a large vessel. The vessel is not a pressure vessel but some features of a pressure vessel design and construction are incorporated, especially for large coppers of this kind. Thus the vertical welds are not in line, but are staggered and no opening into the vessel cuts across a weld. Some external calandria are designed for low pressure dry saturated steam, others for high pressure hot water. Very careful consideration has to be taken in the design of the heat-exchanger to the volume of wort to be boiled, its gravity, the minimum time required to bring the wort to boiling, the amount of water to be evaporated and the frequency of cleaning [4].

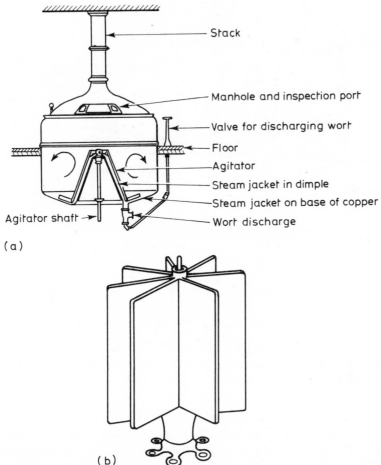

Stack

Manhole and inspection port

Valve for discharging wort

Floor

Agitator

Steam jacket in dimple

Steam jacket on base of copper

Agitator shaft

Wort discharge

(a)

(b)

Fig. 15.4 (a) A symmetrical copper with symmetrically disposed steam jackets, dimple and agitator. (Courtesy of A. Ziemann, GmbH.) (b) A 'star' heater for mounting in the base of a copper.

15.4 *Heat economy* [5]

It will be appreciated that in the initial stages of heating the wort in the copper, the heat energy load is very high. This is because the temperature has to be raised from say 70 to 102°C (158–216°F). From this unsteady state, the steady state is eventually reached when the copper is full, the wort is

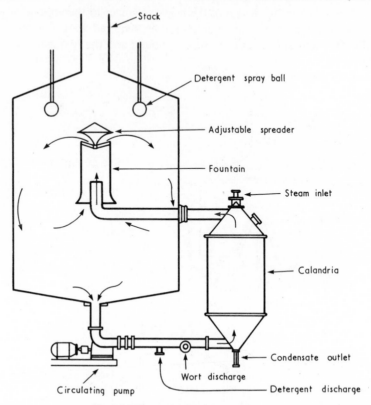

Fig. 15.5 External calandria copper.

boiling and water is being evaporated. At the steady state, the steam or hot water requirements are less and are uniform. The relevant equations are:

$$\frac{dQ}{dt} = U\ A\ \varDelta\ T \tag{15.1}$$

This equation is the simplest for expressing a particular unsteady state. Q is the heat provided, t is time, U is the overall heat transfer coefficient, A is the area for transfer and T is the temperature difference at time t.

$$q = U\ A\ \varDelta\ T_m \tag{15.2}$$

This is the steady-state equation in which q is the heat transfer rate and T_m is the difference between the condensing temperature of steam and the temperature at which the wort boils.

The overall coefficient U_o, referable to the tube outside diameter is calculated from:

$$\frac{1}{U_o} = \frac{d_o}{d_i} \times \frac{1}{h_i} + \frac{1}{h_o} + \frac{d_o}{d_m} \times \frac{x}{k} + R_1 + R_2 \tag{15.3}$$

where d_o, d_i and d_m are the outside, inside and mean diameter of the walls, h_i is the inside film coefficient and h_o the corresponding outside one, x is the thickness of the wall, k the thermal conductivity of the material, R_1 is the resistance relating to the inside fouling coefficient and R_2 the corresponding outside fouling coefficient. For thin-walled tubes, the equation (15.3) can be simplified to:

$$\frac{1}{U} = \frac{1}{h_i} + \frac{1}{h_o} + \frac{x}{k} + R_1 + R_2 \qquad (15.4)$$

Typical resistance values are given in Table 15.2.

TABLE 15.2

Typical heat transfer coefficients ($kW/m^2\ K$)

Steam side (low pressure)	5–6
High pressure hot water side	2·5
Wort side (clean)	1·6
Wort side (dirty)	1·2
Vessel wall (copper) (k/x)	19·25
Vessel wall (stainless) (k/x)	7·5
Overall heat transfer coefficient for clean stainless steel kettle	1·0
Corresponding coefficient for dirty kettle	0·5

Many breweries clean their coppers after 6–12 brews, despite the fact that after say 10 brews only 75% of the maximum evaporation is achieved. The reasons for infrequent cleaning are (*i*) the difficulty of finding 'down time' in an intensive schedule of many brews per day, (*ii*) the cost of cleaning, including fitting cleaning equipment, supplying hot water, detergent and disposing of and paying for effluent produced, (*iii*) the oversizing of the heat exchange surfaces and (*iv*) the tendency of many breweries to require less evaporation because last wort runnings are discarded or recycled.

The boiling of wort in a copper tends to make a brewhouse hot and humid. In order to conserve heat energy and provide acceptable working conditions, the copper is well insulated on the sides and base, but often not on the upper surfaces. Heat recovery from the stack of the copper is well worth considering, although not all breweries are equipped for it. The heat recovered can be used for either raising the temperature of mashing-in water or detergent solutions used for cleaning in-place; 2258 kJ are released for every kg of steam condensed and consequently the temperature of the water to be heated could, for instance, be raised 50°C (122°F), say from 15 to 65°C (59–149°F). Typically in such condensers the heat transfer coefficients are 5 kW/m² K on the steam side and 3 kW/m² on the water side.

Because the steam carries with it wort solids and steam-volatile components, the heat-exchanger becomes fouled and needs periodic cleaning. The heat recovery can be set against the price of steam. For example, assume 1000 hl (10^5 kg) wort is to be boiled for one hour and the evaporation rate is 8 % per hour, the weight of water evaporated is 8000 kg. If the efficiency of heater in the copper is 90 % the steam used will be 8889 kg. At say 0·8 pence/kg, this will be just over £71. In practice, one metric ton of steam is needed for boiling 100–150 hl of wort, and from the boiling of 100 hl of wort, heat can be recovered to raise the temperature of 50 hl of water from 25°C (77°F) to 85°C (185°F) assuming 75 % recovery of the heat energy [3].

15.5 Temperature and pressure [6–11]

The temperature of wort boiling at ambient pressure will depend on a number of factors. Thus, the greater the gravity (extract) of the wort, the higher will be the temperature. Hydrostatic pressure will also increase the boiling temperature. Conversely, breweries situated at high altitudes will have their wort boiling at lower temperatures unless they pressurize the coppers. The use of pressurized coppers is controversial, some authorities claiming better utilization [7] and others poorer utilization of α-acids [6]. In general, pressure coppers are not favoured for producing pale beers because the greater temperatures lead to darker wort colours than with non-pressurized coppers. Undoubtedly even a small increase in pressure within the copper over atmospheric (0·2 bar) will speed the chemical and physical changes taking place in the copper. Thus boiling time can be reduced in a pressure copper from 90 min to something between 45 and 60 min. At the extreme is the claim that 98 s at 150°C (302°F) or 180 s at 140°C (284°F) will give similar results to 90 min at 100°C (212°F), as shown in Table 15.3.

TABLE 15.3

Comparison between conventional boiling and high pressure short time copper boiling [11]

	Boiling conditions	
	90 min, 100°C	98 s, 150°C
% extract (°Plato)	10·6	10·9
pH	5·45	5·34
Colour (°EBC)	9·0	6·9
Total nitrogen (mg/100 ml)	93·3	93·0
Coagulable nitrogen (mg/100 ml)	3·4	1·4
Bitterness (EBU)	46·0	44·7
Iso-α-Acid content (mg/l)	41·0	38·2
α-Acid content (mg/l)	12·3	12·0
Tannins (mg/l)	171	159
Anthocyanogens (mg/l)	65	57

One of the difficulties about pressure boiling is that undesirable volatiles are not steam-volatilized sufficiently, especially when whole hops, powder or pellets are added to the copper. In this connection, many US breweries assist the removal of undesirable essential oils by keeping man-holes open while the coppers boil. The air thus drawn into the vessels improves the draught up the stack and hence volatilization. Some coppers have condensate traps in the throat of the stack to prevent condensed volatiles returning to the boiling wort.

It has long been known that vigorous boiling gives better percentage utilization and enhances other chemical and physical changes during copper boil. Equally, it has been known that rather similar results can be obtained by simmering around 100°C (212°F) providing that there is intense mechanical agitation of the wort [9]. The question arises whether wort treatment could usefully be carried out at temperatures below 100°C. Sweet worts were held for 90 min at 85°C (185°F) in the presence of hop extracts and compared with similar worts held for 90 min under boiling conditions (Table 15.4). The unboiled wort and derived beer were lower in colour and bitter substances and higher in total nitrogen than the standard wort and beer. The unboiled worts were cloudy while the shelf life of the derived beer was lower and its flavour was different from the standard.

TABLE 15.4

The effect of replacing wort boiling by an 85°C hold [10]

		Boiling conditions	
		Standard boil for 90 min	85°C hold for 90 min
Wort	pH	5·06	5·20
	Colour (°EBC)	11·5	10·0
	Total N (mg/100 ml)	74·9	79·4
	Amino N (mg/100 ml)	19·4	19·0
	Bitter substances (mg/l)	45·9	37·5
Beer	pH	3·82	3·84
	Colour (°EBC)	11·0	9·0
	Total N (mg/100 ml)	43·9	47·2
	Amino N (mg/100 ml)	3·7	3·7
	Bitter substances (mg/l)	20·9	16·3
	Head retention (s)	95	96
	Shelf life (weeks)	16	12

15.6 *Operating a copper*

Worts from the mash tun, lauter tun or mash filter may be run directly into the copper. However, with some brewing schedules the copper may be engaged in boiling the wort of the previous brew when first runnings of wort leave the wort separator. Under these circumstances the wort is either diverted temporarily into the mash mixing vessel (if it is free) or into a heated, insulated buffer tank (a sweet wort back or underback). Worts must not be allowed to cool below 55°C (131°F) – preferably 65°C (149°F) – because there may be opportunity for infection by thermophilic bacteria such as *Lactobacillus delbrueckii*. In older breweries in Britain, the coppers were often sited high in the building so that worts from the mash tun had to be pumped a considerable height. With traditional lager breweries, the coppers are usually slightly below the level of the lauter tun, alongside mash conversion vessels and mash coppers. A centrifugal pump is used for transferring wort in contrast to a rotary positive displacement pump (such as a Monopump which could be used for pumping mash).

When the contents of a mash tun or other wort separator are to be divided between two or more coppers, this can be achieved in several ways. The two coppers may be filled simultaneously by means of a split main in which case the gravity and composition of the wort will be the same in each. However, both coppers must wait until the final worts have reached them before the boiling time commences. Even if the wort is simmering at this time, the demand for steam by synchronous operation may be considered excessive. Alternatively, one copper may be filled, and boiling commenced, while the other receives weaker worts. After boiling, when the coppers are cast, the worts can be mixed in various proportions to give rise, after fermentation, to several different beers varying in original gravity. This complex mixing arrangement is known as a parti-gyle system.

Boiling worts in the absence of hop material presents problems to the brewer. The surface tension of the wort is sufficiently high to encourage foaming and there have been catastrophic incidents when coppers have boiled over because hop material has not been added. Hops may be added as whole cones, freshly minced hops, powder, pellets or extract. The choice influences the final beer flavour, the costs of the various forms, the facilities available in the brewery for storing and handling them and finally the percentage utilization achieved. Alternatively, part of the hop bitterness may be added to the copper and the balance provided at the beer treatment stage in the form of isomerized extract [12].

Longer boiling times are normally required for whole hops and there may be problems in getting accurate weights of representative samples into the copper, especially if a complex blend of hops has to be introduced. With whole hops in external calandria coppers, contaminating materials such as string, wire and nails may cause breakdowns of the circulating pump. Pellets are particularly easy to weigh accurately and add to the copper. Extracts are viscous and are introduced either after preheating opened cans of the material or the cans are pierced repeatedly and suspended in or above the hot wort in the copper. Many breweries add hops to vessels containing stronger worts at a rate greater than to coppers holding weaker worts. Better percentage utilization is obtained if this practice is reversed. Many breweries add hops at the beginning of the boil and postpone adding the remainder until part way through the boil. Very commonly, the hops with the most attractive aroma are added very close to the end of the boil (aroma hops). North American breweries usually add their native hops at the beginning of the boil (say 140 g/hl or 0·5 lb/brl). Aroma hops such as Saaz or Hallertau are added some 15 min before cast. Some breweries are convinced that this practice is well worthwhile because of the hoppy aroma imparted to their beers, while others are equally convinced that the practice is either too expensive or even worthless. Very few breweries now reuse their hops in successive brews but, when highly hopped beers were in vogue, this practice was common [13].

The production of high gravity beers can be achieved by adding considerable volumes of syrup before the wort comes to boil – if for instance nine parts of wort of 10°P (SG 1040) were mixed with one part of syrup of 36·4°P (SG 1150), the resultant gravity would be about 12·6°P (SG 1051). Great care must be taken to ensure that the syrup becomes well mixed with the wort before charring of the dense syrup occurs on the heating surfaces. Another consideration is whether the modified wort has the appropriate composition with respect to carbohydrates and amino acids, and whether this will influence yeast growth and final flavour of the beer. Addition of sugar solutions to the copper are common where sugar is cheap or where sweet beers are required. These 'copper sugars' may be produced from cane sugar or beet sugar or a mixture; it is now rare to find the use of inverted sugar for this purpose.

A few breweries add negatively charged colloidal material to their coppers in order to promote hot trub formation. This copper fining material is usually Irish moss, the dried red marine alga *Chondrus crispus* (plus some *Gigartina stellata*). It is added at 4–8 g/hl and fining action arises because polysaccharide called carrageenan is extracted by hot wort. This substance (or substances) is made up of chains of galactose, and occasionally anhydrogalactose, units linked alternately 1–3 and 1–4. Some of the free hydroxyl groups are esterified with sulphate groups, hence the negative charge [14]. Purified preparations of carrageenan may be substituted for the natural product. Alternatively, a few breweries add silica gel.

A further practice which is becoming progressively rare is to add calcium sulphate to the copper, sometimes with other salts, in order to adjust the calcium concentration of the wort. The rationale is presumably to use the circulation and boiling currents to dissolve the salts and bring about a lower pH of the wort. But α-amylase activity in mashing depends on sufficient calcium being present, therefore it seems better to have all the calcium available in the mashing and sparging water.

It used to be considered desirable to have oxidation conditions in the copper but, in recent years the view has swung away from this idea because of adverse effects of oxygen on colour, flavour, flavour stability and haze formation. The absorption of oxygen during mashing-in is low (3–8 mg O_2/l) but later steps in the mashing and lautering process are much greater (25–100 mg O_2/l). However in the copper, oxygen absorption is low again (3–15 mg O_2/l) and the same is true during wort clarification [15]. When wort boiling is carried out in the absence of hops and with gas bubbling through, it was observed that less hot trub formed when oxygen was used than when carbon dioxide or nitrogen was employed [16]. In this connection, it has been suggested that one protein fraction will coagulate during the copper boil, providing that it is not oxidized. If the oxidation occurs, coagulation is delayed until the pH falls during fermentation [33].

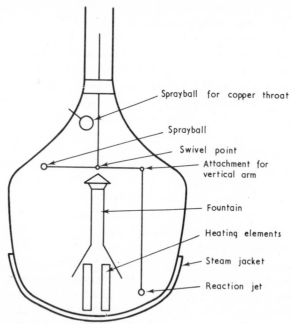

Fig. 15.6 Copper heated by steam jacket and rod-like elements showing arrangements for cleaning in-place. The reaction jet is detached from the revolving horizontal bar after cleaning is completed.

At the end of the boil, the copper is cast and the wort is run to a clarifying unit. The copper may then be used immediately, or rinsed with water, or fully cleaned with detergent. In some respects, coppers are the most difficult vessels in the brewery to clean, especially if they have internal coils, tubes and fountains. The amount of scale after 6–12 brews is very substantial, calling for particularly effective cleaning in-place. The throat of the stack requires spraying, usually with a spray ball. Other spray balls and rotating jet sprays are located so that all surfaces within the copper are sprayed. Some coppers are fitted with a bearing supported just below the throat of the stack. The bearing carries a rotating horizontal branch with a reaction jet at one end and at the other a vertical arm which is attached only during cleaning. This terminates in a spray or jet (Fig. 15.6). As has been mentioned, coppers with external calandria are relatively simple to clean, normally relying on the circulating pump and a single spray ball above the fountain.

15.7 Continuous wort boiling [1, 3, 17–19]

There have been many attempts at continuous wort boiling, with varying degrees of success but few examples are to be seen in large-scale commercial use. In some, the wort boiling is a separate operation from hop extraction [17]. In others, the principle of a continuous belt is adopted, bearing a thin film of hops through boiling wort (and eventually through sparge water to recover extract) [18]. The Centribrew continuous wort production system has been installed in a few breweries [19]. It features a tank receiving shredded hops, hop pellets or extracts which are mixed with wort. From here, the wort is heated to 150°C by steam injection at 6–8 bar but pressurized so that it does not boil. The wort is then led through a special reactor and held for about 2 min and thence to a vacuum vessel with integral condenser, where volatiles are 'flashed off.'

The lack of success of most continuous wort boiling plants may possibly be due to difficulties concerned with inadequate release of undesirable volatiles, leading to abnormal beer flavours and aromas. Fundamentally, this is expressed by the Rayleigh equation which for batch boiling is

$$\frac{x_1}{x_0} = \left(\frac{1 - E}{1}\right)\alpha - 1 \qquad [1]$$

where x_1 = final concentration of volatile component, x_0 = initial concentration of volatile component, E = percentage evaporation, and α = volatility relative to water.

Thus for 10% evaporation, which might be considered the average loss/hr for an open copper, some 86·5% of a component (of relative volatility 20) would be lost. However for continuous boiling the Rayleigh equation becomes:

$$\frac{x_1}{x_0} = \frac{1}{1 + E(\alpha - 1)}$$

and so for 10% evaporation only 65% of a component will be lost. In practice, it may be difficult to achieve 10% evaporation.

15.8 *Wort clarification*

Wort, when boiled in the copper, should be brilliantly clear with suspended large particles of trub and spent-hop material. If whole hops are used in the copper, the amount of spent hops will be 0·7–1·4 kg/hl (2·5–5·0 lb/brl) wet weight. The amount of trub will be in the order of 0·21–0·28 kg/hl (0·75–1·0 lb/brl) wet weight – roughly 80–85% water. The hot trub is made up of protein–tannin material plus insoluble salts, some hop resin material, and a significant proportion of the lipid material that was present in the sweet wort and hops. Trub particles may be as big as 5–10 mm diameter but in any conditions of shear, these break down first into particles of 30–80 μm and then to elementary particles of 0·5–1·5 μm [20]. The latter may look superficially like bacterial cocci but they are irregular in shape, variable in size and dissolve readily in alkali. Table 15.5 gives details of the composition of hot trub and spent hops. It will be seen that the trub has a reasonably high level of digestible protein and is much superior, from a nutritive point of view, than spent hops. In many breweries, the spent hops and trub are returned to the lauter tun or mash tun to cover the spent grains. There they can drain with spent grains and the liquor obtained can either be run to drain or used for mashing-in. No nutritive problems seem to arise when the mixture of spent materials are fed to cattle and such wet feed is extensively used in the UK [21].

TABLE 15.5
Nutritive analysis of spent brewhouse materials [21]

	Spent grain	Spent hops	Hot trub
Dry matter (%)	20·0, 22·0	25·0	—
Crude protein (%)	19·8, 20·5	17·2	35·4
Digestible crude protein (%)	12·0, 14·9	5·2	21·9
Crude fibre (%)	18·0, 18·6	23·6	2·3
Ether extract (%)	6·8, 6·4	7·6	1·5
Ash (%)	4·2, 4·5	6·0	7·4
Oil (%)	not determined	not determined	1·5

When the wort is cast from the copper, it is necessary to remove spent hops and trub, and the method originally used was straining or sieving. With a small brewery, the wort was run into a pipe which was expanded at its end into a perforated ball. The solid material was retained and the clarified wort was run to the cooler. In larger breweries, this same idea was developed for the hop Montejus (Fig. 15.7) and in ale breweries for the hop back (Fig. 15.8). Additional features include equipment for the recirculation of worts, the sparging of extract from the spent hops and trub, and the mechanical discharge of the spent material.

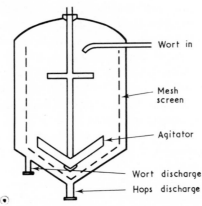

Fig. 15.7 Hop Montejus for sieving wort discharged from the copper.

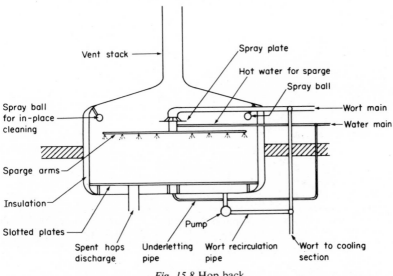

Fig. 15.8 Hop back.

The hop back may be an open vessel but, because of the steam generated during its operation, it is almost invariably covered and the steam plus volatiles extracted by a stack. Wort from the copper is run into the hop back and is strained by the slotted base – the slots are about 1·55 mm (0·06 in) wide and occupy 25–30% of the area of the base plates. As the spent hop material accumulates, it progressively improves the straining action so that hot trub is retained. In order to take advantage of this, the wort which in the earliest stages passed through the slotted base is recycled. A hop back is a large vessel and in many respects resembles an infusion mash tun. It is only applicable where whole hops are used. With general reduction in the amount of hops added to the copper, the depth of spent hops in the back may be insufficient to get efficient clarification. A bed of 30–60 cm (1–2 ft) is considered best, while a 15 cm (6 in) bed is the minimal depth.

Some brewers put fresh hops into the hop back in the hope that this will impart hoppiness to the final beers. From the hop back, the wort is pumped directly to the cooler or held in a buffer tank before cooling. A considerable amount of wort is left entrained in the spent hops and is normally recovered by sparging with hot water (8 l/kg spent hops or 0·8 gal/lb). Finally, spent hops and hot trub are removed from the hop back and cleaning may take place either after every brew or following several brews.

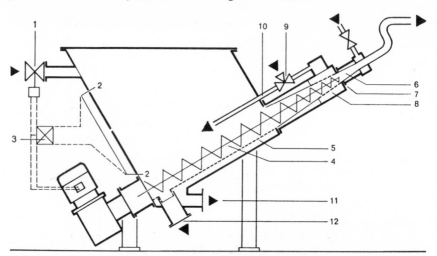

Fig. 15.9 Hop separator. 1. Valve; 2. Level control electrodes; 3. Level control; 4. Screw-conveyor; 5. Strainer area; 6. Compression chamber; 7. Fasteners; 8. Strainer basket; 9. Three-way valve (wort return and sparge water); 10. Return pipe; 11. Wort discharge; 12. Clean-out valve. Spent hops are discharged at the top. (Courtesy of A. Ziemann, GmbH).

In many breweries, the removal of the spent hop material and the hot trub from the wort occurs in two separate stages. Hop separators (Fig. 15.9) receive the wort from the copper and strain it through wire mesh. The separated spent hops are scraped from the mesh by a screw-conveyor and transferred to a part of the separator where they can be compressed and sparged before being ejected.

When breweries use hop pellets, powder or extract, rather than whole hops, hop backs and hop separators are not applicable. The wort from the copper is clarified in much the same way as wort coming out of the hop separators. One old method was to use a shallow sedimentation tank and run off the clear wort at the top of the tank. This method involves not only clarification but wort cooling and will be mentioned later. Filtration to remove hot trub might at first sight be a possibility but because kieselguhr partly dissolves in hot wort and also since wort develops cold trub on cooling, only filtration of cooled wort is normally practised. Centrifugal separation of hot trub (and spent hop powder or ground hops) is employed in some breweries, usually with large continuous, automatic rejection centrifuges. As with other methods of separation, it is often necessary on economic grounds to recover wort from the separated material.

The most popular separation device applicable whatever the method of hopping, developed by the Molson Breweries in Canada, is called the whirl-pool tank [22]. It comprises a vertical cylindrical tank into which the wort is pumped at fairly high velocity (Fig. 15.10). The batch of wort circulates within the tank and eventually the solids are deposited as a heap in the centre of the base. Clear wort can be run off and the trub plus any spent hop material can be recovered. There are considerable variations in the constructional details and modes of operation of whirlpool tanks, often leading to varying success with separation of the solids.

It has recently been stated that the 'mechanics of whirlpool separation, although basically quite simple in concept, do not easily lead to either mathe-matical or experimental analysis' [23]. Whirlpool tanks are normally con-structed of cold-rolled stainless steel and have an insulating jacket. The

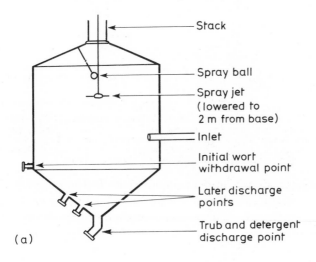

(a)

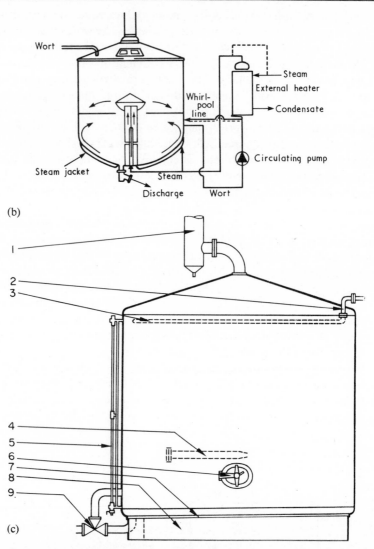

Fig. 15.10 Whirlpool tanks of various designs. (a) With conical base; (b) Combined copper and whirlpool tank; (c) Whirlpool separator with inclined base. 1. Vent stack; 2. Spray-water inlet; 3. Spray ring with nozzles; 4. Tangential wort inlet; 5. Liquid level indicator; 6. Manhole; 7. Water shield ring for concrete base; 8. Concrete base; 9. Three-way valve for discharge of wort and sludge. (Courtesy of A. Ziemann, GmbH.)

height to diameter ratio is in the region 0·67–0·77 : 1 and the head-space is about 20%. There is considerable controversy about the base of the vessel; some are flat, others have a cup or well to retain the solids, others are conical and, finally, some have a cone rising towards the top of the vessel. It is probable that the processes of forming a discrete deposit of solid material, retaining the material while wort is drained from the vessel, and finally removing the material easily and efficiently during cleaning, are to some extent incompatible. There is also controversy about the point at which wort is introduced; some vessels have the pipe about a quarter to a third of the way up the vessel, others have it near the final wort depth. In general, the vessels with lower pipes seem more popular.

Wort velocity varies greatly in the operation of these vessels; in one survey it ranged from 1·4–12 m/s (4·6–40 ft/s), averaging 6·5 m/s (21·5 ft/s) [24]. Some authorities consider that the initial rotational speed must be as high as possible. The entry pipe is usually set approximately tangentially to the vertical wall of the tank, but it has been stated that 20–30° to the tangent gives the maximum efficiency of energy conversion [25].

Recently, vessels have been installed in breweries which can act both as coppers and separators (Fig. 15.10b). This leads to an economy in the number of vessels but it must be remembered that the whirlpool acts as a buffer tank and is relatively inexpensive as a separate vessel.

The wort entering the whirlpool tank initially rotates about the vertical axis. This rotational movement in the upper layers of liquid tends to throw particles radially outwards. As the tank fills up, the wort at the bottom of the vessel will, because of friction with the base of the tank, lose this rotation. A pressure gradient builds up which causes the wort to flow radially inwards at the base where the particles tend to be carried inwards to the centre. The drag of the vessel base reduces the velocity of the wort stream and so the particles tend to be deposited at the centre. From the centre, the wort rises. The circulatory currents appear to assist in the flocculation of hot trub particles because, compared with simple sedimentation, the particles are larger and more granular.

High gravity worts do not give such rapid clarification as worts of lower extract because the difference between the density of particles and the wort is less (Stokes' Law). If no hop material is present, separation is poorer and the best result has been claimed for hop powder [26]. Additions of Irish Moss, polyvinylpyrrolidone, nylon 66 and particularly bentonite, have been stated to improve separation [26]. Anaerobic conditions are also said to increase the amount of material deposited, particularly by injecting carbon dioxide into the wort line when pumping into the whirlpool tank [26].

In order to speed withdrawal of clear wort, there are usually draw-off pipes at various heights. It is normal to run several brews through the whirlpool tank before removing the solids. The consistency of the solids changes with time and eventually the mass will set like concrete due to oxidative copolymerization of proteins and polyphenols. Two methods of removing the solids are the use of a high pressure water spray jet lowered to 2 m (6 ft) from

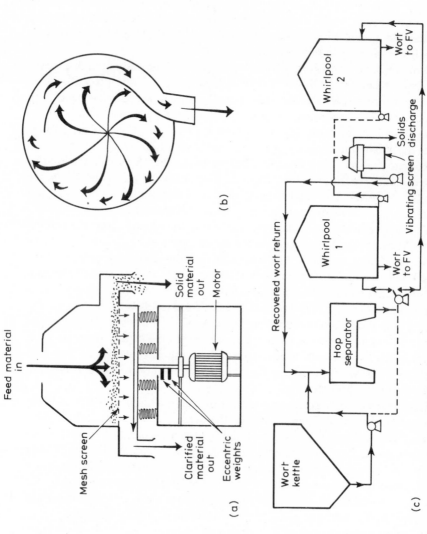

Fig. 15.11 (a) Vertical section of vibrating screen filter; (b) The distribution and movement of solids as seen from above the filter; (c) Arrangement of vessels that may be used for efficient use of the vibrating screen filter [28].

the base, and the incorporation of a 'hedgehog' spray jet in the base of the vessel. The slurry of hot trub material may be transferred to the mash copper, mash tun or lauter tun [27]. Alternatively it can be passed to a vibrating screen and the recovered weak wort pumped back to join wort cast from the copper (Fig. 15.11). The best separation occurs using a 30 μm screen [28]. Trub with a moisture of 80% can be added to spent grains for cattle feed. After removal of the trub, the vessel may be cleaned using 2–4% hot caustic soda solution, usually with additives, and then rinsed.

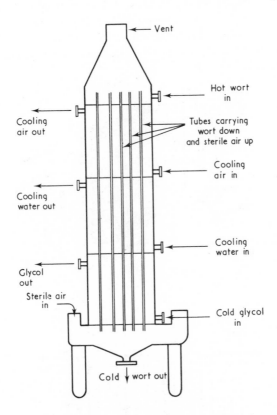

Fig. 15.12 Wort cooler which allows for aeration.

Wort freed from spent hop material and trub is cooled in order that it can be pitched with yeast. In very old breweries, the wort is cooled in shallow open vessels, using only air cooling. These open coolers or coolships had three functions: cooling, aeration of the wort and separation of cold trub.

Originally they were open to the atmosphere, but in order to avoid microbiological contamination it is preferable to use cooled sterile air. In order to have greater economy of space, vertical coolers were introduced in which the wort flowed continuously as a thin film over a vertical metal surface cooled with chilled water (or other coolant). Such coolers aerated the wort as well as cooling, but there was no removal of cold trub. Most breweries now use plate heat-exchangers, which cool, but neither aerate the wort nor separate cold trub. However, coolers involving aeration are still used by some modern breweries (Fig. 15.12). Wort enters at the top of the cooler and flows down through a series of stainless steel tubes. It is cooled progressively, first by air, then water and finally glycol. During its fall, it is exposed to sterilized air introduced at the bottom of the tubes. A unit capable of cooling 450 hl/hr (275 brl/hr) would be about 7 m (23 ft) high and 2 m (6 ft) diameter [34].

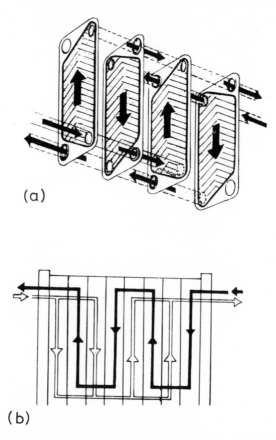

(a)

(b)

Fig. 15.13 (a) Principles of the plate heat-exchanger; (b) A typical flow grouping.

Although there are some shell and tube coolers used, plate heat-exchangers are far more common. They comprise a stainless steel frame carrying a large number of vertically arranged stainless steel plates which are compressed together. Each plate has a series of indentations and a rubber sealant gasket around its periphery. There are four circular holes cut in the corners of the plate. When the plates are pressed together, they seal at the rubber gaskets and the indentations form channels. Between two plates, say a and b, the channels allow coolant to flow in at hole 1 and out at the diametrically opposite one which we will call 3. Between the next pair of plates, b and c the wort enters through hole 4 and passes through channels before leaving at the diametrically opposite hole 2. Coolant would then pass between plates c and d, and so on (Fig. 15.13). The channels are designed to give very turbulent flow and good heat transfer. Any build-up of scale from either the wort or the coolant, or both, seriously reduces the heat transfer. The plate heat-exchanger may comprise two or more stages, so that wort may run counter-current to water in the first section while a second stage may reduce the wort temperature still further by using glycol or alcohol as a refrigerant. In this connection it is usual to cool lager worts to 6–12°C (11–54°F), depending on the fermentation temperature to be employed. Worts for ales are cooled to about 15°C (59°C). Another important consideration of wort coolers is their ability to generate considerable volumes of hot water (at say 70°C) for mashing, and for cleaning equipment.

15.9 *Removal of cold trub*

During the cooling of wort, cold trub progressively precipitates. It is impossible to remove all the potential precipitate because the trub continues to form during fermentation and subsequent beer cooling (Fig. 15.14). However, many breweries, especially those concerned with lager fermentation, remove much of the cold trub; some use kieselguhr filtration (see Chapter 20) while others centrifuge. An additional method involves flotation of cold trub: air is forced through cooled wort by a Venturi tube and mixing pump. After wort has been held a few hours in a collecting vessel, air bubbles plus cold trub collect at the surface and can be skimmed off as a compact layer. This method is claimed to be superior to sedimentation or filtration in the removal of cold trub [29]. It must be emphasized that great care must be taken to ensure that wort held at temperatures in the range 0–60°C (32–140°F) does not become infected.

A recent survey [30] has shown that in Swiss breweries, the cold break content of beers varied over a wide range, independent of separating procedure. The effects on fermentation, maturation and beer clarification were not significant., During the course of successive fermentations, the preference of tasting panels shifted from beers where cold trub had not been removed

to beers where partial removal had been practised. The overall impression
from other studies is that the presence of cold trub may stimulate the rate
of fermentation, possibly by providing nuclei for carbon dioxide release;
on the other hand, with more delicate beers there seems to be more possibility
of having unacceptable sulphury aroma and taste.

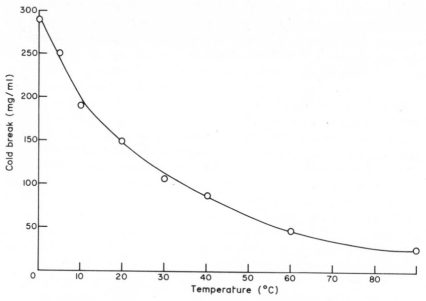

Fig. 15.14 Amount of cold trub formed at various temperatures.

In New Zealand, worts are normally chilled to the point where slush-ice
forms. This procedure permits the short storage of wort, but the main
advantage appears to be the stability of the derived beers from the point of
view of haze formation.

The production of cold trub has received little biochemical study. Many
years ago, it was claimed that to get maximum trub production it was
necessary to cool slowly over the range 49–26°C (120–80°F), at least 30 s
being required, and mechanical agitation being desirable [31]. Later results
[32] described worts where the best cold trub formation occurred when cooling
from 60–21°C (140–70°F) took place in 3 s or less. An hypothesis explaining
the reasons for fast cooling and slow cooling worts states that there are two
or more protein fractions with isoelectric points above pH 6·0, and at least
one with an isoelectric point (IEP) of about pH 3·9, mutual flocculation
between fractions of opposite charge occurring [33]. One of the fractions with
an IEP of over pH 6·0 has the ability to change by oxidation to material with
an IEP of about pH 3·9. Some worts have a high content of this positively

charged material. They should be cooled slowly and aerated so that more of the negatively charged material is produced which can coprecipitate with the positively-charged material present.

15.10 *Wort aeration*

As mentioned previously, wort aeration may occur during cooling of wort. Yeasts vary in their requirements for oxygen (see Chapters 17 and 18) in the range of approximately 4–14 mg/l, dependent *inter alia* on the strain used and the content of unsaturated lipids. Wort saturated with air contains approximately 8 mg/l of oxygen at 15°C (59°F) but wort saturated with oxygen will contain about five-fold this amount. Thus oxygen-saturated *water* at 10°C and standard atmospheric pressure contains 54·3 mg/l. Wort takes up rather less oxygen than water. Breweries may either spray wort to pick up atmospheric oxygen or inject air or oxygen into the wort stream, the injection relating to hot wort or cold wort as appropriate. When injected into wort at the hot end of a cooler, air will give a darker coloured wort than if added at the cold end. Oxygen will have a much more pronounced effect with respect to this and other oxidative reactions. This is due to chemical combination of oxygen with the wort constituents, particularly polyphenolic ones. Physical solution of oxygen will be less than if injection occurred at the cold end and more foaming of wort may occur. It may be that the air or oxygen is sterilized when put in contact with hot wort but this depends on the size of the bubbles. Certainly the turbulence of the wort in its passage through the cooler will aid solution of the oxygen. There are a few breweries that optimize the situation by injecting sterile air or oxygen between two stages of a plate heat-exchanger, with the temperature at 10–15°C (50–59°F). Finally, it should be emphasized that oxygenation must be restricted, otherwise fermentation is too vigorous, yeast growth excessive, and beer quality suffers. Probably the most popular treatment is injection of air or oxygen at the cold end of the wort cooler.

REFERENCES

[1] ROYSTON, M. G. (1966). *J. Inst. Brewing*, **72**, 351.
[2] FARBER, E. A. and SCORAH, R. L. (1948). *Trans. Amer. Soc. Mech. Eng.*, **70**, 369.
[3] ROYSTON, M. G. (1971). *Modern Brewing Technology* (ed. FINDLAY, W. P. K.), Macmillan, London, p. 60.
[4] BARKER, A. J. (1980). Private communication.
[5] COULSON, J. M. and RICHARDSON, J. F. (1977). *Chemical Engineering*, Vol. 1, 3rd edn., Pergamon Press, Oxford, 167.
[6] ST. JOHNSON, J. H. (1952). *Brewers Guardian*, **81** (2), 22.
[7] ROBSON, F. O. (1974). *The Brewer* (2), 59.
[8] HUDSON, J. R. and RENNIE, H. (1971). *Tech. Quart. Master Brewers Assoc. Americas*, **8**, (4), 173.

[9] HUDSON, J. H. and BIRTWISTLE, S. E. (1966). *J. Inst. Brewing*, **72, 46**.

[10] RENNIE, H. (1972). *J. Inst. Brewing*, **78**, 162.

[11] SOMMER, G. and SCHILFARTH, H. (1975). *Proc. Eur. Brewery Conv. Congr.*, *Nice*, p. 233.

[12] HIPWELL, C. R., BUTTON, A. H. and SULLIVAN, M. A. (1975). *Proc. Eur. Brewery Conv. Congr.*, *Nice*, p. 171.

[13] HUDSON, L. E. (1958). *Wallerstein Lab. Commun.* **21**, 183, 323.

[14] PERCIVAL, E. and MCDOWELL, R. H. (1967). *Chemistry and Enzymology of Marine Algal Polysaccharides*, Academic Press, London, p. 137.

[15] LIE, S., GRINDOM, T. and JACOBSEN, T. (1977). *Proc. Eur. Brewery Conv. Congr.*, *Amsterdam*, p. 235.

[16] BREMNER, T. S. (1963). *J. Inst. Brewing*, **69**, 406.

[17] DUMMETT, G. A. (1958). *Brewers Guild J.*, **44**, 419.

[18] DAVIS, A. D., POLLOCK, J. R. A. and GOUGH, P. E. (1962). *J. Inst. Brewing*, **68**, 309.

[19] EHNSTROM, L. (1977). *Tech. Quart. Master Brewers Assoc. Americas*, **14** (3), 159.

[20] VACANO, N. L. (1955). *Wallerstein Lab. Commun.*, **23**, 13.

[21] CHAPMAN, J. (1976). *Disposal of a Brewery Waste with special reference to the Whirlpool Separator*, PhD. Thesis, University of Newcastle-upon-Tyne.

[22] HUDSTON, H. R. (1969). *Tech. Quart. Master Brewers Assoc. Americas*, **6**, (3), 164.

[23] CHAPMAN, J., WOODS, J. L. and O'CALLAGHAN, J. R. (1977). *The Brewer* (4), 130; (5), 164.

[24] Joint Development Committee (1971). *J. Inst. Brewing*, **77**, 334.

[25] MUNCH, H. (1969). *Brewers Guardian*, **98**, (11), 46.

[26] DADIC, M. and VAN GHELUWE, J. E. A. (1972). *Brewers Digest*, (9), 120.

[27] KIENINGER, H. (1977). *J. Inst. Brewing*, **83**, 72.

[28] BUTTON, A. H., STACEY, A. J. and TAYLOR, B. (1977). *Proc. Eur. Brewery Conv. Congr.*, *Amsterdam*, p. 377.

[29] NARZISS, L., KIENINGER, H. and REICHENDER, E. (1971). *Proc. Eur. Brewery Conv. Congr.*, *Estoril*, p. 197.

[30] SCHUR, F. and PFENNINGER, H. B. (1977). *Proc. Eur. Brewery Conv. Congr.*, *Amsterdam*, p. 225.

[31] BROWN, H. T. (1913). *J. Inst. Brewing*, **19**, 84.

[32] CLENDINNEN, F. W. J. (1936). *J. Inst. Brewing*, **42**, 566.

[33] ST. JOHNSON, J. H. (1948). *J. Inst. Brewing*, **54, 305**.

[34] STRAUSS, K. M. (1977). *The Practical Brewer*, Master Brewers Association of the Americas, Madison, Wisconsin, USA.

Chapter 16

BIOLOGY OF YEASTS

16.1 *Yeast taxonomy*

Brewers have repeatedly experienced the need to identify a yeast in order that they can search the appropriate literature for information on the yeast in question, or be able to recognize the yeast on a subsequent occasion. It may be that they wish to be assured that a particular sample of pitching yeast is the strain which they propagated initially from laboratory stocks. On the other hand, they may be anxious to know if a yeast strain which has contaminated their pure culture of pitching yeast is, according to other brewers' experience, likely to cause the beer to spoil. Because yeasts are microscopic in size, and change both their shape and size considerably according to the medium in which they grow, simple microscopic examination rarely suffices and identification is normally based on a range of morphological and biochemical criteria.

It might be expected that identification of a large number of yeasts should lead to an arrangement of these micro-organisms into groups, families, sub-families, genera, species, and varieties in much the same way as higher plants have been classified. Biological classification (or taxonomy) is normally based on probable evolutionary relationships between organisms and, because it is never possible to be absolutely sure of such relationships, the classification may be based on certain logical assumptions. For instance, similarities in mode of reproduction are rated more important than similarities in gross shape and size, since the latter are more prone to be influenced by the age of the cell and the nature of its environment. When groups of organisms that are closely similar are classified, the basis of classification tends to become more and more arbitrary and therefore debatable. An example of this is the classification of strains of brewing yeast where it is clearly a matter of classifying on the basis of industrially useful characters such as rate of growth and the ability to sediment, etc.

Defining the word 'yeast' is very difficult indeed because it is a convenient label for a wide range of fungi where the usual growth form is unicellular [1]. Until 1931, the classification of yeasts was extremely confused and no system

527

gained general acceptance. Since that time, however, a series of monographs has been produced by a group of dedicated research workers in the Netherlands that has helped greatly in achieving a satisfactory system of classification [2–7]. Nevertheless, there are still some rather puzzling arbitrary decisions; thus black yeast-like fungi are excluded from a consideration of yeasts, but red, pink, and yellow forms are included.

Yeasts are Protists. *The Protista* are organisms which possess characteristics of cells of higher organisms, but show a simpler level of biological organization. The yeasts are higher protists because they possess a true nucleus (i.e., are eukaryotic) and cytoplasmic organelles (plastids) e.g., mitochondria. Higher protists comprise the algae, protozoa, fungi and slime moulds. All yeasts are classified as fungi, that is, non-photosynthetic higher protists with a rigid cell wall and existing either as unicellular organisms or as a mycelium. The mycelium is a rigid, branched system of tubes of fairly uniform diameter containing a multinucleate cytoplasm.

The fungi are divided into the following main groups:

1. The Phycomycetes are those in which the vegetative structure normally comprises mycelia which are not divided into cells by cross-walls. The group is subdivided according to the mode of sexual reproduction. Thus those that have male and female sex cells of the same shape and size are termed Zygomycetes, e.g. *Mucor* and *Rhizopus* (bread moulds). Those that have female sex cells which are larger than the male cells are Oomycetes, e.g. *Pseudoperonospora* (downy mildew of hops).

2. The Ascomycetes have mycelia which are divided by cross-walls and their characteristic spores (ascospores) are produced within a sac called an ascus. In many cases these organisms also produce other spores called conidia which, unlike the ascospores, are not produced as a consequence of fusion of sex cells. This is the largest group of fungi (about 35 000 species) and includes many well-known genera of yeasts, and the moulds *Aspergillus* and *Penicillium* that are used extensively in microbiological industries.

3. The Basidiomycetes have mycelia that are divided by cross-walls and their characteristic spores (basidiospores) are produced in tetrads by extrusions arising from the cells (basidia). Fusion of two nuclei occurs in each basidium and the basidiospores are formed after reduction division (meiosis) of this 'fusion nucleus' when the number of chromosomes in each cell becomes halved. The group includes the rust and smut diseases of agricultural crops and species with large fruiting bodies such as bracket fungi of trees, mushrooms, and toadstools.

4. The Fungi Imperfecti. This is a heterogeneous group of fungi in which sexual reproduction is unknown. Some of the examples may have no

sexual phase but in other instances such a phase may not yet have been discovered. From time to time, a species within the group discloses its identity with one of the other groups (usually the Ascomycetes) by producing sexual cells and then it is transferred to the appropriate group. Examples of the Fungi Imperfecti are the organisms causing ringworm and athlete's foot in man, *Verticillium* wilt of hops, *Fusarium* infection of barley, etc.

The yeasts which form ascospores are termed 'ascosporogenous', e.g. *Saccharomyces*, *Pichia* and *Hansenula*. Those that produce external spores, and are probably representatives of the Basidiomycetes, are termed 'ballistosporogenous', e.g. *Sporobolomyces*. Finally, those yeasts which have no known sexual stage and are therefore Fungi Imperfecti, are called 'anascosporogenous.' From this preliminary trichotomy the yeasts, comprising about 350 species in 39 genera, are classified according to a number of morphological and physiological characteristics (Table 16.1) in order to arrive first at the generic name, and then the specific name.

TABLE 16.1

Some criteria used in the classification of yeasts

Morphological characteristics	Physiological characteristics
(a) Growth form on selected solid media.	(a) Production of CO_2 in anaerobic growth in liquid medium in the presence of a single source of carbon (fermentation).
(b) Size and shape of cells in liquid media.	(b) Growth in the presence of a single source of carbon (assimilation).
(c) Mode of reproduction.	(c) Assimilation of single sources of nitrogen, e.g. nitrate, ethylamine.
(d) Ascospore number and shape (or ballistospore formation).	(d) Production of pigments.
(e) Formation of a pellicle (skin) or ring at the surface of liquid media.	(e) Production of esters.
(f) Nature of the sediment in liquid media.	

An indication of the range of morphology encountered amongst the different genera of yeasts is given in Fig. 16.1. Cells may be oval, spherical, apiculate (lemon-shaped) or elongated. Division is most commonly by the process of multilateral budding whereby a bud may be formed at any point on the cell surface e.g., *Saccharomyces* sp. In bipolar budding (e.g., *Nadsonia* sp., *Kloeckera* sp.), only the poles of an elongated cell are sites for bud formation, whereas in binary fission (e.g. *Schizosaccharomyces* sp.), a cross-wall is laid down within the cell after elongation. Following multilateral budding, failure of buds to separate from their parent cell results in the development of branched chains of cells. In yeasts exhibiting polar budding or binary fission, failure of cells to separate produces a single filament. Such branched and unbranched filaments are referred to as pseudomycelia. Some yeasts are capable of producing true mycelia but often only under certain cultural conditions, for example in a thin film of solid medium between glass slides. Also included in the morphological examination of yeasts is the ability to produce spores, the nature of the sexual process, e.g. whether conjugation of cells occurs, and the shape of spores produced, e.g. spherical, hat, saturn (see Fig. 16.1).

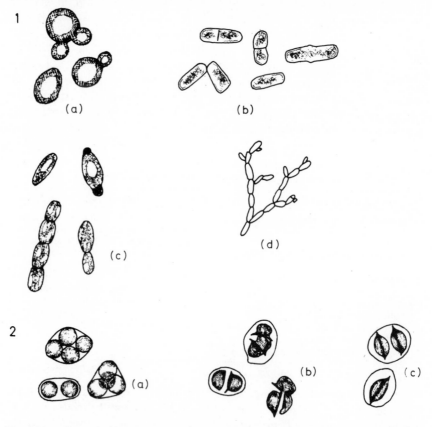

Fig. 16.1 1. Drawings of (a) *S. cerevisiae* (multilateral budding); (b) *Schizosaccharomyces pombe* (binary fission); (c) *Nadsonia* Sp. (bipolar budding); (d) pseudomycelium of *Pichia membranaefaciens*. 2. Asci and ascopores of (a) *Saccharomyces* Sp.; (b) *Pichia* Sp. (hat-shaped spores); (c) *Hansenula saturnus* (saturn-shaped spores).
Magnification: 1(a), (b), (c), ⌣ 6 μm; 1(d), ⌣ 10 μm; 2(a), (b), (c), ⌣ 3 μm.

Classification to genus is often achieved by morphological tests supplemented with a few physiological tests, whereas classification to species level relies heavily on the latter. As an example of the use of physiological criteria for classifying members of a genus to the species level, Table 16.2 shows fermentation reactions of species of the genus *Saccharomyces*. It is important to note that many taxonomists believe that assigning species on the basis of one or a few tests only, such as the difference between *S. cerevisiae* and *S. diastaticus*, is unacceptable and current schemes would name both *S. cerevisiae*. Whilst the 'lumping' process has undoubted merits for the taxonomist, the brewing scientist is required to distinguish between these organisms, therefore, in brewing, the former species names such as *S. diastaticus* are likely to remain in use. This is equally true for the brewing distinction between *S. carlsbergenis* and *S. cerevisiae*, which the taxonomist will in future 'lump' as *S. cerevisiae*. To the brewer however, these are distinct organisms and differ in several important respects in their brewing characteristics (e.g. optimum fermentation temperature). Such characteristics, however, have no place in the criteria used for classical taxonomy.

TABLE 16.2

Fermentation reactions of some species of Saccharomyces*
{Table simplified from reference [7]}

Species	Galactose	Sucrose	Maltose	Melibiose	Starch
S. bayanus	−	+	+	−	−
S. capensis	−	+	−	−	−
S. cerevisiae	+	+	+	−	−
S. diastaticus	+	+	+	−	+
S. inusitatus	−	+	+	+	−
S. uvarum (carlsbergensis) +	+	+	+	−

* These species accepted in reference [7] are all classified as *S. cerevisiae* in reference [9].

From the practical standpoint of identifying yeasts, the classical taxonomic approach suffers from the major disadvantage that assignment to genus often necessitates the demonstration of spore formation. Many yeasts isolated from their natural habitats often fail to sporulate readily and will do so only either at low frequency or on a particular medium. Furthermore the process of sporulation may take up to 4 weeks. Accordingly, schemes for identifying yeasts which do not rely heavily on spore formation are of considerable value. One such scheme employs a computer-made series of keys [8, 9]. It provides two keys specifically related to yeasts encountered in brewing; one uses physiological tests and microscopic examination, and the other physiological tests only [9]. These keys are of great value for identifying 'non-Saccharomyces' yeasts, but no longer accept many specific names, e.g. *diastaticus* and *fermentati*.

Another scheme uses a very small number of simple morphological and physiological tests, together with serological tests using six antisera [10].

This scheme is limited to fourteen genera of yeast; however its principal advantage is that results are obtained in a few days. Agreement with the classical methods is good although, as is to be expected, some differences are found.

Serological tests rely on the highly specific reaction between antibodies and antigens. The antigens used are whole (dead) cells of a particular yeast strain which are injected into experimental animals, particularly rabbits. The rabbit produces antibodies to certain chemical groupings (the antigens) on the surface of the yeast. After a course of injections, some blood is taken from the rabbit and the red blood cells are removed. The resultant serum, when mixed with a suspension of the yeast cells used, causes cell agglutination. The serum is therefore an antiserum to the particular yeast strain used. This antiserum will agglutinate other strains of yeast which bear the appropriate antigen and such strains are said to be serologically related.

An antiserum may be exhaustively reacted with a yeast by separating and discarding agglutinated cells and repeating the process several times. The product is termed an absorbed antiserum. An antiserum raised to a selected yeast when absorbed by a related strain will no longer agglutinate the latter but may still agglutinate the former. This is because there are still present in the absorbed antiserum, antibodies produced to antigens present on the selected strain, but not present on the related strain.

TABLE 16.3

Agglutination of Saccharomyces *species by* S. carlsbergensis *(Strain NCYC 1116)*
antiserum before and after absorption
{Simplified from results of CAMPBELL and BRUDZYNSKI (1966) [19]}

Yeast suspensions under test	Unabsorbed	Agglutination after absorption with:			
		S. carlsbergensis 396, 397, 1116	S. carlsbergensis 399, 511, 519, 529, 530	S. rouxii 170, 381	S. cerevisiae 1006, 1027, 1062
S. carlsbergensis 396, 397, 1116	+	−	+	+	+
S. carlsbergensis 399, 511, 519, 529, 530	+	−	−	−	−
S. rouxii 170, 381	+	−	+	−	+
S. cerevisiae 1006, 1027, 1062	+	−	+	−	−

Antigenic reactions can therefore be exploited in cross-absorption techniques in which a group of yeasts is tested to reveal which are common antigens in the group and which are unique antigens. An example of the cross-absorption technique is given in Table 16.3 which demonstrates that there are two serological groups within the species *S. carlsbergensis*. Antiserum produced using *S. carlsbergensis* 1116 will cause agglutination of strains of *S. carlsbergensis*, *S. cerevisiae*, and *S. rouxii*. There are, therefore, antigens present on the walls of each of these strains which will react to corresponding antibodies in the serum. In other words, since antibodies are specific to particular antigens, the strains referred to above must have certain antigens in common. When the antiserum is mixed with 1116 (or strains 396 and 397) reaction of the antibodies occurs with specific antigens giving agglutination. The agglutinated mass is then removed, but the 'absorbed antiserum' so produced will not now agglutinate any of the yeasts under test. Therefore, agglutination is complete in the case of 1116 and all antibodies have been removed in the process. This represents a confirmatory control. The results for antiserum mixed with 396 and 397 demonstrate their close antigenic similarity to 1116. If fresh 1116 antiserum is absorbed with *S. carlsbergensis* strains 399, 511, etc., and is mixed with cells of 1116, 396, or 397, there is agglutination. This shows that 399 and its group cannot react with all the antibodies of the antiserum. Thus this group lacks one or more antigens present in 1116. The table also shows that (*i*) 1116 antiserum absorbed with *S. carlsbergensis* strains 399, 511, etc., will agglutinate with *S. rouxii* and *S. cerevisiae*. (Therefore the latter two species have antigens in common with the 1116 group of *S. carlsbergensis*, and not present in the 399 group of *S. carlsbergensis*.) (*ii*) The last vertical column in Table 16.3 shows that *S. rouxii* shares antigens with the 1116 group of *S. carlsbergensis* which are not present in *S. cerevisiae* strains.

This technique has been used extensively to discover the antigenic relationships between (*i*) several genera of yeast, (*ii*) species of selected genera, and (*iii*) strains of selected species [11–14]. Because it has been shown that changes in yeast cell-wall composition occurring towards the end of fermentation do not change the antigenic structure of the yeasts, the value of the tests is enhanced [15].

A useful extension of cross-absorption methods involves the coupling of antibodies with a fluorescent dye such as fluorescein. Detection of specific antigen–antibody reaction is then not dependent on agglutination of a large number of cells but on the fluorescence of individual cells that are coated with the specific antibody–dye complex. The fluorescence can be seen under a suitable microscope using quartz–iodine illumination, enabling a single fluorescent cell to be identified among thousands of non-fluorescing cells [16]. This technique has been so developed that it is used in routine microbiological control in breweries to detect extremely small proportions of unwanted 'wild' yeasts in pure-culture brewing yeasts (see Chapter 21).

Other serological methods have been used in examining extracts of yeasts rather than whole cells; a suitable extracting material is phenol. They include the Ouchterlony technique [17] in which the antiserum is placed in a hole cut in the centre of an agar plate. Extracts of various yeasts are placed in a series of holes cut at equal distances from the first. Agglutination lines appear when the antiserum and extracts diffuse, meet, and react, but the ratio of amount of antigen to antibody is critical to get satisfactory agglutination lines. Different antigens will tend to produce agglutination lines at different distances from the central hole in relation to diffusion characteristics.

In immunoelectrophoretic methods [18] two spots of yeast extract are placed on an agar gel covering a microscope slide. They are situated one on either side of a trough cut in the agar and running most of the length of the slide. An electric current is then induced to flow along the gel to electrophorese the two spots of yeast extract. A specific antiserum is then added to the trough and agglutination occurs after diffusion of the antibodies and the antigens which have been separated by electrophoresis.

Strains of *Saccharomyces cerevisiae* and *S. carlsbergensis* used for brewing have been classified for many years on the basis of their performance in brewery fermentations. This classification has been extended by serological analysis, e.g. two serological groups of *S. carlsbergensis* may be recognized [19]. Recently classification of brewing yeasts by numerical taxonomic techniques [20] based on brewing performance has been made. Using a computer and principal coordinate analysis it was found that ale brewing strains could be classified into five groups and each group could be further subdivided into two sub-groups. A comparison of the antigenic composition of the strains by immunoelectrophoresis of cell extracts with the classification based on brewing properties showed significant relationships between the presence of certain antigens and the properties of the yeast head and deposited yeast at the end of a fermentation [21].

Classification of brewing yeasts and selection of suitable strains for brewing receive some treatment in Chapters 18 and 19.

16.2 *Ecology of yeasts* [22–24]

Yeasts depend strictly on the presence of organic carbon compounds as energy and carbon sources because they are not photosynthetic organisms. The organic carbon may be in the form of carbohydrates or polyols or acid derivatives of them. Hydrocarbons, including n-paraffins, provide suitable sources of organic carbon for species of *Candida* and, therefore, oil products can be used to produce yeast that can be incorporated into animal feeds. Species of *Cryptococcus*, *Rhodotorula*, *Candida*, and *Torulopsis* are unable to assimilate a wide variety of carbon compounds, are abundant in fruit juices, sugary plant exudates, and other materials rich in simple sugars.

Certain yeasts are able to grow at very low temperatures and such psychrophiles are common in Arctic soils and waters. Thus *Trichosporon scottii* grows in the range of −10–10°C (14–50°F). Similar adaptation to low temperatures has led to yeasts being important spoilage agents of frozen foods. Other yeasts are only able to grow in the range 28–42°C (82–108°F) because they have adapted to an existence in the gut of warm-blooded animals. Among human and animal pathogens are species of the genera *Candida*, *Cryptococcus*, *Torulopsis*, *Pityrosporum*, *Trichosporon* and *Rhodotorula*. Symbiosis of some yeasts with certain insects is also well documented. Competition for nutrients is a most important factor in the distribution of yeasts. Against bacteria, yeasts have the advantage of growing well at relatively low pH values, but they are suppressed by certain antibiotics secreted by bacteria. In certain cases, a form of symbiosis with bacteria may develop, as in the case of the microbial complexes used for yoghourt and for bees-wine fermentations.

Soil provides a habitat for many yeasts either permanently or as a temporary home to escape desiccation. Desiccation is often prevented by the secretion of extracellular slime by the yeasts. Poor soil, such as seashore sand, may contain few yeasts but rich agricultural soils often have as many as 40 000 viable yeasts per gram of soil. Leaves and other plant material, particularly rotting fruit, are also rich sources of yeasts. From the vegetative layer above the soil surface, yeasts are blown by air currents. The dominant yeasts encountered in one survey of urban New Zealand air were species of *Cryptococcus*, *Rhodotorula*, *Sporobolomyces* and *Debaryomyces*. On average there was one viable yeast cell per 0·56 m³ (per 2 ft³). A wide range of yeasts has also been identified in samples taken in marine areas, including species of *Candida*, *Cryptococcus Rhodotorula* and *Debaryomyces*.

During the ripening of fruits, one group of yeast species gives way to another group. Thus on grapes, species of *Candida*, *Torulopsis*, *Kloeckera* and *Hanseniaspora* are replaced by strains of *Saccharomyces cerevisiae* and *S. cerevisiae* var *ellipsoideus* (which is the variety used for production of wine). In the production of Kaffir beer from sorghum malt, strains of *S. cerevisiae*, *Candida krusei*, and *Kloeckera apiculata* have been isolated from the malt. Cider orchards are characterized by a high level of *Candida pulcherrima*. There is no clear indication from yeast ecology how *Saccharomyces carlsbergensis* and *S. cerevisiae* came to be universally employed for beer production. Strong sugar solutions such as honey and maple syrup tend to be infected by species of *Zygosaccharomyces*, *Hanseniaspora*, and *Candida*; these osmophilic yeasts, along with *Saccharomyces mellis* and *S. rouxii*, are important spoilage organisms of fruit and syrups. The spread of yeasts on ripe fruit is aided by insects and in particular fruit flies (*Drosophila* sp.).

16.3 *Structure of* Saccharomyces cerevisiae [25]

Cells of brewing strains are usually spherical or ellipsoidal in shape and their size varies between species, strains and even within a culture of a pure strain. Some values for mean diameter (assuming spherical cells) and dry cell mass are given in Table 16.4. All members of the genus *Saccharomyces* reproduce by multilateral budding.

TABLE 16.4

Mean diameters and dry cell mass for strains of S. cerevisiae

	Mean diameter* (μm)	Dry mass/cell (pg)
NCYC 1006 (Brewing yeast)	13·4	40
NCYC 738 (Wild yeast)	5·5	10
A8209B (Haploid 'genetic' strain)	7·0	—

* Obtained using a Coulter Counter.

Using a light microscope (magnification $\times$ 1000), unstained cells may be seen to contain a vacuole and various small 'bodies' (inclusions) both within the vacuole and cytoplasm. Specific optical (e.g. phase-contrast) or staining techniques may be used to show the presence of the nucleus and the bud and birth scars on the cell wall. Detailed information on the structure of the cell is obtained only by using the electron microscope. Scanning electron microscopy may be used to examine the cell surface and transmission electron microscopy to observe sections through the yeast cell. Techniques of fixation and staining may induce artefacts and therefore much detailed analysis uses the method of freeze-fracturing of fresh, unfixed material to prepare cells for analysis.

A diagram of a section through a typical yeast cell is shown in Fig. 16.2. The cell is bounded by a wall which may bear one or several scars, and within the wall lies the cell membrane. Connected with the membrane and extending into the cytoplasm is the endoplasmic reticulum. This membranous system also appears to connect with the nuclear membrane which forms the boundary of the nucleus. Other organelles within the cytoplasm are the mitochondria and vacuoles, the latter often containing granular material. Lipid droplets may also be found in the cytoplasm.

During the budding process, division of nucleus and production of new organelles occurs, these are distributed between the mother cell and bud.

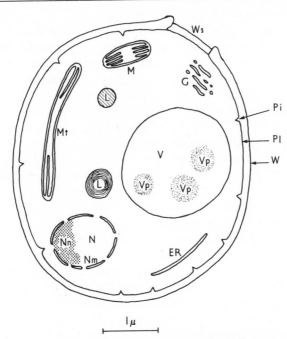

Fig. 16.2 Diagram of an electron micrograph of a section through a resting cell of bakers' yeast (*Saccharomyces cerevisiae*). ER, endoplasmic reticulum; M, mitochondrion; N, nucleus; Nm, nuclear membrane; Nn, nucleolus; Pi, invagination; Pl, plasmalemma; V, vacuole; Vp, polymetaphosphate granule; W, cell wall; Ws, bud scar; L, lipid granule (sphaerosome).

16.3.1 THE NUCLEUS

This organelle is approximately $1 \cdot 5 \, \mu m$ in diameter and is bounded by a double membrane containing pores of some $0 \cdot 1 \, \mu m$ diameter. A dense crescent-shaped area within the nucleus is referred to as the nucleolus. Within the nucleus resides the genetic material. In *Saccharomyces*, clearly-defined chromosomes have not been observed; however genetic evidence shows that the haploid cell nucleus contains at least 17 chromosomes (linkage groups) and several fragments (see Fig. 16.9, p. 554). The difficulties experienced in attempting to make yeast chromosomes visible most probably arise because they are much smaller than those of other eukaryotes. Each chromosome is expected to be composed of a single molecule of double-helical DNA associated with basic (histone-like) proteins. During the S phase of cell growth (see Chapter 18), each chromosome is replicated and during the subsequent phases the duplicated chromosomes are separated. This asexual process involving mitotic nuclear division occurs wholly within the confines of the nuclear membrane, which remains intact throughout the process as two nuclei are formed.

16.3.2 THE MITOCHONDRIA [25, 26]

At all stages of the growth cycle, when growing under aerobic conditions in the presence of low concentrations of glucose, yeast cells contain several mitochondria. However one of these organelles is always highly branched and larger than the others. Rapidly-growing cells contain only a few mitochondria and these are transformed into a population of numerous small organelles in stationary phase cells [27]. Each mitochondrion is bounded by a double membrane, the innermost one is often folded and extends into the lumen of the organelle as invaginations (cristae).

Mitochondria are associated with (*i*) the components of the electron transport system (respiratory chain), (*ii*) the synthesis of ATP during respiration, and (*iii*) the oxidative reactions of the tricarboxylic acid (Krebs') cycle.

To a large extent, mitochondrial development and activity is under the control of mitochondrial genes located in mitochondrial DNA (mtDNA). This single circular molecule has a molecular weight of approximately 50×10^6. For complete mitochondrial development and function, nuclear (chromosomal) genes are also required. Within the mitochondrion mtDNA is transcribed into messenger RNA (mRNA) and translated into protein. Protein synthesis occurs on 70 S ribosomes whose synthesis is under mtDNA control. This protein-synthesizing machinery is quite distinct from that present in the cytoplasm of the cell which uses 80 S ribosomes encoded by yeast nuclear DNA. These differences between cytoplasmic and mitochondrial protein synthesis account for the disruption of mitochondrial function by certain antibiotics, e.g. erythromycin. Mutants whose mitochondrial protein synthesis is resistant to these antibiotics may be isolated and have contributed much to the study of mitochondrial function. Furthermore evidence is available which shows that mitochondrial mutations also affect the permeability of the cytoplasmic membrane [28]. Mitochondria may therefore influence the growth of yeast by affecting the flow of nutrients into the cell.

Under anaerobic conditions or in the presence of high levels of glucose in the medium (see Chapter 17), the mitochondria differ morphologically from those of aerobically-grown cells in that they lack tricarboxylic acid cycle enzymes and some components of the respiratory chain. These changes are reflected in the inability of yeast to respire glucose and, when caused by high levels of this monosaccharide, are manifestations of the Crabtree effect (see Chapter 17). When cells exhibiting the Crabtree effect are given oxygen in a medium containing low levels of glucose ($< 0.4\%$), fully functional mitochondria develop in 6–8 hr. Rapid synthesis of respiratory chain components (e.g. cytochromes) occurs during the first hour and after 3 hr the inner mitochondrial membrane has developed.

Mutant forms of yeast which are incapable of respiring glucose arise spontaneously at frequencies of 0.5% or higher. These strains have mitochondria with permanently impaired activity and arise usually because of mutation of mtDNA, although some nuclear mutations have a similar effect. Such strains produce small colonies when grown on agar media containing glucose, are unable to reduce certain dyes (e.g., tetrazolium salts), and cannot grow on ethanol or glycerol as sole sources of carbon. These mutant forms are called cytoplasmic or nuclear 'petites' (depending on the site of mutation) or respiratory-deficient; the wild types being referred to as 'grande' or respiratory-sufficient. The petite mutation is irreversible and may be induced by agents such as acridine orange or ethidium bromide, the latter substance causing the complete elimination of mtDNA from the cell [29].

16.3.3 THE VACUOLE

Yeast cells in stationary phase of growth often contain a single large vacuole. Within this organelle there are usually several dense 'granules' (volutin granules) of polyphosphate. During exponential growth there may be one or several vacuoles in the cell and they often lack granular inclusions, possibly indicating the mobilization of a phosphate reserve during active growth. Vacuoles are bounded by a single membrane and contain hydrolytic enzymes whose function is to recycle ('turn-over') the macromolecular components of the cell e.g. protein, nucleic acids. The vacuolar membrane isolates these lytic enzymes from the cytoplasm. It is of interest that these enzymes have no substantial carbohydrate moiety, in contrast to extracellular enzymes of yeast. Disintegration of the membrane, which is encouraged by high temperature, alkaline pH, the absence of nutrients and certain organic solvents, results in the autolysis of the cell. Leaving yeast for long periods in contact with beer may also induce autolysis and the products released impart a bitter taste (yeast-bite) to the beverage.

16.3.4 MEMBRANES

Membraneous structures play a crucial role in the organization of the yeast cell. The membrane (plasmalemma) is some 8 nm thick and is invaginated to protrude into the cytoplasm. The plasmalemma is the site of cell wall synthesis, excretion of metabolites, secretion of extracellular enzymes and the regulated uptake of nutrients. Enzymes responsible for transporting nutrients are located in the membrane which also exhibits an ATPase activity which may be involved in the movement of molecules against concentration gradients.

The membrane is composed of lipid and phospholipid and contains proteins and sterols. The absolute requirement for unsaturated fats and sterols in membranes accounts for much of the oxygen requirement of brewing yeast strains (see Chapter 18). The nature of the unsaturated fats in the cell membrane affects its properties, e.g. in relation to ethanol tolerance [30].

The endoplasmic reticulum of the yeast cell is a folded double-membrane structure which permeates the cytoplasm. The lumen between the membranes is 20 nm wide. From the reticulum, spherical vesicles develop, which can penetrate the plasmalemma and release their contents. Such vesicles appear to be involved in the synthesis of the cell wall, particularly that of developing buds.

Other membraneous structures which are either associated with or develop from the endoplasmic reticulum are (*i*) the Golgi bodies, which may be associated with cell wall synthesis, (*ii*) lipid droplets (sphaerosomes) and (*iii*) microbodies containing catalase.

16.3.5 THE CYTOPLASM
Within the free space of the cytoplasm reside all those intracellular enzymes which are not located in organelles. For example, the enzymes of the glycolytic pathway, the fatty acid synthase complex, the protein synthesizing system and all other enzymes involved in the metabolism of the yeast cell. Additionally, metabolic intermediates and storage compounds such as trehalose and starch reside in the cytoplasm.

16.3.6 THE YEAST CELL WALL [25, 31]
The cell wall represents some 30 % of the total dry mass of the cell and is in the range of 100–200 nm thick. Procedures for purifying cell wall material are, of necessity, arbitrary and rely on the differential centrifugation of broken cells. The degree and extent of contamination of wall preparations will therefore be a function of the preparatory methods used. Chemical analysis reveals that 60–85 % of the dry weight of the walls is made up of a mixture of approximately equal proportions of β-glucans and α-mannans. In addition, some 8 % each of lipid and protein, 3 % inorganic material (mainly phosphate) and 2 % hexoseamine are present. A small amount of chitin is also found. The proportions of glucan and mannan vary according to the strain of yeast and are influenced by the conditions of growth. Thus high levels of glucose in the medium and anaerobic conditions give walls of greater glucan content.

The glucan of the yeast wall comprises at least three separate molecular species (*i*) an alkali-soluble β(1-3) glucan [32], (*ii*) an alkali-insoluble β(1-3) glucan which is also insoluble in acetic acid [33] and (*iii*) an alkali-insoluble, acid-soluble β(1-6) glucan [34]. The detailed properties of these molecules are still unknown; however, it seems highly probable that branched β-glucans constitute the fibrillar component of the cell wall, since treatment of cells with β-glucanases produces sphaeroplasts. Much of the hexoseamine is found as chitin (β(1-4) linked *N*-acetyl glucosamine residues) which is the principal component of the bud scars [35], but some hexoseamine is associated with the wall mannan.

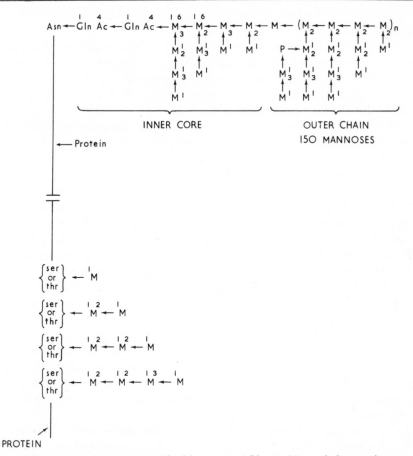

Fig. 16.3 Yeast phosphomanno-protein. M, mannose; Gln Ac, N-acetyl glucosamine; asn, asparagnine; ser, serine; thr, threonine.

The best characterized component of the cell wall is the α-mannan [36] (Fig. 16.3). The molecule is made up of an inner core of a repeating α-(1-6) chain of mannose residues with short side chains of α-(1-2) and α-(1-3) linked residues. At the end of this inner core are two *N*-acetyl glucosamine residues (chitobiose) and the terminal one is attached to the carboxylic acid residue in the side chain of an aspartic acid residue of a protein. Attached to the opposite end of the inner core molecule is an outer chain of 100–150 mannose residues. This unit consists of an α(1-6) backbone with α(1-2) and α(1-3) side chains, some of which contain phosphodiester linkages. In addition to this complex molecule, and attached to the same protein *via* serine and threonine hydroxyl groups, are short α(1-2) and α(1-3) chains of mannose residues. Other observations on the structure of the wall reveal that glucan is also covalently associated with protein [37] and that cross-linking between glucose and mannose may occur.

The biosynthesis of the mannan inner core involves dolichol pyrophosphate derivatives containing N-acetyl glucosamine and several mannose residues [38]. The participation of the polyprenol (dolichol) in the biosynthesis of the mannan inner core in yeast is analogous to its role in animal tissues as a mechanism for the glycosylation of proteins.

The cell wall protein is rich in the amino acids glutamate and aspartate. Its role is two-fold: firstly it acts as a structural molecule and secondly it is found in extracellular enzymes. Treatment of yeast cells with reducing agents (2-mercaptoethanol, dithiothreitol) is often a prerequisite for obtaining successful sphaeroplast formation especially from stationary phase cells [39]. Thus the removal of protein disu'phide br dges increases the accessibility of the β-glucan to enzyme action. In dimorphic yeasts, i.e. those which can change from mycelial to unicellular form, the synthesis of a protein disulphide reductase increases the plasticity of the wall as dimorphic change occurs [40, 41]. The change itself is influenced by temperature, dissolved oxygen concentration and the nitrogen to carbon ratio in the growth medium [42].

The extracellular enzymes of yeast are glycoproteins and include invertase and acid phosphatase. Strains of *Saccharomyces carlsbergensis* but not *S. cerevisiae* also possess melibiase. Yeast invertase has a minimum molecular weight of 27 000 contains 50% mannan and 2–3% glucosamine [43]. The precise location of the extracellular enzymes is still uncertain. They may occupy the space (periplasm) between the membrane and the bulk of the wall components, be anchored to the membrane via protein or covalently associated with other mannan or even glucan molecules.

It is clear that the three-dimensional structure of the yeast wall is highly complex and not likely to exist as a bilayer of inner glucan and outer mannan as earlier proposed [44].

Some information on the chemical nature of the cell wall has been obtained using various enzyme preparations. The most frequent use of enzymic attack on cell walls however is to obtain sphaeroplast preparations. 'Helicase' [45] (a mixed enzyme preparation containing β-glucanase) from the digestive gland of the snail *Helix pomatia* and 'Zymolyase' [46] from cultures of *Arthrobacter luteus* are the most commonly employed. Treatment of washed whole cells (obtained from an exponentially growing culture) at pH 6 in the presence of 1–1·5 M sorbitol or mannitol (as osmotic stabilizer) is used. The cell wall is degraded and sphaeroplasts are formed. Spherical sphaeroplasts are produced irrespective of the shape of the whole cells. Sphaeroplasts are unable to divide but maintain their metabolic functions. e.g., macromolecule synthesis [47] and extracellular enzyme production [48]. Careful lysis of sphaeroplasts in hypotonic media, often in the presence of detergents, is used to prepare nuclei, mitochondria, enzymes and nucleic acids. Sphaeroplasts may regenerate (under suitable conditions) to whole cells – a procedure of considerable importance to techniques for genetically manipulating yeast strains (see below).

In the budding process of *Saccharomyces cerevisiae* [25, 49] there is a local weakening of the yeast cell wall that may possibly be brought about by protein disulphide reductase. The cytoplasm is extruded from this weakened zone and is immediately bounded by new cell-wall material. At all stages during bud development, the cell walls of mother and bud are contiguous. The new cell-wall material can be distinguished by the use of fluorescent antibodies. Vesicles derived from the endoplasmic reticulum congregate at the site of cell-wall synthesis. The plasmalemma is invaginated at the junction of bud and mother cell and after the bud nucleus, mitochondria, etc., have migrated into the bud, the invaginated region fuses to form a septum of two membranes. Two new cell walls are constructed between the membranes, the one closer to the mother cell is particularly rich in mannan-protein and hexoseamine and forms a prominent bud scar when the bud eventually detaches. The scar is delimited by a raised ring of cell-wall material and is easily seen in isolated cell walls viewed by phase-contrast microscopy or when stained with primulin and seen by fluorescence microscopy. In contrast the birth scar on the bud is distinguished only with difficulty. As many as fifty bud scars may be formed on an individual cell [50].

16.4 *The role of the yeast cell wall in brewing*

The yeast cell wall confers certain important properties from the point of view of brewing. Thus, some brewing yeasts rise to the surface of the fermenting wort towards the end of fermentation (top yeasts) while others sediment (bottom yeasts). This distinction is a reflection of differences in composition of the yeast cell wall, although the chemical nature of these differences is not known. The ability of top yeasts to accumulate at the liquid–air interface can be demonstrated in water [51]. Shaken in a very clean tube, the yeast persists so well at the interface that what appears to be a type of skin is visible at the meniscus. Bottom yeasts fail to form such a 'skin' and this simple test is therefore valuable in practice for distinguishing between top and bottom yeasts. Other factors are undoubtedly involved in head-formation such as the transport of yeast clusters to the surface on the interfaces of carbon dioxide bubbles. Chains of cells or loosely-packed flocs are particularly favoured by such flotation.

The generation of a yeast-head or barm is a separate process from the maintenance of the head. Some yeasts form unstable heads and other strains will only barm in vessels over a critical volume and height. Barm stability is possibly akin to the stability of beer foam at dispense, that is, foam-retention.

Carbon-dioxide bubbles are surrounded by thin films of beer in both cases but the barm is complicated by the presence of yeast cells. Yeast cells cling to the outside of the bubble lamellae. The foam is more stable if the bubbles are small and of even size, if the beer viscosity is high, and surface-tension is low. It is known that some top yeasts will form no head in unhopped wort [53]. This may be due to the greater surface tension of unhopped compared with hopped wort. It has also been claimed [54] that high levels of nitrogen in wort result in poor yeast-heads but it is not easy to offer a completely satisfactory explanation for this.

One might expect sedimentary yeasts to be those that increase their effective size by the clumping of cells or by inducing complex charged shells to form around them. It is curious, however, that most bottom yeasts employed commercially have very little ability to group together. This applies both to the formation of chains of cells arising from non-separation of mother cell and buds, and to the aggregation of cells into flocs. Increase in effective size might possibly depend on the existence of electrically-charged shells surrounding the yeast cells but it should be noted that substantial sedimentation of cells of only 5 μm diameter will occur in 2 m (6 ft) depth of beer in 2–4 days. There is also experimental evidence that sedimentation rates do not conform to those calculated from Stokes' Law but are in fact some 50% greater than calculated. According to the Law, the velocity of sedimentation is inversely proportional to viscosity of the liquid and proportional both to the difference of the specific gravities of particles and liquid, and to the square of the radius of the particles. (The specific gravity of yeast has been calculated to be about 1·073.) It is possible that adsorption of protein and polyphenolic material on the surface of the yeast during fermentation may play some part in modifiying the rate of sedimentation.

There are several tests which are concerned with sedimentation rates of yeast samples. The Burns test [55] and its variants [56] measure the volume of yeast which sediments into the base of a conical centrifuge tube from a given volume of defined yeast suspension in a specified time. There have been modifications [57] in which the yeast is suspended in beer under carefully standardized conditions; cell concentrations are measured over a number of hours, just below the surface of beer. Concentrations fall steadily until, at a time and cell count which is characteristic for the yeast, the rate of fall changes abruptly. Sedimentation then proceeds at a steady but much lower rate that is characteristic of single cells; the faster initial rate is that of aggregated cells. Measurement of the increase in cell concentrations, following deflocculation with the enzyme pronase, has also been used [51].

The clumping of certain yeast strains into flocs or aggregates has an influence upon both yeast-head formation and the sedimentation of bottom yeasts by creating larger units. With flocculent strains, the aggregation can be encouraged by gentle rocking of a yeast suspension in a tube, but redispersion of the cells is just as easily achieved, merely by vigorous shaking. All growing cells tend to be non-flocculent but strains differ greatly with maturity in their ability to flocculate in a variety of circumstances [52]. Thus, some strains will flocculate in aqueous suspension, providing divalent ions (particularly calcium) are present. Other strains, while failing under these conditions to flocculate, will do so when ethanol at 3% w/v concentration is added. Some strains are more flocculent at pH 3.5 in weak calcium chloride solution than at pH 5·0; others present the reverse picture. Most strains in a flocculent condition will disperse in the presence of sugars, notably mannose and maltose. Sucrose is inferior in this respect but it is a better dispersant than glucose. Most yeasts therefore disperse when added to wort and will only flocculate when most of the sugar has been used or removed during fermentation.

It appears unlikely that a single mechanism of flocculation exists for all yeast strains, although it is generally agreed that the presence of calcium ions is essential for flocculation to occur [58–61]. One obvious interpretation is that the divalent metal ion forms salt bridges with negative charges on the surfaces of adjacent yeast cells [58]. The observations that (i) 2-epoxypropane (which specifically esterifies carboxylic acid residues) abolishes flocculence [58], (ii) that the electrophoretic mobility of yeasts entering stationary phase increases with flocculent but not non-flocculent yeasts and is characteristic of the presence of charged carboxylic acid, and not phosphate, residues [62], and (iii) that treating flocculent yeasts with the proteolytic enzyme pronase abolishes flocculence [63], indicate that protein carboxylic acid residues (presumably the side chains of glutamate and aspartate) furnish most of the negative charges which react with calcium.

In strains of Saccharomyces cerevisiae, wort peptides rich in glutamic and aspartic acids have been shown to induce flocculence [61]. This phenomenon may be observed either with a single strain or with two strains neither of which is flocculent by itself (co-flocculence). Ale strains have been classified as (i) non-flocculent, (ii) flocculent without inducer, (iii) flocculent only in the presence of inducer, and (iv) co-flocculent. All classes are distinguished from strains which form a head as a result of chain formation [61]. Strains of S. carlsbergensis studied show either non-flocculence or flocculate without the need for an inducer. The wort peptides are envisaged as acting as spacer molecules forming salt bridges with two calcium ions each of which forms an additional bridge with the yeast cell wall.

A limitation of the salt-bridging hypothesis is that at pH values less than 4·6 (i.e., beer pH) carboxylic acid residues are protonated and consequently flocs would be expected to disperse. The fact that dispersal does not occur has led to the view that additional factors, principally hydrogen-bond formation, are responsible for floc stability under acid conditions. Hydrogen bonds could readily form between hydroxyl groups on the cell-wall poly-saccharides of adjacent cells. Agents known to disrupt hydrogen bonds do indeed disperse flocs. Furthermore, the ability of the monosaccharides glucose and mannose to disperse flocs could arise by their competing for sites of hydrogen bonding [58].

Attempts to demonstrate differences in the chemical composition of the walls of flocculent and non-flocculent yeasts indicate an elevated level of mannan [63] and increased phosphorous content in the walls of flocculent strains [64]. In view of the covalent association between mannan, phospho-mannan and protein, both observations could indicate an increase in the amount of a specific protein in the cell wall.

An alternative view of the role of calcium in flocculation arises from very careful observations showing that only very small amounts are required and that strontium and barium ions, but not those of magnesium and manganese, inhibit the effect of calcium [59]. This evidence of a very high specificity shown by the flocculation system for calcium was interpreted as being inconsistent with the salt-bridging hypothesis, and indicating that a protein in the cell wall might require calcium for activity. Proteins called lectins, such as concanavalin A (Con A) (from the Jack-Bean *Canavalia ensiformis*), are well known in higher plants. Each protomer of Con A binds one manganese and one calcium ion in order to form a multimeric molecule which then specifically and strongly binds to $\alpha(1-2)$ linked mannose residues [65, 66]. The ability of one yeast strain to be flocculated by a polysaccharide constituent of wort has also been interpreted as indicating the presence of lectin-like activity in the yeast cell wall.

16.5 *Life cycle and genetics*

Knowledge of the life cycle and genetics of *Saccharomyces cerevisiae* has been obtained using strains selected for their suitability for analysis. Such strains, often termed 'laboratory' or 'genetic', have their origins in commerc-ially used bakers' yeast.

The 'laboratory' strains have been analysed genetically to produce a map denoting the positions of genes on chromosomes, to study gene function, and examine all aspects of yeast biochemistry. Much of the information obtained is of great value in attempting to understand commercial processes and making improvements to commercial yeasts.

The following discussion is supplemented, at the end of this Chapter, with a glossary of the specialized terms used.

16.5.1 LIFE CYCLE

The life cycle of *S. cerevisiae* (Fig. 16.4) may be considered (for convenience) as beginning in the vegetative stage of reproduction. Haploid yeast cells reproduce by budding, during which the chromosomes are duplicated by the process of mitosis. DNA replication occurs during the S phase of the cell cycle (see Chapter 18), separation of the replicated chromosomes and division of the nucleus is completed by the end of the M phase. So long as reproduction continues, the process of budding and mitosis will proceed and the cells are said to reproduce in the vegetative state in the haplophase of the life cycle.

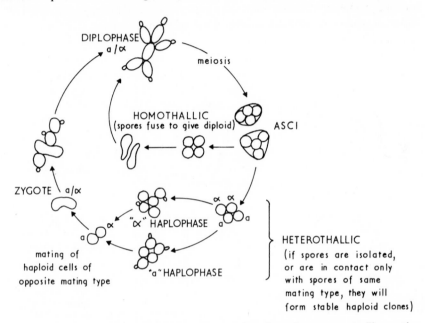

Fig. 16.4 Life cycle of *Saccharomyces cerevisiae*: a and α refer to the genes controlling mating response.

If haploid cells fuse, nuclear fusion follows and a diploid nucleus (one containing two sets, twice the haploid number, of chromosomes) is formed. The immediate product of such a fusion process is termed a zygote. From the zygote develop diploid cells which reproduce vegetatively by budding; the nucleus divides mitotically and the cells are said to be in the diplophase.

When diplophase cells are transferred to a medium deficient in nutrients (sporulation medium) the nucleus undergoes meiosis (reduction division) (Fig. 16.5). Chromosomes come together as homologous pairs, each pair containing the equivalent chromosome of the two haploid sets which formed the diploid nucleus. DNA synthesis is initiated so that each chromosome is replicated. During this process, 'breaking and rejoining' (crossing-over) of replicating DNA may occur, resulting in the reciprocal translocation of segments of the genetic material from one homologue to the other. Separation of the homologous pairs completes the first division of meiosis (Fig. 16.5(6)). Subsequently, separation of the replicas of each individual chromosome completes the second division of meiosis (Fig. 16.5(7) and (8)). The overall effect is to produce four haploid nuclei (in some yeasts a subsequent mitotic division generates a total of eight). Each nucleus, together with a portion of the cytoplasm of the cell, becomes an ascospore (spore) and the group of spores (usually four) is encased in an ascus derived from the original cell. Since it is likely that the genetic make-up of the original haploids differed and that some genetic exchange occurred, then the haploid spores will have different genetic constitutions from those of their parents.

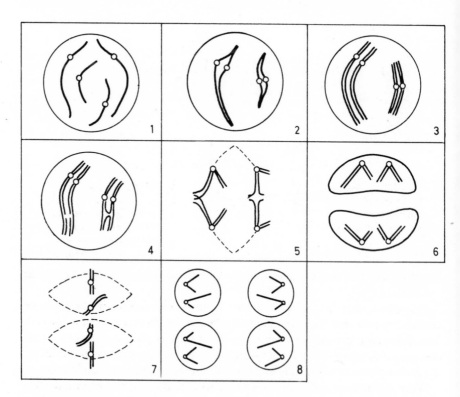

Fig. 16.5 Phases of the reduction division in meiosis showing the behaviour of the chromosomes. 1. Chromosomes as single threads; 2. Chromosomes pair; 3. Chromosomes are replicated, each now comprises two chromatids; 4. Chromosomes break and rejoin; 5. Repulsion of centromeres (small circles): this represents the tetrad stage of meiosis; 6. Two cells formed; 7. Second division; 8. Four haploid cells. 1–6 are events of the first, and 7–8 those of the second meiotic division.

In *S. cerevisiae*, ascospores are not liberated from the ascus and will fuse to produce diploid cells. Physical separation of the spores is therefore necessary for genetic analysis (see below). Separated ascospores will 'germinate' to produce haploid cells.

From the point of view of the life cycle, two types of yeast are apparent (Fig. 16.4): so-called 'homothallic' and 'heterothallic' strains. Spores of homothallic strains even when physically separated from one another will germinate and self-diploidize, i.e. fuse with their mitotic progeny. Homothallism is determined by the presence of a dominant allele *HO*. Heterothallic strains carry a non-functioning form of the *ho* and it is these strains that are most commonly used for genetic analysis.

Heterothallic strains exhibit mating types, designated *a* and α. Only haploid cells of opposite mating type may fuse to form zygotes. The gene for mating type, *MAT*, is located on chromosome III; in α strains it is designated *MATα*, and in *a* strains *MATa*. These genes are responsible for the control of mating specific genes such as those which produce the sex pheromones (*a* and α factors). Each acts upon a cell of opposite, but not the same, mating type. When exposed to α and *a* factors respectively *a* and α cells agglutinate, are arrested in the G1 phase of the cell cycle and produce aberrantly shaped cells (shmoos) [67]. 'Shmoo' formation evidences a number of cell wall structural changes which culminate in wall, membrane and nuclear fusion.

Under certain conditions *S. cerevisiae* strains are able to switch mating type. On chromosome III, *MAT* occupies a medial position and its *a* and α alleles behave as stable genes. In addition to the expressed *MAT* locus, chromosome III carries two 'silent' (unexpressed) copies, thus on the distal left arm is a silent copy of *MATα* designated *HML*, and on the distal right arm a silent copy of *MATa* (*HMR*). Certain mutations in other genes, gross deletions of chromosome III, or the presence of the dominant gene *HO*, all result in the expression of the silent copies. In the presence of *HO* and as often as once every cell division, the *MAT* locus is physically removed from chromosome III and either *HMR* or *HML* inserted in its place. In its new location, the formerly silent copy is now expressed and determines the mating type of the cell [67], *a* if *HMR* is inserted and α with *HML*.

This amazing sequence of events appears to be a means of maintaining diploid cells (since mixed cultures of *a* and α cells will fuse). This would tend to confer a greater degree of genetic stability because, with two copies of every gene, simultaneous mutation of both would be extremely unlikely.

16.5.2 YEAST GENETICS [68–70]

Genetic analysis in *S. cerevisiae* is performed by hybridizing (mating) haploid strains of opposite mating type, selecting the diploids produced and forcing these to undergo meiosis and sporulation. Sporulation is forced by inoculating actively growing diploid cells onto the surface of an agar medium containing 0·1 % or less of glucose, 1 % potassium acetate and 0·25 % yeast extract. After 2–3 days incubation at 30°C, asci may be identified by microscopic examination. A suspension of asci is treated with 'helicase' to degrade the ascus wall and the spores of each ascus (which remain adhered to one another) are separated by micromanipulation. Individual spores are permitted to germinate and the haploid cells produced grow to form colonies, which are subsequently tested for the presence or absence of various traits. This type of procedure is referred to as tetrad analysis because the spores are the products of meiosis, which commences with a tetrad comprising four chromatids of each homologous pair of chromosomes (Fig. 16.6).

In haploid cells, differences in genetic make-up (genotype) have an excellent chance (since only one copy of each allele is present) of being expressed in the properties of the organism (phenotype). Thus auxotrophy (nutritional requirement) may be detected by replica plating colonies of cells grown on complete medium to one lacking a particular nutrient, such as histidine. Failure to grow shows a particular requirement, in this case, histidine. Auxotrophic and other mutations (e.g. colony morphology) are readily obtained by exposing haploid cells to ionizing radiation or chemical mutagens.

Genetic analysis sets out to answer three fundamental questions about the genetic determinant for a given phenotypic character: (*i*) is it located on a chromosome or in the cytoplasm? (i.e., nuclear or cytoplasmic), (*ii*) to which chromosome does it belong and what is its position relative to other genes on the chromosome? (linkage and map position), (*iii*) how many different genes give the same phenotype? (complementation analysis).

If a gene is nuclear, then a diploid carrying two alleles of the gene will produce by meiosis four spores, two of which will carry one allele, and two the other. Thus, tetrad analysis is said to yield 2:2 segregation for nuclear genes. If a genetic determinant is cytoplasmic, and many copies are present, then when spores are formed cytoplasmic elements will be encased in each spore coat. Thus, in the case of cytoplasmic inheritance, tetrad analysis will usually show 4:0 segregation.

In tests of linkage, a haploid strain bearing the allele of interest is crossed with strains of opposite mating type which carry known alleles. In analyses involving allelic pairs of two different genes which reside on different chromosomes (i.e. are unlinked), then two arrangements of chromosomes are possible at meiosis I. Arrangement 1 (Fig. 16.6) will result in the production of an ascus containing 2 spores of the same phenotypes as the parent strains – this is a Parental Ditype (PD ascus). Arrangement 2 will however produce pairs of spores with non-parental phenotypes (ab and AB) – this is a non-Parental Ditype ascus (NPD). Any single genetic exchange which occurs between one pair of alleles on sister chromatids (Fig. 16.6) will generate a

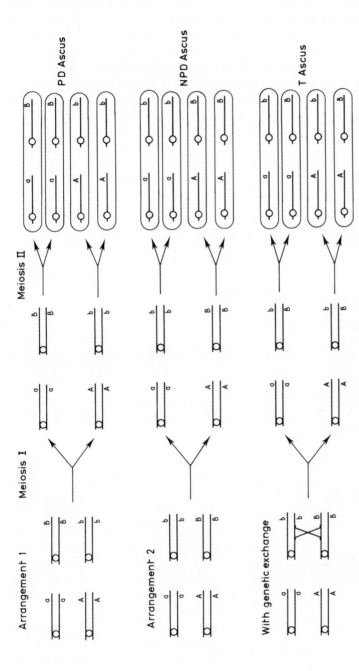

Fig. 16.6 Meiosis in a diploid formed by a hypothetical cross aB × Ab. It is assumed that the genes A and B reside on different chromosomes (i.e. are unlinked). For simplicity only the two relevant homologous pairs of chromosomes are shown. Prior to germination and mitotic cell division (budding) each chromosome in a spore will be replicated to yield a bivalent (two chromatids joined at the centromere, ○). (See text for details.)

tetratype ascus with 4 spores of different phenotypes, one each of the parental types (aB, Ab), and one each of the non-parental types (ab and AB). Since each arrangement (1 or 2, Fig. 16.6) of chromosomes at division I is equally probable, then crosses with unlinked genes will always give a ratio of PD asci/ NPD asci which does not differ significantly from 1:1, irrespective of any genetic exchange which may occur. Data may be tested using the Chi-square test so long as > 5 asci in each class are obtained.

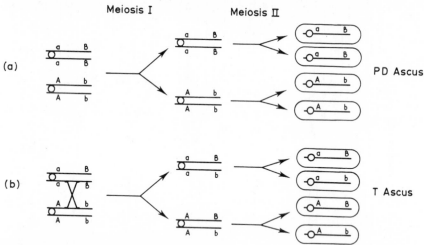

Fig. 16.7 Meiosis in a diploid formed by a hypothetical cross aB × Ab. It is assumed that the genes A and B reside on the same chromosome (i.e. are linked). For simplicity only the relevant homologous pair of chromosomes is shown. (a) No genetic exchange occurs. (b) Genetic exchange – a single crossover between A and B. (See text and legend to Fig. 16.6 for further details.)

Where two genes reside on the same chromosome (Fig. 16.7(a)), they will tend to segregate together, the closer they are, the more likely this will be (Fig. 16.7(a)). Thus, in such a situation the ratio PD:NPD will always be significantly greater than 1:1. If genetic exchange occurs between alleles, a single exchange (Fig. 16.7(b)) will generate a T ascus, and a double exchange (two crossover events) may produce either a T, PD or NPD ascus. If the restriction that no crossovers of greater multiplicity than 2 occur, then the following equation can be used to obtain the distance in centiMorgans (cM) [71].

$$\text{Distance in cM} = \tfrac{1}{2}\left(\frac{T + 6NPD}{T + PD + NPD}\right) 100 \qquad (16.1)$$

Because of the assumptions embodied in formulating this equation, it is only reliable for distances of up to 35 cM. An alternative set of equations is available which take into account all types of multiple crossover; however, their solution requires iteration using a computer [72, 73]. A graph of the relationship between the two methods of calculation is available to enable equation (16.1) to be used and the values corrected [74].

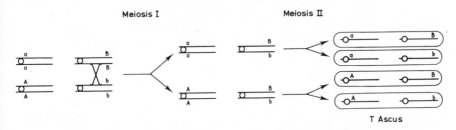

Fig. 16.8 Meiosis in a diploid formed by a hypothetical cross aB × Ab. It is assumed that A is a centromere linked gene and that B is a gene not linked to A. For simplicity only the two relevant homologous pairs of chromosomes are shown. (See text and legend to Fig. 16.6 for further details.)

Mapping in yeast may also be carried out using centromere marker genes. Such genes are so close to the centromere of the chromosome that the probability of crossing-over occurring between the gene and its centromere is very low (Fig. 16.8(A)). Therefore an allele on a different chromosome (Fig. 16.8(B)), which exchanges with its own centromere (i.e., crossing-over occurs between them), will generate a tetratype ascus (Fig. 16.8). Accordingly the distance between the gene and its own centromere is given by:

$$cM = \tfrac{1}{2}\left(\frac{T}{PD + NPD + T}\right) 100 \qquad (16.2)\ [68]$$

This distance calculated using equation (16.2) is referred to as the % second division segregation (%SDS) and the assumptions embodied in its use may be compensated for by use of an appropriate correction [74].

Mapping in yeast may also be accomplished by a random spore procedure avoiding the need to manipulate asci [69, 70] and by analysis of mitotic segregants [68, 70].

The genetic map of *S. cerevisiae* is presented in Fig. 16.9 and a glossary of gene symbols in Table 16.5. Gene symbols are normally assigned three letters. Upper case letters show that the allele is dominant (i.e., in diploids containing the dominant allele, the cells exhibit the trait e.g. *CUP/cup* diploids are copper resistant).

When a series of independently isolated recessive mutants, which have the same phenotype (e.g. *his* mutants; all require histidine), is available the question arises as to whether or not they are alleles of the same gene. Under

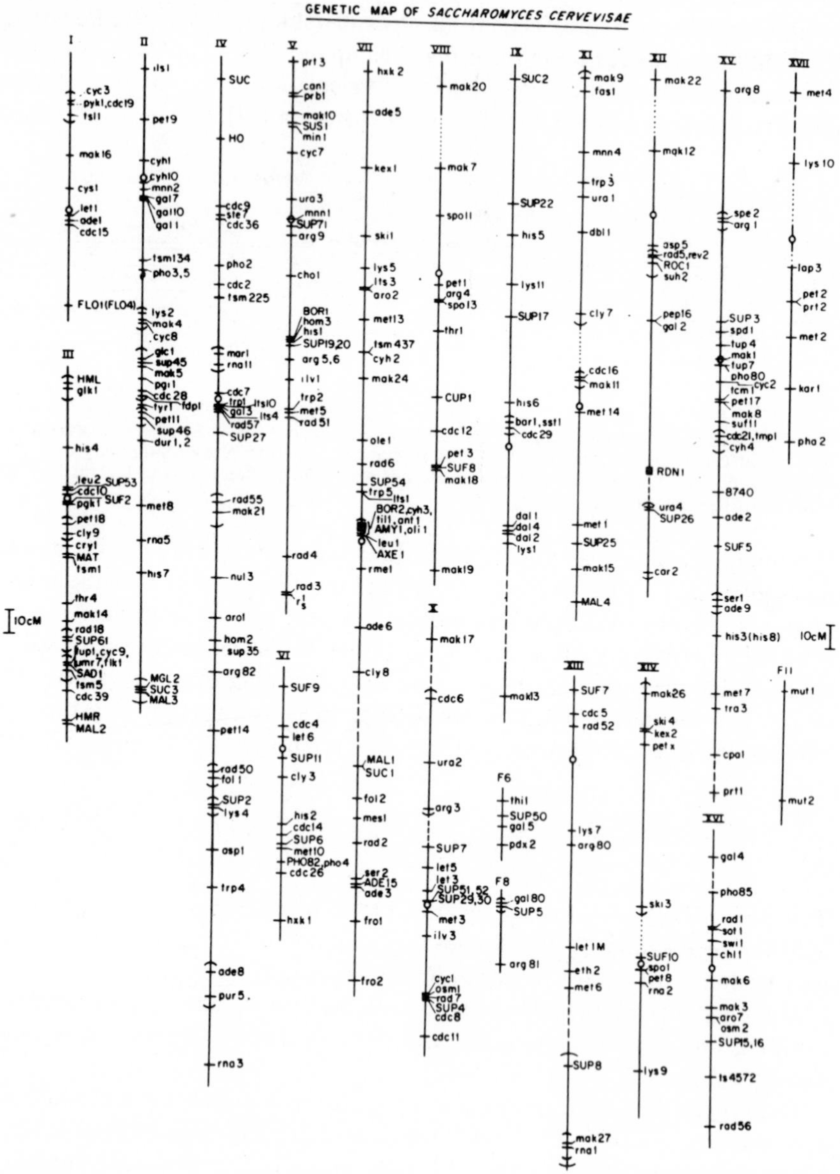

Fig. 16.9 The genetic map of *S. cerevisiae* [74]. Centromeres are represented as circles, the left arm of each chromosome being drawn above the centromere. Dashed and dotted lines represent linkages established other than by tetrad analysis. Parentheses enclose genes where exact orientation is unknown. (Published by kind permission of Dr R. K. Mortimer.)

these circumstances, one uses complementation analysis [69, 70]. Two haploids, each carrying one independently-isolated mutation, are mated and the diploid tested for the presence of the mutant phenotype. If the diploid is mutant, it can be concluded that the original lesions are in the same gene.

TABLE 16.5

Glossary of gene symbols

Gene symbol	Phenotype	Gene symbol	Phenotype
ade	Adenine requiring	hom	Homoserine requiring
AMY	Antimycin resistance	hxk	Hexokinase deficient
ant	Antibiotic resistance	ils	Isoleucyl-tRNA synthetase deficient; no growth at 36°C
arg	Arginine requiring		
aro	Aromatic amino acid requiring	ilv	Isoleucine-plus-valine requiring
asp	Aspartic acid requiring	kar	Nuclear fusion defective
AXE	Axenomycin resistance	kex	Unable to express killer phenotype
bar	a Cells lack barrier effect on α factor	lap	Leucine aminopeptidase deficient
		let	Lethal
BOR	Borrelidin resistance	leu	Leucine requiring
can	Canavanine resistance	lts	Low-temperature sensitive
car	Arginine catabolism defective	lys	Lysine requiring
cdc	Cell division cycle block at 36°C	mak	Maintenance of killer deficient
cen	Centromere	MAL	Maltose fermentation positive
chl	Chromosome loss	mar	Partial expression of mating type cassettes
cho	Choline requiring		
cly	Cell lysis at 36°C	MAT	Mating type locus
cpa	Arginine requiring in presence of excess uracil	mes	Methionyl-tRNA synthetase defective; no growth at 36°C
cry	Cryptopleurine resistance	met	Methionine requiring
CUP	Copper resistance	MGL	α-Methyl glucoside fermenter
cyc	Chytochrome c deficiency	min	Inhibited by methionine
cyh	Cycloheximide resistance	mnn	Mannan synthesis defective
cys	Cysteine requiring	mut	Elevated spontaneous mutation rate
dal	Allantoin degradation deficient		
dbl	Alcian blue dye binding deficient	nul	Non-mater
dur	Urea degradation deficient	ole	Oleic acid requiring
eth	Ethionine resistance	oli	Oligomycin resistance
fas	Fatty acid synthetase deficient	osm	Sensitive to low osmotic pressure
fdp	Unable to grow on glucose, fructose, sucrose or mannose	pdx	Pyridoxine requiring
		pep	Proteinase deficient
flk	Resistance to catabolite repression	pet	Petite; unable to grow on non-fermentable carbon sources
FLO	Flocculation		
fol	Folinic acid requiring	pgi	Phosphoglucose isomerase deficient
fro	Frothing		
gal	Galactose non-utilizer	pgk	3-Phosphoglycerate kinase deficient
glc	Glycogen storage		
glk	Glucokinase deficient (unable to use glucose)	pha	Phenylalanine requiring
		pho	Phosphatase deficient
his	Histidine requiring	prb	Proteinase deficient
HML	Mating type cassette	prt	Protein synthesis defective at 36°C
HMR	Mating type cassette	pur	Purine excretion
HO	Homothallic switching	pyk	Pyruvate kinase deficient

TABLE 16.5 (*continued*)

Gene symbol	Phenotype	Gene symbol	Phenotype
r^1_s	Radiation sensitive	SUF/suf	Suppression of frameshift mutation
rad	Radiation (u.v. or ionizing) sensitive	suh	Suppression of his2–1
		SUP/sup	Suppression of nonsense mutation
RDN	Ribosomal DNA structural genes	SUS	Suppression of ser1
rev	Non-revertible	swi	Homothallic switching deficient
ROC	Roccal resistance	tcm	Trichodermin resistance
rme	Meiosis independent of mating type heterozygosity	thi	Thiamine requiring
		thr	Threonine requiring
rna	Unable to grow at 36°C; block in RNA synthesis	til	Thiaisoleucine resistance
		tmp	Thymidine monophosphate requiring
SAD	Sporulation regulation		
ser	Serine requiring	tra	Triazylalanine resistant
ski	Super-killer	trp	Tryptophan requiring
sot	Supression of dTMP uptake	ts	Lethal, temperature sensitive
spd	Sporulation not repressed on rich media	tsl	Lethal, temperature sensitive
		tsm	Lethal, temperature sensitive
spe	Spermidine resistance	tup	dTMP uptake positive
spo	Sporulation deficient	tyr	Tyrosine requiring
sst	Supersensitive to α factor	umr	Non-u.v. revertible
ste	Sterile	ura	Uracil requiring
SUC	Sucrose fermenter		

If the diploid has non-mutant (wild-type) phenotype, and it can be shown that they map at different positions (random spore analysis is most often used) then the lesions are in different genes. Such genes are named by adding a number after the letter code, e.g. his1, his2. Different genes which influence the same phenotype often produce proteins controlling for example a biosynthetic pathway. In this way the pathway and enzymes involved, in for example, histidine biosynthesis were elucidated.

Fundamental genetic analysis of 'laboratory' strains generates information of commercial significance e.g. the presence of two genes for flocculation, FLO1 (a dominant allele) and flo3 a recessive gene [75, 76]. A full genetic description of yeast is indespensible to the use of newer techniques for manipulating the genotypes of commercial yeast strains.

16.6 *Techniques of strain improvement* [77, 78]

Processes for strain improvement include: (*i*) mutagenesis and selection, (*ii*) hybridization procedures with or without segregation, and (*iii*) transformation with 'naked DNA' or with recombinant DNA vectors.

Mutation may be induced using chemical or physical mutagenic agents or spontaneously occurring mutants selected from a population. Selection of spontaneous mutants has the advantage that undesired mutations which may result from the use of mutagens, are not present. Continuous culture of cells under conditions of nutrient limitation is a useful procedure for selecting mutants which utilize a nutrient more efficiently, e.g. inorganic phosphate [79], and might be used, for example, to increase a cell's ability to utilize maltotriose.

Hybridization of cells using the sexual cycle (i.e. breeding) is a process much exploited with higher plants and animals, and in improving baker's yeast strains, but has not been used extensively with brewing strains. Brewing yeasts, possibly because of their polyploid or aneuploid nature, sporulate poorly, produce few viable spores and difficulty is experienced in isolating stable mating strains. Some success has been obtained in this way in producing: (*i*) hybrids of *S. cerevisiae* and *S. diastaticus*, thus combining brewing properties with the ability to utilize wort dextrins [80] and (*ii*) yeasts with higher rates of attenuation [81]. In order to avoid the necessity of obtaining stable mating strains of brewing yeast, two further hybridization procedures may be adopted, namely rare-mating and protoplast (sphaeroplast) fusion.

In rare-mating, hybrids are formed (at low frequency) between auxotrophic respiratory-sufficient and prototrophic respiratory-deficient strains. The hybrids will grow on defined media lacking the nutritional requirements of the auxotrophic parent and containing a source of carbon (e.g. glycerol) which may only be used by respiratory-sufficient cells. Respiratory-deficient brewing yeasts are readily obtained (e.g. by eliminating mtDNA using ethidium bromide) however strains carrying several auxotrophic mutations are not. Accordingly the procedure used normally employs an auxotrophic laboratory strain. This procedure has been used to hybridize *aa* and *αα* auxotrophic diploids with respiratory-deficient brewing yeasts [81]; some of the hybrids obtained were apparently tetraploid and sporulated freely. It has also been used to generate hybrids between haploid strains and brewing yeasts [82]. If one of the strains contains the nuclear allele *kar* which restricts nuclear fusion in hybrids [83], then cells containing mixed cytoplasms and the nucleus of either one or other parent (heteroplasmons) may be obtained. This method has been exploited to obtain brewing yeasts with the ability to kill wild yeasts [82]. Crosses employing *kar* have also been used to transfer single chromosomes from one yeast to another, thus creating aneuploids [84, 85].

Protoplast fusion is an efficient means of hybridizing yeast strains. Sphaeroplasts are mixed in a medium containing an osmotic stabilizer and fusion induced by the addition of polyethylene glycol and calcium ions. The fused products may be regenerated (i.e. encouraged to form new cell walls) in a medium containing 3% agar [86]. This technique has been used to render a brewing strain amenable to genetic analysis [87] to transfer flocculence from haploids to brewing strains and form hybrids of brewing ale and lager strains [78]. To date, however, most strains produced in this way have proved unsatisfactory for brewing purposes.

The various techniques of hybridization involving nuclear fusion described above may well prove to be the methods of choice when improvements are sought which depend upon the action of many genes, e.g. fermentation rate. Where single-gene changes are concerned, transformation is probably the method of choice for manipulating brewing yeasts.

Transformation is the process whereby naked DNA from one organism (the donor) is introduced into another (the recipient) and becomes part of the heritable genetic material of the latter. Early reports of transformation [88] were criticized for lack of appropriate controls [89]. Subsequently, other workers have reported the successful transformation of whole yeasts [90]; however the current trend is to use sphaeroplasts as recipients. This stems from the unequivocal demonstration (using plasmid DNA) of the presence of donor DNA in recipient cells [91]. Transformation has been used to transfer flocculence to a non-flocculent laboratory strain using a laboratory strain as a source of DNA [92], ability to utilize maltotriose to a laboratory strain using brewing yeast DNA as donor [78] and the ability to utilize wort dextrins to a brewing yeast using wild yeast DNA as donor [93]. Transformation frequencies are low and some means of selecting for transformed cells is essential. When extracellular enzyme activity such as dextrinase is transformed, transformants will grow on dextrin as sole carbon source. In the transformation of the ability to use maltotriose, sphaeroplasts were regenerated and then screened for their ability to use the trisaccharide. In the case of transformation of flocculent ability it was necessary to score for adenine prototrophy (knowing in advance that FLO 1 and ade 1 are linked) and then screen prototrophs for flocculence. This technique of cotransformation demands a detailed knowledge of the yeast genetic map and in this case an adenine auxotroph as recipient, the FLO 1 ADE 1 DNA was shown to have been incorporated (integrated) into chromosome I.

Techniques are now available for recombining DNA molecules *in vitro* and so produce vehicles (hybrid vectors – chimaeras) for the transformation of microorganisms [94]. Fragments of DNA from a donor (or cDNA; a DNA copy of an isolated mRNA) are integrated into vectors. Vectors are usually derived from small bacterial plasmids and are covalently closed circular DNA molecules (cccDNA) capable of replication in bacteria. The plasmids are opened (restricted) using specific restriction endonucleases and mixed with DNA from a donor prepared by restriction or by mechanical shearing. By one of several enzymatic procedures the vector and donor DNA molecules are prepared so that they anneal (base pair) with one another thereby forming hybrid circular molecules. These molecules are then closed (ligated) to produce cccDNA hybrids which may then be used for transformation. In yeasts, transformed cells are usually detected by transforming auxotrophs to prototrophy using hybrid vectors carrying the wild-type allele.

A major problem in recombinant DNA technology is detecting the transformant which contains the donor gene of interest. Several procedures are available and are thoroughly discussed in reference [94]. Once detected the transformant may be grown in pure culture and the clone obtained will possess the hybrid vector containing the desired gene from the donor – hence the term 'gene-cloning'.

Five types of hybrid vector are currently available for gene-cloning in yeast (Table 16.6): (*i*) those containing yeast nuclear alleles (e.g. pY*eleu*10) which when used as transforming agents integrate into the yeast chromosomes, (*ii*) those containing both yeast nuclear and yeast plasmid (2 μm) DNA (e.g. pJDB219); these vectors may integrate but also may exist as cytoplasmic elements, (*iii*) vectors containing the centromere of a yeast chromosome (YRp7) these do not integrate but reside in the nucleus and behave as 'mini chromosomes', (*iv*) a vector comprising wholly yeast DNA sequences (pC504) and (*v*) a hybrid between 2μm DNA and mtDNA. Those vectors containing bacterial plasmid DNA may also be used to clone genes in *E. coli*.

The enormous potential of recombinant DNA technology will undoubtedly be exploited in the near future for the genetic manipulation of brewing yeast strains.

TABLE 16.6

Some hybrid vectors for recombinant DNA techniques in Yeast

Hybrid vector	Bacterial plasmid* component	Yeast nuclear component	Yeast plasmid component
pC504 [101]	None	*HIS4*	2 μm DNA***
p JDB219 [99]	pMB9	*LEU2*	2 μm DNA
p Ye *arg* 1 [102]	ColEl	*ARG4*	None
p Ye *leu* 10 [91]	ColEl	*LEU2*	None
p Ye *trp* 1 [102]	ColEl	*TRP5*	None
YEp6 [98]	pBR322	*HIS3*	2 μm DNA
YIpl [98]	pBR322	*HIS3*	None
YRp7** [95]	pBR322	*TRP1*	
YT 11 [100]	pBR325	*LEU2*	2 μm DNA
Lgt. Sc 2601 [102]	Bacteriophage lambda	*HIS3*	None
Un-named [103]	None	None	mtDNA and 2 μm DNA

* Details of the structure and properties of plasmids are given in reference [94].
** Contains the centromere of chromosome IV.
*** See reference [104] for details of 2 μm DNA.

APPENDIX

Glossary of genetic terms

Allelic	Two or more genes occupying the same relative position (locus) on homologous chromosomes.
Allele	Any one of several forms of a gene which may occupy the same locus on a chromosome.
Aneuploid	Having more or less than an integral multiple of the haploid (qv) number of chromosomes.
Ascus	The body which contains the ascospores (qv).
Ascospore	The haploid (qv) product of meiosis (qv). Usually 4 per ascus.
Auxotroph	A strain requiring a growth factor (e.g. amino acid) not required by the wild type or prototroph (qv).
Centromere	A specialized region of a chromosome, the point of attachment to the apparatus regulating nuclear division.
Complementation	The restoration of wild-type phenotype when different recessive (qv) mutations producing the same mutant phenotype (e.g. *his*-1 and *his*-3) are present in the same cell.
Crossing-over	The exchange of genetic material between homologous chromosomes.
Cytoplasmic	Pertaining to material of a cell which is outside the nucleus but within the plasma membrane.
Deletion	A mutation involving the loss of a segment of DNA
Diploid	Having two homologous sets of chromosomes i.e. twice the haploid (qv) number.
Diplophase	Vegetative growth of diploid cells.
Dominant	The form of a gene expressed in the presence of other forms.
Genome	A complete set of nuclear (qv) and/or cytoplasmic genes.
Genotype	The genetic make-up of a strain.
Grande	Respiratory sufficient (qv)
Haploid	Having a single set of chromosomes.
Haplophase	Vegetative growth of a haploid strain.
Heteroplasmon	A cell containing the cytoplasmic elements of two strains but the nucleus of only one of them.
Heterothallic	Exhibiting 'sexuality' i.e. cells may be either of two mating types.
Heterozygous	The presence of two different alleles of a gene in the same nucleus.
Homologous chromosomes	A pair of chromosomes in a diploid (qv). Each chromosome contains genes governing the same characters and is derived from a different haploid.
Homothallic	Failing to possess mating types.
Homozygous	Having two or more copies of the same allele in a nucleus.

Hybridization	The fusion of two cells often followed by the fusion of nuclei.
Karyogamy	Fusion of nuclei.
Linkage-group	Genes which are found on the same chromosome.
Mating type	In yeast either *a* (MAT*a*) or α (MATα) alleles which determine the ability of cells to hybridize with those of opposite type.
Meiosis	Reduction division where the diploid number of chromosomes is reduced to the haploid number.
Mitosis	Duplication and division of chromosomes during vegetative growth, the number present initially is maintained.
Mutagen	A chemical or physical agent which alters the structure (base sequence) of DNA.
Mutation	A change in the structure (base sequence) of DNA.
NPD	An ascus containing two pairs of spores with different phenotypes from those of either haploid parent – non-parental ditype.
Nuclear	Pertaining to the nucleus – the organelle which contains the chromosomes.
PD ascus	An ascus containing two pairs of spores one pair having an identical phenotype to one parent the other to the other parent – parental ditype.
Petite	Respiratory deficient (qv).
Phenotype	The characteristics expressed by an organism.
Plasmid	Genetic determinants which may replicate independently and separately from the chromosomes – usually a small circular molecule of DNA.
Polyploid	Having three (triploid), four (tetraploid) or more integral sets of the haploid number of chromosomes.
Rare-mating	A low frequency mating event occurring without the involvement of mating type.
Recessive	The form of a gene expressed only in the homozygous state (qv).
Recombinant	The progeny of a cross which contain combinations of alleles different from those of the parents. Result from crossing-over (qv).
Respiratory deficient	Unable to oxidize glucose to CO_2 and H_2O. Lack complete mitochrondrial function. Produce small (petite) colonies on glucose media, do not grow on glycerol or ethanol.
Respiratory sufficient	Able to oxidize glucose to CO_2 and H_2O. Have complete mitochondrial function. Produce large (grande) colonies on glucose media, grow on glycerol and ethanol.
Segregation	The separation of the members of a pair or number of alleles originally present in the same cell into different cells (e.g. spores).
Spore	Ascospore (qv).
Sporulation	The process whereby a vegetative cell is transformed into an ascus and the production of ascospores by meiosis (qv).

Tetrad	The four chromatids of a homologous pair of chromosomes at the first division of meiosis.
T ascus	An ascus containing 4 spores each of a different phenotype – tetratype ascus.
Tetraploid	see Polyploid.
Transformation	The process whereby genetic characters are acquired by one strain from another when the former is treated with DNA prepared from the latter.
Vector	A plasmid (qv) molecule capable of being joined *in vitro* to pieces of DNA to form a recombinant molecule for transformation (qv).
Wild-type	The 'natural' non-mutated form of a strain – used to prepare auxotrophs.

A more comprehensive bibliography may be found in references [96] and [97].

REFERENCES

[1] HENRICI, A. T. (1947). *Molds, Yeasts and Actinomycetes*, 2nd edn., Wiley, New York, Chapter 9.

[2] STELLING-DEKKER, N. M. (1931). *Die Hefesammlung des Centralbureau voor Schimmelcultures. I. Teil. Die sporogenen Hefen*, Amsterdam: Verhandel. Koninkl. Akad. Wetenschap., Afd. Natuurkunde.

[3] LODDER, J. (1934). *Die Hefesammlung des Centralbureau voor Schimmelcultures II. Teil. Erst halfte. Die anaskosporogenen Hefen*. Amsterdam: Verhandel, Koninkl. Akad. Wetenschap.

[4] DIDDENS, H. A. and LODDER, J. (1942). *Die Hefesammlung des Centralbureau voor Schimmelcultures. II. Teil. Zweite halfte:* N.V. Noord Hollandsche Uitgevers Maatschappij.

[5] LODDER, J. and KREGER VAN RIJ, N. J. W. (1952). *The Yeasts, A taxonomic Study*, North Holland, Amsterdam.

[6] KREGER VAN RIJ, N. J. W. (1962). Microbial Classification, *Symp. Soc. Gen Microbiol.*, 196.

[7] LODDER, J. (ed.) (1970). *The Yeasts*, North Holland, Amsterdam.

[8] BARNETT, J. A. and PANKHURST, R. J. (1974). *A new key to the Yeasts*, North Holland, Amsterdam.

[9] BARNETT, J. A., PAYNE, R. W. and YARROW, D. (1979). *A guide to identifying and classifying yeasts*. Cambridge University Press, Cambridge.

[10] CAMPBELL, I. (1971). *J. Gen. Microbiol.*, **67**, 223.

[11] CAMPBELL, I. (1967). *Proc. Eur. Brewery Conv. Congr., Madrid*, p. 145.

[12] SANDULA, J., KOCKOVA-KRATOCHVILOVA, A. and ZAMEKNIKOVA, M. (1964). *Brauwissenschaft*, **17**, 130.

[13] TSUCHIYA, T., FUKAZAWA, Y. and YAMASE, Y. (1961). *Jap. J. Microbiol.* **5**, 417.

[14] RICHARDS, M. (1969). *J. Inst. Brewing*, **75**, 476.

[15] CAMPBELL, I., ROBSON, F. O. and HOUGH, J. S. (1968). *J. Inst. Brewing*, **74**, 360.

[16] RICHARDS, M. and COWLAND, T. W. (1967). *J. Inst. Brewing*, **73**, 552.

[17] OUCHTERLONY, O. (1949). *Acta Pathol., Microbiol. Scand.*, **26**, 507.

[18] GRABAR, P. and BURTIN, P. (1960). *L'analyse immuno-electrophoretique*, Masson, Paris.

[19] CAMPBELL, I. and BRUDZYNSKI, A. (1966). *J. Inst. Brewing*, **72**, 556.

[20] BRYANT, T. N. and COWAN, W. D. (1981). *J. Inst. Brewing*, **85**, 89.

[21] COWAN, W. D. and BRYANT, T. N. (1981). *J. Inst. Brewing*, **87**, 45.

[22] CARMO-SOUSA, L. (1969). *The Yeasts*, Vol. 1 (eds. ROSE, A. H. and HARRISON, J. S.), Academic Press, London, p. 79.

[23] GENTLES, J. C. and LA TOUCHE, C. J. (1969). *The Yeasts*, Vol. 1 (eds. ROSE, A. H. and HARRISON, J. S.), Academic Press, London, p. 107.

[24] LAST, F. T. and PRICE, D. (1969). *The Yeasts*, Vol. 1 (eds. ROSE, A. H. and HARRISON, J. S.), Academic Press, London, p. 183.

[25] MATILE, R., MOOR, H. and ROBINOW, C. F. (1969). *The Yeasts*, Vol. 1 (eds. ROSE, A. H. and HARRISON, J. S.), Academic Press, London. p. 219.

[26] BANDLOW, W., SCHWEYEN, R. J., WOLF, K. and KAUDEWITZ, F. (1977). *Genetics and Biogenesis of Mitochondria*. de Gruyter, Berlin and New York.

[27] STEVENS, B. J. (1977). *Biologie Cellulaire*, **28**, 37.

[28] EVANS, I. H. (1980), *Biochim. Biophys. Acta*, **602**, 201.

[29] SLONIMSKI, P. P., PERRODIN, G. and CROFT, J. H. (1968). *Biochem. Biophys. Res. Commun.*, **30**, 232.

[30] THOMAS, D. S., HOSSACK, J. A. and ROSE, A. H. (1978), *Arch. Microbiol.*, **117**, 239.

[31] ROGERS, H. J., PERKINS, H. R. and WARD, J. B. (1980). *Microbial Cell Walls and Membranes*, Chapman and Hall, London.

[32] FLEET, G. H. and MANNERS, D. J. (1976). *J. Gen. Microbiol*, **94**, 180.

[33] MANNERS, D. J., MASSON, A. J. and PATTERSON, J. C. (1973). *Biochem J.*, **135**, 19.

[34] MANNERS, D. J., MASSON, A. J., PATTERSON, J. C., BJORNAL, H. and LINDBERG, B. (1973). *Biochem J.*, **135**, 31.

[35] CABIB, E. (1975). *Ann. Rev. Microbiol.*, **29**, 191

[36] BALLOU, C. E. (1976). *Advances in Microbial Physiol.*, **14**, 93.

[37] PARODI, A. J. (1977). *Eur. J. Biochem.*, **75**, 171.

[38] PARODI, A. J. (1978). *The Biochemistry and Genetics of Yeasts* (eds. BACILA, M., HORECKER, B. L., and STOPPANI, A. O. M.), Academic Press, London.

[39] SOMMER, A. and LEWIS, M. J. (1971). *J. Gen. Microbiol.*, **68**, 327.

[40] NICKERSON, W. J. and KREGER VAN RIJ, N. W. J. (1949). *Biochim, Biophys. Acta*, **3**, 461.

[41] BROWN, C. M. and HOUGH, J. S. (1965). *Proc. Eur. Brewery Conv. Congr.*, *Stockholm*, p. 223.

[42] MORRIS, E. O. (1958). *The Chemistry and Biology of Yeasts* (ed. COOK, A. H.), Academic Press, New York, p. 251.

[43] LAMPEN, J. O. (1968) *Antonie Van Leeu.*, **34**, 1.

[44] MATILE, P. H., MOOR, H. and ROBINOW, C. F. (1969). *The Yeasts*, Vol. 1 (eds. ROSE, A. H. and HARRISON, J. S.), Academic Press, London. p. 235.

[45] EDDY, A. A. and WILLIAMSON, D. H. (1957). *Nature*, **179**, 1252.

[46] KITAMURA, K. and YAMAMOTO, Y. (1972), *Arch. Biochem. Biophys.*, **153**, 403.

[47] HUTCHISON, T. H. and HARTWELL, L. H. (1967). *J. Bacteriol.*, **94**, 1697.

[48] MCLELLAN, W. L. and LAMPEN, J. O. (1963). *Biochim. Biophys. Acta*, **67**, 324.

[49] MOOR, H. (1967). *Arch. Mikrobiol*, **57**, 135.

[50] COOK, A. H. (1963). *Proc. Eur. Brewery Conv. Congr.*, *Brussels*, p. 477.

[51] CALLEJA, C. B. and JOHNSON, B. F. (1977). *Can. J. Microbiol.*, **23**, 68.

[52] EDDY, A. A. (1958). *J. Inst. Brewing*, **64**, 143.

[53] DIXON, I. J. (1967). *J. Inst. Brewing*, **73**, 488.

[54] OLDFIELD, A. I., ST. JOHNSTON, J. H. and TAYLOR, A. E. (1951). *Proc. Eur. Brewery Conv. Congr.*, *Brighton*, p. 98.

[55] BURNS, J. A. (1937). *J. Inst. Brewing*, **43**, 31.

[56] KATO, S. and MISHIKAWA, N. (1957). *Bull. Brew. Sci.*, **3**, 39.

[57] WOOF, J. B. (1962). *J. Inst. Brewing*, **68**, 315.

[58] MILL, P. J. (1964). *J. Gen. Microbiol.*, **35**, 61.

[59] TAYLOR, N. W. and ORTON, W. L. (1975). *J. Inst. Brewing*, **81**, 53.

[60] FISHER, D. J. (1975). *J. Inst. Brewing*, **81**, 107.

[61] STEWART, G. G., RUSSELL, I. and GARRISON, I. F. (1975). *J. Inst. Brewing*, **81**, 248

[62] BEAVAN, M. J., BELK, D. M., STEWART, G. G. and ROSE, A. H. (1979). *Can. J. Microbiol.*, **25**, 888.

[63] STEWART, G. G. (1975). *Brewers Digest*, **50**(3), 42.

[64] LYONS, T. P. and HOUGH, J. S. (1971). *J. Inst. Brewing*, **77**, 300.

[65] REEKE, G. N., BECKER, J. W., CUNNINGHAM, G. R., GUNTHER, J. L. W. and EDELMAN, G. M. (1974). *Annals. NY Acad. Sci.*, **234**, 369.

[66] GOLDSTEIN, I. J., REICHERT, C. M. and MISAKI, A. (1974). *Annals, NY Acad. Sci.*, **234**, 283.

[67] GOODENOUGH, U. W. (1980). *The Eukaryotic Microbial Cell*, (eds. LLOYD, D. and TRINCI, A. P. J.), Cambridge University Press, Cambridge, p. 313.

[68] MORTIMER, R. K. and HAWTHORNE, D. C. (1969). *The Yeasts.* Vol. 1 (eds. ROSE, A. H. and HARRISON, J. S.), Academic Press, London. p. 386.

[69] FINK, G. R. (1970). *Methods in Enzymology*, Vol. 17A, (eds. TABOR, H. and TABOR, C. W.), p. 59.

[70] SHERMAN, F., FINK, G. R., and LAWRENCE, C. W. (1974). *Methods in Yeast Genetics*—Laboratory Manual, Cold Spring Harbour Laboratory, Cold Spring Harbour, New York.

[71] PERKINS, D. D. (1949). *Genetics*, **34**, 607.

[72] SNOW, R. (1979). *Genetics*, **92**, 231.

[73] SNOW, R. (1979). *Genetics*, **93**, 285.

[74] MORTIMER, R. K. and SCHILD, D. (1980). *Bacteriol. Rev.* **44**, 519.

[75] LEWIS, C. W., JOHNSTON, J. R. and MARTIN, P. A. (1976). *J. Inst. Brewing*, **82**, 158.

[76] RUSSELL, I., STEWART, G. G., READER, H. P., JOHNSTON, J. R. and MARTIN, P. A. (1980). *J. Inst. Brewing*, **86**, 120.

[77] TUBB, R. S. (1979). *J. Inst. Brewing*, **85**, 286.

[78] STEWART, G. G. and RUSSELL, I. (1979). *Proc. Eur. Brewery Conv. Congr.*, *Berlin*, p. 475.

[79] EMEIS, C. C. (1971) *Proc. Am. Soc. Brew. Chem.*, 58.

[80] ANDERSON, E. and MARTIN, P. A. (1975). *J. Inst. Brewing*, **81**, 242.

[81] SPENCER, J. F. T. and SPENCER, D. M. (1977). *J. Inst. Brewing*, **83**, 287.

[82] YOUNG, T. W. (1981). *J. Inst. Brewing*, **87**, 292.

[83] CONDE, J. and FINK, G. R. (1976). *Proc. Natl. Acad. Sci. USA*, **73**, 3651.

[84] NILSSON-TILLGREN, T., PETERSEN, J. G. L., HOLMBERG, S. and KIELLAND-BRANDT, M. C. (1980). *Carlsberg Res. Commun.*, **45**, 113.

[85] GOODEY, A. R., BROWN, A. J. P. and TUBB, R. S. (1981). *J. Inst. Brewing*, **87**, 239.

[86] VAN SOLINGEN, P. and VAN DER PLAAT, J. B. (1977). *J. Bacteriol.*, **130**, 946.

[87] SKATRUD, P. L., JAECK, D. M., HOT, E. J. and HELBERT, J. R. (1980) *J. Am. Soc. Brew. Chem.*, **38**, 49.

[88] OOPENOORTH, W. F. F. (1959). *Proc. Eur. Brewery Conv. Congr.*, Rome, p. 180.

[89] HARRIS, G. and THOMPSON, C. C. (1960). *Nature*, **188**, 1212.

[90] KHAN, N. C. and SEN, S. P. (1974). *J. Gen. Microbiol.*, **83**, 237.

[91] HINNEN, A., HICKS, J. B. and FINK, G. R. (1978). *Proc. Natl. Acad. Sci. USA*, **75**, 1929.

[92] BARNEY, M. C., JANSEN, G. P. and HELBERT, J. R. (1980). *J. Am. Soc. Brew. Chem.*, **38**, 71.

[93] BARNEY, M. C., JANSEN, G. P. and HELBERT, J. R. (1980). *J. Am. Soc. Brew. Chem.*, **38**, 1.

[94] OLD, R. W. and PRIMROSE, S. B. (1980). *Principles of Gene Manipulation* (Studies in Microbiology, Vol. 2) Blackwell Scientific, Oxford.

[95] ABERCROMBIE, M., HICKMAN, C. J. and JOHNSON, M. L. (1973). *Dictionary of Biology*, Penguin Books Ltd., Harmondsworth.

[96] RIEGER, R., MICHAELIS, A. and GREEN, M. M. (1968). *A Glossary of Genetics and Cytogenetics*, George Allen and Unwin, London.

[97] KIELLAND-BRANDT, M. C., NILSSON-TILLGREN, T., HOLMBERG, S., PETERSEN, J. G. L., and SVENNINGSEN, B. A. (1979). *Carlsberg Res. Commun.*, **44**, 89.

[98] STRUHL, K., STINCHCOMB, D. T., SCHERER, S. and DAVIS, R. W. (1979). *Proc. Natl. Acad. Sci. USA*, **76**, 1035.

[99] BEGGS, J. D., (1978). *Nature*, **275**, 104.

[100] COHEN, J. D., ECCLESHALL, T. R., NEEDLEMAN, R. B., FEDEROFF, H., BUCHFERER, B. A. and MARMUR, J. (1980). *Proc. Natl. Acad. Sci. USA*. **77**, 1078.

[101] HOLMBERG, S., PETERSEN, J. G. L., NILSSON-TILLGREN, T. and KIELLAND-BRANDT, M. C. (1979). *Carlsberg Res. Commun.*, **44**, 269.

[102] CARBON, J., CLARKE, L., CHINAULT, C., RATZKIN, R. and WALZ, A. (1978). *Biochemistry and Genetics of Yeasts.* (eds. BACILA, M., HORECKER, B. L. and STOPPANI, A. D. M.), Academic Press, New York. p. 425.

[103] ATCHISON, B. A., DEVENISH, R. J., LINNANE, A. W. and NAGLEY, P. C. (1980). *Biochem. Biophys. Res. Commun.*, **96**, 580

[104] LIVINGSTON, D. M. and KLEIN, H. L. (1977). *J. Bacteriol.*, **129**, 472.

Chapter 17

METABOLISM OF WORT BY YEAST

17.1 *Nutritional requirements* [1]

Yeast will grow fermentatively in simple media which contain fermentable carbohydrates to supply energy and carbon 'skeletons' for biosynthesis, adequate nitrogen for protein synthesis, mineral salts and one or more growth factors. Yeasts also require molecular oxygen (see Chapters 16, 18 and pp. 604–608, this chapter).

Sources of carbon include the monosaccharide hexose sugars D-glucose, D-fructose, D-mannose and D-galactose. *Saccharomyces* strains are able to use xylulose but not other pentose sugars e.g. xylose [3]. Disaccharides may also serve as sources of carbon and energy, thus sucrose and maltose, but not lactose, are utilized by brewing yeasts. The disaccharide melibiose (α-*O*-4-D-galactopyranosyl-D-glucopyranose) is metabolized by *S. carlsbergensis* but not by *S. cerevisiae* and growth on this sugar may be employed to distinguish ale and lager yeasts. The trisaccharides raffinose (used completely by *S. carlsbergensis* and partially by *S. cerevisiae*) and maltotriose may also serve as carbon sources. Higher polymers of glucose such as maltotetraose and dextrins are not metabolized by brewers' yeast.

Under aerobic conditions yeast may also use glycerol, ethanol and lactic acid which are themselves the products of anaerobic (fermentative) growth. Similarly the organic acids acetic, citric and malic are also metabolized by some species. Other compounds, generated by cellular metabolism, which appear in the medium and may be subsequently taken up by the cells, include pyruvic acid and acetaldehyde. In addition yeast cells may 'fix' carbon dioxide to provide up to 5% of their carbon requirement [4].

The nitrogen requirement of the brewing yeast cell may be met by ammonium ions (in which case the cell synthesizes the necessary carbon constituents of amino acids from fermentable sugars), amino acids or low molecular weight peptides [5]. Brewing strains do not appear to produce extracellular proteolytic enzymes and thus are unable to use polypeptides or proteins. Many yeast strains do however possess these abilities [6] and one strain of *Saccharomyces* has been reported to produce an extracellular protease [7]. *Saccharomyces* strains are unable to use either molecular nitrogen or nitrate ions.

The requirement for minerals resembles that of other living cells and a supply of potassium, iron, calcium, magnesium, manganese, copper and zinc is necessary. Many of these metal ions and others are essential for the activity of enzymes. Relatively large amounts of phosphate and sulphate are also needed by brewing yeasts.

17.1.2 GROWTH FACTORS [3, 8]

It is usual for brewing yeasts to require one or more accessory nutrients (nutrilites), and most if not all strains show an absolute requirement for biotin. In the absence of growth factors, the yeast cells may fail to grow, grow very slowly or grow only after a prolonged lag. In many cases addition of nutrilites will stimulate the rate of growth even though there is no absolute requirement for them (Fig. 17.1). Strains vary considerably with respect to their need for growth factors (Table 17.1). In a survey of 61 strains of *S. carlsbergensis* [9], biotin was required by all strains. Pantothentic acid, *meso*-inositol, nicotinic acid, thiamine, *p*-amino-benzoic acid and pyridoxine were found to stimulate the growth of some (but not all) strains. In some cases strains required either thiamine or pyridoxine for growth. The roles of various growth factors in yeast metabolism are indicated in Table 17.2. With the exception of *meso*-inositol they all act as essential cofactors of enzyme function. In addition to the nutrilites already mentioned, some yeast strains require the nucleotides uracil and guanine. Some instances are also known where particular amino acids are required (e.g. methionine) when ammonium ions represent the only major source of nitrogen.

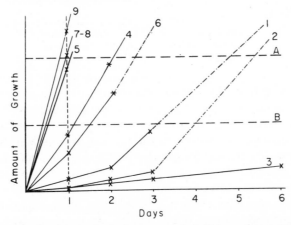

Fig. 17.1 The amount of growth obtained over a period of days when a particular yeast strain was cultured in a series of media differing in the accessory growth factors present. Medium 1 is deficient in inositol, 2 in pantothenic acid, 3 in biotin, 4 in thiamine, 5 in pyridoxine, 6 in thiamine plus pyridoxine, 7 in nicotinic acid, 8 in *p*-aminobenzoic acid, and 9 is a complete medium. A represents moderate, B poor growth levels.

TABLE 17.1

The requirement of some strains of Saccharomyces carlsbergensis *for growth factors* [9]

Strain No.	Biotin	Pantothenic acid	Inositol	Thia-mine	Pyri-doxine	Nicotinic acid	Uracil and guanine
9	+	+	S	−	−	−	+
26	+	+	−	−	S	−	S
34	+	+	−	−	−	−	S
44	+	+	−	−	--	−	S
59	+	+	+	S	S	−	S
66	+	S	S	−	−	−	S
71	+	+	+	−	S	−	+
G	+	+	−	S	S	S	−

+ Definitely essential or markedly stimulatory for growth; S stimulatory; − not essential.

TABLE 17.2

Nutrilites (vitamins) required for full growth on synthetic media by a range of yeasts

Nutrilite required	Active form within cell	Function
Biotin	Biotin	Coenzyme in carboxylation and transcarboxy-lation
(*meso*) Inositol	Phospholipids	Numerous effects upon carbohydrate and lipid metabolism, membrane integrity
Pantothenic acid	Coenzyme A	As above
Thiamine	Thiamine pyrophosphate	Coenzyme in oxo-acid decarboxylation and oxidation
Pyridoxine	Pyridoxal phosphate	Coenzyme for transamination, decarboxyla-tion and racemization
Nicotinic acid (Niacin)	NAD and NADP	Coenzymes for dehydrogenases
p-Aminobenzoic acid	Folic acid and tetrahydrofolate compounds	Coenzymes for transfer of one carbon units e.g. glycine→serine

Brewers' wort normally contains all the nutrients required by the yeast cell. The principal source of carbohydrate is maltose although significant amounts of glucose, fructose, sucrose, maltotriose as well as non-metabolizable pentoses, oligosaccharides and dextrins are also present (Volume 1, Chapter 9). The yeasts' requirement for nitrogen is satisfied by ammonium ions, amino acids and peptides. Ample quantities of minerals and nutrilites are also available in malt wort. Worts of low assimilable nitrogen content, prepared using carbohydrate adjuncts, may be deficient in nitrogen and also in growth factors, particularly biotin. Worts may be supplemented by adding 'yeast foods' containing yeast extract (and hence a supply of nutrilites), metal ions (e.g. Zn^{2+}), ammonium and phosphate. More complex formulations may also be employed [10].

17.2 *Permeation of the yeast cell* [2, 11–15]

Most substances dissolved in the medium surrounding yeast cells diffuse freely through the cell walls to the plasma membranes. There is adsorption of certain materials by the outer layers of the cell walls during the diffusion. For instance, hop bitter substances, polyphenols, and nitrogenous compounds of wort tend to be adsorbed. The plasma membrane isolates the living cell or protoplast from its environment and controls the movement of materials in and out of the cell. Substances which are soluble in lipid, an important constituent of the membrane, tend to penetrate readily. Thus, unbranched long-chain fatty acids and α-oxo-acids penetrate more quickly than the corresponding short-chain acids which are less soluble in lipid. If the acids are dissociated, they enter the cell either slowly or not at all.

In addition to lipid, the plasma membrane also contains protein and carbohydrate, and most low molecular weight compounds penetrate because of their association with these constituents. There is some evidence also for minute pores in the membrane which sieve the ions and molecules bombarding its surface. Three methods of entry have been recognized: (*i*) simple net diffusion involving a concentration gradient, (*ii*) facilitated diffusion or catalysed diffusion which is probably enzymic in nature (this brings about entry of a substance faster than would be expected from simple diffusion but is motivated by a concentration gradient), and (*iii*) methods which involve the expenditure of metabolic energy by the yeast cell to concentrate the substance within the cell, sometimes against the concentration gradient to a level far in excess of that in the medium. This is called active transport and is believed in at least some instances to be mediated by specific transport enzymes or permeases.

A permease (carrier [16]) is assumed to have the characteristics of an enzyme and thus exhibits stereospecificity for the transported solute. It can traverse the cell membrane, thus transporting the solute from the outside to the inside of the cell, and both influx and efflux of solute occur. The transport will usually exhibit saturation (Michaelis–Menten) kinetics. Enzymes involved in facilitated diffusion or active transport (i.e. permeases and molecules responsible for the intracellular modification of the transported solute) may be either constitutive or inducible. This means that the system may be present at all times (constitutive) or developed by the cell only in the presence of the transported solute (inducible). Clearly for induction to occur some of the solute must enter the cell either by way of a small (constitutive) amount of the transport system or by another means (e.g. diffusion). When the inducer concentration falls to zero or below a critical level, the transport system fails to operate; thus a degree of control on the entry of the inducer is exercised. The presence of glucose in the medium may prevent the synthesis of the transport system (catabolite repression) thereby enabling glucose to be utilized and preventing unnecessary synthesis of the enzymes of the transport system.

Simple diffusion probably accounts for the uptake of undissociated organic acids by the yeast cell. Facilitated diffusion may be involved in the transport of sugars [17], although the fact that some are taken up against a concentration gradient could indicate that active transport occurs [18]. Active transport processes are used to transport amino acids and the ions of potassium, magnesium, phosphorus and sulphate.

17.2.1 UPTAKE OF WORT SUGARS

The glucose, fructose and sucrose present in wort are rapidly utilized by brewers' yeast. Sucrose is hydrolysed, at the outer surface of the cell, to glucose and fructose by an external invertase. The monosaccharides produced, as well as those already present, are transported into the cell by a constitutive permease (glucose permease). The transport system shows that many monosaccharides (Table 17.3) have a somewhat higher affinity (lower K_m value) for glucose than for fructose, which is utilized more slowly. In some strains of yeast two different carriers may be present, each showing different stereospecificities with regard to the transported monosaccharides [19]. Consequently, sugars with the same stereospecific grouping will compete for the same carrier.

TABLE 17.3

Specificity of the constitutive hexose transport in Saccharomyces cerevisiae. *The hexoses are listed in order of their apparent affinities with the order of magnitude of the Michaelis constants in mol/l, assuming no major differences in maximal rate among substrates* [12]

10^{-3}	D-Glucose
	2-Deoxy-D-glucose
	D-Glucosone
10^{-2}	D-Fructose
	D-Mannose
	D-Allose
	N-Acetyl-D-glucosamine
10^{-1}	D-Xylose
	D-Arabinose
	3-O-Methyl-D-glucose
	L-Sorbose
	D-Lyxose
	1, 5-Anhydro-D-glucitol
1	L-Fucose
	D-Mannoheptulose
	D-Galactose
	L-Xylose
10	D-Ribose
	D-Fucose
> 20	L-Rhamnose, L-Arabinose, Sorbitol

The uptake of maltose and maltotriose is mediated by specific inducible permeases [20, 21], A coordinated induction of an α-glucosidase (maltase) also occurs, so that on entering the cell both sugars are hydrolyzed to glucose [22, 23]. Neither the permeases nor the maltase are synthesized in the presence of glucose ($>0.4\%$ w/v for brewing yeasts [24]) and hence are said to be catabolite repressed [25].

In bacteria, enzymes which are subject to catabolite repression are only synthesized when an addition complex between cyclic adenosine mono-phosphate (cAMP) and a specific protein (cAMP binding protein) is present. This complex interacts with the genome to permit transcription of the DNA and hence, ultimately, the synthesis of the enzyme(s). (With inducible enzyme systems, transcription remains blocked unless the inducer is also present.) When cells are grown on glucose, low levels of cAMP are present, therefore catabolite repression occurs because the addition complex is either not formed, or is present at too low a concentration to be effective. When cells are grown on 'non-repressing' sugars, e.g. galactose, high levels of cAMP are produced and catabolite repression is relieved by the complex of cAMP and specific protein [26, 27].

In yeast, increased levels of cAMP are found when glucose grown cells adapt to growth on maltose [27, 28]. Consequently cAMP relieves the cata-bolite repression of α-glucosidase [29]. It seems, therefore, that cAMP has a similar regulatory function in yeast to that in bacteria.

In addition to acting as a catabolite repressor, glucose (or its catabolites) may also act as a catabolite inactivator. Catabolite inactivation describes a rapid disappearance of enzyme activity, in contrast to the 'diluting out' which follows catabolite repression, when the cells continue to multiply. Maltose permease is inactivated by this process, which is probably the result of proteolytic enzyme action [30].

The half-life of maltose permease is approximately 1·2 hr [19], therefore in (i) the presence of repressing concentrations of glucose, (ii) the absence of inducing concentrations of maltose or (iii) the absence of protein synthesis, the level of permease will fall by 90% in some 5 hr.

In a brewery fermentation, pitched with viable yeast cropped from the active stage of growth on wort, the yeast cells will be able to utilize all the fermentable carbohydrates immediately. This is in fact the situation observed with laboratory fermentations of brewers' wort [22, 31]. However, the rate of maltose utilization may decline (because of catabolite repression of the synthesis of new permease and α-glucosidase), until the level of glucose falls from its initial level (approx. 1% w/v) to a level below that required to repress enzyme synthesis. Where exceptionally high levels of glucose are present (e.g. when using glucose syrup adjuncts) this effect will be more pronounced. Fructose also acts as a catabolite repressor [25] so that adjuncts such as invert sugar or sucrose (since it is rapidly hydrolyzed to glucose and fructose by the yeast external invertase) will have similar effects.

When pitching yeast is stored for prolonged periods of time in the absence of inducing concentrations of maltose, or under conditions where protein synthesis is restricted (e.g. in the absence of assimilable nitrogen), it will lose its maltose permease activity. Under these circumstances, fermentation might be prolonged by the time taken for cells to synthesize new enzymes. Repression of maltose uptake is not expressed by all brewing strains [23]. However, the phenomenon of catabolite repression would be expected to prolong fermentation time, whereas strains which no longer exhibit the phenomenon would be expected to attenuate at greater rates, and more extensively, than repressed cells.

Analysis of the uptake of wort sugars shows that glucose, fructose and sucrose are most rapidly consumed (24–28 hr) followed by maltose (70–72 hr) and finally maltotriose (after 72 hr) [21, 30]. This order of uptake reflects the fact that glucose, fructose and sucrose are present in low concentrations and are utilized rapidly; maltose is present at much higher concentrations but used at a similar rate and maltotriose, present in lower concentration than maltose, is used at a much lower rate [21, 22, 31, 32].

17.2.2 UPTAKE OF WORT NITROGEN

All yeasts are able to use ammonium ions as a source of nitrogen. Growth with ammonium salts as sole source of nitrogen is better than when any single amino acid is used. Indeed, brewing yeasts are unable to use certain amino acids (e.g. lysine) as sole sources of nitrogen, and this is used as the basis of a test to detect the presence of wild yeasts (see Chapter 21). When mixtures of amino acids are present, as in brewers' wort, growth is more rapid than when ammonium ions are the sole source of nitrogen [33].

Brewers' yeast can assimilate some 50% of the amino nitrogen in wort [34]; in general, bottom yeasts use the amino acids less completely than top yeasts [35]. The bulk of the yeast's nitrogen requirement is met by amino nitrogen (amino acids, peptides) rather than ammonium ions.

The uptake of wort amino acids by brewers' yeast occurs in a sequential manner, which is largely independent of the conditions of fermentation and strains of yeast used [36]. Four groups of amino acids were described based upon their order of removal from wort [36, 37]:

Group A. Absorbed immediately and consumed during the first 20 hr of fermentation – glutamate, aspartate, asparagine, glutamine, serine, threonine, lysine and arginine.
Group B. Absorbed gradually during the whole course of fermentation – histidine, valine, methionine, leucine and isoleucine.

Group C. Absorbed after an appreciable lag – glycine, phenylalanine, tyrosine, tryptophan, alanine, ammonia.

Group D. Negligible net absorption – proline.

The basis for this orderly sequence of events appears to involve the nature and specificities of amino acid permeases. Thus, two general permeases may be involved, one showing specificity for group A and group C amino acids, since members of the former group compete with those of the latter [37], and one transporting group B amino acids.

The process of uptake of amino acids by yeasts appears to be very complex. At least ten systems of different specificities are capable of transporting amino acids against considerable concentration gradients [38, 39]. There is no clear evidence as to either the ultimate source of the energy required for transport, or to the mechanism of coupling of energy to transport. There appear, however, to be two different energy reserves supporting amino acid uptake [40], one involving mitochondrially generated ATP, the other, polyphosphate derived from glycolysis at the level of 1,3 diphosphoglycerate. Presumably, in the absence of oxidative phosphorylation, this latter source is the one primarily used by brewing yeast.

17.2.3 EXCRETION OF NITROGENOUS METABOLITES

Yeast in aqueous suspension gradually excretes amino acids, nucleotides and other low molecular weight substances. Suspension of yeast in glucose solution causes a rapid release of amino acids which are subsequently re-absorbed in 2–3 hr [41]. This phenomenon (termed 'shock excretion') does not occur when maltose rather than glucose solutions are used and apparently does not require energy [42].

Shock excretion is thought to involve changes in membrane function and is more apparent in mature yeast cells [43]. The significance of this process in practical terms is unknown, however it might be expected to contribute to lag in fermentation, particularly if mature yeast is pitched into worts with relatively high glucose contents. Similarly, priming beer might induce excretion of metabolites which may then support the growth of beer spoilage organisms such as lactic acid bacteria.

17.3 *Metabolism* [44, 45, 46]

Metabolism encompasses all enzymic reactions which occur in a cell and the organization and regulation of those reactions. It is often convenient to consider individual aspects of metabolism in terms of biochemical pathways; it should never be forgotten, however, that such pathways do not exist in isolation, but are merely parts of a whole integrated metabolic process.

A biochemical pathway consists of a series of chemical reactions catalysed by enzymes. The catalytic moiety of enzymes is invariably protein, although lipid and carbohydrate may be covalently associated with particular protein molecules. The function of an enzyme is to increase the rate of a chemical reaction and enable it to occur at the physiological temperatures and pH values within the living cell. As the enzyme is a catalyst only minute quantities need to be present. Because of the protein nature of enzymes they are inactivated by extremes of pH, temperature and other 'denaturing' agents.

Enzymes show stereospecificity towards their substrates, and often require cofactors to assist and/or participate in their catalytic activity. Cofactors include divalent metal ions, e.g. Mg^{2+}, Zn^{2+} and many low molecular weight molecules derived in part from growth factors (vitamins), e.g. nicotinic acid and biotin (see Table 17.2).

The extent to which any chemical reaction proceeds is determined by the sign and magnitude of the free energy change (ΔG). Reactions which proceed to completion have large negative values of ΔG. A large positive value on the other hand is typical of reactions which occur only to a very limited extent. It is usual to quote the standard free energy change (when all reactants and products are at 1 M concentration at equilibrium at pH 7), i.e. $\Delta G^{\circ\prime}$. The sign and magnitude of the free energy change of a reaction however do not indicate how quickly a reaction proceeds. For example, the complete oxidation of glucose:

$$C_6H_{12}O_6 + 6O_2 \rightarrow 6CO_2 + 6H_2O$$

has a standard free energy change $\Delta G^{\circ\prime}$ of 2·9 MJ (-688 kcal); however, glucose can be left in contact with oxygen at room temperature indefinitely without significant reaction occurring. Most living organisms carry out this reaction using the catalytic properties of the enzymes of the glycolytic pathway, tricarboxylic acid cycle and oxidative phosphorylation. Each enzyme accelerates the rate at which a particular chemical reaction occurs it does not influence the equilibrium constant or the overall change in ΔG.

Biochemical pathways may be described as catabolic, anabolic (biosynthetic), amphibolic or anaplerotic. The principal function of a catabolic sequence is to degrade (usually by an oxidative process) simple organic molecules derived from the breakdown of polymers (e.g. amino acids from proteins) and retain some of the free energy released in a 'biologically useful' form. Anabolic pathways consume energy and synthesize (usually by a reductive process) the simple molecules which are assembled into proteins, nucleic acids, carbohydrate polymers and lipids. Amphibolic pathways, such as the tricarboxylic acid cycle, have both catabolic and anabolic properties. They are central metabolic pathways which furnish, from catabolic sequences, the intermediates which form the substrates of anabolic processes. The removal of intermediates (essential to the operation of the catabolic processes) from a central metabolic pathway would result in cessation of the production of biologically useful energy. These essential compounds are replaced by anaplerotic reactions, thus ensuring the continued operation of the amphibolic pathway.

The biologically useful energy produced during catabolism and consumed in anabolism is stored chemically in the form of adenosine triphosphate (ATP). This so-called high energy compound has a large negative free energy of hydrolysis. Hydrolysis of ATP to adenosine diphosphate (ADP) and inorganic phosphate (Pi) liberates some 30·5 kJ (7·3 kcal) under standard conditions. The free energy of hydrolysis is a function of pH, temperature and the concentrations of ATP itself and the ADP and Pi produced. In the conditions obtaining inside living cells, the hydrolysis of 1 mol ATP may yield as much as 52 kJ (12·5 kcal). During the course of a catabolic sequence, intermediates containing phosphate are synthesized, these may then be hydrolysed with the simultaneous formation of ATP from ADP. Thus by enzyme action, the energy of catabolism can be packaged into ATP molecules.

Oxidative reactions in catabolic sequences involve the removal of electrons from an intermediate. This process is controlled by dehydrogenases and often involves the participation of the cofactor nicotinamide adenine dinucleotide (NAD or NAD^+). Electrons from the donor are transferred to NAD in the form of the hydride ion $[:H^-]$ to produce reduced NAD (NADH). In many reactions two 'hydrogen atoms' are 'removed' from the substrate, one in the form of the hydride ion, the other liberated as a proton; accordingly, the reduction of NAD^+ is often written as

$$NAD^+ + [2H] \rightarrow NADH + H^+ \text{ (or } NADH_2\text{)}.$$

Anabolic (biosynthetic) reactions are driven by ATP energy, and the process of reduction is mediated by enzymes most of which utilize nicotinamide adenine dinucleotide phosphate (NADP or $NADP^+$) as cofactor. The specificity of catabolism for NAD^+ and anabolism for $NADP^+$ is an example of 'chemical compartmentation' and enables some degree of metabolic regulation to be exerted through control of the levels of the two cofactors. The relative concentrations of the oxidized and reduced forms of a particular cofactor may also serve a regulatory role.

Metabolic regulation also involves 'biological compartmentation' whereby metabolic sequences are localized within subcellular organelles, e.g. the location of the tricarboxylic acid cycle in mitochondria. In addition control of biochemical pathways may be achieved by (i) regulating the synthesis of enzymes at the level of the gene or protein synthesis, e.g. catabolite repression; (ii) regulating the degradation of enzymes thereby changing their steady-state concentration within the cell e.g. catabolite inactivation; (*iii*) influencing the rate of enzyme activity by allosteric inhibition, e.g. the ability of the end product of a pathway to 'feed-back' inhibit enzymes in the pathway, or by allosteric activation, i.e. increasing the affinity of an enzyme for its substrate; these processes change the catalytic activity exhibited by a given amount of enzyme; (*iv*) the presence of isozymes, e.g. alcohol dehydrogenase (ADH 1) used when yeast grows on ethanol has a high affinity for ethanol and low affinity for acetaldehyde whereas ADH 2 used when yeast grows on glucose, has the opposite affinities.

17.3.1 AEROBIC CARBOHYDRATE METABOLISM

The principal pathway for the fermentation of glucose and fructose is the Embden–Meyerhof–Parnas route (alternatively named EMP or glycolytic sequence). Wort sucrose is hydrolysed extracellularly and maltose and maltotriose intracellularly. Intracellular storage carbohydrates such as glycogen and trehalose may also serve as sources of intracellular monosaccharide.

The monosaccharides produced are phosphorylated: the EMP pathway (Fig. 17.2) commences with the phosphorylation of glucose using the high energy bond of ATP and the production of glucose-6-phosphate (G-6-P) a reaction mediated by the enzyme hexokinase. In the case of glycogen utilization, phosphorolytic degradation yields glucose-1-phosphate which may be enzymically isomerized to G-6-P. G-6-P is converted to its isomer fructose-6-phosphate (F-6-P) by the enzyme phosphohexose isomerase (a readily reversible reaction). Intracellular fructose is phosphorylated by hexokinase to yield F-6-P directly. The third enzyme of the glycolytic sequence, phosphofructokinase, is responsible for the phosphorylation, using ATP, of F-6-P to yield fructose-1,6-diphosphate. In common with other 'kinase' reactions, i.e. those consuming or producing ATP, Mg^{2+} ions are essential cofactors of the enzyme reaction.

Aldolase then catalyses the reversible cleavage of the six-carbon molecule into two three-carbon molecules, triose phosphates. Yeast aldolase is inactivated by cysteine and may be reactivated by Zn^{2+}, Fe^{2+} or Co^{2+} ions. The triose phosphates are a mixture of dihydroxyacetone phosphate and D-glyceraldehyde-3-phosphate. Only the latter undergoes further change in the EMP pathway, but an equilibrium between the two is maintained by enzymic conversion of some of the dihydroxyacetone phosphate into glyceraldehyde-3-phosphate, catalysed by the enzyme triose-phosphate isomerase.

The D-glyceraldehyde-3-phosphate is converted into 1,3-diphosphoglyceric acid using inorganic phosphate, and electrons are transferred to the coenzyme NAD^+. The enzyme complex involved is called phosphoglyceraldehyde dehydrogenase. The reaction is the first in the EMP pathway to involve

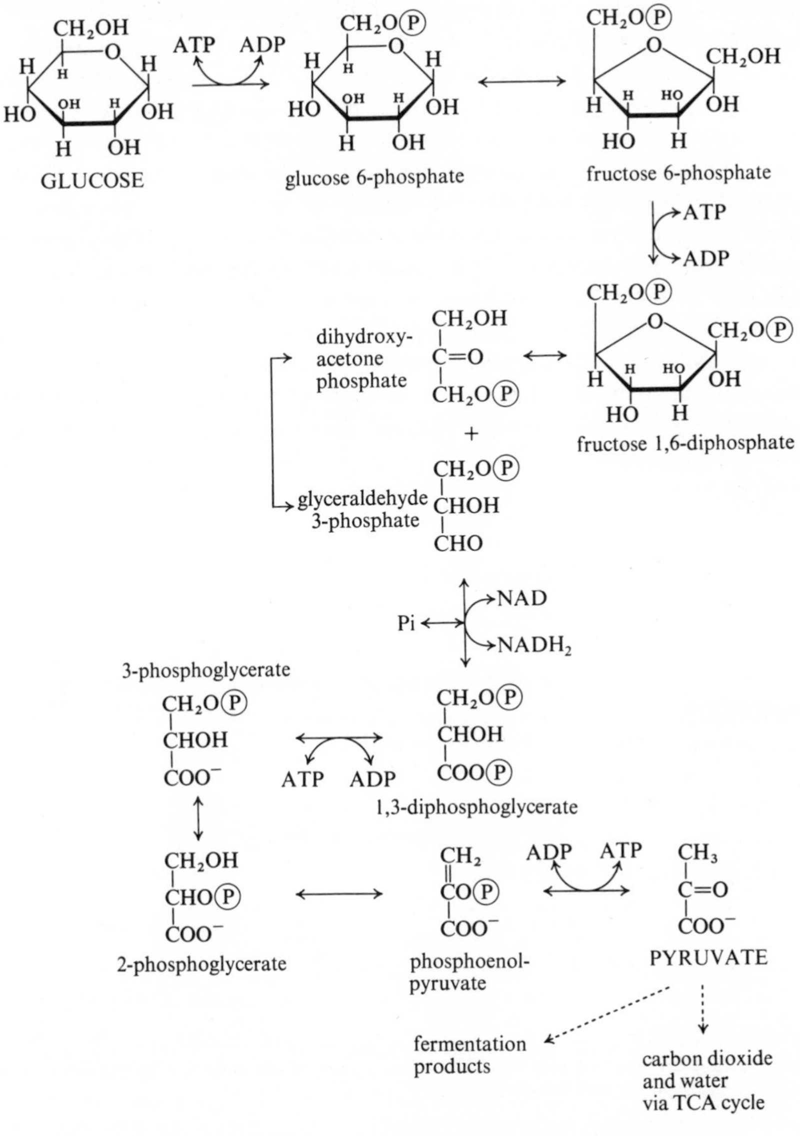

Fig. 17.2 The Embden–Meyerhof–Parnas pathway (glycolytic pathway).

oxidation/reduction and also the first in which a high energy phosphate compound is formed where none previously existed. Thus the phosphate bond formed at position 1 in 1,3-diphosphoglyceric acid has a standard free energy of hydrolysis of $-49 \cdot 3$ kJ ($-11 \cdot 8$ kcal). The next step is the transfer of this energy-rich phosphate to ADP to give ATP and 3-phosphoglyceric acid, a reaction catalysed by phosphoglycerate kinase with Mg^{2+} ions acting as cofactor. Because each molecule of glucose yields two triose molecules, two molecules of ATP are generated at this stage and balance out the ATP used in the phosphorylation of glucose (or fructose) and of F-6-P. 3-Phosphoglyceric acid is converted to 2-phosphoglyceric acid by the enzyme phosphoglycero-mutase. Enolase then mediates the removal of water to give phosphoenol-pyruvic acid, a step which requires magnesium ions and is inhibited by fluoride ions. The energy-rich phosphate bond of the phosphoenol-pyruvic acid ($\Delta G^{\circ\prime} = -61.9$ kJ; -14.8 kcal) is used to transfer phosphate to ADP to yield ATP and pyruvic acid. Thus, overall, two molecules of ATP are produced for each molecule of hexose converted to pyruvate. At the same time, two molecules of NAD^+ are reduced. The supply of NAD^+ is normally limited and therefore oxidation of the reduced form is necessary for the EMP pathway to continue.

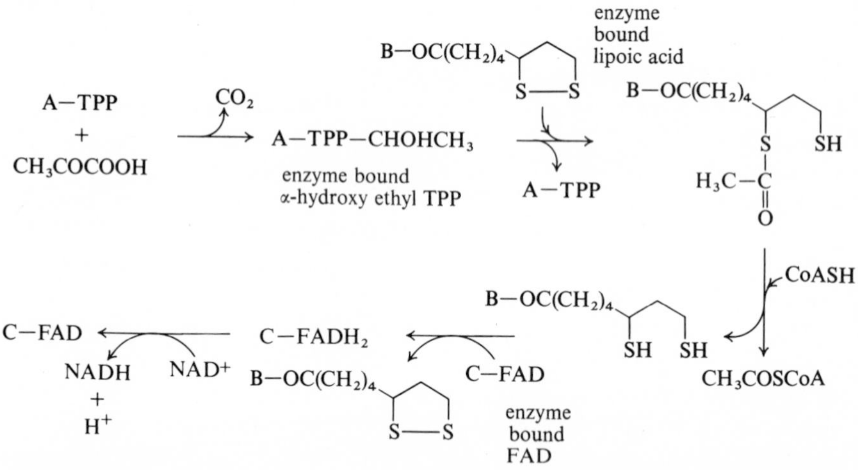

Fig. 17.3 Conversion of pyruvate to acetyl Coenzyme A by the mitochondrial pyruvate dehydrogenase complex of enzymes. A, pyruvate dehydrogenase; B, dihydrolipoyl trans-acetylase; C, dihydrolipoyl dehydrogenase.

Under aerobic conditions and in the absence of high concentrations of glucose, yeast respires glucose. Under these circumstances pyruvic acid is oxidized and decarboxylated by the so-called pyruvate dehydrogenase complex. This system comprises three separate enzyme activities and is located within mitochondria. The three separate enzymes are pyruvate dehydrogenase, dihydrolipoyl transacetylase and dihydrolipoyl dehydrogenase (A, B and C in

Fig. 17.3). Participating in the reaction are thiamine pyrophosphate (TPP), Coenzyme A (CoASH), flavin adenine dinucleotide (FAD), NAD^+ and dihydrolipoic acid:

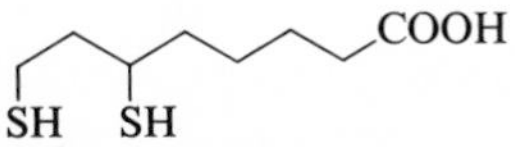

The overall reaction produces, from one molecule of pyruvic acid, one molecule of CO_2, one of acetylated Coenzyme A (acetyl-S-CoA) and one of NADH.

$$\text{Pyruvate} + NAD^+ + \text{CoA-SH} \rightarrow \text{Acetyl-S-CoA} + CO_2 + NADH + H^+$$

$$\Delta G^{\circ\prime} = -33 \cdot 4 \text{ kJ} (-8 \text{ kcal})$$

This reaction is essentially irreversible and the thioester bond of acetyl-S-CoA ($CH_3CO \cdot SCoA$) has a high free energy of hydrolysis ($\Delta G^{\circ\prime} = -31$ kJ; $-7 \cdot 5$ kcal). This energy is utilized in a condensation reaction of acetyl CoA with the *enol* form of oxaloacetic acid to produce citric acid and CoASH is liberated. The enzyme mediating this reaction, citrate synthase (condensing enzyme), is the first enzyme of the tricarboxylic acid cycle (Krebs' cycle) (Fig. 17.4).

Citric acid is isomerized by aconitase to yield isocitric acid (*cis*-aconitic acid is an intermediate). The oxidation of isocitrate by isocitrate dehydrogenase to α-oxoglutarate involves the formation of NADH (an $NADP^+$ linked enzyme is also found) and the oxalosuccinic acid produced is decarboxylated to yield α-oxoglutarate.

The 5-carbon α-oxoglutaric acid is decarboxylated by an oxidative step, involving Coenzyme A, thiamine pyrophosphate, lipoic acid and NAD^+, by α-oxoglutarate dehydrogenase to produce succinyl CoA. Succinyl CoA is converted to succinic acid by the action of succinyl thiokinase; during this reaction Coenzyme A is released and guanosine diphosphate plus inorganic phosphate combine to give energy-rich guanosine triphosphate (GTP), a process which is called 'substrate level phosphorylation'. Succinic acid is oxidized to fumaric acid by succinate dehydrogenase, with flavin adenine dinucleotide (FAD) acting as electron acceptor. Fumarase catalyses the reversible hydration of fumarate to L-malate which in turn is oxidized to oxaloacetate by the action of malate dehydrogenase, with NAD^+ as hydrogen acceptor.

The effect of the Krebs' cycle is to produce (by oxidizing the acetate moiety derived from pyruvic acid) two molecules of CO_2, 3 NADH, 1 FADH, 4 H^+ and 1 GTP.

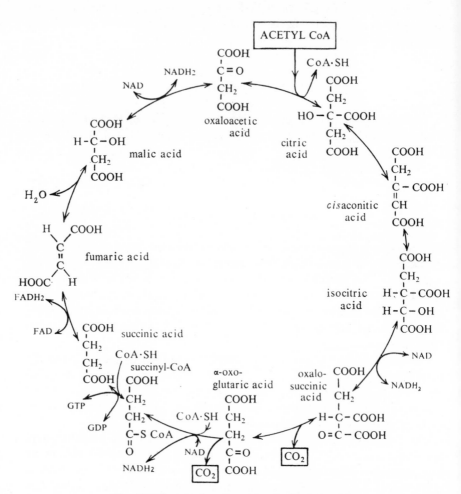

Fig. 17.4 The tricarboxylic acid cycle (Krebs' cycle).

The final stage of glucose catabolism by respiring yeast also occurs within the mitochondria where the reduced cofactors NADH and FADH, formed by the complete oxidation of glucose, are themselves oxidized to regenerate NAD⁺ and FAD respectively. In contrast to fermentation, where acetaldehyde acts as the oxidizing agent, molecular oxygen is used in respiration. Electrons, donated by the coenzymes are shuttled along a chain of carrier molecules (including ubiquinone, iron–sulphur-containing carriers and cytochromes) which constitute the electron transport or respiratory chain (Fig. 17.5).

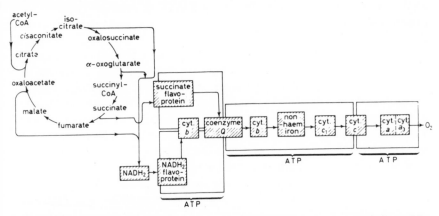

Fig. 17.5 Diagrammatic representation of the complete electron transport chain and its relationship with the Krebs' cycle.

Each electron of a pair is in turn received by a ferric ion (Fe^{3+}) in the haem centre of cytochrome b, the ferrous ion (Fe^{2+}) produced then donates the electron to a non-haem iron carrier, which in turn passes it on to cytochrome c_1; it is finally passed to molecular oxygen and water is produced. The overall reaction is therefore:

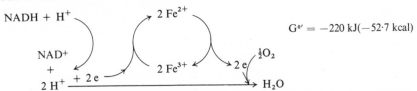

$$G^{o'} = -220 \text{ kJ}(-52\cdot7 \text{ kcal})$$

At certain positions within the electron transport chain (Fig. 17.5), namely: site I (NADH → CoQ); site II (CoQ → cyt. c); and site III (cyt. a/a_3 → O_2), sufficiently large changes in free energy occur to drive the synthesis of ATP from ADP and Pi. The mechanism whereby electron transport is *coupled* to phosphorylation of ADP (oxidative phosphorylation, cf. substrate-level phosphorylation) is still the subject of debate and remains one of the major unsolved problems in biochemistry (see [45]).

The enzymes of Krebs' cycle are located within the contents of the mitochondria, while the components of the electron transport chain are situated in or on the inner membranes. It is thought that each of the components of the respiratory chain are assembled together in the precise sequence in which they interact. There are clearly many such assemblies on the inner mitochondrial membrane.

The oxidation by electron transport of each molecule of NADH produced by the citric acid cycle may generate up to 3 molecules of ATP, whereas oxidation of a molecule $FADH_2$ yields 2 ATP molecules. There is some evidence [47] that yeast cannot phosphorylate at site I and therefore only 2 molecules of ATP are produced from the oxidation of 1 molecule of NADH. The NADH produced during the operation of the EMP pathway cannot be oxidized directly within the mitochondria because these organelles are impermeable to the reduced cofactor. Accordingly, cytoplasmic enzymes utilize NADH to reduce organic molecules which may enter the mitochondria whereupon mitochondrial enzymes oxidize them to yield reduced cofactor. Two of these so-called 'shuttle' mechanisms, which effectively transfer reducing power from the cytoplasm to the mitochondria, may be used. The necessary enzymes for both mechanisms have been shown to occur in yeast [48, 49]. The first, the glycerophosphate shuttle, oxidizes NADH by reducing dihydroxyacetone phosphate to glycerol-3-phosphate which enters the mito-chondria where it is oxidized by an FAD-dependent glycerol phosphate dehydrogenase. The FADH produced reacts in turn with the respiratory chain. In the second shuttle system (the malate shuttle) cytoplasmic oxalo-acetic acid is reduced to malic acid by an NADH-dependent, cytoplasmically located, malate dehydrogenase. The malate produced enters the mitochondrion to be oxidized to oxaloacetic acid by the mitochondrial NAD^+-dependent malate dehydrogenase. The NADH produced is then oxidized by the electron transport chain.

Respiration of 1 molecule of glucose by yeast generates 28 molecules of ATP (2 from the EMP, 2 from the Krebs' cycle and 24 from oxidative phosphorylation of 10 NADH and 2 $FADH_2$). The $G^{\circ\prime}$ for hydrolysis of ATP is 30·5 kJ (7·3 kcal) therefore one mole of glucose oxidized yields the equi-valent (under standard conditions of) $28 \times 30\cdot5$ kJ, i.e. 854 kJ (204 kcal). The standard free energy change for the complete oxidation of glucose is 2·9 MJ, therefore the efficiency of respiration by yeast is $(0\cdot854/2\cdot9) \times 100\%$, i.e. 29%. In animal tissues up to 38 molecules of ATP may be produced with a corresponding efficiency of 40%. The proportion of energy not retained by the cell as ATP is largely dissipated as heat.

Although glycolysis represents the major pathway for glucose catabolism, some glucose is metabolized by an alternative route, the hexose monophos-phate (HMP) pathway (also called the pentose phosphate pathway) (Fig. 17.6). There is no general agreement as to how much glucose is metabolized by this route. The function of this pathway is two-fold, namely (i) to provide a source of NADPH for anabolic reduction reactions and (ii) to supply pentose sugars for biosynthesis (e.g. nucleotide synthesis).

The first step in the HMP pathway (Fig. 17.6) is the oxidation of glucose-6-phosphate by an $NADP^+$-dependent dehydrogenase. The product, 6-phospho-gluconolactone, is converted to 6-phosphogluconic acid by a lactonase. A second oxidative step mediated by 6-phosphogluconic acid dehydrogenase,

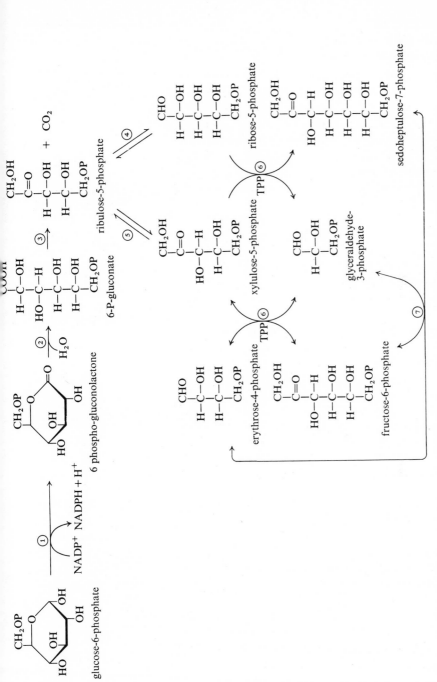

Fig. 17.6 Hexose monophosphate pathway. 1, glucose-6-P-dehydrogenase; 2, 6-P-gluconolactonase; 3, 6-P-gluconate dehydrogenase; 4, phosphoribose isomerase; 5, phosphoketopentose epimerase; 6, transketolase; 7, transaldolase; TPP, thiamine pyrophosphate.

and NADP$^+$-dependent enzyme, liberates carbon dioxide and produces the ketopentose ribulose-5-phosphate. From ribulose-5-phosphate an isomerase yields ribose-5-phosphate and an epimerase xylulose-5-phosphate. The enzyme transketolase with thiamine pyrophosphate as cofactor, catalyses the transfer of the two-carbon keto-fragment of xylulose-5-P to the aldehyde group of ribose-5-P, thereby forming sedoheptulose-7-P and glyceraldehyde-3-P. The enzyme transaldolase catalyses the transfer of carbon atoms (1, 2 and 3) of a keto sugar to the aldehyde group of an aldo sugar. Thus from sedoheptulose-7-phosphate and glyceraldehyde-3-phosphate, fructose-6-phosphate and erythrose-4-phosphate are formed. This HMP pathway may be considered to oxidize glucose:

$$\text{G-6-P} + 12\ \text{NADP}^+ \rightarrow 6\ \text{CO}_2 + 12\ \text{NADPH} + 12\ \text{H}^+ + \text{Pi} + 6\ \text{H}_2\text{O}$$

and, if transhydrogenation of NADPH and NAD occurs within the cell, clearly, under aerobic conditions, ATP could be generated by oxidative phosphorylation.

Some yeasts, e.g. *Candida utilis* produce all their pentose sugar requirements by the HMP pathway [50]. When the specific activities of the key enzymes of the pathway are compared with those in *S. cerevisiae* (Table 17.4) it is seen that in the latter yeast they are markedly lower. This is particularly so for glucose-6-phosphate dehydrogenase. In *S. cerevisiae* therefore it is thought that most of the pentose sugar requirement is met by the action of transketolase on glyceraldehyde-3-phosphate and fructose-6-phosphate derived from the glycolytic pathway.

TABLE 17.4

Enzymes of the pentose phosphate pathway in Candida utilis *and* Saccharomyces cerevisiae [50]

Enzyme	S. cerevisiae	C. utilis
	(μmol/min/mg protein)	
Glucose 6-phosphate dehydrogenase	0·06	2·15
6-Phosphogluconic dehydrogenase	0·12	0·35
Transketolase	0·20	1·45
Transaldolase	0·02	0·20
Aldolase	3·0	1·1

Although of limited importance in *Saccharomyces* sp. the enzyme glucose-6-phosphate dehydrogenase is used in the metabolism of glucose by the bacterium *Zymomonas* (Entner–Doudoroff pathway) and lactic acid bacteria (phosphoketolase pathway) (see Chapter 21).

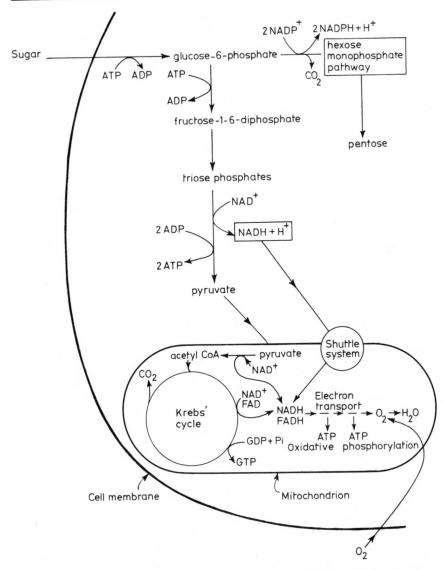

Fig. 17.7 Summary of aerobic metabolism (respiration) of sugar.

The major routes for glucose catabolism by respiring yeast are shown in Fig. 17.7. The EMP pathway and Krebs' cycle are amphibolic and several intermediates of these pathways are used for the biosynthesis of the monomers, e.g. fatty acids and amino acids, used to produce high molecular weight compounds such as fats and proteins. The importance of these pathways in furnishing the starting points of anabolism is indicated in Fig 17.8. Since the

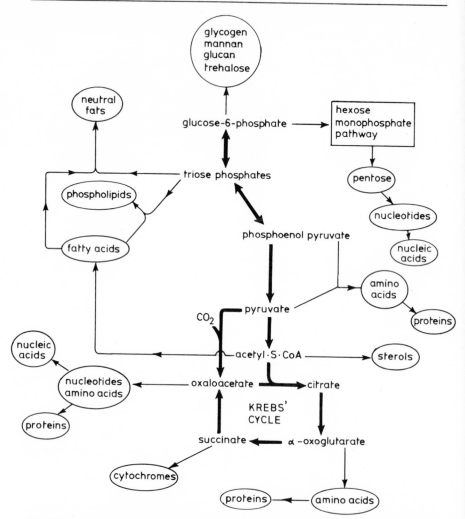

Fig. 17.8 The participation of the EMP pathway and Krebs' cycle in furnishing intermediates for biosynthetic reactions. (Heavy lines show major routes of carbohydrate catabolism.)

cells are supplied with a fermentable sugar, intermediates as far along the pathway as acetyl CoA are readily produced. However, the intermediates of the tricarboxylic acid cycle need to be replenished if withdrawn for biosynthetic purposes. They may be derived from amino acids in the medium, e.g. α-oxoglutarate from glutamate, but are more reliably furnished by anaplerotic sequences. In yeast, the main anaplerotic system involves a single enzyme, pyruvate carboxylase. This biotin-dependent enzyme mediates a reaction in which ATP is expended and CO_2 fixed. The substrates, pyruvate and CO_2 are condensed to yield oxaloacetic acid which in turn may enter and hence 'top up' the Krebs' cycle, The reaction is:

$$CH_3CO \cdot COOH + CO_2 \xrightarrow{\text{Biotin}} HOOC \cdot CO_2CO \cdot COOH$$

pyruvate $\qquad\qquad$ ATP $\quad$ ADP + Pi $\quad$ oxaloacetate

Yeast can supply some 5% of its carbon requirement by fixing CO_2 in this manner.

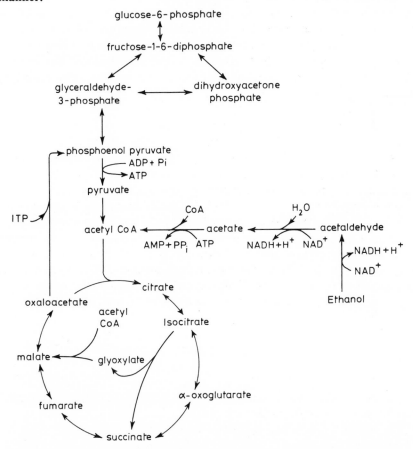

Fig. 17.9 Growth on ethanol or acetate, the glyoxylate cycle and gluconeogenesis.

When yeast cells are respiring carbon sources which cannot furnish pyruvic acid, e.g. acetate or ethanol, then although energy may be furnished by the use of the Krebs' cycle and oxidative phosphorylation, a different anaplerotic system must operate. This system needs to be capable of furnishing both intermediates of the tricarboxylic acid cycle and enabling cells to synthesize glucose (gluconeogenesis). The anaplerotic pathway used under these circumstances is the glyoxylate cycle, Fig. 17.9. When yeast respires ethanol, an alcohol dehydrogenase (ADH 1) is used to oxidize ethanol to acetaldehyde and two key enzymes are induced, isocitrate lyase and malate synthase. Acetyl coenzyme A is synthesized from ethanol or acetate and citric acid produced and converted to isocitrate. The enzyme isocitrate lyase produces glyoxylate (CHO·COOH) and succinate from isocitrate. Malate is synthesized from glyoxylate and acetyl CoA. In this way the intermediates of the tricarboxylic acid cycle are supplied from acetyl CoA. Reversal of the EMP pathway to hexose phosphate is achieved from phosphenol pyruvate which may be supplied by phosphorylation of oxaloacetic acid in a reaction using the free energy of hydrolysis of inosine triphosphate. The enzyme mediating this react on, phosphoenolpyruvate carboxylase, is repressed by glucose.

17.3.2 ANAEROBIC CARBOHYDRATE METABOLISM

Yeasts growing in media containing high concentrations of fermentable carbohydrate invariably metabolize it fermentatively to produce ethanol and CO_2. If air is present, and when the sugar concentration has been lowered, the ethanol is respired using the metabolic routes described above. Under the anaerobic conditions of a brewery fermentation the hexoses derived from wort fermentable carbohydrates are catabolized by the EMP pathway (Fig. 17.2) to pyruvic acid. The pyruvate produced is decarboxylated by the enzyme pyruvate decarboxylase, with the formation of acetaldehyde and CO_2. The enzyme requires the cofactor thiamine pyrophosphate (TPP) for activity and the reaction is shown in Fig. 17.10. The acetaldehyde formed acts (in the absence of the respiratory chain) as an electron acceptor and is used to oxidize NADH with the formation of ethanol:

$$NADH + H^+ \quad NAD^+$$
$$CH_3CHO \longrightarrow CH_3CH_2OH$$

The formation of ethanol occurs solely in order that the cell may regenerate NAD^+, so that ATP synthesis may proceed.

The standard free energy change for fermentation is:

$$C_6H_{12}O_6 \rightarrow 2\ CO_2 + 2\ C_2H_5OH \qquad \Delta G^{\circ\prime} = -234\ kJ\ (-56\ kcal)$$

The EMP pathway yields 4 molecules of ATP, 2 are consumed early in the pathway therefore there is a net gain of 2 ATP. This is equivalent under standard conditions to 61 kJ (14·6 kcal) free energy and the efficiency of fermentation is therefore 26%.

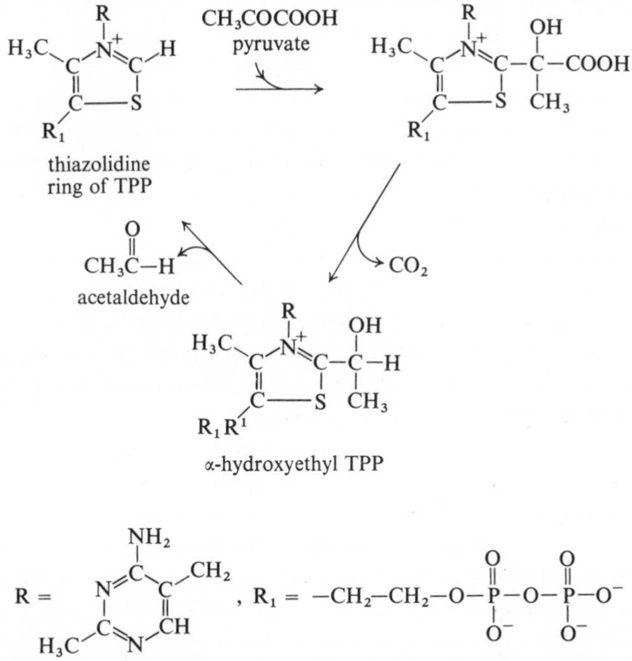

Fig. 17.10 Steps in the conversion of pyruvic acid to acetaldehyde by pyruvate decarboxylase using the cofactor thiamine pyrophosphate (TPP).

Lactic acid bacteria and muscle tissue also catabolize glucose by the EMP pathway but regenerate NAD^+ by reducing pyruvic acid to lactic acid using the enzyme lactate dehydrogenase:

$$NADH + H^+ \quad NAD^+$$

$$CH_3COCOOH \longrightarrow CH_3CHOHCOOH$$

pyruvic acid   lactic acid

Early in fermentation when yeast is growing, removal of pyruvate for biosynthesis might be expected to lead to a build up of NADH and thus to a halt in catabolism. To avoid this, cells reduce dihydroxyacetone phosphate to glycerol phosphate. This, in turn, is dephosphorylated to produce glycerol which is excreted.

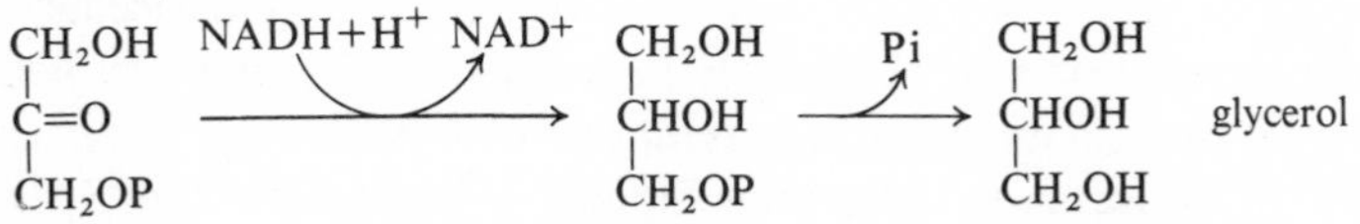

$$
\begin{array}{lll}
CH_2OH & CH_2OH & CH_2OH \\
C{=}O & CHOH & CHOH \quad \text{glycerol} \\
CH_2OP & CH_2OP & CH_2OH
\end{array}
$$

with $NADH + H^+ \quad NAD^+$ over the first arrow and Pi over the second arrow.

This reaction was exploited in Germany in 1914–1918 by adding compounds (e.g. bisulphite) to complex acetaldehyde. Under these conditions glycerol was produced for the manufacture of explosives such as trinitroglycerol.

Under anaerobic conditions, the levels of Krebs' cycle enzymes in yeast are greatly lowered. The question arises therefore as to how cells synthesize the organic acids (e.g. succinic, oxoglutaric, malic, oxaloacetic) essential for biosynthetic reactions and cell growth. Two mechanisms have been proposed, the first envisages a limited operation of the Krebs' cycle with the oxidative formation of succinic acid, whereas the second involves the synthesis of additional enzymes leading to the production of succinate by a reductive pathway.

In both mechanisms, pyruvate is converted to acetyl CoA by pyruvate dehydrogenase and also to oxaloacetate by pyruvate carboxylase. In the oxidative pathway the citric acid cycle operates (see Fig. 17.4) and it is argued [53] that the level of α-oxoglutarate dehydrogenase in anaerobic cells is sufficient to account for the succinate formed. Furthermore, added glutamate is converted to succinate (a reaction dependent upon α-oxoglutarate dehydrogenase). It is claimed that during fermentation a balance between NAD+ and NADH (essential to the continued operation of catabolism) is only achieved if succinate is produced by an oxidative process [53]. The excretion of succinate into the medium is presumed to arise following its formation by the activity of low levels of succinate dehydrogenase. Apparently the activity of this enzyme of the Krebs' cycle is sufficient to account for the succinic acid excreted by yeast growing under anaerobic conditions [53].

In the reductive pathway, the Krebs' cycle enzymes are assumed to operate as far as α-oxoglutarate, thus forming a linear pathway. A second linear pathway, from oxaloacetate to malate to fumarate to succinate, is suggested to account for the formation of succinic acid [46]. In support of this 'new pathway' are the observations that (*i*) yeast contains cytoplasmic malate dehydrogenases capable of converting oxaloacetate to malate, (*ii*) several fumarate reductases (FAD-dependent) have been found in the yeast cytoplasm which have high affinity for fumarate and are unable to oxidize succinate [52] and (*iii*) succinate is a significant product of fermentation, i.e. an 'end product'.

A summary of the major catabolic and amphibolic reactions for the anaerobic metabolism of glucose is presented in Fig. 17.11.

17.3.3 CARBOHYDRATE POLYMERS [54]
Yeast cells produce two storage polymers, trehalose (a disaccharide) and glycogen. In addition they synthesize the mannan and glucan components of the cell wall (see Chapter 16). The synthesis of both storage polymers commences with the formation of uridine diphosphate glucose (UDPG) catalysed by UDPG-pyrophosphorylase:

UTP + glucose-1-phosphate $\longrightarrow$ UDPG + pyrophosphate

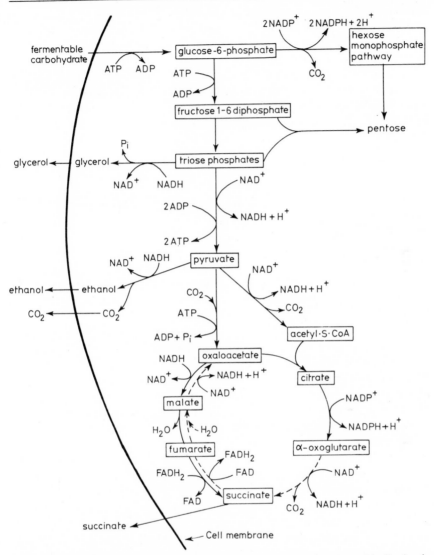

Fig. 17.11 Summary of carbohydrate metabolism in yeast growing anaerobically, i.e. in fermentation. The dotted lines represent the *oxidative pathway* for the formation of succinate (and possibly fumarate and malate) from pyruvate. The alternative *reductive pathway* is indicated by solid lines.

Trehalose phosphate is synthesized from G-6-P and UDPG by trehalose phosphate synthetase and converted to trehalose by a phosphatase.

Glycogen synthetase catalyses the sequential addition of glucose from UDPG to a polysaccharide acceptor. The residues are linked $\alpha(1-4)$. These linear chains are joined together by the action of branching enzymes which break α(1–4) links in adjacent chains and link the chains together with short α(1–4) chains. The attachment of the short α(1–4) bridging chains to the longer chains is by α(1–6) links.

Trehalose and glycogen are accumulated by the brewing yeast cell towards the end of fermentation to be used for maintenance metabolism when yeast is stored (see Chapter 18). Their role is presumably to furnish ATP (by glycolysis) necessary for maintaining cell viability.

17.3.4 REGULATION OF CARBOHYDRATE METABOLISM [14, 46]

(a) *The Pasteur effect*

It has been found that in most living organisms the cells can survive without oxygen, although in some instances only for brief periods. Energy is derived from the glycolytic pathway and the pyruvic acid formed is usually converted to ethanol or lactic acid. When oxygen is admitted, anaerobic metabolism declines. At the same time aerobic respiration, giving complete oxidation of the carbon source begins. In yeast, therefore, growth on glucose in the presence of oxygen, is diauxic, i.e. fermentation proceeds in the presence of glucose then the ethanol produced is respired.

Because aerobic respiration leads to greater energy production for each molecule of glucose or other suitable carbon source used, less substrate is required for the release of a given amount of energy and less is metabolized for energy production. This phenomenon has been termed the 'Pasteur effect'. If low glucose levels (say 50 mg/100 ml) are present in the growth medium, the 'Pasteur effect' operates in brewers' and bakers' yeasts. At higher glucose levels, the position is somewhat different and is considered later

The mechanism responsible for the Pasteur effect appears complex. At least five steps in the uptake and metabolism of hexose have been said by various workers to be implicated: (*i*) Hexose transport seems to be inhibited by high concentrations of glucose-6-phosphate; (*ii*) phosphofructokinase also seems to control the rate of hexose breakdown: the enzyme is inhibited by ATP in high concentrations and by citrate, but in contrast is stimulated by adenosine monophosphate (AMP). If the TCA cycle operates, ATP and citrate are generated. If they are able to diffuse to phosphofructokinase they will tend to inhibit its action and the flow of intermediates through the EMP pathway will, therefore, be restricted; (*iii*) there has also been some suggestion that phosphate deficiency occurs during aerobic respiration because of the intense ATP production: this restricts the oxidative phosphorylation in the EMP pathway leading to 1,3-diphosphoglyceric acid; (*iv*) another enzyme in the EMP pathway of interest in the Pasteur effect is pyruvate kinase, operating at the point where the ATP is generated from the phosphate of *enol* pyruvic acid. The reaction mediated by pyruvate kinase is stimulated by fructose diphosphate but inhibited by ATP. Thus fructose diphosphate has a 'feed forward' effect upon pyruvate kinase, in contrast to the 'feedback' effect of the ATP; (v) a further point of regulation is isocitrate dehydrogenase which, like phosphofructokinase, is stimulated by AMP. The general view is that the Pasteur effect arises from the feedback mechanisms associated with hexose transport, phosphofructokinase, and isocitrate dehydrogenase (Fig. 17.12).

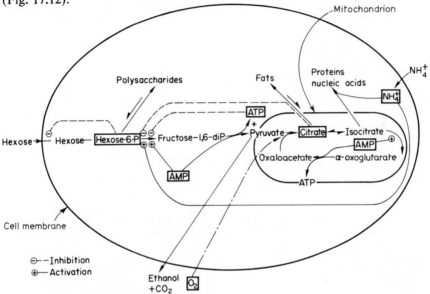

Fig. 17.12 Schematic diagram showing feedback and feed-forward mechanisms involved in the Pasteur effect. (Modified from reference [46].)

(b) *The Crabtree effect* (*glucose effect; catabolite repression*)

Glucose in excess of 0·4 w/v even in the presence of molecular oxygen is metabolized by the brewing yeast via the glycolytic pathway with the production of ethanol and CO_2, i.e. fermentation rather than respiration occurs. This effect of 'high' concentrations of glucose on yeast produces changes in enzymic composition and influences cell structure, e.g. the formation of mitochondria (Chapter 16). This process has been termed the Crabtree effect, the glucose effect and, more recently, catabolite repression.

The Crabtree effect does not operate in all species of the genus *Saccharomyces* and is absent in *Hansenula* sp. and *Candida* sp. (Table 17.5). The effect is expressed in the presence of fructose as well as glucose but is less marked when maltose, mannose or galactose is the fermentable carbohydrate (Table 17.6).

TABLE 17.5

Presence of the Crabtree effect in various yeast strains [51]

Organism	Ratio glucose fermented/ glucose respired	Crabtree effect
Saccharomyces cerevisiae	49·0	+
S. chevalieri	250·0	+
S. fragilis	0·23	−
S. pastorianus	93·0	+
S. turbidans	57·0	+
S. carlsbergensis		+
Schizosaccharomyces pombe		+
Candida utilis	0	−
Hansenula anomala	0	−
Debaryomyces globosus	5·4	+
Pichia fermentans	0·16	−
Brettanomyces lambicus	23·0	+
Torulopsis colliculosa	11·0	+
T. sake	0	−

TABLE 17.6

Rates of fermentation, respiration, and growth, of Saccharomyces cerevisiae *on various hexoses* [51]

Carbon Source	Rate of fermentation as % of glucose value	Rate of respiration as % of glucose value	Rate of growth as % of glucose value
Glucose	100·0	100·0	100·0
Fructose	88·4	127·0	100·0
Mannose	59·0	221·0	84·0
Galactose	19·6	416·0	74·0

The differences in carbohydrate metabolism depicted in Figs 17.7 and 17.11 are largely the result of catabolite repression. Thus, enzymes of the Krebs' cycle have greatly lowered activites and α-oxoglutarate and succinic dehydrogenases are barely detectable. Mitochondrial malate dehydrogenase appears to be inactivated as well as repressed by glucose. Enzymes of the inducible reductive pathway from oxaloacetate to fumarate may be synthesized under these conditions. The major difference observed however, is the lack of a functional respiratory chain. Cells grown anaerobically in the presence of high concentrations of glucose lack cytochromes a, a_3, b, c and c_1 [55]; these essential components of the electron transport system are only synthesized when the glucose concentration falls and when molecular oxygen is available. Thus, molecular oxygen also has a regulatory role in carbohydrate metabolism. The mechanism whereby catabolite repression is effected is still unknown but may be related to the levels of cyclic adenosine monophosphate (see p. 571).

17.3.5 MINOR METABOLIC PRODUCTS OF CARBOHYDRATE METABOLISM

(a) *Organic acids* [56, 57]

In addition to ethanol and CO_2, (the main end products of the metabolism of maltose) and the minor product glycerol, several organic acids are also produced. Organic acids (e.g. citrate and succinate) are imporant in contributing to the sourness (acidity) of beer and several have distinctive tastes. The non-volatile acids include oxo-acids such as pyruvate and α-oxoglutarate which are excreted by yeast in their reduced forms: lactate and 2-hydroxyglutarate. Malic acid, the product of the carboxylation of pyruvate, and succinic acid, the 'end product' of the reductive pathway from oxaloacetate (or formed via a restricted Krebs' cycle, Fig. 17.11) are also excreted.

The factors regulating the production of acids are unknown. Different yeast strains produce different amounts, and vitamin deficiencies increase the excretion of some organic acids e.g. thiamine deficiency leads to increased pyruvate levels. Many oxo-acids are produced as the result of amino acid metabolism (see below) therefore, the wort amino acid content is important.

Volatile organic acids such as acetic and higher fatty acids are also found in beer. Acetic acid presumably arises from the hydrolysis of acetyl CoA and higher fatty acids result from lipid biosynthesis (see below).

(b) *Diacetyl and 2,3-pentane dione* [58]

Of the pyruvic acid formed during glycolysis, a proportion is used for biosynthetic reactions (see Fig. 17.8). Pyruvate is converted to α-acetolactate by the enzyme acetohydroxy acid synthetase. The substrates for this reaction are pyruvate and hydroxyethyl thiamine pyrophosphate. In a similar reaction involving hydroxyethyl TPP and α-oxobutyrate, α-acetohydroxybutyrate is formed (Fig. 17.13). Both acetohydroxy acids are excreted by yeast and are non-enzymically converted, in the medium, to vicinal diketones.

The precise mechanism of these reactions is unknown, however an oxidizing agent is required. Molecular oxygen is not necessary for this oxidation and other electron donors, e.g. Cu^{2+}, Al^{3+} or Fe^{3+} also increase the formation of diacetyl from α-acetolactate. Under the conditions pertaining in beer freed of yeast, 4% of acetolactate is converted to diacetyl [59]. This proportion is increased by raising the temperature [60] or exposing beer, containing yeast, to air. The level of acetohydroxy acids in beer is a function of yeast strain and is enhanced by conditions leading to rapid yeast growth (increased production of pyruvic acid). Yeast cells cannot use acetohydroxy acids, but readily take up and reduce diacetyl and 2,3-pentane-dione; the rate and extent of this reaction are dependent on yeast strain, the age of the yeast and the conditions under which it is stored.

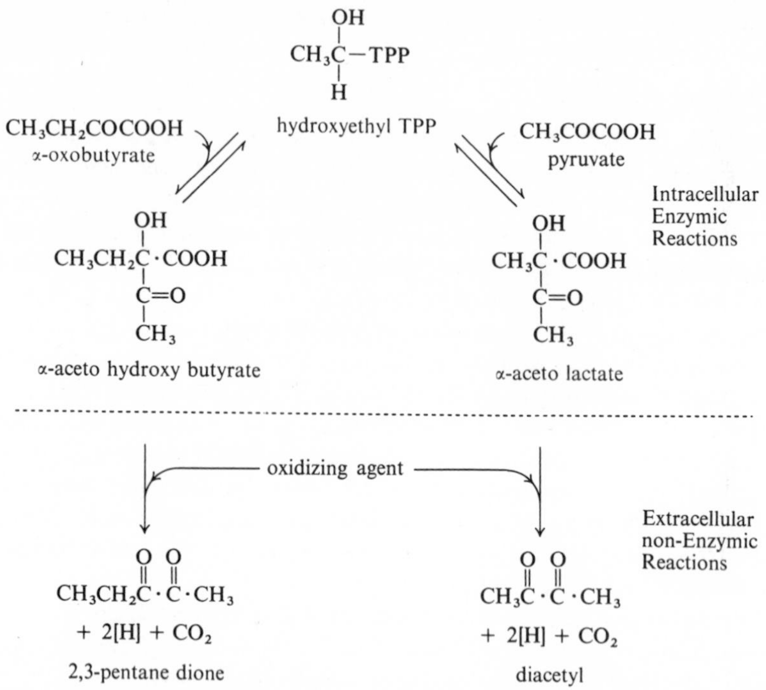

Fig. 17.13 The formation of α-acetohydroxy acids and their non-enzymic oxidative decarboxylation to diacetyl and pentane dione.

Because these compounds have extremely low taste thresholds and impart a strong toffee, honey or butter-like aroma to beer, considerable attention is paid to controlling their levels. The practices used encourage the breakdown of acetohydroxy acids and the subsequent reduction of diketones to inocuous diols (Chapter 19).

There is some evidence [57] that towards the end of fermentation, α-acetolactate forms a complex with as yet unknown substances. This complex is more stable than the free acetohydroxy acid and may present problems when attempting to use short (rapid) conditioning processes.

Acetoin ($CH_3CHOH \cdot CO \cdot COOH$) is produced enzymically by yeast from hydroxyethyl TPP and acetaldehyde. This compound has a higher taste threshold than the diketones and is also reduced to a diol by yeast cells.

17.3.6 METABOLISM OF WORT NITROGEN AND FORMATION OF FUSEL ALCOHOLS [1, 37]

In fermentation, the amino acids present in wort are preferentially used to supply nitrogen to the cell. Ammonium ions may or may not be used depending on the particular yeast strain [61]. The assimilated nitrogen is used for the synthesis of amino acids which are then incorporated into protein. The complex series of reactions which make up the protein synthesizing system is beyond the scope of this Chapter. Yeasts exhibit both cytoplasmic and mitochondrial protein synthesis. Details of the mechanism of protein synthesis may be found in references [44] and [45].

Although yeast cells were considered to incorporate up to 50% of wort amino acids directly into protein [62], analysis of the utilization of ^{15}N and ^{14}C labelled amino acids by brewers' yeast show that negligible assimilation of complete amino acid occurs [63]. Thus, when amino acids enter the cell their amino groups are removed by a transaminase system and their carbon skeletons assimilated. Transaminases catalyse readily reversible reactions dependent upon the presence of the cofactor pyridoxal phosphate. The general mechanism of the reaction is depicted in Fig. 17.14.

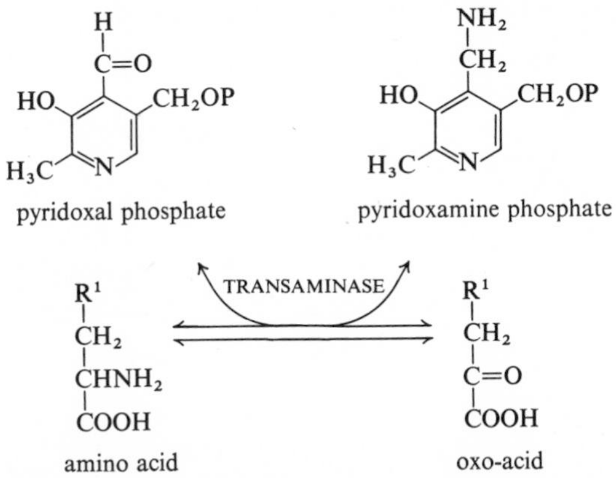

$$
\begin{array}{cc}
\text{pyridoxal phosphate} & \text{pyridoxamine phosphate}
\end{array}
$$

Fig. 17.14 Participation of the cofactor pyridoxal phosphate in the process of transamination.

The available evidence indicates that in brewing yeast the main acceptor for amino groups is α-oxoglutarate [61]. The products of the reaction, glutamic acid and an oxo-acid (the carbon skeleton of the amino acid) enter the cell's metabolic pools. The synthesis of amino acids by the yeast cell then proceeds by transfer of the amino group of glutamic acid to oxo-acids in the pools. The oxo-acids may be derived from amino acids present in wort or from carbohydrate metabolism. In the latter instance, de novo synthesis of amino acids is said to occur and the penultimate reaction is usually transamination [see Fig. 17.16].

The nitrogen of the basic amino acids lysine, histidine and arginine is not derived from wort amino acids but possibly from ammonium ions. In these cases intracellular oxoglutarate is aminated with 'ammonia' to produce glutamate for biosynthesis. The imino acid proline is synthesized, without a transamination step, directly from glutamic acid. Fig. 17.15 is a summary of the metabolism of wort amino acids.

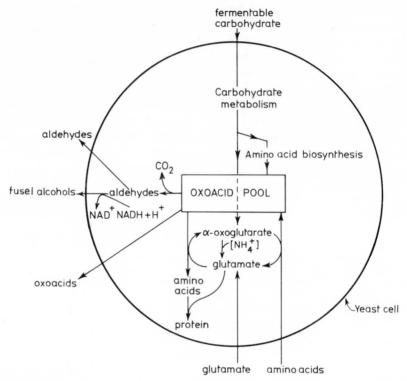

Fig. 17.15 Amino acid metabolism and the production of beer oxo-acids, aldehydes and fusel alcohols.

The manner in which amino acids are utilized by yeast has important implications in practical brewing. Thus when an amino acid is synthesized by the yeast from its carbon skeleton provided (from the same amino acid) in wort then the wort content of the particular amino acid will influence the metabolism of the yeast. Amino acids have therefore been classified according to the 'essential' (i.e. not provided by carbohydrate metabolism) nature of their oxo-acid analogues in yeast metabolism.

The concentration in wort of the amino acids: isoleucine, valine, phenylalanine, glycine, alanine, tyrosine, lysine, histidine, arginine and leucine, are considered important [37]. Changes in the concentrations of amino acids in wort will undoubtedly influence nitrogen metabolism because the yeast amino acid is principally derived from the wort amino acid.

The yeast oxo-acid pool is also the source of substrates for the synthesis of aldehydes and fusel alcohols. Fusel alcohols are so named because they are found in fusel oil, the fluid remaining after the distillation of ethanol from a fermented liquid. These substances have higher boiling points than ethanol and are potently aromatic, exerting a considerable influence on beer flavour/aroma. Since the yeast oxo-acid pool is derived from both carbohydrate metabolism and wort amino acids, both may serve for generating these precursors of fusel alcohols (Fig. 17.15).

The production of oxoisovaleric acid and oxoisocaproic acids, intermediates in the biosynthesis of valine and leucine respectively, is shown in Fig. 17.16. The decarboxylation and reduction (NAD^+ dependent) of these oxo-acids yields the fusel alcohols isobutanol and isoamyl alcohol (Fig. 17.16). Presumably, some oxo-acids in beer result from excretion from the pool and some aldehydes by excretion prior to reduction to the corresponding alcohol. Table 17.7 shows the chemical relationships between alcohols, aldehydes, oxo-acids and corresponding amino acids.

TABLE 17.7

Alcohols, aldehydes, oxo-acids, and amino acids identified in yeast [1]

Alcohols	Aldehydes	Oxo-acids	Amino acids
Ethanol	Acetaldehyde	Pyruvic acid	Alanine
Glycol	Glyoxal	Hydroxypyruvic acid	Serine
Propanol	Propionaldehyde	α-Oxobutyric acid	α-Aminobutyric
Isopropanol	—	—	—
Butanol	Butyraldehyde	—	—
Isobutanol	Isobutyraldehyde	α-Oxoisovaleric acid	Valine
Sec-butanol	—	—	—
Tert-butanol	—	—	—
Isoamyl alcohol	Isovaleraldehyde	α-Oxoisocaproic acid	Leucine
2-Methylbutanol	2-Methylbutanal	α-Oxo-β-methyl valeric acid	Isoleucine
Hexanol	Hexanal	—	—
Heptanol	Heptanal	—	—
—	—	Oxaloacetic acid	Aspartic acid
—	—	α-Oxoglutaric acid	Glutamic acid
Phenethyl alcohol	—	Phenylpyruvic acid	Phenylalanine
Tyrosol	—	Hydroxyphenyl pyruvic acid	Tyrosine
Tryptophol	—	—	Tryptophan

Fusel alcohol formation is linked to amino acid biosynthesis, and the presence of an amino acid in wort may inhibit the formation of the corresponding fusel alcohol. This usually results from the end product of an anabolic pathway (e.g. valine, Fig. 17.16) inhibiting the operation of the first step (α-acetolactate synthetase) and thus preventing synthesis of the oxo-acid (oxoisovaleric). In defined media, such regulatory effects are

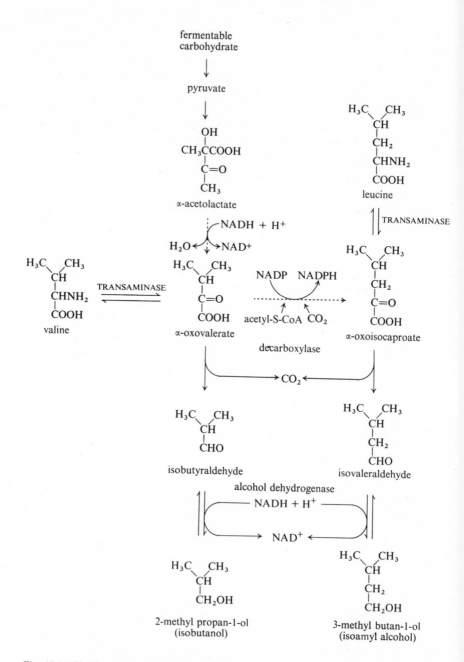

Fig. 17.16 The formation of fusel alcohols from carbohydrate metabolism and the bio-synthesis of amino acids.

well documented [64], however their significance in a brewery fermentation is unclear. On the other hand an amino acid concentration in wort in excess of that required by the brewing yeast, will often lead to elevated levels of the corresponding fusel alcohol [65]. Thus the fusel alcohol content and hence the flavour of beer is related to the balance of amino acids present in wort.

Apart from the particular properties of yeast strains, the principal factors leading to elevated levels of fusel alcohols in brewery fermentations are: (*i*) elevated levels of amino acids in wort, (*ii*) anaerobic conditions, (*iii*) high temperatures, (*iv*) continuous agitation, (*v*) large amount of yeast growth, and (*vi*) high ethanol concentration [66].

17.3.7 METABOLISM OF LIPIDS AND ESTER FORMATION [67]

The bulk of yeast lipid is represented by three different classes of chemical compound, (*i*) triacylglycerols (triglycerides), (*ii*) phospholipids and (*iii*) sterols. Triglycerides are triesters of glycerol and long chain fatty acids. In yeast lipid the major fatty acid residues contain 16 or 18 carbon atoms (C_{16} or C_{18}; palmitic or stearic acids) although C_8 to C_{24} acids are found. Unsaturated fatty acids are also found and include the monoenoic acids (which have single double bonds) such as palmitoleic ($C_{16:1}$) and oleic ($C_{18:1}$) and dienoic acids such as linoleic ($C_{18:2}$). Triacylglycerols are important membrane constituents (as indeed are phospholipids and sterols) and experiments in which yeast membranes are artifically enriched in lipid containing unsaturated fatty acids produce yeast cells with altered characteristics, e.g. ethanol tolerance [68] and uptake of pyruvic acid [69]. Triglycerides may also be found in the form of lipid droplets within the cell.

Phospholipids are substituted diacylglycerophosphates, the substituents (at the phosphate residue) most commonly found are choline ((CH_3)$_3$N$^+$CH$_2$ CH$_2$OH) ethanolamine (NH$_2$CH$_2$CH$_2$OH) serine (HOOCCHNH$_2$CH$_2$OH) and inositol.

The two most commonly encountered yeast sterols are ergosterol and zymosterol; other sterols e.g. lanosterol are also found in lesser amounts.

17.3.8 CATABOLISM OF FATS

Triacylglycerols are hydrolysed by lipolytic enzymes (lipases) in a step-wise fashion ultimately to yield glycerol and long chain fatty acids. In *S. cerevisiae*, lipase action is located in the plasma membrane [70]. Phospholipid hydrolysis is catalysed by phospholipases yielding glycerol and fatty acids, as well as products such as choline etc. Glycerol may be phosphorylated, oxidized and enter the EMP pathway as dihydroxyacetone phosphate. The long chain fatty acids are presumed to be converted to acetyl CoA by the β-oxidation pathway (Fig. 17.17). This pathway may be located either within the mitochondria or microbodies.

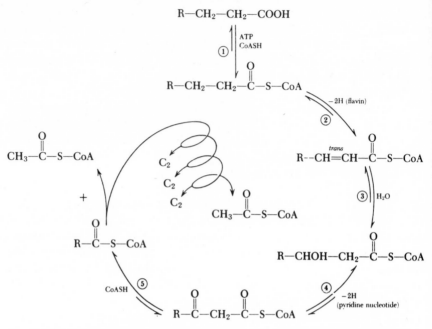

Fig. 17.17 The mechanism for the breakdown of fatty acids. (The β-oxidation mechanism.)

In a reaction catalysed by the enzyme fatty acid thiokinase (1 in Fig. 17.17) each fatty acid is converted to an acyl CoA molecule with the expenditure of ATP. This is followed by: (*i*) oxidation, catalysed by an FAD-dependent acyl CoA dehydrogenase (2 in Fig. 17.7); (*ii*) removal of water by enoyl hydrase (3); (*iii*) oxidation *via* an NAD⁺-dependent enzyme (4), hydroxyacylCoA dehydrogenase and finally (*iv*) liberation of acetyl CoA and the formation of a long chain fatty acid, two carbon atoms shorter than the original molecule. This terminal step is catalysed by β-ketoacylthiolase (5 in Fig. 17.17). The long chain fatty acid re-enters the pathway at the level of acyl CoA dehydrogenase and in this way fatty acids with an even number of carbon atoms are wholly degraded to acetyl CoA by the sequential removal of two-carbon (acetate) units. In the case of fatty acids with an odd number of carbon atoms, the final product is propionyl CoA ($CH_3CH_2COSCoA$).

In respiring yeast the acetyl CoA could be oxidized by the tricarboxylic acid cycle, and oxidative phosphorylation would yield additional energy from the FADH and NADH derived from the β-oxidation pathway.

Under fermentative conditions the pathway probably operates only in the 'turn-over' of fats and the acetyl CoA generated is probably used for the synthesis of fatty acids.

Synthesis of Malonyl CoA:

$$1)\ CH_3COSCoA + CO_2 + ATP \xrightarrow{\text{biotin}} \overset{\text{COOH}}{\overset{|}{C}}H_2COSCoA + ADP + Pi$$

Priming Reaction:

$$2)\ CH_3\text{–}COSCoA + \left.\begin{array}{l} HS \\ HS \end{array}\right\rangle \text{Enzyme} \rightleftharpoons \left.\begin{array}{r} HS \\ CH_3COS \end{array}\right\rangle \text{Enzyme} + HSCoA$$

Chain Lengthening Reactions:

$$3)\ \overset{\text{COOH}}{\overset{|}{C}}H_2\text{–}COSCoA + \left.\begin{array}{r} HS \\ CH_3\text{–}(CH_2\text{–}CH_2)_n\text{–}COS \end{array}\right\rangle \text{Enzyme} \rightleftharpoons \left.\begin{array}{r} \overset{\text{COOH}}{\overset{|}{C}}H_2\text{–}COS \\ CH_3\text{–}(CH_2\text{–}CH_2)_n\text{–}COS \end{array}\right\rangle \text{Enzyme} + HSCoA$$

$$4)\ \left.\begin{array}{r} \overset{\text{COOH}}{\overset{|}{C}}H_2\text{–}COS \\ CH_3\text{–}(CH_2\text{–}CH_2)_n\text{–}COS \end{array}\right\rangle \text{Enzyme} \rightleftharpoons \left.\begin{array}{r} CH_3\text{–}(CH_2\text{–}CH_2)_n\text{–}\overset{O}{\overset{\|}{C}}\text{–}CH_2\text{–}COS \\ HS \end{array}\right\rangle \text{Enzyme} + CO_2$$

$$5)\ \left.\begin{array}{r} CH_3\text{–}(CH_2\text{–}CH_2)_n\text{–}\overset{O}{\overset{\|}{C}}\text{–}CH_2\text{–}COS \\ HS \end{array}\right\rangle \text{Enzyme} + NADPH + H^+ \rightleftharpoons \left.\begin{array}{r} CH_3\text{–}(CH_2\text{–}CH_2)_n\text{–}\overset{OH}{\overset{|}{C}}H\text{–}CH_2\text{–}COS \\ HS \end{array}\right\rangle \text{Enzyme} + NADP^+$$

$$6)\ \left.\begin{array}{r} CH_3\text{–}(CH_2\text{–}CH_2)_n\text{–}\overset{OH}{\overset{|}{C}}H\text{–}CH_2\text{–}COS \\ HS \end{array}\right\rangle \text{Enzyme} \quad \left.\begin{array}{r} CH_3\text{–}(CH_2\text{–}CH_2)_n\text{–}CH{=}CH\text{–}COS \\ HS \end{array}\right\rangle \text{Enzyme} + H_2O$$

$$7)\ \left.\begin{array}{r} CH_3\text{–}(CH_2\text{–}CH_2)_n\text{–}CH{=}CH\text{–}COS \\ HS \end{array}\right\rangle \text{Enzyme} + NADPH + H^+ \xrightarrow{\text{(FMN)}} \left.\begin{array}{r} CH_3\text{–}(CH_2\text{–}CH_2)_{n+1}\text{–}COS \\ HS \end{array}\right\rangle \text{Enzyme} + NADP^+$$

$$8)\ \left.\begin{array}{r} CH_3\text{–}(CH_2\text{–}CH_2)_{n+1}\cdot COS \\ HS \end{array}\right\rangle \text{Enzyme} \rightleftharpoons \left.\begin{array}{r} HS \\ CH_3\text{–}(CH_2\text{–}CH_2)_{n+1}.COS \end{array}\right\rangle \text{Enzyme}$$

Terminal Reaction:

$$9)\ \left.\begin{array}{r} CH_3\text{–}(CH_2\text{–}CH_2)_{n+1}.COS \\ HS \end{array}\right\rangle \text{Enzyme} + HSCoA \rightleftharpoons \left.\begin{array}{r} HS \\ HS \end{array}\right\rangle \text{Enzyme} + CH_3\text{–}(CH_2\text{–}CH_2)_{n+1}.COSCoA$$

Fig. 17.18 The mechanisms of fatty acid synthesis. The boldly printed 'S' refers to the central sulphydryl group of the fatty acid synthetase. The peripheral sulphydryl groups are in normal print.

17.3.9 BIOSYNTHESIS OF FATTY ACIDS

Yeast fatty acid synthetase is a multienzymic complex of seven distinct enzyme units [71]. The synthesis of fatty acids with even numbers of carbon atoms proceeds by the sequential addition, to an acyl CoA, of two carbon atom fragments from malonyl CoA. All reactions proceed with the intermediates bound to thiol groups on the acyl carrier protein in the enzymic complex (Fig. 17.18). The enzyme acetyl CoA carboxylase with biotin as cofactor catalyses, with the expenditure of ATP, the synthesis of malonyl CoA from acetyl CoA and CO_2 (1 in Fig. 17.18). In the priming reaction (2 in Fig. 17.18), the acetate moiety of acetyl CoA is transferred to a peripheral thiol group on the multi-enzyme; this is followed by the attachment of the malonate moiety of malonyl CoA to a central thiol group on the complex (reaction 3). The transfer of acetate to the β-carbon atom of malonate forms acetoacetyl enzyme (CH_3COCH_2COS-E-SH), reaction 4 (n = 0). Reduction of this substrate in an NADPH-dependent reaction (reaction 5) generates a β-hydroxyacyl intermediate. A dehydratase (reaction 6) produces an unsaturated intermediate which, in turn, is reduced in a second NADPH-dependent reaction to produce a saturated acyl enzyme (n = 1). Transfer of this derivative to the peripheral thiol group and attachment of malonate to the central thiol group (reaction 3) permits a repeat of the cycle and generates a six carbon acyl fragment (n = 2) and so on. The terminal reaction involving CoASH results in the liberation of an acyl CoA molecule with an even number of carbon atoms and the regeneration of the central thiol group of the enzyme. The synthesis of fatty acids with an odd number of carbon atoms probably involves propionyl CoA in the priming reaction. Free fatty acids may be excreted by yeast (e.g. caprylic acid; C_8) and have a marked effect on beer flavour [73].

The synthesis of unsaturated fatty acids (Fig. 17.19) requires the participation of molecular oxygen and involves a mixed function oxidase (NADP-dependent) [72].

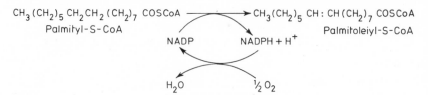

Fig. 17.19 Synthesis of unsaturated fatty acids.

17.3.10 BIOSYNTHESIS OF TRIACYLGLYCEROLS AND PHOSPHOLIPIDS

The overall reactions leading to the biosynthesis of triglycerides and phospholipids are shown in Fig. 17.20. All are derived from α-glycerophosphate produced either by reduction of dihydroxyacetone phosphate (generated by the EMP pathway), or from glycerol by ATP dependent phosphorylation. Acylation of this molecule leads to the formation of phosphatidic acid which, following phosphorylase action and acylation with saturated or unsaturated acyl CoA molecules, leads to triacylglycerol formation. Reaction of phosphatidic acid with cytosine triphosphate (CTP) produces CDP diacyl glycerols to which serine or inositol or ethanolamine is added (with the elimination of CDP) to produce phospholipids.

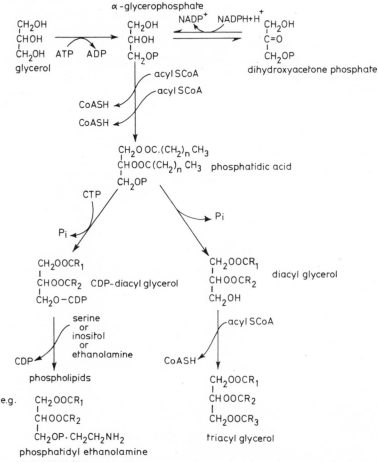

Fig. 17.20 Biosynthesis of triacylglycerols and phospholipids.

17.3.11 BIOSYNTHESIS OF STEROLS [74]

The key reaction in the biosynthesis of sterols is the formation of mevalonic acid (Fig. 17.21). The unsaturated C_5 isoprenoid, isopentenyl pyrophosphate, is formed from mevalonic acid, with the expenditure of 2 ATP. This C_5 isoprenoid is readily isomerized to dimethylallyl pyrophosphate. The two isomers interact to form a C_{10} compound (geranyl pyrophosphate) which, on reaction with the C_5 units, produces farnesyl and nerolidol pyrophosphates.

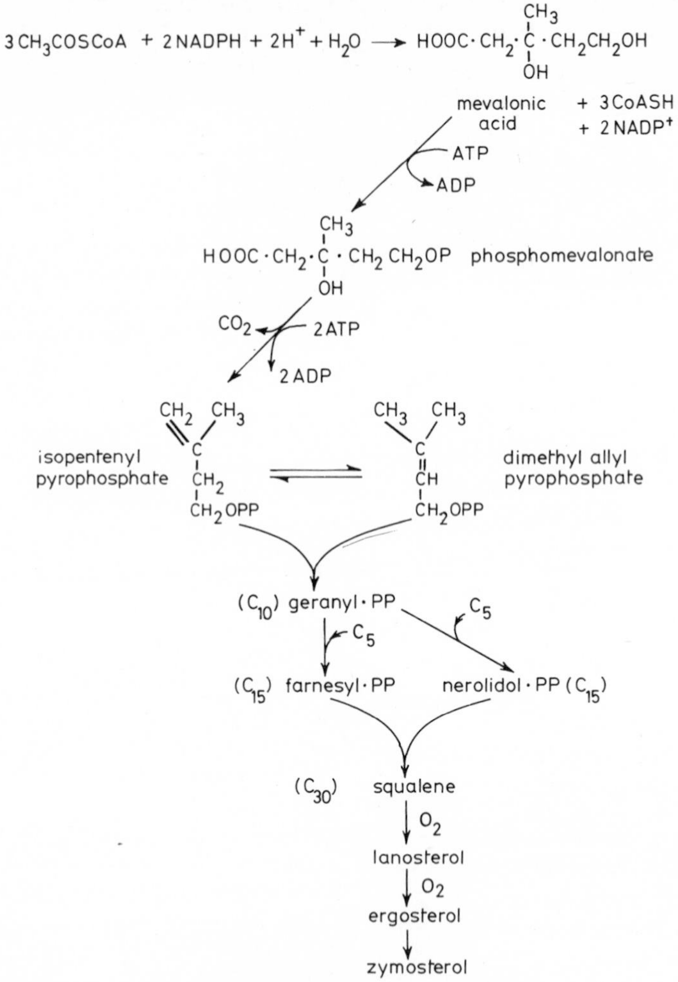

$$3\,CH_3COSCoA \;+\; 2\,NADPH + 2H^+ + H_2O \;\longrightarrow\; HOOC \cdot CH_2 \cdot \underset{\underset{OH}{|}}{\overset{\overset{CH_3}{|}}{C}} \cdot CH_2CH_2OH$$

mevalonic   + 3 CoASH
acid   + 2 NADP$^+$

ATP
ADP

$$HOOC \cdot CH_2 \cdot \underset{\underset{OH}{|}}{\overset{\overset{CH_3}{|}}{C}} \cdot CH_2\,CH_2OP \quad \text{phosphomevalonate}$$

CO_2 — 2 ATP
2 ADP

isopentenyl pyrophosphate

dimethyl allyl pyrophosphate

(C_{10}) geranyl·PP C_5

C_5

(C_{15}) farnesyl·PP   nerolidol·PP (C_{15})

(C_{30}) squalene

O_2

lanosterol

O_2

ergosterol

zymosterol

Fig. 17.21 Biosynthesis of sterols.

These two C_{15} molecules combine to yield the C_{30} squalene in a reaction requiring the presence of molecular oxygen. Squalene is the precursor of the principal yeast sterols: lanosterol, ergosterol and zymosterol. During fermentation, these compounds become esterified once wort oxygen has been utilized [75]. The formation of lanosterol is conducted by a mixed function oxidase ($NADP^+$-dependent) which requires iron for its activity and uses molecular oxygen. Other reactions in this pathway also utilize O_2. The requirement by yeast for molecular oxygen in sterol biosynthesis is greater than that for the synthesis of unsaturated fatty acids [76].

17.3.12 BIOSYNTHESIS OF ESTERS [1, 77, 78]
Esters are formed in a reaction between an alcohol and fatty acid:

$$R_1CH_2OH + R_2COOH \rightleftharpoons R_1CH_2OOCR_2 + H_2O$$

Fatty acids and alcohols are products of yeast metabolism but the uncatalysed rate of chemical reaction between these substances is 1000 times too slow to account for ester formation in fermentation. Pantothenic acid (a precursor of coenzyme A) stimulates ester production [79] and factors which influence acetyl CoA metabolism affect ethyl acetate synthesis [77]. The biosynthesis of esters in yeast was therefore proposed to occur by the alcoholysis of acyl CoA compounds [77]. The alcohols involved in these reactions are ethanol and the fusel alcohols. The acyl CoA molecules used may be derived in one of several ways:

1. Activation of wort fatty acids

$$RCOOH + CoASH \xrightarrow{\hspace{1cm}} RCOSCoA + H_2O$$
$$ATP \quad AMP + PPi$$

2. From oxo-acids by oxidative decarboxylation

$$RCOCOOH + CoASH \xrightarrow{\hspace{1cm}} RCOSCoA + CO_2$$
$$NAD^+ \quad NADH + H^+$$

3. From the catabolism of fats (see p. 601).
4. From the biosynthesis of fatty acids (Fig. 17.18).

Enzymes capable of synthesizing esters and requiring coenzyme A for activity have been identified in cell free extracts [80], as have preparations apparently showing no requirement for coenzymes [81]. Yeast esterase activity has been located both within the cell membrane and on its external surface [82].

The alcohol in greatest concentration in fermentation is ethanol and the predominant acyl CoA molecule in the yeast cell is acetyl CoA. It is not surprising therefore that the ester of highest concentration in beer is ethyl acetate:

$$CH_3CH_2OH + CH_3COSCoA \longrightarrow CH_3CH_2OOCH_3 + CoASH$$

Ethanol   Acetyl CoA   Ethyl acetate

The synthesis of acetate esters is clearly related to the intracellular levels of acetyl CoA as well as to the availability of fusel alcohols. Fig. 17.22 is a diagrammatic representation of these interrelationships. Any factors which increase the intracellular pool of acetyl CoA will elevate ester production provided that a supply of fusel alcohols (i.e. amino acids, see p. 598) is available. Because acetyl CoA occupies a central position in anabolism, (see Fig. 17.8) any restriction of cell growth will lead to elevated levels of acetate esters.

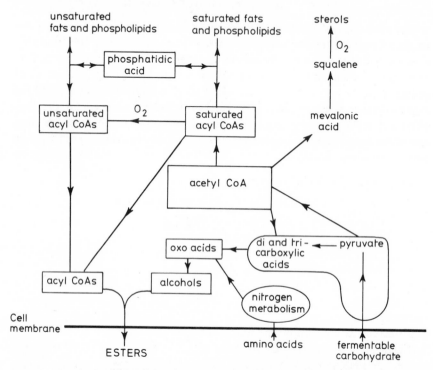

Fig. 17.22 Metabolic inter-relationships leading to ester formation.

When yeast growth is restricted by oxygen supply (e.g. in high gravity brewing – see Chapter 18), cells are unable to synthesize unsaturated fatty acids and sterols (Fig. 17.22), and hence cease to grow. Under these circumstances, provided that adequate amino nitrogen is present in the wort, elevated ester levels ensue [88]. The addition of oleic acid and ergosterol to 'oxygen starved' yeast restores ester production to normal levels, because cell growth is able to proceed.

17.3.13 SULPHUR METABOLISM
Brewers' wort contains very variable amounts of sulphur partly because of

the range of sulphate ion concentrations in the brewing water (see Volume I, Chapter 7). Hydrogen sulphide levels in wort have been reported as 13 to 37 μg/l and these are greatly affected by aeration of hot wort and removal of wort sediment. Organic compounds in wort containing sulphur include methionine (6 mg S/l), cysteic acid (6 mg S/l), biotin (10 μg S/l), thiamine (500 μg S/l), along with sulphur-containing proteins, polypeptides and peptides, totalling approximately 50 mg S/l. A similar amount of sulphur is present as sulphate ion.

Yeast needs sulphur for the synthesis of proteins, certain coenzymes, and vitamins, and the sulphur content is between 0·2 and 0·9% of the cell dry weight. The amino acids, cysteine and methionine, are represented in the cell protein of brewers' yeast while the tripeptide glutathione in the cytoplasm incorporates the bulk of the yeast's supply of cysteine. Glutathione accounts for about 20% of the total sulphur in the cells and is the coenzyme for glyceraldehyde-3-phosphate dehydrogenase. Other important sulphur-containing compounds include coenzyme A and the vitamins thiamine, biotin, and lipoic acid. Biotin is important in the process of incorporating carbon dioxide into organic molecules while thiamine in the form of its pyrophosphate (TPP) is the prosthetic group for carboxylase and is important in the decarboxylation of oxo-acids such as pyruvic acid. Lipoic acid, TPP, and CoA are involved in the production of acetyl CoA from pyruvate. Sulphur compounds are also involved in the change of shape of yeast cell walls (see Chapter 16), especially in connection with the change from disulphide linkages to unattached pairs of thiol groups between polypeptide chains. The source of sulphur in the wort preferred by yeast is methionine but other organic forms are also used. Sulphate ions will serve but are little utilized in the presence of sulphur-containing amino acids and their uptake requires a source of energy and a supply of nitrogen. Colloidal elemental sulphur is also used by yeasts under certain conditions.

Hydrogen sulphide is generated during yeast metabolism, and during a brewery fermentation the maximum rate of production coincides with the maximum rate of yeast growth. The amount produced depends not only on the composition of the wort but also on temperature and on the yeast strain employed; thus, top-fermentation yeasts tend to produce less than bottom yeasts under the same conditions. In normal brewery worts the hydrogen sulphide arises from organic sulphur compounds, either from the metabolism of those present in the wort or from the breakdown of yeast proteins. Thus, cysteine from either source encourages hydrogen sulphide production through the action of the enzyme cysteine desulphydrase (Fig. 17.23).

In the absence of organic sulphur compounds in wort, hydrogen sulphide arises from sulphate ions. The metabolism of sulphate ions by yeast is indicated in Fig. 17.24. Leakage of sulphide ions from the pathway is the origin of the hydrogen sulphide produced. Pantothenate, which is present in wort, suppresses the production.

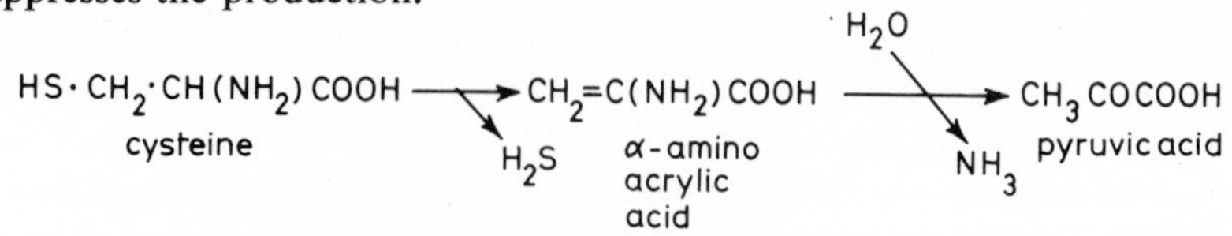

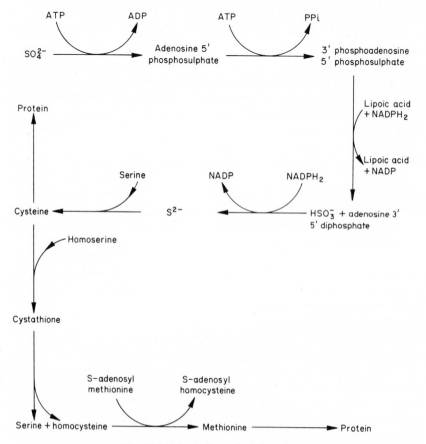

Fig. 17.23 The production of pyruvic acid, ammonia and hydrogen sulphide from cysteine by cysteine desulphydrase.

Fig. 17.24 Metabolism of sulphate ions.

Dimethyl sulphide (DMS, $CH_3 \cdot S \cdot CH_3$) is recognized as making a significant contribution to beer flavour, particularly in lagers [87]. DMS is derived from a heat-labile precursor in malt; it is also produced during fermentation. The heat-labile precursor of the DMS derived from malt is S-methyl methionine [88]. The DMS produced during fermentation appears to arise from the enzymic (NADP$^+$-dependent) reduction by yeast of dimethyl sulphoxide (DMSO) [89]. DMSO is a product of the oxidation (during malt kilning and wort boiling) of DMS. The enzymic conversion is incomplete and the extent to which it occurs is a function of the yeast strain used, the composition of the wort and the fermentation temperature [90]. The fact that ale and lager worts contain similar levels of DMSO, yet lagers contain higher levels of DMS, is most likely explained by the observation that more DMS is produced at lower fermentation temperatures [90].

Volatile sulphur compounds may also arise as a result of the metabolic processes of contaminant micro-organisms. Thus wild yeasts may produce both H_2S and DMS, *Zymomonas* produces H_2S and *Enterobacter* sp. generate DMS.

Under the reducing conditions of a brewery fermentation, sulphur dioxide is formed (up to 10 mg/l). Other volatile sulphur compounds have been reported in beer, e.g. thiols and mercaptans. Many of these may be derived from hops or other materials rather than from yeast metabolism.

17.3.14 PRODUCTS OF NUCLEIC ACID METABOLISM

Nucleotides are excreted by yeast early in fermentation [91] and also under certain conditions of storage [91, 92]. Yeast is not the sole source of these compounds, malt being a particularly rich source. Free bases are reported to modify beer flavour, thus xanthine, guanine and cytidine enhance bitterness whereas adenine slightly depresses flavour [93].

A high proportion of yeast dry weight is made up of nucleic acids (principally ribonucleic acid). This renders yeast unsuitable for use as a primary foodstuff because of the undesirable physiological effects produced by the end-products of nucleic acid metabolism. Much research has been directed towards lowering the levels of nucleic acids (in for example yeast autolysates) with only limited success.

Details of the biosynthesis and degradation of nucleic acids may be found in references [44] and [45].

REFERENCES

[1] RAINBOW, C. (1970). *The Yeasts*, Vol. 3, (eds. ROSE, A. H. and HARRISON, J. S.), Academic Press, London and New York, p. 147.
[2] SUOMALAINEN, H. and OURA, E. (1971). *The Yeasts*, Vol. 2, (eds. ROSE, A. H. and HARRISON, J. S.), Academic Press, London and New York, p. 3.
[3] WANG, P. Y., JOHNSON, B. F. and SCHNEIDER, H. (1980). *Biotechnol. Lett.*, 3, 273.
[4] MORRIS, E. O. (1958). *Chemistry and Biology of Yeasts*, (ed. COOK, A. H.), Academic Press, London and New York, p. 251.

[5] NIELSEN, N. (1943). *Ergebn. Biol.*, **19**, 375.

[6] AHEARNS, D. G., MAYERS, S. P. and ÑICHOLS, R. A. (1968). *Appl. Microbiol.*, **16**, 1370.

[7] MADDOX, I. S. and HOUGH, J. S. (1970). *Proc. Eur. Brewery. Conv. Congr.*, *Interlaken*, p. 315.

[8] KOSER, S. A. (1968). *Vitamin requirements of Bacteria and Yeasts*, Thomas, Springfield Illinois, USA.

[9] WEINFURTNER, F., ESCHENBECHER, F. and BORGES, W. (1959). *Zbl. Bakt. Parasit.*, II, abt, p. 113.

[10] HSU, N. P., VOGT, A., and BERNSTEIN, L. (1980). *Tech. Quart.*, MBAA, **17**, 85.

[11] SUOMALAINEN, N. (1968). *Aspects of Yeast Metabolism*, (eds. MILLS, A. K. and KREBS, H.), Blackwell, Oxford, p. 1.

[12] KLEINZELLER, A. and KOTYK, A. (1968). *Aspects of Yeast Metabolism*, (eds. MILLS, A. K. and KREBS, H.), Blackwell, Oxford, p. 33.

[13] SOLS, A. (1968). *Aspects of Yeast Metabolism*, (eds. MILLS, A. K. and KREBS, H. J., Blackwell, Oxford p.47.

[14] ROSE, A. H. (1968). *Chemical Microbiology*, Butterworth, London.

[15] SUOMALAINEN, H., NURMINEN, T. and OURA, E. (1973). *Prog. Ind. Microbiol.*, **12**, 109.

[16] CIRILLO, V. P. (1961). *Ann. Rev. Microbiol.*, **15**, 197.

[17] HEREDIA, C. F., SOLS, A. and DE LA FUENTE, G. (1968). *Eur. J. Biochem.*, **5**, 321.

[18] VAN STEVENINCK, J. (1968). *Biochim. Biophys. Acta*, **150**, 424.

[19] KOTYK, A. (1967). *Folia Microbiol.*, **12**, 121.

[20] SOLS, A. and DE LA FUENTE, G. (1961). *Membrane Transport and Metabolism*, (eds. KLEINZELLER, A. and KOTYK, A.), Academic Press, London, p. 361.

[21] HARRIS, G. and THOMPSON, C. (1960). *J. Inst. Brewing*, **66**, 293.

[22] STEWART, G. G., ERRATT, J., GARRISON, I., GORING, T., and HANCOCK, I. (1979). *Techn. Quart.*, MBAA, **16**, 1.

[23] HARRIS, G. and MILLIN, D. J. (1963). *Biochem. J.*, **88**, 89.

[24] GRIFFIN, S. R. (1970). *J. Inst. Brewing*, **76**, 45.

[25] LOVGREN, T. and HAUTERA, P. (1977). *Brewers Digest*, Aug., p. 43.

[26] RICKENBERG, H. V. (1974). *Ann. Rev. Microbiol.*, **28**, 353.

[27] VAN WIJK, R. and KONIJN, T. M. (1971), *FEBS Letters*, **13**, 184.

[28] DELLWEG, H., SCHLANDERER, G. and MEGNET, R. (1973). *Proc. Eur. Brewery. Conv. Congr.*, *Salzburg*, p. 241.

[29] WISEMAN, A. and LIM, T-K. (1974). *Biochem. Soc. Trans.*, **2**, 932.

[30] HOLTZER, H. (1978). *Biochemistry and Genetics of Yeasts*, (eds. BACILA, M., HORECKER, B. L. and STOPPANI, A. O. M.), Academic Press, New York, p. 224.

[31] BUDD, J. A. (1975). *J. Gen. Microbiol.*, **90**, 293.

[32] ALONSO, A. and KOTYK, A. (1978). *Folia Microbiol.*, **23**, 118.

[33] THORNE, R. S. W. (1949), *J. Inst. Brewing*, **55**, 201.

[34] NIELSEN, N., and LUND, A. (1936), *C. R. Trav. Lab. Carlsberg. Ser. Physiol.*, **21**, No. 13, 239.

[35] BARTON-WRIGHT, E. C. (1949). *Proc. Eur. Brewery. Conv. Congr.*, *Lucerne*, p. 19.

[36] JONES, M. and PIERCE, J. S. (1964). *J. Inst. Brewing*, **70**, 307.

[37] JONES, M. and PIERCE, J. S. (1970). *Proc. Eur. Brewery. Conv. Congr.*, *Interlaken*, p. 151.

[38] GRENSON, M., HOU, C. and CRABEEL, M. (1970). *J. Bacteriol.*, **103**, 770.

[39] KOTYK, A., PONEC, M. and RIHOVA, L. (1971). *Folia Microbiol.*, **16**, 445.

[40] HORAK, J., KOTYK, A. and RIHOVA, L. (1978). *Folia Microbiol.*, **23**, 286.

[41] LEWIS, M. J. and PHAFF, H. J. (1964). *J. Bacteriol.*, **87**, 1389.

[42] LEWIS, M. J. and PHAFF, H. J. (1965). *J. Bacteriol.*, **89**, 960.

[43] LEWIS, M. J. and STEPHANOPOULOS, D. (1967). *J. Bacteriol.*, **93**, 976.

[44] CONN, E. E. and STUMPF, P. K. (1976). *Outlines of Biochemistry*, John Wiley, New York.

[45] LEHNINGER, A. L. (1975). *Biochemistry*, Worth Inc., New York.

[46] SOLS, A., GANCEDO, G. and DE LA FUENTE, G. (1971). *The Yeasts*, Vol. 2, (eds. ROSE, A. H. and HARRISON, J. S.), Academic Press, London, p. 271.

[47] CHANCE, B., LEE, C. P. and MELIA, L. (1967), *Fedn. Proc. Fedn. Am. Socs., Exp. Biol.*, **26**, 1341.

[48] GANCEDO, C., GANCEDO, J. M. and SOLS, A. (1968). *Eur. J. Biochem.*, **5**, 165.

[49] ATZPODIEN, W., GANCEDO, J. M., DUNTZE, W. and HOLZER, H. (1968). *Eur. J. Biochem.*, **7**, 58.

[50] HORECKER, H. *Aspects of Yeast Metabolism* (1968). (eds. MILLS, A. K. and KREBS, H.), Blackwell, Oxford, p. 71.

[51] DE DEKEN, R. H. (1966). *J. Gen. Microbiol.*, **44**, 149.

[52] ROSSI, C., HAUBER, J. and SINGER, T. P. (1964), *Nature, London*, **204**, 167

[53] OURA, E. (1977). *Process Biochem.*, **12**, (3), p. 19.

[54] MANNERS, D. J. (1971). *The Yeasts*, Vol. 2 (eds. ROSE, A. H. and HARRISON, J. S.), Academic Press, London, p. 419.

[55] EPHRUSSI, B. (1950). *Harvey Lect.*, **46**, 45.

[56] WHITING, G. C. (1976). *J. Inst. Brewing*, **82**, 84.

[57] LIE, S. (1978). *EBC Fermentation and Storage Symp.*, Monograph V, Zoeterwoude, p. 40.

[58] WAINWRIGHT, T. (1973) *J. Inst. Brewing*, **79**, 451.

[59] SUOMALAINEN, H. and RONKAINEN, P. (1968). *Nature*, London, **220**, 792.

[60] INOUE, T. and YAMAMOTO, Y. (1970). *Proc. Am. Soc. Brew. Chem.*, 198.

[61] AYRAPAA, T. and PALMQVIST, U. (1970). *J. Inst. Brewing*, **76**, 144.

[62] THORNE, R. S. W. (1949). *J. Inst. Brewing*, **55**, 201.

[63] JONES, M., PRAGNELL, M. J. and PIERCE, J. S. (1969). *J. Inst. Brewing*, **75**, 520.

[64] SCHULTHESS, D. and ETTLINGER, L. (1977). *Proc. Eur. Brewery Conv. Congr. Amsterdam*, p. 471.

[65] AYRAPAA, T. (1965). *J. Inst. Brewing*, **71**, 341.

[66] LIE, S., SKJELDAM, M. and JACOBSEN, T. (1979). *Proc. Eur. Brewery Conv. Congr., West Berlin*, p. 715.

[67] HUNTER, K. and ROSE, A. H. (1971). *The Yeasts*, Vol. 2 (eds ROSE, A. H. and HARRISON, J. S.), Academic Press, London, p. 211.

[68] THOMAS, D. S., HOSSACK, J. A. and ROSE, A. H. (1978). *Arch. Microbiol.*, **117**, 239.

[69] SUOMALAINEN, H. and NURMINEN, T. (1976). *J. Inst. Brewing*, **82**, 218.

[70] NURMINEN, T. and SUOMALAINEN, H. (1970). *Biochem. J.*, **118**, 759.

[71] LYNEN, F. (1967). *Biochem. J.*, **102**, 381.

[72] BLOOMFIELD, D. and BLOCH, K. (1960). *J. Biol. Chem.*, **235**, 337.

[73] CLAPPERTON, J. F. (1978). *J. Inst. Brewing*, **84**, 90.

[74] RATTRAY, J. B. M., SCHIBECI, A. and KIDBY, D. K. (1975), *Bacteriol. Rev.*, **39**, 197.

[75] ARIES, V. and KIRSOP, B. H. (1977). *J. Inst. Brewing*, **83**, 220.

[76] DAVID, M. H. (1974). *J. Inst. Brewing*, **80,** 80.

[77] NORDSTROM, K. (1964). *Svensk. Kemisk. Tidskr.*, p. 550.

[78] NORDSTROM, K. (1966). *J. Inst. Brewing*, **72,** 38, 324.

[79] NORDSTROM, K. (1962). *J. Inst. Brewing*, **68,** 398.

[80] HOWARD, D. and ANDERSON, R. G. (1976). *J. Inst. Brewing*, **82,** 70.

[81] SCHERMERS, F. H., DUFFUS, J. H. and MACLEOD, A. M. (1976). *J. Inst. Brewing*, **82,** 170.

[82] PARKINEN, E., OURA, E. and SUOMALAINEN, H. (1978), *J. Inst. Brewing*, **84,** 5.

[83] WHITE, F. H. and PORTNO, A. D. (1979). *Proc. Eur. Brewery Conv. Congr., West Berlin*, p. 447.

[84] ANDERSON, R. J., HOWARD, G. A. and HOUGH, J. S. (1971). *Proc. Eur. Brewery Conv. Congr., Estoril*, p. 253.

[85] WAINWRIGHT, T. (1971) *Proc. Eur. Brewery Conv. Congr., Estoril*, p. 437.

[86] ANDERSON, R. J. and HOWARD, G. A. (1974). *J. Inst. Brewing*, **80,** 245.

[87] ANDERSON, R. J., CLAPPERTON, J. F., CRABB, D. and HUDSON, J. R. (1975). *J. Inst. Brewing*, **81,** 208.

[88] DICKENSON, C. J. (1979). *J. Inst. Brewing*, **85,** 329.

[89] ANNESS, B. J., BAMFORTH, C. W. and WAINWRIGHT, T. (1979). *J. Inst. Brewing*, **85,** 346.

[90] ANNESS, B. J. (1980). *J. Inst. Brewing*, **86,** 134.

[91] KAMIMURA, M. (1973). *Bull. Brew. Sci. Tokyo*, **19,** 19.

[92] MASSCHELEIN, CH. A., VAN DE MEERSSCHE, J., HABOUCHA, J. and DEVREUX, A. (1973). *Proc. Am. Soc. Brew. Chem., New Orleans*, p. 114.

[93] CHARALAMBOUS, G., BRUCKNER, K. J., HARDWICK, W. A. and LINNEBACK, A. (1974). *Techn. Quart.*, MBAA, **11,** 150.

Chapter 18

YEAST GROWTH

A growing yeast cell increases in volume and mass until, at the attainment of a critical size, bud formation is initiated. Initiated buds increase in size and eventually separate from the parent cell. As the growth of a yeast culture therefore encompasses both an increase in total mass (biomass) and number of cells, both parameters may be used for its measurement.

18.1 *Measurement of growth* [1–3]

The procedures commonly employed to measure the growth of cultures may also be used to estimate the amount of yeast in a sample. In brewing practice, such measurements are used to control, for example, the pitching rate of a fermenter, or estimate the amount of yeast in suspension during conditioning.

A direct estimation of the biomass present may be made by determining the dry weight of a sample. In breweries, however, less direct but more rapid methods are used. Examples of such techniques are the measurement of the packed cell volume of a sample after centrifugation under precisely controlled conditions, determination of wet weight after filtration, and the measurement of the optical opacity of a sample by turbidimetry or spectrophotometry. Alternatively, where pressed yeast or yeast slurry of consistent quality are available, the weight or volume of such samples may be measured. The accuracy of all of these procedures is impaired where non-yeast matter such as trub or haze is present.

Indirect estimates of biomass present may also be obtained from the measurement of the chemical constituents of cells, e.g. protein or nucleic acid, the levels of individual enzymes, or the rate of oxygen uptake. These techniques have application in research but are of no practical value in the brewery.

Cell number is most conveniently measured, after suspending cells in a suitable electrolyte, with a particle counter. This technique however cannot distinguish between single cells and budding cells, chains of cells, cell aggregates or non-yeast particles which are all recorded as single counts. Brief exposure of samples to ultrasound prior to analysis may be used to disrupt aggregates, and this technique is of particular value when flocculent yeasts are encountered.

Cell counts may be obtained microscopically using a counting chamber

615

and this procedure enables the numbers of cells in chains and small aggregates to be counted. This process is, however, considerably more time consuming than using a particle counter. Furthermore it is necessary to exercise great care in the setting up of the chamber if reproducible counts are to be obtained [1].

The measurements of biomass and cell number described cannot, by themselves, discriminate between living and dead cells, and are therefore made in conjunction with a procedure for estimating the viability of the cells in the sample.

18.2 *Measurement of viability* [2, 3]

The most direct method involves the serial dilution of a yeast suspension and either spreading an aliquot on the surface of a nutritionally rich medium or mixing it with molten medium at 47–49°C and pouring the mixture into a petri dish. Isolated viable cells grow to form colonies which are counted, thus giving the number of viable cells in the aliquot taken. This technique has proved unacceptable for use with brewing yeast since the estimate of viability even when corrected for the presence of budding cells, chains and aggregates, is invariably lower than that obtained with other methods [45].

The presence of ATP in living but not dead cells forms the basis of a recent technique for estimating viability which is claimed to give highly reproducible results [6]. The procedures most routinely used however employ the microscopic analysis of stained preparations. In the UK, the dye methylene blue at pH 5 is used; dead cells stain blue whereas living cells remain colourless. Whether this reaction is the result of the inability of living cells to absorb the dye, or their ability to chemically reduce it to the colourless form, is unclear [7]. Methylene blue is considered to be inaccurate when viabilities of less than 85% are encountered [3, 8]. When carried out using a counting chamber, total cell number and viability are obtained simultaneously.

Fluorescence microscopy may also be used to estimate viability. The compound fluorescein diacetate is hydrolysed by esterases in living cells; the fluorescein released is then visualized by its characteristic yellow/green fluorescence on illumination with blue light [9]. Because viable cells fluoresce, this procedure is most suitable for detecting contaminating yeasts, for example in beer. Samples are filtered onto black membranes of 0·22 or 0·46 μm pore size. The membranes are then scanned using a microscope equipped with an epifluorescence lighting system. Fluorescent vital stains (stains absorbed by dead but not living cells) may also be used [10].

For accurate estimates with yeast populations of low viability the slide culture technique is the preferred method [3, 11]. A suitably diluted suspension of yeast is mixed with just molten wort gelatin and applied to a microscope slide or counting chamber. A coverslip is lowered into position and sealed with sterile paraffin wax. After incubation for 8–16 h in a humidity chamber, microscopic examination reveals the production of microcolonies by viable cells; those cells not producing microcolonies are dead.

18.3 *Growth in batch culture* [2, 12]

A batch culture is produced when a number of viable cells is inoculated into a suitable growth medium and incubated. The population of cells which makes up the inoculum contains individuals at various stages of growth therefore the development of the culture is asynchronous.

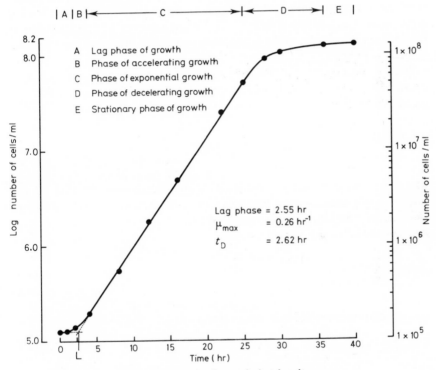

Fig. 18.1 Growth of yeast in batch culture.

A typical batch growth curve for yeast is presented in Fig. 18.1. For convenience the curve may be subdivided into five regions or phases (A to E, Fig. 18.1) namely: lag phase, phase of accelerating growth, exponential phase, phase of decelerating growth and stationary phase. Provided that no substances inhibitory to growth are present in the medium, and that the inoculum is of high viability, then a lag phase indicates that the inoculum is experiencing a change in the nutritional status or physical composition of its environment.

Thus an inoculum consisting of cells grown on nutritionally depleted medium or a medium of different composition will exhibit a lag in growth. This lag reflects the time required for the biosynthesis of enzyme systems necessary to cope with the different nutrients present or to achieve levels of enzymes necessary to support growth at a higher rate. Changes in the physical nature of the environment such as temperature or osmolarity may also induce a lag in growth probably through their effect upon the integrity of the cell membrane.

Once adaptation to the new conditions commences then the rate of growth increases until the cells enter the exponential phase. Since the transition from lag to exponential phases is not sharp, the problem as to where the lag phase ends is solved graphically [1, 2]. This is achieved by extrapolating to the abcissa the intercept of the exponential phase with the initial biomass level (L in Fig. 18.1).

During the exponential phase of growth the population increases at a constant rate (Fig. 18.1). Thus, one expects the rate of increase of biomass (dx/dt) to be proportional to the amount of biomass (x) present:

$$\frac{dx}{dt} = \mu x \qquad\qquad (18.1)$$

where the proportionality constant μ is the specific growth rate of the culture; μ is a constant for a given medium, organism and growth conditions and has the dimensions of reciprocal time (h^{-1}).
Rearrangement of Equation 18.1 gives:

$$\frac{dx}{x} = \mu dt \qquad\qquad (18.2)$$

and integration gives the following expression:

$$\ln_e x - \ln_e x_0 = \mu t \qquad\qquad (18.3)$$

or

$$\ln_e\left(\frac{x}{x_0}\right) = \mu t \qquad\qquad (18.4)$$

and

$$x = x_0 e^{\mu t} \qquad\qquad (18.5)$$

Growth according to this law is therefore said to be exponential, and when the culture is growing exponentially, a plot of $\ln x$ vs. t is linear and the slope of such a plot is the specific growth rate, μ. It is often more convenient to plot $\log_{10} x$ vs. t, in which case Equation 18.3 becomes:

$$\log_{10} x - \log_{10} x_0 = \mu t/2 \cdot 303 \qquad (18.6)$$

and thus the slope is $\mu/2 \cdot 303$.

The growth rate of a culture is often expressed in terms of the doubling time t_D, the latter being readily derived from Equation 18.4 by putting $x/x_0 = 2$. Thus:

$$t_D = \frac{\log_{10} 2}{\mu} = \frac{0 \cdot 301}{\mu} \qquad (18.7)$$

When expressing growth in terms of t_D, great convenience may be gained by expressing biomass concentration in terms of logarithms to the base 2, since for a unit increase in the ordinate ($\log_2 x$) there is a doubling of the population. Tables giving logarithms to the base 2 have been published for this purpose [13]. In a batch culture growth rate eventually declines usually because some product of microbial metabolism accumulates and the cells enter the stationary or resting phase. In unagitated cultures, the biomass concentration in the medium may decline as cells flocculate and, even in shaken cultures, the concentration of biomass will decline after a period of stationary phase. However, no change in cell number occurs and this phenomenon results from the depletion of stored carbohydrate reserves [14]. After a prolonged period in stationary phase, cells may die and autolyse.

The total amount of yeast produced in a culture is a function of the size of the inoculum and the nutritional status of the medium. For purposes of comparing brewing yeasts, the number of doublings which occur during fermentation are often determined. One doubling of biomass is equivalent to a 2^1 fold increase and n doublings to an increase of 2^n times. Thus for n doublings:

$$x/x_0 = 2_n \qquad (18.8)$$

and

$$n = \log_2 \frac{x}{x_0} \qquad (18.9)$$

or

$$n = 3 \cdot 32 \log_{10} (x/x_0) \qquad (18.10)$$

Commercial fermentations generally result in between two and three doublings of the yeast population.

It is a simple matter to ensure that cells enter the stationary phase of growth as a result of the exhaustion of a constituent of the medium. This is achieved by designing a medium such that all nutrients except one (the limiting nutrient) are in excess of the requirements for growth [15]. The measurement of μ for cultures grown on media with different concentrations of the limiting nutrient shows that the specific growth rate (μ) is dependent upon the limiting nutrient concentration $[s]$ as shown in Fig. 18.2. The relationship obtained for both a brewing (A) and non-brewing (B) strain of *S. cerevisiae* has the form:

$$\mu = \mu_m \frac{[s]}{K_s + [s]} \qquad (18.11)$$

K_s is a saturation constant corresponding to the concentration of limiting nutrient at which μ is equal to one half its maximal (μ_m) value. K_s is of the order of mg/l for carbohydrates and μg/l for amino acids.

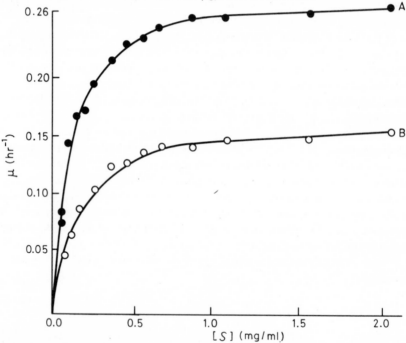

Fig. 18.2 Specific growth rate (μ) vs. glucose concentration $[S]$ for two strains of *S. cerevisiae*. A, a wild yeast; B, a brewing yeast.

Substituting the right hand term of Equation 18.11 for μ in Equation 18.1 gives:

$$\frac{dx}{dt} = \mu_m \, x \left\{ \frac{[s]}{K_s + [s]} \right\} \qquad (18.12)$$

Thus the rate of increase in biomass is a function of the maximal specific growth rate (μ_m), the biomass concentration (x) and the concentration of limiting nutrient. Where the latter is high (e.g. 10 times K_s) then the right hand term approaches unity and the culture grows at near maximal specific growth rate. This case applies therefore when all nutrients are in excess.

The amount of biomass produced for the consumption of an amount of substrate is defined as the growth yield Y. Thus:

$$Y = \frac{dx}{ds} \tag{18.13}$$

Substitution of Yds for dx in equation 18.12 gives

$$-\frac{ds}{dt} = \mu_m \frac{x}{Y} \left\{ \frac{[s]}{K_s + [s]} \right\} \tag{18.14}$$

The negative sign indicating that the nutrient is consumed.

Monod [15] showed, for bacterial cultures, that when conditions of culture were maintained constant, Y was constant. This relationship does not always hold true [16]. For instance an extracellular product such as alcohol, lactic acid or butane-2,3-diol may be produced in varying amounts rather than cell substance. Alternatively changes in Y may arise as the result of the accumulation of intracellular storage compounds such as glycogen, trehalose or lipid. Yield may also be influenced by the requirement of the yeast cell for threshold levels of nutrient to carry out endogenous metabolism or to provide so-called maintenance energy, for example the osmotic work required to maintain concentration gradients between the cell and its environment. The total rate of substrate consumption is therefore equal to the rate of consumption for growth, plus the rate of consumption for maintenance:

$$\frac{ds}{dt} = \left(\frac{ds}{dt} \right)_G + \left(\frac{ds}{dt} \right)_M \tag{18.15}$$

and from 18.11 and 18.14:
$$\frac{\mu x}{Y} = \frac{\mu x}{Y_G} + mx \tag{18.16}$$

where Y is the yield constant Y_G is the true yield constant and m the maintenance coefficient $(ds/dt)_M = mx$.

Dividing equation 18.16 by μx gives

$$\frac{1}{Y} = \frac{1}{Y_G} + \frac{m}{\mu} \tag{18.17}$$

Therefore a plot of $\dfrac{1}{Y}$ vs. $\dfrac{1}{\mu}$ will be a straight line of slope m and intercept

$\dfrac{1}{Y_G}$. For the yeast *Debaryomyces subglobosus*, m is approx. 0·08 and for the
bacterium *Escherichia coli*, it is of the order of 0·02 [17].

It is also possible to relate the growth yield to the energy made available
by the substrate. The values obtained (Y_{ATP}) are expressed in terms of
adenosine triphosphate (ATP), a concept explained in Chapter 17. When the
substrate is used both as a source of energy as well as biomass, the net energy
available is related to the growth yield [18]. This approach has been used to
evaluate the various factors in the growth of brewing yeasts [19]. The constants
μ_m, K_s and Y are readily ascertained and may be used to compute the batch
growth curve at least for certain bacterial cultures [2]. Application of these
conventional kinetics to brewery fermentations is of limited value. This is
because the data are usually obtained with homogenous fermentations, on
defined media and often with aeration. These conditions are far removed from
brewing practice where the yeast separates out during fermentation; wort is a
very complex medium and anaerobic conditions obtain. Nevertheless it
does make it easier to recognize more clearly the important characteristics of
brewery fermentations, gives incentive to express them in quantitative terms,
and so construct mathematical models of brewery fermentations.

18.4 *Growth in continuous culture* [2, 15, 20, 21]

The same parameters of μ_m, Y and K_s can be applied to describe the behaviour
of continuous cultures. Such cultures may readily be established in a homogeneously mixed fermenter where fresh medium is continuously supplied to
replace outflowing culture. A system in which medium containing a limiting
nutrient is used is referred to as a chemostat. Consideration of Equation 18.11
and Fig. 18.2 will show that for any concentration of limiting nutrient there
is a corresponding value of μ until the limiting nutrient is in excess of that
needed to attain maximal possible value of μ (μ_m). In the chemostat, therefore,
if the rate of nutrient supply is in excess of the rate of consumption, then [s]
will rise and a new (higher) value of μ will obtain. The converse is true where
the rate of supply of limiting nutrient is less than the rate of consumption.
The system is therefore autoregulatory and produces a steady state where the
substrate concentration, growth rate and biomass concentrations in the
fermenter are constant. Any net growth of biomass in the vessel would result
from the difference between the rate of increase and the rate of output of
biomass:

$$\frac{dx}{dt} = \mu x - Dx \qquad (18.18)$$

where D (the dilution rate) is the ratio of the culture volume to the flow rate of culture from (or medium into) the vessel.

Since the system is autoregulatory towards the steady state condition where $dx/dt = 0$ then:

$$\mu x - Dx = 0$$

and hence

$$\mu = D \tag{18.19}$$

Substituting μ from equation 18.11 we have:

$$D = \mu_m \frac{[s]}{K_s + [s]} \tag{18.20}$$

The important features of this system are therefore that the flow rate may be used to set the rate at which the cells grow, and that steady state conditions apply to the population size and metabolism of the culture. This latter feature enables time independent studies of levels of cellular intermediates, activities of enzymes, formation of end products of metabolism such as ethanol, CO_2 etc to be made. Given that Y is a constant, at different growth rates the yield of biomass in the vessel is a function of the level of limiting nutrient (s_R) in the inflowing medium thus:

$$x = Y(s_R - [s]) \tag{18.21}$$

Clearly if the dilution rate exceeds μ_m, $[s]$ rises to $[s_R]$ and x becomes 0; thus the population will wash out the vessel. Consequently any value of μ obtained in continuous culture in a chemostat is always less then μ_m, determined in a corresponding batch culture. Furthermore the dilution rate at which washout occurs (the critical dilution rate, D_c) is always less than that corresponding to μ_m. Continuous cultures at values of D approaching μ_m may be achieved in a turbidostat where the biomass concentration as represented by optical turbidity is measured and used to control D [20].

Laboratory studies on continuous fermentation of wort by brewers' yeast demonstrated that satisfactory beers could be produced only when a number of stirred fermenters were used in series (cascade system) or in tubular (tower) fermenters (Chapter 19). In both cases satisfactory throughputs were only obtained by ensuring a high concentration of yeast remained in the system. To achieve this, in a cascade system, yeast was recycled from the outflow back into the fermenter. Under such conditions in a single vessel homogeneously mixed system at steady state we have:

$$\frac{dx}{dt} = \mu x_1 - Dx_2 \tag{18.22}$$

where x_1 the concentration of biomass in the vessel is greater than x_2, its concentration in the outflow. This may be achieved by using a highly flocculent strain of yeast and or by physically recycling yeast after concentration (e.g. by using a settling tank) back into the fermenter.

From Equation 18.22 it follows that at steady state

$$\mu = \frac{x_2 D}{x_1} \qquad (18.23)$$

and thus a higher throughput may be achieved for a given growth rate as compared to an unrecycled system. Consequently values of D in excess of μ_m may be used, and therefore more output may be obtained before wash-out occurs. Rearranging Equation 18.23 and substituting for μ from Equation 18.11 we have:

$$D = \frac{x_1}{x_2} \times \mu_m \frac{[s]}{K_s + [s]} \qquad (18.24)$$

Therefore, for a given dilution rate, the level of limiting nutrient is lower than that obtained in a system without recycle. Put another way, the recycled system permits a more efficient utilization of substrate. The mathematics of recycled systems and cascades of continuous fermenters have been studied [22, 23].

18.5 *Pure culture practice and brewing yeast propagation*

From 1880 onwards Emil Christian Hansen devised methods for isolating single cells of brewery yeasts by repeated dilutions of a yeast suspension. He was therefore in a position to separate the component strains of a yeast mixture and study them in isolation. Because sexual reproduction occurs rarely in brewery yeasts, a single cell repeatedly cultured yields a clone, or in other words, all the cells have the same genetic constitution (with the exception of any mutants which arise during yeast reproduction). Hansen could, therefore, take a commercial brewing yeast (which was most likely to be a mixture of strains), isolate a number of single yeast cells into separate tubes of sterile wort and from each cell produce a pure culture strain. The technique also provided an opportunity to free the yeast from attendant bacteria and wild yeasts because only uncontaminated cultures were accepted as stocks, and propagation was conducted in sterile wort in sterile containers.

The strains could be examined in small-scale fermentations and selected for pilot-scale fermentations. By cultivation in successively larger quantities of sterile wort, a selected pure culture could be used on a full commercial scale. When, for various reasons, the yeast no longer gave satisfactory results in the brewery, it could be replaced by propagating stocks either of the same clone from the laboratory, or of another selected clone. The Hansen techniques were therefore concerned with (*i*) selecting a suitable strain, (*ii*) maintaining that strain indefinitely, and (*iii*) reducing the incidence of bacteria and wild yeast in brewing pitching yeast. Hansen and Kuhle devised a yeast propagator based on semicontinuous methods. The equipment (Fig. 18.3) comprises a wort receiver and a yeast propagation vessel (both of which can be steam-sterilized). The latter receives sterile wort, laboratory yeast culture and air which has been filtered sterile. Rousing is achieved by a hand-cranked impellor. The yeast and beer produced are withdrawn periodically for pitching the brewing fermentation vessels, but a portion of the yeast is retained for seeding fresh wort run into the propagator. The system is the basis of many yeast propagators for bottom yeast production [27].

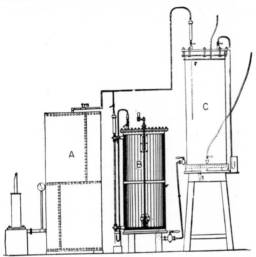

Fig. 18.3 Yeast propagating apparatus devised by Hansen and Kühle. A is the boiler, B is the propagator, and C the wort sterilizer.

In breweries using pure yeast cultures, the yeast may be isolated, selected and maintained at each brewery or by a central laboratory. Yeast may be transported in refrigerated containers in quantities sufficient to pitch a propagator or in small amounts for laboratory cultivation prior to propagation. Some companies rely on commercial laboratories to isolate and maintain their yeast.

There has always been controversy as to whether the entire yeast in a brewery should be derived from a single cell or a number of cells. The various practices include: (*i*) culturing from a single cell, (*ii*) culturing from a mixture of several single cell isolates, (*iii*) culturing from a single colony (clone) isolated from a streak of yeast on a culture plate, or (*iv*) using several isolated colonies as the inoculum. Some breweries isolate two or more strains of yeast which they employ either in mixture or in separate fermentation vessels. In favour of the single cell culture is the smaller chance of variaton since all cells, with the exception of the occasional mutation, will have the same genetic constitution [28]. Mixed cultures, however, are not only susceptible to mutation but also to environmental changes, e.g. changes in wort composition and type of fermenter used, which may induce uncontrolled variation in the proportions of yeast strains present. Such variation may affect the palate of the finished beer, and in extreme cases may result in the loss of one of the component strains of the mixture. It is conceivable however that a mixed culture, because of its genetic diversity, may adapt more successfully to environmental or process changes than a single strain system.

The successful maintenance of a pure culture system requires that isolated cultures are given the minimum exposure to conditions which either induce mutation, propagate mutant cells, or encourage sporulation. Furthermore the method chosen should maintain the cells in a state of high viability.

Accordingly, cultures are generally kept in glass containers in the dark to reduce exposure to radiation, e.g. ultraviolet light, which induces mutation. Cultures may be maintained on wort agar slopes (slants) at 10–20°C (50–68°F) because at lower temperatures (0–4°C; 32–39°F) there is an increased chance of sporulation. Cultures may be overlayed with sterile mineral oil, to maintain anaerobic conditions and lower the rate of growth. Many laboratories hold stock cultures in liquid media such as wort, Wickerham's medium (MYGP) [22], or 10% sucrose. Liquid stocks are usually held at 4°C (39°F). Whether sloped or liquid cultures are used, regular subculturing at intervals of 3–6 months is necessary to preserve culture viability. Since the culture is growing at each stage of sub-culture, there is the chance of selecting and propagating any mutant strain which may arise in the stock culture. Furthermore, the dividing yeast cell is more prone to mutation, resulting from copying errors during the replication of its genetic material, than a non-growing cell. An additional problem with subculturing procedures is the possibility of introducing contaminant organisms into the master culture. In all cases therefore it is advisable to maintain at least two cultures of each strain. It is clearly preferable to keep yeast in a way which dispenses with the need for subculture. Freeze-drying (lyophilization) is such a process; however it has not proved popular because of the high mortality of some yeasts during the freeze-drying process; different yeast strains are affected differently and higher viabilities are generally obtained if the process is carefully controlled [30]. There is also some concern about selection of mutants when using the process [31, 32], although it has been reported that whereas routine subculture over a period of 10 to 20 years caused marked changes in the brewing characteristics of ale yeasts, no such changes were produced when freeze-dried cultures were examined [33].

An alternative to freeze-drying as a means of culture preservation is to store suspensions of yeast in medium containing glycerol and serum, in vials which are sealed and then submerged in liquid nitrogen at $-196°C$ $(-321°F)$ [4]. The viability of many cultures is maintained and consequently this technique is most successful. It does of course suffer from the disadvantage of requiring a supply of liquefied gas since this evaporates and needs regular replacement.

It is common practice to maintain yeast cultures used for genetic analysis in dried form using silica gel as a desiccant [35]. This procedure which is far simpler than either freeze-drying or storing under liquid nitrogen has apparently not been examined as a means of maintaining brewing yeast cultures.

The selection of yeast cultures for the brewery is normally from the pitching yeast in use. In fact, some breweries isolate cultures from their pitching yeast prior to each major propagation programme. This process clearly avoids both maintaining laboratory cultures, and any changes in properties which might arise during storage. The selection is based upon the results of small scale fermentations or simple laboratory tests concerned with flocculation, attenuation of brewery wort, yeast crop, rate of fermentation, etc. [36–43]. The performance of 153 top fermenting yeasts in 2 litre fermentations has been recorded in respect of yeast distribution at the end of fermentation, the degree of attenuation and the degree of clarification [44].

Fermentation tests on a larger scale (0·5–5 brl; 0·8–8 hl) would be conducted with a small number of selected cultures. The strain is selected on the basis of flavour and aroma of beer produced, degree of attenuation achieved, the amount of yeast in suspension and the amount of yeast growth. In British practice the ease with which the yeast reacts with isinglass finings may also be taken into account.

Before using yeast grown from a laboratory stock culture, it is common practice to conduct simple tests to ensure that is is a typical sample. Thus any or all of the small scale laboratory tests described above might be used, together with an analysis of colony morphology using wort gelatin [45] or other media.

The selected yeast would be grown from laboratory stocks using sterile wort. Provided that great care is taken, the size of the inoculum may be very small. Nevertheless it is usual practice for the inoculum to represent 5–10% of the total volume at each stage of culture.

In British practice, the use of pure cultures and propagators met severe opposition. Possibly because it was regarded merely as a means to reduce infection by wild yeasts and bacteria, it was rejected [46]. This is not surprising in view of the poor standards of hygiene, methods of fermentation and type of beer produced [24]. In modern breweries, where standards of hygiene are high, and pitching yeast often represents the major source of contaminant microbes, propagation of yeast is a routinely practised procedure. Furthermore the production of clean, highly viable culture yeast is a major factor in ensuring consistent fermentation performance.

The yeast propagation system in the brewery must be designed to a high standard to limit the possibility of the culture becoming contaminated with wild yeasts or bacteria. Clearly such undesirable organisms, on gaining access to the system, would be propagated along with the culture yeast and subsequently would be transferred at high levels to the brewery fermenters. Accordingly, propagation is best conducted in an area isolated from other plant, particularly that associated with fermentation, yeast processing and yeast storage. Under ideal circumstances the room would be maintained at a positive pressure relative to adjacent areas, and access would be restricted to a few personnel. Self-closing doors and disinfectant mats in doorways are also an advantage.

Vessels used for yeast propagation are closed and are capable of being effectively cleaned and sterilized. Cleaning may be in-place, either with a combined detergent sanitizer, or employ separate cleaning and sterilizing routines, live steam often being used as a sterilant. The wort used may either be sterilized by boiling and transferred via a plate heat-exchanger to the vessel or sterilized in situ. This is achieved by fitting steam-jackets to the vessel (or by injecting live steam into the wort). As the wort boils, air and steam are allowed to vent from the vessel, the vent is then closed and sterilization occurs under pressure of steam. After sterilization, the wort may be permitted to cool naturally or force-cooled by circulating coolant through jackets fitted to the vessel. During the cooling cycle, the vacuum generated is relieved by admitting sterile air into the vessel by way of a sterilizing filter. Most propagation vessels are fitted with a sparge ring to enable the culture to be aerated or oxygenated with air or oxygen sterilized by filtration. All vessels are also fitted with cooling jackets to enable the culture to be attemperated during propagation.

Transfer of the laboratory-grown culture to the propagator is usually effected by making an aseptic connection, and using sterile gas to 'blow' the culture over. Propagation systems typically employ two or more vessels of increasing volume. A system used to propagate S. cerevisiae in a British brewery is shown in Fig. 18.4, and a modern propagation vessel is shown in Fig. 18.5. When the primary aim of propagation is to produce yeast mass, wort of higher specific gravity, temperatures in excess of those normally used in fermentation, and intermittent aeration during the whole of the cycle are used. The growth of yeast in such a system follows the form shown in Fig. 18.1, although the culture would not normally exhibit a lag phase and the contents would be transferred while still in exponential phase. The concentration of yeast produced would be approximately 10-fold that required to achieve a normal pitching rate and the contents of the propagator would be pitched into 9–10 volumes of wort. The beer produced from this first generation would usually be blended. The yeast crop (2nd generation yeast) would however produce a beer with typical flavour.

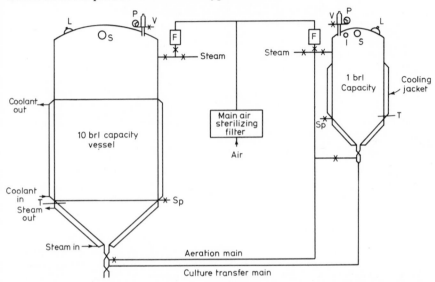

Fig. 18.4 Two-stage yeast propagation system. F, Secondary filters; L, Inspection lamp/ manway/dip-point; S, Sight glass; Sp, Sample point; P, Pressure gauge/safety valve; V, Vent; I, Inoculation point; T, Temperature probe. (Courtesy of Davenports, Birmingham.)

Some breweries employ identical conditions to those employed in fermentation, to propagate their yeast. This type of propagation may eliminate the necessity of blending off the first beer and is claimed to produce more consistent fermentations [47]. In general however, because the yeast yield will be lower, larger propagators will be required.

As a result of their superiority in terms of yeast handling, when compared to traditional fermenters, cylindroconical fermentation vessels may be used as yeast propagators.

In most breweries the practice of propagation is used to replace pitching yeast after 8–10 generations, or earlier if problems of yeast performance or unusual levels of infection are encountered. Where the propagation system is designed to hold an inoculum of yeast (e.g. the 1 brl vessel in Fig. 18.4) this is used to propagate the next batch. Recourse to a laboratory culture may or may not be practised on a regular basis, and usually at intervals of one year or longer.

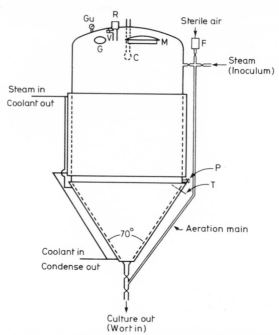

Fig. 18.5 A modern yeast propagator of 49 hl (30 brl) capacity. C, CIP sprayball; F, Secondary air filter; G, Sight glass; Gu, Pressure gauge; M, Manway (dip-point); P, Sample point; R, Pressure/vacuum relief valve with air sterilizing filter; T, Temperature probe; V, Vent with shut-off valve. (Courtesy of Shobwood Engineering Ltd., Burton-on-Trent.)

18.6 *Propagation of bakers' yeast* [48, 49, 50]

The Assize of Bread and Ale in England in 1236 ensured that brewers' yeast was supplied to bakers for breadmaking. This practice was still operating until the middle of the 19th century. Subsequently, however, special processes were developed for producing bakers' yeast using unhopped malt worts. These practices being superseded by the use of molasses and salts as a nutrient medium for yeast production. The introduction of air into the fermentation system greatly increases the amount of yeast produced and lowers the level of alcohol (Table 18.1). Furthermore if the level of fermentable sugar is maintained at a low value in the fermenter (by supplying it as the culture requires it), greater yields of yeast are obtained (Table 18.1). This batch-feeding, or Zulauf process (also called incremental feeding), is commonly employed and enables the metaboli m of the yeast to proceed wholly aerobically. Under these circumstances, far more energy is available to the yeast cell than under fermentative conditions. The effects of air and fermentable carbohydrates on yeast metabolism, the so-called Pasteur and Crabtree effects, are considered more fully in Chapter 17.

TABLE 18.1

Yields of yeast and ethanol from 100 kg substrate on different media under different conditions of culture

| Medium | Conditions | Mass (kg) | |
		Yeast	Ethanol
Wort	Unaerated	2·7	17·5
Wort	Aerated	8·6	10·5
Wort	Aerated incremental feed	23	0·7
Molasses	Aerated and with incremental feed	50	0

The practice of incremental feeding has not found favour in the production of brewers' yeast as it has with bakers' yeast. In bakers', in contrast to brewers' yeast propagation, the growth medium is relatively inexpensive, the spent medium has little value and attemperation and aeration costs are high. Bakers' yeast propagators tend to be large and fully utilized, unlike the small, intermittently used ones found in brewing.

Bakers' yeast is cultivated in media based on beet molasses, refiners' cane molasses (residues after sugar is separated from cane pulp) [50]. Beet molasses are higher in assimilable nitrogen but lower in biotin than cane molasses. These two types of molasses are usually blended to yield the production medium. The molasses are diluted with water, pasteurized, blended and supplemented with: (*i*) ammonia and ammonium sulphate to a pH of 4·0–4·5 (acidic conditions inhibit the growth of many potential contaminant microbes), (*ii*) diammonium hydrogen phosphate, and (*iii*) magnesium sulphate. In addition, biotin, thiamine, pantothenic acid or yeast extract are added. Inoculated medium is aerated with sterile air and as the nutrients are utilized, fresh medium and increasing quantities of air are added exponentially, in step with yeast growth. The rapidly growing, vigorously aerated culture generates foam which is supressed by the addition of antifoams. The optimum temperature for the process is 30°C (86°F) and this is maintained by an attemperation system. The pH of the culture is held at 4·0–4·5 by addition of ammonia and ammonium sulphate, or ammonia and sulphuric acid. The overall process can be presented as:

Sucrose + Ammonia + Oxygen → Yeast + Water + Carbon dioxide
200 g   10·4 g   102·5 g   100 g   77·2 g   145·6 g

The overall heat output is 1600 kJ (357 kcal) per 100 g yeast produced.

This may be compared with the growth of yeast on maltose under anaerobic conditions:

$$\text{Maltose} + \text{Ammonia} \rightarrow \text{Yeast} + \text{Ethanol} + \text{Carbon dioxide}$$
$$\quad\text{200 g}\qquad\text{1 g}\qquad\quad\text{10 g}\quad\ \ \text{97·5 g}\qquad\ \ \text{93·6 g}$$

which liberates 240 kJ (100 kcal) heat per 10 g yeast produced.

TABLE 18.2

Composition of bakers' yeast (100 g) [49, 52]

Constituent	Composition in gram molecular equivalents				
	C	H	O	N	S
Carbohydrate	1·7	2·84	1·42		
Protein	1·77	2·76	0·50	0·46	0·017
Nitrogen bases	0·12	0·12	0·02	0·10	
Ammonia		0·15		0·05	
Fats	0·13	0·24	0·01	0·01	
Yeast	$C_{3\cdot72}H_{6\cdot11}O_{1\cdot95}N_{0\cdot61}S_{0\cdot017}$ $+ P_{0\cdot035} + K_{0\cdot056} + 5\cdot7$ g of other elements				

Constituent	% of yeast dry matter	Normal average % of dry matter
Carbon (C)	45·0–49·0	47·0
Hydrogen	5–7	6·0
Oxygen (O)	30–35	32·5
Nitrogen (N)	7·1–10·8	8·5
Total ash	4·7–10·5	6·0
Phosphate (as P_2O_5)	1·9–5·5	2·6
Potash (as K_2O)	1·4–4·3	2·5
Calcium (as CaO)	0·005–0·2	0·05
Magnesium (as MgO)	0·1–0·7	0·4
Aluminium (as Al_2O_3)	0·002–0·02	0·005
Sulphate (as SO_4)	0·01–0·05	0·03
Chloride (Cl)	0·004–0·1	0·02
Iron (as Fe_2O_3)	0·005–0·012	0·007
Copper (Cu)	10–100 μg/ml	20 μg/ml
Silica (SiO_2)	0·02–0·2	0·08

Towards the end of the propagation the pH is allowed to rise to dissociate adsorbed coloured matter from the yeast; nutrient addition ceases, and the yeast is 'ripened' by holding at 30°C (86°F) for 30–60 min. During the ripening period, cell division proceeds and the number of budded cells falls.

Yeast containing more than 20% budded cells keeps poorly [51]. The yeast is separated from the liquor and the resultant yeast cream is washed, centrifuged and dried on rotary vacuum filters. Additives may be used to facilitate drying and cake formation. The final product in the form of blocks is stored at a temperature of approximately 4°C (39°F). This so-called pressed bakers' yeast is gradually being replaced by the manufacture of active dried yeast. The production processes are similar with the following exceptions: (i) yeast strains are used which have been selected by hybridization to maintain viability during drying, (ii) the nitrogen and sugar feeds are restricted towards the end of fermentation, (iii) the yeast cream is processed to give a product of 35% dry matter, and (iv) the yeast mass is extruded through a screen and chopped to yield pellets which are dried in tunnel- or rotary-driers. Dried yeast has less bulk than pressed yeast, it may be stored at ambient temperatures and is readily reconstituted by dispersion in warm water. Its main disadvantage is its lower viability (65% of that of pressed yeast). Typical analyses for bakers' yeasts are given in Table 18.2. Many of the commercially useful properties of bakers' yeasts (e.g. high yields on molasses, cells easy to filter and capability of retaining viability on prolonged storage) have been achieved by exploiting the yeast's sexual cycle (Chapter 16) and breeding new lines. This genetic manipulation, so successfully exploited with baking yeast has had little success and been little used as a means of improving brewing yeast strains (Chapter 16).

18.7 Oxygen requirements for yeast growth [1, 53, 54, 55, 56]

The role of oxygen in the production of bakers' yeast necessitates a study of the mass transfer of oxygen during propagation of the yeast. Oxygen is sparingly soluble in aqueous solutions and only 0·1 mM dissolves in such growth media as nutrient broth at 25°C (77°F). Under laboratory and commercial conditions, bakers' yeast may be propagated so intensively that, even if the medium were fully saturated with oxygen, it might only afford some 15–20 s supply of oxygen if the aeration were cut off. Clearly there is a considerable problem in maintaining sufficient oxygen to support a rapid growth of yeast with such small reserves of oxygen available.

To increase the oxygen content, air is often bubbled into the medium, but this has little or no effect if the bubbles escape rapidly. Small bubbles provide a larger surface area for oxygen transfer, while baffles built onto the walls of the vessel help to arrest the loss of bubbles. Shaking or swirling the medium has the effect of increasing the effective surface area of the liquid presented to the atmosphere. Furthermore, a vortex produced by an agitator has the same effect.

The rate at which oxygen passes from atmosphere into solution depends on: (i) the degree to which the medium is saturated with oxygen, (ii) the area of the interface between atmosphere and medium and (*iii*) the ease with which oxygen passes through the interface. The rate is expressed by $K_L a$ (C^*–C_L) where K_L is the ease of passage through the interface, a is the area of interface, C^* is the oxygen concentration at which atmosphere and medium are in equilibrium, and C_L is the actual concentration of oxygen in the med·um. The resistance to oxygen transfer between the liquid and the enzyme sites within the micro-organism is known to be very small indeed.

The measurement of absorption rates in a fermenter can be achieved indirectly. Table 18.3 gives $K_L aC^*$ values for a variety of vessels. It should be noted K_L is reduced by foam, wetting of cotton plug filters, and by oil at the interface. If pure oxygen is used rather than air, C^* is increased according to Henry's Law (which applies to oxygen in the range of pressures used for culturing). Pure oxygen at high pressures can have strongly inhibitory effects upon a wide range of micro-organisms, including yeast [56].

TABLE 18.3

Oxygen absorption rates in laboratory cultures [1]

Vessel	Volume of medium		Air flow (l/min)	$K_L aC^*$ (mM–O_2/l/min)
18 × 150 mm test-tube	10 ml	Stationary	—	0·03
Erlenmeyer flask 500 ml	20 ml	Stationary	—	0·32
Erlenmeyer flask 500 ml	20 ml	Eccentric shaker (250 rev/min)	—	1·1
Indented Erlenmeyer flasks 500 ml	20 ml	Eccentric shaker (250 rev/min)	—	2–9·5
100 ml	50 ml	Reciprocal shaker (80–100 strokes/min)	—	0·78–1·5
1000 ml	200 ml	Reciprocal shaker (80–100 strokes/min)	—	0·22–0·78
Baffled tank 3·5 l	1460 ml	Stirred: 750 rev/min 1100 rev/min	5·8 6·1	3·6 6·33

The role of oxygen in brewery fermentations has received study using fermenters of 49 hl (30 brl) capacity [59]. Wort of 11° Plato (SG 1044) was pitched at 55 g/hl (0·2 lb/brl) at 18°C (64°F) and the degree of oxygenation prior to pitching was selected in the range 5–100% saturation. The weight of yeast crop was hyperbolically related to the initial oxygen concentration of the wort. Above about 20% oxygen saturation, little is achieved if the wort is completely saturated with air. Below this level, the yeast crop is greatly influenced by the initial level of oxygen and, with the strain of yeast used, it seemed likely that no growth of yeast would occur in the absence of oxygen (Fig. 18.6). The μ_m was calculated from the results obtained for various levels of initial oxygen saturation, and a straight line of negative slope obtained for the relationship between μ_m and oxygen saturation. It is interesting that the overall amount of ethanol formed during the fermentations was independent of the degree of oxygenation prior to pitching. The rate of fermentation was related to oxygen saturation in a manner very similar to that shown in Fig. 18.6. In contrast, the incidence of dead cells falls markedly as oxygen saturation increases, the curve obtained is inverse to those relating to growth and fermentation.

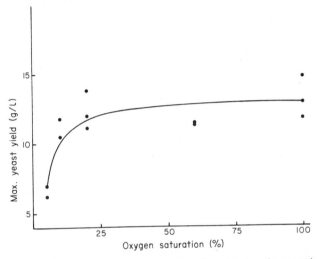

Fig. 18.6 Relationship between % oxygen saturation of wort before fermentation and the yeast yield obtained.

It is now well established that different strains of brewing yeast have different requirements for molecular oxygen [26]. Furthermore, most, if not all, of the molecular oxygen consumed by the brewing yeast (which occurs during the very early stages of fermentation) is used for the production of unsaturated fatty acids and sterols, which are essential constituents of the yeast cell membrane, and not as with aerobically grown bakers' yeast for the additional process of energy production (see Chapter 17). Where insufficient O_2 is available for membrane synthesis, yeast cells fail to grow and loss of membrane integrity results in cell death. These changes are also associated with an increased production of esters (Chapter 17) and therefore have a marked effect on beer flavour. A yeast with a high oxygen requirement, i.e. one approaching air saturation, in worts of 10° Plato (SG 1040) will be unable to satisfactorily ferment air-saturated high gravity worts because lower amounts of oxygen will be available. The concentration of oxygen at 100% air saturation is inversely proportional to the specific gravity; thus an air saturated wort of 10° Plato (SG 1040) contains 8·5 mg/l O_2, whereas a wort of 17° Plato (SG 1070) contains 7·9 mg/l O_2 [57]. Oxygen saturated worts will clearly contain 4- to 5-fold more oxygen than those saturated with air.

18.8 Use of yeast [59, 60]

In addition to its use in baking and fermentation industries, yeast is also used as a food supplement and in animal feeds. Both whole and extracted yeast is a valuable source of protein and vitamins. However, large quantities in the diet are undesirable, for although it is rich in protein, it contains very high levels of nucleic acids. Table 18.4 shows the partial composition of unfortified molasses-grown yeast and debittered surplus brewers' yeast. The 40–50% material unaccounted for in Table 18.4 is mainly carbohydrate and lesser amounts of nucleic acids. When used for medicinal purposes, yeast is often 'fortified' by the addition of vitamins during processing, to give levels some 50-fold those naturally present in the yeast.

TABLE 18.4

Partial composition of unfortified yeast powders

	Molasses grown	Debittered brewers' yeast
Moisture (%)	5	6
Fat (%)	6	6
Protein (%)	50	45
Ash (%)	7	8
Thiamine (ppm)	150	150
Riboflavin (ppm)	70	45
Niacin (ppm)	500	400
Pyridoxine (ppm)	30	40

For use specifically as a food additive, yeast is dried and powdered; the processing kills the cells. In addition to providing a source of vitamins this material forms an ideal carrier for food flavouring materials, e.g. on potato crisps.

Dried yeast is also used to produce yeast extracts by acid hydrolysis, by refluxing a slurry of 65–80% solids with hydrochloric acid for 6–12 hr. On completion of hydrolysis, the material is neutralized, clarified and concentrated to yield syrups (45% solids), pastes (55% solids) or spray dried to 95% solids. Although acid hydrolysis is the most efficient means of obtaining yeast extracts, it does destroy some vitamins.

Viable yeasts in pressed or slurried form may be autolysed or plasmolysed to yield extracts. Surplus brewers' yeast is usually debittered (the adsorbed hop bitter substances removed) by treatment with alkali before processing.

Although autolysis occurs fairly readily when yeast is stored (and consequently is of importance in influencing beer flavour (see Chapters 16 and 17), the process used to make extracts is accelerated by raising the temperature to 45°C (113°F) in the presence of small amounts of ethyl acetate or chloroform, and often in the presence of zinc salts. After a period of 6–12 hr, the autolysed (self digested) yeast is clarified and concentrated. The autolytic procedure involves the disintegration of the vacuole and the release of lytic enzymes (see Chapter 16). During the process the yeast cells are killed.

Plasmolysates are produced by mixing viable yeast in high concentration with salts, sugar or certain acetate esters to produce a slurry. This process extracts low molecular weight substances (e.g. vitamins, nucleotides, amino acids) from the cells but does not extract high molecular weight substances such as carbohydrate polymers and proteins. The plasmolysate is separated from the yeast cells, concentrated and dried. The final product has a strong meat-like flavour. As in the case of autolysis, plasmolysis is lethal to yeast cells.

18.9 *Growth of yeast in synchronous culture* [61, 62]

Synchronous division of yeast cells may either be induced or cells at the same state of growth may be selected from an asynchronous population. Induction synchrony is most readily achieved by subjecting cells to starvation, exposing them to X-rays, hydroxyurea or mating type pheromones (*a* or *α* factors). The properties of certain temperature-sensitive cell division cycle mutants may also be exploited in order to induce synchrony. The principal advantage of induction is that large numbers of cells may be obtained in the induced state. The main disadvantage is that the process itself might so alter cellular metabolism that measurements made subsequently during synchronous growth may result from the induction process used rather than from the mode of growth. Selection synchrony exploits differences in physical properties of cells, e.g. size or density. Thus centrifugation in sucrose gradients is the most commonly used technique. However, this process too can affect cellular metabolism because of the osmotic effects produced by high concentrations of sucrose. These effects may be reduced by using substituted tri-iodo benzenes (e.g. renografin [63]) to form gradients.

Others compounds, e.g. Ludox (a colloidal silica) may be used to separate cells by their density differences alone [64]. The main disadvantage with selection synchrony is that only relatively small numbers (10% of an asynchronous population) of cells are obtained.

Synchronous cultures are used to study the detail of the biochemical processes which occur during the cycle of yeast cell growth and division. This study is greatly enhanced by the isolation and characterization of cell division cycle mutants (e.g. *cdc*) [65]. Synchrony, once attained, usually decays rapidly, the population being eventually asynchronous after 3 cycles.

The cell division cycle is shown in Fig. 18.7. The cycle is usually considered from the G1 phase which encompasses cell separation to bud emergence. This is followed by the S phase during which DNA is replicated, bud size continues to increase and the S phase moves to the G2 phase as DNA synthesis is completed. The G2 phase extends to the point where the nucleus migrates towards the bud, and the M phase encompasses the division of the nucleus. The total cell mass increases continuously throughout the cell cycle, DNA synthesis occurs during the S phase, whereas the RNA and protein accumulate continuously throughout the cycle. Carbohydrate content also increases throughout the cycle. However, when synchrony is induced by starvation, the cellular glycogen and trehalose levels, but not those of glucan and mannan, decrease sharply as the cells commence budding.

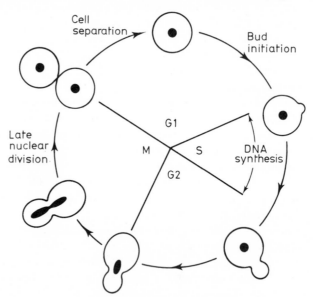

Fig. 18.7 Cell cycle of *S. cerevisiae*.

Although total protein accumulates throughout the cell cycle, many individual enzymes show step synthesis. Step synthesis is a rapid doubling of the level of enzyme activity. The time during the cell cycle at which the step synthesis of a particular enzyme occurs is always the same; however stepping occurs at different times with different enzymes. It is thought that this phenomenon might relate to the order of genes on chromosomes [67] and the sequential transcription of these genes.

The study of synchronized growth may well be of value in understanding the events during fermentation where the stationary phase cells used as an inoculum tend to reproduce in a synchronous manner in the early stages of fermentation.

18.10 *Growth of surface colonies*

Although the growth of surface colonies does not take place in a brewery fermentation there is considerable interest in connection with giant colonies whose morphology is used for distinguishing between yeast strains.

The kinetics of surface growth have attracted far less attention than that of growth in liquid culture. Again,

$$\frac{dx}{dt} = \mu x \qquad (18.1)$$

and $\log_e x = \mu t + \log_e x_0$.

Assume x, the mass of microorganisms, to be a hemisphere of radius r, and therefore of volume $2/3\ r^3$ arising from a mass x_0 of radius r_0,

then:
$$\log_e r = \frac{\mu}{3}\ t + \log_e r_0$$

which means that the radius should increase exponentially. In the few examples where this situation has received reasonable study, the increase per unit time was linear rather than exponential and can be expressed:

$$rt = K_r t + r_0$$

(where K_r is the constant for radial growth, r the colony radius at time t and r_0 is the radius at zero time).

As has been mentioned, yeast colonies growing on solid media develop characteristic margins, textures, and contours (Fig. 18.8). This is particularly so if they are grown on wort-gelatin at temperatures below 20°C, for periods up to six weeks [67]. The morphological characters are extremely complex and can often be of diagnostic value in *S. cerevisiae* and *S. carlsbergensis* for distinguishing strains [46]. If a giant colony is sectioned vertically, it can be seen to comprise an outer zone of resting cells (sometimes with asci), a zone beneath them of autolysed cells, and finally a large number of apparently healthy cells. With chain-forming yeasts the rough margin of the colony and the undersurface may have pseudomycelia [68].

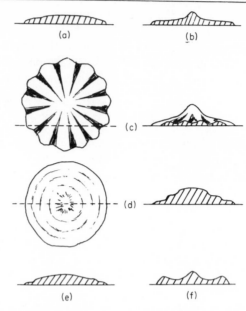

Fig. 18.8 Component features of Giant Colonies. (a) Free from convolutions, flatly convex (section). (b) Flatly convex with central dome (section). (c) Radial valleys, well-developed dome (section and plan view). (d) Concentrically ringed, poorly-defined dome (section and plan view). (e) Peripheral concentric rings, featureless convex centre (section). (f) Raised edge and dome (section).

18.11 *Kinetics of the death of cells* [1, 2, 69, 70]

The effects of toxic materials, excessive temperatures, and abnormal pH levels upon micro-organisms have received considerable study. From a kinetic point of view, the speed of killing is similar to the velocity of a unimolecular reaction. It is the product of the concentration of toxic substance and a constant that depends on the toxic substance used. The position is, however, rather more complex than this and at least three phases of death of the population of micro-organisms may occur.

1. Some of the metabolic activities of the cells are impaired without loss of viability.
2. Death-rate increases until it is exponential. The survival times of individual cells cannot be predetermined because survival depends on chance events, with surviving cells being no more adapted to the toxic material than the cells that succumb.
3. When a considerable proportion of the population of cells has died, the death-rate may slow down and cease to be exponential. This is due in part to dead organisms protecting living ones. It may also be due to adaptation of some surviving cells to the toxic material. Because of these complications, it is hazardous to predict results for a particular set of conditions from experience with other conditions.

Temperature has a profound effect upon sterilization with chemical substances and at higher temperatures less of the toxic material is required. Thus

$$t_2 Q \ (T_2 - T_1) = t_1$$

where T_1 and T_2 are two temperatures and t_1 and t_2 the corresponding periods of applications. Q is the temperature quotient for the temperature change. Similar dramatic effects may arise from changes in pH but the relationships tend to be more complex.

REFERENCES

[1] MEYNELL, G. G. and MEYNELL, E. (1965). *Theory and Practice in Experimental Bacteriology*, Cambridge University Press.

[2] PIRT, S. J. (1975). *Principles of Microbe and Cell Cultivation*, Blackwell Scientific Publications, Oxford

[3] Inst. Brew. Analysis Committee (1971). *Recommended Methods of analysis*, *J. Inst. Brewing*, 77, 181.

[4] MILLS, D. R. (1941). *Food Research*, 6, 361.

[5] HALL, J. F. (1954). *J. Inst. Brewing*, 60, 482.

[6] MILLER, L. F., MABEE, M. S., GRESS, H. S. and JANGAARD, N. O. (1977). *Proc. Am. Soc. Brew. Chem.*, p. 59.

[7] CHILVER, M. J., HARRISON, J. and WEBB, T. J. B. (1977). *Proc. Am. Soc. Brew. Chem.*, p. 13.

[8] EBC Yeast Group (1962). *J. Inst. Brewing*, 68, 14.

[9] MOLZAHN, S. W. and PORTNO, A. D. (1975). *Proc. Eur. Brewery Conv. Congr.*, Nice, p. 479.

[10] PARKINNEN, E., OURA, E. and SUOMALAINEN, H. (1976). *J. Inst. Brewing*, 82, 283.

[11] GILLILAND, R. B. (1959). *J. Inst. Brewing*, 65, 424.

[12] MANDELSTAM, J. and MCQUILLEN, K. (1973). *Biochemistry of Bacterial Growth*, Blackwell Scientific Publications, Oxford.

[13] FINNEY, D. J., HAZELWOOD, T. and SMITH, M. J. (1955). *J. Gen. Microbiol*, 12, 222.

[14] QUAIN, D. E., THURSTON, P. A. and TUBB, R. S. (1981). *J. Inst. Brewing*, 87, 108.

[15] MONOD, J. (1949). *Ann. Rev. Microbiol*, 3, 371.

[16] HOUGH, J. S. and WASE, D. A. J. (May 1966). *Process Biochem.*, 1, 1.

[17] WASE, D. A. J. and HOUGH, J. S. (1966). *J. Gen. Microbiol*, 42, 13.

[18] BAUCHOP, T. and ELSDON, S. R. (1960). *J. Gen. Microbiol.*, 23, 457.

[19] LIE, S. and GETHER, J. J. (1967). *Proc. Eur. Brewery Conv. Congr.*, Madrid, p. 167.

[20] HERBERT, D., ELSWORTH, R. and TELLING, R. C. (1956). *J. Gen. Microbiol.*, 14, 601.

[21] HOUGH, J. S. (1962). *Brewers' Guard.*, 91, 17.

[22] LUEDEKING, R. (1967). *Biochemical and Biological Engineering Science*, Vol. 1 (ed. BLAKEBROUGH, N.), Academic Press, London.
[23] HERBERT, D. (1961). *Continuous Culture of Micro-organisms*, SCI Monograph No. 12, Society of Chemical Industry, London, p. 21.
[24] BURNS, J. A. (1964). *Brewers' Guild J.*, p. 589.
[25] HANSEN, A. (1948). *Jorgensen's Micro-organisms and Fermentation*, Griffin, London.
[26] BERG, R. van den (1978). *EBC Fermentation and storage symposium*, Zoeterwoude.
[27] CURTIS, N. S. and CLARK, A. G. (1957). *Proc. Eur. Brewery Conv. Congr., Copenhagen*, p. 249.
[28] BRADLEY, S. G. (1962). *Ann. Rev. Microbiol*, **16**, 35.
[29] WICKERHAM, L. J. (1951). *Tech. Bull. US Dept. Agr.*, No. 1029.
[30] BARNEY, M. C. and HELBERT, J. R. (1976). *J. Am. Soc. Brew. Chem.*, **34**, 61.
[31] KIRSOP, B. (1955). *J. Inst. Brewing*, **61**, 466.
[32] WYNANTS, J. (1962). *J. Inst. Brewing*, **68**, 350.
[33] KIRSOP, B. (1974). *J. Inst. Brewing*, **80**, 565.
[34] WELLMAN, A. M. and STEWART, G. G. (1973). *Applied Microbiol.*, **26**, 577.
[35] FINK, G. R. (1970) in *Methods in Enzymology*, Vol. XVIIA (eds. TABOR, H. and TABOR, C. W.), Academic Press, London, p. 59.
[36] BISHOP, L. R. and WHITLEY, W. A. (1938). *J. Inst. Brewing*, **44**, 70.
[37] BURNS, J. A. (1941). *J. Inst. Brewing*, **47**, 10.
[38] GILLILAND, R. B. (1957). *Wallerstein Labs. Commun.*, **20**, 41.
[39] HOGGAN, J. (1963). *Proc. Eur. Brewery Conv. Congr., Brussels*, p. 370.
[40] HOUGH, J. S. (1957). *J. Inst. Brewing*, **63**, 483.
[41] THORNE, R. S. W. (1954). *J. Inst. Brewing*, **60**, 227; 238.
[42] WEINFURTHNER, F., WILLINGER, F. and PIENDL, A. (1961). *Brauwissenschaft*, **14**, 281.
[43] STEVENS, T. J. (1966). *J. Inst. Brewing*, **72**, 369.
[44] WALKEY, R. J. and KIRSOP, B. H. (1969). *J. Inst. Brewing*, **75**, 393.
[45] RICHARDS, M. (1967). *J. Inst. Brewing*, **73**, 162.
[46] BROWN, H. T. (1916). *J. Inst. Brewing*, **22**, 267.
[47] HOGGAN, J. (1977). *J. Inst. Brewing*, **83**, 133.
[48] HARRISON, J. S. (1967). *Process Biochem.*, **2**, 41.
[49] WHITE, J. (1962). *Proc. Annu. Meet. Am. Soc. Brew. Chem.*, p. 119.
[50] BURROWS, S. (1970) in *The Yeasts*, Vol. 3 (eds. ROSE, A. H. and HARRISON, J. S.), Academic Press, London, p. 349.
[51] FRIES, H. von (1904). *German Pat.*, **1**, 174; 733.
[52] WHITE, J. (1954). *Yeast Technology*, Wiley, New York.
[53] FINN, R. K. (1967). *Biochemical and Biological Engineering Science*, Vol. 1 (ed. BLAKEBROUGH, N.), Academic Press, London. p. 69.
[54] CALDERBANK, P. H. (1967). *Biochemical and Biological Engineering Science*, Vol. 1 (ed. BLAKEBROUGH, N.), Academic Press, London, p. 102.
[55] DAVID, M. H. and KIRSOP, B. H. (1973). *J. Inst. Brewing*, **79**, 20.
[56] HENNESY, J. P. (1964). *J. Inst. Brewing*, **70**, 337.
[57] BAKER, C. D. and MORTON, S. (1977). *J. Inst. Brewing*, **83**, 348.
[58] MARKHAM, E. (1969). *Wallerstein Labs. Commun.*, **32**, 5.
[59] NAY, E. V. (1954). *Brewers' Digest*, **29** (5), 51.
[60] PEPPLER, H. J. (1970) in *The Yeasts*, Vol. 3 (eds. ROSE, A. H. and HARRISON, J. S.), Academic Press, London, p. 421.

[61] DUFFUS, J. H. (1971), *J. Inst. Brewing*, **77,** 500.
[62] HARTWELL, L. H. (1974). *Bacteriol. Rev.*, **38,** 164.
[63] CULOTTI, J. and HARTWELL, L. H. (1971). *Exptl. Cell Research*, **67,** 389.
[64] SHULMAN, R. W., HARTWELL, L. H. and WARNER, J. R. (1973). *J. Mol. Biol.*, **73,** 513.
[65] HARTWELL, L. H., MORTIMER, R. K., CULOTTI, J. and CULOTTI, M. (1973). *Genetics*, **74,** 267–286.
[66] HALVORSON, H. O., CARTER, B. L. A. and TAURO, P. (1971). *Advan. Microbial Physiol.* **6,** 47.
[67] HALL, J. F. (1954). *J. Inst. Brewing*, **60,** 482.
[68] MORRIS, E. O. and HOUGH, J. S. (1956). *J. Inst. Brewing*, **62,** 466.
[69] SYKES, J. (1965). *Disinfection and Sterilization*, 2nd ed., Spon, London.
[70] RIVIERE, J. (1977). *Industrial Applications of Microbiology*, Surrey University Press.

Chapter 19

BREWERY FERMENTATIONS

19.1 *Historical introduction*

The making of beer is one of the oldest crafts known to man and it is therefore surprising that the nature of fermentation was not understood unt.l the latter half of the nineteenth century. Yeast was for long regarded as an undesirable scum which had to be disposed of as quickly as possible. Nevertheless, in the seventeenth century at least, some brewers were reusing yeast although failing to understand the significance of their practice. C. Cagniard-Latour expressed the belief in 1836 that fermentation of sugar was due to vital activity of yeast. In the following year, T. Schwann recognized the fungal nature of yeast and gave the organism the name Zucherpilz, which translates to *Saccharomyces* [1].

The secrets of using bottom-fermentation yeast were held by Bavarian brewers, notably in Munich, and until the middle of the nineteenth century the rest of the world was using top-fermentation yeast [2]. Yeast and fermentation techniques were smuggled to Czechoslovakia by a Bavarian monk in 1842 and so helped to establish Pilsen as a premier brewing centre. Only three years later, a Danish brewer, Jacobsen, in a less clandest.ne but just as exciting a journey, took bottom-fermentation yeast from Munich to Copenhagen and improved Danish beer so that Copenhagen, too, became a world-renowned centre of brewing. About the same time, bottom fermentation was introduced into Pennsylvania, USA and spread through the country, largely because of the immigration of German brewmasters.

While bottom fermentation spread, Pasteur began his microbiological research and developed not only a reasonable theory of fermentation [3] but also principles of sterilization, and culture techniques for micro-organisms. His special contributions to brewing microbiology are described in the volume *Études sur la Bière* [4]. Pasteur's work was extended by Hansen and methods were developed for isolating single yeast cells [5]. Selected single cells were propagated, each to give clones or pure-strain cultures suitable for pitching (see Chapter 18).

Improvements in the microbiological aspects of fermentation went hand in hand with those involving engineering technology. Thus, maintenance of low temperatures for storage or lagering of bottom-fermentation beer was difficult without the use of large amounts of ice until the compression refrigerator was developed in Australia and Germany and appeared in breweries from 1873 onwards. The gradual improvement in centrifuges has also had an important bearing on fermentation technology and in some breweries, the separation of yeast from beer is achieved by centrifugation rather than by sedimentation or flotation. After the spread of bottom fermentation, the traditional top-fermentation techniques were largely discarded except in Britain. However, a small proportion of the beer produced in Australia, Belgium, Canada, the USA, and West Germany is of the top-fermentation type and in the last few years the use of this technique has increased. Within the last 20 years, new methods of fermentation have been developed where the distinction between top and bottom fermentation largely disappears. These techniques substantially reduce the time required for fermentation by using more yeast, higher temperatures, and maintaining yeast in a highly active state.

19.2 *Factors affecting fermentation* [6–9]

The main factors influencing fermentation performance and beer quality are as follows:

1. The choice of yeast strain.
2. The condition of the yeast at the time of pitching.
3. The amount of yeast added to the wort.
4. The distribution of the yeast in the fermenting wort throughout the fermentation, and the size and geometry of the fermentation vessel.
5. Aeration (rousing or stirring usually involves (4) and (5)).
6. Wort composition and pH.
7. Fermentation temperature and pressure.

The order of importance of these factors will vary from one type of beer to another and from brewery to brewery. Some consideration has already been given to selection of yeast strain in Chapter 18. It will be appreciated that the choice depends on many parameters. The requirements can be summarized as a yeast which will produce a beer of desired taste, aroma, flavour stability and brilliance, within an acceptable period of time in the equipment available, and without undue losses of beer during processing.

The condition of the yeast on pitching depends on its previous history. It has been shown that lack of contact between yeast and oxygen over successive fermentations has a cumulative and deleterious effect. Thus in a series of three fermentations in which the wort used had only 0·5 μl/l of dissolved oxygen, the percentage apparent attenuation:

$$\left(\frac{\text{SG Wort} - \text{SG beer}}{\text{SG Wort} - 1000} \times 100 \right)$$

fell successively from 67 to 65·5 to 44%; the balance of fusel alcohols, esters, and diketones was abnormal [6]. In some instances, increasing dissolved oxygen levels over 6 mg/l has little effect, but with other yeasts, there is advantage in oxygenating the wort rather than aerating to achieve values over 8 mg/l. The requirement for oxygen may in some cases be satisfied by the presence of unsaturated fatty acids or sterols at concentrations as low as 5 μg/ml. Lack of oxygen, particularly coupled with a shortage of unsaturated fatty acids (see Chapters 17 and 18), leads to a progressive fall in viability [10]. Yeasts of low viability when pitched have long lag phases in most instances. A further influence on the length of lag phase relates to the complement of enzymes and permeases. In certain strains the maltose permease and maltase are inducible [11]. They may be either absent or provide little activity in either yeast used for pitching or yeast that has completed fermentation of glucose in a wort particularly rich in this particular sugar. The cells therefore have to synthesize these enzymes to utilize the principal fermentable carbohydrate of wort.

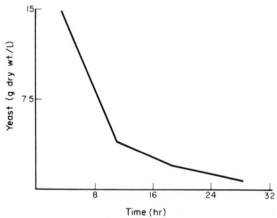

Fig. 19.1 The relationship between the amount of yeast present in a semicontinuous fermentation and the time taken for the SG of wort to fall from 1040–1010 (10–4°P).

The amount of yeast added to the wort at the time of pitching greatly influences the speed of fermentation. For instance top yeast pitched at 0·3 kg/hl (1 lb/brl) into wort at 17°C (63°F) attenuated to 75% in 84 hr. At four times this pitching rate the same attenuation was reached in 44 hr [6]. Using a similar wort, temperature and attenuation with a semi-continuous or accelerated batch procedure, the results given in Fig. 19.1 show the relationship between the amount of yeast present at the beginning of fermentation and the time required for fermentation [12]. The amount of yeast produced by growth during a fermentation is dependent on the pitching rate. At very high concentrations of yeast, the individual cells multiply slowly. The result is that the crop of yeast at the end of the fermentation is almost independent of pitching rate in the conventional range of 0·09–0·3 kg/hl (0·3–1 lb/brl).

The distribution of yeast throughout the fermentation depends on (*i*) the behaviour of the yeast strain in relation to sedimentation, flocculation, and yeast-head formation (*ii*) the agitation provided by convection currents, carbon-dioxide evolution, rousing, and stirring, and (*iii*) the size and geometry of the fermentation vessel. In connection with yeast strain, six types of behaviour have been recognized [7]:

Group A. Yeasts that sediment very early in the fermentation because of flocculation, but fermentation proceeds because of the continued action of the sedimented yeast.

Group B. Yeasts that only sediment when the wort is well attenuated and simultaneously fermentation is substantially arrested.

Group C. Yeasts that sediment only to a small degree at the end of fermentation, leaving much of the yeast in suspension.

Group D. Yeasts that pass out of suspension into a yeast-head early in fermentation and fermentation is prematurely arrested.

Group E. Yeasts that form a yeast-head to some extent but much is left in suspension. When the wort is well attenuated, the suspended yeast sediments.

Group F. Yeasts that form a yeast-head to some extent but the greater part of the yeast remains suspended and does not sediment.

It is difficult to generalize with regard to vessel geometry but some observations are made on the use of cylindro-conical tanks (see pp. 659–668). Probably the most important dimension is depth because this affects not only (*i*) yeast sedimentation but also (*ii*) carbon-dioxide bubble generation per unit area, (*iii*) hydrostatic pressure effects on carbon-dioxide evolution and (*iv*) circulation currents in the vessel.

The effects of rousing or agitating fermentation vessels include aeration and mixing. Both tend to hasten fermentation, aeration by supplementing the dissolved oxygen supplied by the wort, and mixing by bringing yeast in the head and yeast that has sedimented into suspension. The overall action is to increase yeast crops and speed fermentation. For some yeast strains agitation influences beer flavour and the shape of the yeast cells. Thus diacetyl and ester levels may be higher [13] while propagated cells may be elongated [14].

Wort composition greatly influences the speed of fermentation, the extent of fermentation, the amount of yeast produced, and the quality of the beer produced. The wort constituents which play a major role include fermentable carbohydrates, assimilable nitrogenous compounds (and in particular amino acids, purines, and pyrimidines), and accessory food factors. Amino acids normally limit growth and the spectrum of these acids is important [15] (see Chapter 17). Another important factor is the level of Zn^{2+} ions. Many fermentations are accelerated by the addition of zinc chloride (0·2 mg/l) to the wort. Zinc ions do however tend to promote yeast autolysis and are toxic if the concentration of manganese ions is less than 0·01 mg/l [16]. Wort composition is itself influenced by the mash temperature employed. Low mash temperatures give rise to more fermentable worts and therefore better attenuation. Fusel oil levels also tend to be higher [6]. The presence of suspended solids also affects fermentation by increasing yeast growth and beer constituents such as fusel alcohols and glycerol. Suspended solids can, however, accelerate yeast autolysis and depress yeast-head formation [17]. Fermentation and more particularly the quality of the final beer are influenced by pH. In this connection, some yeast strains will cause a much greater fall of pH than others when fermenting the same wort. This may well be due to a difference in either their uptake of phosphate ions from the wort, or their excretion of organic acids and nitrogenous compounds [18].

The use of elevated temperatures for fermentation has been advocated by many workers. Providing that there is no bacterial or wild yeast contamination, acceptable beers can be produced at comparatively high temperatures, say 20°C (68°F) for bottom yeasts and 27°C (81°F) for top yeasts. The quality of these beers is different however from those fe mented at normal temperatures in connection with lower pH, bitterness, shelf-life, foam stability, and ease of filtration. Ester and fusel alcohol contents are higher [6]. Fermentation temperatures of around 25°C (77°F) are used for the manufacture of certain Trappist beers [19].

19.3 *Fermentation rooms and vessels* [20–25]
In order to minimize the risk of microbiological contamination, surfaces must be clean and therefore smooth and accessible. Walls are often tiled or painted while floors are of asphalt, terrazo, or other suitable material. There must be a sufficient fall to the floor to permit efficient drainage. The drains themselves must be well constructed so that they are easy to maintain and trap all odours. Ceilings are so designed that condensation does not fall into the body of the room. Alternatively, air conditioning should ensure that no condensation forms.

Particularly with open vessels it is usual to have a false floor between vessels, some 2 m (6ft) above the true floor and about 60–90 cm (2–3 ft) below the tops of the vessels. Under the false floor and between vessels, the space may be exploited for circulating attemperated air and for various mains or pipes. Air heated by fermentation and adulterated by released carbon dioxide is aspirated into these spaces, where it is mixed with fresh air, blown through an air-cooling heat-exchanger and re-enters the room near the ceiling (Fig. 19.2). In the case of bottom fermentation the temperature of the room is usually maintained around 7°C (45°F). Moisture in the air condenses and freezes on the heat-exchanger used; a standby unit may be necessary, therefore, for defrosting periods. To prevent the fermentation room gaining heat from its surroundings, the walls, ceiling, and floors are insulated. Top fermentation rooms are usually at 15–18°C (59–64·4°F).

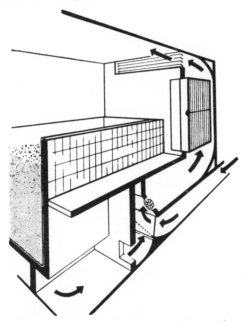

Fig. 19.2 Circulation of air around an open-fermentation vessel.

Fermentation vessels are usually 2–6 m (6·5–18·6 ft) deep, although deeper ones are used successfully. The material of construction should present an internal surface which is smooth, easy to clean, and hard to scratch or pit. It must not corrode, be subject to electrolysis, release toxic material, or deform. It should be chemically inert to wort, beer and to cleansing and sterilizing solutions. Expensive or deformable materials which are otherwise suitable for vessel construction are often used as liners for less expensive or more durable materials (Tables 19.1 and 19.2).

TABLE 19.1

Characteristics of materials used for the construction of fermentation vessels

Material	Possible lining materials	Adverse features
Wood	Copper, aluminium, or stainless steel	There is restriction on size. Unless lined, wood presents a surface which is difficult to clean.
Cast iron/mild steel	Vitrified enamel	Fragile lining, which is very difficult to repair.
Cast iron/mild steel	Bonded resin	Lining difficult to repair. Sometimes fragile. Care needed with hypochlorites.
Cast iron/mild steel	Plastic (with or without fibreglass)	Relatively soft surface which scratches. Must ensure no leaching of plasticizer.
Aluminium	(or as liner)	Needs support, corroded by alkalis and mercury, forms electric couples with fittings of other metals.
Copper	(or as liner)	Releases toxic ions when burnished. Needs support. May form electric couples with fittings of other metals.
Stainless steel	(or as liner)	Chloride plus acid causes corrosion; thin sheet requires support.
Reinforced concrete	Pitch or ebon*	Fragile lining but fairly easy to repair.
Plastic reinforced by fibreglass	(or as liner)	Relatively soft surface which scratches. Must ensure no leaching of plasticizer.

* Proprietary name for a pitch-like substance formulated for lining concrete vessels.

TABLE 19.2

Heat transmission of various materials used in construction of fermentation vessels [48]

Material	Thickness (mm)	Coefficient of conductivity	Loss of heat W/m² K
Oak	50	0·17	3·95
Concrete FVs	150	0·65	5·00
Concrete tanks	250	0·65	3·02
Steel	10	56·0	6 513
Aluminium	6	175·0	33 960
Stainless steel	10	36·0	4 187

Ethanol and carbon dioxide production accounts for the utilization of about 92 % of the carbohydrate metabolized and heat released amounts to $0·59 \times 10^3$ kJ/kg of glucose equivalent. In contrast, yeast growth accounts for about 8 % of the carbohydrate metabolized and the heat energy released from this source is 6×10^3 kJ/kg of glucose equivalent. Other calculations show that the overall fermentation and yeast growth occurring in a fermenter yields 3·60 kJ/l/hr or 560 BTU/brl/hr [20].

The temperature required for bottom fermentation is in the region 7–14°C (45–57°F) and therefore cooling devices are normally required to maintain it. The cooling fluid is usually brine or a mixture of water and alcohol. Brine is cheaper but encourages corrosion of steels particularly under acidic conditions. The attemperation is carried out by mounting, in the fermentation vessel, pipework carrying the refrigerant fluid and made of copper, aluminium or stainless steel. Alternatively, the refrigerant is passed through a jacket to the wall, sometimes called a 'cold wall'. In vessels constructed of reinforced concrete, it is possible to build the attemperator pipes into the concrete. There are very many designs of attemperators but for comparatively small vessels of new construction (say up to 500 hl or 300 brl), the jacket type or 'cold wall' seems to be favoured.

For conventional rectangular open fermenters, the distance between opposite cooling walls should not exceed about 5 m (16 ft), assuming that the depth is not greater than 2·75 m (9 ft). Any increase in these measurements requires additional cooling surfaces – as a vertical panel or series of tubes just below the wort surface [22]. It has been suggested that similar requirements may apply to very tall vessels. Thus with a cylindroconical vessel of 4·2 m (13·8 ft) diameter of 1640 hl (1000 brl), it was noted that the beer was warmer at the central axis than nearer the walls, despite vigorous convection currents [23].

The refrigeration plant is traditionally a huge centralized bank of compressors. But some breweries prefer a number of smaller local compressors which serve a restricted number of vessels, have much shorter runs of pipework carrying refrigerant, and may provide a cheaper, more flexible system of cooling.

Enclosed vessels have several desirable features. Less cooling is needed because the heating of the beer by air is minimized. It has been calculated that refrigeration of enclosed vessels is about 15% of that needed for open fermenters [22].

Carbon dioxide evolution is not dangerous in enclosed vessels (except for those who enter them) whereas it can be a continual hazard in those fermentation rooms having both open vessels and poor air circulation. About 4% of carbon dioxide in air by volume can be a danger, even for short periods and legislation may limit levels in some countries to below 0·5%.

The carbon dioxide can of course be recovered readily from the enclosed vessels. For one unit weight of sugar, about half this weight is theoretically recoverable as carbon dioxide and, considering the cost of the gas and the great use for it in the post-fermentation period of beer treatment, the escape from open fermenters appears to be an expensive waste. In practice, the percentage of carbon dioxide recovered is rarely above 50% of the theoretical (see Chapter 20). There is, however, considerable debate on the economics of recovering carbon dioxide from fermentation gases, or for that matter from flue gases.

Enclosed vessels are more easily cleaned by in-place methods and indeed some open vessels are covered temporarily by a light metal or plastic canopy, in order to clean them in-place. Again fermentations in enclosed vessels are less likely to become infected by air-borne or water spray-borne micro-organisms. The advantages of open vessels are that they are somewhat less expensive, are easier to clean manually, and permit easier 'dipping' of the vessel to judge the volume of wort present. The latter procedure is required by Excise authorities in Britain unless the volume of wort is measured in a collecting vessel used specially for this purpose.

19.3.1 BOTTOM FERMENTATION [26–37]

Wort arriving from the coolers at about 7–11°C (45–52°F) is not absolutely sterile and, if left unpitched with yeast, will soon become infected with bacteria. It is therefore essential to provide conditions for rapid fermentation. Yeast is mixed intimately with the wort using about a quarter of the crop provided by the previous fermentation (say 0·22 kg/hl or 0·8 lb/brl). This is equivalent to about 8–16 × 10^6 cells/ml. Low pitching rates result in extensive yeast growth and tend to give more aromatic beers. High rates may lead to sub-sequent yeast autolysis. If there is an excessive lag period before the yeast begins to multiply then more yeast must be used.

Filling is carried out by allowing the wort to enter gently through a port in the bottom of the vessel, aeration of the wort having been carried out during cooling. If the vessel is an open one, it is never filled to within more than 30·5 cm (1 ft) from the top, in order that the head of yeasty froth which forms be accommodated. About 8–16 hr after pitching, a fine white head appears near the side of the vessel and above any attemperating coils. In some breweries, particularly those in North America, the beer is run off after 6–24 hr into another vessel, leaving trub and other solids. The first vessel is referred to as a starter or settling tank and may be open. The second vessel is normally enclosed. On the third day, 'rocky' or cauliflower' heads of foam appear which are called 'krausen' and reach maximum development called 'high krausen' from the fourth to the seventh day. At this time, the temper-ature of the fermenting wort tends to rise because of the intense metabolism of the yeast but it is restrained by attemperation so that it does not normally exceed 10–12°C (50–54°F). Abrupt reductions in temperature tend to arrest fermentation completely. From the eighth day onwards the fermentation subsides as judged by production of heat and is usually complete on the ninth to fourteenth day depending on the choice of yeast and operating temperatures. The head gradually collapses, leaving a dark-coloured, bitter-tasting scum which should be separated from the beer by skimming or suction.

Some breweries arrange for this scum to stick to the roof of the fermenter and then be removed by special chutes at the side of the vessel. Another suggestion is that plastic balls floating in the fermenter will retain the scum while the fermenter is drained. The course of a typical traditional bottom fermentation is portrayed in Fig. 19.3.

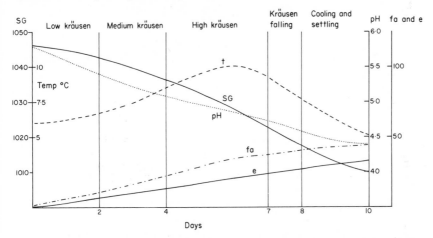

Fig. 19.3 The course of a typical traditional bottom-fermentation. SG, t, pH, fa and e refer to specific gravity of the wort, temperature (°C), pH of the wort, fusel alcohol content (μg/ml), and ester content (μg/ml).

Traditional practice requires that the beer passing on to the lager tank can sustain a secondary fermentation by having some 1·1% remaining fermentable extract (4° of gravity) and also about 1–4 million yeast cells/ml in suspension. With a powdery yeast, it may be necessary to cool the beer to about 4°C (30°F) so that the yeast both sediments more readily and ferments more slowly, thus reducing the yeast concentration and preventing the remaining fermentable extract being utilized. Alternatively the powdery yeast may be removed by passing the beer through a centrifuge while the correct level of extract remains in the beer. Still another possibility is to use a powdery yeast and, after the primary fermentation has removed all fermentable extract, to add to the lager tank fermenting wort at the krausen stage. This addition of fermentable extract at the rate of 5–10% by volume is called 'krausening'. If the yeast is sedimentary, then it must be kept fermenting by agitation in order that no more than about 4° of fermentable extract (1° Plato) is left in the beer. Some breweries use a known mixture of a sedimentary and a powdery strain but other breweries have been fortunate in selecting a strain of yeast which, after a normal period of sedimentation, leaves the correct content of yeast and fermentable matter in the beer for secondary fermentation. Still another practice involves the use of a sedimentary yeast for fermenting a proportion of the wort while the remainder is pitched with a powdery strain. The two beers are then mixed in the lagering tanks, ensuring adequate yeast and fermentable material.

A wide range of conditions of fermentation are used in different countries. It has been reported that in Denmark [27] it is usual to ferment for 8 days at 9–10°C (48–50°F). In Western Germany [28] the time of fermentation may range from 5 to 14 days and the temperature 5–9°C (41–48°F). American practice is to ferment for 6–9 days at temperatures of 10–13°C (50–55°F) but being reduced on the last 1–2 days to as low as 5°C (41°F) before the completion [29].

What is clear is that fermentation rates are being accelerated in most breweries. This can be brought about in many ways but the most common is by using higher temperatures. However, such a change often brings about differences in flavour and aroma and therefore great care has to be exercised. Some authorities believe that the unfavourable effects of temperature can be offset, at least in part, by applying pressure to the fermenting wort [30]. But pressure vessels are more expensive than normal ones. Another method of speeding fermentation is to agitate the contents of fermenters but again caution is necessary otherwise there is excessive yeast growth and the lag phase of fermentation is virtually eliminated. This is achieved either by activating the yeast with wort in a 'starter tank' before pitching it into the main body of wort or by blending actively fermenting wort with fresh wort. The most popular method however, is, to adjust carefully the dissolved oxygen and amino acid contents of the wort so as to control yeast growth [8].

In the lager fermentat ons of many years ago there were not the same intense economic pressures to have a speedy process. Because there was no refrigeration equipment it was necessary to brew in the colder months of the year. Again, because there were no means of removing yeast and trub except by sedimentation, the beer was maintained for many months at low temperatures in shallow vessels. Traditional practice is only slightly modified from these old methods but in the past 20–30 years, economic pressures have created the need for acceleration. Thus in North America, many breweries pitch at 11°C (52°F) using $15–20 \times 10^6$ cells/ml and hold the temperature at 12°C (54°F) for some 7 days [29]. They may leave fermentable extract for secondary fermentation (a true lagering process) or completely ferment out and use what is called an 'ageing' process (see Chapter 21). At the end of the primary fermentation, the temperature is brought down quickly to say 4°C (39°F). The complete range of possibilities is indicated in Table 19.3 but many more variants of these methods are practised.

The beer from the primary fermentation is run slowly and without turbulence (thus ensuring no uptake of air) into lagering tanks which are usually cylindrical and horizontally disposed (Fig. 19.4). The traditional lagering

TABLE 19.3

Comparison of fermentation and maturation systems used in Germany [31–33] and North America [29]

Method	Primary fermentation	Transfer	Post fermentation storage
Traditional lagering	7 days at 9°C (48°F)	Beer with 3·5°P residual extract (SG 1014) cooled to 4°C (39°F)	35–50 days with temperature gradually falling to 0°C (32°F). Secondary fermentation occurs
Krausening	7 days at 9–10°C (48–50°F)	Beer with 2°P residual extract (SG 1008) cooled to 4°C (39°F). Krausen added at rate of 10–12% by volume, containing 8°P (SG 1032)	14–28 days with temperature reducing from 4°C (39°F) to 0°C (32°F). Secondary fermentation occurs
High temperature pressurized fermentation (as in Weissbier)	3 days at 16°C (61°F) or 4 days at 14°C (57°F) under pressure (2 bar)	Beer with 2°P residual extract (SG 1008) at 2 bar cooled to 0°C (32°F)	7–14 days stabilization at 0°C (32°F). Little secondary fermentation occurs
Modern system	7 days at 12–14°C (54–57°F) with CO₂ collection; fermented to limit	Fully attenuated beer already carbonated is cooled to 0°C (32°F)	14–21 days stabilization at 0°C. No secondary fermentation occurs
North American lagering system	7 days at 12°C (54°F)	Beer with 2·6°P residual extract (SG 1010) cooled to 4°C (39°F) in fermenter. Krausen added by some brewers on transfer	14–28 days with temperature reducing from 4°C (39°F) to 0°C (32°F). Secondary fermentation occurs
North American modern ageing system (temperature-time programme)	7 days at 13°C (55·5°F)	Yeast is removed from beer of 2°P (SG 1008) with no fermentable extract	6 days with temperature falling from 13°C slowly to 0°C (32°F). No secondary fermentation
North American system variant to above	Temperature arising rapidly from 10° to 17°C (50 to 63°F) then held	Beer at 2°P (SG 1008) chilled rapidly to 0°C (32°F) and yeast removed by centrifuge	3–4 days at 0°C (32°F). No secondary fermentation

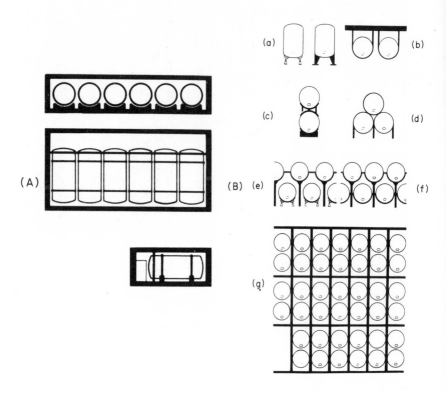

*Fig. 19.*4 (A) Tanks suitable for fermentation and beer maturation; elevation, plan and side elevation. (B) Methods of installing storage tanks. (a) Vertical tanks; (b) Strap mounting of suspended horizontal tanks; (c) Bottom tank on concrete cradle, upper tank saddled; (d) Bottom tanks on legs, upper tanks offset saddled; (e) Bottom tanks on jacks, upper tanks interspaced and mounted on centre column; (f) Bottom tanks ring mounted and suspended, upper tanks mounted on offset centre columns; (g) Ring suspended multi-tier installation.

process extends over several months beginning at 5°C (41°F) and then dropping to about 0°C (32°F) [31]. During this period, both the remaining yeast and chill haze settle out. At the same time, the yeast continues to attack the residual fermentable material and the carbon dioxide produced is effective in purging any air out of the beer and also much of the hydrogen sulphide and other volatile materials. As has been mentioned, some breweries add to the lagering vessel 'krausen'. A further reason for lagering is said to be the improvement of flavour of the beer which results. The maturation process is complex and probably involves reactions featuring esterification and redox changes. In one method of hastening these chemical changes, the beer is irradiated in thin films with light of wavelength near ultra violet. During lagering, polyphenols and proteins coprecipitate giving improved beer stability. There is, however, an increasing number of brewers who do not believe that lagering is strictly necessary [9, 30, 31], although they do stress the importance of primary fermentations being sufficiently long, so that all excreted α-acetohydroxy acids can be oxidatively decarboxylated to vicinal diketones and subsequently reduced, by the yeast present, to alkane-2,3,-diols (see Chapter 17). Other brewers subject beer, after primary fermentation, to warm conditioning (20°C for 2–3 days) to achieve the same changes, a process referred to as 'diacetyl rest'.

At the end of the primary fermentation and subsequent steps in post fermentation treatments it is imperative that there is no dissolved oxygen present in the beer and this is especially so if there is no traditional lagering. Unwanted volatiles are purged from the beer by carbon dioxide either by the natural secondary fermentation process or artificially by introducing a stream of the gas into the base of the vessel. Clarification may be hastened by centrifugation or by accelerating sedimentation using isinglass finings or gelatin, aided by chilling. At the low temperatures of lagering or ageing, the protein–polyphenol complexes come out of solution more readily; moreover convection currents and fermentation currents are minimized.

Whether beer is subject to lagering or to accelerated post fermentation treatment, tanks are required to hold the beer until it is packaged. As will be mentioned in greater detail later, it is possible to use a single tank for both primary fermentation and subsequent post fermentation treatment. Such tanks are referred to as 'Unitanks' [23, 36, 37]. The tanks are sometimes constructed and disposed so that they form a self-supporting block, the building's walls and roof being little more than a light covering (Fig. 19.4). Alternatively, they may be massive free-standing outdoor tanks. The vessels are always insulated, and frequently they have either jacket or internal tube attemperators. There is, however, a tendency to dispense with the attemperators and circulate the beer in closed circuit through a refrigerating heat exchanger either continuously or spasmodically. A further possibility is to use one series of tanks at 4°C (39°F) until secondary fermentation is virtually complete and then give the beer a rough prefiltration before it enters a second series of tanks held at just below 0°C (32°F).

After lagering, the beer is filtered. Traditionally filtration was carried out using long-fibre pulp filters but these have several disadvantages including cost. Thus, the pulp needs to be washed and pressed into filter-pads before use and when the pads are blinded, they are shredded prior to rewashing of the pulp. In many breweries therefore, rough clarification is carried out using kieselguhr filters or centrifuges while final clarification is achieved by filtration with sheet filters. Lagers are in some cases bulk pasteurized, or pasteurized in bottle. In other instances, sterilization is brought about by careful filtration, or by means of sheet filters followed by membrane filters. Considerable care has to be exercised during handling to avoid uptake of air by the beer, otherwise flavour and stability are jeopardized (see Chapter 20).

Yeast recovered from bottom fermentation is normally passed through an oscillating fine sieve and then washed in cold water to remove trub or break, bacteria, and dead yeast cells. The denser living yeast cells are retained and are stored under water at about 2°C (36°F). Yeast rooms are usually refrigerated but sometimes water-jacketted storage vessels are used for the yeast. Only a proportion of the yeast is retained for repitching, and only the middle layer of yeast sediment in the fermentation vessel normally receives the above treatment. Before repitching, the yeast is slurried in either wort or water and injected into the wort main leading to the fermenters.

19.3.2 MODERN SYSTEMS OF BATCH FERMENTATION [8, 23, 31, 36–47]

One of the early changes in fermenter design was the move to enclosed vessels. Nathan in 1908 and 1927 patented designs of enclosed vertical cylindrical vessels with conical bases. He claimed faster fermentation, that the same vessel could be used for fermentation and lagering, that fermentation could be controlled by temperature and dissolved oxygen and that carbon dioxide could be readily collected [41]. Nathan vessels, constructed of aluminium, were installed in few breweries. However, other types of stainless steel enclosed fermenters of 5200–11 500 hl (3100–6900 brl) were built just before 1960 in Ireland; ones of 1000–4000 hl (600–2400 brl) were constructed outdoors in Japan (Fig. 19.5) from 1965 [38]. Larger ones were built in the USA soon afterwards (4700–10 600 hl or 2620–6360 brl) [36] All these vessels had gently sloping bases (Fig. 19.6). Some were used for both fermentation and lagering and almost all were equipped with in-place cleaning systems.

An important feature of these vessels is that they can accommodate many brews. They are therefore filled over many hours and there is considerable choice with respect to which brews are pitching with yeast and which are oxygenated. Somewhat different results occur with regard to fermentation speed and chemical characteristics of the beers resulting from these various practices. The Rainier Unitank is a variant of these large outdoor fermenters in that it has a conical base with a slope of not more than 25° from the horizontal (Fig. 19.6). It is used for both fermentation and lagering as its name suggests. The cooling jackets are sized for maximum rates of fermentation and there are means of injecting carbon dioxide to wash the green beer free of unwanted volatiles [36].

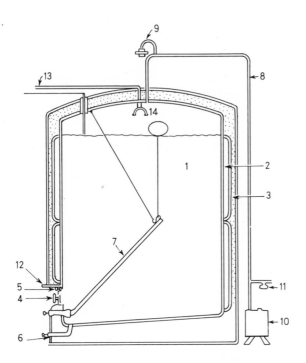

Fig. 19.5 Large outdoor fermentation vessel (USP 3, 374, 726). 1. Tank; 2. Cooling jacket; 3. Foamed-synthetic resin; 4. Manhole; 5. Beer drainage cock; 6. Beer feed pipe; 7. Beer discharge pipe (pivoted); 8. Exhaust pipe; 9. Siphon breaker; 10. Pressure relief valve; 11. Vacuum breaker; 12. Thermometer and liquid depth senser; 13. Water and detergent supply pipe; 14. Water and detergent spray.

Probably the most popular of the modern vessels are the cylindroconical fermenters, direct descendants of the Nathan vessels [8, 23, 31, 40]. They range in size from 100 to 4800 hl (60–2880 brl). An important characteristic of most of these vessels is the steep angled cone at the base (Fig. 19.7). It has been discovered that an included angle of 70° is the best compromise angle for bringing the yeast into the base at the vessel. This compacting permits the yeast to be run off discretely, leaving beer comparatively free from yeast in the vessel. The consequences are that lagering can then proceed in the same vessel without the need for centrifuging. However, not all yeast strains compact efficiently, leaving some need for centrifuging. Cylindrical vessels with dished bottoms are usually satisfactory for lagering but because of poorer yeast separation are less well adapted to primary fermentation.

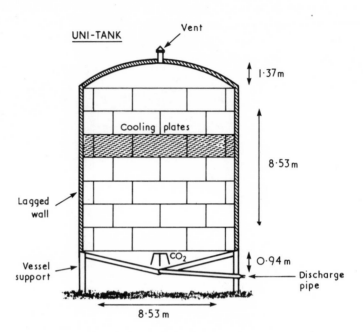

Fig. 19.6 The Unitank, a dual purpose fermenter/maturation vessel designed by the Rainier company [36].

The advantages claimed for cylindroconical fermenters are (*i*) reduced capital and operating costs, (*ii*) reduced beer losses because of excellent drainage and good yeast separation, (*iii*) increased speed and flexibility of operation, (*iv*) improved and more consistent beer quality, (*v*) better utiliz- ation of vessels, (*vi*) easy collection of carbon dioxide, (*vii*) efficient in-p ace c'eaning, (*viii*) improved utilization of bitter substances, (*ix*) efficient and hygienic yeast handling, and (*x*) better foam retention of the beer. Modern vessels are constructed of cold-rolled stainless steel sheet which is particularly easy to clean. The vessels are lagged and protected with a fibre glass skin incorporating a phenolic foam; the whole may be sheathed if necessary in aluminium or stainless steel. Lagging must be fireproof, resistant to mould growth and non-corrosive to stainless steel under any working conditions.

It is usual to leave 25–33 % of the volume as headspace so as to accommo- date foam during fermentation. However, many breweries are able to decrease headspaces dramatically by the use of an antifoam – of either unsaturated lipids or silicone [42, 43]. The question of the location of jackets and temper- ature probes is complex [6, 23, 44]. The recommendations of one authority are set out in Table 19.4. It appears that other brewers do not necessarily subscribe to these views and many use a single jacket some two-thirds up the vertical wall; they say that cone cooling is only required if yeast is to be stored in the cone [8]. Cooling duty should preferably be about 1°C/hr, but many vessels are incapable of more than half this duty.

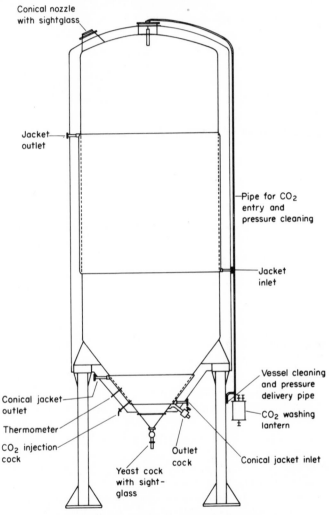

Conical nozzle with sightglass

Jacket outlet

Pipe for CO_2 entry and pressure cleaning

Jacket inlet

Vessel cleaning and pressure delivery pipe

Conical jacket outlet

Thermometer

CO_2 injection cock

CO_2 washing lantern

Outlet cock

Yeast cock with sight-glass

Conical jacket inlet

Fig. 19.7 Cylindro-conical fermentation vessel.

There is also considerable debate about the circulatory currents in these vessels. The driving forces are evolution of carbon dioxide during fermentation and convection currents. Carbon dioxide is released during fermentation at the deepest part of the vessel [45]. It is the relatively long distance to the surface which causes the particularly strong upward current of beer along the central axis of the vessel. The return of the beer is mainly near the walls and will be greatly aided by cooling jackets placed high up the wall of the fermenter. Circulatory patterns have been studied in detail [20, 40] and appear to vary somewhat according to the rate of fermentation, the position of the coolers and the speed of cooling. Hydrostatic pressure will tend to lead to a greater content of dissolved carbon dioxide near the base, but during active fermentation and/or cooling the gradient up the tank tends to be lost. When circulatory currents are weak, surprising variations in temperature occur, some being caused by beer having its greatest density around 3°C (37°F). Ice can therefore form at the surface when beer of 3°C is at the base and colder beer rises. Several probes at different depths are therefore needed to detect this stratification [30, 44].

TABLE 19.4

Suggested positioning of cooling jackets and temperature probes in beer tanks [23]

Vessel	Duty	Jackets	Temperature probe
Fermenter	Ferment	2 side jackets	Low in vessel
Fermenter	Chill to temperature above 3°C (37°F)	2 side jackets; top jacket high	Low in vessel
Maturation	Chill to 3°C	Jacket on cone and jacket two-thirds up the side	Below side jacket
Bright beer tank	Hold at 0°C (32°F)	Jacket on cone	Two-thirds up the vessel

The vessels are usually 3–4 times taller than their diameter and working pressures of 1–1.3 bar above atmospheric can usually be accommodated. Increasing size of the vessels leads to economies in terms of cost per unit volume. According to several authorities [23, 36], the cost of large fermenters rises with size by something close to the equation:

$$\text{cost ratio} = \text{volume ratio}^{0.65}$$

Thus, doubling the volume of a fermenter leads to a cost increase of about 30–37%. However, very large vessels may provide a variety of problems. They may be so large that they have to be accommodated in the open; even then their height may be unacceptable to local authorities. Unless the brewery is very large, vessels of say 20 m (66 ft) high are only applicable to particular brands of beer sold in very large volumes. As mentioned, filling may require several brews and take many hours. Emptying is also slow, but the fermentation tends to be very rapid because of the strong circulatory currents.

The logistical situation may therefore be complex. Another feature of the large vessels is the need for very efficient pressure release mechanisms to avoid explosion or implosion. Thus, emptying such vessels without balancing pressure will lead to implosion.

Returning to the question of costs of vessels, in general the greater the volume to surface area, the less expensive the unit volume cost should be. Fig. 19.8 illustrates this with respect to several types of large fermenting vessel. It was originally believed that spheroconical vessels would be prohibitively expensive to construct because of special fabrication difficulties. However such vessels have been successfully manufactured and used in Spain [39].

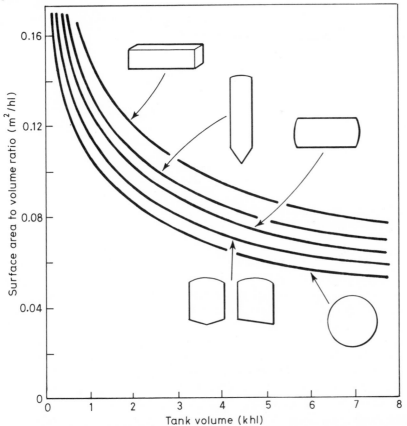

Fig. 19.8 The relationship between volume and surface area for a variety of shapes of fermenting vessels [36]. (Reproduced by kind permission of the Master Brewers Association of America.)

Under British conditions, lager primary fermentations are carried out in cylindroconical tanks at about 12°C (54°F) in some 4–7 days, the time being only slightly dependent on the original gravity of the wort [46, 47]. For ale the corresponding figures are 2–3 days at 20°C (68°F). The yeast pitching rate is around 20×10^6 cells/ml. High gravity brewing greatly benefits from the fact that in the range 8–12°P (SG 1032–1050), the time taken to 80% apparent attenuation is approximately the same (Fig. 19.9). It is usual to use bottom-cropping (sedimentary) strains of *Saccharomyces cerevisiae* for ale production.

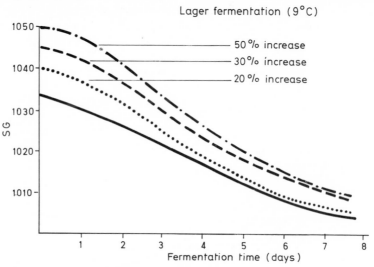

Lager fermentation (9°C)

50% increase
30% increase
20% increase

SG

Fermentation time (days)

Fig. 19.9 The relationship between fermentation time and increasing the original gravity of wort from 1033.3 in cylindro-conical fermenters [73].

Foam production during fermentation tends to be excessive and is one of the reasons why antifoams are used by some breweries. The early generations of a new yeast culture are particularly prone to overfoam, especial!y if high aeration rates are used in the yeast propagator. Some control can also be exercised by using lower levels of dissolved oxygen in the cylindroconical for worts of greater extract. Thus if a 7·8°P (SG 1031) wort can tolerate in this respect 8 mg O_2/l, the equivalent for 11·9°P (SG 1048) wort is 4–5 mg O_2/l. There were no abnormal effects using dissolved oxygen contents as low as 4 mg O_2/l reported by the brewery concerned [8]. Clearly, other yeast strains may not be so accommodating. The use of pressure is another method of controlling foam height.

With respect to the main fermentation, the control on the speed of attenuating to satisfactory gravities depends on (*i*) wort composition, especially the level of α-amino nitrogen and the spectrum of fermentable sugars, (*ii*) dissolved oxygen, (*iii*) temperature, (*iv*) pressure, and (*v*) yeast concentration.

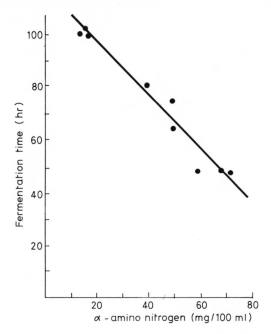

Fig. 19.10 Relationship between fermentation time and α-amino nitrogen of the wort [74].

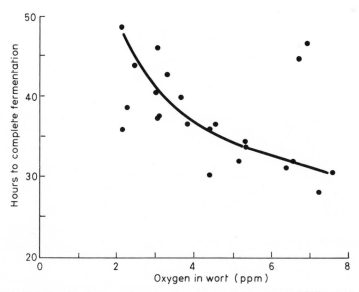

Fig. 19.11 Relationship between fermentation time and the content of dissolved oxygen (hl/l) in the wort [74].

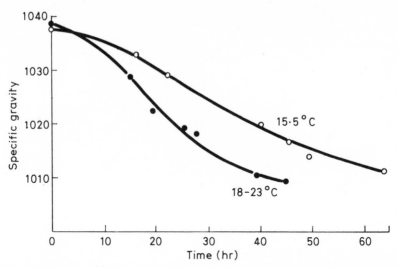

Fig. 19.12 The rates of fall in wort specific gravity for two temperatures of fermentation [74].

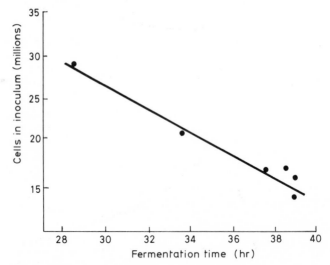

Fig. 19.13 The influence of fermentation time and the number of yeast cells (10^6/ml) inoculated [74].

With respect to α-amino nitrogen, 400 mg/l present in a wort of 19·3°P (SG 1080) allows one brewery to ferment in 40 hr. For worts in the range 9–10·5°P (SG 1036–1042), the same fermentation time can be achieved with α-amino nitrogen levels of around 150 mg/l [8, 46]. Pitching yeast concentrations for the lower gravities just mentioned would be 10×10^6 cells/ml. For worts in excess of 14·7°P (SG 1060), 15×10^6 cells/ml would be necessary to achieve fermentations in the same time [8]. The importance of these factors is illustrated in Figs 19.10–19·13. With respect to the effect of these variables on flavour, it has been shown that dissolved oxygen content can be important. Reducing the level from 8 to 3 mg O_2/l causes significant increases (2–4-fold) in the esters ethyl acetate, isoamyl acetate and ethyl caproate. Acetaldehyde rises seven-fold [46]. Levels of zinc ions up to 0·08 mg/l may be necessary for satisfactory fermentations [46].

Details of the cycle times required for cylindroconical vessels, using one vessel for both fermentation and maturation against using separate vessels for these two processes, is given in Table 19.5. The advantages of a two vessel process have been given as (i) better utilization of the capacity available, (ii) faster and more uniform chilling, (iii) easier to blend beers and make additions, and (iv) better yeast separation. Against this, there are (i) higher beer losses, (ii) danger of picking up dissolved oxygen during transfer from one vessel to the other, (iii) an additional vessel and mains to clean, and (iv) a less flexible ratio of times for fermenting and maturation [23]. With a two vessel system, it is common to have centrifuge and chiller in the main connecting the two vessels.

TABLE 19.5

Cycle times (hr) for 3000 hl (1800 brl) cylindroconical vessels; single vessel system for fermentation and maturation of ale versus two vessel system [23]

	Single vessel system	Two vessel system	
		Vessel 1	Vessel 2
Fill	6	6	
Pitch	2	2	
Ferment at 18°C (64·4°F)*	48	48	
Chill to 8°C (46·4°F)*	16	16	
Warm condition	72	72	
Chill to 0°C (32°F)	36	6	6
Store at 0°C (32°F)	72	—	72
Empty	6	—	6
Clean	3	3	3
Subtotals		153	87
Totals	261	240	

* These temperatures were not given in the original reference and are estimates.

Where cylindroconical vessels are used in the UK as wort collecting vessels, it is still required by the Excise authorities at the present time to obtain a measure of volume using a dip-stick. It is to be hoped that this practice, undesirable from the microbiological viewpoint, can soon be abandoned.

Because of the possibility of stratification, it is necessary to have various temperature probes in the vessels (Table 19.4) and sampling points. If the vessels are outside, it may be necessary to offer weather protection to quality control workers. The sampling systems may involve rubber septa through which samples can be withdrawn using hypodermic needles. Alternatively they may be sample cocks that can be sterilized before and after sampling. A recent sampling system uses loops of pipework through which the samples can thus be taken at the depths where the loops originate (after the pump has been operating for a short time).

19.3.3 TRADITIONAL TOP FERMENTATION [48–52]

The most popular system of top fermentation uses a single vessel, which until recently was usually open, but now enclosed vessels have tended to oust them. In very deep vessels such as cylindroconical fermenters, the yeast forms little top crop and is mainly harvested at the base. However with open vessels and the more shallow enclosed fermenters, the yeast rises to the top of the beer at the end of fermentation and is either removed by suction or by skimming. The method is therefore called the 'skimming system'. If during the fermentation, the beer is fed by gravity from one vessel to another, the method is called a 'dropping system'.

The skimming system, and its variant the dropping system, have the advantages of using simple equipment, being suitable for a wide range of beers, and in keeping beer losses to a minimum (under 2%). The vessels are either square or round in plan view and are usually 2–4 m (6–13 ft) deep. Traditional wooden vessels were normally of small capacity (say 82·5 hl or 50 brl), but modern stainless steel vessels are often over 825 hl (500 brl) capacity. The largest vessel built – a stainless steel enclosed fermenter – is 13 225 hl (8016 brl) capacity. The usual range is 165–412 hl (100–250 brl). Materials of construction and the advantages of enclosed fermenters have received mention earlier in this chapter.

Oxygenated or aerated wort with a dissolved oxygen content in the range 5–15 mg O_2/l is introduced from above. The wort is pitched as soon as possible with 0·15–0·30 kg/hl (0·5–1·0 lb/brl) pressed yeast. It is common practice to pitch at 15–16°C (59–61°F) and allow the temperature to rise gently to 20°C (68°F), or rarely to 22°C (72°F), as fermentation proceeds (Fig. 19.14). The first indication of fermentation is the production of gas bubbles which collect as a froth. Gradually the froth builds up to a substantial foam. If the dropping system is adopted, after 24–36 hr the fermenting wort may be transferred into another vessel. Dropping the fermenting wort has the advantages of (i) cold trub and other undesirable materials (see Chapter 15) being left in the first vessel, called a collecting vessel, and (ii) mixing and aeration. Many brewers with or without facilities for dropping, mix and

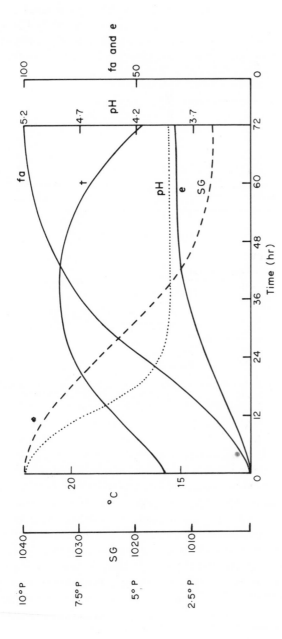

Fig. 19.14 The course of a typical top-fermentation. SG, t, pH, fa and e refer to specific gravity of the wort (or extract in °P), temperature (°C), pH of wort, fusel alcohol content (μg/ml), and ester content (μg/ml).

aerate by 'rousing'. This was traditionally carried out with paddles but today is achieved by circulating the fermenting wort through a pump and back through a spray to discharge over the surface of the beer. Opinions are very divided about the need to rouse during a fermentation, but in the case of yeasts which flocculate and sediment strongly it is normally essential.

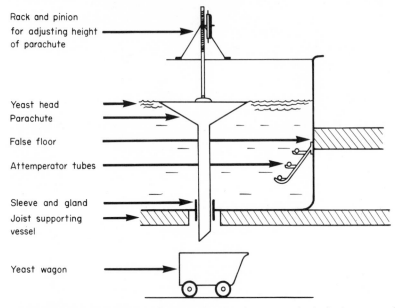

Rack and pinion
for adjusting height
of parachute

Yeast head
Parachute

False floor

Attemperator tubes

Sleeve and gland
Joist supporting
vessel

Yeast wagon

Fig. 19.15 Skimming system of top fermentation showing one method of using a parachute that can be adjusted for height.

As fermentation proceeds, a substantial crop of yeast collects in the head. This is removed by either suction or by a conical collector in the vessel (Fig. 19.15). Removal of the yeast may take place once, twice, or three times during fermentation depending on the yeast strain used and the type of beer produced. If attenuation is insufficient or is proceeding too slowly the fermenting wort is roused. When the degree of attenuation is satisfactory, the yeast is removed by skimming or by suction. The first crop to emerge on the surface is yeast which tends to be less attenuative and the last crop of top yeast is the most attenuative. A brewer takes for repitching the crop which gives him the best results, namely a yeast which attenuates rapidly and rises from the beer readily into the head at the completion of the primary fermentation. To some extent the requirements are difficult to meet because a powdery yeast tends to ferment rapidly but does not separate well. In contrast, a yeast forming flocs tends to move into the head before primary fermentation is completed (see Chapter 16). There are, however, no hard and fast rules in this matter and the situation is greatly complicated by the use of mixtures of strains.

Yeast can be encouraged to come out of suspension by cooling and it is common practice to reduce the temperature of the beer to 14–15°C (57–59°F) by the end of fermentation. For British beers, it is usual to have 0·5–2 million cells/ml at the time the beer is run from the fermentation vessels. About 0·5–1·0°P (2–4 degrees of gravity) in the form of fermentable carbohydrate is left in the beer for secondary fermentation. In some breweries continuous discharge centrifuges are used to reduce the level of yeast to a desired value. Using centrifuges, powdery yeasts may be employed without having high yeast counts during secondary fermentation, which would mean difficulty in fining or filtration and possibly too rapid secondary fermentation.

Yeast removed from the fermenter by suction is usually collected in an enclosed cylindrical vessel called a yeast back. The yeast is usually pumped from the back to a sheet filter press where entrained beer (barm ale) is recovered and after pasteurizing it is blended with racked beer (Fig. 19.16). Sometimes the yeast is held in the filter which is cooled by water or brine circulating in a jacket around it. In other cases, the yeast is discharged from the filter into trays or trucks which are placed in a refrigerator until it is required for pitching.

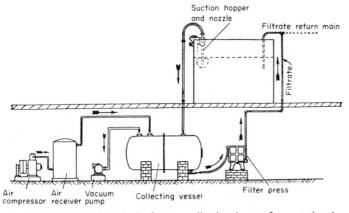

Fig. 19.16 A frequently used method of yeast collection in top-fermentation breweries.

Where yeast is removed by skimming, it collects in the conical parachute which is placed either in the centre or at the edge of the fermenter. The parachute leads to a yeast main which in turn discharges into a yeast back or yeast wagon. If yeast is held in the back until it is required for repitching, the temperature is kept low, say, 10°C (50°F). The barm ale is allowed to run away from the yeast and is blended. An alternative procedure is to transfer the yeast to a filter press as mentioned previously for suction systems, or the yeast may be held at 2–4°C (36–39°F) under water. Repitching can be carried out with either pressed yeast or yeast slurried in water or wort.

The growing use of centrifuges for clarifying beer between fermenting
vessels and racking vessels has had a profound effect upon the design of
modern fermenters. The traditional open fermenter with an almost flat bottom
is shallow in order to facilitate almost complete sedimentation of the yeast
which fails to rise into the head. With a suitable centrifuge available it is not
necessary to achieve clarification within the fermenter and therefore beer can
be discharged as soon as fermentation is judged to be complete. The time
needed for sedimentation is therefore saved, and cooling of the beer to hasten
sedimentation is reduced. Furthermore, there is no reason to use shallow
vessels, rather than deep vessels which are more economical in space, and no
reason for using flat-bottomed vessels instead of conical-based vessels which
drain more readily. The cylindroconical vessel (Fig. 19.17) therefore comes
into its own for top fermentation. Whatever the type of fermenter used, it is
logical to match the capacity of the fermenters with the volume of wort
produced by each brew (the brew length), and the size and number of vessels
to receive the green beer.

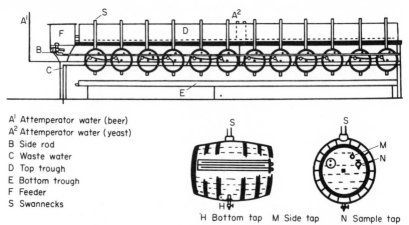

A^1 Attemperator water (beer)
A^2 Attemperator water (yeast)
B Side rod
C Waste water
D Top trough
E Bottom trough
F Feeder
S Swannecks

H Bottom tap   M Side tap   N Sample tap

Fig. 19.17 Burton Union system of fermentation.

The Burton Union system of fermentation is practised in Burton upon
Trent, England, and formerly in other areas of the English Midlands [51].
Fermenting wort is dropped from collecting vessels at the peak of fermentation
into a set of Union vessels (Fig. 19.17). The latter are of oak, arranged in two
adjacent rows each of 12. The individual vessel is a cask of about 7 hl (153 gal)
equipped with tubular internal attemperators. At the top of each cask
is a swan-neck pipe which during active fermentation discharges yeast and
beer into a trough that is constructed above the casks. The trough is held at
a temperature lower than the casks and it is slightly inclined. Yeast tends to
sediment in it but the beer collects at the lower end and is returned by 'side

rods' to the casks. As the fermentation comes to completion, nearly all the yeast has found its way to the trough. The beer in the casks is then discharged into a trough immediately below them and run into racking backs. The Union system gives yeast of excellent quality and is reputed to give characteristic flavour to the beer. Disadvantages of the Union system include the space required, the high cost of the equipment itself, the maintenance and cleaning. Stainless-steel Union systems have been made in which the Union casks are replaced by a single horizontal cylindrical vessel running beneath the top trough.

Yorkshire Stone Squares were originally vessels made of stone and later, slate. They were therefore of small capacity – 46 hl (28 brl) was a common capacity. Like the Burton Unions, modern materials have largely replaced the traditional ones and modern Yorkshire Squares are of stainless steel. They are characterized by having a lower compartment separated from the upper open portion by a deck (Fig. 19.18). The deck gives entry to the lower vessel by a series of pipes and by a central manhole with a flange 15 cm (6 in) around the rim. The lower compartment is filled with wort and yeast and the upper to a depth of about 2·5 cm (1 in). Yeast rises through the manhole and remains on the deck while the beer drains back through the pipes. Strongly flocculent yeast strains are used with this system of fermentation and the fermenting wort has to be roused vigorously by a pumping system of circulation. Eventually the yeast on the deck is recovered by stopping the circulation and skimming it away from the deck. The beer is racked off from the lower compartment. The system tends to be more expensive than the skimming system but less expensive than the Union method. It is claimed to give a characteristic type of beer.

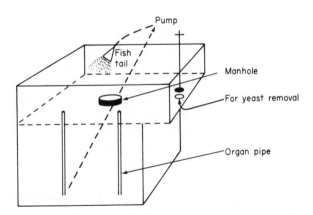

Fig. 19.18 Yorkshire Stone Square system of fermentation.

19.4 *Accelerated fermentations* [9, 12, 30, 53, 54]

There are many traditional fermentation processes which are based on the idea of partly emptying a vessel, in which fermentation is active, into a second vessel and replenishing the first with fresh medium. In this way, the lag period of growth of the micro-organism is reduced or even eliminated in the replenished vessels. This has found expression in the Hansen and Kühle yeast propagator (Chapter 18), the Schalk process for primary fermentation [53]; and such systems operate on a semicontinuous basis. Reduction or elimination of the lag period cuts down the fermentation time and minimizes the risk of bacterial infection. Further increases in fermentation rate can often be achieved as has previously been mentioned by (*i*) keeping the yeast free of infection, (*ii*) stirring so that the yeast is kept in suspension, (*iii*) raising the temperature to a maximum of about 28°C (82°F), (*iv*) increasing the yeast concentration, (*v*) increasing the dissolved oxygen content of the wort, and (*vi*) optimizing the composition of the wort maximum rate of fermentation.

In the past decade, many of these methods of speeding fermentation have been employed on laboratory and pilot-scale plant and several adopted for full-scale processes.

Infection-free yeast is obtained using well designed propagators (see Chapter 18). By careful yeast management and adoption of microbiological principles in the construction of the fermenters, the yeast should remain free of infection. Stirring is not obligatory if powdery yeasts are used, and in any case can be replaced by sparging of suitable gas mixtures or by recirculation devices. The choice of temperature is dependent on the flavour and other characteristics of the beer required but in practice, temperatures above 20°C (68°F) are not used. Increasing yeast concentration is achieved by separating the yeast from the discharged beer and returning it to the fermenter. Either a centrifuge or settling tank would serve for such separations. Alternatively a flocculent or sedimentary yeast may be used which will settle in the fermenter itself, allowing beer to be withdrawn relatively free of yeast. The dissolved oxygen content of the wort may be increased by oxygenating rather than aerating on the cold side of the wort chillers. Optimization of wort composition is clearly a complex undertaking. It will depend in part on the yeast strain because strains differ in their quantitative requirement for individual carbohydrates, amino acids, and other nutrients [6]. There are, however, differences in requirements for a single strain when used at different temperatures, for instance in the need for accessory food factors [55]. With increasing yeast concentration, the optimal wort composition is also likely to change [8, 56].

Speeding up fermentation rates is relatively simple for most breweries but achieving it without change or even deterioration of the quality of the beer is far more difficult. The acceleration is quite likely to alter the levels of beer constituents which are important in beer flavour and aroma. This is particularly true of such substances as esters, diketones, fusel alcohols, and hydrogen sulphide. General experience appears to indicate that if the amount of yeast produced, per unit volume of beer, is changed significantly then there are important alterations in the character of the beer [12, 56]. This does not mean that acceptable beer cannot be produced if the yeast crop is smaller or greater than normal, but the beer will tend to differ appreciably from the normal beer in taste and aroma.

Semicontinuous systems may be fed with wort either continuously or batchwise. In either case the beer can be discharged in batches. There are logistic reasons for preferring such a system to the less flexible fully-continuous methods requiring continuous feed and discharge. Thus it may not be convenient or economic to produce wort continuously or to store it. Additionally, it may be inconvenient to rack off beer on a continuous basis. Especially if the dwell-time in a semicontinuous fermenter fits in well with both the time required to produce wort and the programme of wort production, this method of fermentation appears attractive. In one example of a semicontinuous system [54] cylindroconical vessels are 5% filled with wort of 12·5°P (SG 1050) at 10–12°C (50–54°F) and seeded with yeast at a rate of 40 kg/hl (144 lb/brl). After 4–5 hr, which is the time needed for 75% attenuation, fresh wort is fed in at such a rate that the vessel is full in a further 44–48 hr. Providing that the yeast is kept in suspension, the attenuation of the beer is satisfactory. Beers produced in this manner are similar to those derived from traditional fermentation processes. It is known from other studies [12] that the wort may be fed at a uniform rate into the partly filled vessel, or at a variable rate to maintain a given degree of attenuation. A flocculent strain may be selected so that sedimentation of the yeast is rapid when the vessel is full. The beer can then be run off comparatively free of yeast leaving a large charge of yeast for the next delivery of wort into the vessel. There is, however, considerable concern among brewing scientists about the relatively high percentage of dead cells when high concentrations of yeasts are maintained. It is not known why viability is low under these conditions, but it would appear likely that (i) yeast cells in high concentrations do not bud because the wort is not a suitable medium for such cell numbers [56] and (ii) yeast cells which fail to bud for a considerable period of time, become effete although fermenting actively. It must be emphasized, however, that this explanation is highly conjectural.

19.5 Continuous fermentations [12, 30, 57–72]
Patented methods of continuous fermentation have existed since the beginning of the century [63]. In many respects, they resemble the more recent methods but advances in vessel design and construction and in microbiological

techniques have given these new methods better chances of survival. Continuous fermentation systems may be classified in three ways: (*i*) Stirred tank reactors may be contrasted with unstirred reactors. (*ii*) Single-vessel systems versus a number of vessels connected in series. (*iii*) Vessels which allow yeast to overflow freely with the beer (an 'open system') versus vessels which have abnormally high yeast concentrations (a 'closed' or 'semi-closed system') [64]. The high yeast concentration is achieved by preventing yeast from overflowing with the beer or by recycling yeast separated from overflowed beer [12] (Fig. 19.19).

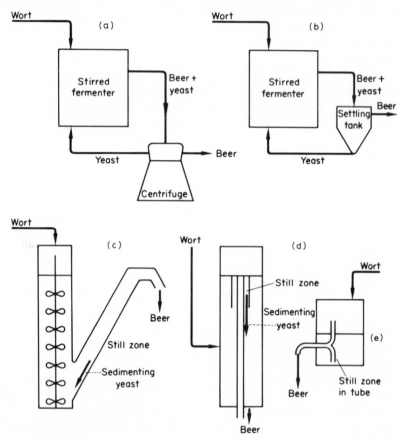

Fig. 19.19 Methods of achieving high yeast concentrations in continuous fermentation by: (a) Centrifuge; (b) Settling tank; (c) Inclined tube; (d) Concentric tubes; (e) Riser tube.

Stirred tank reactors have received a great deal of fundamental study [60, 64]. As single vessel, open systems, the principles of their operation were described in 1950 [65, 66]. Unfortunately, most research has been carried out with simple media in which one essential nutrient in the media is deliberately in short supply. Growth is therefore largely controlled by the supply of this foodstuff. While it is possible to apply these studies to some extent to fermentation of wort, it is unlikely that any one substance is restricting growth throughout the fermentation. With closed fermenters the position is probably rather different; assimilable carbohydrate may be a limiting factor in this case, controlling not only the amount of growth but also the uptake of proline and other amino acids which are not readily assimilated by yeast [56].

The idea of applying continuous culture to brewery fermentations was born in 1892 and the possibility of using high concentrations of yeast was mooted [67]. Equipment for continuous fermentation was patented in Paris in 1899 [68] and in Singapore in 1906 [63]. The latter process is of particular interest because it foreshadowed the cascade systems in which fermentation tanks are connected in series using an open system of fermentation; partly fermented beer cascades from one tank to the next until fermentation is complete.

The recent developments of continuous fermentation in the brewing industry began with a process which involved a number of fermentation tanks connected in series [69]. This cascade system was comparatively slow; it was maintained at low temperatures, and fairly high carbon dioxide pressures were used. Patent specifications for continuous brewery fermentations became common from 1957 onwards, especially ones from New Zealand [70]. The New Zealand method of continuous fermentation is an integral part of a continuous brewing system (Fig. 19.20) and comprises (*i*) a hold-up vessel, (*ii*) two stirred fermenters, and (*iii*) a yeast separator. In the hold-up vessel the wort is aerated and mixed with beer, along with yeast recycled from the first fermenter. The dwell time is about 4 hr and considerable yeast growth occurs. The volume of the hold-up tank is about 230 hl (140 brl) while those of succeeding fermenters are approximately 1637 hl (1000 brl) and 409 hl (250 brl) respectively. The temperature is maintained at 15°C (59°F) and hourly throughput at 68 hl (41·7 brl). Wort of 17·5°P (SG 1072) is fed to the hold-up vessel but dilution with water occurs in the first fermenter to reduce it to the equivalent of 12·9°P (SG 1052). The specific gravity of the beer emerging is 3·1°P (SG 1012) and the total residence time is about 30 hr. Runs of up to one year without closing down the process are achieved [59].

It is unnecessary to recycle yeast if a sedimentary strain of yeast is used. (Fig. 19.19). Very high yeast concentrations may be achieved by the use of inclined tubes, still zones around outlet pipes and by holding the yeast in a filter. Growth of the sedimentary yeast may be controlled by the amount of air injected, while carbon dioxide is used to cause some mixing. Parallel to these developments is the tower fermenter system [58, 61, 71] which comprises a vertical tube into the base of which wort is pumped (Fig. 19.21).

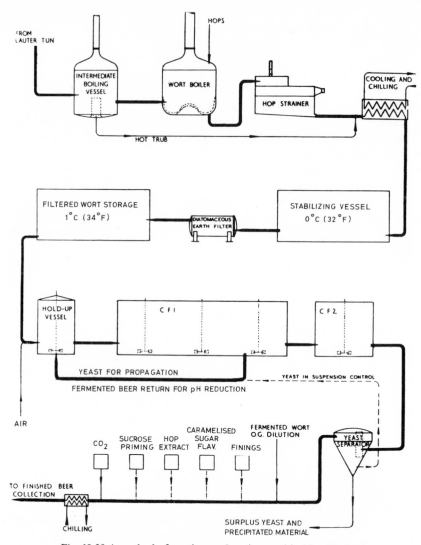

Fig. 19.20 A method of continuous brewing used in New Zealand.

The sedimentary yeast forms a solid plug at the base of the vessel and through it the wort permeates. Some of the yeast is carried upwards by the flow of wort and by the dispersing of the yeast flocs by maltose. Fermentation proceeds as the wort rises, with the rate of wort injection being so adjusted that at the top of the tower the wort is completely fermented. Yeast tends to fall from suspension in this region aided by an inclined chute provided near the beer outflow. Baffles are provided to check yeast being carried up in considerable quantities by large bubbles of carbon dioxide evolved near the base of the tower.

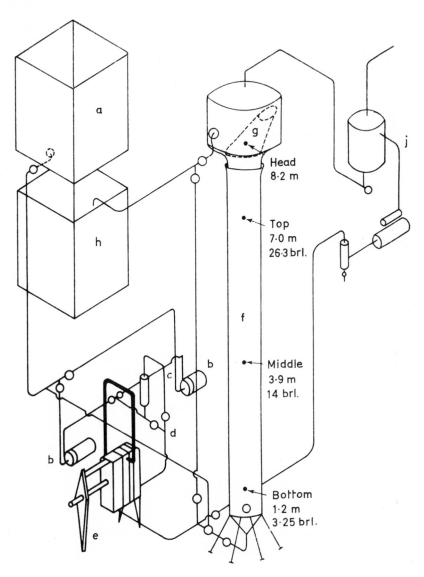

Fig. 19.21 Continuous tower fermenter. (a) Wort-collecting vessels; (b) Impellor-type pump; (c) Flowmeter; (d) Control valve; (e) Flash pasteurizer; (f) Tower; (g) Yeast separator; (h) Beer receiver; (j) CO_2-Collecting vessel.

In systems using high yeast concentrations brought about by trapping the cells, the strains selected have to be highly sedimentary and usually highly flocculent. It is normally not possible to use powdery strains, and adoption of these systems may therefore exclude a yeast strain traditionally used by a particular brewery. As has been mentioned previously it is important to achieve the same crop of yeast as in conventional fermentation if beers from the continuous system have to match those from the conventional plant. Yeast in high concentrations tends to grow slowly and therefore does not abstract from the wort the usual amount of nitrogenous nutrients. It may therefore be necessary to use worts with high levels of fermentable carbohydrate and low concentrations of assimilable nitrogenous compounds in order to obtain beers of normal composition. It is, however, possible to obtain normal yeast crops in a tower fermenter by permitting more yeast to escape from the top of the vessel and operating at high flow rates. There are also dangers with regard to abnormal production of acids, esters, fusel oils and diacetyl but again beers having normal concentrations have been produced. A further difficulty is that the conditions within the tower fermenter are conducive to the development of lactic acid bacteria which are particularly dangerous contaminants in that they spoil the beer and grow very rapidly. If their numbers become too high it may be necessary not only to empty the fermenter but also pasteurize the beer before it receives further processing. Because of the danger of chance infection, the wort entering a continuous fermenter is normally pasteurized in a plate heat-exchanger. Other danger points are sample cocks, the glands of the metering pumps and of the impeller. Further disadvantages include the complexity and expense of the plant and its inflexibility – a rapid change from one type of beer to another is difficult, if not impossible. The performance of tower fermenters is well documented [58]. With a total capacity of approximately 65·4 hl (40 brl) rates of beer production up to 16·4 hl (10 brl) per hour can be achieved. The temperature of the tower shows a gradient with wort entering at the base at 16°C (60°F) and attaining at the top of the tower 21–23°C (70–74°F). A flocculent yeast which sediments well is employed; it is a top-fermentation strain when used in batch fermentation. To start up the tower fermenter, laboratory-grown yeast is propagated within the fermenter under gentle aeration and wort is added in batches over a seven-day period until the vessel is full. Continuous pumping starts slowly at first at 3·27 hl/hr (2 brl/hr) but attains full production rate within a week. Table 19.6 shows the gradient of SG at different levels in the tower (Fig. 19.21). The average amount of yeast produced is about 1·1 kg/hl (4 lb/brl) of pressed yeast.

Recent studies on continuous fermenters [62] and in particular the tower fermenters have identified the main requirements (Table 19.7). High concentrations of yeast promote rapid fermentation but if these concentrations can only be attained using very flocculent or sedimentary yeasts, the system has less commercial attraction. Flexibility is also required with respect to flow rate to accommodate different yeast concentrations and various levels of trade demand for beer. A fermentation gradient involving a progressive transformation of wort to beer over a period of time has also been identified as a desirable feature. A single stirred tank does not achieve this, nor is it fully satisfied in the present tower fermenter where much of the fermentation takes place at the base. Multivessel cascade systems approach this situation and it has been proposed that the tower fermenter would be improved if it were modified by horizontal septa. These septa would create five separate chambers with little back-mixing so that the tower becomes a five vessel cascade system with wort flowing upwards. This establishment of a fermentation gradient gives lower levels of acetate esters and also reduces the difficulties encountered with yeast strains that readily deadapt to maltose fermentation. The latter is particularly relevant where glucose levels in the wort are high.

TABLE 19.6

Gravity gradient in a production tower fermenter operating at different flow-rates [58]

Flow rate		Present gravity (SG − 1000)				
(hl/hr)	(brl/hr)	Bottom	Middle	Top	Head	Effluent
8·2	5	13·0	7·1	6·2	6·2	6·3
9·8	6	16·0	7·8	6·3	6·2	6·3
11·5	7	16.9	8·4	6·5	6·2	6·1
13·1	8	17·3	9·1	6·2	6.1	6·2
14·8	9	19·1	17·6	7·2	6·6	6·6
16·4	10	22·1	17·6	9·1	7·2	7·6

There is considerable difficulty in maintaining normal growth and a population of vigorous young cells in a continuous tower fermenter. This arises chiefly from the requirements of the huge plug of yeast for oxygen and by dissolving oxygen into the inflowing wort, these needs are met in part. Unless yeast growth rates match those of batch fermentations, it is difficult if not impossible to obtain similar beers with respect to flavour and aroma.

Other approaches to continuous fermentation involve the entrapment of yeast so that wort can be passed through a reactor of yeast and be fermented. Immobilization on calcium alginate, wood and other materials has been achieved for a wide variety of yeast strains, including non-flocculent ones. Rather more attention has been paid to the construction of a yeast reactor containing both yeast and kieselguhr [72]. Such a system can be used either for primary fermentation or for biochemically reducing diacetyl present in green beer. The reactor gives 80 % attenuation with less than 2 hr dwell-time. The wort is not aerated and therefore no or little yeast growth occurs, but it is claimed that satisfactory beer is produced.

TABLE 19.7

Requirements for efficient operation of continuous fermentation systems [based on 62]

Operating condition	Reason required	How achieved	Cascade systems	Tower systems
High yeast concentration	Rapid fermentation	Restriction of cells escaping or yeast recycling	No (but maybe by some recycling)	Yes
Correct yeast growth (unit weight produced/unit weight yeast present/hour)	Regulation of mean cell age Maintenance of active culture	Control of cell concentration Control of level of growth	Yes	In part
Selected level of growth (unit weight of yeast/ unit volume of throughput)	Low losses of extract by minimizing cell growth Production of aroma compounds in desired concentrations	Rate of oxygen availability Wort composition adjusted	Yes	Yes
Steady state conditions	Constant flow Trouble free operating Consistent product	Maintenance of constant operating conditions, e.g. temperature	Yes	In part
Fermentation gradient	Avoiding excess ester formation Elimination of unstable conditions	Use of several stirred vessels in series, or long tube, or segmented tower	In part	In part
Good mixing	Maximum efficiency Exposure of cells to maximum substrate levels Elimination of 'stagnant' zones	Adequate agitation, either by stirrer or by gas bubbling	Yes	No

The vessels of continuous fermenters are nearly always full, fermentation times may be lower than 6 hr and there is an even demand on services such as cooling. The highly efficient use of the vessel means that the cost of the fermenter is lower per unit of beer produced than it would be for conventional plant [67]. Ancillary equipment is, however, expensive. A great saving in space arises from the rapid throughput and, in the case of tower fermenters, their shape. The shape of most continuous fermenters makes carbon dioxide collection simple. Continuous runs of 6–18 months are achieved without any emptying and cleaning of the fermenter. Process advantages result if a small crop of the yeast is produced. The losses of hop bittering substances during fermentation are then lower than in conventional processing because less bitter material is adsorbed on to the yeast. Again, the utilization of carbohydrate for ethanol production is higher, with less being transformed into yeast constituents. This means that calculation of original gravity from (*i*) estimations of alcohol and (*ii*) the assumption that the amount of carbohydrate used in the production of yeast cells is equivalent to that in conventional fermentations, leads to a spuriously high result.

The disadvantages of continuous fermenters relate to (*i*) infection, (*ii*) supervision, (*iii*) cost of ancillary equipment and (*iv*) logistics. Infection due to bacteria and wild yeast is likely unless wort is stored hot or chilled. If infection occurs, processing of the beer and starting up again is lengthy and expensive. Supervision of the plant has to be skilled and vigilant. Finally, because wort production and beer processing are not continuous, problems of logistics arise and ancillary equipment such as wort pasteurizers can be relatively expensive.

The development of continuous processing has had a profound effect upon brewery fermentations. Attention was focused on chemical engineering parameters and exact measurements made on rates of fermentation, yeast growth, heat production and generation of flavour components. This has led to enormous studies in batch processing, giving rise to better quality beers in general, more rapid and economical fermentations and lower beer losses. As one authority puts it 'The development of continuous systems has improved brewing science and deepened the understanding of fermentation. Nevertheless the future of continuous fermentation as a production method seems doubtful, [30].

19.6 *Light beer and shandy*
A number of beers are marketed which have a low content of non-fermentable carbohydrate. Where the ethanol content is normal, such beers are usually referred to as 'light' or 'lite' beers but where both ethanol and residual carbohydrate levels are reduced, the beverages may be labelled 'low calorie beers'. A reduction in non-fermentable carbohydrate may be achieved by providing the yeast with a highly fermentative wort. The latter may be produced using high levels of an adjunct that is completely fermentable, e.g. sucrose, or by enhancing amylolysis during mashing. More commonly, manufacture of light beers involves the addition of the fungal enzyme amyloglucosidase (glucamylase) to the fermenter so that both the $\alpha(1,6)$ and $\alpha(1,4)$ links of the non-fermentable carbohydrate are broken. The glucose

produced is readily fermented by the yeast. In practice, fermentation to the attenuation limit takes approximately one day more where amyloglucosidase is added to the fermenter. The only problem which is normally encountered is when the yeast employed is subject to glucose repression, but this is far more serious where high levels of glucose or sucrose are added to wort rather than having gradual release of glucose in the fermenter by amyloglucosidase action.

In the manufacture of shandy in Britain, it is common to produce a 'light' beer using amyloglucosidase and to dilute the beer with lemonade or ginger ale to give a final ethanol content of just below 0·5%v/v. From the point of view of trades description, this is considered non-alcoholic and not subject to excise duty.

REFERENCES

[1] BROCK, T. (1961). *Milestones in Microbiology*, Prentice Hall, Englewood Cliffs, New Jersey.

[2] CHRISTIAN, A. H. R. (1959). *Brewers' Guardian.*, **88**, 43.

[3] PASTEUR, L. (1860). *Annales de Chimie et de Physique*, 3ᵉ serie, **58**, 323.

[4] PASTEUR, L. (1876). *Études sur la bière*, Gauthier-Villars, Paris.

[5] LAUFER, S. and SCHWARZ, R. (1936). *Yeast Fermentation and Pure Culture Systems*, Schwarz Laboratories, New York.

[6] HUDSON, J. R. (1967). *Proc. Eur. Brewery Conv. Congr.*, Madrid, p. 187.

[7] WALKEY, R. J. and KIRSOP, B. H. (1969). *J. Inst. Brewing*, **75**, 393.

[8] HOGGAN, J. (1977). *J. Inst. Brewing*, **83**, 133.

[9] DROST, B. W. (1977). *Proc. Eur. Brewery Conv. Congr.*, Amsterdam, p. 519.

[10] THOMPSON, C. C. and RALPH, D. J. (1967). *Proc. Eur. Brewery Conv. Congr.*, Madrid, p. 177.

[11] HARRIS, G. and MILLIN, D. J. (1963). *Biochem. J.*, **88**, 89.

[12] HOUGH, J. S. (1961). *Proc. Eur. Brewery Conv. Congr.*, Vienna, p. 160.

[13] NORDSTROM, K. (1964). *J. Inst. Brewing*, **70**, 328.

[14] CURTIS, N. S. and CLARK, A. G. (1957). *Proc. Eur. Brewery Conv. Congr.*, Copenhagen, p. 249.

[15] JONES, M. and PIERCE, J. S. (1969). *Proc. Eur. Brewery Conv. Congr.*, Interlaken, p. 151.

[16] HELLIN, T. R. M. and SLAUGHTER, J. C. (1977). *J. Inst. Brewing*, **83**, 17.

[17] MERRITT, N. R. (1967). *J. Inst. Brewing*, **73**, 484

[18] COOTE, N. and KIRSOP, B. H. (1976). *J. Inst. Brewing*, **82**, 149.

[19] MERCIER, P. (1969). *Wallerstein Lab. Commun.*, (4), 15.

[20] FRICKER, R. (1978). *Brewers Guardian*, **107**, (5), 28.

[21] PETERSEN, H. (1969). *Ziemann Information*, No. 6, 26.

[22] VERMEYLEN, J. (1962). *Traité de la fabrication du malt et de la bière*, Vol. 2, Assoc. Roy. des Anciens Élèves de l'Institut Sup. des Fermentation, Gand, Belgium.

[23] MAULE, D. R. (1977). *The Brewer*, **63** (6), 204.

[24] RICKETTS, R. W. (1971). *Modern Brewing Technology* (ed. FINDLAY, E. P. R.), Macmillan, London, p. 83.

[25] STARKIE, G. L. (1974). *Chem. and Ind.*, Feb. 16th, 142.

[26] DE CLERK, J. (1957). *A Textbook of Brewing* (translated by K. BARTON-WRIGHT), Chapman and Hall, London.

[27] MAYFIELD, A. J. (1960). *J. Inst. Brewing*, **66**, 494.

[28] NARZISS, L. (1966). *J. Inst. Brewing*, **72**, 13.

[29] KNUDSEN, F. B. (1977). *The Practical Brewer* (ed. BRODERICK, H. M.), Master Brewers Assoc. Americas, Madison, p. 160.

[30] DROST, B. W. (1979). *Proc. Eur. Brewery Conv. Congr., Berlin*, p. 767.

[31] KIENINGER, H. (1977). *J. Inst. Brewing*, **83**, 72.

[32] MIEDANER, H. (1978). *The Brewer*, **64** (2), 33.

[33] KIENINGER, H. (1975). *Tech. Quart., Master Brewers Assoc. Americas*, **12**, 256.

[34] HLAVCEK, I. (1977). *Tech. Quart., Master Brewers Assoc. Americas*, **14**, 94.

[35] BECKLEY, R. F. (1974). *Inst. Brew. (Aust. and NZ) Proc. 13th Conv.*, 1.

[36] LINDSAY, J. H. and LARSON, J. W. (1975). *Tech. Quart, Master Brewers Assoc., Americas*, **12**, 264.

[37] HAAG, O. G. (1974). *Inst. Brew. (Aust. and NZ) Proc. 13th Conv.*, 81.

[38] AMAHA, M. NAKAKOJI, S. and KOMIYA, Y. (1977). *Proc. Eur. Brewery Conv. Congr., Amsterdam*, p. 545.

[39] MARTIN, S., BOSCH, J., ALMENAR, J. and POSADA, J. (1975). *Proc. Eur. Brewery Conv. Congr., Nice*, p. 301.

[40] KNUDSEN, F. B. (1978). *Tech. Quart. Master Brewers Assoc. Americas*, **15**, 132.

[41] NATHAN, L. (1930). *J. Inst. Brewing*, **36**, 538.

[42] BUTTON, A. H. and WREN, J. J. (1972). *J. Inst. Brewing*, **78**, 443.

[43] HALL, R. D. and EVANS, J. I. (1972). *British Patent*, 1 290 444.

[44] MAULE, D. R. (1976). *The Brewer*, **62** (5), 140.

[45] LADENBURG, K. (1968). *Tech. Quart., Master Brewers Assoc. Americas*, **5**, 81.

[46] AWFORD, B. B. (1977). *Tech. Quart., Master Brewers Assoc. Americas*, **14**, 129.

[47] LINLEY, P. A. (1977). *Brewers Guardian*, **106** (1), 23.

[48] LLOYD-HIND, (1950). *Brewing Science and Practice*, Vol. 2, Chapman and Hall, London.

[49] PAINE, S. W. T. (1948). *J. Inst. Brewing*, **54**, 245.

[50] LASMAN, W. C. (1955). *J. Inst. Brewing*, **61**, 192.

[51] PEARD, G. T. (1955). *J. Inst. Brewing*, **61**, 196.

[52] CHALCRAFT, M. (1978). *The Brewer*, **64** (9), 354.

[53] HLAVACEK, F., KLAZAR, G. and KAHLER, M. (1959). *Brauwissenschaft*, **12**, 10.

[54] HABOUCHA, J., JENARD, H., DEVREUX, A. and MASSCHELEIN, C. A. (1969). *Proc. Eur. Brewery Conv., Interlaken*, p. 241.

[55] AMAHA, M. and TAKEUCHI, M. (1961). *J. Inst. Brewing*, **67**, 339.

[56] WATSON, T. G. and HOUGH, J. S. (1969). *J. Inst. Brewing*, **75**, 359.

[57] PURSSELL, A. J. R. and SMITH, M. T. (1969). *Proc. Eur. Brewery Conv. Congr. Madrid*, p. 155.

[58] AULT, R. G., HAMPTON, A. N., NEWTON, R. and ROBERTS, R. H. (1969). *J. Inst. Brewing*, **75**, 260.

[59] COUTTS, M. W. (1967). *Internat. Brewer and Distiller*, **1** (6), 33.

[60] MALEK, I. (ed.) (1964). *Continuous Cultivation of Micro-organisms Proc. 2nd Symp.*, Czechoslovak Academy of Scienee.

[61] SEDDON, A. W. (1975). *Tech. Quart. Master Brewers Assoc. Americas*, **12**, 130.

[62] PORTNO, A. D. (1973). *Brewers Guardian*, **102** (7), 33.
[63] VAN RIJN, L. A. (1906). *British Patent*, 18 045.
[64] HERBERT, D. (1961). *Continuous Culture of Micro-organisms*, SCI Monograph, No. 12, Soc. Chem. Ind., London, p. 21.
[65] MONOD, J. (1950). *Ann. Inst. Pasteur*, **79**, 390.
[66] NOVICK, A. and SZILARD, L. (1950). *Proc. Natl. Acad Sci., Washington*, **36**, 708.
[67] DELBRÜCK, M. (1892). *Wochshr. Brau.*, **9**, 695.
[68] BARBET, E. (1905). British Patent, 16 233.
[69] WELLHOENER, H. J. (1954). *Brauwelt*, **94**, 44; 624.
[70] COUTTS, M. W. (Dominion Breweries) (1957). *British Patents*, 872 391–872 400.
[71] ROYSTON, M. G. (1966). *Process Biochem.*, **1**, 215.
[72] NARZISS, L. and HELLICH, P. (1972). *Int. Brew. and Distill.*, **6**, 33.
[73] WHITEAR, A. L. and CRABB, D. (1977). *The Brewer*, **63** (2), 60.
[74] HOGGAN, J. unpublished results.

Chapter 20

BEER TREATMENT

20.1 *Introduction*

Beer which has completed primary fermentation is said to be 'green', it contains little carbon dioxide and its taste and aroma are inferior to those of mature beer. The maturation process (sometimes called 'conditioning', 'lagering', or 'ruh storage') is carried out in closed containers, and up to recent times was a process occupying weeks and in some cases, months. Traditionally, maturation involves a secondary fermentation and is brought about by the action of the small charge of yeast remaining in the beer after racking from the fermentation vessels. The yeast attacks either (*i*) fermentable carbohydrates which have escaped degradation in the primary fermentation, (*ii*) small quantities of fermentable carbohydrates added in the form of 'priming sugars', (*iii*) added wort, or (*iv*) added actively fermenting wort, a process called 'krausening'. The carbon dioxide produced largely dissolves in the beer because the vessel is closed, and thus the beer 'comes into condition'. Occasional release of pressure leads to the loss not only of carbon dioxide but also undesirable gases and volatile substances including air, hydrogen sulphide, some diketones, and esters.

Long-term chemical changes also take place in the maturation vessel such as esterification and certain reductions. During the post-fermenting treatment of beer it is necessary to promote clarification of the beer and, by stabilizing treatment, ensure that turbidity due to chemical precipitation or growth of micro-organisms does not occur.

Beer treatment may be considered to involve six processes:

1. Carbonation.
2. Flavour/aroma changes.
3. Additions of colouring and flavouring materials (see Chapter 23).
4. Stabilization against non-biological haze and flavour change (see Chapter 22).
5. Clarification.
6. Biological stabilization (see Chapter 21)

20.2 *Cask beers* (*conditioned and fined in cask*) [1]

The oldest processes involve oak casks with storage for long periods, preferably at 12–15°C (54–59°F) during which there is controlled venting.
Venting or release of fermentation gases is controlled by the use of porous
and non-porous wooden plugs called 'spiles'. Rapid release of gas is permitted
by removing the spile; a porous spile in position permits slow escape of gas
through the microscopic vessels and tracheids of its structure. A non-porous
spile is constructed so that the run of the grain of the wood virtually prevents
gas diffusing through. With the advent in the UK of weaker beers (particularly
after 1939) there were demands for brilliantly clear beers, and because of
increasing costs of storage, more complex and rapid procedures for cask beer
evolved. Only in Britain is there still a substantial volume of cask-conditioned
beer. It was rapidly being replaced by brewery-conditioned keg beer until some
10 years ago when its popularity was restored. However wooden casks are
rare, most casks being constructed of aluminium. The advantages of cask-
conditioned beers to the consumer is that they tend to be rich in flavour and
low in carbon dioxide. Their advantages to the brewer include the low costs
of equipment and energy involved in the production of cask-conditioned
beers. Disadvantages of this kind of beer include its variability, its proneness
to infection if consumed slowly and the skill and time that the publican has
to devote to it.

Beer is racked either directly from fermenting vessels or via racking backs
into casks. This is done when fermentation is judged sufficiently complete and
when the correct charge of yeast is present (0·25–4·00 million cells/ml).
Various additions may be made at this stage including (*i*) priming sugars of
approximately 34°P (SG 1150) at 0·35–1·75 l/hl (1–5 pints/brl) and (*ii*) hops,
hop pellets at 8·5–49 g/hl (0·5–3·0 oz/brl) or lupulin at about 5–10% this rate,
(*iii*) isinglass finings to promote clarification and formation of beer foam, and
(*iv*) potassium metabisulphite which is a bacteriostat at pH values below 4·2.
The finings are added at 0·36–1·08 l/hl (1–3 pints/brl) either in the racking
back, in the cask at the same time as the primings, or at any stage up to
putting the cask on stillage at the public house (stillage is merely wood or
metal for supporting the barrel in a horizontal position for dispense). Settling
of the finings requires 2–20 hr, depending on the yeast strain.

The beer is stored at the brewery for widely varying periods, often seven
days or even less, preferably at a temperature between 13–16°C (55–60°F). If
too much yeast is suspended in the beer or the temperature too high, the
secondary fermentation may be too violent. When the casks are vented the beer
foam gushes out of the cask and is lost. If too little yeast is present in the
beer, secondary fermentation is too slow and insufficient carbon dioxide is
dissolved in the beer at dispense. The volume of finings used depends on the
amount of yeast present in the cask (see p. 698 *et seq.*)

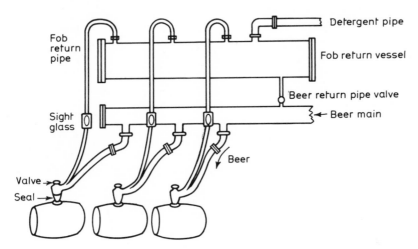

Fig. 20.1 A typical racking back for a traditional ale brewery.

In recent years there have been several developments in the production of traditional cask beer. The racking backs may be pressurized either with carbon dioxide or air, and beer led into the cask through counterpressure fillers. The fillers automatically stop the flow of beer when the cask is full; the cask is pressurized at a level like that of the racking backs into which all fob or excess beer in the filler is returned (Fig 20.1). A further development is the use of amyloglucosidase (or more rarely fungal α-amylase) as a complete or partial replacement of primings [2]. The enzyme degrades unfermentable dextrins and both $\alpha(1\rightarrow4)$ and $\alpha(1\rightarrow6)$ linkages may be severed to produce fermentable sugars, notably maltose and glucose. The evolution of the sugars is controlled by the amount of enzyme added, the temperature and the spectrum of dextrins present. Because time and temperature are variable in storage, the method leads to problems of gas content in the beer. Yeast present in the cask ferments some of the sugar produced, but that remaining contributes to sweetness. Another development is the use of cylinders of carbon dioxide in the dispense of cask beer. The cask is subjected to a top-pressure of carbon dioxide and beer is thus gently blown out of the cask into the dispense beer mains. Alternatively, a small top-pressure of carbon dioxide is maintained on the cask contents and beer is induced to flow by a centrifugal pump through the beer pipe to the dispense tap. One brewery company has run traditional ale into kegs (vessels with a single outlet) rather than the traditional cask which has two (Fig. 20.2). The fined yeast and hop material is retained in the keg by the use of a small plastic filter which enshrouds the spear or extractor. Casks are washed using equipment depicted in Fig. 20.3.

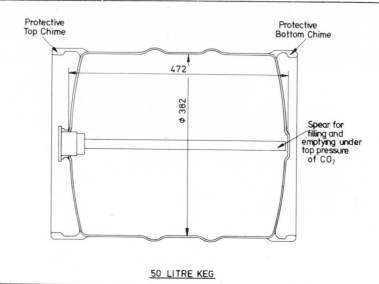

50 LITRE KEG

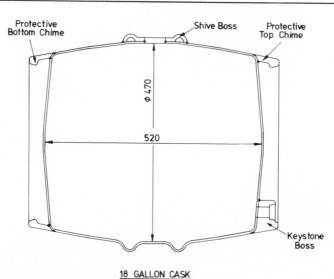

18 GALLON CASK

Fig. 20.2 Vertical sections of typical aluminium keg and cask. (Courtesy of Alumasc Ltd.)

High quality beers were traditionally treated with dry hops; normally Golding hops or other hops with an excellent 'nose' were added at racking to the cask. The hops gave excellent aroma to the beer but washing out the spent hops completely from emptied casks was difficult. Hop pellets, enriched hop powder, or lupulin have replaced normal dry hops in some breweries but in

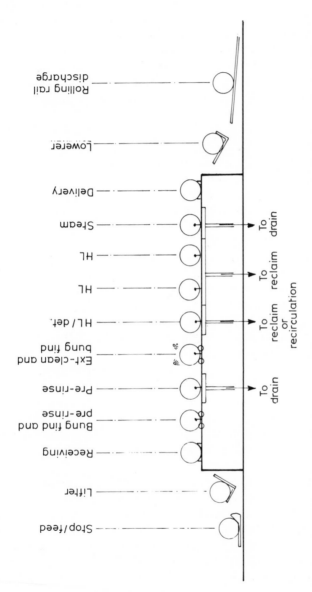

Fig. 20.3 Typical cask washing equipment: Nine station indexing chain machine, with vertically moving centre beam. HL is hot water (liquor). Det. refers to detergent applied to outside of cask. Maximum output 240 brl/hr. Pressure jets give 1000 psig (66.7 bar). (Courtesy of Porter Lancastrian Ltd.)

other instances, the aroma arising from essential oils of hops is provided by direct addition of hop oil or emulsion of essential oils of hops (Chapter 13).

In order to remove beer from the cask, a tap must be hammered into the recess of the keystone plug. The tap is left partly open during this operation so that air is not forced into the beer; it is of course closed again when firmly in position. In order that the finings may resettle, the taps are normally driven in 24–48 hr before the beer is required. When about a quarter of the beer has been withdrawn, the cask is very gently tilted by lifting the rear end of the cask. Either a mechanical tilting device is used or wedges (thralls) are employed.

20.3 Conditioning in bottle

In the past many beers were racked from wooden casks into bottles and the various maturation and clarification processes continued within the bottles. With a few notable exceptions beers are not now produced in this way. Beers conditioned in bottle have a sediment and tend to have distinctive flavours and aromas.

20.4 Beer conditioned in brewery tanks [3, 4]

There are many ways of maturing beers destined for bulk delivery, keg, bottled or canned product, but there is a universal tendency to reduce the time required. In this connection it has been estimated that between 25–40% of the capital required for building a new brewery would be used for providing beer conditioning and storage [4]. Bottom-fermented beers have by tradition a secondary fermentation at temperatures which fall from 10 to 0°C (50 to 32°F). Under these conditions, yeast, cold break, and chill haze tend to settle and subsequent clarification is thereby made simpler. The secondary fermentation used to require months and subsequent cold storage also needed long periods. Now the time involved varies very much from brewery to brewery, on the original gravity of the wort from which the beer was derived, and on the shelf-life required of the beer, but has generally been cut to about 7–28 days.

Although many breweries have achieved satisfactory results by simply reducing the period of lagering to say 21 days, others have found it necessary to modify the process because the flavour changes required were incomplete (Fig. 20.4). In particular, the need to reduce the level of vicinal diketones in the packaged product has led to a period of warm conditioning, sometimes called ruh storage or 'diacetyl rest'. This period of a few days at 14–16°C (57–61°F) encourages the oxidative decarboxylation of α-acetohydroxy acids to vicinal dike ones, followed by reduction to the corresponding diols (see Chapter 17). Essentially it involves intense yeast activity to carbonate the beer, purge undersirable volatiles, reduce many compounds chemically (hence the trade name 'Redox' for one process) and to take up all dissolved oxygen. This leads not only to immediate improvement in flavour and aroma but also to flavour stability. The cylindrical tanks used are either vertical or horizontal and may be constructed of (*i*) stainless steel, (*ii*) mild steel with glass, enamel, or plastic (phenolic epoxy-resin) linings, or less often (*iii*) aluminium. They are usually of 100–500 hl (61–305 brl) but the vertical ones may be as large as 5700 hl (3500 brl) capacity. Conditioning tanks are normally fitted with impellors for mixing, with attemporator jacket or coils and with devices for maintaining a selected gas pressure – usually up to 1·4 bar gauge pressure (20 lb/in²). Implosion (antivacuum) devices are fitted (Fig. 20.5). Unitanks used for both fermentation and maturation are vertical cylindrical tanks with shallow conical bases. The height is usually equal to the diameter and the capacity may be as much as 7000 hl (4300 brl). Alternatively vertical cylindroconical tanks similar to those used in fermentation (Chapter 19) may be used. Conical bases make cleaning of vessels much easier.

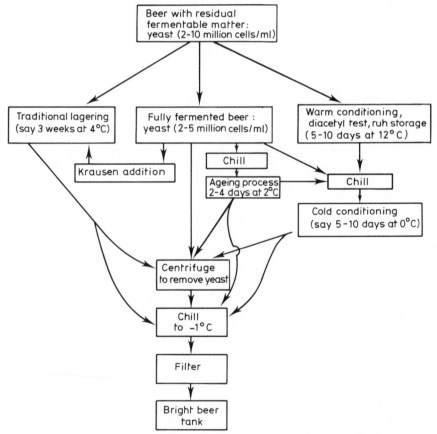

Fig. 20.4 An outline of the relationship between various post-fermentation systems. Despite the complexity of the diagram it is not entirely comprehensive of all systems practised.

In Table 19.3 and Fig. 20.4 details are given of maturation processes including traditional lagering, the use of krausen in lagering, the use of pressure in high temperature fermentation and maturation systems and finally 'ageing' systems. In the latter, it is essential to ferment the beer completely, leaving no residual fermentable extract at the end of primary fermentation. Furthermore there must be every opportunity before transfer to ageing tank for the oxidative decarboxylation of α-acetohydroxy acids, using relatively high fermentation temperatures and sufficient time for this process (see Chapter 17). Ageing as a process varies in detail from one brewery to another but typically involves holding fully fermented beer for 3–6 days in the presence of yeast (2–4 million cells/ml) with the temperature falling progressively from 13°C (55°F) to 0°C (32°F). In Britain, some beers receive no post-fermentation treatment in contact with yeast. These beers are centrifuged as they are emptied from the fermenter.

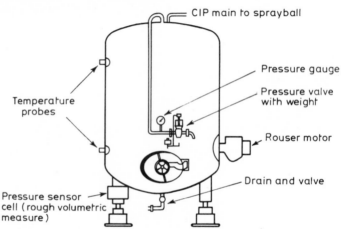

Fig. 20.5 A typical vertical maturation tank.

When the diacetyl rest, ruh storage, or warm conditioning is complete, the beer is chilled to —1 to 1°C (31–34°F) by the use of a plate heat-exchanger between warm and cold conditioning tanks. Alternatively the beer may be chilled within the tank used for warm conditioning by having the exchanger in a loop of pipework or by using attemperators. During the chilling operation of beer containing or free of yeast, the level of carbon dioxide dissolved in the beer may be increased by artificial carbonation (Fig. 20.6). This takes advantage of the turbulence of the beer as it passes through the plate heat-exchanger and also the final low temperature.

Considerable care has to be taken not to get more carbon dioxide into the beer than specification permits; it is difficult to reduce carbon dioxide levels without creating froth or fob. If this has to be achieved then bubbling nitrogen gas (oxygen free) through the beer is probably the best approach. Where beer has to have a shelf-life of several months, great care is taken not to reintroduce air after conditioning. Another consideration is that overcarbonating in no way reduces the uptake of oxygen if beer is exposed to air. This uptake is primarily a function of the difference in partial pressures between the beer and the air in contact with it. Furthermore, it is important that there is little turbulence of beer during its movement. Turbulence, particularly in air, causes the beer to (i) lose its carbon dioxide, (ii) become oxidized, and (iii) reduces its shelf-life and its foaming potential because of the intensive chemical actions occurring at the gas-liquid interfaces.

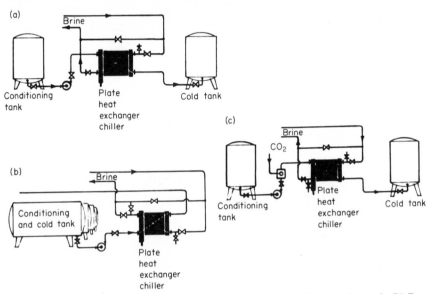

Fig. 20.6 Refrigeration of beer by plate heat-exchanger (a) Chilling 'on the run'; (b) Recirculation; (c) Carbonation and chilling 'on the run'.

Movement from one tank to another is sometimes encouraged by applying top-pressure of carbon dioxide to the donor tank after the mains and recipient tank have been filled with the same gas. But carbon dioxide is expensive and economies are achieved by exploiting the high density of the gas Thus a thin blanket of carbon dioxide may be readily produced above the beer in the donor tank, and a top-pressure of air used to move the beer out of the tank. A small amount of carbon dioxide may be injected into the main as the beer passes to the recipient tank, in such a way that it readily escapes as a gas when the beer enters the tank. Again a thin blanket of carbon dioxide covers the beer, this time in the recipient tank. As the tank fills, the air within it is displaced upwards. Alternatively a recipient tank is filled first with deaerated water which is discharged by top pressure of carbon dioxide. When the tank receives the beer, the carbon dioxide is recovered in a gas balloon. Further information on carbon dioxide saturation is given on p. 735 *et seq.*

During maturation, there is a deposition of yeast and trub. This is enhanced by various additions which may be made at this stage such as isinglass finings or tannic acid. When the conditioning vessel is emptied these solids usually remain. It may be that entrained with them is sufficient beer to warrant recovery so that slurrying the solids would be avoided. In any case slurrying and disposing the slurry to drain is expensive in terms of both water use and effluent costs. However, to remove the tank bottoms manually also presents a problem because the carbon dioxide in the vessel is difficult to exhaust. The concentration of the gas must be lower than 0·5% v/v and two people must be present for safe working conditions.

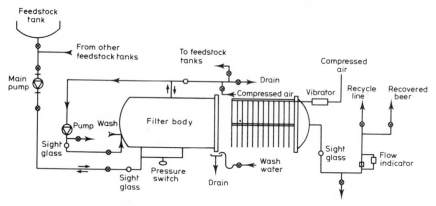

Fig. 20.7 Typical flow-line diagram of an open mud discharge (OMD) filter system.

New forms of filter have become available recently which are effective in recovering beer from tank bottoms and spent kieselguhr (diatomaceous earth) powder even when the solids content is 30% v/v (Fig. 20.7). The equipment comprises a horizontal tank fitted with vertical circular filter leaves, each covered with heavy-weight synthetic fibre textile septa. The leaves are mounted into side drainage manifolds so as to promote the discharge of the filter cake. Feedstock slurry is pumped into the filter to fill it, there is then recirculation to build up a cake on the septa, followed by normal continuous flow of the feedstock until the space (5 cm, 2 in) between the septa is completely filled. Prior to discharge, the cake is compressed and dewatered by air pressure exerted on impermeable elastomeric diaphragms mounted opposite each leaf face. The cake is discharged by opening up the filter and vibrating the leaves. Alternative equipment includes rotary vacuum filters or self-cleaning centrifuges. (Figs 20.8, 20.9 and 20.12). The rotary vacuum filters are often used to recover beer from surplus yeast after primary fermentation. In the UK, the yeast is sold for yeast extracts and for whisky manufacture.

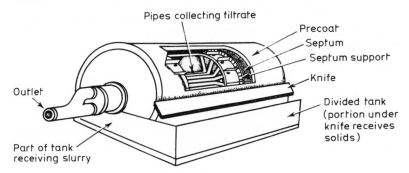

Fig. 20.8 Rotary vacuum filter.

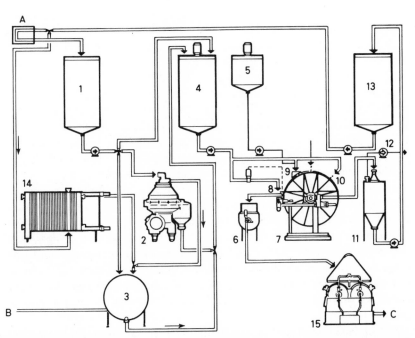

Fig. 20.9 A beer and yeast recovery system. 1. Fermenter; 2. Beer clarifier; 3. Surge tank; 4. Yeast suspension tank; 5. Filter aid mixer; 6. Yeast (autolysis) tank; 7. Rotary vacuum filter; 8. Top feed applicator; 9. Precoat applicator; 10. Yeast suspension spray; 11. Defoamer; 12. Vacuum pump; 13. Beer recovery tank; 14. Pasteurizer; 15. Yeast drier; A. Wort preparation; B. Beer treatment; C. Dried yeast. (Based on drawing of Alfa-Laval Ltd.)

20.5 *Beer Clarification*

Beer tends to be considerably more stable with respect to flavour when some yeast is suspended in it. This is mainly because the yeast promotes strongly reducing conditions. This applies to a lesser degree when yeast is sedimented by finings and remains in contact with the beer. Total removal of yeast should only be effected when the beer is virtually ready for packaging. The clarification of beer may be achieved by one or more of the following methods: (*i*) finings, (*ii*) centrifuging, and (*iii*) filtering.

20.5.1 FINING [5–7]

Isinglass finings comprise dried swim-bladders of selected fishes (less commonly the gills) which have been soaked and dissolved for up to six weeks in dilute solutions of cold tartaric and sulphurous acids [4]. The turbid, colourless, viscous solution so produced consists of (*i*) solubilized collagen, (*ii*) gelatine (which is a denaturation product of collagen), and (*iii*) some insoluble material. Only the solubilized collagen contributes to the fining action. This action occurs because of its molecular configuration and positive electrical charge. Insoluble particles do increase the viscosity and therefore total viscosity is not a reliable guide to the efficiency of batches of finings [5]. Round Saigon and Long Saigon finings are examples of excellent material with low overall viscosity. Breweries may purchase either solutions from finings manufacturers or shredded swim-bladders ready for acid soaking.

Larger molecules of solubilized collagen are likely to be more effective than smaller molecules in finings. They will probably (*i*) have more charged sites per molecule and therefore react more readily with negatively charged material, and (*ii*) protrude from yeast cells and create bridges between cells. The molecules have both positive and negative charges but the overall charge is positive at the pH of beer. They react very effectively therefore with yeast cells whose overall charge is negative, with negatively charged proteins, and also react to some extent with positively-charged proteins [6]. In addition they will take up lipids and antifoams (see Chapter 19).

Specimens of finings do not appear to differ from each other significantly with regard to total charge and charge distribution, but the constituent molecules do differ significantly in size and size distribution. The size distribution is a function of the ease with which collagen is broken down by acid and to the survival of aggregates held together by weak physical or chemical forces [5].

The collagen molecule is made up of three coiled polypeptide chains (coiled around each other) forming a long, fairly rigid rod of 1·5 nm diameter. The coils of the individual chains are given frequent sharp twists due to the presence of adjacent imino acids, proline, and hydroxyproline. The total content of hydroxyl groupings is high and therefore there is strong hydrogen bonding between the three chains (and hydrogen bonding may also occur between the chains and appropriate substances in beer). Young tissues contain monomers of 300 nm length and have molecular weights of about 300 000 (in old tissues, the molecules are more complex because of polymerization).

The molecular size of the soluble component of finings can be assessed by measuring the so-called intrinsic viscosity [5].

$$\text{Intrinsic viscosity } [\eta] = KM\alpha$$

where K is a constant, depending on the particular solute solvent system, M is the average molecular weight, and α is a constant dependent on molecular shape and rigidity – for insinglass α is approximately 2,

$$\therefore \sqrt{\eta} = KM$$

Intrinsic viscosities for finings are high compared with the average for proteins. They have been calculated for many samples of finings and some examples are shown in Table 20.1. With easily fined beer, where $[\eta]$ in citrate solution needs to be over 16 to achieve its purpose, various types of isinglass show little difference in response. With beer which is more difficult to fine and where $[\eta]$ of the finings needs to exceed 20, differences between the performance of different types of isinglass finings are readily seen.

TABLE 20.1

Comparison of finings prepared by procedure No. 1 from different forms of isinglass [5]

Type of leaf	Form	Source	Soluble nitrogen % (A)*	Soluble collagen % (B)*	Intrinsic viscosity $[\eta]$ (dl/g)
Karachi	Shredded	C	78	96	21·9
	Flock	C	80	86	15·4
Brazil lump	Shredded	C	84	93	18·7
	Flock	C	81	97	18·2
	Shredded	A	93	95	20·2
	Ribbon	A	54	79	10·6
Long Saigon	Shredded	C	57	92	2·6
	Flock	C	62	87	16·5
	Shredded	A	98	93	22·9
Round Saigon	Shredded	A	97	94	26·5
Saigon	Ribbon	A	34	59	11·9
Purse	Shredded	C	83	93	18.1
	Flock	C	80	87	17·4
Indian pipe	Shredded	C	57	91	21·4
	Flock	C	59	89	19·6
Penang character	Shredded	A	20	98	16·8
	Ribbon	A	18	56	9·3

* Proportion of 'effective' finings derived from isinglass $= \dfrac{A \times B}{100}$ %.

The temperature at which the collagen fibres show abrupt shrinkage and the temperature at which half the collagen is denatured in a fixed time, provide other measurements that are useful in characterizing different samples. The first temperature indicates when both intra- and intermolecular forces holding the fibres together have been overcome by the thermal agitation of the molecules. The second is a reflection of the breakdown of the intramolecular bonds. Isinglass finings must have reasonable stability at ambient temperatures for draught cask beer; for other types of beer they are usually added at lower temperatures. Finings are stored at temperatures between 4–10°C (39–50°F) and seriously deteriorate in a few hours at 25–30°C (77–86°F). For reasons not properly understood, finings work poorly if the temperature of the beer is falling.

The reaction between finings and brewers' yeast is seriously retarded by cations of salts, those of higher valency inhibiting more effectively the reaction. The best pH level for fining action is 4·4, but at 4·0 the reaction is almost as good. The reaction leads to the aggregation of yeast cells and finings and the larger particles so formed sink more readily, as postulated by Stokes' Law.

$$V = \frac{2r^2 (S - S_2) g}{9\eta}$$

where V is the settling rate, r is the radius of the particle, S is the density of the particle, S_2 the density of the surrounding medium, η the viscosity coefficient of the medium, and g the gravitational constant. Rapid settling is important but, particularly for cask beers, the production of a compact coagulum is essential. Otherwise, this coagulum (the lees) will rise into the beer with every minor disturbance caused by convection or by drawing beer off from the cask.

Some beers do not clarify satisfactorily by simple treatment with isinglass finings. This may be due to using too little or too much finings. The yeast may have a relatively small negative charge, or the concentration of yeast may be too high – say over 2 million cells/ml. Again, the poor fining action may be caused by an excess of positively charged colloidal material in the beer. In the last instance, auxiliary finings, derived from alginates, carrageenin, or silicic acid and having a negative charge, are added to the beer in carefully predetermined amounts before normal finings, in order to precipitate the positively charged colloids [7]. If possible, the flocs produced with the auxiliary finings should be separated before isinglass finings are added.

The use of finings is not universal and finds its widest employment in Britain, but there is renewed interest in North America. It has a secondary but important benefit in improving the foam-stability of many beers by removing fats and other foam-negative material. The finings are themselves foam-forming. Another important use of finings is to spare filter media by removing material from beer before it is pumped to the filter. Accordingly filter runs may be extended significantly. Increasingly in Britain, clarification is partly accomplished by centrifugation so that yeast concentration can readily be adjusted to achieve efficient fining.

Gelatin derived from alkaline degradation of slaughter-house by-products is used in some American breweries for clarification of beer. Its action is similar to that of finings but it is slower and less effective; five days is required to clarify a large conditioning tank. One large US company adds beechwood chips to conditioning tanks to promote clarification and flavour maturation of their beers.

20.5.2 CENTRIFUGATION [8]

It follows from Stokes' Law that settling speed can be enhanced by increasing the particle size, by increasing the gravitational force applied and by increasing the differential density between the particle and the medium. Alteration of the last is rarely applicable in brewing and the same applies to adjusting the viscosity coefficient. Nevertheless, the following parameters may by usefully varied: (*i*) particle size adjustment is employed in fining and exploited when yeast flocculates and (*ii*) gravitational force may be augmented

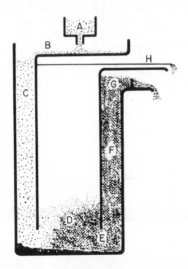

Fig. 20.10 Balanced column tank for separating two liquids, indicating a principle used in centrifuges. The efficiency of the process depends on the rate of flow, the settling rate of the heavier liquid, and the dimensions of the tank. (A) Mixed liquids; (B) Trough containing mixed liquids; (C) Inlet passage to main tank; (D) Main tank body where separation occurs; (E) Opening to outlet column; (F) Column taking the heavier liquid; (G) Overflow for the heavier liquid; (H) Overflow for the lighter liquid. (Based on drawing of Alfa-Laval Ltd.)

by centrifugation. Sedimentation can be completed more rapidly if the settling distance is reduced and such reduction is an important feature of centrifuges. If, for instance, a solid separates at the rate of one unit distance/hr and it takes five hours to clarify liquid in a tank of five units depth, when horizontal trays stacked at single unit intervals of depth are put in the tank, clarification is completed in one hour.

Continuous separation is feasible with the balanced column tank shown in Fig. 20.10 either of particles from a liquid, or of two liquids differing in density. If such a balanced tank is rotated about its vertical axis, centrifugal force can be used to supplement gravitational force.* In this way the centrifuge was developed. To exploit the principle referred to in the previous paragraph of using horizontal trays, conical discs representing tiers of trays are inserted in certain types of centrifuge. Four main kinds of centrifuge are to be found in breweries, namely:

1. Cylindrical bowl clarifiers, mainly confined to small breweries for clarification of wort (Fig. 20.11). Throughput is up to 107 hl/hr (65 brl/hr).

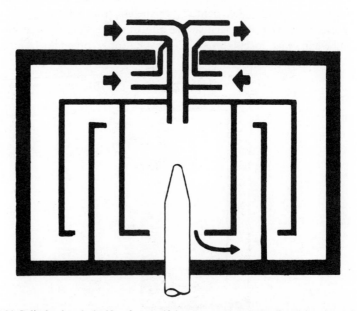

Fig. 20.11 Cylinder bowl clarifier for clarifying wort. The sludge bowl has large holding capacity and hot break is well packed. Centrifugal force increases as the suspension moves to the more peripheral chambers. (Based on drawing of Alfa-Laval Ltd.)

* Force developed in kg = 0·104 [weight of loaded centrifuge head × radius of head (mm) × rev/min²].

2. Self-cleaning clarifiers, in which the solids are discharged at intervals while the centrifuge is operating at full-speed (Fig. 20.12). They are available for both wort and beer clarification with throughputs of up to 600 hl/hr (370 brl/hr). The same machines used for beer recovery from fermenters and tank bottoms operate at up to 40 hl/hr (25 brl/hr). Many of these machines used for beer treatment are hermetically sealed so that neither carbon dioxide is lost nor oxygen taken up.

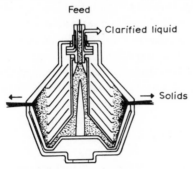

Fig. 20.12 Self-cleaning clarifier.

3. Nozzle clarifiers, in which the solids are discharged through a nozzle when the speed of rotation is allowed to fall. They are used for clarifying rough beer from fermenting vessels or racking tanks. Throughput is up to 492 hl/hr (300 brl/hr). They have largely been superseded by the self-cleaning clarifiers.
4. Decanter clarifiers. These are used for clarifying worts and beers containing high contents of yeast or trub, for instance beer recovery from fermenter or tank bottoms where the solids concentration is as high as 60 % by volume (Fig. 20.13). Throughput is up to 40 hl/hr (25 brl/hr).

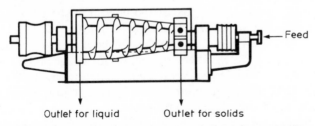

Fig. 20.13 Decanter centrifuge. (Based on drawing of Alfa-Laval Ltd.)

The advantages of centrifuges are: (*i*) small requirement for space, (*ii*) they can be sterilized and maintained sterile, (*iii*) there is no requirement for kieselguhr of other filter aids, (*iv*) using hermetic clarifiers there is no contact with air, (*v*) there is no removal of material by adsorption to active surfaces, and (*vi*) in self-cleaning clarifiers and nozzle clarifiers, it is possible to operate continuously for an indefinite period. The self-discharging clarifiers operate by the spinning bowl separating momentarily at the rim into two parts so that the solids are ejected. In so doing, the speed of rotation falls somewhat but is quickly restored. Some of these clarifiers eject on a predetermined time basis; such machines are simpler and less troublesome than the more sophisticated self-sensing type. The latter use a hydraulic differential pressure system for sensing the accumulation of solids in the bowl, or alternatively use a photo-electric scanner on the discharge lines. It is desirable with all the self-discharging clarifiers to get a reasonably constant concentration of solids in the feed. Balance tanks help to achieve this.

Disadvantages of centrifuges include (*i*) the high cost of electrical energy to operate them and (*ii*) excessive noise so that machines are often operated remotely when frequent visual inspection would be desirable. The most sophisticated machines are costly and complex; spares, maintenance and repair may pose problems. During centrifugation, the beer is raised in temperature by say 3°C (5°F) and may require rechilling. Yeast recovered from a centrifuge is often inferior for repitching purposes than yeast collected by other methods available.

20.5.3 FILTRATION [9–12]

In order for filtration to have its maximum effect it is necessary to chill beer as much as is practicable. The lower the temperature, the more cold trub and chill haze will form; fine filtration will remove this material providing that the beer temperature does not rise in the filter itself. Some breweries consider that better results are obtained if the beer is cooled gradually and held at low temperatures for at least several hours. Many are satisfied, on the grounds of economy and convenience, to flash-cool the beer immediately prior to filtration. Without using a scraper-chiller that some wine bottlers employ, considerable care has to be exercised to prevent the beer freezing because of local over-cooling. In practice, beers of 8–12°P (SG 1032–1048) are chilled to the range 0°C (32°F) to −1°C (30·2°F) while higher gravity beers may be chilled to −2°C (28·4°F). There is therefore advantage in this respect in high gravity brewing. With respect to the clarity of beer emerging, this must be less than 0·5° EBC and there must be no significant loss of colour, extract, bitterness, and foaming ability. Care must be taken not to introduce oxygen; many filtration steps increase the dissolved oxygen level by 0·2 to 2 mg/l.

In 1850 a study was made of eddyless flow of liquid in capillary tubes and the following relationship was revealed:

$$V = \frac{Pgr^4}{8LM}$$

where V is the velocity of flow, P is the pressure differential, g is the gravitational constant, r is the internal capillary radius, L is the length of the tube, and M is the viscosity of the liquid. It is interesting that the radius of the capillary tubes has a profound effect upon the pressure differential, all other things being constant. For instance, by reducing the radius to an eighth, the pressure differential has to be increased 4000-fold to achieve the same velocity. This relationship has obvious application to filtration where the fine pores in the filter correspond to the capillaries, but the relationship is not a very close one.

A further study made in 1856 applies more directly to filters and gave the relationship:

$$Q = \varphi \frac{PA}{LM}$$

where Q is the flow rate in ml/s, φ is the permeability factor, P is the pressure differential in dyn/cm^2, A is the area of the filter medium in cm^2, M is the viscosity of liquid in poises, and L is the thickness of the filter medium in cm. One may therefore increase throughput by increasing φ – a question of the composition of the filter material. Alternatively, the applied pressure may be increased, the filter area may be increased, the filter thickness may be decreased or the liquid viscosity decreased. (The latter may usually be brought about by increasing the temperature.) Normal sheet filters do more than sieve, they also adsorb material. Thus yeasts and bacteria fail to penetrate sheets whose mean pore size should permit it. This is because the fibres hold the negatively charged micro-organisms electrostatically. Naturally, if the flow rate is increased too much, the pressure forces the micro-organisms off the fibres and through the pores. For this reason, pressure differentials not exceeding 0·7 bar on fine filters are maintained. (Coarse filters are capable of removing larger suspended particles from the beer and although they deplete any bacterial or yeast population in the beer, the removal is usually not complete. Fine or polishing filters remove all suspended particles remaining after coarse filtration.) When the normal range of pressure differentials are exceeded, the sheets are cleaned by back-washing or are replaced. Steam (less than 0·6 bar) may be passed through the filter sheets fitted between the filter-plates of a frame press, and thus sterilize them. Many breweries rely on sterilized fine sheet filters to remove all micro-organisms from the beer prior to bottling.

The standard filter sheet in breweries is 60 × 62 cm (approx. 23·6 × 24·4 in) and the largest is normally 100 × 100 cm (39·4 × 39·4 in). Some large single-ended filter presses have 240 filter-plates which permit an hourly flow rate of about 120 hl/hr (73 brl/hr). Such small throughput capacity means that sheet filtration has lost popularity except for second stage filtration in which they are designed to polish and in some cases sterile-filter. Considerable attention has recently been paid to the design of filter-plates so as to ensure that the maximum area of filter sheet is presented to the beer (Fig. 20.14). Ribbed and rifled aluminium alloy plates have given way to stainless-steel plates with expanded metal inserts acting as sheet supports and even more recently to stainless-steel plates with deeply corrugated inserts as supports. Flow-rates are in the range $0.8–2.0$ hl/m²/hr, depending on the retentivity of the sheet.

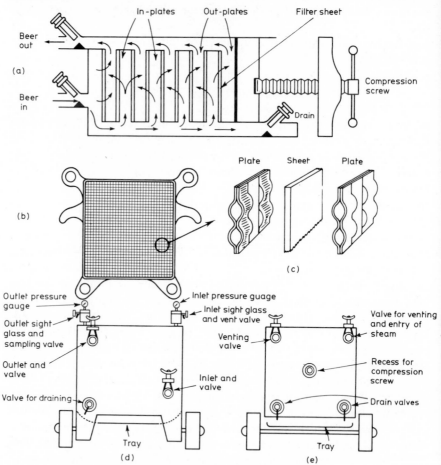

Fig. 20.14 Details of a sheet filter. (a) Vertical section; (b) Single plate front view; (c) Relationship between plates and sheets; (d) Control end of machine; (e) Compression end.

The first sheet filters for use in breweries were made of a mixture of cellulose and asbestos fibres but kieselguhr has been represented as a third constituent for the last fifty years. Filter sheets are not made to constant composition but to constant filtration performance. The constituent materials afford the possibility of a wide range of performance because fibres of asbestos may be altered in length and specific surface, the cellulose modified by wetting the fibre, and the kieselguhr varied in particle size (Fig. 20.15 and Table 20.2).

TABLE 20.2

Grades of filter sheet relating to Fig. 20.15 [11]

Grade	Average density	Permeability	Mean pore size	Water output $(l/hr/m^2)$
EKS2	0·352	0·00744	10·0	560
EKS	0·344	0·00713	13·7	750
EK	0·322	0·01116	15·4	1100
S10	0·320	0·01069	18·5	1400
S9	0·294	0·02433	27·3	2150
8	0·300	0·03441	24·8	2200
7	0·304	0·03131	24·6	2500
7A	0·297	0·03177	23·6	2900
6	0·282	0·05812	37·0	3400
6A	0·291	0·08137	29·2	3400
6B	0·309	0·05874	22·2	2400
5	0·279	0·08773	32·9	3750
5A	0·271	0·3278	39·2	5000
4	0·263	0·1219	38·0	4600
3	0·264	0·5133	40·6	6000
2	0·243	0·8900	47·2	6600
2A	0·235	0·3376	39·3	5600
1	0·238	1·3950	42·2	8000
1A	0·224	1·6290	48·9	8000
0	0·216	1·6290	58·5	8000

Two major developments have occurred in sheet manufacture. The first relates to concern about the carcinogenic properties of certain types of asbestos. In Britain, although most wines and spirits are now filtered through sheets free of asbestos, such replacement has been slower in the case of beers. Alternatives to charged asbestos fibres include aluminium oxide fibres and zirconium oxide fibres. A second development has been the incorporation of insoluble polyvinyl pyrrolidone (PVPP) into the sheet material which adsorbs phenolic materials from the beer, especially the tannin materials associated with beer haze. The PVPP can be regenerated by washing the sheet in a 0·5 % solution of sodium hydroxide at ambient temperatures.

Prior to the introduction of filter sheets, many breweries used cellulosic pulp filters or 'filter mass'. A small number of breweries still use them for rough filtration and remarkable strides have been made in reducing the manpower required to maintain them. The pulp is compressed by the breweries into circular thick pads which are fitted into a type of filter frame.

Filtration is achieved by the thickness of the pads and the tortuous path that beer has to take through the fibre. When the pressure required to force the beer through the filter rises beyond specification, the filter is dismantled, the pads broken up for washing and finally the pads are reconstituted.

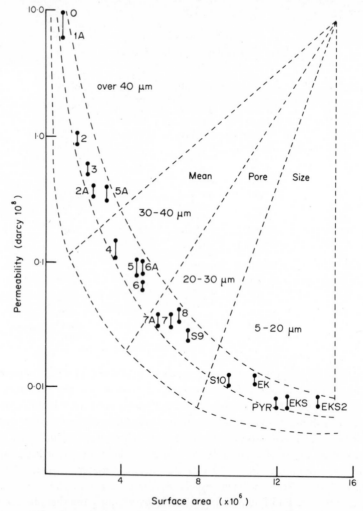

Fig. 20.15 Filter sheet performance. The relationship with Table 20.2 is apparent from the permeability data. Surface area refers to the gross area of asbestos fibres presented to liquid on filtration and is measured in cm²/g. on a Rigden apparatus [11].

At the other extreme, membrane filters of cellulose acetate have been developed in which there are pores of specified uniform diameter. Such filters readily clog and therefore are normally only applicable to microbiological quality control and in rare cases to sterile beer filtration where they follow the sterilizing sheet. They tend to be expensive, fragile and inconvenient on large scale but excellent for quality control purposes. A further type of plastic filter for large scale final filtration (often in the form of a candle) has a fibrous consistency on the upstream side of the beer, while on the down stream side the sheet becomes progressively like a membrane filter. The fibrous portion ensures that the filter does not clog easily.

Over the past thirty years, powder filters have become increasingly popular, either as a complete filtration system or as the first step of a two-stage filtration in which sheet filtration follows. The most popular powder for this purpose is kieselguhr or diatomaceous earth which is mined from Miocene deposits in a number of areas in Europe and the Americas. An alternative is the volcanic material called Perlite obtained from certain Greek islands. Very recently it has been shown that silica hydrogel can substitute for kieselguhr and at the same time stabilize the beer against chill haze [13].

Most kieselguhr is flux-kilned and is very effective in beer filtration. It comprises silicious skeletons of diatoms which are milled to the degree required. Unfortunately calcined kieselguhr is classed as very dangerous to anyone inhaling it; workmen are therefore required to wear face masks when working with it in the dry form. Large breweries may have equipment for automatically slitting the bags and transferring the powder to silos from which it is pumped as required to the slurry tanks. Uncalcined kieselguhr represents a moderate risk but it often contains undesirable traces of iron and other metals; it has been said to readily pick up taints. Perlite is a lower risk but, with only 60% of the density of kieselguhr, tends to disperse in the air very readily and spread as dust. Silica gel is considered to present no risk.

The principle on which all powder filters operate is similar to that of sheet and pulp filtration, namely the beer is made to pass through a comparatively long tortuous passage and there is more or less an opportunity for adsorption of particles. In all powder filters it is necessary to build up on a sheet or perforated septum a thickness of powder which will permit filtration of particles from the beer. Normally a coarse variety of powder is slurried with water (sometimes beer) and pumped into the filter where it forms an even layer called a first precoat on the permeable septa. The operation is repeated with a finer powder to form a second precoat. Recycling of the slurries occurs until the emerging water is clear. Beer is then pumped in avoiding pressure surges. At frequent predetermined intervals, an accurately determined volume of kieselguhr slurry is introduced into the beer flowing into the filter. This body feed slurry builds up progressively on the precoat, presenting a fresh surface to the beer requiring filtering (Fig. 20.16); of course, eventually the cavities of the filter become completely filled with kieselguhr. Filtration is terminated if either this happens, or for other reasons the pressure required to pump beer into the filter rises above a specified figure. Dosing of precoat slurry is normally about 500 g/m², body feed at about 100 g/hl (0.36 lb/brl). The disposal of kieselguhr may present a problem; not all breweries are permitted to discharge the slurry to sewer. Much of it has to be tipped on waste ground or is buried where it tends to be an unsatisfactory uncompacted infill.

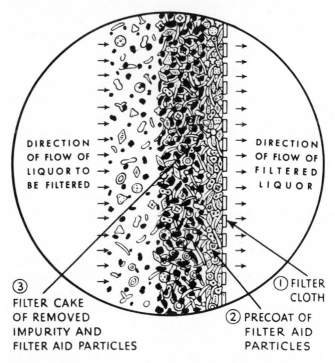

DIRECTION OF FLOW OF LIQUOR TO BE FILTERED

DIRECTION OF FLOW OF FILTERED LIQUOR

③ FILTER CAKE OF REMOVED IMPURITY AND FILTER AID PARTICLES

① FILTER CLOTH

② PRECOAT OF FILTER AID PARTICLES

Fig. 20.16 Kieselguhr filtration diagram showing a section through sheet or leaf, precoat, and normal kieselguhr.

There are several types of powder filter, namely (*i*) plate and frame, (*ii*) vertical leaf, (*iii*) horizontal leaf and (*iv*) candle or edge filters. The plate and frame filter is more popular in Europe than America [4, 12]. It comprises a succession of vertically dispersed plates each covered with a cellulose sheet folded at the top of the plate. Each plate alternates with a frame which will receive in succession the precoats and the beer plus body feed. The beer passes through the kieselguhr bed, then the sheet and into the plate from which it discharges (Fig. 20.17). Leaf filters have a series of stainless steel leaves disposed either vertically or horizontally inside a filter body. Both surfaces of vertical leaves are used for filtration (Fig. 20.18) but only the upper surfaces in the case of horizontal leaves (Fig. 20.19). The kieselguhr adheres to the septa because of the pressure at which the beer is forced into the filter. At the completion of filtration, release of pressure frees the spent kieselguhr. Complete cleaning may be aided by either spraying of the leaves and filterbody or in the case of the horizontal filters, revolving the leaves. The candle filters have a filter body containing many vertical filter elements (Fig. 20.20). Each element comprises a rod of Y-section on which annular discs are stacked. The discs are so fabricated that liquid can penetrate between them and then flow along the channels between the holes in the discs and the recesses of the Y-section rod. Kieselguhr is made to build up between adjacent filter discs in a manner similar to that described for other forms of filter.

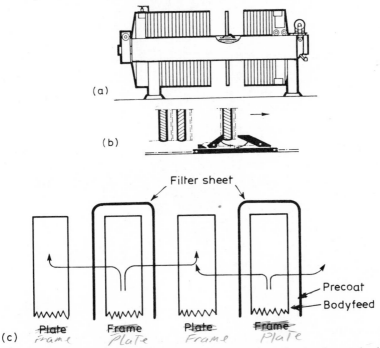

Fig. 20.17 Plate and frame filter. (a) Side view; (b) Automatic mechanism for moving individual plates for opening and closing; (c) Arrangement of plates and frames (vertical section) and the flow of beer. ((a) and (b) by courtesy of Alfa-Laval Ltd.)

It is convenient to compare performances of powder filters on the basis of (*i*) filtration efficiency, (*ii*) ease of sterilizing the unit, (*iii*) ease of automation, (*iv*) avoiding beer dilution, (*v*) ease of spent powder removal and (*vi*) dryness of the spent powder discharged [12]. Table 20.3 gives details of such a comparison. Flow rates are usually about 4–5 hl/m² but slower rates ensure more efficient particle removal. The average pore size of filter sheets is 4–6 μm, that of leaf septa is 45–70 μm and the slits in a candle are 50–90 μm.

Plate and frame filters are therefore more readily precoated and less susceptible to malfunction due to pressure surges. Again, the effective filtration area in a cellulose sheet represents 50% of the total while corresponding values for leaf septa and candles are 35% and 10% respectively. This means that localized flow rates in leaf and candle filters are undesirably far greater than in plate and frame filters.

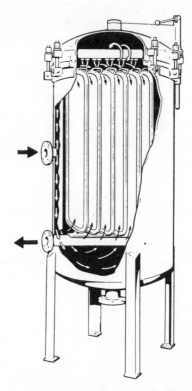

Fig. 20.18 A vertical leaf type filter.

With respect to sterilization, the plate and frame and leaf filters have a large mass of metal to heat and in comparison the candle filter would seem to have an advantage. Similarly candle filters appear to be the most readily automated. Turning to beer dilution the plate and frame rates best with less than 0·25 hl/m² of beer to filter area whereas the other types of filter have at least 0·5 hl/m².

Kieselguhr removal is easiest with the rotary horizontal leaf filter and the plate and frame filters are most difficult. However considerable strides have been made in reducing the complexity and labour requirement of the latter.

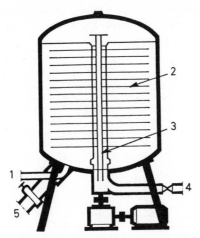

Fig. 20.19 Horizontal pressure leaf filter. 1. Inlet for beer; 2. Filter carrier; 3. Perforated shaft; 4. Outlet for filtered beer; 5. Outlet for sediment. (Based on drawing of Alfa-Laval Ltd.)

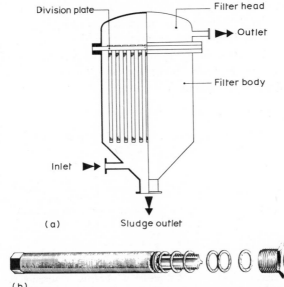

Fig. 20.20 (a) Candle filter or Metafilter; (b) Details of a single candle or element.

The plates may be separated mechanically and the spent kieselguhr caused to fall into a conveying screw set below the filter. Sheets of paper (called nappy liners) are sometimes used to cover the filter sheets proper and facilitate kieselguhr removal. Certainly the dryness of the spent powder from the plate and frame filter is superior to that of the other filters. Capital and revenue costs are lowest for the candle filter, highest for the horizontal leaf filter and intermediate for the other two.

TABLE 20.3

Performance of four types of beer filter [12] (*Scoring: best = 1, worst = 4*)

Filter performance parameter	Fixed vertical screen	Rotary horizontal screen	Candle	Plate and frame
Filtration	4	3	2	1
Sterilization	2	2	2	1
Automation	2	2	1	2
Dilution	2	2	2	1
Kieselguhr removal	2	1	2	2
Kieselguhr dryness	3	2	2	1
Total	15	12	11	8

The design of a filtration plant concerns not only the filter itself but also the provision of suitable pipework, pumps, buffer tanks and dosing units so that the beer is brought to as low a temperature as practicable before filtration and that no oxygen is taken up by the beer from maturation tank to 'sterile' beer tank. An example of a two stage filtration plant is given in Fig. 20.21. The buffer tanks have an important secondary function of guarding against pressure shocks and, in the case of the one before the filter, evening out variations in beer turbidity.

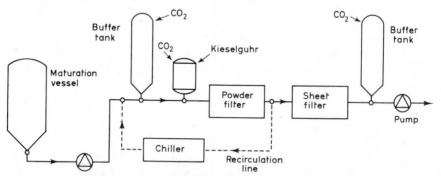

Fig. 20.21 Flow diagram for two stage filtration of beer from maturation vessel (0 to $-1°C$, 32 to 30°F) to bright beer tank. This arrangement is suitable for sterile filtration.

20.6 *Pasteurization* [14–16]

While some breweries rely on filtration to sterilize beer, many others pasteurize the beer either before or after bottling. The basis for pasteurization involves establishing the minimum times and temperatures required to destroy all expected biological contaminants at the highest concentrations that might be anticipated in bright (filtered) beer.

With food which may carry spore-forming bacteria, the levels of heat treatment have to be considerably higher than for beer. For this reason, temperature/time units of pasteurization for milk or food canning do not have the same value as those units of the same name in brewing. However non-alcoholic beers, low alcohol beers and shandies may support the growth of mould spores, or even some bacterial spores. In these cases there are good grounds for sterile filtration and pasteurization.

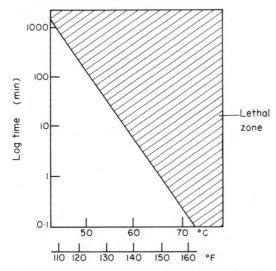

Fig. 20.22 The effect of time and temperature on the viability of a mixed population of yeasts and brewery bacteria. The hatched area represents the range of conditions where all cells are killed.

Mixed populations of common brewery contaminants, in beer subjected to a range of temperatures of various times, were examined for viability (Fig. 20.22). Typically with temperatures over 50°C (122°F) an increase in temperature of 7°C (12·6°F) accelerated the rate of cell-kill ten-fold. Thus at 60°C (140°F) the minimum time required for the population to be killed may be 5·6 min, but at 53°C (127·4°F) it would be 56 min and at 67°C (152·6°F) would be 0·56 min. One Pasteurization Unit (PU) has been defined arbitrarily for the beer as the biological destruction obtained by the holding of a beer for one minute at 60°C (140°F). The effect is a product of (*i*) the 'lethal rate' (dx/dt, where x is the number of viable micro-organisms per wort volume and t is time in min) and (*ii*) the time of application. Thus $PU/min = 1·39a$ where a is the temperature (in °C) minus 60°C. Pasteurization Units have been shown to be additive in their effects in a complex treatment where temperature

TABLE 20.4

Relationships between temperature and lethal rate or pasteurization units per minute of treatment

Temperature (°C)	Lethal rate and PU	Temperature (°C)	Lethal rate and PU	Temperature (°C)	Lethal rate and PU	Temperature (°C)	Lethal rate and PU	Temperature (°C)	Lethal rate and PU
46	0·01	53	0·1	60	1	67	10	74	100
46·5	0·012	53·5	0·12	60·5	1·2	67·5	12	74·5	119
47	0·014	54	0·14	61	1·4	68	14	75	139
47·5	0·016	54·5	0·16	61·5	1·65	68·5	16·5	75·5	166
48	0·019	55	0·19	62	1·9	69	19	76	196
48·5	0·023	55·5	0·23	62·5	2·3	69·5	23	76·5	231
49	0·027	56	0·27	63	2·7	70	27	77	268
49·5	0·032	56·5	0·32	63·5	3·2	70·5	32	77·5	320
50	0·037	57	0·37	64	3·7	71	37	78	373
50·5	0·045	57·5	0·45	64·5	4·5	71·5	45	78·5	445
51	0·052	58	0·52	65	5·2	72	52	79	519
51·5	0·062	58·5	0·62	65·5	6·2	72·5	62	79·5	620
52	0·072	59	0·72	66	7·2	73	72	80	720
52·5	0·086	59.5	0·86	66·5	8·6	73·5	86	80·5	860

is changing. When assessing the number of PU applied, a time/temperature curve may be used in conjunction with Table 20.4. In this way a curve can be constructed for PU per min against minutes of application and the areas under the curve calculated (Fig. 20.23). For measuring pasteurizing temperatures within bottles and cans, thermocouples have to be inserted and it has to be established that all bottles, etc., receive identical time/temperature treatments in the pasteurizer. Methods are available for receiving signals from the thermocouples by radio waves; thermographs are used to check controls [17]. Laboratory tests on bottled beers indicate that 5–6 PU are reasonably effective in achieving sterility, when cell numbers are low – say less than 100 per ml but to allow a considerable margin of safety, 15–30 PU is the generally-used range [18].

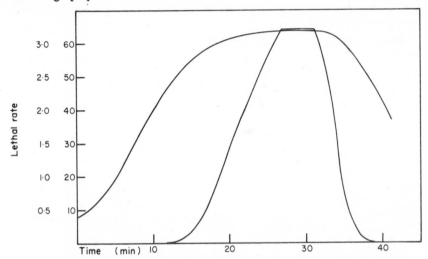

Fig. 20.23 The upper curve represents a sequence of temperatures 8–62·5°C (46·5–144·5°F) typical of a pasteurization process. The lower curve is the corresponding number of pasteurization units delivered (ordinate 0–3·2). Total pasteurization units = 40.

It has been claimed that the lethal rate is enhanced when carbonated instead of noncarbonated beer is used. The most resistant of the normal brewery contaminants are members of the lactic acid bacteria and certain species of *Saccharomyces*, e.g. *S. pastorianus*. Special difficulties attend the pasteurization of returned beer where the level of contaminants may be very high. However since such beer may be filtered before pasteurization and is usually blended into conditioning tank at low rates, the adverse effect on flavour of using a large number of pasteurization units may be discounted. With normal beers, excessive pasteurization leads to cooked, biscuity flavours, especially when the dissolved oxygen content of the beer is high (say in excess of 0·3 mg/l).

20.6.1 TUNNEL PASTEURIZATION [19]

Tunnel pasteurizers are employed after bottles and cans have been filled and closed (Fig. 20.24). They comprise a large compartmented metal casing enclosing a continuous chain-conyeyor or walking beam type of conveyor (Fig. 20.25). The bottles are loaded at one end of the pasteurizer and are passed under sprays of water. The sprays are so arranged that the bottles are subjected to increasingly hot water until the pasteurization temperature is reached by the beer in the bottles. This temperature (usually 60°C (140°F)) is then held for about 20 min before the bottles move under other water sprays, which cool them gradually until they are discharged from the end of the pasteurizer (Fig. 20.24). Some pasteurizers have one deck or tier while others have two decks; in the latter case it may be that the bottles travel to the end of the pasteurizer and then return on the lower deck. Consequently the sequence of sprays which have given gradual heating on the upper deck then afford gradual cooling on the lower deck. With single-deck pasteurizers, the discharge point can be remote from the entry station. Alternatively, the pasteurizers may be U-shaped in plan so that discharge and entry stations are adjacent. Recycling of water between the preheat and precooling section is normally practised. Outputs are normally in the range 2000–60 000 bottle/hr.

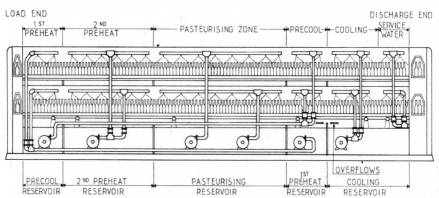

Fig. 20.24 A tunnel pasteurizer (double deck). Typical times and temperatures for the various zones are 35–50°C for 5 min for first preheat, 50–62°C for 13 min for second preheat 60°C for 20 min for pasteurization, 60–49°C for 5 min precool, 49–30°C for cool and 30–20°C for 2 min at discharge. For can pasteurization the preheat and cooling zones may be appreciably shortened in length and therefore in time because the containers withstand thermal shock.

It is important that the water used in the pasteurizer is clean and is maintained at a pH close to 8 otherwise the pasteurizer may become grossly infected with a variety of bacteria and moulds, jets become blocked and bottles emerge soiled. Inhibitors such as chlorinated compounds are often added to the water. Any hardness must be softened, or at least the calcium ions sequestered to ensure that the sprays do not block and that the bottles do not dry with a coating of salts over them. An economy of water and heat energy is essential in operating a tunnel pasteurizer. In recent years there has been considerable interest in providing insulation to pasteurizer walls and to using solar energy for heating the water. Another consideration is the alarming rate at which some pasteurizers corrode. In order to reduce this, the mild steel is protected to some degree by the use of cathodic protection.

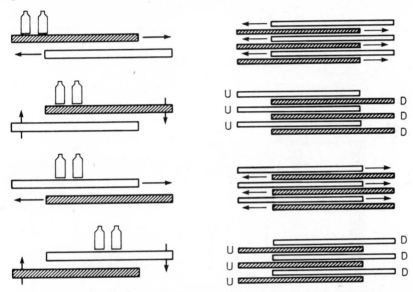

Fig. 20.25 'Walking beam' principle for moving bottles through a tunnel pasteurizer [15]. Left-hand sequence of diagrams represent side elevations showing successive movements of shaded grid of beams in relation to unshaded grid. The right-hand sequence represents corresponding plan views. (D indicates downward movement, U upward movement.)

During pasteurization, pressure builds up in the head-space of the bottles and cans if carbon dioxide is released from its supersaturated conditions by violent shaking or knocking. With defective containers leakage of carbon dioxide may occur or the containers may burst if the carbon dioxide comes out of solution. If the carbon dioxide content of beer is 0·38% and the percentage head-space in a bottle is 1·7%, the pressure would exceed 10 atmospheres during pasteurization if supersaturation did not pertain. Correspondingly with a head-space of 3·6% the pressure would be 5·8 bar (75 psig).

20.6.2 FLASH PASTEURIZATION [15, 20]
Flash pasteurization is typically carried out in a plate heat-exchanger in which there are four sections: (*i*) a regeneration section, (*ii*) a heating section,

(*iii*) a holding tube, and (*iv*) a cooling section (Fig. 20.26). Beer is pumped to (*i*) where it flows counter-current to hot beer and is therefore heated. In (*ii*) it is brought up to the pasteurizing temperature by passing counter-currently to hot water or steam and is then held for a predetermined period in the holding tube (*iii*). It then passes back to (*i*) where it loses heat to the incoming beer, and subsequently it runs counter-current to cold brine or alcohol in section (*iv*). The maximum temperature achieved is between 71 and 79°C (160 and 175°F) and the holding periods range from 15 to 60 s.

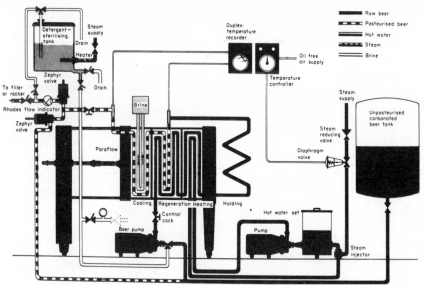

Fig. 20.26 Flash pasteurizing equipment. (Courtesy APV Co. Ltd.)

It is important that all beer flowing through the heat-exchanger receives the same pasteurization treatment. If the rate of flow through the exchanger is too slow, beer close to the metal plates will flow very much more slowly than beer in the middle of the stream because of drag and stratification. The Reynolds number provides a useful guide in choosing conditions that do not permit laminar flow. The number is the product of liquid density, velocity, and tube diameter, divided by liquid viscosity (where the terms are in consistent units). At Reynolds number values below 2000 the flow is laminar but above 3000 the flow becomes increasingly turbulent. Turbulent flow through the heat-exchanger ensures that all the beer receives the same treatment. Holding efficiency is the ratio of the residence time of the fastest particle or drop within the heat-exchanger to the corresponding residence time for the average particle, expressed as a percentage. For laminar flow, it could well be 50% as against 80% for turbulent flow.

In order to alter the number of Pasteurization Units given to the beer, it is the temperature rather than the flow-rate which is adjusted. The heat-exchanger is designed for a particular flow-rate to achieve maximum efficiency. There is a very substantial pressure drop through the pasteurizer and, in order to keep carbon dioxide in solution, it is normal to pump beer in at around 8·5–10 bar gauge pressure with a back pressure of say 1 bar gauge pressure. The provision of balance tanks before and after the pasteurizer is desirable to prevent interruption of flow and pressure surges on the beer in bright beer tanks and the fillers or rackers.

Heat transfer in the exchanger is achieved mainly by convection and the surface area required for transfer to heat is given by the expression $A = Q/HT$, where Q is the heat load in joules/hr., A is the area in m^2, H is the overall heat transfer coefficient in watts/m^2/K, and T is the logarithmic temperature difference.

In order to define T, it is convenient to cite an example of a heat-exchanger with liquid in at 87·5°C and out at 15·5°C, as against coolant entering at 11°C and out at 69°C.

$$T = \frac{(87\cdot5-69) - (15\cdot5-11)}{\log_e \dfrac{(87\cdot5-69)}{(15\cdot5-11)}} = 9.9$$

If the coolant entered at 13°C, T would equal 8·0 and the heat-exchanger area would have to be increased by at least 24 % to achieve the same cooling effect. The overall heat transfer coefficient (H) is made up of the sum of the reciprocals of the heat resistances including those of (i) the thin liquid layer dragging on the surface of the plate, because the Reynolds number is low or the surface is rough, (ii) the plate itself, and (iii) any scale deposited on the plate and derived from protein or water hardness. Very significant reductions in the coefficient arise from (i) and more so from (iii). Therefore, from this standpoint, it is desirable to have very turbulent flow and clean plates.

The advantages of flash pasteurizers compared with conventional 'tunnel' pasteurizers have been listed as: (i) less space required, (ii) cheaper equipment, (iii) cheaper operation (less coolant, steam, etc), (iv) shorter periods in the temperature ranges where chemical changes are rapid but in which pasteurization is very slow. When dissolved oxygen levels are relatively high (say over 0·3 mg/l), but not where they are lower, more marked flavour changes may take place during flash pasteurization than conventional pasteurization. This is possibly due in some part to the higher temperatures used and the turbulent flow, but mainly arises from recycling of beer back to the buffer tank when either process conditions fail to be met or beer cannot flow forward because of stoppage in packaging. This leads to excessive pasteurization. Good practice is to circulate water instead of beer when stoppages are prolonged but this is difficult to predict, leads to beer losses and possibly some dilution. An acknowledged disadvantage of flash pasteurization is that the bottles, cans, and kegs must be sterile and filled under sterile conditions. Strict microbiological checks downstream of the pasteurizer are therefore essential.

20.7 *Other methods of sterilization* [16]

It has been claimed that cold sterilization can be achieved by the addition of diethyl pyrocarbonate, n-heptyl *p*-hydroxybenzoate, or octyl gallate (3,4,5-trihydroxylbenzoic acid) to beer. Diethyl pyrocarbonate (DEPC) reacts with water to given carbon dioxide and ethanol but there is reason to believe that in alcoholic solutions such as beer, the breakdown is incomplete and DEPC reacts with amino acids. At 70–100 µg/ml DEPC is effective in sterilizing beer but its fruity aroma lingers in the beer [16]. Heptyl *p*-hydroxybenzoate at 10–12 µg/ml is also an effective sterilant but there have been reports about adverse effects upon both foam-retention and brilliance. Octyl gallate at 10–50 µg/ml has also been advocated and has been employed for beers with a very low level of microorganisms. The use of sterilants is controlled in most countries and the range of sterilants permitted tends to vary from country to country. In Britain sulphur dioxide, usually in the form of bisulphites, is permitted at levels of 70µg/ml or less. This compound is a weak bacteriostat at the pH of beer.

Gamma radiation has proved to be effective in the sterilization of certain foodstuffs but when applied to beer, the colour, aroma, and flavour suffers. This may be due to the production of peroxide, especially if the content of oxygen in the head-space is high. Radiation methods for sterilization of beer are not permitted in many countries. Other methods such as treatment with ultra-high frequency vibrations or ultra-sonication have not been fully evaluated.

The only effective and acceptable methods of sterilization of beer are therefore sterile filtration and pasteurization.

20.8 *Bottling* [19, 21–28]

(a) *Bottle washers*

Two types of bottle are used, namely those which are non-returnable to the brewery (single-trip bottles) and the heavier, more durable returnable bottles (multi-trip bottles). The cleaning treatment for non-returnable bottles is relatively simple; they are virtually sterile when received by the brewery but are usually jetted with sterile compressed air and then sterile water.

Multi-trip bottles on return to the brewery require a complex sequence of soaking and jetting in bottle washers using detergent solutions (Fig. 20.27).

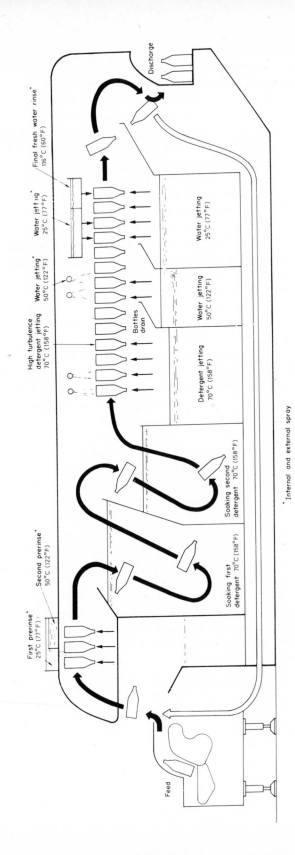

Fig. 20.27 Bottle washing machine with soak tanks and jets.

Discharge

Final fresh water rinse*
116°C (60°F)

Water jetting*
25°C (77°F)

Water jetting*
50°C (122°F)

High turbulence
detergent jetting
70°C (158°F)

Bottles
drain

Water jetting
25°C (77°F)

Water jetting
50°C (122°F)

Detergent jetting
70°C (158°F)

Second prerinse*
50°C (122°F)

First prerinse*
25°C (77°F)

Sooking second
detergent 70°C (158°F)

Sooking first
detergent 70°C (158°F)

*Internal and external spray

Feed

The multi-trip bottles are normally unloaded automatically from crates and placed in individual pockets or carriers on an endless chain of the washer. The bottles are carried through a series of compartments in which the conveyor belt may take successive downward and upward directions to enable soaking, jetting, and draining operations to occur in each compartment. Thus the bottles are washed both internally and externally at temperatures rising in steps from 25–70°C (77–158°F). They are then sterilized in a caustic detergent solution by holding for some 5–10 min at 60–80°C (140–176°F). Finally, the temperature of the bottles is lowered stepwise and the bottles washed free of detergent with clean, sterile water. The dwell-time in the washer is in the order of 30 min. During the process labels are washed away (preferably in one piece) and some bottles break. It is therefore necessary to have efficient discharge of these materials and adequate filtration of the various solutions so that the jets do not become blocked. The washer also requires careful checking to ensure that sprays operate properly and that there is neither undue corrosion nor microbial infection of the water tanks.

The strengths of the various detergent solutions have to be maintained and these are usually gauged by conductivity cells, but titratable alkalinity would be a better parameter to measure. In the USA, some states require bottles to be washed in at least 3 or more rare y 3·5% caustic soda. Other countries find better results with 2% caustic soda and elevated temperatures; thus raising the temperature of the 2% solution from 65·5°C (150°F) to 71°C (160°F) brings its killing power to that of 3% at 65·5°C. Chelating agents such as gluconates are added to the caustic soda to keep calcium salts in solution. Wetting agents and sequestering solutions such as polyphosphates help to remove moulds and other soils from the bottles, eliminate foaming, reduce scuffing of bottles and improve bottle rinsing. Aluminium foil or aluminized labels on bottles will react with caustic soda and release hydrogen gas which has to be vented.

Bottles emerging from the washer onto the conveyors are monitored for carry-over of caustic. They are also inspected for solids present by automatic scanning of the bottles from beneath as the bottles are caused to spin. In order that interruptions in the working of individual items of plant may be compensated without stopping all operations up-stream, it is common at strategic positions for conveyor lines to lead to 'accummulation tables' in which a supply of bottles may build up ready for resumption of normal operation.

A typical sequence of events is:

1. Preliminary hot water rinse at 25°C (77°F)
2. Second hot water rinse at 50°C (122°F)
3. Caustic soak at 70°C (158°F)
4. Caustic spray at 70°C (158°F)

5. Hot water rinse at 50°C (122°F) – this is recycled to the preliminary rinse.
6. First cold water rinse at 25°C (77°F) – hypochlorite (5 µl/l) may be added as a further sterilant.
7. Second cold water rinse at 15°C (60°F) – mains water (preferably deionized and sterilized) is fed in here.

It should be emphasized, however, that washing programmes and temperatures are often decided by the brewery concerned and the washing machine is manufactured to these specifications. Bottle washing machines with jets but no soak tanks are called 'hydrowashers'. Those with both jets and soak tanks are called 'soaker-hydrowashers.'

(b) *Fillers* [24–26]

Filling machines are complex and some are capable of filling 2000 bottles per minute. There is thus a need to feed bottles in very carefully and, in all operations, timing is crucial. All machines have (*i*) an enclosed bright beer tank which commands the bottle filling heads which in turn have a passage to apply pressure of air (or carbon dioxide) to the bottle equal to that above the beer in the tank, (*ii*) a tube for carrying beer, and (*iii*) a passage for scavenging excess beer and fob (foam) from the bottle. In some with short filler tubes, there is opportunity to evacuate the bottle of air before counter-pressurizing with carbon dioxide. The beer in the tank is maintained at a gauge pressure of up to 2 bar. A constant level of beer is achieved by means of a float control.

A bottle is raised on an air-pressurized bottle lift into position for filling under the 'bell', or cover. The bell forms an airtight seal between the bottle and filling head. In some instances the bottle is evacuated to remove air. In all cases the bottle is counter-pressured, then by a sequence of valve operations the counter-pressure passage is closed and the beer is delivered from the filling tube. Short filler tubes are so constructed that the beer is caused to flow quietly down the bottle from holes in the tube near the bottle neck while the atmosphere in the bottle is evacuated through the tube. Beer stops flowing when the holes in the tube are covered. In contrast long filler tubes deliver the beer at the base of the bottle and air in the bottle is snifted from the neck between the tube and the neck wall (Fig. 20.28). In part, the final volume delivered depends on the displacement of the full filler tube. The returned air passage receives the dispensed air and fob until the beer reaches a predetermined height. (Alternatively, the bottle is completely filled and then a standardized volume is withdrawn by displacement.) The valve assembly then cuts off entry to all pipes. The filling heads are arranged in a ring and normally revolve with the beer tank. The bottles are automatically conveyed and spaced so that each filling head receives a bottle at one station, the bottle is raised to the bell, the filling sequence is carried out and the bottle lowered from the machine at a second station towards the 'crown' closure equipment.

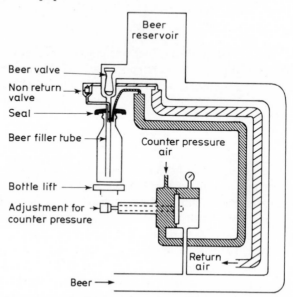

Fig. 20.28 A single filling head of a bottle filler, showing the three chamber system. (Based on drawing of Seitz Werke GmbH.)

Many machines incorporate a mechanical or ultrasonic 'fobber' or a jetter, using either beer or water, which induces beer in the filled bottle to rise as foam or fob and displace air in the space above the beer. In another device used to reduce air-content of the beer, the return of fob and displaced air to the beer tank is eliminated by the use of a second tank, which collects the fob. When the foam has broken down the beer so produced is conveyed to a pasteurizer and ultimately blended with other beer.

When sterile filling is called for, the sterile bottles are conveyed in sterile tunnels, the filling head is shrouded and ideally the filler and crown closure machine are housed in separate, but adjacent, air-conditioned rooms. In hot-filling, the beer is dispensed at 65°C (149°F) which tends to sterilize the bottle. Care has to be taken to ensure that bottles are scrupulously clean and free of flaws otherwise uncontrollable fobbing occurs. Fillers are cleaned in-place, usually at the end of a large batch of beer. Bell housings and filler tubes are often sprayed continuously with a mist of either a chlorinated solution or an iodophore (see Chapter 21). Provision is also made on some machines to jet water at high pressure if a bottle breaks while on the filler.

(c) *Crown closure* [26]

The crown closure machine (crowner or capper are alternative names) is placed close to the filler. It is charged with crown corks and these closures are delivered one by one from a slide. The bottle is raised to the crown cork and pressure is applied to the top of the crown in order to seal the liner to the bottle, then the crimped edges of the closure are pressed tightly over the top of the bottle. In many cases the crowns are jetted with a blast of air to remove foreign matter from inside the closure, especially chips of lacquer and cork dust in the case of closures with cork seals. The crown is made of steel, coated with resin or enamel, and the seal embedded in it is either cork or plastic. In some cases the cork is partly covered by a plastic or aluminium disc.

(d) *Labelling and packaging* [26–28]

The bottles are inspected for fill-height and then are conveyed to the labeller (Fig. 20.29). Bottle labels are made of (*i*) sized machine-coated paper, (*ii*) wet-strength paper, (*iii*) foil, or (*iv*) metallized paper. The first is cheapest and the range of grades is 70–85 g/m^2. Wet-strength paper is paper treated with either melamine–formaldehyde or urea–formaldehyde resins. Compared with the machine-coated paper it is marginally more expensive and is less likely to be pulped in modern bottle washers. Aluminium foil is 4–5-fold more expensive

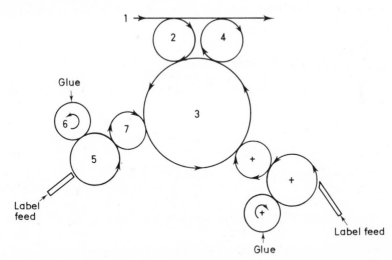

Fig. 20.29 A typical labeller in plan view. Bottles from conveyor (1) are withdrawn by rotating table (2) and introduced onto the labelling carousel (3); they are withdrawn by table (4) and fed back onto conveyor (1). Labels for the fronts of bottles are fed onto arms attached to disc (5). The arms are made sticky by glue fed onto disc (6). Disc (7) receives the labels from (5) with the sticky side outwards and applies them to bottles rotating on carousel (3). The other label station offers the opportunity to apply labels to the neck of the bottles.

and the caustic soda strength in the washer has to be 3% or more. Unfortunately, the caustic soda reacts with the aluminium, not only losing its causticity but generating hydrogen. Modern metallized paper is about twice as expensive as machine-coated paper and is produced by spraying aluminium particles in a vacuum chamber to coat paper. The amount of aluminium on each label is small [27]. Labels that are peelable and self adhesive are becoming available. Bottles may receive a front label, back label, neck label and foil cap over the crown but costs of labels and applying them escalate greatly with increasing complexities.

It is important that the grain of the label paper is correct and that the appropriate adhesive is applied. The label has to adhere readily and effectively, remain in place during its journey to the customer and in dry or wet storage. Finally the label must detach easily in the bottle washer. Adhesives include (*i*) dextrins, (*ii*) jelly gums and (*iii*) casein which will retain the label even if the bottle is immersed in ice-cold water.

A typical arrangement of equipment in a bottling hall is shown in Fig. 20.30. The bottles arrive in plastic (rarely wooden) crates and the crates are arranged on wooden pallets. After the crates have been removed from the pallets, the bottles are automatically lifted from the crates and proceed towards the washer. The crates are normally cleaned and moved into position to be automatically loaded with full bottles. Similarly the pallets are transferred to the station where they can be loaded with the appropriate number of full crates.

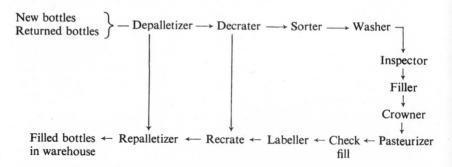

Fig. 20.30 Arrangement of equipment in a bottling hall.

On a line such as this, the speed of operation is normally determined by the speed of the filler. All equipment is therefore selected so that the filler is not held up for lack of empty bottles or because the equipment downstream cannot cope with the flow of filled bottles. In order to provide some flexibility, the conveyors lead at strategic points to accumulation tables where bottles can be temporarily held when there are hold-ups.

20.9 *Canning* [19, 29]

The canning operation has close similarities with the packaging of non-returnable bottles. Empty cans arrive at the packaging hall in large compression packs, often mounted on pallets. A depalletizer sweeps each layer of cans onto a conveyor system on which the cans are arranged in a single line. The cans are moved into the inverted position so that when they are air-jetted, any dust falls from them; also when sprayed with clean cold water, they readily drain. After the spray, cans are filled in a rotating filler generally similar to those used for filling bottles. Indeed there are fillers that can be quickly changed from bottles to cans and *vice-versa*. Can filling is usually carried out on a 72 or 100 head filler capable of filling 500–2000 cans/min. There is no pre-evacuation of the cans and the filler tube has similarities to a short (bottle) filler tube. Thus beer is caused to flow quietly down the sides of the can and air present is induced to flow from the can to a special annular tank above the separate annular filler bowl. Beer ceases to flow when a ball valve in the counter-pressure return floats in the beer to block the tube at a seating, the height of which may be adjusted. Little fob is developed so that recovery of it from the evacuated air is not justified. Naturally, a thin-walled can will not withstand high thrust pressures when the cans are lifted to seal them during filling. In some filler units, the can is not lifted; instead the sealer comes down to the can. Change of the size of can to be filled means that each filling head requires adjustment. In the UK, two sizes are in common use, 9·68 and 15·5 fluid oz or 275 and 440 ml respectively. Most North American breweries use exclusively 12 (US) fluid oz (335 ml).

Immediately following the filler any bubbles of carbon dioxide or air are broken by jetting carbon dioxide over the beer surface. Cans are then engaged in a large horizontal star wheel of the seamer machine and carbon dioxide is blown over the surface of the beer as the ring-pull can end is being slid into position. This means that most of the air is blown out and displaced by carbon dioxide (under-cover gassing) so that air contents are less than 1·5 ml. The can-end is sealed onto the can by two rolling operations in the seamer. Some units check fill-heights at this stage using a beam of gamma radiation which penetrates the cans and discerns whether the true level is within specification. At this point also, cans are regularly sampled to ascertain whether the cans and beer are meeting other quality control specifications. The cans are then introduced into a tunnel pasteurizer and a typical programme is set out below providing approx 20 PU:

Preheat	46°C (115°F)	1 min
Superheat	62°C (144°F)	3–4 min
Pasteurize	60°C (140°F)	15 min
Precool	46°C (115°F)	2 min
Cool	32°C (90°F)	2 min

One large US brewery does not pasteurize canned beer and therefore has to have special sterile rooms and aseptic techniques to contain each filler plus seamer. The same applies to certain large cans in the UK (4 and 7 pints or 2·27 and 3·97 l); corresponding pasteurized packs are considered to have superior shelf-lives. Following pasteurization, the cans are dried with jets of compressed air, checked for fill-height by gamma radiation and then the base of the can is date coded. Finally cans are packaged, sometimes with plastic sheet perforated with holes, each of which accurately accommodates a can. Usually the cans are packed onto trays and may be enveloped in thin plastic film which shrinks when exposed to heat. This shrink-wrapping is one of the most expensive operations in the brewery in terms of energy costs per unit of beer volume. Finally the trays are loaded onto pallets and conveyed to the 'full' warehouse.

Microbiological checks are usually centred on the bright beer tank, the filler and seamer units, and particularly on the canned beer emerging from the pasteurizer. The latter is membrane-filtered and the membranes are incubated on nutrient medium; there should be no colonies after 3–4 days at 25–30°C (77–86°F). Some cans are held for 14 days at 30°C (86°F) before being subjected to the membrane-filtration and incubation tests. Again there should be no development of colonies.

In the past 5 years, two-piece cans have steadily become more popular than the older three-piece. The older three-piece resin-coated steel can involves the rolling and seaming of the can body and the spraying of lacquer on the inside of the seam. It is then fitted with the 'maker's end'. Finally the canner's end, usually aluminium, is fitted after filling. Aluminium cans do not need to be resin-coated. The two piece can is made from a disc of aluminium (or less usually, steel) which is pressed and ironed into a cup. To strengthen the can, its diameter at the canner's end or rarely at both ends is slightly less than the rest of the body; this practice has been adopted for many three-piece cans because such 'necked-in' cans scuff less than the cans of simpler shape. In contrast to the three-piece can, the 2–4-colour labelling and artwork is applied after the body has been made. Finally the canner's end is made in the same way as for the three-piece; it may be ring-pull or push-tab and is likely to be improved over the next few years time. Aluminium cans require a great deal of electrical energy to manufacture from ore; reforming used cans only requires 10% of this energy. In order to conserve energy and aluminium, and avoid unsightly accummulation of litter, there are active programmes in many countries to collect and recycle used aluminium cans.

20.10 *Kegging* [30–33]

The kegging operation is concerned with filling carbonated pasteurized beer into sterile aluminium or stainless steel containers. In British practice, the kegs usually have a stainless steel spear or extractor screwed into the single opening or neck (Fig. 20.2). Some other countries fill pasteurized or sterile-filtered beer into casks with two openings, one for gas top-pressurizing and the other for beer withdrawal. Compared with traditional cask ale, keg beer is more resistant to haze formation, and is more likely to remain free of microbial contamination. It therefore has a shelf life of 1–3 months compared with the 2–4 weeks for traditional cask beer. Because the spear is difficult to remove except with a specialized tool, keg beer is less likely to be adulterated by water or inferior beer.

Aluminium kegs, of an alloy with magnesium and silicon, are generally more popular than stainless steel ones because they are lighter, more resistant to minor damage and may be factory-repaired in many instances. However they must not be washed with caustic soda as is the case with stainless steel kegs. Acid or weakly alkaline detergents are used instead, for instance 10% phosphoric acid, polycarboxylate sequestrant and a non-foaming surfactant such as sodium xylene sulphonate. In many instances, the internal surfaces of aluminium kegs are either coated with epoxy resin or oxidized. Common sizes of kegs are 0·41 hl (9 gal), 0·5 hl (11 gal), 0·82 hl (18 gal) or 1·0 hl (22 gal). The spear or extractor screws into a closely-threaded 'Barnes' neck; it completely seals the container. Spring-loaded valves may be released by clamping on a specially-designed tapping head which permits carbon dioxide top pressure to induce beer to rise out of the extractor through a beer dispense pipe.

Beer destined for kegging, either ale or lager, is normally conditioned (to provide 1·5 to 2·5 vol. CO_2), treated to reduce the incidence of haze and clarified, for instance through a kieselguhr filter. The bright beer is then fed to a continuous-flow pasteurizer at high pressure (say 10 bar) against a back pressure of 1 bar. A substantial pressure fall therefore occurs in the pasteurizer and care must be taken to prevent carbon dioxide from breaking out of solution at the temperature of pasteurization and the turbulence of the beer in the plate heat-exchanger. A typical pasteurizer will hold the beer at 75°C (165°F) for about 20 s which is equivalent to 50 Pasteurization Units. Modification of the number of units is achieved by altering temperature rather than flow-rate. In many instances, any failure to achieve this specified temperature leads to recycling of the beer back to a point between bright beer tank and the pressurizing pump. However in some breweries any delay downstream from the pasteurizer leads to recycling so that beer may become grossly overpasteurized.

Kegs are washed externally and then fed to the internal washers. In modern equipment, there is completely automated feed of kegs, washing, deterging, steam-sterilizing and filling with the spear in place. Internal cleaning normally takes place with the keg inverted because drainage is

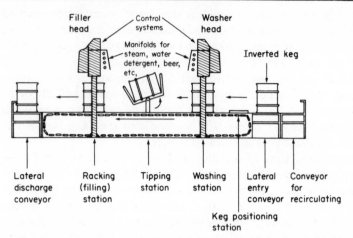

Fig. 20.31 Automatic internal keg washing machine and filler. Sequences of operations are indicated in Table 20.5.

TABLE 20.5

Time (s) to carry out automated cleaning and sterilization of kegs of two sizes

	0·5 hl (11 gal)	1·0 hl (22 gal)
Lift delay	3	3
Gas relief	6	6
First water rinse 70°C (158°F)	10	10
Steam purge 105°C (221°F)	22	35
Steam pressure (1·33 bar)	2	8
Head cool	2	2
Transfer of keg	9	9
Total	122	165
Apply steam	7	11
Steam hold 105°C (221°F)	15	15
Carbon dioxide purge (2 bar)	2	2
Counterpressure	2	2
Fill (4–5 bar)	55	110
Scavenge fob and beer	4	4
Transfer	7	7
Total	92	151

quicker and more complete, water forced up the spear cleans the sides and base of the keg more effectively. The kegs may be filled very rapidly in the inverted position but any misalignment of filler and neck leads to large beer losses. It is therefore usual to restore the keg to the upright position for filling (Fig. 20.31). A typical sequence of timings is presented in Table 20.5 for the various automatic operations before filling. Temperature probes must record 105°C (221°F) within the keg before a keg is deemed to have been steamed. All beer mains and filling equipment are cleaned and steam-sterilized before pasteurized beer is passed through. Carbon dioxide used is sterile-filtered. After filling, kegs have the Barnes neck washed and air-dried; they are weighed, capped, labelled, palletted and stored in warehouses. A typical arrangement of kegging equipment is shown in Fig. 20.32.

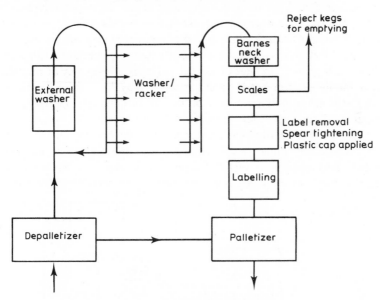

Fig. 20.32 Arrangement of equipment of a kegging line.

20.11 *Tank beer* [34]

Some breweries deliver pasteurized beer, similar to that dispensed into kegs, in tanker wagons directly to the point of sale. The beer is pumped through a hose from the wagon into cellar tanks in the inn cellar. Such cellar tanks (usually about 8 hl or 5 brl) may be aluminium or stainless steel and may be equipped with cleaning-in-place facilities and also with means of maintaining constant pressure. Other cellar tanks of similar size are of mild steel construction and the beer is filled into a disposable plastic bag which acts as a liner to the tank. In such tanks, the beer may be emptied from the bag by applying gas pressure (usually air) within the top of the tank upon the plastic bag. It is not normal to use tank beer systems unless the beer within the tank is likely to be held for 4 days or less.

A further system of delivery involves the filling at the brewery of mild steel vessels with plastic bag inserts of the type described. The vessels are carried on a flat-bed wagon to the inn where the vessels are emptied by pumping the beer to cellar tanks. The advantage of delivery- and cellar-tank beer systems for large inns is the labour saving at both the brewery and the inn.

20.12 *High gravity brewing* [35–37]

In earlier chapters, reference has been made to high gravity brewing. To summarize, worts of higher than normal extract (usually 15–40% greater) are fermented and are diluted with water at the latest possible step before packaging. The advantages include (*i*) smaller vessels are required, (*ii*) energy requirements for heating, chilling and pumping are proportionately reduced, (*iii*) final filtration may be carried out at a lower temperature, (*iv*) there may be less yeast growth per unit of extract, (*v*) more consistency of products and (*vi*) a family of beers of different extracts may be readily prepared. Disadvantages are usually (*i*) poorer utilization of hops or hop products in the copper (although post-fermentation bittering operation is not affected), (*ii*) beer lost in processing has greater SG, (*iii*) flavour differences in the final beer, particularly higher levels of esters and (*iv*) additional equipment is needed. This equipment includes either weak worts storage or additional syrup storage; in either case a water deaerator/carbonator is required.

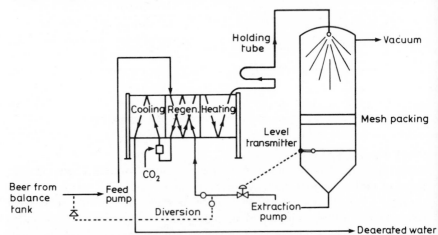

Fig. 20.33 A typical water deaeration plant involving pasteurization. Equipment for producing chilled, carbonated, deaerated, pasteurized water for beer dilution after high gravity brewing. Alternative systems lead water to the spray chamber either at 15°C or at temperatures above 100°C. In these, the holding tube is omitted. The system with the highest temperature of water relies on flash action within the spray vessel which eliminates the need for vacuum. (Based on diagrams of APV Co., Crawley.)

There are several types of water deaerator available. A simple form has water (often deionized) charged with nitrogen gas spraying into an enclosed vessel. Gas (nitrogen-enriched air) is permitted to escape from the vessel while the water is sprayed in a second tank similar to the first. Water emerges from the second tank with an oxygen content of approx. 0·2 mg/l. More sophisticated deaerators have water passing through the following, successively: (*i*) a plate heat-exchanger, (*ii*) a spray into an evacuated pressure tank, and (*iii*) back to the plate heat-exchanger where it is chilled and carbonated. If the water is raised in the plate heat-exchanger to a temperature in excess of 100°C (212°F), the pressure tank does not require evacuation, because the flashing-off action in the tank vents dissolved air from the water (Fig. 20.33). Dissolved oxygen contents of 0·1 mg/l or even below can be achieved. Stripping of oxygen when water trickles through a packed bed tower and when carbon dioxide is forced up the bed has also been investigated [36].

The deaerated carbonated water, which has been sterilized either by the heating in the plate heat-exchanger or by filtration, has to be blended accurately with beer. Errors at this stage are serious; too high a final extract may mean a serious loss of revenue to the company while too low a value may prejudice beer quality. A microprocessor is often employed in the adjustment of valves controlling the ratio of beer and of water, using electromagnetic flow meters to gain the required information.

20.13 *Carbon dioxide saturation* [38]

Enclosed fermenters, maturation tanks and bright beer tanks are normally fitted with automatic carbon-dioxide pressure regulators which can be set at a predetermined pressure (Fig. 20.5). Unless these regulators become frozen or become fouled by substances ejected with foam, they will maintain the beer at the predetermined pressure. Assuming that the gas above the beer is pure carbon dioxide, the content of carbon dioxide that will dissolve in the beer at equilibrium is indicated in Fig. 20.34. This concentration is often expressed in terms of volumes of gas at standard temperature and pressure per volume of beer. If a gram molecule of gas occupies 22·4 l, then 1 vol. of carbon dioxide is equivalent to 0·196% carbon dioxide by weight.

The amount of carbon dioxide which dissolves is a function of time, the rate decreasing exponentially as equilibrium is approached. In order to speed up the rate of dissolution, the surface exposed to the gas may be increased. Thus a very shallow layer of beer picks up gas more readily; alternatively a given surface may be increased by making waves or by creating bubbles. A fine mist of bubbles presents a very large surface area for gas to transfer into the surrounding beer. Temperature and pressure play a most important role (as shown in Fig. 20.34) in determining the equilibrium concentration of carbon dioxide. Thus, at a given pressure and temperature, a particular equilibrium concentration will be reached. An

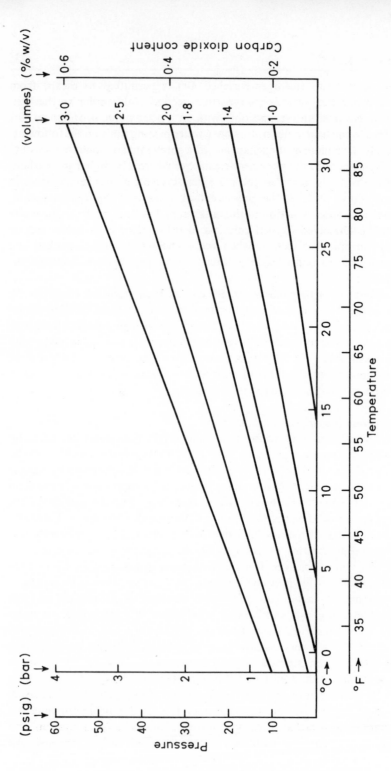

Fig. 20.34 Relationship between equilibrium values for dissolved carbon dioxide, temperature and pressure.

increase in pressure leads to a linear increase in weight of carbon dioxide dissolving in beer or water. However an increase in temperature gives a non-linear decrease in the amount dissolving (Fig. 20.35). Henry's Law states that the concentration of gas in the liquid phase is equal to the imposed pressure of gas divided by Henry's constant (which is temperature dependent). However in deep beer tanks, the content of dissolved carbon dioxide at the base tends to be greater than at the beer surface because of hydrostatic pressure (roughly 0·5 vol./m). This graduation is of course greatly reduced by any convection or other circulatory currents.

Beer is capable of holding carbon dioxide in a supersaturated state so that rapid release of pressure or increase in temperature does not lead to the immediate attainment of the appropriate equilibrium. This has the advantage that when bottled beer with 3 vol. of carbon dioxide is poured into a glass, the gas does not normally gush uncontrollably but releases its carbon dioxide slowly. Considerable energy is required to create bubbles but they arise normally because of the presence of suspended solids, imperfections of the container, or mechanical agitation.

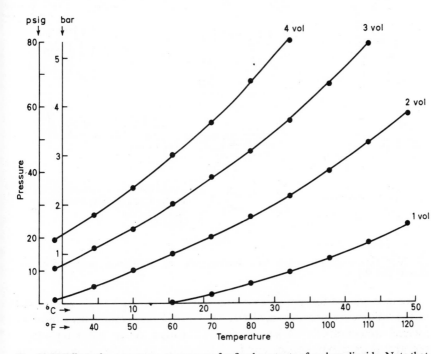

Fig. 20.35 Effect of temperature on pressure for fixed contents of carbon dioxide. Note that rise in temperature at a fixed pressure, say 3 bar, the equilibrium occurs for 4 vol. at 15°C, 3 vol. at 26°C, and 2 vol. at 41°C. Thus increase in temperature gives a non-linear decrease in the amount of gas that dissolves.

In the dispense of keg beer, the relationship between gas content, temperature and pressure is very important. If for example a beer at 10°C (50°F) has to have a carbon dioxide content of 2 vol., the equilibrium pressure is 0·7 bar over-pressure (or 10·5 psig). Were the temperature to fall to 4·4°C (40°F) and the pressure maintained, the content would rise to 2·4 vol. so that the beer may be difficult to dispense. On the other hand if the temperature rose to 15·5°C (60°F), the gas content would fall to 1·65 vol. at the dispense tap and the beer would foam uncontrollably. Fobbing of this kind is usually a result of having an incorrect balance of temperature, pressure and carbon dioxide content. However, compensation has to be made when gas pressure has to force beer along long runs of dispense pipe or up a vertical pipe. Thus for every horizontal metre an additional 0·011 bar is required and for each vertical metre, an extra 0·108 bar. If, however, the pressure required to take the beer to the dispense tap is, because of height or distance, in excess of the equilibrium pressure then a pump must be installed.

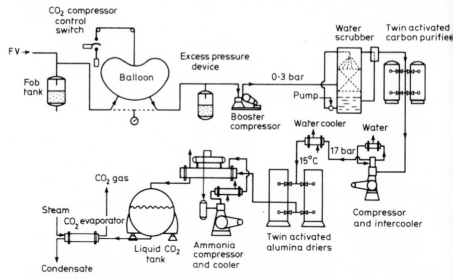

Fig. 20.36 Typical equipment used for collecting, purifying, storing and releasing of carbon dioxide [39, 40].

Some beers are top-pressurized with nitrogen and carbon dioxide mixed in the volumetric proportion of 60: 40. To this end, certain kegs have an integral doughnut-shaped gas chamber. Nitrogen is far less temperature sensitive than carbon-dioxide and far less soluble. The rationale of using the mixture is that (*i*) nitrogen is extremely effective in inducing beer foam without undue nitrogen dissolving, (*ii*) on dispense the nitrogen tends to stay in solution while the carbon dioxide is released as fine bubbles, (*iii*) thus the partial pressure of nitrogen in the bubbles is low and therefore some capture of nitrogen by the bubbles occurs and (*iv*) the nitrogen-rich gas left in the beer has less of a 'pricking' sensation to the tongue and mouth.

Carbon dioxide used in a brewery may be purchased from suppliers of industrial gases or may be recovered from fermentation vessels. The equipment shown in Fig. 20.36 is typical of that required for collection, purification and storage. Approximately 40–50 % of the theoretical production of carbon dioxide may be readily recovered using this technique.

REFERENCES

[1] CHALCRAFT, M. (1978). *The Brewer*, **64** (9), 354.
[2] WOODWARD, J. (1972). *Brewers Guardian*, **101** (6), 43.
[3] MIEDANER, H. (1978). *The Brewer*, **64** (2), 33.
[4] COORS, J. H. (1977). *The Practical Brewer* (ed. BRODERICK, H. M.) Master Brewers Assoc., Americas, Madison, Wisconsin.
[5] LEACH, A. A. and BARRETT, J. (1967). *J. Inst. Brewing*, **73**, 8; 246.
[6] WOODHEAD-GALLOWAY, J. (1980). Collagen: *The Anatomy of a Protein*, Studies in Biology No. 117, Edward Arnold, London.
[7] VICKERS, J. C. and BALLARD, G. (1974). *The Brewer*, **60** (1), 19.
[8] OHLSEN, D. (1978). *Brewers Guardian*, **108** (12), 33.
[9] JOHNSTONE, J. T. and WHITMORE, D. J. (1971). *Modern Brewing Technology* (ed. FINDLAY, W. P. K.), Macmillan, London, p. 233.
[10] HARRIS, J. O. (1968). *J. Inst. Brewing*, **74**, 500.
[11] OSGOOD, G. (1969). *Brewers Guild. J.*, **55**, 298.
[12] HARDING, J. A. A. (1977). *Brewers Guardian*, **106** (9), 90.
[13] CLARK, B. E., CRABB, D., LOVELL, A. L. and SMITH, C. (1980). *The Brewer*, (6), 168.
[14] DALLYN, H. and FALLOON, W. C. (1976). *The Brewer*, **62** (11), 354.
[15] COLEMAN, M. (1976). *Brewers Guardian*, **105** (10), 51.
[16] PORTNO, A. D. (1968). *J. Inst. Brewing*, **74**, 291.
[17] DROST, B. W., BEUMER, L. A., MASTENBROECK, G. G. A. and PELT, V. B. (1969). *Proc. Eur. Brewery Conv. Congr., Interlaken*, p. 539.
[18] WILLOX, I. C. (1966). *J. Inst. Brewing*, **72**, 236.
[19] DEYOUNG, R. E. (1977). *The Practical Brewer*, p. 253 (ed. BRODERICK, H. M.), Master Brewers Assoc. Americas, Madison, Wisconsin, p. 253.
[20] CLARKE, D. F. (1976). *The Brewer*, **62** (1), 8.
[21] SCHOENKE, D. F. (1975). *Tech. Quart. Master Brewers Assoc. Americas*, **12** (4), 228.
[22] MILLER, S. (1978). *Tech. Quart Master Brewers Assoc. Americas*, **15** (4), 207.
[23] PERMENTER, P. (1976). *Brewers Guardian*, **105** (10), 48.
[24] MICKLEM, D. R. (1978). *Brewers Guardian*, **107** (7), 43.
[25] HACKSTAFF, B. W. (1981). *The Brewer*, **67** (3), 76.
[26] RUFF, D. G. and BECKER, K. (1955). *Bottling and Canning of Beer*, Siebel, Chicago.
[27] PEARSON, J. (1978). *Brewers Guardian*, **107** (2), 25.
[28] WILSON, G. (1978). *The Brewer*, **64** (4), 126.

[29] FELTHAM, R. (1976). *Brewers Guardian*, **105** (10), 45.
[30] BABCOCK, D. R. and HOLMER, C. (1977). *The Practical Brewer* (ed. BRODERICK, H. M.), Master Brewers Assoc. Americas, Madison, Wisconsin, p. 272.
[31] HARDING, J. A. (1976). *The Brewer*, **62** (12), 392.
[32] COLEMAN, M. J. (1974). *Brewers Guardian*, **103** (1), 23.
[33] GRIFFIN, S. R. (1980). *The Brewer*, **66** (2), 37.
[34] KNIGHT, R. J. V. (1973). *The Brewer*, **59** (3), 105.
[35] SKINNER, K. (1977). *Brewers Guardian*, **106** (6), 41.
[36] WILSON, R. J. H. (1977). *Proc. Eur. Brewery Conv. Congr., Amsterdam*, p. 343.
[37] HOGGAN, J., RUST, F., SPILLANE, M. H., WILLEMS, E. J. and WREN, J. J. (1979). *Proc. Eur. Brewery Conv. Congr., Berlin*, p. 245.
[38] CARROLL, T. C. N. (1979). *Tech. Quart. Master Brewers Assoc. Americas*, **16** (3), 116.
[39] TURVILL, W. R. (1973). *Brewers Guardian*, **102** (12), 38.
[40] EIKER, J. (1977). *The Practical Brewer* (ed. BRODERICK, H. M.), Master Brewers Assoc. Americas, Madison, Wisconsin, p. 336.

Chapter 21

MICROBIOLOGICAL CONTAMINATION IN BREWERIES

21.1 *Introduction*

There has always been a measure of disagreement among brewers on the degree of microbiological control needed in breweries. On the one hand, there are those who wish to eliminate all micro-organisms from the brewery except for pure culture yeast and thereby help to achieve a consistently satisfactory quality of extremely uniform beer. There are however those who, while wishing to restrict rampant growth of other micro-organisms, nevertheless emphasize the distinctive, desirable flavours which these organisms can on occasion impart to beer. As with wines and ciders, outstanding flavours in beers are often associated with the metabolic activities of a mixed microbial population. Because there is no detailed knowledge available on achieving a desirable balance of strains, usually involving both bacteria and yeasts, such a balance can be achieved only fortuitously. A change in the proportions of the organisms in the balanced mixture may, and usually does, lead to beer with inferior taste and aroma. It is particularly true of modern beers of comparatively low original gravity (say under 10° Plato and SG 1040), undergoing a very short maturation treatment. This is because in stronger beers the bacterial strains are inhibited to different degrees by (*i*) low pH values, (*ii*) high concentrations of alcohol, (*iii*) high contents of hop resins, and (*iv*) in some cases the yeast strains used.

Fortunately for brewers, microbiological control has to be exercised only over a limited range of bacteria and yeasts; in bottled or canned mixtures of beer and soft drink (such as shandies), the range of organisms encountered is much greater and may include moulds. Pathogenic micro-organisms fail to grow in beer, or even survive for extended periods. Nevertheless, the possibility of spread of pathogens, by glassware becoming infected in bars, must be borne in mind. Clear-cut evidence of this actually happening however has not been reported.

On first consideration, the isolation and identification and counting of bacteria associated with breweries would seem straightforward. On the whole this is true. Nevertheless difficulties do not arise because of the variability of bacteria. For instance, a strain of an acetic acid bacterium or a lactic acid bacterium isolated from wort or beer can change profoundly both in morphological and biochemical characteristics under laboratory conditions of culture. This is due in part to the propensity of bacterial cultures for adaptive change and in part to mutation. Indeed, it has been suggested that the concept of a species, as known in botanical and zoological taxonomy, is inapplicable to bacteria [1]. Although reference will be made in this chapter to species, these doubts as to the validity of the species concept should be borne in mind. Another feature is that on rare occasions, unexpected genera of bacteria are encountered in wort, e.g. *Pseudomonas*, or in beer, e.g. *Bacillus*.

21.2 *General classification of brewery bacteria* [2–11]

Bacteria are classified according to their shape, flagellation, Gram-staining, other structural features and biochemical characteristics. Important biochemical information is provided when the strain under test is inoculated into a series of media comprising (*i*) a selected carbohydrate, or other carbon source, plus (*ii*) nutrient broth (meat extract, enzyme-degraded meat or milk, and sodium chloride), and (*iii*) neutral red to detect by colour change the production of acid during growth. Gas production during growth is indicated by bubble accumulation in a small inverted tube (a Durham tube) which is placed below the level of the medium and filled with the medium. Hydrogen peroxide (10 volumes) is used in a test to indicate the presence of catalase, by the intense liberation of oxygen from a slope culture. Other tests include noting the liberation of hydrogen sulphide with lead acetate papers, the formation of acetoin by the Voges-Proskauer test and other tests referred to in the identification of coliform organisms (Chapter 7).

It has already been mentioned that the number of bacterial genera usually encountered in brewing is small. An indication of the shape of these bacteria is given in Fig. 21.1. The identification of a genus from within the normal restricted range is therefore relatively simple and is summarized below:

(a) **Gram-positive bacteria**

    1. Catalase-negative rods, e.g. *Lactobacillus* [5]

    2. Catalase-negative cocci or cells in cubical packets, e.g. *Pediococcus* [6]

(b) **Gram-negative bacteria**

    1. Capable of oxidizing ethanol; grows well on glucose but not lactate; if motile, then polar flagellation, e.g. *Acetomonas* [7]

    2. Capable of oxidizing ethanol, grows well on both glucose and lactate; if motile, then peritrichous flagellation, e.g. *Acetobacter* [7]

3. Incapable of oxidizing ethanol; produces carbon dioxide, ethanol, acetaldehyde, and usually H_2S when grown on a glucose medium, e.g. *Zymomonas* [8, 9].

4. Capable of producing ethanol from glucose; will grow in the presence of bile salts; some will multiply in competition with actively growing yeast in a brewery fermentation, e.g. genera of *Enterobacteriaceae* [10, 11].

5. Incapable of producing ethanol from glucose, anaerobic, flagella emanating from one side of the rod-like cell, e.g. *Pectinatus* [12]

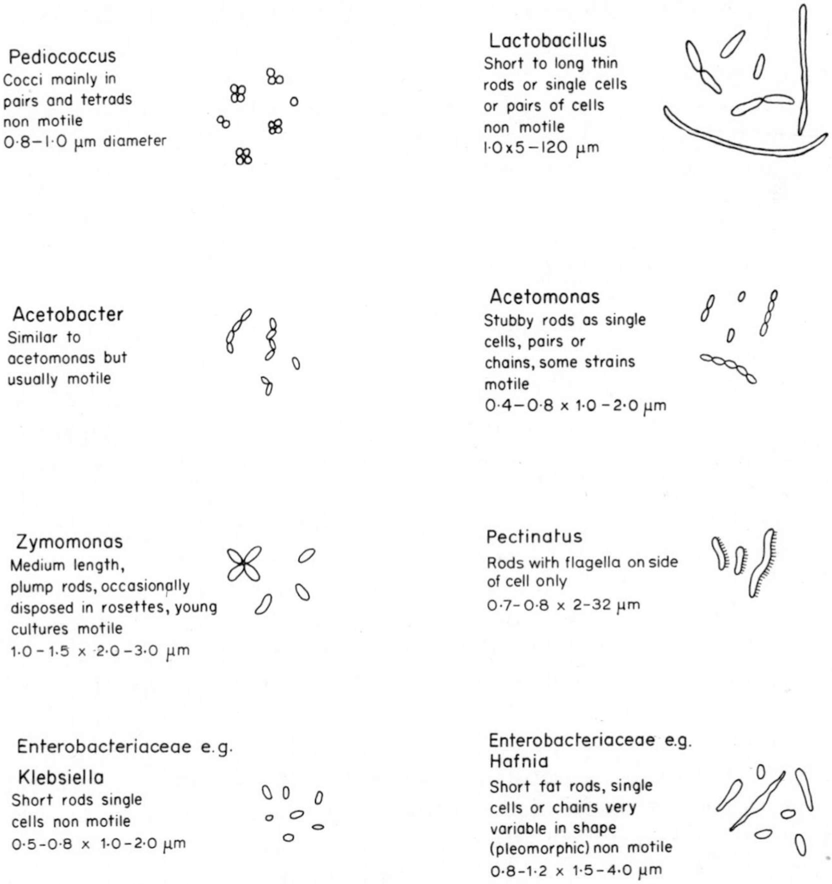

Pediococcus
Cocci mainly in pairs and tetrads non motile
0·8–1·0 μm diameter

Lactobacillus
Short to long thin rods or single cells or pairs of cells non motile
1·0 x 5–120 μm

Acetobacter
Similar to acetomonas but usually motile

Acetomonas
Stubby rods as single cells, pairs or chains, some strains motile
0·4–0·8 x 1·0–2·0 μm

Zymomonas
Medium length, plump rods, occasionally disposed in rosettes, young cultures motile
1·0–1·5 x 2·0–3·0 μm

Pectinatus
Rods with flagella on side of cell only
0·7–0·8 x 2–32 μm

Enterobacteriaceae e.g.
Klebsiella
Short rods single cells non motile
0·5–0·8 x 1·0–2·0 μm

Enterobacteriaceae e.g.
Hafnia
Short fat rods, single cells or chains very variable in shape (pleomorphic) non motile
0·8–1·2 x 1·5–4·0 μm

Fig. 21.1 Types of bacteria encountered in brewing (approx. ×1000).

21.2.1 GRAM-POSITIVE BACTERIA [5, 6]

The gram-positive bacterial genera *Lactobacillus* and *Pediococcus* encountered in the brewery (often termed the lactic acid bacteria) are always non-motile and have complex nutritional requirements, for instance a range of amino acids is required as nitrogen source. (Some species, such as *Lactobacillus arabinosus*, are used for the bioassay of nicotinic acid or other nutrilites while biotin, riboflavin, pyridoxin are required by some [13].) They ferment sugars strongly, attack proteins weakly, and fats hardly at all. Their respiratory abilities are limited and growth is favoured by microaerophilic and occasionally anaerobic conditions. The growth of some strains is encouraged by the presence of carbon dioxide. It is desirable therefore to add this gas when hydrogen or nitrogen are used to provide anaerobic conditions. The optimum pH level for growth is about 5·5, but some strains are capable of developing in media of pH 3·5. Curiously, these bacteria once isolated often show extreme reluctance to grow again in their native environment without the pH level being raised and additional nutrients supplied. It is usual to refer to these microorganisms as lactic acid bacteria because of their propensity for producing lactic acid from simple sugars. *Pediococcus* strains and some strains of *Lactobacillus* convert a high proportion of the sugar to lactic acid and are termed homofermentative. In contrast those strains which in addition produce acetic acid, ethanol, and carbon dioxide are said to be heterofermentative.

Many names have been assigned to the lactic acid bacteria associated with brewing. It is probable however that most rod-shaped isolates may be classified as the heterofermentative species *Lactobacillus brevis*, the homofermentative species *L. casei* and *L. plantarum*, and the homofermentative thermophilic species *L. delbrueckii* [14]. Cocci are also encountered, notably the homofermentative *Pediococcus damnosus*. (Less common because they are more sensitive to hop resins are *P. pentosaceus/acidilactici*, *Streptococcus saprophyticus*, *S. epidermis* and *Micrococcus varians*.) *Micrococcus kristinae* is however resistant to hop resins and low pH, but requires oxygen for growth [15]. An American report states that many breweries encounter *L. brevis*, *L. plantarum* and *P. damnosus*. When the primary fermentation is complete, *Pediococcus* continues to grow at the bottom of the fermenter in the deposited yeast [16].

The biochemistry of the lactic acid bacteria has received attention [4, 17–20]. Homofermentative strains such as the *Pediococci* use the glycolytic pathway for the dissimilation of carbohydrates, such as glucose, to yield pyruvic acid. Pyruvic acid acts as a hydrogen acceptor and is converted to lactic acid by means of an NADH-dependent lactic dehydrogenase. It is believed that the homofermentative strains use in addition the hexose monophosphate pathway and possibly a phosphoketolase pathway (Fig. 21.2) when pentoses are degraded. The heterofermentative strains on the other hand lack both aldolase and hexose isomerase, essential for the operation of the glycolytic pathway, while pyruvic acid will not readily function as a

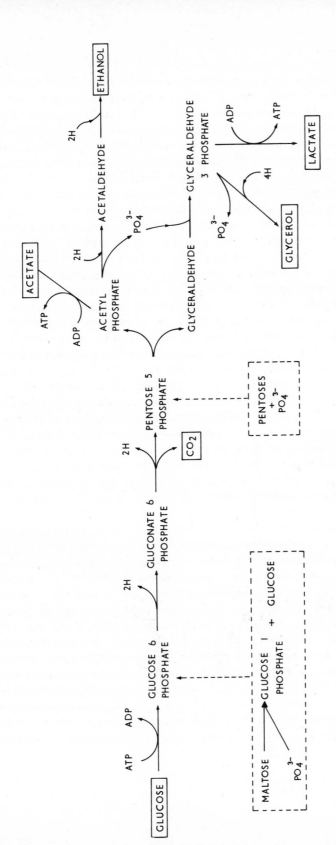

Fig. 21.2 Phosphoketolase pathway incorporating the phosphorolysis of maltose [20].

hydrogen acceptor for the regeneration of NAD. Breakdown of hexoses and pentoses by the heterofermentative strains is achieved by the phosphoketolase pathway (Fig. 21.2). From glucose or maltose, lactic acid plus a range of other end products are produced such as ethanol, glycerol, acetic acid, and carbon dioxide. The pivotal reaction is the cleavage of pentose-5-phosphate to acetyl phosphate and glyceraldehyde, mediated by the enzyme phosphoketolase. It is a reaction which is virtually irreversible. Fructose usually affords a better substrate for growth than glucose for heterofermentative strains and when a mixture of glucose and fructose is present, the latter acts as a hydrogen acceptor and is reduced to mannitol. Maltose is readily used by certain heterofermentative strains although no maltase is present. A maltophosphorylase permits the formation of β-glucose-1-phosphate wi hout the use of ATP; the rest of the maltose molecule is excreted as glucose [20]. Pentoses may also serve as substrates after a period of adaptation and are metabolized to yield acetate and lactate (*L. brevis*). From a brewing standpoint it is significant that maltose and pentoses are often present in considerable amounts in many beers and may encourage growth of any contaminant present. Beers low in fermentable sugars are therefore less prone to infection by lactic acid bacteria, especially when the level of simple nitrogenous compounds is also minimal. It also appears that the metabolic products of particular strains of brewing yeast are able to restrict the growth of lactic acid bacteria. Thus when 13 strains of *Lactobacillus* and three of *Pediococcus*, isolated from wort to beer, were added to 31 different sterile beers, only in three beers did they all grow. In five beers none grew while diverse results were obtained with the remaining 23 beers. Resistant beers could be made susceptible if heated at 80°C (176°F) for 15 min, but not if heated at only 60°C (140°F). A heat-labile metabolite of yeast is therefore thought to be responsible for resistance [21].

Both homofermentative and heterofermentative lactobacilli are auxotrophic for a range of specific amino acids (that is they require them for growth) and are often unable to sustain growth if a single amino acid is lacking including arginine, aspartic acid, glutamic acid, isoleucine, leucine, phenylalanine, proline, serine, threonine, tryptophan, and valine. In addition some strains require alanine, glycine, histidine, lysine, methionine, and tyrosine [6]. It has been shown that for *L. brevis*, L-arginine plays a role not only in protein synthesis but also in the production of energy. Arginine is hydrolysed to citrulline and ammonia, the citrulline then reacts with inorganic phosphate to give L-ornithine and carbamyl phosphate [6]. The latter converts ADP to ATP and by hydrolysis is broken down to carbon dioxide and ammonia in the process. In this connection it has been shown that arginine is present in both continuously produced and in batch-fermentation beer. Growth of lactobacilli in beer is usually not possible because essential amino acids such as isoleucine, leucine, phenylalanine, serine, threonine, and tryptophan are removed during fermentation by the yeast. Nevertheless, excretion of amino acids and other nitrogenous compounds [22] by yeast under conditions of osmotic shock and temperature shock is important in this context and should be avoided by preventing abrupt osmotic changes during fermentation. Various lactic acid bacteria require particular vitamins such as p-amino-benzoic acid, folic acid, and also certain purines and pyrimidines [6].

The heterofermentative strains normally have long rod-shaped cells but considerable variation in shape (pleomorphism) occurs, and short rods may develop. They grow best at 30°C (86°F) and in the pH range 4·0–5·0. With an extended lag period, they can adapt to grow in a medium of lower pH, in the presence of hop resins and of ethanol. Beer may support growth when suitable nitrogenous compounds are present. The quantity of lactic acid produced usually reflects the concentration of carbohydrates in the beer available for assimilation by these organisms.

Hop resins and isomeric compounds inhibit the growth of lactic acid bacteria in general but, possibly because of adaptation to their environment, strains encountered in breweries are relatively uninhibited. It has been shown that resistance to humulone derivatives develops rapidly in a number of strains and two to five subculturings give rise to between eight- and twenty-fold greater resistance to humulone at concentrations over 100 mg/ml. Bioassay of hop resins and their isomers is therefore carried out with suscep-tible lactic acid bacteria isolated from cheese and other dairy products. The length of lag period is, in very general terms, proportional to the level of the hop antiseptics [23].

All the strains mentioned can spoil beer by causing turbidity and acidity and off-flavours due to the range of metabolic products. Some strains are notable for their ability to produce extracellular slime, thus giving rise to 'ropey' beer. The slime produced by these bacteria is thixotropic and disappears temporarily on vigorous shaking. 'Rope'-forming strains seem to arise on occasion from strains without slime covering and conversely the ability to form 'rope' is often lost because of mutation. The rope is made up of a complex heteropolymer containing units of glucose, mannose, and nucleic acid.

The most important off-flavour and aroma associated with the lactic acid bacteria is the sweet, butterscotch or honey note provided by diacetyl and related vicinal diketones. It can be discerned readily in lager beers at concentrations as low as 0·5 μg/ml. The defect was formerly called 'Sarcina sickness' after *Sarcina*, the outdated generic name for brewery gram-positive bacteria.

If mash temperatures in the brewhouse fall or sweet wort is held at temper-atures below 60°C (140°F), there is a danger that thermophilic bacteria will grow. *Lactobacillus delbrueckii* is homofermentative and readily grows in the range 45–55°C (113–131°F). Its growth may be encouraged in those countries, notably West Germany, where acidification of bicarbonate in the brewing water is normally not carried out because of purity laws. Hence the D-(−) lactic acid production is a valuable aid to reduce pH to those levels where amylase action is optimal. Other thermophilic bacteria associated with malt may also be present in the mash tun, especially species of *Bacillus* such as *B. coagulans* and *B. stearothermophilus* [24, 25]. These produce considerable amounts of L-(+)lactic acid, have an optimum growth temperature of 60–63°C (140–145°F) and will survive at least 70°C (158°F). The rod-shaped cells are gram-positive, catalase-positive, 0·5–0·8 μm by 2·5–5·0 μm in size, sometimes disposed in chains, and with certain cells containing a single elliptical spore. As far as is known, all thermophilic bacteria associated with the mash tun and sweet wort are inhibited by isohumulones at say 12 μg/ml.

It is convenient to mention briefly that isolates of spore-forming bacteria are sometimes encountered in beer, especially in maturation or ruh tanks. They are variously identified as strains of *Bacillus* or *Clostridium* but have not been described in detail in the literature. It is not clear whether they are growing in the beer or merely surviving. Their numbers are normally very small.

Strains of *Pediococcus* are common in breweries practising bottom-fermentation and rare in top-fermentation breweries. Whether this distinction arises because of the lower temperatures used in bottom fermentation or because of the use of *Saccharomyces carlsbergensis* rather than *S. cerevisiae* is not clear. The spoilage caused by *Pediococcus* is very similar to that caused by other lactic acid bacteria, giving rise to acidity, turbidity, and off-flavours. *Pediococcus* strains have an optimum temperature range for growth of 21–25°C (70–77°F) but are capable of developing at low temperatures. The cocci may be disposed as single cells, in pairs, tetrads, short chains, or irregular clumps. There are various strains differing in the way they attack glucose, fructose, maltose, and sucrose. The diastatic variety of *P. damnosus* is able to degrade both dextrins and starch but unlike the other strains, it fails to produce diacetyl. The varieties *viscosus* and *limosus* of *P. damnosus* produce 'ropiness' in beer, using glucose, fructose, sucrose, or maltose as their source of carbohydrate. The complex polysaccharide 'rope' has already been referred to above [26, 27]. The varieties differ in their need for an atmosphere of carbon dioxide. Some have a pseudo-catalase which will break down hydrogen peroxide but is insensitive to cyanide and azide, and has no haem group [28, 29].

The difficulty of isolating lactic acid bacteria from brewing environments and culturing them successfully has led to the development of many culture media. A list of these and of other media commonly used in brewing microbiology is given in Table 21.1. Although there are claims that one medium will support the growth of all brewery lactic acid bacteria, many microbiologists dispute this. Some progress has been made in serological identification [14].

TABLE 21.1

Media commonly used in microbiological quality control

Reference	Medium	Comments
[30]	MYGP*†	Contains malt extract, yeast extract, glucose and peptone. General nutrient medium (particularly for yeasts) which supports growth of many brewery microorganisms.
[31]	Wallerstein Lab. nutrient medium (WLN)*†	General non-selective medium for many brewery microorganisms. Bromocresol green indicator enhances differences between appearance of colonies of various strains.
[32]	Lee's multidifferential medium (LMD)*†	General non-selective medium. Acid-producing bacteria detected by dissolution of calcium carbonate present in medium and by colour change of bromocresol green indicator.
[33]	Hsu's rapid medium (HRM)*†	General non-selective medium.
[34]	Lysine medium†	Lysine is sole source of nitrogen, *Saccharomyces* does not grow but other yeasts do.
[35]	Crystal violet medium†	Crystal violet (20 µg/ml) suppresses culture yeasts particularly, but variable response by all yeasts.
[36]	Schwarz differential medium†	Contains *inter alia* fuchsin-sulphite which tends to suppress culture yeast when plates held at 37°C (99°F) for 24 hr, then 30°C (86°F) for about 72 hr.
[37]	Lin's medium†	Contains *inter alia* fuchsin-sulphite and crystal violet and therefore has properties like previous two media.
[38]	Longley's medium†	A modification of Lin's medium.
[39]	Actidione medium†	Contains actidione (2–4 µg/ml). Tends to suppress culture yeast. Variable results with other yeasts.
[40]	Williamson's deep-liver medium*	Contains yeast extract, liver extract, casein hydrolysate, glucose and pot. monohydrogen phosphate. Encourages some acetic acid bacteria and *Hafnia*.
[40]	Williamson's medium A*	Contains beer, yeast extract, citrate–phosphate buffer. Supports acetic acid bacteria.
[40]	Williamson's medium L*	Contains unhopped beer, maltose, yeast extract, liver extract, casein hydrolysate, either polymyxin or phenylethanol; with CO_2 atmosphere (25°C), supports lactic acid bacteria. Polymyxin suppresses gram-negative bacteria. Phenylethanol supports *Pediococcus* rather than *Lactobacillus*
[41]	Universal liquid medium*	Contains tomato juice and peptonized milk to encourage lactic acid bacteria.

TABLE 21.1 (*continued*)

Reference	Medium	Comments
[42]	Sucrose agar*	General purpose medium to which may be added specific inhibitors such as actidione, polymyxin and phenylethanol which make it specific for lactic acid bacteria.
[43]	Universal beer agar*	Like above but contains beer and agar.
[44]	MacConkey's medium*	Contains *inter alia* bile salts and neutral red indicator. Reasonably selective for brewery enterobacteria. *Hafnia* takes an extra day to grow at 25°C (77°F) on solid medium.
[45]	Acetic acid bacteria differential medium*	Contains *inter alia*, ethanol and indicator (powdered chalk might be added). Suppresses most brewery microorganisms except acetic acid bacteria.
[46]	Zymomonas detection medium*	Has low pH. Most brewery microorganisms are suppressed except *Zymomonas*.

* Actidione (5–25 μg/ml) may be added to suppress yeast growth.
† Chlortetracycline (25–50 μg/ml) may be added to suppress growth of gram-positive bacteria. Polymyxin may be added to suppress the growth of gram-negative bacteria.

21.2.2 GRAM-NEGATIVE BACTERIA
(a) *Acetic acid bacteria* [7]

The acetic acid bacteria are normally divided into two groups and thirty years ago it was suggested that a new genus called *Gluconobacter* be created for those members of the genus *Acetobacter* which were 'scarcely able to oxidize ethanol but which nevertheless produce considerable amounts of gluconic acid [47]. Subsequently it was shown that these acetic acid bacteria which oxidize ethanol no further than acetic acid had polar flagellation (in contrast to the strong oxidizers with peritrichous flagellation). This led to be suggestion that the genus *Acetomonas* be ascribed to the polar flagellated strains [48] and this name for the genus is now widely accepted. A distinction on bio-chemical grounds had been made between (*i*) lactophiles which grow well on lactate, have simple growth requirements and whose resting cells transform glutamic acid and (*ii*) glucophiles which grow well on glucose, but not on lactate, have complex growth requirements and their resting cells transform amino acids related to glutamate feebly or not at all [49]. Lactophiles can in general terms be equated with *Acetobacter* species and glucophiles with *Acetomonas*. Subsequently, it has been shown that the glucophiles lack certain enzymes of the citric acid cycle [50, 51]. Other support for two distinct genera of acetic acid bacteria has been given by infrared spectro-photometric studies [52].

In some *Acetobacter* species, glucose is metabolized via the hexose mono-phosphate pathway and then the tricarboxylic acid cycle. In other strains, the entry to these pathways may follow the oxidation of glucose to gluconate, when gluconokinase gives rise to gluconate-6-phosphate. In still others, the ability to phosphorylate is completely lost and glucose is oxidized through gluconate to a 2- or 5-oxogluconate or even further to diketogluconate or a γ-pyrone [51]. (A pyrone is a six-membered oxygen heterocyclic compound with a carboxyl group in the α or γ position.) One species, *Acetobacter liquefaciens*, is able to carry out most of these changes but in most strains of *Acetobacter*, there is severe restriction of metabolic routes when glucose is the carbon source. In *Acetomonas*, the hexose-monophosphate shunt may operate but the tricarboxylic acid cycle fails to do so, due to lack of activity of isocitrate dehydrogenase and possibly other enzymes. Glucose may be oxidized to gluconate but usually no further and the major metabolic route (HMP) leads to acetic acid, the principal metabolite.

The strong oxidizing ability of acetic acid bacteria is exploited commercially, for instance in the production of gluconates and oxogluconates from glucose, and in the oxidation of sorbitol to sorbose – a precursor of ascorbic acid [53]. By far the most important application and indeed the original one is the manufacture of vinegar [54] from fermented malt wort, from wine, or from cider using *Acetobacter rancens* or *A. operans*. Strains used in the quick vinegar process have been reported to be unable to grow at a pH greater than 4·3 [55].

Industrial use for other strains which have special powers of synthesizing polysaccharides is also likely to be achieved [56]. Thus *A. xylinum* and *A. acetigenum* yield a cellulose, while *A. capsulatum* and *A. acidum-mucosum* give rise to a non-cellulosic polyglucose with α(1 → 6)linkages, an average chain length of 13 glucose units and branches stemming from α(1 → 4)linkages. Some strains produce rope in vinegar and beer, the rope comprising dextran which could substitute for the serologically identical product from *Leuconostoc* species used as a blood plasma extender. Yields of cellulose may be greatly increased by the use of stirred, aerated fermenters [57]. Regarding the spoiling of beer, it must be emphasized that the rope produced can be very substantial from a small number of bacteria.

The nitrogen metabolism of acetic acid bacteria has not received a great deal of attention but it is clear that *Acetobacter* strains can make their entire complement of nitrogenous compounds from ammonia, suitable sources of energy and appropriate carbon fragments [58, 59]. Possibly glutamate is synthesized from ammonia and 2-oxoglutarate generated from the tricarboxylic acid cycle. From glutamate, enzymic transamination with oxaloacetate yields aspartate. Alanine possibly arises from the β-decarboxyl-ation of aspartate; it does not apparently arise from transamination with pyruvate. *Acetomonas* fails to operate the tricarboxylic acid cycle and therefore requires the presence of glutamate, proline or aspartate or the corresponding oxo-acids.

Acetic acid bacteria are either aerobic or micro-aerophilic and develop best in wort and beer when these media are exposed to air. They are particularly prevalent on bar dispense taps and other fittings exposed to beer and air. Beer dispense lines in public houses are also often grossly contaminated by these bacteria. It is thought that aerial infection by these organisms may occur but it is just as likely that infection is spread by flies, particularly the fruit-fly, *Drosophila*. It is usually possible to control the growth of acetic acid bacteria in beer by imposing anaerobic conditions but at least one strain is able to continue growth and produce a marked turbidity and rope [60]. This ability is also familiar in one form of cider spoilage [61].

There is no restriction of growth of the acetic acid bacteria by low pH, or by hop resins or their isomers. Ethanol is, of course, a source of carbon for strains of *Acetobacter*. The simple nutritional requirements of the acetic acid bacteria permit them to be almost ubiquitous in the brewery and be the most frequent cause of acidity, off-flavours, turbidity, and ropiness. Growth of the bacteria often gives rise to a greasy-looking covering or pellicle at the surface of liquid so that when drawing beer from a traditional ale cask, the acidity may appear excessive for the few bacterial cells in suspension. Recently a strain resembling *A. rancens* was shown to kill yeasts in bottled beer so that natural conditioning could not take place [62]. It was demonstrated that the toxin produced would pass through dialysis membranes but was extremely labile.

The distinction between genera of acetic acid bacteria appears to be reasonably well founded but Shimwell has repeatedly stressed that variability is so widespread that classification into species is of little value. This viewpoint has not been given whole-hearted support but it is likely that there is a continuous range of strains within a genus, with immediate neighbours in the series differing in their ability to produce one or two particular enzymes [1].

(b) *Zymomonas* [8, 9, 63]

This contaminant is a gram-negative organism, often highly motile with the rod-like cells having 1–5 polar flagella, but under some circumstances the cells may group into rosette-like clusters. *Z. mobilis* grows under micro-aerophilic conditions. It was formerly called *Achromobacter anaerobium*. The optimum temperature is 30°C (86°F) but it can develop extremely rapidly at 15°C (59°F) in cask beer. It can grow over a wide pH range (3·5–7·5). The organism is comparatively rare and this is fortunate because it can spoil beer in cask id a few hours. Glucose and fructose, sometimes sucrose, but not maltose, are utilized for the production of energy through a modified Entner–Doudoroff pathway [9] (Fig. 21.3). A wide range of amino acids are necessary for heavy growth, as are lipoic acid and biotin. Differences between strains with respect to carbohydrate and nitrogenous requirements has suggested that two species are to be found in beer, *Z. anaerobia* and *Z. mobilis*. However interconversion of the two 'species' by modifying culture conditions strongly indicates that only one species can be admitted [63].

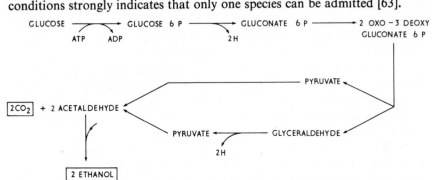

Fig. 21.3 Entner–Doudoroff pathway in *Zymomonas*. (It is of biochemical interest that in this pathway the carboxyl groups of the pyruvate arise from the carbon atoms 1 and 4 of the glucose. In the glycolytic pathway, the pyruvate comes from atoms 3 and 4.)

Hydrogen sulphide and acetaldehyde may cause a most unpleasant stench. The only methods of arresting spoilage are rigorous cleaning of brewery and plant, pasteurization or filtration of the beer. *Z. mobilis* may be introduced by dirty keg fillers or by the brushes at cask-washing or from soil and dust during brewery reconstruction.

It is clear that this organism is normally confined to sugar-primed un-pasteurized beer. In some breweries there is a chronic infection of traditional cask-conditioned ales which is normally at a low level except during long warm periods.

(c) *Enterobacteriaceae* [10, 11]

A range of species from this family of gram-negative, facultative anaerobic bacteria, many of which are motile, have been encountered in breweries. Some are closely related to the most well-known example of the family, *Escherichia coli*, strains of which are present in large numbers in the gut of mammals (see Chapter 7). They are therefore termed coliforms and include species of *Citrobacter*, *Enterobacter*, and *Klebsiella*. It is probable that they were first described by Lindner in 1895 as *Termobacterium album*, *T. iridescens* and *T. lutescens*, bacteria known to grow readily in wort and produce a variety of flavours and aromas ranging from sweet, honey and fruity through to vegetable and faecal.

The wort bacteria were considered by some as unimportant provided that wort was pitched with yeast promptly [64]. However it has been established that these bacteria are able to continue their growth in wort after the yeast has begun to multiply [10, 11, 65, 66]. Many are severely inhibited during the progress of fermentation and may die as the pH falls below 4·4 and the ethanol content rises about 2·0% (v/v). Their metabolic products are however present in the beer and may modify taste and aroma adversely. Thus phenolic and medicinal off-flavours arising from volatile phenols and chlorophenols have been caused by some species [10, 67]. Volatile organo-sulphur compounds are released, such as dimethyl sulphide and related compounds. Levels of acetaldehyde and various esters and fusel alcohols are also higher in beer when enterobacterial numbers are high. Although diacetyl is not produced directly in appreciable amounts by the bacteria, they do appear to be able to influence yeast metabolism so that abnormally high levels are present.

While many enterobacterial species fail to survive to the end of a fermentation of a normal beer, they may well do so in the case of beers with a pH over 4·4 and with a low content of alcohol (say under 2% v/v). Other enterobacterial species on the other hand persist through fermentation of a normal beer and are transferred to fresh wort by being present in the harvested pitching yeast. One example recently recognized is *Enterobacter agglomerans* [65, 66] which gives rise to increased levels of acetaldehyde, methyl acetate, diacetyl-2,3-pentane dione and dimethyl sulphide in the final beer. A result of the metabolism is that the pH of the beer is greater than normal.

The most striking example of a bacterium which is capable of surviving fermentation and being transmitted by the pitching yeast is the familiar 'short fat rod'. This organism was probably that named by Lindner *Termobacterium lutescens* and commonly recognized during microscopic examination of brewery pitching yeast subsequently [10]. The same bacterium was later called *Flavobacterium proteus* on the rather negative grounds that the organism could not be readily placed in another genus [68]. Later it was placed in a specially created genus, *Obesumbacterium proteus* with no named family [69]. Its claimed distinction was the ability to grow alongside yeast in a brewery fermentation. This claim was shown to be invalid because the enterobacterial *Hafnia alvei* was demonstrated to share this property [10], as was later the enterobacterial *E. agglomerans* [65]. It was then shown on the basis of (*i*) guanine and cytosine content of the cell DNA, (*ii*) DNA base sequence comparison and (*iii*) numerical taxonomy, that *O. proteus* was very closely related to *H. alvei*. A new name *Hafnia protea* was proposed [10]. Phage typing indicated that there were two strains, differing in the amount of dimethyl sulphide and dimethyl disulphide that they produced [70]. Increased levels in beers of n-propanol, isobutanol, isopentanol and butane-2,3-diol were associated with the presence of the organism. When the bacterium and brewing yeast were both present, the level of diacetyl could be high [10] as could the final pH and gravity of the beer [71]. Thus the bacterium appears to influence yeast metabolism in a way that encourages the survival of both it and other enterobacteria.

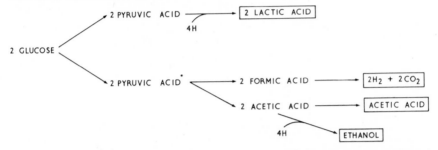

Fig. 21.4 Fate of pyruvic acid in *Escherichia* strains. * Involves a phosphoroclastic split of pyruvic acid in which inorganic phosphate and ADP give rise to ATP.

The enterobacteria have a considerable range of biochemical accomplishments. They have, for instance, the ability to degrade glucose by either the EMP (glycolytic), the hexose-monophosphate or the Entner–Doudoroff pathway [17]. Pyruvic acid formed by these different routes can, under acidic conditions, be transformed into lactic acid, acetic acid, ethanol, carbon dioxide, and hydrogen (Fig. 21.4). *Klebsiella* strains differ from those of *Escherichia* in producing, instead of equimolecular amounts of carbon dioxide and hydrogen, more carbon dioxide. This is because in *Klebsiella* two molecules of pyruvic acid condense to give acetoin and carbon dioxide [17]. The acetoin so formed normally acts as a hydrogen acceptor to give rise to butane-2,3-diol (Fig. 21.5). *Klebsiella* therefore tends to form less lactic acid and acetic acid and so the methyl red test is negative (see Chapter 7). Many of the *Enterobacteriaceae* can grow in a simple salts medium supplemented with one of a range of carbohydrates to supply carbon and energy. Other species of the family however require additionally certain amino acids and vitamins, such as glutamate, methionine, lysine and thiamin. With regard to nitrogen metabolism, *E. coli*, but not *K. aerogenes*, produces ammonia under starvation conditions following the oxidation of cellular proteins and their degradation products.

Hafnia (*Obesumbacterium*) grows under aerobic conditions in defined media containing arginine plus either glutamate or aspartate. Glucose, fructose, mannose and galactose are rapidly utilized; maltose and soluble starch give slower growth. Products of metabolism include acetic, formic, 2-oxoglutaric, pyruvic and succinic acids [72]. The organism appears to have both EMP and HMP pathways and a terminal electron transfer chain.

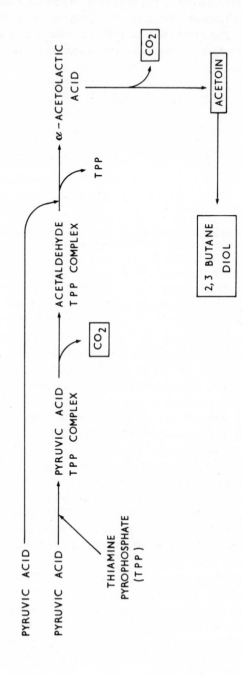

Fig. 21.5 The formation of acetoin and butane-2,3-diol by *Klebsiella* strains.

Like brewers' yeast, it readily adapts to microaerophilic conditions and terminal oxidation is repressed [72].

Another feature of the enterobacteria is their ability to use nitrate under anaerobic or microaerophilic conditions as a hydrogen acceptor instead of oxygen. The consequence is that if a brewery fermentation is conducted in the presence of enterobacterial contaminants and nitrate is present, an unacceptable level of nitrite may be produced [73].

Wort bacteria not belonging to the family *Enterobacteriaceae* may be present in small numbers, such as species of *Achromobacter*, *Acinetobacter* and *Pseudomonas*. They are more sensitive to pH and ethanol than the majority of the brewery enterobacterial strains. Still other bacteria may be present in sweet wort, sometimes in appreciable numbers, arising from the microbial flora of raw materials, particularly malt. Most of these bacteria fail to grow in the wort.

(d) *Pectinatus* [12, 74]

This organism, *Pectinatus cerevisiiphilus*, a member of the family *Bacteroidaceae*, is an anaerobic, gram-negative, non-sporing mesophile, producing rod-shaped cells with flagella developing only on one side of the cell body. Young cells move actively and appear X-shaped as they swim. Older cells in contrast display snake-like movement. It has been isolated from bottled beer in which it can grow strongly but, because it is a strict anaerobe, it is not easily grown in simple media such as glucose agar without the inclusion of a reducing substance such as thioglycollate. It grows vigorously when inoculated into fresh beer and produces copious quantities of hydrogen sulphide and acetic and propionic acids. The beer becomes turbid and may take a year to clear as the cells die and settle. Pasteurization readily kills the bacterium, say one minute at 58°C (136°F); it is easily controlled by iodophors and chlorinating agents. The mode of transmission of the organism has not been established but it has been isolated from lubrication oil mixed with beer and water, and from a drainage system.

21.3 *Bacterial spoilage at various stages in the brewing process*

The spoilage caused by bacteria at the various stages of the brewing process are outlined in Table 21.2. The infection of sweet-wort by thermophilic lactic acid bacteria has already been mentioned. Because these bacteria are sensitive to isohumulones, they do not survive in hopped wort.

Coliform bacteria are able to develop in both unhopped and hopped wort and are somewhat thermophilic; some strains are capable of growth at 40°C (104°F). Unfortunately, these organisms may be present in very small numbers in the water supply and, if such water is used for washing or rinsing, infection may occur. It may be that coliform infection is sometimes picked up when paraflow gaskets need replacing and allow some seepage of water into the wort. The greatest difficulty arises when wort is stored, as for example for continuous fermentation.

TABLE 21.2

Brewery spoilage organisms and the stage of production at which they occur [64]

Stage	Organisms present
I Mashing and sweet-wort	Thermophilic lactic acid bacteria†
II Cooling to pitching	Coliform bacteria
	Acetic acid bacteria*
	Lactic acid bacteria*
	Obesumbacterium (*Hafnia*)*
III Fermentation	*Obesumbacterium* (*Hafnia*)
	Acetic acid bacteria
	Lactic acid bacteria
IV Conditioning and	Acetic acid bacteria
dispensing in trade	Lactic acid bacteria
	*Zymomonas mobilis**

* Rare.   † Extremely rare, unless encouraged.

A very small inoculum of coliform bacteria is able to grow at an alarming pace. The cells may divide approximately every 20 min under appropriate culture conditions, thus giving a million-fold increase in numbers in less than 7 hr. Once a pocket of coliform bacteria has developed in an area which cannot easily be scoured clean, for instance certain fittings associated with the wort lines, it is extremely difficult to free the plant from infection. Low pressure steaming is often ineffective as a sterilization procedure because the bacteria are thermophilic and, protected by condensate and dead bacteria in the outer layers of the pocket, some cells survive.

Growth of lactic acid and acetic acid bacteria in wort is usually slow in comparison with enterobacteria, including *Hafnia* (*Obesumbacterium*). Normally, however, cells of *Hafnia* are not introduced into wort until pitching, when large numbers may be present in the pitching yeast. Very few pitching yeasts are free from *H. protea* and it is quite common to find this bacterium in proportions ranging from 0·1 to 4·0% of the total cell population [75]. On pitching, this gives a viable cell count of *H. protea* ranging from a few thousand to over a million per ml. (At a pitching rate of 0·28 kg/hl (1 lb/brl), a yeast bearing 1000 living bacteria per million yeast cells will give an immediate contribution of about 25 000 bacteria per ml.) The bacterial flora of fermenting wort normally reflects therefore the organisms present in the pitching yeast rather than the wort. This is emphasized further by the coliform bacteria failing to grow appreciably once fermentation is under way. The open type of continuous fermentation (see Chapter 19) will support the growth not only of yeast but also contaminating acetic acid bacteria and *H. protea*. In the closed type where the conditions are more anaerobic, the chief contaminants are lactic acid bacteria. The difficulty of removing this type of infection from Tower continuous fermenters of the closed type has been stressed and rapid development of a lactobacillus contamination over a three-day period has been recorded in which the final concentration was three million rods per ml [64].

In conventional fermentation the growth of yeast hinders the development of many coliform organisms; before fermentation is complete the growth of *Hafnia protea* and *Enterobacter agglomerans* also ceases. Pitching yeast often contains cells of acetic acid or lactic acid bacteria and growth of these can occur during fermentation. The development of lactobacilli in three breweries gave maximum cell counts at racking ranging from approximately 100–10 000 per ml. At two breweries, the wort and fermentation conditions were identical but in one of these the average count per ml for twelve brews was 4740 while in the other brewery it was 135 [64].

Microaerophilic strains of acetic acid bacteria may develop in some instances during fermentation. More commonly, however, they multiply during racking, and subsequently the most striking growth is when air is allowed to accumulate above the beer, for instance when casks stand partly-emptied for some time. Infection may occur in keg beers if the keg or its component spear is not sterilized effectively. Contamination of cask and keg beer may also be caused by lactic acid bacteria and by *Zymomonas mobilis*. The possible results as already mentioned include turbidity, acidity, off-flavours, and ropiness.

Bottled and canned beers will normally only develop infection if pasteurization of filtration has not been effective, or if the containers are not sterile. Naturally conditioned bottled beer is however prone to the same dangers as cask beer.

21.4 *Prevention of spoilage*

The most important factor is cleanliness, not only of the parts of equipment and plant that can be seen, but the parts that are out of sight. Bacteria will find suitable sites for growth wherever residues of sugar, wort, beer or yeast lodge. Special attention must therefore be given to the inclination of supply pipes, to the bends, valves, junctions and joints that may harbour infection. Rough internal surfaces must be avoided. In vessels, difficulties arise from poor location of drainage points, from beer stone, and from every implement dipped into the vessel contents including attemperators, rousing equipment and hoses, temperature probes, skimmers or suction devices. Absolute sterility may not be attainable but cleanliness can be. It is

possible to sterilize wort, beer, or yeast residues in plant, but they greatly
increase the vulnerability of the plant to future infection because they are
potential media for microorganisms.

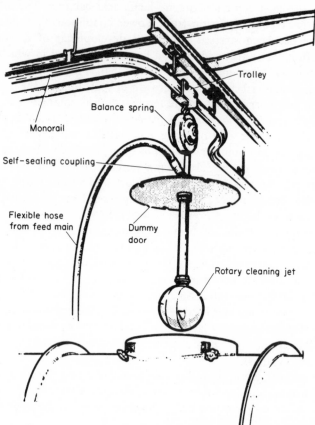

Fig. 21.6 Rotary cleaning jet equipment for top-entry fermenting vessels and road tankers.

In-place cleaning has developed greatly over the past decade [77–80]
mainly because of the high cost and variability of manual cleaning. Both
sprayball and high pressure rotating jets are employed and, with correct
siting, cleaning liquid impinges on all surfaces. Portable equipment has also
been developed which can be transferred from one vessel to another in an
orderly sequence of cleaning operations (Figs 21.6 and 21.7). Because in-place
cleaning is most satisfactory with closed vessels, open fermenters are being
gradually replaced by closed fermenters even in top-fermentation breweries.
The development of spraying equipment has gone hand in hand with automated systems which allow standardized programmes of cleaning and

rinsing to be carried out. The cleaning fluids are made up and stored in a special tank and are pumped, or gravity fed, to and from the vessel being sprayed (Fig. 21.8).

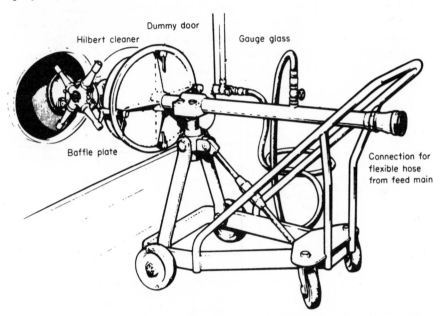

Fig. 21.7 In-place cleaning rotary jet equipment for cleaning vessels with manholes near ground level.

A typical cleaning sequence for plate heat-exchangers, enclosed fermenters, conditioning or lagering tanks, bright beer tanks and associated pipework is given below:

1. First cold water rinse (and thence to drain).
2. Hot or cold detergent spraying (and thence to detergent collection tank).
3. Second cold water rinse (and then recovered to be used on other vessels as first cold water rinse).
4. Cold sterilant spraying (and then to sterilant collection tank).
5. Final cold water rinse (and then recovered to be used on other vessels as second cold water rinse).

Some breweries will discard all rinses, detergent and sterilant spray solutions after using them once. Other breweries use their detergent and sterilant (sanitizer) solutions many times before sending them to the drains. It may be possible to keep the effective strength reasonably constant by topping-up with concentrated solution but this is only cost-effective if the effective strength can be monitored readily. Still other breweries will use a combined detergent sterilant so that the programme comprises three or four steps, not five. However, a very good case for separating cleaning from sterilizing (sanitizing) can be made on the grounds that sterilants are used up unnecessarily on the soil that is being removed. Some breweries insist on using saturated steam for sterilizing but this is usually expensive in energy, especially if the vessel has to be cooled immediately afterwards. The use of a non-sterile water spray to cool at this stage is to be deplored. Steam sterilizing of kegs is a special case because the time available for sterilizing is so short.

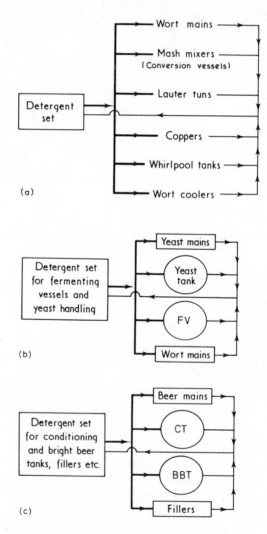

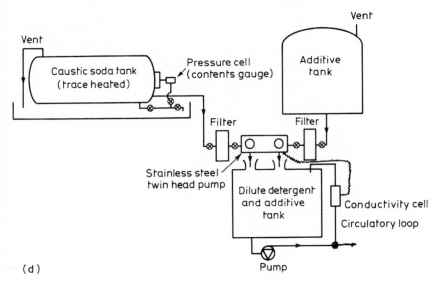

(d)

Fig. 21.8 Diagrammatic representation of the arrangements for cleaning-in-place within a modern brewery.

The problems of cleaning the brewhouse vessels are rather different from those in the fermentation and post-fermentation areas. Thus the amount of soil is much greater and the accent is on cleanliness rather than sterilization. Another factor is that the brewhouse vessels are not chilled. Thus, use of caustic soda (plus compounds that are capable of wetting and sequestering calcium salts) is widespread for stainless steel equipment. It is usual to employ the detergent mixture at 80–85°C (176–185°F) and with caustic concentrations in the range 1–3 % w/v. Thus there is in most instances a completely separate system for cleaning the brewhouse equipment as against that dealing with the wort receiver, whirlpool, wort cooler, fermenters and other beer tanks where sterilization is necessary.

Caustic soda, without sequestering agents, is used by some breweries to clean stainless steel equipment but this normally leads to problems with residues of calcium salts that cling tenaciously to the metal. It is therefore normal to formulate a detergent mixture capable of removing, readily and entirely, the various soils encrusted on the stainless steel internal surface. Hot caustic soda solution itself will dissolve protein, lipid, cellulose, hemicellulose, mucilage, gums, pectins and tannins. The effects of caustic soda and the various compounds that may be added to it in solution are indicated in Table 21.3.

TABLE 21.3

Properties of components of commercial cleaning mixtures. (The strength of various properties is indicated by a scale in which 5 is the maximum strength.) [76]

	Organic dissolving power (wort beer and yeast residues)	Wetting power (penetration of detergents)	Dispersing power (hold insoluble particles of dirt in suspension)	Rinsing power	Germicidal power	Calcium sequestering power (keep carbonate in solution)	Calcium dissolving power (dissolve Ca salts in alkaline solution)
Caustic soda	5	1	1	1	3		
Sodium carbonate	2	1	1	1	1		
Sodium metasilicate	3	3	4	3	2		
Sodium orthosilicate	3	2	4	3	3		
Trisodium phosphate	2	2	4	3	2		
Wetting agents		5	4	5			
Sodium tripolyphosphate	2	1	3	2		3	
Sodium hexametaphosphate			4	2		4	1
Ethylene diamine tetraacetic acid						5	5
Sodium gluconate						5	3

Mixture of caustic soda, sodium metasilicate, wetting agent, and sodium tripolyphosphate will cover most requirements. EDTA and gluconates are included for mixtures required to remove beerstone and heater-scale, the former in acidic and weakly alkaline solutions, the latter in alkaline solutions.

It may be necessary to spray a stainless steel vessel occasionally with 2% nitric acid to remove the scale that builds up from silica and calcium salt deposition. Where vessels are copper, it is necessary to add to the caustic solution a corrosion inhibitor. Aluminium vessels require cleaning with acidic detergents, usually involving phosphoric acid. There is, however, also interest in the use of acidic detergents for cleaning fermenters, lagering and conditioning tanks, and bright beer tanks. Such detergents would not dissolve carbon dioxide present in the vessels to any appreciable extent, as caustic detergents would, and can therefore be used without carbon dioxide being scavenged from the vessel before cleaning and returned after it. (It is possible to spray caustic-based detergents carefully so that carbon dioxide within the vessel being treated is not appreciably depleted; the caustic soda in solution is however substantially transformed into sodium carbonate and bicarbonate.)

Sterilization of the surfaces of vessels, pipes and valves may be achieved by heat, radiation or chemicals [81]. The use of steam has already been mentioned; apart from cost it tends to be a slow procedure for sterilizing brewery vessels when steam pressures are low. Furthermore, it may carry undesirable particles and odours while the condensate is often drained unsatisfactorily. Radiation sterilization is rare although ultraviolet light irradiation is used for the treatment of water on a continuous basis. One of the simplest chemicals used for sterilization is ozone but this has proved corrosive [82]. More widely employed is hydrogen peroxide which, with peracetic acid, is added to soak baths for flexible pipes and items of fermentation equipment.

The most common sanitizers yield chlorine, such as sodium hypochlorite solutions, chlorinated trisodium phosphate or trichloro-isocyanuric acid. Hypochlorites must not be added to acidic solutions because chlorine gas generated is poisonous to people and corrosive to stainless steel. In alkaline solutions however, the biocidal effects are strong, the hypochlorite is stable and corrosion of stainless steel (type 316) does not occur [79]. For the less resistant type 304, it is necessary to restrict temperatures to 60°C (140°F) and available chlorine to a maximum of 250 ppm (Fig. 21.9). Like other sanitizers, chlorine donating compounds react with organic soil and in the presence of such soil, are less effective in sterilizing. With 200 ppm available chlorine, alkaline detergents are adequately bactericidal in clean solutions. (One disadvantage of these sanitizers is their ability to react with the phenolic resin coatings used on some beer tanks. They produce chlorophenols which may be identified at a few parts per 10^9 in beer as medicinal flavours.)

Iodine is a halogen, like chlorine, but does not produce an acid analogous to hypochlorous acid. In alkali, iodine dissolves to yield the iodate ion which is not bacteriocidal. However iodine may be formulated with certain acids such as phosphoric acid to form an 'iodophor'. Such iodophors, incorporating surface active agents, are effective biocides in the pH range 2·5–3·5, with about 50 ppm available iodine. At 0°C (32°F), they require about 15 min contact time. The maximum temperature of use is 49°C (120°F), otherwise iodine is liberated and will stain. Another feature is that iodine is readily absorbed by rubber [79].

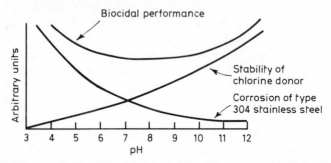

Fig. 21.9 The influence of pH on hypochlorite solutions with respect to biocidal performance, chemical stability and corrosion of type 304 stainless steel.

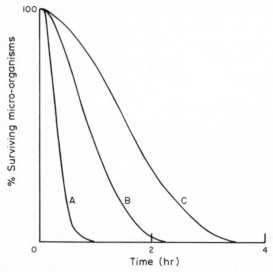

Fig. 21.10 Effect of a sterilizing agent on bacterial populations A, B, and C having 100, 1000 and 100 000 cell/ml medium.

Anionic surfactants are little used in breweries while cationic surfactants such as quaternary ammonium compounds are employed for certain biocidal applications. Ampholytic (amphoteric) surfactants are also used as biocides and like the quaternary ammonium compounds they have to be rigorously rinsed from beer tanks because they have a strongly adverse effect on beer foam. Surfactants normally have molecules with a short hydrophilic head and a long hydrophobic tail. The tails tend to be adsorbed by metal surfaces and also by soil surfaces. Hence the chemical attractions between soil and metal is lost.

The killing of microorganisms by sanitizers has been studied at length [83]. It is not proposed in this volume to discuss the dynamics of sterilization except to stress the significance of (*i*) soil being present, (*ii*) the numbers of viable microorganisms exposed and (*iii*) the temperature and pH of the medium. It is often forgotten that the smaller the number of organisms present on a surface, the more quickly and effectively a bacteriocide operates. The number of viable microorganisms falls at first exponentially and then decreases asymptotically (Fig. 21.10). There can therefore be no certainty that all microorganisms are killed during a sterilization treatment. The chances are less if (*i*) soil is present, (*ii*) microbial numbers are initially high, and (*iii*) the temperature and pH are inappropriate for the sanitizer employed.

21.5 *Pitching yeast*

Pitching yeast is, in terms of the number of contaminant cells introduced into the process stream, the most important reservoir of infection in the brewery. The bacterial content of the yeast should therefore be kept low. Proper attention to handling and storage of the yeast should prevent bacterial contamination from increasing, and may even decrease it. There are, however, examples where careful management has not been sufficient. Under these circumstances, the yeast may be replaced by either one from another brewery or by one propagated from laboratory stocks. The imported yeast may be inferior to the one it replaces, from the point of view of the types of bacteria present. The propagated yeast should on the other hand be free of infection.

Another, but less desirable, possibility is to wash the yeast with either bisulphite preparations or with dilute acid such as tartaric, phosphoric or sulphuric acids. The pH of the wash should never fall below 2·5. Acidified ammonium persulphate (0·75 % at pH 2·8) has also been used with success [84]. Antibiotics such as polymyxin, neomycin, and penicillin have been evaluated for yeast washing but have not been generally adopted because they will not inhibit the full spectrum of brewery contaminants, and because they could possibly cause the building up of stocks of antibiotic-resistant strains. The washing of yeast presents some difficulties; the choice of sanitizer, its concentration, the length and temperature of application offer a complex problem. Furthermore, the ability of the yeast to ferment and to flocculate is usually changed during the fermentation immediately after washing. It is often observed that the viability of the yeast after acid washing is markedly reduced.

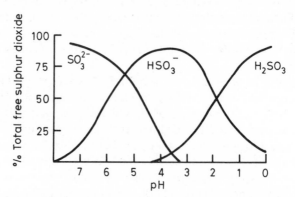

Fig. 21.11 The influence of pH on the ionization of sulphurous acid.

In wine-making and cider-making, sulphur dioxide plays a vital role in restricting the growth of unwanted organisms. The importance of sulphites in brewing is possibly not so great, but many breweries rely on them. Roughly, the length of the lag phase imposed on the bacteria is proportional to the concentrations of sulphite used up to 40 μg/ml [64]. In Britain, where sulphites are the only bacteriostats that may be legally added to beer, the statutory limit for sulphur dioxide in beer. is 70 μg/ml. Sulphite is rapidly taken up by a variety of compounds in beer including carbonyls so that the level of uncombined or 'available' sulphur dioxide falls appreciably. The undissociated sulphurous acid is more potent than the bisulphite ion, but the concentration of the former is very low at the pH of beer, namely 4·0. The bisulphite ion is however more effective than the sulphite ion (Fig. 21.11). It is undesirable to add bisulphite to wort because, not only is the pH too high for effective bacteriostasis but the yeast reduces the material to hydrogen sulphide.

21.6 *Estimation and identification of brewery bacteria*
Samples to be evaluated may be liquid such as water, wort, sugar, beer, finings, primings, etc. Alternatively the samples may be solid and need dispersing (for example, yeast). Swab samples from vessels, pipes, and casks will also be taken and spread on to media in petri dishes. Alternatively, frozen cylinders of solid medium can be applied to the surfaces to be tested, the medium cut with a sterile knife and placed in a sterile petri dish for culturing.

When there are few viable bacteria in a liquid sample it may be necessary to concentrate either by centrifugation or by membrane filtration. The latter is particularly valuable because the organisms left on the membrane can be either stained *in situ* and examined microscopically, or the membrane can be cultured on a solid medium in a petri dish. An example of a scheme for microbiological control in a bottling or kegging installation is shown in Fig. 21.12.

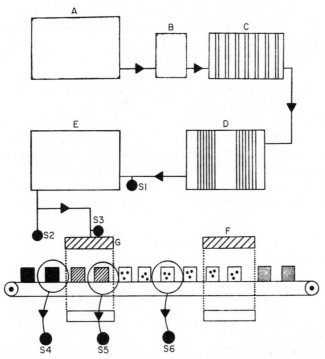

Fig. 21.12 Scheme for microbiological control in a bottling or kegging installation [81]. A. Cold-storage tank; B. Dosing tank; C. Powder filter; D. Flash pasteurizer; E. Sterile beer tank; F. Washer; G. Filler.

Sample point	Sample	Treatment
S1	Beer leaving pasteurizer	Membrane filter samplers
S2	Beer leaving sterile beer tank	Filters plated-out on to hopped-wort agar
S3	Beer entering filler	
S6	Empty washed container	Saline solution added and subsequently plated out
S5	Empty steamed container	
S4	Completely filled container	Forcing test

For simple detection of contamination, the sample is cultured in wort or beer at 25°C (77°F) or 37°C (99°F) to discover whether a growth of microorganisms occurs. It is valuable in many situations however to get an indication of numbers of organisms and therefore it is preferable to plate the sample on to a solid medium at an appropriate known dilution in order to count the colonies which develop. If the medium were beer or wort agar, a small proportion of bacteria in a large yeast population might go undetected. Fortunately it is possible to inhibit yeast growth by incorporating actidione at 10 μg/ml into the medium. Growth of bacteria is virtually unaffected by this concentration of actidione and therefore a relatively small number of bacteria can be estimated.

If cold medium in petri dishes is streaked, rather than mixing the inoculum with the warm medium before pouring into the dishes, the colonies can be more easily removed for further tests. A scheme for selective media and confirmatory tests is given in Table 21.1. Results are given in Table 21.4 for bacterial numbers in pitching yeasts. When lactic acid bacteria are suspected, the plates are held in an atmosphere of carbon dioxide because these bacteria often fail to grow unless the gas is present. Selective media may also be used for slide culture [85, 86]. Microcolonies develop from the individual bacterial cells and may be detected in a few hours by microscopical examination – long before colonies could be seen by the naked eye on the medium in a petri dish.

TABLE 21.4

Representative results from the pitching yeasts of fifteen ale breweries in Britain using certain selective media described in Table 21.3 [40]

Sample from brewery no.	Total bacterial count (living and dead) per 10^6 yeast cells	Viable cell count (per 10^6 yeast cells)			
		Lacto-bacillus	*Obesum-bacterium*	Acetic acid bacteria	% viable to total bacteria
1	3000	p*	400	3	13
2	3000	2	900	9	30
3	3900	p*	2300	18	59
4	7500	20	6400	720	95
5	8000	p*	5700	1800	94
6	9000	p*	2200	0·5	25
7	10 000	1	650	150	8
8	12 000	7	450	12	4
9	18 000	0·3	13 000	4	73
10	29 000	15	2400	0·3	86
11	40 000	p*	2500	1	60
12	50 000	0·5	2500	15	100
13	68 000	50	2200	50	3
14	74 000	0·5	12 000	3	16
15	82 000	350	1200	2	2

p* Not detected by plating 10^7 yeast cells but shown to be present by using larger samples in liquid media.

21.7 *Wild yeasts*

A survey of wild yeasts encountered in British breweries nearly 30 years ago showed that the number of potential sources of such yeasts is large because many non-sterile materials and pieces of equipment were used. A wide variety of species and strains were isolated but not all caused spoilage to materials or to beer [87]. Certain of these yeasts however frequently recur in spoiled beer. Of 27 species isolated, hops had 12 and brewing yeast 11, but many of the species have no known technical significance. With yeasts known to affect beer quality, four species were detected in washed casks, three in hops, and four in brewing yeast. It was considered however that pitching yeast, and to a far lesser extent, priming sugars, were chiefly responsible for the incursion into beer of dangerous wild yeasts, such as wild *Saccharomyces cerevisiae*, *S. carlsbergensis*, *Pichia membranaefaciens*, *Torulopsis* spp., and *Candida* spp. [87]. Nevertheless dirty equipment and particularly casks must account for many outbreaks of beer spoilage by wild yeasts.

In a large proportion of traditional draught ales purchased in public houses, *Pichia* and *Candida* species were encountered. Wild strains of *Saccharomyces carlsbergensis* were detected in almost a third of the samples while less frequent were species of *Hanseniaspora*, *Kloeckera*, *Rhodotorula*, and *Torulopsis* [88].

An examination of the wild yeast flora of pitching yeasts from a number of breweries showed that *Pichia membranaefaciens*, *Candida mycoderma*, *Torulopsis colliculosa*, and *T. inconspicua* were of common occurrence. Other yeasts encountered less commonly were species of *Candida*, *Debaryomyces*, *Hansenula*, and *Rhodotorula* [89]. The wild yeasts were isolated by plating out pitching yeast (in order of 1–10 million pitching yeast cells per plate) on *Hansenula*, and *Rhodotorula* [89]. The wild yeasts were isolated by plating out pitching yeast (in the order of 1–10 million pitching yeast cells per plate) on to a medium containing lysine as the sole source of nitrogen. *Saccharomyces* species fail to grow (including wild strains of the genus) but the cells of other genera produce colonies [90]. Usually the frequency was 1–30 wild yeast cells per 10 million cells of pitching yeast and the greatest recorded level of contamination was 410 per 10 million. Other methods may be used to differentiate wild strains of *Saccharomyces* from culture strains of the same genus; they exploit the greater tolerance of the wild strains to temperature or to actidione or to crystal violet or to a combination [35, 38, 39].

The speed at which wild yeasts can grow in beer should not be underestimated. *S. cerevisiae* var. *turbidans* in commercial beer may give rise to turbidity of draught beers when the ratios of the wild yeast cells to culture yeast cells in the pitching yeast are as low as one in 1.6×10^8 [91].

In recent years, serological techniques have been developed for identifying and enumerating wild yeasts in the presence of culture yeast (see Chapter 16) [92, 93]. It is now possible by fluorescent antisera to detect under an ultraviolet microscope certain wild yeasts (including those in the genus *Saccharomyces*) at levels as low as one cell per 10^6 culture yeasts.

Spoilage caused by wild yeasts includes turbidity, off-flavours, and pellicle formation on the surface of the beer [94]. Turbidity from this source is caused by growth of wild yeasts remaining after the culture yeasts have been removed by filtering or by fining. Wild yeasts often sediment very slowly indeed and are usually insensitive to isinglass finings because they do not have a strong negative charge. Sometimes the wild yeast is particularly resistant to the normal pasteurization treatment. Common offenders in this category include *Saccharomyces cerevisiae* var. *turbidans* and var. *ellipsoideus*, *S. carlsbergensis* and *S. pastorianus*. Turbidity may also arise from species of *Torulopsis* which comprise very small cells and are therefore slow in sedimenting. Breaking up of the film or pellicle produced by *Pichia* and *Candida* sp. may also produce turbidity.

Off-flavours may arise from the activities of all the wild yeasts encountered. *Pichia* and *Candida* species will oxidize ethanol in a vessel exposed to air to produce acetic acid, while *Saccharomyces diastaticus* will attack malto-tetraose and often dextrins to produce ethanol. There are also differences between culture yeast and wild yeast with respect to the production of esters, fusel alcohols, organo-sulphur compounds, hydrogen sulphide, vicinal diketones and other products important in beer flavour. Phenolic flavours are known to be produced by certain wild yeasts. [95].

Certain strains of yeast including *S. cerevisiae* and *S. carlsbergensis* have developed the ability to secrete protein material which, over a particular range of pH values, is capable of killing sensitive strains of yeast (Chapter 16). Under certain circumstances therefore these killer yeasts are able to dominate fermentation. Several killer strains, otherwise suitable for brewing, are characterized by the production of unacceptable medicinal flavours [96].

Respiratory-deficient mutant forms of brewing yeast arise from time to time. Because they produce a different balance of metabolic products than the parent strain, they tend to influence the flavour of the beer. For instance they may produce unacceptable levels of vicinal diketones, notably diacetyl. They arise spontaneously but may be induced by a variety of substances, including copper salts [97] and formaldehyde [98].

Elimination of wild yeasts, or at least holding their numbers low, is princi-pally a matter of using pitching yeast free of wild yeasts and keeping equipment sterile. Yeast propagation equipment can help greatly in this matter but regular microbiological checks need to be carried out on cooled worts, sterile air lines, pitching yeast, finings, primings and dry hops as well as all equipment used for storage, transport, treatment, and dispense of beer [99, 100]. Absolute sterility can be achieved but many breweries are willing to accept slightly lower standards which are sufficient to ensure that very few bottles, cans and kegs become contaminated. Thus it has been stated [101] that the critical level is around 4–10 yeast cells per bottle of beer, but for reasons not sufficiently understood, many yeasts will not grow at this low level of contamination. However, there is no such safe level [102] for *Saccharomyces diastaticus* (or for lactic acid bacteria).

REFERENCES

[1] SHIMWELL, J. L. (1959). *Antonie van Leeuwenhoek J. Microbiol. Serol.*, **25**, 49.

[2] BREED, R. S., MURRAY, E. G. D. and SMITH, N. R., eds. (1951). *Bergey's Manual of Determinative Bacteriology*, Ballière Tindall and Cox, London.

[3] SKERMAN, V. B. D. (1967). *A Guide to the Identification of the Genera of Bacteria*, 2nd Edn., Williams and Wilkins, Baltimore, USA.

[4] INGLEDEW, W. M. (1979). *J. Am. Soc. Brew. Chem.*, **37** (3), 145.

[5] RAINBOW, C. (1975). *Lactic Acid Bacteria in Beverages and Food* (eds. CARR, J. G., CUTTING, C. V. and WHITING, G. C.), (Fourth Long Ashton Symposium), Academic Press, London.

[6] LAWRENCE, D. R. and LEEDHAM, P. A. (1979). *J. Inst. Brewing*, **85**, 119.

[7] RAINBOW, C. (1966). *Wallerstein Labs. Commun.*, **29**, 5.

[8] DADDS, M. J. S. and MARTIN, P. A. (1973). *J. Inst. Brewing*, **79**, 386.

[9] SWINGS, J. and DE LEY, J. (1977). *Bact. Reviews*, **41** (3), 1.

[10] PRIEST, F. G., COWBOURNE, M. A. and HOUGH, J. S. (1964). *J. Inst. Brewing*, **80**, 342.

[11] ESCHENBECHER, F. and ELLENRIEDER, M. (1975). *Proc. Eur. Brewery Conv. Congr., Nice*, p. 497.

[12] LEE, S. Y., MABEE, M. S., JANGAARD, N. O. and HORIUCHI, E. K. (1980). *J. Inst. Brewing*, **86**, 28.

[13] SOLBERG, O. and CLAUSEN, O. G. (1973). *J. Inst. Brewing*, **79**, 231.

[14] DOLEZIL, L. and KIRSOP, B. H. (1975). *J. Inst. Brewing*, **81**, 281.

[15] LAWRENCE, D. R. and PRIEST, F. G. (1981). *Proc. Eur. Brewery Conv. Congr., Copenhagen*, p. 217.

[16] VAN ENGEL, E. L. (1971). *Proc. Annu. Meet. Am. Soc. Brew. Chem.*, p. 89.

[17] BEXON, J. and DAWES, E. A. (1970). *J. Gen. Microbiol*, **60**, 421.

[18] HURTWITZ, J. (1958). *Biochim. Biophys. Acta*, **28**, 599.

[19] RAINBOW, C. (1965). *Brewers' Digest*, p. 50.

[20] WOOD, J. B. and RAINBOW, C. (1961). *Biochem. J.*, **78**, 204.

[21] DOLEZIL, L. and KIRSOP, B. H. (1980). *J. Inst. Brewing*, **86**, 122.

[22] LEWIS, M. J. and PHAFF, M. J. (1963). *Proc. Annu. Meet. Am. Soc. Brew. Chem.*, p. 114.

[23] KULKA, D. (1958). *J. Inst. Brewing*, **64**, 331.

[24] MCMURROUGH, I. and PALMER, V. (1979). *J. Inst. Brewing*, **85**, 11.

[25] HEALY, P. and ARMITT, J. (1980). *J. Inst. Brewing*, **86**, 169.

[26] DUNICAN, L. K., and SEELEY, H. W. (1965). *J. Gen. Microbiol.*, **40**, 297.

[27] WILLIAMSON, D. H. (1959). *J. Appl. Bact.*, **22**, 392.

[28] DEIBEL, R. H. and EVANS, J. B. (1960). *J. Bact.*, **79**, 356.

[29] DELWICHE, E. A. (1961). *J. Bact.*, **81**, 416.

[30] WICKERHAM, L. J. (1951). *Tech. Bulletin* 1029, US Dept. Agric.

[31] GREEN, S. R. and GRAY, P. P. (1950). *Wallerstein Lab. Commun.*, **13**, 357.

[32] LEE, S. Y. (1975). US Patent 3 878 050.

[33] HSU, W. P., TOPAROWSKY, J. A. and BRENNER, M. W. (1975). *Brewers' Digest*, **50** (5), 52.

[34] MORRIS, E. O. and EDDY, A. A. (1957). *J. Inst. Brewing*, **63**, 34.
[35] KATO, S. (1967). *Bulletin Brewing Science, Tokyo*, **13**, 19.
[36] BRENNER, M. W., KARPISCAK, M., STEM, H. and HSU, W. P. (1969). *Proc. Annu. Meet. Am. Soc. Brew. Chem.*, pp. 79–86.
[37] LIN, Y. (1974). *Proc. Annu. Meet. Am. Soc. Brew. Chem.*, p. 69.
[38] LONGLEY, W. P. (1980). *J. Am. Soc. Brew. Chem.*, **38**, 18.
[39] HARRIS, J. O. and WATSON, W. (1968). *J. Inst. Brewing*, **74**, 286.
[40] WILLIAMSON, D. G. (1959). *J. Inst. Brewing*, **65**, 154.
[41] VAN VUUREN, H. J. J., LOVW, H. A., LOOS, M. A. and MEISEL, R. (1977). *Appl. and Env. Microbiol.*, **33** (2), 246.
[42] BOATWRIGHT, J. and KIRSOP, B. H. (1976). *J. Inst. Brewing*, **82**, 343.
[43] KOZULIS, J. K. and PAGE, H. G. (1968). *Proc. Annu. Meet. Am. Soc. Brew. Chem.*, p. 52.
[44] MACKIE, T. J. and MCCARTNEY, J. E. (1953). *Handbook of Practical Bacteriology*, 9th Edn., Churchill Livingstone, Edinburgh.
[45] CARR, J. G. (1968). In *Identification Methods for Microbiologists* (eds. GIBBS, B. M. and SHAPTEN, D. A.), Academic Press, London.
[46] SWINGS, J. and DE LEY, J. (1977). *Bacteriological Reviews*, **41**, 1.
[47] ASAI, T. (1934). *J. Agr. Chem. Soc., Japan*, **10**, 621, 731, 932, 1124; (1935), **11**, 50, 331, 377, 499, 610, 674.
[48] LEIFSON, E. (1954). *Antonie van Leeuwenhoek J. Microbiol. Serol.*, **20**, 102.
[49] RAINBOW, C. and MITSON, G. W. (1953). *J. Gen. Microbiol.* **9**, 371.
[50] WILLIAMS, P. J. C. B. and RAINBOW, C. (1964). *J. Gen. Microbiol.*, **35**, 237.
[51] DE LEY, J. (1961). *J. Gen. Microbiol.*, **24**, 31.
[52] SCOPES, A. W. (1962). *J. Gen. Microbiol.*, **28**, 69.
[53] HALL, A. N. (1963). *Biochemistry of Industrial Micro-organisms* (eds. RAINBOW, C. and ROSE, A. H.), Academic Press, New York, p. 607.
[54] WHITE, J. (1966). *Process Biochem.*, **1**, 139.
[55] SUOMALAINEN, H., KERANEN, A. J. and KANGASPERKO, J. (1965). *J. Inst. Brewing*, **71**, 41.
[56] RAINBOW, C. (1961). *Progress in Industrial Microbiology* (ed. HOCKENHULL, D. J. D.), Vol. 3, p. 43, Wiley-Interscience, New York.
[57] DUDMAN, W. F. (1960). *J. Gen. Microbiol.*, **22**, 25.
[58] BROWN, G. D. and RAINBOW, C. (1956). *J. Gen. Microbiol.*, **15**, 61.
[59] COOKSEY, K. E. and RAINBOW, C. (1962). *J. Gen. Microbiol.*, **27**, 135.
[60] HAMPSHIRE, P. (1922). *Bureau of Biotechnology*, Bull. No. 6, p. 179.
[61] CARR, J. G. (1959). *Report Long Ashton Res. Station* (1958). p. 16.
[62] GILLILAND, R. B. and LACEY, J. P. (1966). *J. Inst. Brewing*, **72**, 291.
[63] RICHARDS, M. and CORBEY, D. A. (1974). *J. Inst. Brewing*, **80**, 241.
[64] AULT, R. G. (1965). *J. Inst. Brewing*, **71**, 376.
[65] THASTUM, S. and JAKOBSEN, M. (1982). *Psychrotrophic Microorganisms in Spoilage and Pathogenicity* (ed. ROBERTS, T. A.), Academic Press, New York, p. 325.
[66] VAN VUUREN, H. J. J., COSSER, K. and PRIOR, B. A. (1980). *J. Inst. Brewing*, **86**, 31.
[67] WEST, D. B., LAUTENBACH, A. F. and BRUMSTEAD, D. D. (1963). *Proc. Annu. Meet. Am. Soc. Brew. Chem.*, 194.
[68] SHIMWELL, J. L. and GRIMES, M. (1936). *J. Inst. Brewing*, **42**, 348.
[69] SHIMWELL, J. L. (1964). *J. Inst. Brewing*, **70**, 247.
[70] PRIEST, F. G. and HOUGH, J. S. (1974). *J. Inst. Brewing*, **80**, 370.
[71] CASE, A. C. (1965). *J. Inst. Brewing*, **71**, 250.

[72] THOMAS, M., COLE, J. A. and HOUGH, J. S. (1972). *J. Inst. Brewing*, **78**, 332.

[73] WEINER, J. P., ROLPH, D. J. and TAYLOR, R. (1975). *Proc. Eur. Brewery Conv. Congr., Nice*, p. 565.

[74] LEE, S. Y., MABEE, M. S. and JANGAARD, N. O. (1978). *Internat. J. Syst. Bact.*, **28** (4), 582.

[75] STRANDSKOV, F. B. and BOCKELMANN, J. B. (1957). *Proc. Annu. Meet. Am. Soc. Brew. Chem.*, p. 94.

[76] RICKETTS, R. W. (1965). *Brewers' Guild J.*, **51**, 160.

[77] PARRY, D. (1970). *J. Inst. Brewing*, **76**, 443.

[78] PARRY, D. (1974). *Process Biochem.*, (4), 27.

[79] BARRETT, M. (1979). *Brewers' Guardian*, (8), 35.

[80] HAMILTON, G. (1979). *Brewers' Guardian*, (7), 53.

[81] PORTNO, A. D. (1968). *J. Inst. Brewing*, **74**, 291.

[82] EGAN, L. H., TAYLOR, K. E. and HAHN, C. W. (1979). *Tech. Quart. Master Brewers Assoc. Americas*, **16**, 164.

[83] SYKES, J. (1965). Disinfection and Sterilization, 2nd Edn., Spon, London.

[84] BRUCH, C. W., HOFFMAN, A., GOSINE, R. M. and BRUENE, M. W. (1964). *J. Inst. Brewing*, **70**, 242.

[85] POSTGATE, J. R., CRUMPTON, J. E. and HUNTER, J. R. (1961). *J. Gen. Microbiol.*, **24**, 15.

[86] AULT, R. G. and WOODWARD, J. D. (1965). *J. Inst. Brewing*, **71**, 36.

[87] WILES, A. E. (1953). *J. Inst. Brewing*, **59**, 265.

[88] HEMMONS, L. M. (1954). *J. Inst. Brewing*, **60**, 288.

[89] BRADY, B. L. (1958). *J. Inst. Brewing*, **64**, 304.

[90] MORRIS, E. O. and EDDY, A. A. (1957). *J. Inst. Brewing*, **63**, 34.

[91] ELLISON, J. and DORAN, A. H. (1961). *Proc. Eur. Brewery Conv. Congr., Vienna*, p. 224.

[92] RICHARDS, M. (1968). *J. Inst. Brewing*, **74**, 433.

[93] HAMMOND, J. R. M. and JONES, M. (1979). *J. Inst. Brewing*, **85**, 26.

[94] BOURGEOIS, C. (1969). *Biotechnique*, p. 2.

[95] RYDER, D. S., MURRAY, J. P. and STEWART, M. (1978). *Tech. Quart. Master Brewers Assoc. Americas*, **15** (2), 79.

[96] MAULE, A. P. and THOMAS, P. D. (1973). *J. Inst. Brewing*, **79**, 137.

[97] HOGGAN, J. (1963). *Proc. Eur. Brewery Conv. Congr., Brussels*, p. 370.

[98] COWAN, W. D., HOGGAN, J. and SMITH, J. E. (1975). *Tech. Quart. Master Brewers Assoc. Americas*, **12** (1), 15.

[99] GREENSPAN, R. P. (1965). *Proc. Annu. Meet. Am. Soc. Brew. Chem.*, p. 57.

[100] LAKOIS, G. C. (1965). *Proc. Annu. Meet. Am. Soc. Brew. Chem.*, p. 60.

[101] BRUMSTEAD, D. D. and GLENISTER, P. R. (1962). *Proc. Annu. Meet. Am. Soc. Brew. Chem.*, p. 72; (1963). p. 12.

[102] VAN DER BOGAERT, X., HASSAN, S. and QUESADA, F. (1967). *Proc. Eur. Brewery Conv. Congr., Madrid*, p. 227.

Chapter 22

CHEMICAL AND PHYSICAL
PROPERTIES OF BEER

22.1 *Chemical composition of beer*

Beer is a complex mixture; over 400 different compounds have been characterized in beer which, in addition, contains macromolecules such as proteins,
nucleic acids, carbohydrates and lipids. Some of the constituents of beer
are derived from the raw materials and survive the brewing process unchanged.
Others are the result of chemical and biochemical transformation of the
raw materials during malting, mashing, boiling, fermentation and conditioning. Together all these constituents make up the character of beer
but, in general, different beers and lagers contain different proportions
of the same compounds rather than novel constituents. Nevertheless, acci-
dental or deliberate contamination of beer with micro-organisms other than
yeast may well produce new metabolites.

In this chapter the compounds that have been identified in beer are reviewed but the influence which they have on flavour is not discussed until
Chapter 23. However, in order to avoid duplication, data on the taste
threshold of compounds are included in the tables given in this chapter.
Beer constituents can be divided into volatile and non-volatile components.
The volatile constituents have greater vapour pressure and are responsible
for the aroma or bouquet of beer. They are concentrated in the headspace
above the beverage in a closed container and will pass into the distillate
if the beverage is distilled. The complex mixture of volatile constituents,
either in the headspace or a solvent extracts of beer, can be resolved by
gas–liquid chromatography (GLC) and the components identified by mass
spectrometry. The non-volatile constituents of beer include inorganic salts,
sugars, amino acids, nucleotides, polyphenols, and the hop resins, together
with macromolecules such as polysaccharides, proteins, and nucleic acids.
Non-volatile constituents can only be resolved by gas chromatography after
conversion into volatile derivatives so the technique is limited to compounds
with fairly low molecular weight. High precision liquid chromatography
(HPLC) is being used increasingly to resolve the mixture of non-volatile
components in beer.

TABLE 22.1

Representative analyses of beers

	British Fined Draught Beer [4]	British Ale and Lager		Pilsner Urquell [5]	Germany Premium [6]	Bavarian Bright [7]	American Lager [7]	US Lager [8]	Australian Bottled [9]
		Bulk and Keg [4]	Bottle and Can [4]						
OG	1030–1045	1030–1045	1030–1090	12·1	11·5–12·4	11·8	11·5		
Original extract (%)	(7·5–11·2)	(7·5–11·2)	(7·5–21·5)						
PG	1006–1013	1006–1013	1006–1020						1006–1011
Apparent extract (%)	1·5–3·3	1·5–3·3	1·5–3·1	3·7				2·0–3·1	
Real extract (%)	2·8–5·0	2·8–5·0	2·8–7·5	5·4				3·7–4·8	
Apparent attenuation (%)	68–82	65–82	50–82	69·0	74–83	78·6	76·6		
Real attenuation (%)	53–67	50–67	38–67	55·0					
Attenuation limit	1005–1008	1005–1008	1005–1015			84·0%	80·3%		
Alcohol (% v/v)	2·8–4·4	2·6–4·5	2·5–9·5	3·45 w/w	3·69–4·21 w/v	3·7	3·6	3·4–3·9 w/v	4·38–4·98 w/v
Reducing sugars (%)			(2·4–4·5)	1·4				0·8–1·5	1·09–2·44
pH	3·9–4·2	3·9–4·2	3·9–4·2	4·6	4·2–4·6	4·51	4·32	3·8–4·7	
Acidity (mg/l)	—		2·2	0·15	1·9–4·4			0·9–1·5	
Diacetyl (mg/l)		0·2–0·5	0·2–0·5		0·02–0·15	0·12	0·04	0·8	
Bitterness (BU)	28–38	17–35	17–40	43	20–37	27	18	10–23	
Tannins (mg/l)				240	89–230	170	122	120–210	
N × 6·25 (%)	0·25–0·4	0·25–0·4	0·25–0·4	0·45	0·45–0·62	0·44	0·30	0·25–0·37	0·21–0·39
α-Amino N (mg/l)	40–80	40–80	40–100		93–197	87	32		34–109
CO$_2$ (vols)	0·8–1·3	1·1–2·3	1·5–3·0			0·46 w/v	0·55 v/v	2·4–2·8	
SO$_2$ (mg/l)	30	20	20		0–12·6				
Dissolved O$_2$ (mg/l)	<0·5	<0·5	0·5		0–0·76				
Colour	15–60*	6–90*	6–90*	10	7–11·5	8·6*	5·3*	2·4–3·8†	
Haze	2*	0·5–1·5*	0·5–1·5*		0·12–0·45				
Head retention $t_{\frac{1}{2}}$	—	>95	>95		112–146	(233)	(234)		

* EBC. † SRM.

Another way to classify the organic constituents of beer is with regard to the heteroatoms present. Beer contains only traces of hydrocarbons; the majority of the constituents contain carbon, hydrogen and oxygen. Small amounts of nitrogen-containing constituents are present and phosphorous is associated with some of these. Only trace amounts of sulphur-containing compounds are present but some of these are very potent flavouring agents. Volatile sulphur derivatives are studied by gas chromatography using a flame photometric detector which is specific for sulphur-containing compounds.

Methods for beer analysis have been published by *inter alia* the European Brewery Convention-*Analytica-EBC* [1], the American Society of Brewing Chemists (ASBC) [2], and the Institute of Brewing [3]. There is increasing collaboration between the authorities to agree 'International methods'. Not all of the methods described refer to the estimation of specific constituents. Some give methods for other chemical and physical parameters found useful in the quality control of the brewing process. Some analytical data for a range of beers are collected in Table 22.1. In the Tables which follow, listing beer constituents and their concentration, the references refer to the bulk of the information but additional data have been added without citation.

22.1.1 INORGANIC CONSTITUENTS

The most abundant constituent of beer is water, the medium in which, in bright beer, all the other constituents are dissolved. Brewing liquor normally contains only trace amounts of organic matter and the desirable inorganic cations and anions are reviewed in Chapter 7. During the brewing process other salts will be extracted from malt and hops, some ions may be precipitated with the break and others may be absorbed by the yeast so that the inorganic salts present in beer are very different from those in the liquor used. Data for the inorganic constituents of beer are collected in Table 22.2.

The major ions are the cations potassium, sodium, magnesium and calcium with the anions chloride, sulphate, nitrate and phosphate. The level of toxic metals may be limited by law. In Britain the level of arsenic (1959) and lead (1979) may not exceed 0·2 mg/kg (ppm) and the Food Standards Committee have recommended limits of 7·0 ppm for copper and 5·0 ppm for zinc in both wine and beer. The EBC, ASBC and the Institute of Brewing all describe methods for the estimation of iron and copper in beer. In addition the EBC gives methods for calcium, nickel, potassium, sodium and zinc; the ASBC for calcium and phosphorous; and the Institute of Brewing for arsenic, lead and zinc.

Carbon dioxide is a natural product of fermentation and beers should contain 3·5–4·5 g/l. Supersaturated beers and naturally conditioned beers may contain more than 6 g/l but the gas will be evolved as soon as the pressure is released. The Institute of Brewing recommend a manometric method of analysis. The CO_2 in the beer is absorbed into 40% sodium hydroxide solution and an aliquot of this solution is introduced into the apparatus. After evacuation, the carbon dioxide is liberated with 50% sulphuric acid and the pressure of the gas liberated measured. The results are expressed as g CO_2/l. The ASBC method is dependent on the reading of a pressure gauge at a given temperature. The CO_2 content (v/v) can then be determined from the published chart which also allows results to be expressed as % by weight. For bottles and cans measurements should be made at 25°C.

TABLE 22.2

Inorganic constituents of beer

Constituent	Source	Concentration range (mg/l (ppm)) (mean value in parentheses)
Potassium	British [10]	330–1100
	German [6]	396–562 (476)
	Mexican [11]	220–358
	Lagers [12]	253–680 (362)
Sodium	British [10]	40–230
	German [6]	9–120 (35)
	Lagers [12]	15–170 (58)
Magnesium	British [10]	60–200
	German [13]	75–250 (114)
	Lagers [12]	34–162 (82)
Calcium	British [10]	40–140
	German [13]	3·8–102 (32·7)
	Lagers [12]	10–135 (46)
Iron	British [10]	0·1–0·5
	German [14]	0·02–0·84 (0·02)
	Lagers [12]	0·04–0·44 (0·12)
	Wheat beer [14]	(0·63)
Copper	British [10]	0·3–0·8
	German [15]	0·04–0·80 (0·19)
	Lagers [12]	0·01–0·41 (0·11)
Zinc	German [16]	0·01–1·48 (0·10)
	Lagers [12]	0·01–0·46 (0·06)
Manganese	German [17]	0·04–0·51 (0·20)
Lead	Lagers [12]	0.06
Arsenic	Lagers [12]	0·02
Chloride	British [10, 18]	150–984
	German [6]	143–365 (210)
Sulphate	British	150–400
	German [6]	107–398 (182)
	African lager [19]	125–260
Phosphate	British	260–400
	German [6]	624–995 (860)
Phosphorous	British [10]	90–400
	Australian [9]	96–304 (196)
Nitrate	German [20]	1·4–101·3 (34·0)
Fluoride	German [21]	0·08–0·64 (0·15)

The gauge is connected to a piercing device with a hollow steel spike. The CO_2 may be collected in an absorption burette containing 15% sodium hydroxide thus allowing measurement of the residual air.

22.1.2 ALCOHOL AND ORIGINAL EXTRACT

The alcoholic content of beer is usually regarded as a measure of its strength and, since excise duty has been levied on alcoholic beverages for many years, official methods for measuring the alcoholic content have been laid down. Since 1980 most European countries have adopted the OIML (International Organization for Legal Metrology) system of measurement by reference to the percentage of ethyl alcohol by volume at 20°C. For example, in the United Kingdom excise duty must be paid on beers that contain more than 1·8% v/v of ethyl alcohol. Before 1980 British legislation was based on proof spirit – originally that strength of alcohol in water which, when poured on to gunpowder and lighted, just allowed the gunpowder to ignite. Later it was defined as 57·06% v/v of ethyl alcohol in water at 60°F. In the United States proof spirit contains 50·0% v/v of ethanol (SG 0·7939) at 60°F (15·6°C). In Tables 22.1 and 22.3 it can be seen that the majority of beers contain between 2·5% and 5·0% of ethanol although strong ales and barley wines may contain up to 10% of alcohol. In Germany bock beers must contain more than 6·0% and double bock beers more than 7·5% of alcohol. Weaker beers and shandies (mixtures of beer and lemonade) are produced, on which excise duty does not have to be paid and alcohol-free beers are produced for Muslim countries [23]. Unlike distillers, few brewers declare the alcohol content of their products on the label, except with beers specially brewed for supermarket chains.

TABLE 22.3
Analyses of beers [22]

Quality	OG	Alcohol by volume (%)	Unfermented matter (%)	Isohumulones (mg/l)
Draught bitter	1030·9–1045·3	3·0–4·6	27–45	20–40
Draught mild	1030·7–1036·5	2·5–3·6	29–48	14–37
Light ale (bottle or can)	1030·6–1038·9	2·9–4·0	30–40	16–38
Best pale ale	1040·3–1050·3	4·3–6·6	21–43	19–55
Brown ale	1030·2–1040·6	2·5–3·6	43–55	16–28
Stout—Guinness	1040·0–1046·1	4·4–5·1	30	55–62
—Mackeson	1044·3–1047·6	3·7–3·8	49	27–31
Strong ales	1065·9–1077·7	6·1–8·4	32–44	25–43
Lagers	1029·7–1036·3	3·3–3·6	35–39	20–32

To estimate the alcoholic content of a beverage, or any complex biological fluid, it is usually necessary to separate the alcohol from the medium either by distillation, microdiffusion, dialysis, or gas–liquid chromatography.

The alcohol in a distillate can be estimated from its specific gravity or re-fractive index or more occasionally by chemical or enzymatic analysis. These last methods are more sensitive and are usually reserved for measuring small quantities of ethanol. For example, the alcohol in blood may be estimated by microdiffusion into a dilute acidified solution of potassium dichromate where it is oxidized to acetaldehyde while the orange–red di-chromate is reduced to a green chromous salt:

$$K_2Cr_2O_7 + 4H_2SO_4 + 3C_2H_5OH \rightarrow$$

$$3CH_3CHO + K_2SO_4 + Cr_2(SO_4)_3 + 7H_2O.$$

This colour change is the principle on which the breath analyser operates. Instrumental methods of breath alcohol analysis have recently been reviewed [24]. Enzymatic methods are usually based on alcohol dehydrogenase which catalyses the oxidation of ethanol to acetaldehyde:

$$C_2H_5OH + NAD \underset{\text{dehydrogenase}}{\overset{\text{Alcohol}}{\rightleftharpoons}} CH_3CHO + NADH + H^+$$

when the reduction of the cofactor NAD can be measured spectrophoto-metrically [25]. This method can also be applied to beer directly without distillation. The alcoholic content of beer and other biological fluids can be rapidly estimated by gas–liquid chromatography using a stationary phase and detector not affected by excess water [26, 27].

However, it is excise practice in the United Kingdom, Belgium, and some other countries to levy duty not on the measured alcoholic content of the beer but on the extract or gravity of the wort fermented – the potential alcohol. In Britain the excise officer measures the volume and specific gravity of the wort before fermentation, and records must be kept of any later addition of priming sugars to the beer. These are added to the wort gravity to assess the duty payable. It will be seen from Table 22.3 that the original gravities (OG) of normal beers lie in the range 1029–1050 while with strong ales the OG may be as high as 1100. Elsewhere, the specific gravity measurements are converted into % extract or degrees Plato using the tables originally calculated for sucrose solutions by F. Plato (see p. 881). For normal lager beers the original extract lies between 10·0 and 13·0% (°P) but for strong beers, for example, doppelbock, the original extract may be as high as 20·0%.

Most excise authorities have laid down procedures for determining the original extract or gravity of partly fermented worts and beers. In the British system 100·0 ml of filtered beer at 20°C is distilled until about 85 ml

TABLE 22.4

A table for determining the original gravity of worts of beer [29]

Spirit indication	Corresponding degrees of gravity lost (tenths)									
	0	1	2	3	4	5	6	7	8	9
0	0·00	0·42	0·85	1·27	1·70	2·12	2·54	2·97	3·39	3·81
1	4·24	4·66	5·08	5·51	5·93	6·35	6·78	7·20	7·62	8·05
2	8·47	8·91	9·35	9·79	10·23	10·66	11·10	11·53	11·97	12·40
3	12·84	13·27	13·71	14·15	14·58	15·02	15·46	15·90	16·34	16·78
4	17·22	17·67	18·11	18·56	19·00	19·45	19·90	20·35	20·80	21·25
5	21·70	22·16	22·61	23·06	23·51	23·96	24·42	24·87	25·31	25·76
6	26·21	26·66	27·11	27·57	28·02	28·48	28·93	29·39	29·84	30·29
7	30·75	31·20	31·66	32·12	32·57	33·03	33·48	33·94	34·40	34·85
8	35·31	35·77	36·22	36·68	37·14	37·59	38·05	38·51	38·97	39·43
9	39·88	40·34	40·80	41·26	41·72	42·18	42·64	43·10	43·56	44·02
10	44·48	44·94	45·41	45·88	46·35	46·82	47·29	47·77	48·24	48·72
11	49·20	49·68	50·16	50·65	51·13	51·62	52·10	52·59	53·08	53·57
12	54·06	54·55	55·04	55·53	56·03	56·52	57·01	57·51	58·00	58·50
13	58·99	59·48	59·98	60·47	60·97	61·46	61·96	62·45	62·94	63·44
14	63·97	64·47	64·96	65·46	65·96	66·46	66·96	67·47	67·97	68·47
15	68·97	69·48	69·98	70·49	70·99	71·50	72·01	72·51	73·02	73·53
16	74.04	—	—	—	—	—	—	—	—	—

of distillate is collected. Both distillate and residue are then diluted to 100·0 ml at 20°C and the specific gravity of each measured. The number of degrees of gravity by which the distillate is less than the gravity of distilled water is called the spirit indication of the distillate. From the 'mean brewery table' (Table 22.4) the degrees of extract which must have been fermented to produce the spirit indicated is read off and added to the gravity of the residue to give the original gravity. The 'mean brewery table' was constructed for the authorities by Sir Edward Thorpe and Dr H. T. Brown from the results of brews in ten breweries carried out in 1909–10 [28]. It was recalculated in 1979 [29] to allow for working at 20°C. Such a table is necessary since, as carbohydrates are utilized for yeast growth and the production of metabolites other than ethanol in a brewery fermentation, the yield of ethanol will always be less than that predicted by Gay–Lussac's equation:

$$C_6H_{12}O_6 \rightarrow 2\,C_2H_5OH + 2\,CO_2$$

Nevertheless the alcoholic content of beer (%v/v) can be estimated by multiplying the drop in SG during fermentation by 0·102.

Any radical change in the ratio of yeast growth to alcohol production from that used in the production of the 'mean brewery table' could result in beers in which the actual original gravity differs from that arrived at by the above procedure. Thus, the use of larger fermentation vessels and methods of continuous fermentation result in beers in which the measured original gravity is slightly higher than that actually employed. Similarly the production of large amounts of secondary metabolites can alter the results. Belgian lambic beer contains a high level of volatile acids and accordingly this is taken into account in the official Belgium method for determining the original extract.

Both the EBC and the ASBC describe methods for determining the original extracts of beers. The apparent extract ($E\%$ w/w) is determined from the specific gravity of the filtered beer. Then 100·0 g of beer is distilled and the alcoholic content ($A\%$ w/w) is determined from the specific gravity of the distillate diluted to 100·0 g and the real extract ($E_R\%$ w/w) is determined from the specific gravity of the residue diluted to 100·0 g.

From Balling's equation:

The extract in the original wort (% w/w) (= °Plato) = p

$$p = 100\left[\frac{2{\cdot}0665\,A - E_R}{100 + 1{\cdot}0665A}\right]$$

or

$$\frac{p = E_R + E}{q} + E_R$$

where q is a correcting factor.

The ASBC also define:

$$\text{Real degree of fermentation} = \frac{100\,(p - E_R)}{p}$$

$$\text{Apparent degree of fermentation} = \frac{100\,(p - E)}{p}$$

22.1.3 CARBOHYDRATES

The total carbohydrates remaining in beer can be estimated as the colour produced by anthrone in 85% sulphuric acid [30]. For a range of beers, values between 0·89–5·98% w/v as glucose were found [31]. Fully attenuated low carbohydrate 'lite' beers, which have been brewed in the past for diabetic patients, are now generally available with carbohydrate contents between 0·4–0·9% w/v as glucose.

TABLE 22.5

Sugar content of commercial beers [34]

Type of beer	OG	SG	Fructose	Glucose	Sucrose	Maltose (hydrate)	Malto-triose	Malto-tetraose	Total
1 Pale ale	1050	1011	nil	0·06	nil	0·54	0·28	0·04	0·92
2 Brown ale (primed)	1032	1012	1·0	1·0	trace	trace	0·2	0·4	2·6
3 Stout (primed)	1033	1013	0·53	0·61	trace	trace	0·08	0·06	1·28
4 Sweet stout (primed)	1045	1022	0·6	1·2	trace	trace	0·6	0·3	3·6*
5 Pale ale	1068	1019	0·01	0·01	nil	0·7	1·7	0·4	2·9
6 Strong ale	1085	1026	trace	trace	nil	0·16	0·21	0·12	0·49
7 Lager	1032	1007	nil	nil	nil	trace	trace	trace	trace
8 Lager export	1045	1008	nil	trace	nil	trace	0·28	0·18	0·46
9 Stout (conditioned)	1044	1008	nil	nil	nil	nil	trace	nil	trace
10 Ale	1038	1002	trace	0·8	nil	nil	trace	trace	0·8
11 Lager	1040	1003	0·18	0·49	nil	nil	nil	nil	0·67
12 Lager	1046	1003	nil	trace	nil	trace	trace	trace	trace
13 Lager	1045	1004	nil	0·27	nil	0·17	0·24	0·09	0·77
14 Lager	1052	1011	trace	0·15	nil	0·13	0·16	0·14	0·58
15 Lager	1045	1008	nil	nil	nil	0·25	0·33	0·20	0·78

* Contained also lactose (hydrate) 0·9%.

Of the carbohydrates present in wort, glucose, fructose, maltose and maltotriose will normally be fermented. Unattenuating yeast strains will not ferment maltotriose and super-attenuating strains will partly ferment maltotetraose but, in general, beers will only contain low levels of sugars other than those added as primings (Table 22.5). Nevertheless, trace amounts of many sugars have been characterized in beer including: D-ribose, L-arabinose, D-xylose, D-glucose, D-fructose, D-mannose and D-galactose [32] (see Chapter 4 for structures). In addition to maltose the disaccharides isomaltose, cellobiose, and kojibiose have been found. The beer produced by a super-attenuating strain of *S. cerevisiae* (NCYC 422) also contained maltulose and nigerose [33]. The trisaccharides present include maltotriose, panose and isopanose. Data for these and higher oligosaccharides are given in Table 22.6.

TABLE 22.6
Oligosaccharides in beer (g/100 ml as glucose)

	Lager (Danish) [35]	Lager (German) [36]	Diabetic Lager [36]
Pentose	—	0·019	0·052
Fructose	} 0·02	0·015	—
Glucose		—	0·008
Isomaltose	0·08	0·102	0·098
Maltose	0·07	0·188	0·143
Panose	—	0·036	0·066
Maltotriose	0·17	0·315	0·193
4α-Isomaltosyl-D-maltose	—	0·049	0·100
Maltotetraose	0·30	0·187	0·043
Maltopentaose	0·08	0·144	0·100
Maltohexaose	0·15	0·130	0·039
Maltoheptaose	0·15	0·063	0·035
Malto-octaose	0·17 }	} 1·560	0·065
Maltonoaose	0·15		
Higher dextrins	1·06	—	—
Total	2·40	2·830	0·962

Analyses, made by paper chromatography followed by elution and colorimetry with anthrone, gave values for maltotriose in the range 0·13–0·74% w/v and for dextrins in the range of 0·70–4·05 w/v [31]. Sugars can also be estimated by gas chromatography as their trimethysilyl ethers [34] but partition chromatography is necessary to resolve the oligosaccharides [35]. A detailed study of the dextrins in Tuborg lager has been made using gel chromatography [37]. The carbohydrates present were resolved into the following fractions (degree of polymerization – glucose units, percentage of total carbohydrate): DP 1–3, 7·4%; DP 4, 13·1%; Group I (DP 5–10),

27·7%; Group II (DP 11–16), 16·7%; Group III (DP 17–21), 9·7%; Group IV (DP 22–27), 6·2%; Group V (DP 28–34), 4·0%; and Higher Dextrins (DP > 35), 15·2%. Debranching studies with pullanase established that the dextrins in Group I are either linear or singly-branched while those in Groups II, III, and IV contain two, three and four $\alpha(1,6)$linkages respectively. The majority of the $\alpha(1,6)$linkages in amylopectin appear to survive the brewing process. By colorimetric methods beers were found to contain 0·13–0·21% of fructose and fructosans and 0·25–0·39% of pentosans. The level of β-glucans were also estimated; beers, 0·29–0·58%; low carbohydrate beers, 0·18–0·44%; stouts, 0·9–1·03%; and malt liquor, 0·79–1·00% w/v as glucose. Over 50% of the β-glucan fraction passed through a dialysis membrane and has a molecular weight < 3000. The β-glucan that is mainly responsible for the viscosity of beer has a mol. wt. > 300 000 [31].

22.1.4 OTHER CONSTITUENTS CONTAINING CARBON, HYDROGEN AND OXYGEN

(a) *Non-volatile*

Many of these components are products of yeast metabolism. Most of the components of the metabolic pathways discussed in Chapter 17 have been detected in beer. Quantitatively glycerol is important: German beers contain 1·5–1·95 g/l [38] and values of 2·7–3·4 g/l are given for Canadian beers [39]. Significant amounts of higher polyols are absent [32]. It is noteworthy that cyclic acetals, formed between acetaldehyde and glycerol, are important flavour constituents of Australian flor sherries [40]. Beers also contain butane-2,3-diol (10–128 ppm) and smaller amounts of pentane-2,3-diol which, together with acetoin (3-hydroxybutan-2-one) (3–26 ppm) and 3-hydroxy-pentan-2-one, are reduction products of vicinal diketones (see later). Another non-volatile alcohol is tyrosol which is closely related to the volatile β-phenylethanol and the nitrogen compound tryptophol. Canadian lagers contained 22·1–29·4 mg/l of tyrosol while ales had 3·0–13·6 mg/l [41]. In the past tyrosol has been thought to be a potent flavouring component of beer but when purified the taste threshold (200 ppm) is well above the levels reported.

Beer contains trace amounts of lipids. A Swedish beer (12° Plato) was found to contain (mg/l): triglycerides, 0·1–0·2; diglycerides, 0·1; mono-glycerides, 0·1–0·3; sterol esters, 0·01; free sterols, 0·01–0·02; and free fatty acids, C_4–C_{10}, 10–15; C_{12}–C_{18}, 0–0·5 [42]. Similar data were found for American beers. The role that lipids play in head formation is discussed later. The free fatty acids are volatile and more detailed values are given below. Whereas unsubstituted fatty acids are volatile, the addition of a further substituent usually results in loss of volatility. Data for hydroxy-, keto, di-, and tri-basic acids are given in Table 22.7.

Autoxidation of linoleic acid gives rise to three isomers of trihydroxy-octadecenoic acid. The concentrations found in beer (Table 22.7) are higher than those found for linoleic acid itself [47]. All three acids are potential precursors of 2-*trans*-nonenal which is an important component of the cardboard or paper flavour of stale beer.

TABLE 22.7

Non-volatile acids in beer

Acid	Concentration (ppm)				
	Berlin Pilsner [43]	German [38]	British [44]	American [45]	Flavour threshold (ppm) [46]
C₂ Glycolic	—	—	—	—	
Oxalic	—	9·9–22·8	—	0·5–3·0	
C₃ D-Lactic	—	20–200	—	—	
L-Lactic	—	40–152	—	—	
Lactic	188	—	44–292	—	(400)
Pyruvic	—	42–75	10–104	—	(300)
Malonic	0·02	—	—	—	
C₄ Succinic	48	—	36–166	—	
Fumaric	—	—	—	—	
Malic	—	55–105	14–97	—	
Oxaloacetic	—	—	—	—	(500)
Tartaric	—	—	—	—	(600)
C₅ 2-Hydroxy-3-methylbutyric	0·26	—	—	—	
Levulinic	—	—	—	—	
2-Methylfumaric (Mesaconic)	—	—	—	—	
Glutaric	0·01	—	—	—	
2-Hydroxyglutaric	—	—	0–17	—	
Citramalic	—	—	—	[5·9–15·2]	
2-Oxoglutaric	—	—	0–20		
C₆ 2-Hydroxy-3-methylpentanoic	0·29	—	—	—	
2-Hydroxy-4-methylpentanoic	0·33	—	—	—	
Adipic	—	—	—	—	
Kojic	—	—	—	5–78·2	
Citric	—	130–230	56–158	—	
Isocitric	—	—	—	—	
Oxalosuccinic	—	—	—	—	
C₇ Benzoic	0·45	—	—	—	
2-Hydroxybenzoic	0·02	—	—	1·0–9·0	
4-Hydroxybenzoic	0·13	—	—	4·0–28·5	
2-Hydroxyheptanoic	0·06	—	—	—	
3,4-Dihydroxybenzoic	2·4	—	—	6·3–29·0	
2,5-Dihydroxybenzoic (Gentisic)	—	—	—	2·8–12·7	
Pimelic	0·01	—	—	—	
Gallic	—	—	—	12·0–30	360

TABLE 22.7 (continued)

Acid	Concentration (ppm)				Flavour threshold (ppm) [46]
	Berlin Pilsner [43]	German [38]	British [44]	American [45]	
C$_8$ Phenylacetic	0·93	—	—	—	2·5
2-Hydroxyoctanoic	0·04	—	—	—	
3-Hydroxyoctanoic	0·07	—	—	—	
4-Hydroxyphenylacetic	0·04	—	—	—	
Suberic	0·15	—	—	—	
Vanillic	2·4	—	—	0·3–1·5	80
Phthalic	0·02	—	—	—	
C$_9$ Phenylpropionic	0·01	—	—	—	
trans-Cinnamic	0·50	—	—	} 1·0–8·3	
cis-Cinnamic	<0·01	—	—		
Phenyl-lactic	1·2	—	—		
4-Hydroxyphenylpropionic	0·02	—	—	—	
trans-p-Coumaric	1·9	—	—	} 8–21	520
cis-p-Coumaric	0·02	—	—		
Caffeic	—	—	—	1·4–8·0	690
Azelaic	1·5	—	—	—	
C$_{10}$ 3-Hydroxydecanoic	0·16	—	—	—	
trans-Ferulic	4·6	—	—	} 1·7–20·8	660
cis-Ferulic	1·1	—	—		
C$_{11}$ Undecanedioic	0·13	—	—	—	
Sinapic	—	—	—	0·7–3·6	
C$_{12}$ Dodecanedioic	0·18				
C$_{16}$ Chlorogenic	—	—	—	1–11·2	
C$_{18}$ Trihydroxyoctadecenoic		see Ref. [47]			
9,12,13–10-trans		4·9–9·0			
9,10,13–11-trans		1·0–2·4			
9,10,11–12-trans		0·4–0·7			

Table 22.7 also includes data for the phenolic acids in beer which are extracted from malt and hops (Chapter 14). In addition to the phenolic acids beers were found by HPLC to contain quercetin (36–148 ppm), rutin 1·5–7·7 ppm, catechin (26–141 ppm) and epicatechin (8·5–127 ppm) [45]. These values for catechin are considerably higher than those found earlier (0·5–8·0 ppm) by a procedure involving adsorption, elution and GLC [48]. Beers also contain smaller amounts of gallocatechin and epigallocatechin. More important with regard to the formation of haze are the dimeric procyanidins of which B-3 (0·5–4·0 ppm) predominates. Tri-, tetra-, penta- and oligomeric procyanidins are present in beer but are less well characterized [208]. Numerous methods have been described to estimate the total polyphenols or tannins in beer but all are comparative and calibrated against polyphenol fractions of unknown complexity or typicality. The EBC recommend measurement at 600 nm of the colour formed with ferric citrate, when the

concentration of polyphenols (ppm) is given by OD (1 cm cell) $\times$ 820 [49]. Other reagents which give characteristic colour reactions with polyphenols have been used including diazotized p-nitroaniline, Fast Blue Salt B, 4-aminopyrine, p-dimethylaminocinnamaldehyde, and Folin's reagents. In many cases the yield of colour decreases as the molecular weight of the polyphenol increases. Total polyphenols can also be estimated in the ultra-violet as the absorption of an ethyl acetate extract of beer at 270 nm [50] after removal of the bittering substances into iso-octane. Comparable work with cider procyanidins indicate that dimeric and higher oligomeric procyanidins have similar $E_1^1 \%$ cm values but that not all of the polyphenols are extracted into ethyl acetate.

By definition procyanidins and anthocyanogens, on treatment with acid, give anthocyanidins which show maximum light absorption at about 545 nm. By measurement at 455 nm estimates of the amount of catechin present can also be obtained [51]. The yield of anthocyanidin from different procyanidin fractions varies and anthocyanogen values do not correlate with the shelf life of beers. In many cases the yield of anthocyanidin released by acid decreases as the procyanidins polymerize while the level of total polyphenols (EBC) remains roughly constant. Accordingly the

$$\text{Polymerization index} = \frac{\text{Total polyphenols present (EBC)}}{\text{Total anthocyanogens present}}$$

increases during storage. However, the reaction is not straightforward as in other fields polymeric anthocyanogens are known which give higher yields of anthocyanidins than the corresponding monomers [52].

Much of the interest in estimating the polyphenols in beer stems from their involvement in haze formation (see later); thus, methods which simulate this role have been used to predict beer stability. They include precipitation with cinchonidine sulphate or polyvinylpyrrolidine 700 followed by nephelo-metry. Closely related to the polyphenols are the derivatives of the hop resins which provide the bitter principles of beer. As discussed in Chapter 14, in beer brewed from fresh hops these are principally the iso-α-acids: the *cis*- and *trans*-isomers of isohumulone, isocohumulone, and isoadhumulone. These are routinely estimated together on the basis of the light absorption of an iso-octane extract at 275 nm and the results expressed in bitterness units (BU). In beers brewed from fresh hops bitterness units are approximately equal to mg iso-α-acids/l. Some values are given in Tables 22.1 and 22.3. It was because of the lack of knowledge of the nature of the bittering prin-ciples in beer brewed from old hops that the EBC simplified the regression equation and adopted bitterness units [53]. HPLC has been used to estimate the proportion of (*cis* + *trans*) isocohumulone in the iso-α-acids in beer (32·3–45·8%) [54] while other systems have resolved the *cis*- and *trans*-isomers [55] but the optimum conditions have probably not yet been found. By TLC the *cis*- and *trans*-iso-α-acids were resolved and shown to account for 88–100% of the light absorption of iso-octane extracts of beer. The beers contained 12·0–18·4 ppm *cis*-iso-α-acids, 4·7–7·7 ppm *trans*-iso-α-acids, 1·1–4·8 ppm hulupones, and α-acids (< 5·0 ppm). The ratio of *cis/trans* iso-α-acids showed real variation [56].

The nature of the other bittering principles in beer brewed from old hops is still largely unknown. These substances probably contain more oxygen than the iso-α-acids, are more polar, and incompletely extracted into iso-octane. The *abeo*-iso-α-acids (p. 487) are such compounds, the concentration of which in lager beers was reported to be 88–160 mg/l. Subsequent work established the presence of polyphenols in the extracts analysed and found that the concentration of *abeo*-iso-α-acids in English beers was less than 6 ppm [57]. Many other oxidation products of the hop resins have been detected in beers (see Chapter 12) but in most cases it has not been established that they are normal constituents.

(b) *Volatile*

Although small amounts of the volatile constituents of malt and hops survive wort boiling the bulk of these constituents are fermentation products. After ethanol, discussed above, the largest group of volatile constituents are the higher alcohols; those identified in beer are listed in Table 22.8A. By distillation the higher alcohol fraction can be isolated when it is known as fusel oil. Thus the distiller has a closer control over the higher alcohol content of his beverage than the brewer. For example, gin, vodka, and grain whisky have low levels of higher alcohols while malt whisky and brandy, produced in pot stills, are rich in such congeners.

The principal higher alcohols found in beer are 3-methylbutanol (isoamyl alcohol), 2-methylbutanol (*active*-amyl alcohol), 2-methylpropanol (isobutyl alcohol), propanol, and phenethyl alcohol (Table 22.9). It is noteworthy that the levels of higher alcohols in home-brewed beer and wines is at least 10 times higher than those in the commercial products [61]. The major volatile constituents of beer are most conveniently examined by gas chromatography either of the beer directly or of the gas in the head space above the beer in bottle. The ASBC recommend direct injection on to a 20% Carbowax 20M column at 80°C. In order to identify and estimate the minor volatile constituents it is usually necessary to prepare a solvent extract of the beer or a distillate. It may be desirable to fractionate the solvent extract by adsorption chromatography before examination by capillary gas chromatography–mass spectrometry [43, 59].

TABLE 22.8

Volatile constituents of beer

A. *Alcohols* [58]	Concentration (ppm) [59]	Flavour threshold (ppm) [46]
C_1 Methanol	—	10 000
C_2 Ethanol	—	14 000
C_3 Propanol	—	800
Propan-2-ol		1 500
C_4 Butanol	—	450
Butan-2-ol	—	16
2-Methylpropanol	4·8	200
C_5 Pentanol	0·15	(80)
Pentan-2-ol	—	45
2-Methylbutanol	} 84·0	70
3-Methylbutanol		65
Furfuryl alcohol	1·20	3 000
C_6 Hexanol	0·33	4·0
Hexan-2-ol	—	4·0
Hex-2-enol	0·025	13
Hex-3-enol	0·020	15
C_7 Heptanol	—	1·0
Heptan-2-ol	0·015	0·25
Benzyl alcohol	—	900
C_8 Octanol	—	0·9
Octan-2-ol	0·005	0·04
Oct-1-en-3-ol	0·030	0·2
2-Phenylethanol	1·8	125
Tyrosol	see text	200
4-Vinylphenol	0·025	—
C_9 Nonanol	—	0·08
Nonan-2-ol	0·01	0·075
4-Vinylguaiacol	0·10	0·30
C_{10} Decanol	—	0·18
Decan-2-ol	0·005	0·015
Linalool	—	0·08
α-Terpineol	—	2·0
Nerol	—	0·50
C_{12} Dodecanol	—	0·4
Dodecan-2-ol	—	—

B. *Aldehydes* [58]	Concentration (ppb) [203]	Flavour threshold (ppm) [46]
C_2 Acetaldehyde	see Table 22.10	10
Glyoxal	—	—
C_3 Propanal	—	30
Prop-2-enal (Acrolein)	1·6	15
Pyruvaldehyde	—	—
C_4 Butanal	10·9	(1·0)
2-Methylpropanal	—	(1·0)
But-2-enal (Crotonal)	1·33	8
C_5 Pentanal	2·7	0·5
2-Methylbutanal	—	1·25

TABLE 22.8 (*continued*)

B. *Aldehydes* [58]	Concentration (ppb) [203]	Flavour threshold (ppm) [46]
3-Methylbutanal	7·0	0·6
Pent-2-enal	0·59	—
Furfural	(25.0)	150
C_6 Hexanal	1·6	0·3
Hex-2-enal	0·36	0·5
5-Hydroxymethylfurfural	see text	1 000
C_7 Heptanal	1·2	0·05
Hept-2-enal	0·08	0·0005
Benzaldehyde	10	2
C_8 Octanal	1·4	0·04
Oct-2-enal	0·03	0·0003
2-Phenylacetaldehyde	(5)	1·6
C_9 Nonanal	3·7	0·015
Non-2-enal	0·07	0·0003
C_{10} Decanal	0·9	0·005
Dec-2-enal	trace	0·001
C_{11} Undecanal	0·4	0·002
C_{12} Dodecanal	0·2	0·002

C. *Acids* [58]	Concentration (ppm) [43]	Flavour threshold (ppm) [46]
C_1 Formic	—	—
C_2 Acetic		175
C_3 Propionic		150
C_4 Butyric	0·62	2·2
2-Methylpropionic	1·1	30
Crotonic	—	—
C_5 Pentanoic (Valeric)	0·03	8
2-Methylbutyric	—	—
3-Methylbutyric	1·3	1·5
Pentenoic	—	—
C_6 Hexanoic (Caproic)	2·5	8
Hex-2-enoic	} 0·01	—
Hex-3-enoic		1·3
4-Methylpent-3-enoic	0·32	—
3-Carbethoxypropionic	0·22	—
C_7 Heptanoic (Oenanthic)	0·03	—
Hept-2-enoic	<0·01	—
4-Methylhex-2-enoic	—	—
Benzoic	0·45	—
C_8 Octanoic (Caprylic)	6·1	13/15
6-Methylheptanoic	—	—
Oct-2-enoic	<0·01	—
Phenylacetic	0·93	2·5
C_9 Nonanoic (Pelargonic)	0·02	
Non-2-enoic	<0·01	17
Phenylpropionic	0·01	—
Phenyllactic	1·2	—
trans-Cinnamic	0·50	—
cis-Cinnamic	<0·01	—

TABLE 22.8 (*continued*)

C. *Acids* [58]	Concentration (ppm) [43]	Flavour threshold (ppm) [46]
C_{10} Decanoic (Capric)	0·70	10
Dec-4-enoic	0·23	—
Dec-4,8-dienoic	0·03	—
Geranic	—	—
C_{11} Undecanoic	<0·01	—
C_{12} Dodecanoic (Lauric)	0·11	6·1
Dodecenoic acid	0·01	—
C_{13} Tridecanoic	<0·01	—
C_{14} Tetradecanoic (Myristic)	0·02	—
Tetradecenoic	—	—
C_{15} Pentadecanoic	<0.01	—
C_{16} Hexadecanoic (Palmitic)	0·05	—
Hexadec-9-enoic (Palmitoleic)	0·02	
C_{17} Heptadecanoic	<0·01	—
C_{18} Octadecanoic (Stearic)	0·02	—
Octadec-9-enoic (Oleic)	0·02	—
Octadeca-9,12-dienoic (Linoleic)	0·01	—
Octadeca-9,12,15-trienoic (Linolenic)	<0·01	—

D. *Esters* [58]	Concentration (ppm) [59]	Flavour threshold (ppm) [46]
C_3 Ethyl formate	—	(150)
Methyl acetate	—	550
C_4 Ethyl acetate	see Table 22.9	33
C_5 Ethyl propionate	0·08	—
Propyl acetate	—	30
Methionol acetate	0·025	—
C_6 Ethyl butyrate	—	0·4
Ethyl 2-methylpropionate	0·48	5·0
Butyl acetate	—	7·5
But-2-yl acetate	—	12
2-Methylpropyl acetate	—	1·6
3-Methylbutyl formate	—	5.0
C_7 Methyl hexanoate	—	—
Ethyl 3-methylbutyrate	—	1·3
Amyl acetate	—	—
3-Methylbutyl acetate	6·3	1·6
Methyl hexenoate	—	—
Furfuryl acetate	0·060	—
C_8 Methyl heptenoate	—	—
Ethyl hexanoate	0·95	0·23
3-Methylbutyl propionate	0·15	0·7
Hexyl acetate	0·025	1·4
Methyl 4-methylhex-2-enoate	0·060	—
Ethyl hexenoate	—	—
Ethyl nicotinate	1·400	—
C_9 Methyl octanoate	—	—
Ethyl heptanoate	—	—
Amyl butyrate	—	0·6

TABLE 22.8 (*continued*)

D. *Esters* [58]	Concentration (ppm) [59]	Flavour threshold (ppm) [46]
3-Methylbutyl butyrate	—	—
3-Methylbutyl 2-methylpropionate	0·140	—
Heptyl acetate	0.025	1·4
Ethyl heptenoate	—	—
Ethyl benzoate	0.010	—
C_{10} Ethyl octanoate	1·500	0·9
Butyl hexanoate	—	—
2-Methylpropyl hexanoate	0·025	—
Amyl 3-methylbutyrate	—	—
3-Methylbutyl 3-methylbutyrate	0·040	—
Hexyl butyrate	—	—
Octyl acetate	0·030	0·5
2-Phenylethyl acetate	1·625	3·8
C_{11} Ethyl nonanoate	—	1·2
Amyl hexanoate	—	—
Pent-2-yl hexanoate	—	—
3-Methylbutyl hexanoate	0·420	0·9
Heptan-2-yl butyrate	—	—
Nonyl acetate	0·005	—
Ethyl nonenoate	0·045	—
2-Phenylethyl propionate	0·010	—
Ethyl cinnamate	0·005	—
C_{12} Ethyl decanoate	0·190	1·5
Butyl octanoate	—	—
3-Methylbutyl heptanoate	0·020	—
Hexyl hexanoate	—	—
Octyl butyrate	—	—
2-Phenylethyl butyrate	—	—
2-Phenylethyl 2-methylpropionate	0·015	—
3-Methylbutyl benzoate	—	—
Ethyl dec-4-enoate	0·035	—
Ethyl deca-4,8-dienoate	0·015	—
C_{13} 2-Methylbutyl octanoate	0·015	—
3-Methylbutyl octanoate	0·830	2·0
2-Phenylethyl 3-methylbutyrate	0·015	—
C_{14} Ethyl dodecanoate	0·030	3·5
3-Methylbutyl nonanoate	—	2·0
Hexyl octanoate	—	—
Octyl hexanoate	—	—
2-Phenylethyl hexanoate	0·075	—
2-Phenylethyl hexenoate	—	—
C_{15} 2-Methylbutyl decanoate	0·005	—
3-Methylbutyl decanoate	0·095	3·0
3-Methylbutyl dec-4-enoate	0·020	—
C_{16} Ethyl tetradecanoate	—	2·5
Hexyl decanoate	—	—
2-Phenylethyl octanoate	0·015	—
C_{17} 3-Methylbutyl dodecanoate	0·010	—

TABLE 22.8 (*continued*)

E. *Lactones* [58]	Concentration (ppm) [59]	Flavour threshold (ppm) [46]
C_4 4-Butanolide	1·300	—
C_6 4-Hexanolide	0·020	—
4,4-Dimethylbutan-4-olide	0·160	—
4,4-Dimethylbut-2-en-4-olide	1·750	—
C_7 4-Heptanolide	0·015	—
C_8 4-Octanolide	0·020	—
C_9 4-Nonanolide	0·320	—
C_{10} 4-Decanolide	0·020	0·4
C_{11} Dihydroactindiolide	0·030	—

F. *Ketones* [58]	Concentration* (ppm) [59]	Flavour threshold (ppm) [46]
C_4 Butan-2-one	0·018	(80)
Butane-2,3-dione	0·058	0·15
3-Hydroxybutan-2-one	0·420	(50)
C_5 Pentan-2-one	0·020	(30)
Pentan-3-one	—	(30)
Pentane-2,3-dione	0·012	0·9
3-Hydroxypentan-2-one	0·050	—
2-Methyltetrahydrofuran-3-one	0·025	—
2-Methyltetrahydro-thiophen-3-one	0·005	—
C_6 Hexan-2-one	—	4·0
3-Methylpentan-2-one	0·060	0·4
4-Methylpentan-2-one	0·12	—
2-Acetylfuran	0·040	—
C_7 Heptan-2-one	0·110	2·0
C_8 Octan-2-one	0·010	(0·25)
6-Methylhept-5-en-2-one	0·050	
C_9 Nonan-2-one	0·030	(0·20)
C_{10} Decan-2-one	—	0·25
C_{11} Undecan-2-one	0·001	0·4

G. *Hydrocarbons* [58]	Concentration (ppm) [59]	Flavour threshold (ppm) [46]
C_6 Cyclohexane	—	—
C_7 3,4-Dimethylpent-2-ene	—	—
Toluene	—	—
C_8 2,2-Dimethylhexane	—	—
o-Xylene	0·020	—
Styrene	0·070	—
C_9 Methylethylbenzene	0·020	—
C_{10} *i*-Butylbenzene	—	—
α-Pinene	—	—
Limonene	—	—
Myrcene	—	0·013
Naphthalene	0·015	—
C_{15} Caryophyllene	—	—

* See also [203].

TABLE 22.9
Principal volatile constituents of beer [60]

		Concentration range			
Ethanol (% v/v)	b.p. (°C) 78	Stout 2·0–8·9	Pale ale 3·4–4·0	Brown ale 2·1–4·5	Lager 2·8–3·2
		(mg/l)			
n-Propanol	97	13–60	31–48	17–29	5–10
2-Methylpropanol	108	11–98	18–33	11–33	6–11
2-Methylbutanol	128	9–41	14–19	8–22	8–16
3-Methylbutanol	131	33–169	47–61	28–77	32–57
β-Phenylethanol	220	20–55	36–53	19–44	25–32
Ethyl acetate	77	11–69	14–23	9–18	8–14
Isoamyl acetate	139	1·0–4·9	1·4–3·3	0·4–2·6	1·5–2·0

From consideration of the metabolic pathways discussed in Chapter 17 it will be recalled that ethanol and the higher alcohols are formed by reduction of the corresponding aldehydes by the enzyme alcohol dehydrogenase. Thus, only low levels of aldehydes will be found in beer (Table 22.8B). The major aldehyde is acetaldehyde and some concentrations are given in Table 22.10. Acetal has also been detected in beer. During the storage of bottled beer higher alcohols are oxidized to aldehydes by melanoidins; high levels of these aldehydes produce stale off-flavours [65]. The cardboard flavour of stale beer is thought to be due to 2-*trans*-nonenal and 2-methylfurfural [66]; 2-*trans*-nonenal has a very low threshold value (0·11 ppb) and is derived from linoleic acid *via* trihydroxyoctadecenoic acid (Table 22.7). Among the heterocyclic compounds formed during wort boiling (Fig. 14.2) 5-hydroxy-methylfurfural, furfural, and 5-methylfurfural occur in beer. One survey of over 300 German Beers [67] reported 0·5–4·0 ppm of 5-hydroxymethyl-furfural (maximum value: 7·8 ppm) but other workers found higher levels increasing with beer colour: one dark German beer contained 71·5 ppm [68]. Lower levels of furfural are found (< 15 µg/l) but these increase markedly during pasteurization and storage at 40°C: the maximum level of furfural found was 1843 µg/l [69].

TABLE 22.10
Acetaldehyde content of beer

Beer	Acetaldehyde content (ppm) (mean value in parentheses)
British lager [62]	2·3–28·2 (8·7)
Foreign lager [62]	0–13 (5·4)
Light and pale ales [62]	3·8–33·8 (8·2)
Primed beers [62]	3·0–37·2 (15·2)
Irish stout [63]	0·5–10 (4·0)
American beers [64]	2–18 (9·1)

Acetaldehyde is a metabolic branching point: it can either be reduced to ethanol or oxidized to acetic acid. This acid is the principal volatile acid of beer; lager beers contain 57–145 mg/l [70, 71]. The ASBC describe methods for determining the total acidity of beer either by potentiometric titration or using phenolphthalein as indicator. The results may be expressed either as ml 1·0 N alkali per 100 g beer or as percentage of lactic acid. *Lactobacillus* spp. growing in beer produce lactic acid. Belgian lambic and gueuze beer, produced by spontaneous fermentation contain 460–1210 ppm of acetic acid and 1890–3434 ppm of lactic acid [72]. Many other volatile acids have been detected in beer (Table 22.8C). As would be expected from their mode of biosynthesis fatty acids with an even number of carbon atoms predominate [73, 74, 75].

Each of the acids listed in Table 22.7 and 22.8C is theoretically capable of esterifying each of the alcohols named in Table 22.8A to give well over 3700 esters in beer. Those which have been identified are given in Table 22.8D. Ethyl acetate is the major ester and some concentrations in a range of beers is given in Table 22.9. The concentrations found exceed that expected from the equilibrium constant ($K = 4$) of the reaction:

$$CH_3COOH + C_2H_5OH \rightleftharpoons CH_3COOC_2H_5 + H_2O$$

showing that esters are biosynthesized during fermentation (Chapter 17). Of the other esters present in beer ethyl esters predominate but the acetates of the higher alcohols (the so-called 'banana esters') are also important (Table 22.9). The esters undoubtedly contribute to the overall flavour of beer and abnormally high levels may be regarded as off-flavours. The wild yeasts *Hansenula* and *Pichia* produce large quantitites of ethyl acetate by aerobic fermentation. Lambic and gueuze beers contain 33·4–167·0 ppm of ethyl acetate and 107–483 ppm of ethyl lactate [72]. Esters are important constituents of hop oil (Table 13.4) but the majority of those in beer are fermentation products. Nevertheless it has been shown that methyl dec-4-enoate and methyl deca-4,8-dienoate, present in hop oil, are transesterified during fermentation to the corresponding ethyl esters which are found in beer (Table 22.8D). No doubt other esters derived from hop oil into wort undergo transesterification to give ethyl esters in beer. Lactones are cyclic esters of hydroxyacids, those identified in beer (Table 22.8E) are all γ-lactones with five membered rings. Ketones like aldehydes are carbonyl compounds but they are not major fermentation products. Those present in beer (Table 22.8F) are probably derived from hop oil or hop resin degradation products. Vicinal diketones contain two carbonyl groups on adjacent carbon atoms [76]. Those in beer include diacetyl (butane-2,3-dione) and pentane-2,3-dione which are potent flavouring agents. Quantities in excess of 0·5 ppm of diacetyl are regarded as an off-flavour in lager beers. The level of diacetyl and pentane-2,3-dione in a range of commercial beers is given in Table 22.11. Many methods have been proposed for the analysis of diacetyl and vicinal diketones. The most specific involves gas-liquid chromatography using an electron capture detector which is sensitive to vicinal diketones but not to the majority of other beer constituents [77]. The ASBC gives four methods for the analysis of diacetyl or vicinal diketones. One of these, based on the colour formed at 530 nm with α-naphthol, potassium hydroxide, and creatinine, is also adopted by the Institute of Brewing. The EBC prefer to measure the formation of 2,3-dimethylquinoxaline with o-phenylenediamine. The ASBC reference method involves the formation of the Fe^{II} complex of dimethyl-glyoxime which is measured at 520 nm, or alternatively, the absorption of dimethylglyoxime itself at 230 nm can be used. Diacetyl production in beer is related to the biosynthesis of valine (Chapter 17). One of the intermediates, α-acetolactate, decomposes to diacetyl on heating so analytical methods which involve a preliminary distillation, especially those of fermenting wort, give high results. Headspace analysis avoids distillation and using this technique, with electron capture detection, it was found that during fermentation of an Irish stout the maximum level of vicinal diketones (0·6 ppm) occurred about 44 hr after pitching but thereafter the level fell to about 0·1 ppm. Yeast strains differ in the amount of diacetyl they produce and the choice of yeast strain is probably the most important factor in controlling the level in beer [78]. In particular, respiratory deficient 'petite mutants' of yeast produce large quantities of diacetyl and the off-flavour produced in beers infected with *Pediococci* (the so-called beer sarcina) is due to diacetyl.

TABLE 22.11

Levels of diacetyl and 2, 3-pentanedione in commercial beers (mg/l) [77]

Quality*	Diacetyl	Pentane-2,3-dione
Barley wine (4)	0·11–0·40	0·04–0·08
Lager (9)	0·02–0·08	0·01–0·05
Ale (9)	0·06–0·30	0·01–0·20
Stout (5)	0·02–0·07	0·01–0·02
Stout (1)	0·58	0·26

* Number of samples in parentheses.

There has been some debate concerning the occurrence of hop oil constituents in beer (see Chapter 13). Obviously some constituents will go into solution in beer that is dry-hopped but in the copper few components will survive the full period of wort boiling. Consequently many brewers make late additions of hops to the copper. Analysis of a Bavarian beer so treated, which had a fine hop aroma, failed to reveal terpene and sesquiterpene hydrocarbons but gave a fraction with an intensive pleasant hoppy aroma, which contained oxygenated terpenoids and sesquiterpenoids. The same compounds have been detected in American beers and the concentrations found are given in Table 13.6.

22.1.5 NITROGENOUS CONSTITUENTS

(a) *Non-volatile*

The total nitrogen content of beer, determined by Kjeldahl digestion, multiplied by the factor 6·25 is often expressed as protein: the ASBC describe such a method. Thus most beers contain 300–1000 ppm of total N equivalent to 0·19–0·63% protein while an all-malt Burton strong ale (OG 1106) contained 1840 ppm N equivalent to 1·15% protein. However, only a small percentage of the total nitrogen of beer is true protein (mol. wt. > 17 000) [79]. Free α-amino nitrogen is determined by an internationally agreed method by measuring the purple colour formed with ninhydrin at 570 nm. The EBC also describe a method using 2,4,6-trinitrobenzenesulphonic acid (TNBS) which gives a colour at 340 nm. The TBNS method is quicker but less precise and gives higher values with beers than those obtained with ninhydrin. Neither method includes proline.

During fermentation nitrogenous compounds are assimilated from the wort for yeast growth and, in addition, some proteins or polypeptides may be precipitated as the pH falls. Beer therefore contains less nitrogen than the wort from which it is obtained. For example [80] malt with 1·3% N produced worts (SG 1044) which contained 728–862 ppm N. After fermentation, the beers contained 342–426 ppm N. Similarly, using malt which contained 1·8% N, the worts contained 958–1154 ppm N and the beers 541 and 736 ppm N. Thus one-third to a half of the wort nitrogen is lost during fermentation. Less, proportionally, of high nitrogen worts are assimilated and beers brewed at higher original gravities will obviously contain more nitrogen.

With regard to the nature of the nitrogenous constituents of beer, the bulk of the amino acids of wort are assimilated during fermentation so that beers contain only low levels of amino acids. For example, beers from all-malt worts contained 32·6–44·7 ppm α-amino-N equivalent to 8·2% of the total N and beers brewed from a grist containing 22·8% of wheat flour contained 21·3–26·7 ppm α-amino-N, 5·8% of the total N [81]. In a range of Australian bottled beers the mean content of α-amino N was 69 ppm or 14·9% of the total N [9]. In Table 22·12 are collected some analyses of the amino acids in beer obtained by ion-exchange chromatography; similar data are obtained by gas–liquid chromatography [83]. It will be seen that proline predominates: this imino acid is scarcely metabolized during fermentation so that the level in beer is between 121–354 ppm or between 4 and 10% of the total N. The ethyl esters of valine, leucine and isoleucine have been detected in beer [206]. In dialysis experiments Visking tubing retains compounds with molecular weights greater than 5000. In the all-malt beers mentioned above, 45% of the total N was retained and with the beers brewed from the grist containing 22·8% of wheat flour, 49% of the total N was non-dialysable [81]. With another beer, 75% of the total N was dialysable and of this 30% was classified as polypeptide (mol. wt. 1500–5000), 12% as peptide, and 19% as amino acids and proline. The peptides were fractioned by chromatography on DEAE-cellulose and by electrophoresis. This showed that about 40% of the wort peptides were assimilated during fermentation but, in addition, beer contained peptides not presesent in the wort [84].

TABLE 22.12

Amino acid analyses of beers

OG	Amino acids as µg α-amino N/ml					
	Indian pale ale 1042·8	Brown ale 1031·5	Draught bitter 1040·8	Mild ale 1036	Stout 1045	
Alanine	—	0·19	0·43	—	0·2	—
Ammonia	1·07	0·92	1·88	1·36	1·7	1·8
Arginine	—	—	0·18	—	—	—
Aspartic acid	—	0·04	0·16	0·04	0·2	0 2
Glutamic acid	—	0·04	0·14	0·02	—	—
Glycine	0·21	0·01	0·08	0·19	—	—
Histidine	0·14	—	—	—	—	—
Isoleucine	—	—	0·01	—	0·4	—
Leucine	—	—	0·03	—	0·4	—
Lysine	0·42	0·31	0·50	0·32	0·2	0·6
Methionine	—	—	0·24	—	—	—
Phenylalanine	—	0·04	0·49	0·07	—	—
Serine	—	—	0·15	0·05	0·2	0·3
Threonine	—	—	0·66	—	0·2	0·2
Tryptophan	1·77	1·62	2·06	1·62	0·5	1·2
Tyrosine	—	0·50	0·35	0·07	—	—
Valine	—	—	0·03	—	0·4	0·7
Total α-Amino N	3·61	3·74	7·39	3·88	4·4	5·0
Proline	28·25	13·32	28·53	22·05	38·0	40·1
α-Amino N and proline	31·86	17·06	35·92	25·93	42·4	45·1
Total N	276	336	459	—	—	—

The methods used in the investigation of wort, malt and barley proteins such as Lundin fractionation, gel filtration, and electrophoresis have been applied to beer proteins, principally with the aim of characterizing the fractions associated with foam stability and haze formation. The malting and mashing methods employed will affect the degree of proteolysis which the barley proteins undergo and thus determine the nature of the high molecular weight nitrogen compounds in beer. Detailed studies have been carried out with Danish lager [85, 86]. Gel filtration of beer indicates the presence of a small amount of 'protein' with molecular weight above 100 000 but the majority of the complex nitrogen is in the mol. wt. 5000–12 000 range [79]. Most of these 'protein' fractions contain more carbohydrate than protein. The fractions with the highest mol. wt. reacted immunologically with yeast antibodies, the remainder with barley antibodies. By isoelectric focusing the proteins can be resolved into at least 30 discrete bands with isoelectric points (pI) between 3·5 and 10, the majority in the acidic range about pI 5 [85]. The dominant protein in beer occurs in this region and has a mol. wt. about 40 000 but still contains tightly bound carbohydrates. It is immunochemically identical with barley protein Z and thus the 'core' of this protein survives the brewing process. Barley protein Z is associated with β-amylase and may play a role in the formation and solubilization of bound β-amylase [86]. The influence that these protein fractions have on head retention and haze formation is discussed later.

TABLE 22.13

Nucleotides in beer [45, 87]

	Concentration (μg/ml)	Taste threshold (ppm)
5'-Cytidine monophosphate	1·8–7·8	
2'-Cytidine monophosphate	2·3–7·3	
3'-Cytidine monophosphate	16·8–73·3	
5'-Adenosine monophosphate	12·4–67·6	
5'-Guanosine monophosphate	1·1–4·9	35
3'-Adenosine monophosphate	1·6–10·7	
5'-Uridine monophosphate	2·8–9·1	1·7–4·5
2'-Adenosine monophosphate	1·3–5·5	
3'-Uridine monophosphate	1·5–10·3	
2'-Uridine monophosphate	9·3–26·2	
3'-Guanosine monophosphate	1·6–5·1	
5'-Thymidine monophosphate	2·0–11·9	
5'-Inosine monophosphate	1·5–4·7	120
3'-Inosine monophosphate	1·3–8·1	
3'-Thymidine monophosphate	1·4–6·6	
2'-Guanosine monophosphate	2·4–6·7	

Few of the nucleic acids present in barley are thought to survive malting and mashing. Their degradation products, the phosphorous-containing nucleotides (Table 22.13), nucleosides, purine and pyrimidine bases (Table 22.14) are present in beer. Guanosine, cytidine and uridine are the major constituents [88].

TABLE 22.14

Purines, pyrimidines and nucleosides in beer [45]

	Concentration (μg/ml)
Cytosine	11–24·6
Cytidine	18–41·0
Guanine	0·2–3·2
Adenine	0·8–5
Uracil	1·0–4·6
Uridine	21–70·3
Adenosine	12·5–24·3
Xanthine	2·8–9·7
Inosine	1·0–2·4
Guanosine	45–139·0
Thymidine	7–19·8

TABLE 22.15

Some heterocyclic bases present in beer [89]

	Concentration (ppm) [45]	Threshold in light ale (ppb) [89]
Pyridine		
2-Acetylpyridine		100
3-Acetylpyridine		
Pyrazine	19–48·5	
Methylpyrazine	201–279 (410–419)	1 000
2,3-Dimethylpyrazine	0·9–6·5	20
2,5-Dimethylpyrazine	3·4–12·3	50
2,6-Dimethylpyrazine	2·3–16·2	100
Ethylpyrazine	5·9–11·7	
2-Ethyl-5-methylpyrazine	5·4–35	
2-Ethyl-6-methylpyrazine	0·5–3·4	
Trimethylpyrazine	0·7–7·7	100
2-Ethyl-3,5-dimethylpyrazine	6·5–24·6 ⎱	50
2-Ethyl-3,6-dimethylpyrazine	1·9–13·8 ⎰	
2-Ethyl-5,6-dimethylpyrazine		
Tetramethylpyrazine	9·2–62·0	200
Acetylpyrazine	8·1–19·2	100
6,7-Dihydro-5H-cyclopentapyrazine		
2-Methyl-6,7-dihydro-5H-cyclo-pentapyrazine		
Thiazole		
2-Furanmethanol		
Furfural		
2-Acetylfuran	4–97	80 000
Dihydro-2(3H)-furanone		
Dihydro-5-methyl-2(3H)-furanone		
5-Methyl-2-furfural		
2-Thiophenecarboxaldehyde		
2-Acetylthiophene		
5-Methyl-2-thiophenecarboxaldehyde		

Other non-volatile nitrogenous compounds characterized in beer include tryptophol (0·8–3·6 ppm), choline (200–250 ppm), tyramine (0·15 ppm), and hordenine (2 ppm). Patients being treated for depression with monoamine oxidase inhibitors must not take alcoholic drinks (especially chianti) and yeast products, due to the build-up of toxic levels of tyramine.

Nitrogen, oxygen and sulphur heterocycles formed during malt kilning and wort boiling are given in Fig. 14.2 and Tables 14.7 and 14.8. Most of these compounds survive into beer (Table 22.15); indeed the level of pyrazines increases during fermentation. Some data on the concentration of pyrazines in beer, obtained using GLC is given in Table 14.8 but higher values were obtained by HPLC (Table 22.15). Many of these later values exceed the taste threshold level. Also included in Table 22.15 are derivatives of furan and thiophene. The level of furfural and hydroxymethylfurfural found in beer was mentioned earlier. Similar levels of furfural and 2-formylthiophene (2-thiophenecarboxaldehyde) are found in both ales and lagers but 2-acetylfuran occurs at higher levels in ales (70–97 ppb) than in lagers (4–12 ppb). 2-Acetylthiophene, 2-furanmethanol, 5-methylfurfural, and 5-methyl-2-thiophenecarboxaldehyde also occur at higher levels in ales than lagers [90].

TABLE 22.16

Pyrrole derivatives in beer [91]

	Concentration (ppb)
Pyrrole	+
2-Methylpyrrole	1 800
2-Formylpyrrole	30
2-Acetylpyrrole	1 400
2-Acetyl-5-methylpyrrole	10
2-Formyl-5-methylpyrrole	110
2-Pyrrolidone	10
1-Methyl-2-pyrrolidone	+
1-Acetylpyrrole	+
1-Furfurylpyrrole	10
Indole	+

Some data for pyrrole derivatives in beer are given in Table 22.16 and the occurrence of pyridine derivatives is noted in Tables 14.7 and 22.15. One pyridine derivative is noteworthy; pyridine-3-carboxylic acid (nicotinic acid) is a B-vitamin essential for human growth. Beer contains 4500–8600 ppb and about 1500 ppb of ethyl nicotinate. Traces of the methyl, 3-methylbutyl, and phenethyl esters of nicotinic acid are also present in beer [91]. Ethyl nicotinate and o-aminoacetophenone, also present in beer (10 ppb), have also been associated with stale grainy flavours in beer at 2000 and 5 ppb respectively [92]. The level of some amides in beer is given in Table 22.17 [91]. Most of the heterocyclic compounds and amides discussed are sufficiently volatile to be analysed by GLC and may contribute to the aroma of beer but they are much less volatile than the amines discussed below.

TABLE 22.17

Amides in dark German beer [91]

		Concentration (ppb)
N,N-Dimethylformamide	H·CONMe$_2$	15
N,N-Dimethylacetamide	CH$_3$·CONMe$_2$	10
N-Methylacetamide	CH$_3$·CONH·Me	+
N-Ethylacetamide	CH$_3$·CONH·CH$_2$Me	20
N-(2-Methylbutyl) acetamide	CH$_3$·CONH·CHMe·CH$_2$Me	10
N-(3-Methylbutyl) acetamide	CH$_3$·CONH·CH$_2$CHMe$_2$	25
N-Furfurylacetamide		120
N-(2-Phenylethyl) acetamide	CH$_3$·CONH·CH$_2$CH$_2$C$_6$H$_5$	15

TABLE 22.18

Volatile amines present in beer [94]

	Concentration (ppm)
Methylamine	
Ethylamine	0·03–2·12 [95]
n-Propylamine	
n-Butylamine	
Isobutylamine	0·05–0·10 [96]
sec-Butylamine	
n-Amylamine	
Isoamylamine	
Hexylamine	
1,3-Diaminopropane	
1,4-Diaminobutane	
1,5-Diaminopentane	
N,N-Dimethyl-1,4-diaminobutane	
Dimethylamine	0·07–0·78 [96]
Diethylamine	
Di-isobutylamine	
Pyrrolidine	
Trimethylamine	0·02–0·06 [96]
Tripropylamine	
N,N-Dimethylbutylamine	
Ethanolamine	
p-Hydroxybenzylamine	0·16–0·72 [97]
Tyramine	
Histamine	0·08–0·55 [98]

(b) *Volatile*

At the pH of beer ammonia and the other volatile amines in beer (Table 22.18) will be present as their non-volatile salts. Ammonia is the most abundant volatile nitrogenous constituent: the mean value in a range of US beers was 14·6 ppm (3–33 ppm) compared with 21·3 ppm (0–33 ppm) in imported beers [93]. At the low concentrations found, the volatile amines will have little influence on the flavour of beer. Dimethylamine is commonly the major constituent. Secondary amines such as dimethylamine react with nitrogen oxides to form carcinogenic N-nitrosamines:

$$2 \underset{R^2}{\overset{R^1}{N}}H + N_2O_3 \longrightarrow 2 \underset{R^2}{\overset{R^1}{N}} \cdot NO + H_2O$$

N-Nitrosodimethylamine has been detected in beer and other foodstuffs. German beers contained 0–68 ppb (mean 2.7 ppb) [99] and American beers 0–14 ppb (mean 5·9 ppb) [100]. The higher levels were found in dark strong German lager beer (maximum 47 ppb) and in 'Rauchbier' (maximum 68 ppb) made from smoked malt. N-Nitrosodiethylamine was detected in two samples of the German beers (0·5 and 3·0 ppb) but not in the American or Australian beers [204]. N-Nitrosoproline is also present in beer [205]. Although the carcinogenic activity of N-nitrosodimethylamine has been extensively demonstrated in animals, the minimum dose in the human diet that poses a hazard is not known. Nevertheless the Food and Drug Administration of the USA imposed a limit of 5 ppb of N-nitrosodimethylamine in beer from 1st January, 1980. N-Nitrosodimethylamine does not appear to be formed during the brewing process but is present in the malt used. It is absent from barley and green malt and is formed during malt kilning. In particular, nitrosating agents are present in the flue gases of direct-fired kilns. These include nitrous anhydride N_2O_3, the most potent, nitrogen dioxide NO_2, dinitrogen tetroxide N_2O_4, and mixtures of NO_2 and NO known as NO_x. The amine substrate is thought to be hordenine [209], and possibly gramine, formed in the rootlets of barley during germination. Methods for reducing the level of N-nitrosodimethylamine (NDMA) in malt and thus in the beer produced therefrom include [210]:

1. Low drying temperatures and shorter drying periods. Ale malts contained higher levels of NDMA than lager malts.
2. Indirect firing or the use of low NO_x emission burners for direct-fired kilns. Even using low NO_x burners low levels of NDMA were not always obtained in high kilned malts.
3. Acid spraying or acid steeping before kilning reduced NDMA.

4. Burning of sulphur in the kiln, to produce SO_2, reduced the level of NDMA, probably because of the acid conditions produced on the surface of the malt.

5. Malting procedures which reduce root and shoot growth and thus limit the amine precursor.

22.1.6 SULPHUR-CONTAINING CONSTITUENTS [101]

Beer contains 150–400 ppm of sulphate (Table 22.2). The major non-volatile organic sulphur compounds in wort are the amino acids cyst(e)ine and methionine and the peptides and proteins which contain them. Some of these compounds will survive into beer. In addition malt contains S-methyl-methionine and dimethyl sulphoxide which are precursors of dimethyl sulphide. Hops may be a source of sulphur: they are often dusted with elemental sulphur or sprayed with dithiocarbamate insecticides. In addition sulphur is usually burnt in the oast. The sulphur compounds present in hop oil are discussed in Chapter 13.

The analysis of volatile sulphur compounds is difficult as additional compounds may be formed if the sample is heated or exposed to light or oxygen. Headspace analysis by gas–liquid chromatography using a flame photometric detector is the most satisfactory technique although solvent extraction may be necessary for the less volatile compounds. The sulphur compounds which have been identified in beer are listed in Table 22.19.

Much of the sulphur dioxide present in beer is in a bound form, for example, as the acetaldehyde bisulphite compound. The classical (Monier–Williams) method for the estimation of sulphur dioxide, adopted by the Institute of Brewing, involves the removal of SO_2 from acidified beer in a stream of carbon dioxide and nitrogen at 100°C. The gas is absorbed in hydrogen peroxide and the sulphuric acid formed titrated. In Britain sulphur dioxide is a permitted preservative in beers ($\not> 70$ ppm), ciders, and wines ($\not> 150$ ppm) and the Monier–Williams method is official. The EBC-ASBC adopt a more sensitive colorimetric method in which the colour restored to acid-decolourized rosaniline hydrochloride is measured.

Much of the hydrogen sulphide in beer is also in a bound form so that, except in the presence of wort spoilage organisms, the level in beer seldom exceeds 1 ppb. Thiols (mercaptans) occur in beer at similar levels (Table 22.19). The major volatile sulphur constituent in beer is dimethyl sulphide (DMS) and the range of concentrations reported is given in Table 22.20. British ales have low levels of dimethyl sulphide, usually below the taste threshold, but continental lagers contain significant amounts so that dimethyl sulphide is a feature of lager flavour [107]. The precursor of dimethyl sulphide in barley and malt is S-methylmethionine [115]. The degree of kilning determines the amount of precursor present in the malt. There

TABLE 22.19

Volatile sulphur compounds in beer

Compound	Structure	Concentration (ppb)	Reference	Flavour threshold (ppb) [101, 109]
Hydrogen sulphide	H₂S	0·0-0·9	[102]	30 (ale) 10 (lager)
Sulphur dioxide	SO₂	1000-16 000	[103]	20 000
Carbon oxysulphide	COS		[104]	
Thioformaldehyde	H·CHS		[105]	
Methanedithiol (dithioformaldehyde)	HS·CH₂·SH		[105]	
Thioacetone	CH₃CS·CH₃		[105]	
Methanethiol	CH₃SH	0·5-3·4	[102, 106]	3
Ethanethiol	CH₃CH₂SH		[102]	2·5
tert-Butylthiol	(CH₃)₃C·SH		[109]	0·5
Dimethyl sulphide	CH₃·S·CH₃	0·1-0·4	[107]	33
Dimethyl disulphide	CH₃·S·S·CH₃	0·1-0·4	[102]	3
Dimethyl trisulphide	CH₃·S·S·S·CH₃		[108]	0·1
Diethyl sulphide	CH₃CH₂·S·CH₂CH₃			3
Diethyl disulphide	CH₃CH₂·S·S·CH₂CH₃		[109]	30 (ale) 20 (lager)
Methyl n-butyl sulphide	CH₃·S·CH₂CH₂CH₂CH₃	1		
Methional	CH₃SCH₂CH₂CHO	345-3175	[110]	40
Methionol	CH₃S·CH₂CH₂CH₂OH		[110]	
3-Methylthiopropionic acid	CH₃S·CH₂CH₂COOH		[110]	
Ethyl 3-methylthiopropionate	CH₃S·CH₂CH₂COOC₂H₅	5-180	[110]	
3-Methylthiopropyl acetate	CH₃S·CH₂CH₂O·COCH₃		[110]	
2-Methyltetrahydrothiophen-3-one				
S-Methyl 2-methylbutanethiolate	CH₃CH₂CH(CH₃)CO·S·CH₃		[108]	1
S-Methyl 4-methylpentanethioate	(CH₃)₂CH·CH₂CH₂CO·S·CH₃		[108]	15
S-Methyl hexanethioate	CH₃(CH₂)₄CO·S·CH₃		[108]	1
4-(4-Methylpent-3-enyl)-3,6-dihydro-1,2-dithiine				10
3 Methylbut-2-enyl-thiol	(CH₃)₂C=CH·CH₂SH		[111]	1

should be negligible loss of S-methylmethionine during infusion mashing but in boiling wort the compound decomposes to dimethyl sulphide with a half life of 40 min. Free dimethyl sulphide is lost by evaporation but as the boiled wort cools more S-methylmethionine is broken down to dimethyl sulphide. In some cases the level of DMS does not change appreciably during fermentation, in others it may fall or it may increase. Infection by wort spoilage organisms usually results in DMS formation [109].

TABLE 22.20
Dimethyl sulphide content of beers (ppb)

British ales [112]	14
British lagers [112]	16–27
Continental lagers [112]	44–114
Beer from green malt [107]	80
German lagers [113]	32–205 (av. 94)
Diet bier [113]	46–98 (av. 63·5)
Canadian ale [114]	92
Canadian lager [114]	114
Canadian low alcohol [114]	82
British	41–75
German	141–153
United States	59–106

Some of the dimethyl sulphide in barley and malt is oxidized to dimethyl sulphoxide $(CH_3 \cdot SO \cdot CH_3)$ together with a trace of dimethyl sulphone $(CH_3 \cdot SO_2 \cdot CH_3)$. Malt contains 1·42–3·7 ppm of dimethyl sulphoxide. Yeasts are capable of reducing dimethyl sulphoxide back to DMS and this may be one source of DMS present in finished beer [116]. Late addition of hops during wort boiling also contributes dimethyl sulphide, and dimethyl trisulphide, to wort.

22.2 *Nutritive value of beer*
The calorific (caloric) value of beer is due to ethanol, residual carbohydrate, and protein and can be calculated from the equation:

Calorific value (kcal/100 ml) = 4(%w/v solids) + 7(%w/v ethanol).

The ASBC describe such a method. Some representative values for British beers are given in Table 22.21 where the results are also expressed in kilojoules (1 kcal = 4·184 kJ). Many brewers of low carbohydrate 'lite' beers declare the calorific value (e.g. 26–29 kcal/100 ml) on the label. Beer is also a source of B vitamins containing (values in ppb for lagers and top fermentation beers): biotin (7–18; 11–12), nicotinic acid (4494–8607; 7500–7753), pantothenic acid (1093–1535; 1375–1808), pyridoxine (329–709; 341–546), riboflavin (219–420; 331–575), and thiamine (15–58; 59–181) [117]. Folic acid and vitamin B_{12} are also present [10].

TABLE 22.21

Composition and nutritive value of beer [10]

	Alcohol (g/100 ml)	Solid (g/100 ml)	Carbohydrate (g/100 ml)	Protein (N × 6·25) (g/100 ml)	Energy value (kcal/100 ml)	Energy value (kJ/100 ml)
Brown ale (bottled)	2·2	4·2	3·0	0·3	28	117
Canned beer (bottled)	3·1	3·3	2·3	0·3	32	132
Draught bitter	3·1	3·3	2·3	0·3	32	132
Draught mild	2·6	2·5	1·6	0·2	25	104
Keg bitter	3·0	3·6	2·3	0·3	31	129
Lager (bottled)	3·2	2·4	1·5	0·2	29	120
Pale ale (bottled)	3·3	3·3	2·0	0·3	32	133
Stout (bottled)	2·9	5·8	4·2	0·3	37	156
Stout extra	4·3	3·6	2·1	0·3	39	163
Strong ale	6·6	8·0	6·1	0·7	72	301

22.3 *Colour*

The colour of beer is largely determined by the melanoidins and caramel present in the malt and adjuncts used but further caramelization occurs during wort boiling. Minor adjustments of the colour of beer can be made by the addition of caramel either to the copper or with primings. The chemistry of melanoidin and caramel formation is discussed in Chapter 14.

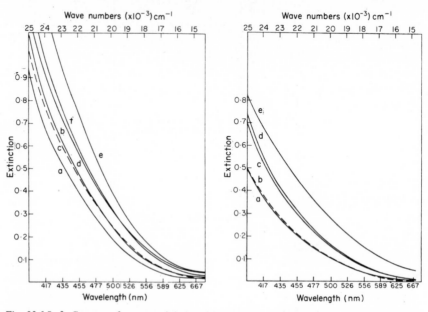

Fig. 22.1 Left. Spectra of commercial ales: (a) Pale ale 1; (b) Pale ale 2; (c) Pale ale 3; (d) Light ale 1; (e) Light ale 2; (f) Pale ale 4. Right. Spectra of lagers and stout: (a–d) Lagers; (e) Stout.

The measurement of the colour of worts, beers and caramel solutions is difficult as the absorption spectrum of, for example, beer (Fig. 22.1) shows no maximum in the visible range. The balance between red and yellow varies from lagers, through pale ales, to stouts. Thus, neither direct visual comparison nor photometric methods are entirely satisfactory. The EBC has established a series of comparison standards as coloured glasses ranging in intensity from 2 to 27 units. The colour match is with yellower pale worts at the low end of the scale and the redder colours of dark worts, beers, and caramel at the upper end of the scale. A good colour match, using solutions free of turbidity, is achieved using cells of varying thickness and the result calculated for a path length of 25 mm. It is essential that the operator should be free from colour blindness: 10% of the male and 1% of the female population do not have perfect colour vision. Operators should also measure the colour of Hartong's solution (0·100 g $K_2Cr_2O_7$ and 3·500 g Na_2 [Fe(CN)$_6$·NO] 2H$_2$O per litre), which would read 15 units in a 40 mm cell, and correct their results accordingly.

The Institute of Brewing use the EBC method for malts but have adopted a photometric method for worts and beers based on measurements at 530 nm. The photometer is previously calibrated with a standard potassium dichromate solution and the result is expressed directly in EBC units of colour [118].

The ASBC also use a spectrophotometric method and define beer colour as 10 times the absorbance of beer measured in a 12·7 mm (0·5 in.) cell with monochromatic light of wavelength 430 nm. The absorbance at 430 and 700 nm is measured. If the absorbance at 700 nm is equal to or less than 0·039 times the absorbance at 430 nm, the beer is judged free of turbidity and the colour calculated from the reading at 430 nm. Otherwise the sample must be clarified before the colour can be measured. Comparisons of wort colours on EBC and ASBC mashes of the same malts gave the following regression equations:

$$\text{EBC colour} = 2\cdot65 \text{ ASBC colour} - 1\cdot2$$

$$\text{ASBC colour} = 0\cdot375 \text{ EBC colour} + 0\cdot46$$

Based upon an ammonia caramel of 20 000 EBC colour units, it has been estimated [207] that dark mild ales and stouts contain up to 15 000 mg/l of caramel.

22.4 Viscosity

The viscosity of beer can be a useful figure reflecting the content and degradation states of various contributory factors, such as β-glucan, derived from the wort. Measurement is made from the time of flow in an Ostwald viscometer at 20·0°C. At this temperature the dynamic viscosity of water is 1·002 cP (centipoises) and the kinematic viscosity is 1·0038 cS (centistokes). The EBC use a 20% w/w sucrose solution as an additional standard (1·96 cP at 20·0°C) but the Institute of Brewing, following British Standard 188: 1957, use a 3·0% w/v solution of glycerol [119]. Some values are: worts (SG 1030–1100) 1·59–5·16; lager (SG 1007) 1·45; and stout (SG 1009) 1·96 cP. The method can be extended to measure the viscosity of liquid sugars and brewing syrups using a viscometer of the appropriate range.

22.5 Foam characteristics and head retention

One of the properties of beer appreciated by many consumers is the head of foam that develops as the glass is filled. It is generally reckoned desirable that this head should persist and not collapse while the beer is being drunk. Most bottled beers produce a good head but the foaming characteristics of draught beers show local variation. Those from Burton-on-Trent traditionally have no foam, but in the North-east a rich creamy foam that overflows the glass is expected. Brewers therefore wish to maintain or improve the foam characteristics of their beers. The theory and industrial application of foams have been well reviewed [120, 121].

22.5.1 METHODS OF ASSESSING FOAM CHARACTERISTICS

The physical properties which are responsible for beer foam behaviour are: (*i*) foam or head formation, (*ii*) foam collapse, foam drainage, or head retention, (*iii*) bubble collapse, and (*iv*) bubble cling, lacing, or foam adhesion. At least 80 different procedures have been described to measure these various parameters, indicating that none is entirely satisfactory. Currently neither the EBC nor the Institute of Brewing publish a recommended method. The factors which influence foam stability are discussed below but it should be noted that it is very sensitive both to temperature and traces of grease or detergents. For example, the time taken for a beer foam to collapse 10 mm was 100, 93 and 77 s at 15°, 20° and 25°C respectively [122]. Thus, as far as possible, measurements should be made in a temperature-controlled room using scrupulously clean apparatus, for example, that washed with 2% trisodium phosphate solution.

The head-forming capacity of beer is directly related to its carbon dioxide content and within the normal range of 0·35–0·42% w/w carbon dioxide, this has no effect on head retention [163]. However, beers foamed with other gases show different behaviour.

It is obvious that by pouring a bottle of beer into a glass one can make a rapid good/bad assessment of the foam stability and in attempts to quantify this process Hartong [124] devised a machine which lifts and pours bottles into scrupulously clean glasses. By measuring the time from the start of pouring until the foam has collapsed, as judged by the appearance of a grey spot in the centre of the head, an estimate of the foam stability is obtained. de Clerck and de Dijcker [125] modified Hartong's method and evaluated the collapse of foam using a travelling microscope. They suggested that foam stability depended more on the fineness of the bubbles than the composition of the beer.

Earlier, Helm [126] allowed the beer to flow through a special pourer from a bottle mounted a fixed height above a cylindrical separating funnel. After two minutes the beer which had separated was drawn off (volume *a*) and after a further eight minutes this process was repeated (volume *b*). The residual foam was then collapsed with ethanol (3 ml) and the volume measured (*c*) after allowing for the ethanol. From these results are calculated:

$$\text{Total head} = \frac{100 \ (b + c)}{(a + b + c)}$$

$$\text{Head retention capacity} = \frac{100c}{(a + b + c)}$$

The ASBC describe a modification of the Helm–Carlsberg method.

In Blom's method [127] foam is produced in a tared separating funnel by passing carbon dioxide through a Chamberland candle. The method is therefore applicable to worts and aqueous fractions containing foam-stabilizing substances. When the funnel is full of foam the beer is run off and the foam weighed. The residual foam is reweighed after intervals of 1, 2, 3, and 4 min. Blom observed that the collapse of foam was analogous to a first-order chemical reaction so that the foam stability (K) was given by

$$K = \frac{1}{t} \log \left[\frac{x}{(a - x)} \right]$$

where t = time (min), a = initial weight of foam, x = final weight of foam after time t. By substituting $a/2$ for x in this equation K can be calculated from the half-life of the foam, $t_{\frac{1}{2}}$. Blom found (no doubt using continental beers) that beers which have a half-life of 90 s have excellent retention and that values less than 80 s indicate poor head retention. Head retention values for a range of British beers are given in Table 22.22. In Table 22.23, the changes in head retention throughout the brewing process are recorded.

TABLE 22.22

Head retention (Blom) for production beers (1958) [128]

	OG	$t_{\frac{1}{2}}$(s)
Pale ale	1035	75
Pale ale	1055	77
Brown ale	1035	77
Strong ale	1080	73
Sweet stout	1046	89

TABLE 22.23

Changes in head retention through brewing process (Blom) [128]

	OG	
	1035	1055
Wort	115	—
Beer at rack	86	94
Fined beer	82	88
One day in bottle	78	—
One week	—	79
One month	80	—

If air is passed continuously through a porous membrane into a liquid there is a correlation between the volume of air (V) passing in time (t) and the average amount of foam produced (v) so that

$$\Sigma = \frac{vt}{V}$$

and Σ is a measure of the life of a bubble in the foam [129]. Applying this to beer foam Ross and Clarke [130] calculated that:

$$\Sigma = \frac{t}{2 \cdot 303 \log \dfrac{b + c}{2}}$$

where t is time in seconds of stationary phase of head, b is volume, in ml, of beer formed in this period, c is the volume of beer given by the residual head and:

$$\Sigma = 1 \cdot 44 t_{\frac{1}{2}}.$$

They concluded that Σ was a property of beer foam independent of the method used to produce it, the dimension of the container and the temperature within the limit of 2°C. This relationship has been widely accepted: the ASBC give the results of their modified Helm method in terms of the sigma value. Nevertheless, many workers have found deviations from the linear logarithmic decay proposed by Blom and by Ross and Clarke. Klopper [131] showed that the linear relationship broke down when 95% of the foam had returned to the liquid phase. Rudin [132] constructed a simple foam meter with a sintered glass base to a cylinder and found that when beer (60 ml) was foamed to 3·5 times its original volume, 90% of the decay was logarithmic. He therefore measured the time of decay from 50 to 75% giving the half-life directly. Bishop et al [133] slightly modified Rudin's apparatus and confirmed that with pure CO_2 beer foam, in both Blom's and Rudin's apparatus, showed a straight line logarithmic decrease. They also confirmed that the rate of collapse depends on the nature of the gas forming the foam. In particular, the logarithmic rectilinear collapse of foams formed with CO_2 was four times faster than foams formed with air or nitrogen. In consequence traces of air in the CO_2 used for foaming or introduced into the beer by pouring can cause departures from the linear logarithmic decay. In 1968 the Institute of Brewing recommended the method of Schuster and Mischke [134] in which the beer was foamed by the addition of 2·5 g of carborundum powder (100 mesh). This will also introduce variable amounts of air and the method was deleted from the 1977 edition of *Recommended Method of Analysis*.

In addition to the modified Helm-Carlsberg method, the ASBC describe a foam flashing method for bottled beers. Under a positive pressure of 29 lb CO_2 the beer is foamed through an 0·79 mm (0·031 inch) orifice and 200 ml of foam are collected. The volume of beer collapsed from the foam in 90 s is measured (B_1) and the remaining foam is collapsed with isopropyl alcohol (2 ml). If the total volume of beer produced from the collapse of 200 ml of foam, after subtraction of 2 ml of isopropyl alcohol, is B_2, then:

$$\text{Foam Value Units (FVU)} \qquad \frac{200(B_2 - B_1)}{B_2}$$

Several workers prefer to use a standard orifice since it has been observed that the porosity of Chamberland candles and of sintered glass discs influences the observed head retention. Ault and his co-workers [135] have designed an apparatus in which the beer (100 ml) is foamed in a cylinder with similar dimensions to a beer glass by an injection of carbon dioxide under pressure through a standardized orifice (5/1000 inch diameter). From readings taken over four minutes they measured head formation, adhesion, and collapse of foam. Klopper [122, 136] has automated the measurement of foam stability and by means of needle electrode system automatically records the time taken for the foam to collapse 10, 20, and 30 mm. Klopper [136] has also designed a cling meter whereby the internal surface of the test glass is scanned by a light source and a photocell which measures the light reflected by the clinging foam. Ault *et al.* [135] also measure % adhesion as part of their method of foam assessment.

22.5.2 FACTORS INFLUENCING HEAD RETENTION [137]

Pure liquids do not give stable foams and many investigations have been carried out to characterize the surface-active substances in beer responsible for good head retention but it is obvious, for example, from the use of alcohols to collapse foams, that beer contains both positive and negative foam factors. 'The behaviour of beer foam can be explained by assuming that beer proteins are the major foaming agents and that any variations in foaming behaviour are due to interaction of the protein with other materials including lipids, hop substances, metal ions, and charged polysaccharides' [138]. Many workers have shown that the complex nitrogenous substances and the iso-α-acids are concentrated into beer foam [139]. As discussed earlier, beer contains few true proteins but a range of peptides and polypeptides. However it is the larger molecules that are most important for head retention. A good correlation was found between foam stability (Ross and Clarke) and the content of nitrogenous material with mol. wt. > 12 000 determined by gel filtration [140]. In other work gel filtration of the protein concentrated in the foam gave three fractions with mol. wt. 150 000, 90 000 and 10 000 [141]. By immuno-electrophoresis two or three components, which originated from barley, were shown to be concentrated in foam. Two of these components also appear to be present in chill haze [142]. Most of these nitrogenous fractions contain tightly bound carbohydrate and are probably glycoproteins. The use of unmalted cereal adjuncts, such as wheat and barley, give beers with improved head retention [143] no doubt due in part to the high mol. wt. glycoproteins which they contain.

In ales, the amount of surface-active proteins present well exceeds that necessary for a reasonable head retention, but in lagers the amount is only adequate for satisfactory foam stability [144]. Thus, in dilution experiments (Fig. 22.2) the head retention of an all-malt ale (10° Plato) did not fall appreciably until it was diluted (with aqueous alcohol) to contain 20% of the original beer. This shows that, in the absence of inhibitors, the original beer contained about four times the amount of protein necessary to provide a reasonable foam. Thus, provided there is a reasonable proportion of malt in the grist, poor foam is more likely to be due to the presence of an inhibitor than shortage of foaming agent [138]. Reducing proteolysis during mashing or reducing the period of wort boiling improves head retention but at the same time causes a large reduction in the shelf life of the beer. Thus, although there may be differences, there is a great overlap of haze and foam proteins.

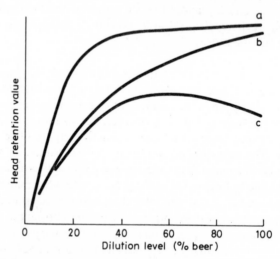

Fig. 22.2 Effect of the state of lipids on the head retention of beer at different dilutions (diluted with approximately 4% aqueous ethanol). (a) No lipid; (b) Dispersed lipid; (c) Non-dispersed lipid [138].

Lipids (fatty acids, glycerides and phospholipids) are also surface-active materials and will form a mixed surfactant system in beer in competition with the surface-active proteins for space in the surface film. If the lipid exists in discrete clusters in the surface film, the film will lose its uniformity, much of its elasticity, and will collapse rapidly. On the other hand, if the lipid is dispersed evenly throughout the film in association with the foaming agent the ensuing foam can have either better or poorer stability. The state of the foam-inhibiting lipid in the beer can be determined from the head retention-dilution curves (Fig. 22.2).

Experiments with individual lipids (1 ppm) showed the order of efficiency in destroying head retention to be: dipalmitin, palmitic acid, and monopalmitin [145]. Short chain fatty acids (C_6–C_{12}) produced during fermentation can affect foam but they are much less harmful than the longer chain acids found in wort. Malt contains 1–2% of lipid but only traces of this are carried into wort and survive into beer. Nevertheless, the addition of 0·5 or 1 ppm whole malt lipids to beer caused a loss in head retention. The malt lipids were fractioned into phospholipid, free fatty acid, and mono-, di-, and triglyceride fractions when, individually, only the diglycerides had significant foam-depressant activity. However, massive head-negative effects were shown by mixtures of the phospholipids and triglycerides [144].

The hop iso-α-acids are also concentrated into the foam. For example, when lager containing 25–26 ppm iso-α-acids (50 l) was foamed, the collapsed foam (2 l) contained 93–120 ppm iso-α-acids [139].

Of the individual iso-α-acids, isohumulone is concentrated into the foam to a greater extent than isocohumulone and unhopped beer bittered (21·0 BU) with isohumulone had a better head retention ($\Sigma = 132$) than that bittered with isocohumulone ($\Sigma = 115$) [146]. Addition of iso-α-acids to beer increases head retention but, in particular, the iso-α-acids are responsible for foam adhesion, cling or lacing. Unhopped beer does not show these effects. Traces of heavy metal ions (iron, cobalt, nickel and copper) also improve the head retention of beers but only in the presence of iso-α-acids [139].

The physical properties of the surface film relevant to foam formation are surface tension, surface elasticity, and surface viscosity. The surface tension should be low since it is a measure of the energy required to form a new surface. The film should be elastic so that local deformations do not need to create a new surface. With an elastic film the ingress and egress in the film is relatively slow so that the surface viscosity is high. The surface viscosity is a direct measure of the adhesion between molecules in a film and it increases in the presence of iso-α-acids [139].

For a foam to be stable, once formed, some change must occur in the surface-active molecules within the film. Such changes could be brought about either by changes in the conformation of the protein or by cross-linking of the protein with small molecules such as the iso-α-acids or by metal ions [138]. Oxidation is not thought to be important in the time concerned in foam formation. On the other hand it has been pointed out that, at the concentration present in the foam, the heavy metal salts of the iso-α-acids may be present in the surface film in the solid state. In the same manner the polypeptide (proteoses) may be precipitated with the iso-α-acids as insoluble salts. Such materials in the interface would obviously increase the rigidity of the foam [139]. In the body of the foam we are concerned with the gas–liquid interface but there is a solid–liquid interface at the wall of the drinking vessel. Most beer glasses and laboratory glassware has a hydrophobic surface on which the surface-active material remains when the beer drains away to show lacing or cling. The rate at which the liquid drains away from the capillaries between the bubbles is governed by the beer viscosity. Thus large molecules without surface-active properties, such as glucans, can influence head retention. When dextrans with mol. wt. in the range 10 000 to 2 000 000 were added to beer, the increase which they caused in the head retention was proportional to the increase in beer viscosity. The larger dextrans gave the largest increase in viscosity for the same concentration [138].

The foam stabilizer most commonly used in the brewing industry is propylene glycol alginate. The major function of such charged polysaccharides as foam stabilizers is to overcome the detrimental effects of lipids. Propylene glycol alginate gives a greater increase in head retention than the same amount of a neutral dextran (mol. wt. 2 000 000). This is due to an electrostatic interaction between the carboxyl groups in the alginate and the amino groups in the protein in the bubble wall. The binding of the alginate to the bubble wall serves to protect the foam against the harmful effects of lipids [147].

22.5.3 HEAD RETENTION IN THE BREWING PROCESS

As mentioned above an all-malt wort should provide ample foam-positive material so that dilution of the grist with nitrogen-free adjuncts and the use of sugars should not affect the head retention significantly. The use of unmalted cereals such as wheat flour or flaked barley in the grist improves head retention in the beer but maize and rice must be processed before use to eliminate excess lipid. The introduction of foam-negative lipids into the wort is largely dependent on brewhouse procedures, especially on the wort run-off. Strainmasters and Nooter tuns are known to give worts with high lipid contents [148]. The last runnings from the mash tun, which could contain malt fat, should be rejected. Alternatively, in production scale brews, the head retention of the beers was much improved when mash worts were recycled to minimize their lipid content [144]. Hop boiling improves head retention but too prolonged boiling may cause coagulation of the foam-stabilizing proteins. For eliminating lipids the hop back was more effective than the hop separator and these differences persisted into the finished beer [144].

During the brewing process the largest loss of head retention occurs during fermentation (Table 22.23). This is due to the loss of foam stabilizing material into the foam and yeast crop and to the formation of ethanol, higher alcohols, C_6-C_{12} fatty acids, and other negative foam factors. The loss of head retention during fermentation can be minimized by the choice of yeast strain and controlling the foam. More foam-stabilizing factors are obviously lost with top-fermenting yeasts than on bottom-fermenting strains. Foam can be controlled by the use of enclosed fermentation vessels or by recirculating part of the fermenting wort and using it to sparge the yeast head and foam [149]. Experimental worts which contained an excess of phospholipids were found to foam less during fermentation and after fining, when the excess phospholipids were removed, give beers with superior head retention to the controls. This protective action of the lipids is more pronounced with bottom yeasts than top yeasts [150]. Yeast should not be allowed to autolyse in contact with beer as the fatty acids liberated will destroy the foam stability.

After fermentation, in order to conserve foam-stabilizing factors, it is desirable to minimize foaming in pipes and vessels. Fining by means of isinglass always improves head retention. Finished beers should be handled gently and finally the maximum head retention will be observed in a beer that is cool and poured fairly vigorously into scrupulously clean tall narrow glasses [151]. Quaternary ammonium detergents remaining on the glassware can reduce head retention.

22.6 *Gushing* [152–153]

Gushing, wild, overfoaming or jumping beer, as it is variously called, is an undesirable quality in packaged beer. A beer is said to gush when, on releasing the overpressure, innumerable minute bubbles appear throughout the volume of the beer, rapidly expand, and displace the contents of the bottle. In severe cases as much as three-quarters of the contents may be lost. Outbreaks of gushing may be of two types: (*i*) sporadic or transitory and (*ii*) epidemic or serious. Transitory gushing may often be related to minor changes in the normal production process and are usually susceptible to specific cures. Epidemic outbreaks of gushing may affect several breweries in any area and *inter alia* are due to the use of weathered barley (see below). Many factors have been implicated in gushing especially shaking and exposure to low temperatures and there is no doubt that such rough handling will aggravate the gushing of sensitive beers but it is unlikely to induce gushing in normal beers. Similarly, excessive carbonation will increase gushing in sensitive beers, but not cause it in normal ones.

Krause suggested in 1936 that prolonged shaking beats many microbubbles from the head space into the beer and that these attract surface-active constituents into their interfaces. When the gas dissolves in the beer, the hydrophobic surface-active shells may not redissolve or disperse, but remain to act as dry spots for CO_2 evolution. These ideas have generally been confirmed by subsequent work although the nature of the nuclei is still not understood [153]. Turbid beers do not have an increased tendency to gush and although a precipitate from gushing beer was reported to contain sharp-edged particles when examined by electron microscopy in later studies no difference could be observed between the precipitates from normal and gushing beers [154]. A correlation is found between surface viscosity and gushing. Addition of substances known to promote gushing in beer causes a large increase in the viscosity which is reduced when anti-gushing agents are added. A high surface viscosity does not 'cause' gushing but appears to correlate with the existence of stable nuclei [155].

Transitory outbreaks of gushing have been observed due to the precipitation of microcrystals of calcium oxalate while other outbreaks have been associated with the presence of heavy metals, in particular, iron, nickel, tin, and molybdenum. Such outbreaks can often be cured by the addition of EDTA to the beer which forms complexes with calcium and heavy metals. The balance of heavy metals in beer is obviously critical for it was observed that iron and nickel only caused gushing when complexed with isohumulone. Cobalt, on the other hand, shows little tendency to cause gushing and, indeed it was found during one severe epidemic of gushing that the addition of 0·2–1·0 ppm of cobalt dramatically reduced the incidence of the complaint. However, in another case it was without effect.

Severe epidemics of gushing have been associated with the introduction of new season's malt especially when this has been produced from barley harvested under wet conditions. In particular it was found that malt produced from grain with damaged husks from such a crop gave beer with a strong tendency to gush. The deterioration of weathered barley is largely due to its microflora and, accordingly, individual micro-organisms isolated from the grain were used to inoculate the steep liquor during malting.

Among the organisms found to cause gushing were *Fusaria* [152], *Alternaria*, *Stemphylium*, *Aspergillus* [156], *Penicillium*, and *Rhizopus* spp. [157]. Addition of *Fusarium* cultures to the mash did not produce gushing beers so it appears that the promoter, probably a polypeptide, is produced from the barley by the micro-organism [152]. Obviously it is undesirable to use weathered barley for málting but if it is necessary the addition of formaldehyde to the steep liquor has been found to prevent gushing in beers brewed from *Fusarium* infected grain. Other successful treatments of wild beer include the use of absorbents such as kaolin (1000 g/l), bleaching earth (200 g/l), fullers' earth (200 g/l), and nylon (140 g/l) or an increase in the hop rate.

The observation that certain isomerized hop extracts provoked gushing caused detailed studies of the gushing potential of individual components.

The α-acids and hulupones suppressed gushing while the iso-α-acids and humulinic acid had no influence on gushing behaviour. The most potent gushing agent found was dehydrated humulinic acid (2-isovaleryl-4-(3-methylbut-2-enylidene)cyclopentane-1,3-dione). This only occurred rarely in isomerized extracts but 25 ppm provoked gushing in most commercial beers [158]. Certain oxidation products of humulone (*abeo*-iso-α-acids) and derivatives with saturated side-chains also provoke gushing. Hop extracts contain variable amounts of fatty acids [159] of which the long chain saturated fatty acids promote gushing while the unsaturated acids are powerful gushing suppressants [160]. Hop oil (1 ppm) also suppresses gushing; the most active constituent found was the hydrocarbon caryophyllene [161].

22.7 *Haze*

Beers infected with bacteria or wild yeast will rapidly go turbid and develop a biological haze but with the widespread use of pasteurization and sterile filtration such infections are fairly rare. However, uninfected beers when stored for any length of time, usually in bottle, also become cloudy and deposit a haze. Such beers are usually unacceptable and the rate of development of this non-biological haze determines the shelf-life of bottled beer. Before a beer shows any permanent haze at room temperature it may form a chill haze if suddenly cooled to 0°C. Such hazes redissolve when the beer is warmed up again to room temperature (20°C). Chill hazes are obviously a more serious problem with lager beers which are served at a lower temperature than ales.

22.7.1 COMPOSITION OF HAZE

Early investigations established that hazes were rich in proteins: indeed they were originally called protein hazes, but later they were also shown to contain phenolic constituents, carbohydrates and metallic elements [162, 163]. It soon appeared that both protein and polyphenol was essential for haze formation. The EBC Haze group set up collaborative studies of a series of chill hazes, the results of which were reported in 1965 [164–166]. The hazes contained 45·5–66·8% protein and revealed similar amino acid patterns on hydrolysis. In particular glutamic acid, proline, arginine and aspartic acid were the principal constituents. As discussed earlier (p. 801) beer contains few undegraded proteins, with mol. wt. in excess of 150 000, the bulk of the complex nitrogen fraction occurs in the mol. wt. 5000–12 000 range [79]. Electrofocusing studies of beer 'proteins' show the presence of 26–30 peaks with pI between 3·5 and 10 [85, 167]. In the hazes thrown by the beers all but the most basic 'proteins' are present but the acidic 'proteins' (pI < 5) appear to be concentrated [167]. Earlier immunoelectrophoretic studies showed that two 'proteins', which reacted with barley antibodies, were present in both foam and haze [142].

The polyphenolic constituents of malt and hops which go into solution during the brewing process are discussed in Chapter 14. Alkaline hydrolysis of beer hazes leads to the formation of a group of phenolic acids including: ferulic, sinapic, vanillic, syringic, gallic, protocatechuic and caffeic acids, demonstrating the part played by polyphenols in haze formation [164]. On the other hand, treatment of hazes with mineral acids affords the pigments cyanidin and delphinidin showing the presence of anthocyanogens in beer hazes; flavonols are also present. The conversion of anthocyanogens into cyanidin pigments is a very inefficient process and may only proceed with 10% yield. 3,3',4,4' 5,7-Hexahydroxyflavan (a monomeric anthocyanogen obtained by reduction of taxifolin) affords cyanidin in 20% yield and by applying this factor it was estimated that beer hazes contained 20–30% of anthocyanogens [168]. However, the occurrence of monomeric anthocyanogens (flavan-3,4-diols) in beer is now thought unlikely [52]. No anthocyanogen has been found in malt, hops, or beer which contain methoxy groups and so the ferulic, sinapic, vanillic and syringic acids obtained by an alkaline hydrolysis must come from another source, most probably lignin. A characteristic reaction of lignin is oxidation with alkaline nitrobenzene to give the aromatic aldehydes, syringaldehyde, vanillin, and p-hydroxybenzaldehyde. These products are also obtained by similar oxidation of beer hazes. Barley straw lignin contains 16·4% methoxyl. On the assumption that all the methoxyl in haze is derived from lignin and that this has the same composition as that of barley straw, hazes contain 5·7–9·7% lignin [164].

The hazes examined gave 0·7–3·3% of ash on combustion and contained comparatively large amounts of aluminium, barium, calcium, chromium, copper, iron, lead, magnesium, manganese, molybdenum, nickel, phosphorous, silicon, silver, strontium, tin, vanadium, and zinc [169]. The mineral content of the hazes differed appreciably from the parent beer showing selective precipitation. In particular, copper, iron and aluminium are concentrated by a factor of 4000–80 000 in hazes as compared with the residual beer. Other metals, e.g. lead, nickel, tin, vanadium, and molybdenum are concentrated 1000–4000 times while manganese, calcium and magnesium are only concentrated about 100 times. Of the metals present in haze, copper and iron appear to be the most significant in view of their activity as oxidation catalysts. Both are originally present in beer in a complexed form. Complexed copper has no catalytic activity, with regard to the oxidation of ascorbic acid, and this only develops as the complexes break down on ageing and liberate free copper ions. In contrast, iron complexes exhibit more catalytic activity than the free ions. At the present time the importance of the metallic constituents of haze is not known. They may be active initiators of haze formation or just passively involved either by association with proteins and polyphenols that form the haze as cations or chelates or by adsorption on the newly precipitated material [165].

In addition to proteins, polyphenols, and metallic ions, hazes contain 2–4% of glucose and traces of the pentoses, arabinose and xylose [162]. Occasionally, however, hazes are encountered which are essentially different from the protein–polyphenol hazes discussed so far. These include hazes due to microcrystals of calcium oxalate (the solubility of which is 6·07 mg/l at 13°C) and hazes which are composed largely of carbohydrates. α-Glucans (dextrins) [170], β-glucans [171] and pentosans [172] have been found in beer sediments.

22.7.2 MEASUREMENT OF HAZE

The amount of chill haze isolated for the EBC collaborative analyses from three different breweries was between 1·4 and 8·1 mg/l while the permanent haze accounted for 6·6–14·6 mg/l [160]. The amount of permanent haze increases with the time of storage and yields of up to 44 mg/l have been reported [162], but beers are commercially unacceptable long before the haze can conveniently be estimated by gravimetry. When light is passed through a suspension of a coloured precipitate and the amount of reflection is negligible, the light absorption gives a measure of the turbidity according to Lambert's law. With white precipitates, such as beer haze, however, much of the light is reflected and measurements are made of the light reflected at a given angle to the incident light (nephelometry). The angle chosen and the size of the haze particles are the two most important factors which determine the amount of haze perceived (for a theoretical discussion see [173]). Electron micrographs show that although chill haze particles are small and irregular in young beers, they become larger and more regular as the beers age and spherical particles up to 0·5 μm diameter may develop. Permanent haze, on the other hand, remains a heterogeneous, structureless, agglomeration of particles with differing light-scattering properties [174].

In the early methods used to estimate haze, samples, viewed at 45° to the incident light, were compared visually with a suitable standard such as Fuller's earth or barium sulphate [175]. It was usually necessary to transfer the sample to a suitable cell so that only one measurement could be made. More precise measurements are made using either the Zeiss Pulfrich nephelometer [162, 176] or the Radiometer hazemeter [162, 169]. Measurements are made in the former 45° to the incident light but at 90° in the latter. In both, the sample is held in a cell which is immersed in distilled water in a cylindrical chamber in the instrument to eliminate irregularities in the cell's construction. Accordingly the cell can be replaced by standard colourless beer bottles and measurements can be taken on the same sample at regular intervals. In the Zeiss instrument the sample is visually matched by the operator but in the Radiometer instrument the light falling on two photoelectric cells is matched by means of a null-point galvanometer. Both instruments measure relative turbidities but the Zeiss instrument can be supplied with a translucent glass body of known absolute turbidity from which it can be calibrated in absolute units [176]. Nevertheless, relative units are usually quoted and on the Zeiss scale (used in BIRF publications) a reading below 30 is given by a clear beer and the haze is unacceptable above 80. The haze standards used in the early investigations, barium sulphate and Fuller's earth, etc., are not very stable and sediment with time. Formazin hazes, produced by the reaction of hexamethylene tetramine with hydrazine are more stable and have been adopted as standards.

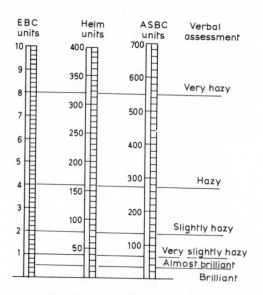

Fig. 22.3 Comparison of haze scales.

Unfortunately the EBC and the ASBC have adopted different scales. The EBC mix equal volumes of a 10% (w/v) solution of hexamethylene tetramine and a 1% (w/v) solution of hydrazine sulphate. After 24 hr this stock suspension (10 ml) is diluted to 100 ml to give a solution which contains 100 EBC Formazin Haze units. In a similar manner the ASBC regard the haze formed from 0·0725 g hydrazine sulphate and 0·725 g hexamethylene tetramine diluted to 100 ml as equivalent to 10 000 Formazin Turbidity units. It must be remembered that haze is not a quantity of substance but an appearance which can vary with the angle of illumination, the colour of the beer, and other factors. Nevertheless:

10 000 ASBC Formazin Turbidity units = 145 EBC Formazin Haze units

1 EBC unit = 69 ASBC units.

A nonogram showing the relationship between these scales, Helm (BaSO$_4$) units, and equivalent verbal assessments is given in Fig. 22.3.

Using the Zeiss Pulfrich nephelometer with a green filter, the following relationships were found [177]:

1 Absolute unit = 9000 Helm (BaSO$_4$) units
= 10 000 ASBC Turbidity units
= 225 EBC Formazin Haze units

The absolute turbidity varies with the wavelength so that the turbidity of formazin in water is 3·2 times greater in violet light ($\lambda = 410$ nm) than red light ($\lambda = 690$ nm). The ASBC take measurements at 580 nm. The colour of the beer will also affect the turbidity measured but between 6 and 10 EBC colour units the discrepancy is negligible [176]. If for control work, the haze of beers is measured in coloured bottles the colour of the bottle will interfere with the measurement in some cases eliminating the effect of beer colour (Fig. 22.4) [177]. Larger random errors occur due to bottle imperfections. A mean of readings on six bottles is recommended.

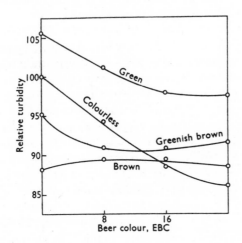

Fig. 22.4 Influence of bottle colour and beer colour on relative turbidity [177].

22.7.3 MECHANISMS OF HAZE FORMATION

Haze is formed by aggregation of polymerized polyphenols and proteins but the detailed mechanisms are still largely unknown. There are obvious analogies with the tanning of hides to produce leather where condensed tannins (mol. wt. 700–1000) are the most effective in cross-linking the major protein collagen. Haze is polydisperse; the average molecular weight has been estimated at 30 000 but molecules in the range of 10 000–100 000 are present. It would thus appear that molecular size is not the major factor in haze formation but that the hydrophilic groups which confer solubility on the proteins are blocked by interaction with the polyphenols. Proteins and polyphenols initially associated together by hydrogen bonding which is comparatively weak and the complexes readily dissociate. It may be represented by the equation:

$$\text{protein} + \text{polyphenol} \rightleftharpoons (\text{protein–polyphenol complex}).$$

Such bonding may be sufficient to account for chill haze formation but it is generally believed that the formation of permanent hazes involves oxidation and the production of covalent bonds.

Fractionation of wort and beer by gel filtration indicates that much of the protein is present as hydrogen-bonded complexes with polyphenols [178]. Whereas proteins and protein–polyphenol complexes are excluded from *Biogel* columns purely on the basis of their molecular size, on *Sephadex* columns phenolic constituents are retarded by hydrogen bonding with the column material. Thus, when a sample of sweet-wort was fractionated on *Sephadex* G-25 four fractions were obtained, the first of which contained 20% protein and 50% carbohydrate together with polyphenol and had a mol. wt. in excess of 5000. The protein constituents of this fraction were examined further by disc electrophoresis followed by staining with Amido black and showed, with the exception of one slow-running band, the same pattern of proteins as that given by the whole wort. Rechromatography of the first fraction, from the *Sephadex* G-25 separation on the same absorbent showed the absence of any low molecular weight polyphenols but after solution 8 M urea, which dissociates hydrogen bonds, several such compounds were observed. In this fraction the protein and polyphenol must be bound together by hydrogen bonds in such a way that there are no free phenolic hydroxy groups available to interact with the molecular sieve. The second fraction from the *Sephadex* G-25 separation of sweet-wort consists mainly of low molecular weight compounds; but it still contains 0·5% protein, characterized by disc electrophoresis, which is complexed with phenols. These were liberated by solution in 8 M urea or by incubation with rutin. In this case the free phenolic groups in the protein–polyphenol complex must have retarded the flow of the complex through the molecular sieve. The polyphenols liberated from the complexes by treatment with 8 M urea have not been characterized but it is believed that all of the polyphenolic constituents of beer take part in haze formation. The role of the anthocyanogens has probably been over-emphasized. There is no correlation between the level of anthocyanogens and the haze potential of the beer.

Treatment of beers with polyamides, such as nylon (see later) removes anthocyanogens and other polyphenols and improves the shelf life of bottled beers. Examination of the polyphenols removed from beers by polyamide treatment shows the presence of a range of phenolic acids and anthocyanogens [179, 180]. Of the anthocyanogens Gramshaw [179] reported the presence of monomeric (mol. wt. approx. 300), dimeric, and more highly polymerized compounds. The occurence of monomeric flavan-3,4-diols in beer is now thought unlikely [52] but procyanidin B-3 has been characterized as the major dimeric anthocyanogen in beer (0·5–4·0 ppm) [180, 181]. Smaller amounts of a gallocatechin–catechin dimer also occur [52]. However, when added back to unstabilized beer, only the polymerized fraction caused an immediate turbidity [182]. Hazes developed slowly after the addition of the dimeric compounds but more rapidly in beers with high air contents. It thus appears that only polymerized polyphenols act as haze precursors. Further work with polyphenols of known structure showed that the monomeric compounds, at the concentration present in beer, have no significant effect on haze formation but the dimeric and polymeric polyphenols cause a large increase in the rate of haze formation [183]. In particular, additions (1–8 ppm) of procyanidin B-3, which is already present in beer, did not cause an immediate precipitation but markedly increased the rate of haze formation.

Two mechanisms of haze formation have been discussed [52]. The most widely accepted theory is that simple phenolics undergo polymerization by various mechanisms (see Chapter 14) to give complex phenolics or 'tannins'. These then react with complex nitrogenous materials to give 'tannin-nitrogen complexes' which combine and grow to give haze. An alternative scheme regards the dimeric proanthocyanidins as the direct precursors of haze which have to be 'activated' (e.g. by oxidation) before they can react with complex nitrogenous material to give 'phenol–nitrogen complexes'. These could then undergo further 'activation' and growth to form haze. The major distinction between the two mechanisms is that the second does not involve the polymerization of the polyphenols. Although polyphenols do polymerize under acid conditions it has not been demonstrated that this reaction occurs in beer during storage. Oxygen, on the other hand, is known to influence haze formation. Beers bottled with high air spaces throw haze more rapidly than those with low air contents. Enrichment of the headspace with $^{18}O_2$ leads to the incorporation of this isotope into the polyphenol fraction [184]. As discussed above, the polyphenols in beer are probably present as complexes with protein which would have to dissociate before polymerization could occur. In contrast, it can be visualized that bound polyphenols could still be oxidized, for example by the mechanisms given in Fig. 14.4, to give larger molecules which could grow into haze.

22.7.4 PREDICTION OF BEER STABILITY

The conditions to which any particular beer package will be subjected in trade cannot be known beforehand; therefore two types of test are adopted by most breweries:

1. Longterm storage at a temperature related to that likely in trade with an examination for biological and non-biological haze at the end of a defined (e.g. three and six month) period.
2. Accelerated haze production under defined high temperature conditions, to give an early estimate of liability to non-biological haze [1].

Customarily the beer is chilled (either overnight or 24 hr at 0°C) before measurements are made at 0°C. Normal lager beers remain bright on initial chilling. The EBC recommend an accelerated forcing test of 48 hr at 60°C after which the bottles are cooled overnight at 0°C and the final haze reading taken the following day at the same temperature. The initial and final haze reported in EBC Formazin units.

The ASBC recommend Room Temperature Storage at 22°C $\pm$ 2°C for 12–13 weeks. The haze is first measured after 8 weeks storage and thereafter at weekly intervals on each occasion after 24 hr at 0°C. Accelerated haze formation is carried out for one week at 40°, 50° and 60°C. The temperature at which the accelerated haze after chilling most closely corresponds with the haze on chilling after 13 weeks storage at room temperature is chosen for routine testing. Changes in raw materials or in processing methods make it necessary to check the correlation from time to time. Hazes are measured in Formazin Turbidity units.

Accelerated shelf life tests take at least 48 hr or one week to provide results. More rapid predictions of beer stability are sometimes obtained using chemical precipitants such as ethanol [185] or formaldehyde [186]. Proteins can be precipitated with ammonium sulphate [187], magnesium sulphate, or gallic tannic acid [188].

22.7.5 PRACTICAL ASPECTS OF IMPROVING BEER STABILITY

As discussed above the presence of complex proteins and polymerized polyphenols in beer is likely to lead to haze formation. Conversely, the removal of part of either group of macromolecules is likely to improve beer stability. However, it is neither practical nor desirable to remove all of the proteins or polyphenols. It will be recalled that certain proteins are essential for the head retention of a beer, others contribute to 'palate fullness', etc., so that some proteins are necessary to preserve the fundamental character of beer. The polyphenols also contribute to beer flavour: the anthocyanogens are probably responsible for the astringency of foodstuffs, including beer [189] and the bitter principles derived from hops may be regarded as a special class of polyphenols. It will be useful to survey the factors in the brewing process that can influence beer stability.

(a) *Malt*

The use of low nitrogen malts results in less soluble protein being available. The addition of caustic alkali to the steep liquor in malting destroys anthocyanogens [190] while the use of formaldehyde reduces their level in the finished beer [191]. At the same time the use of formaldehyde prevents the growth of micro-organisms in the steep. Some large proteins will be destroyed when the malt is kilned but high kiln temperatures may also deactivate the proteolytic enzymes and reduce their action in the mash tun.

(b) *Mashing*

A low mashing temperature, e.g. 40–50°C (104–122°F) (decoction mashing), will favour proteolysis and reduce the level of high molecular weight proteins in the wort. Mash pH is also important as tannins are less soluble at low pH values. The use of adjuncts in mashing will usually result in lowering the nitrogen level of the grist. In particular, wheat flour has a low polyphenol content and contains some proteins of a much higher molecular weight than those found in barley. These react very strongly with polyphenols but, after their removal, the remaining wheat proteins seem fairly insensitive to polyphenol. If green malt is used in the grist, the polyphenols are rapidly polymerized due to the presence of polyphenol oxidase and peroxidase in the unkilned grain [192]. The peroxidase activity of normal grists may also be stimulated by the use of a low concentration of hydrogen peroxide in the mashing liquor [193]. Polyphenols polymerized at this stage react rapidly with proteins and form insoluble complexes which are not extracted into the wort. The addition of formaldehyde into the mashing liquor results in wort with a reduced level of anthocyanogens [194]. Formaldehyde is toxic but less than 0·2 mg/l survives into the finished beer. It presumably reacts by cross-linking the polyphenols and proteins in an analogous way to the formation of phenol-formaldehyde resins (Bakelite). The addition of charcoal to the mash tun (50 mg/kg grist) improves beer stability presumably by removing a portion of the sensitive proteins and/or polyphenols by adsorption [186]. At the end of mashing it is advisable to discard the last runnings as they have a high polyphenol content.

(c) *Wort boiling*

Much of the sensitive protein and protein-polyphenol complexes will be coagulated at wort boiling and given a vigorous boil, will be deposited as break. Prolonged boiling will therefore increase stability. In normal practice, however, further polyphenols together with a small amount of protein will be extracted from the hops. At a given gravity the shelf-life of a beer declines as the hop rate increases. If hop extract is used the solvent employed in its preparation determines the amounts of polyphenol in the extract. Polyphenols are not very soluble in hydrocarbon solvents but more soluble in polar ones. Aeration at wort boiling, and during cooling, will increase the oxidative polymerization of the polyphenols.

(d) *Fermentation*

There is no evidence that the phenolic constituents of the wort are affected by fermentation, but more high molecular weight protein and protein–polyphenol aggregates will be lost due to the change in pH and adsorption on to the yeast-head, cold break and deposited yeast.

(e) *Conditioning*

After fermentation, as many as possible of the remaining haze precursors are removed by chilling and filtration. The techniques employed depend on the type of beer. Draught beers may be flash cooled, taking only a few minutes, but beers destined for bottling are stored at low temperature for several weeks, or even months in the case of lager beers. As far as possible the oxygenation of the beer during filtration should be avoided and the head space in bottling should be kept as low as possible. Contamination of the beer with metallic ions should also be particularly avoided at this stage. Wort and beer contain a group of compounds called reductones which are largely responsible for maintaining the oxidation–reduction balance of a beer. They are by-products of browning reactions (see Chapter 14) and are more plentiful in dark beers. In the absence of heavy metal catalysts they will compete with the polyphenols for any available oxygen but in the presence of metallic ions they behave as oxygen carriers and hasten the oxidation of the polyphenols. Ascorbic acid, a typical reductone, is sometimes added to beer as a stabilizing agent or oxygen scavenger. It, too, in the presence of metallic ions, may act as an oxygen carrier and operate in the reverse manner to that intended. Ascorbic acid is therefore used in conjunction with a reducing agent such as potassium metabisulphite.

As mentioned above, beer treatments may be classified as additive or adsorptive. Ascorbic acid and potassium metabisulphite are permitted additives in most countries. Other additives used include tannic acid and proteolytic enzymes. Addition of tannic acid to beer had no effect on the head retention but was shown, by isoelectric focusing studies, to remove the more acidic proteins (pI 3·7–4·4) and thus stabilize the beer [195]. The proteolytic enzymes used include papain (from the latex of papaya), bromelain (from pineapple), ficin (from figs), and enzymes from *Bacillus subtilis* which have greater heat stability. Use of papain resulted in a substantial fall in the head retention value (Blom) with considerable loss in the amount of protein precipitated with ammonium sulphate. Isoelectric focusing showed the loss of the same acidic proteins as those lost by tannic acid treatment and, in addition the loss of two basic proteins (pI 8·0 and 8·2). A new band (pI 7·4) appeared in the isoelectric focusing pattern [195]. The ASBC describes a qualitative test for the detection of chill proofing enzymes in beer. A recent development is the coupling of enzymes to insoluble inert supports which prevents them being carried into the final bright beer.

Adsorptive treatments of beer involve the use of kieselguhr, bentonite, silica gel or polyamide resins. Such treatments have been compared [196]. In general the inorganic adsorbants remove protein and the polyamides remove polyphenols, in particular anthocyanogens, from beer. Of the inorganic adsorbents there are many different forms of silica gel available. They are mostly aqueous silicas prepared by acidification of sodium silicate solutions. This forms a hydrosol which sets to a hydrogel; the gelling time, the specific surface area, and the pore volume of the gel are all a function of the pH of formation. The hydrogels may be milled to give free flowing powders or dried to give xerogels. The optimum type of silica for beer stabilization was found to be an S-type hydrogel with a pore volume of 2 ml/g, a surface area of about 1000 m²/g, and a mean pore diameter of 8 nm. Electrofocusing studies showed that acidic polypeptide material (pI 3·0–5·0) containing both carbohydrate and polyphenols was removed from the beer and could be eluted from the spent silica gel [197]. Silicas are considerably cheaper than the polyamides discussed below and the disposal of spent silicas presents no problem.

During fundamental research into the phenolic constituents of brewing materials it was found that anthocyanogens are selectively adsorbed on to nylon powder and that beers treated with nylon showed a greatly enhanced shelf-life [198]. Nylon 66, the grade usually employed, is a linear polymer of adipic acid and hexamethylenediamine which contains the amide or peptide linkage, –CO·NH–, found in all proteins. It thus appears that the bonding between polyphenols and nylon is similar to that between polyphenols and proteins. It was found that it is not essential to remove all the anthocyanogens to obtain an improvement in the shelf-life, for example, the addition of 138 g nylon powder/hl (0·5 lb/brl) removed 30% of the anthocyanogens and increased the shelf-life in fobbed bottles to 200 days and to 40 days in bottles containing 10–12 ml of air. This treatment, however, also resulted in the loss of 17·5% of the isohumulones and slightly depressed the head retention of the beer.

In a commercial trial, nylon paste with a larger surface area, was found superior and 55 g dry nylon/hl (0·2 lb/brl) removed 30% of the anthocyanogens, but 333 g/hl (1·2 lb) were necessary to remove 60% [199]. Better results were obtained by adding the nylon to the beer in cask or conditioning tank followed by filtration than by filtering the beer through a bed of the polymer. The nylon could be regenerated for further use by treatment with 0·1 N sodium hydroxide. It is, of course, necessary to use a grade of nylon that contains no water soluble constituents and all may not be suitable. Similarly polyvinylpyrrolidone has been used to remove polyphenolic constituents from beer. The soluble polymer (mol. wt. 8000–12 000) was used experimentally to precipitate polyphenols but could not be used in production in case unreacted molecules remained in the beer. This objection does not apply to the insoluble polymer (mol. wt. > 700 000), known as Agent AT or Polyclar, which compared favourably with Nylon 66 in commercial trials [200]. For example, treatment of a beer with 16 g/hl (1 oz/brl) of Agent AT 496 at 36°F for 48 hr resulted in the removal of 39% of the anthocyanogens with the corresponding increase in shelf-life.

Treatment of beer with AT powder resulted in a substantial fall in the oxidizable tannin value [201] but there was no loss of head retention. Compared with tannic acid and proteolytic enzyme treatment less 'sensitive protein' was removed and that lost was not due to the removal of any particular protein as the isoelectric profile did not differ from that of the control beer [193]. Filter sheets which incorporate polyvinylpyrrolidone are commercially available. The natural polyamides keratin and casein have been used for stabilizing beer but they are not superior to the synthetic polyamides.

REFERENCES

[1] European Brewery Convention (1975). *Analytica—EBC*, 3rd Edn., Schweizer Brauerei-Rundschau, Zurich.

[2] American Society of Brewing Chemists (1976). *Methods of Analysis*, 7th Edn., American Society of Brewing Chemists, St. Paul, Minesota.

[3] Institute of Brewing (1977). *Recommended Methods of Analysis*, The Institute of Brewing, London.

[4] ANDERSON, R. G. and LOWE, C. M. (1981). Unpublished results.

[5] HLAVACEK, I. (1977). *Tech. Quart. Master Brewers Assoc. Americas*, **14**, 94.

[6] KIENINGER, H. (1978). *Brauwelt*, **18**, 616.

[7] PIENDL, A. (1977). *Brewers Digest*, April, p. 58.

[8] COMPTON, J. (1977). In *The Practical Brewer*, 2nd Edn. (BRODERICK, H. M. (ed.)), Master Brewers Assoc. Americas, Madison, Wisconsin.

[9] BOTTOMLEY, R. A. and LINCOLN, G. J. (1958). *J. Inst. Brewing*, **64**, 50; 53.

[10] PAUL, A. A. and SOUTHGATE, D. A. T. (eds.) (1978). *McCance and Widowson's The Composition of Foods*, 4th Edn., HMSO, London.

[11] CANALES, A. M., DE BANCKS, N. M. and GARZA, T. L. I. (1970). *Proc. Annu. Meet. Am. Soc. Brew. Chem.*, p. 75.

[12] BINNS, F., ENSOR, R. J. and MACPHERSON, A. L. (1978). *J. Sci. Food Agric.*, **29**, 71.

[13] POSTEL, W., DRAWERT, F. and GÜVENC, U. (1974). *Brauwissenschaft*, **27**, 11.

[14] POSTEL, W., DRAWERT, F. and GÜVENC, U. (1972). *Brauwissenschaft*, **25**, 341.

[15] POSTEL, W., DRAWERT, F. and GÜVENC, U. (1972). *Brauwissenschaft*, **25**, 391.

[16] POSTEL, W., GORG, A., DRAWERT, F. and GÜVENC, U. (1975). *Brauwissenschaft*, **28**, 301.

[17] POSTEL, W., DRAWERT, F. and GÜVENC, U. (1973). *Brauwissenschaft*, **26**, 46.

[18] PREEN, M. A. and WOODWARD, J. D. (1975). *J. Inst. Brewing*, **81**, 307.

[19] SHAH, S. K. (1975). *J. Inst. Brewing*, **81**, 293.

[20] POSTEL, W. (1976). *Brauwissenschaft*, **29**, 39.

[21] POSTEL, W., GORG, A. and GÜVENC, U. (1976). *Brauwissenschaft*, **29**, 132.

[22] Anon. (1960). *Which*, p. 167; (1967), p. 366.

[23] JAGER, P. and PÜSPÖK, J. (1978). *Mitteilungen der Versuchsstation für das Gärungsgewerbe in Wein*, p. 36.

[24] DENNY, R. C. (1980). *Chemistry in Britain*, **16**, 428.

[25] BÜCHER, T. and REDETZKI, H. (1951). *Klin Wochschr.* **29**, 615.

[26] ASHURST, P. R. (1963). *J. Inst. Brewing*, **69**, 457.

[27] HUNTER, I. R., COLE, E. W. and PEACE, J. W. (1960). *J. Off. Agric. Chem.*, **43**, 769.

[28] THORPE, E. and BROWN, H. T. (1914). *J. Inst. Brewing*, **20**, 569.

[29] Statutory Instrument (1979). No. 1146, HMSO, London.

[30] WEINER, J. (1978). *J. Inst. Brewing*, **84**, 222.

[31] BUCKEE, G. K. and HARGITT, R. (1977). *J. Inst. Brewing*, **83**, 275.

[32] HAVLICEK, J. and SAMUELSON, O. (1975). *J. Inst. Brewing*, **81**, 466.

[33] MACWILLIAM, I. C. and PHILLIPS, A. W. (1959). *Chem. and Ind.*, p. 364.

[34] OTTER, G. E. and TAYLOR, L. (1967). *J. Inst. Brewing*, **73**, 570.

[35] GJERTSEN, P. (1955). *Proc. Eur. Brewery Conv. Congr.*, Baden-Baden, p. 37.

[36] SILBEREISEN, K. and BIELIG, K. (1961). *Proc. Eur. Brewery Conv. Congr.*, Vienna, p. 421.

[37] ENEVOLDSEN, B. S. and SCHMIDT, F. (1974). *J. Inst. Brewing*, **80**, 520.

[38] MANDL, B. and PIENDL, A. (1971). *Proc. Eur. Brewery Conv. Congr.*, Estoril, p. 343.

[39] PARKER, W. E. and RICHARDSON, P. J. (1970). *J. Inst. Brewing*, **76**, 191.

[40] WILLIAMS, P. J. and STRAUSS, C. R. (1978). *J. Inst. Brewing*, **84**, 144.

[41] MCFARLANE, W. D. and THOMPSON, K. D. (1964). *J. Inst. Brewing*, **70**, 497.

[42] ÄYRÄPÄÄ, T., HOLMBERG, J. and SELLMANN-PERSSON, G. (1961). *Proc. Eur. Brewery. Conv. Congr.*, Vienna, p. 286.

[43] TRESSL, R., KOSSA, T., RENNER, R. and KÖPPLER, H. (1975). *Monatsschrift für Brauerei*, **28**, 109

[44] COOTE, N. and KIRSOP, B. H. (1974). *J. Inst. Brewing*, **80**, 474.

[45] QURESHI, A. A., BURGER, W. C. and PRENTICE, N. (1979). *J. Am. Soc. Brew. Chem.*, **37**, 153.

[46] MEILGAARD, M. C. (1975). *Tech. Quart. Master Brewers Assoc. Americas*, **12**, 151.

[47] ESTERBAUER, H. and SCHAUENSTEIN, E. (1977). *Z. fur Lebensmittel-Untersuchung und Forschung*, **164**, 255.

[48] MCGUINNESS, J. D., LAWS, D. R. J., EASTMOND, R. and GARDNER, R. J. (1975). *J. Inst. Brewing*, **81**, 237.

[49] BISHOP, L. R. (1972). *J. Inst. Brewing*, **78**, 37; 372.

[50] OWADES, J. L., RUBIN, G. and BRENNER, M. W. (1958). *J. Agric. Food Chem.*, **6**, 44.

[51] DADIC, M. (1971). *Proc. Annu. Meet. Am. Soc. Brew. Chem.*, 149; 159.

[52] GARDNER, R. J. and MCGUINNESS, J. D. (1977). *Tech. Quart. Master Brewers Assoc. Americas*, **14**, 250.

[53] BISHOP, L. R. (1967). *J. Inst. Brewing*, **73**, 525.

[54] WHITT, J. T. and CUZNER, J. (1979). *J. Am. Soc. Brew. Chem.*, **37**, 41.

[55] SCHWARZENBACH, R. (1979). *J. Am. Soc. Brew. Chem.*, **37**, 180.

[56] AITKEN, R. A., BRUCE, A., HARRIS, J. O. and SEATON, J. C. (1968). *J. Inst. Brewing*, **74**, 436.

[57] MCGUINNESS, J. D. (1973). *J. Inst. Brewing*, **79**, 44.

[58] DRAWERT, F. and TRESSL, R. (1972). *Tech. Quart. Master Brewers Assoc. Americas*, **9**, 72.

[59] TRESSL, R., FRIESE, L., FENDESACK, F. and KOPPLER, H. (1978). *J. Agric. Food Chem.*, **26**, 1422.

[60] MORGAN, K. (1965). *J. Inst. Brewing*, **71**, 166.

[61] GREENSHIELDS, R. N. (1974). *J. Sci. Food Agric.*, **25**, 1307.

[62] OTTER, G. E. and TAYLOR, L. (1971). *J. Inst. Brewing*, **77**, 467.

[63] HARRISON, G. A. F. (1963). *Proc. Eur. Brewery Conv. Congr.*, Brussels, p. 247.

[64] VAN DER KLOOT, A. P. and WILLCOX, F. A. (1959). *Proc. Annu. Meet. Am. Soc. Brew. Chem.*, p. 76.

[65] HASHIMOTO, N. (1972). *J. Inst. Brewing*, **78**, 43.

[66] DROST, B. W., VAN EERDE, P., HOEKSTRA, S. F. and STRATING, J. (1971). *Proc. Eur. Brewery Conv. Congr.*, Estoril, p. 451.

[67] THALACKER, R. and KALTWASSER, I. (1978). *Monstsschrift für Brauerei*, **31**, 20.

[68] KIENINGER, H. and BIRKOVA, V. (1975). *Brauwelt*, **115**, 1250.

[69] BERNSTEIN, L. and LAUFER, L. (1977). *J. Am. Soc. Brew. Chem.*, **35**, 21.

[70] ENEBO, L. (1957). *Proc. Eur. Brewery Conv. Congr.*, Copenhagen, p. 370.

[71] OWADES, J. L. and DANN, J. M. (1965). *Proc. Annu. Meet. Am. Soc. Brew. Chem.*, p. 157.

[72] VAN OEVELEN, D., DE L'ESCAILLE, F. and VERACHTERT, H. (1976). *J. Inst. Brewing*, **82**, 322.

[73] MACPHERSON, J. K. and BUCKEE, G. K. (1974). *J. Inst. Brewing*, **80**, 540.

[74] SANDRA, P. and VERZELE, M. (1975). *J. Inst. Brewing*, **81**, 302.

[75] KLOPPER, W. K., TUNING, B. and VERMEIRE, H. A. (1975). *Proc. Eur. Brewery Conv. Congr.*, Nice, p. 659.

[76] WAINWRIGHT, T. (1973). *J. Inst. Brewing*, **79**, 451.

[77] HARRISON, G. A. F., BYRNE, W. J. and COLLINS, E. (1965). *J. Inst. Brewing*, **71**, 336; (1965). *Proc. Eur. Brewery Conv. Congr.*, Stockholm, p. 352.

[78] PORTNO, A. D. (1966). *J. Inst. Brewing*, **72**, 193; 458.

[79] BISHOP, L. R. (1975). *J. Inst. Brewing*, **81**, 444.

[80] HUDSON, J. R. and BIRTWISTLE, S. E. (1966). *J. Inst. Brewing*, **72**, 46.

[81] LEACH, A. A. (1968). *J. Inst. Brewing*, **74**, 183.

[83] OTTER, G. E. and TAYLOR, L. (1976). *J. Inst. Brewing*, **82**, 264.

[84] CLAPPERTON, J. F. (1971). *Proc. Eur. Brewery Conv. Congr., Estoril*, p. 323.

[85] SORENSEN, S. B. and OTTESEN, M. (1978). *Carlsberg Res. Commun.*, **43**, 133.

[86] HEJGAARD, J. (1977). *J. Inst. Brewing*, **83**, 94.

[87] PICKETT, J. A. (1974). *J. Inst. Brewing*, **80**, 42.

[88] ZIEGLER, L. and PIENDL, A. (1976). *Tech. Quart. Master Brewers Assoc. Americas*, **13**, 177.

[89] HARDING, R. J., NURSTEN, H. E. and WREN, J. J. (1977). *J. Sci. Food Agric.*, **28**, 225.

[90] PICKETT, J. A., COATES, J., PEPPARD, T. L. and SHARPE, F. R. (1976). *J. Inst. Brewing*, **82**, 233.

[91] TRESSL, R., RENNER, R., KOSSA, T. and KOPPLER, H. (1977). *Proc. Eur. Brewery Conv. Congr., Amsterdam*, p. 693.

[92] PALAMAND, S. R. and GRIGSBY, J. H. (1974). *Brewers Digest*, Sept., p. 58; 90.

[93] OWADES, J. L. and JACEVAC, J. (1959). *Proc. Annu. Meet. Am. Soc. Brew. Chem.*, p. 18.

[94] SLAUGHTER, J. C. and UVGARD, A. R. A. (1971). *J. Inst. Brewing*, **77**, 446.

[95] PALAMAND, S. R., HARDWICK, W. A. and MARKL, K. S. (1969). *Proc. Annu. Meet. Am. Soc. Brew. Chem.*, p. 54.

[96] KOIKE, K., HASHIMOTO, N., KITAMI, H. and OKADA, K. (1972). *Report of Research Laboratories of the Kirin Brewery Co. Ltd.*, **15**, 25.

[97] SLAUGHTER, J. C. and UVGARD, A. R. A. (1972). *J. Inst. Brewing*, **78**, 322.

[98] CHEN, E. C.-H. and VAN GHELUWE, G. (1979). *J. Am. Soc. Brew. Chem.*, **37**, 91.

[99] SPIEGELHALDER, B., EISENBRAND, G. and PREUSSMANN, R. (1979). *Food Cosmetic Toxicology*, **17**, 29.

[100] SCANGAN, R. A., BARBOUR, J. F., HOTCHKISS, J. H. and LIBBEY, L. M. (1980). *Food Cosmetic Toxicology*, **18**, 27.

[101] WAINWRIGHT, T. (1972). *Brewers Digest*, July, p. 78.

[102] JANSEN, H. E., STRATING, J. and WESTRA, W. M. (1971). *J. Inst. Brewing*, **77**, 154.

[103] STONE, I. and LASCHIVER, G. (1957). *Proc. Annu. Meet. Am. Soc. Brew. Chem.*, p. 46.

[104] RICHARDSON, P. J. and MOCEK, M. (1973). *J. Inst. Brewing*, **79**, 26.

[105] HASHIMOTO, N. and KUROIWA, Y. (1966) *Proc. Annu. Meet. Am. Soc. Brew. Chem.*, p. 121.

[106] HABOUCHA, J. and MASSCHELEIN, C. A. (1979). *Cerevisia*, **3**, 97.

[107] ANDERSON, R. J., CLAPPERTON, J. F., CRABB, D. and HUDSON, J. R. (1975). *J. Inst Brewing*, **81**, 208.

[108] PEPPARD, T. L. and DOUSE, J. M. F. (1979). *J. Chromatog.*, **176**, 444.

[109] ANDERSON, R. J. and HOWARD, G. A. (1974). *J. Inst. Brewing*, **80**, 357.

[110] SCHREIER, P., DRAWERT, F. and JUNKER, A. (1974). *Brauwissenschaft*, **27**, 205; (1975). **28**, 73.

[111] GUNST, F. and VERZELE, M. (1978). *J. Inst. Brewing*, **84**, 291.

[112] SINCLAIR, A., HALL, R. D., THORBURN-BURNS, D. and HAYES, W. P. (1970). *J. Sci. Food Agric.*, **21**, 468.

[113] NARZISS, L., MIEDANER, H. and BOURJAU, T. (1979). *Brauwissenschaft*, **32,** 62.

[114] HYSERT, D. W., MORRISON, N. M. and JAMIESON, A. M. (1979). *J. Am. Soc. Brew. Chem.*, **37,** 30.

[115] DICKENSON, C. J. (1979). *J. Inst. Brewing*, **85,** 329.

[116] ANNESS, B. J., BAMFORTH, C. W. and WAINWRIGHT, T. (1979). *J. Inst. Brewing*, **85,** 346.

[117] PIENDL, A. and MULLER, K. (1977). *Proc. Eur. Brewery Conv. Congr.*, *Amsterdam*, p 683.

[118] HUDSON, J. R. (1969). *J. Inst. Brewing*, **75,** 164.

[119] HUDSON, J. R. (1970). *J. Inst. Brewing*, **76,** 341.

[120] BIKERMAN, J. J. (1953). *Foams; Theory and Industrial Application*, Reinhold, New York.

[121] AKERS, R. J. (ed.) (1976). *Foams – Proceedings of a Symposium organized by the Society of Chemical Industry*, 1975, Academic Press, London, pp. x 301.

[122] KLOPPER, W. J. and VERMEIRE, H. A. (1977). *Brauwissenschaft*, **30,** 276.

[123] HELM, E. and RICHARDT, O. C. (1936). *J. Inst. Brewing*, **42,** 191.

[124] HARTONG, B. D. (1941). *Woch. Brau.*, **58,** 183.

[125] DE CLERK, J. and DE DIJCKER, G. (1954). *Brauwelt*, p. 700; (1957). *Proc. Eur. Brewery Conv. Congr.*, *Copenhagen*, p. 43.

[126] HELM, E. (1933). *Woch. Brau.*, **50,** 241.

[127] BLOM, J. (1937). *J. Inst. Brewing*, **43,** 251.

[128] CURTIS, N. S., CLARK, A. G., and OGIE, P. J. (1963). *J. Inst. Brewing*, **69,** 30.

[129] BIKERMAN, J. (1938). *Trans. Faraday Soc.*, **74,** 634.

[130] ROSS, S. and CLARKE, C. L. (1939). *Wallerstein Labs. Commun.*, **6,** 46.

[131] KLOPPER, W. J. (1954). *J. Inst. Brewing*, **60,** 217.

[132] RUDIN, A. D. (1958). *J. Inst. Brewing*, **64,** 238.

[133] BISHOP, L. R., WHITEAR, A. L. and INMAN, W. R. (1975). *J. Inst. Brewing*, **81,** 131.

[134] SCHUSTER, K. and MISCHKE, W. (1937). *Woch. Brau.*, **54,** 177.

[135] AULT, R. G., HUDSON, E. J., LINEHAN, A. J. and WOODWARD, J. D. (1967). *J. Inst. Brewing*, **73,** 558.

[136] KLOPPER, W. J. (1973). *Proc. Eur. Brewery. Conv. Congr.*, *Salzberg*, p. 363.

[137] COOK, A. H. (1971). *Proc. Eur. Brewery Conv. Congr.*, *Estoril*, p. 469.

[138] ROBERTS, R. J. (1977). *Brewers Digest*, June, p. 50.

[139] BISHOP, L. R., WHITEAR, A. L. and INMAN, W. R. (1974). *J. Inst. Brewing*, **80,** 68.

[140] NARZISS, L. and ROTTGER, W. (1973). *Brauwissenschaft*, **26,** 261.

[141] SCHULZE, W. G., HERWIG, W. C., FLY, W. H. and CHICOYE, E. (1976). *J. Am. Soc. Brew. Chem.*, **34,** 181.

[142] GRABAR, P. and DAUSSANT, J. (1971). *J. Inst. Brewing*, **77,** 544.

[143] BIRTWISTLE, S. E., HUDSON, J. R. and MACWILLIAM, I. C. (1962). *J. Inst. Brewing*, **68,** 467.

[144] ISHERWOOD, N. D., KIRBY, W., WHEELER, R. E. and JONES, M. (1977). *Proc. Eur. Brewery. Conv. Congr.*, *Amsterdam*, p. 457.

[145] ROBERTS, R. T., KEENEY, P. J. and WAINWRIGHT, T. (1978). *J. Inst. Brewing*, **84,** 9.

[146] DIFFOR, D. W., LIKENS, S. T., REHBERGER, A. J. and BURKHARDT, R. J. (1978). *J. Am. Soc. Brew. Chem.*, **36,** 63.

[147] JACKSON, G., ROBERTS, R. T. and WAINWRIGHT, T. (1980). *J. Inst. Brewing*, **86,** 34.

[148] THOMPSON, C. C. (1974). *Eur. Brewery Conv., Monograph – I, EBC Wort Symposium, Zeist.*

[149] THOMPSON, C. C., CURTIS, N. S., GOUGH, P. E. and RALPH, D. J. (1965). *Proc. Eur. Brewery Conv. Congr., Stockholm,* p. 305.

[150] EDWARDS, R. and THOMPSON, C. C. (1968). *J. Inst. Brewing*, **74,** 257.

[151] COMRIE, A. A. D. (1959). *Brewers Digest*, **34** (2), 42.

[152] GJERTSEN, P. (1967). *Brewers Digest*, **42,** May, 80.

[153] GARDNER, R. J. (1973). *J. Inst. Brewing*, **79,** 275.

[154] CURTIS, N. S. and MARTINDALE, N. (1961). *J. Inst. Brewing*, **67,** 417.

[155] GARDNER, R. J. (1972). *J. Inst. Brewing*, **78,** 391.

[156] GYLLANG, H. and MARTINSON, E. (1976). *J. Inst. Brewing*, **82,** 182.

[157] AMAHA, M., KITABATAKE, K., NAKAGAWA, A., YOSHIDA, J. and HARADA, T. (1973). *Proc. Eur. Brewery. Conv. Congr., Salzberg,* p. 381.

[158] LAWS, D. R. J. and MCGUINNESS, J. D. (1972). *J. Inst. Brewing*, **78,** 302.

[159] SANDRA, P., CLAUS, H. and VERZELE, M. (1973). *J. Inst. Brewing*, **79,** 142.

[160] CARRINGTON, R., COLLETT, R. C., DUNKIN, I. R. and HALEK, G. (1972). *J. Inst. Brewing*, **78,** 243.

[161] GARDNER, R. J., LAWS, D. R. J. and MCGUINNESS, J. D. (1973). *J. Inst. Brewing*, **79,** 209.

[162] BENGOUGH, W. I. and HARRIS, G. (1955). *J. Inst. Brewing*, **61,** 134.

[163] MACFARLANE, W. D., WYE, E. and GRANT, H. L. (1955). *Proc. Eur. Brewery Conv. Congr., Baden-Baden,* p. 298.

[164] HARRIS, G. (1965). *J. Inst. Brewing*, **71,** 292.

[165] CHAPON, L. (1965). *J. Inst. Brewing*, **71,** 299.

[166] DJURTOFT, R. (1965). *J. Inst. Brewing*, **71,** 305.

[167] SAVAGE, D. J. and THOMPSON, C. C. (1972). *J. Inst. Brewing*, **78,** 472.

[168] HARRIS, G. and RICKETTS, R. W. (1959). *J. Inst. Brewing*, **65,** 252.

[169] HUDSON, J. R. (1955). *J. Inst. Brewing*, **61,** 127.

[170] LETTERS, R. (1969). *J. Inst. Brewing*, **75,** 54.

[171] GJERTSEN, P. (1966). *Proc. Annu. Meet. Am. Soc. Brew. Chem.,* p. 113.

[172] COOTE, N. and KIRSOP, B. H. (1976). *J. Inst. Brewing*, **82,** 34.

[173] THORNE, R. S. W. and NANNESTED, I. (1960). *J. Inst. Brewing*, **66,** 388.

[174] CLAESSON, S. and SANDEGREN, E. (1963). *Proc. Eur. Brewery Conv. Congr., Brussels,* p. 221.

[175] HELM, E. (1934). *Woch. Brau.,* **51,** 105.

[176] JANSEN, H. E. (1957). *J. Inst. Brewing*, **63,** 204.

[177] THORNE, R. S. W. and BEAKLEY, R. F. (1958). *J. Inst. Brewing*, **64,** 38.

[178] WOOF, J. B. and PIERCE, J. S. (1968). *J. Inst. Brewing*, **74,** 262.

[179] GRAMSHAW, J. W. (1967). *J. Inst. Brewing*, **73,** 258.

[180] GRACEY, D. E. F. and BARKER, R. L. (1976). *J. Inst. Brewing*, **82,** 72; 78.

[181] EASTMOND, R. (1974). *J. Inst. Brewing*, **80,** 188.

[182] GRAMSHAW, J. W. (1967). *J. Inst. Brewing*, **73,** 258.

[183] EASTMOND, R. and GARDNER, R. J. (1974). *J. Inst. Brewing*, **80,** 192.

[184] OWADES, J. L. and JAKOVAC, J. (1966). *Proc. Annu. Meet. Am. Soc. Brew. Chem.,* p. 180.

[185] CHAPON, L. and CHEMARDIN, M. (1967). *Proc. Eur. Brewery Conv. Congr., Madrid,* p. 389.

[186] WHATLING, A. J., PASFIELD, J. and BRIGGS, D. E. (1968). *J. Inst. Brewing*, **74,** 525.

[187] HOUGH, J. S. (1967). *Tech. Quart. Master Brewers Assoc. Americas*, **13**, 34.
[188] CHAPON, L. (1962). *Int. Tijds. Brouw. Mout.*, **22**, 32.
[189] BATE-SMITH, E. C. and SWAIN, T. (1953). *Chem. and Ind.*, p. 377.
[190] STEVENS, R. (1958). *J. Inst. Brewing*, **64**, 470.
[191] WHITLEY, J. S. and BRIGGS, D. E. (1966). *J. Inst. Brewing*, **72**, 474.
[192] REYNOLDS, T., ATTERTON, R. M., KIRSOP, B. H. and POOL, A. A. (1961). *Proc. Eur. Brewery Conv. Congr., Vienna*, p. 267.
[193] PASFIELD, J. and BRIGGS, D. E. (1967). *J. Inst. Brewing*, **73**, 524.
[194] MACEY, A., STOWELL, K. C. and WHITE, H. B. (1966). *J. Inst. Brewing*, **72**, 29.
[195] SAVAGE, D. J. and THOMPSON, C. C. (1971). *J. Inst. Brewing*, **77**, 371.
[196] ROTTGER, W. (1974). *Brauwelt*, **114**, 1527.
[197] HOUGH, J. S. and LOVELL, A. L. (1979). *Tech. Quart. Master Brewers Assoc. Americas*, **16**, 90.
[198] HARRIS, G. and RICKETTS, R. W. (1959). *Proc. Eur. Brewery Conv. Congr., Rome*, p. 290; (1959). *J. Inst. Brewing*, **65**, 418; (1960). **66**, 313.
[199] CURTIS, N. S. and CLARK, A. G. (1960). *J. Inst. Brewing*, **66**, 226.
[200] MCFARLANE, W. D. and BOYRNE, P. D. (1961). *Proc. Eur. Brewery Conv. Congr., Vienna*, p. 278.
[201] THOMPSON, C. C. and FORWARD, E. (1969). *J. Inst. Brewing*, **75**, 37.
[202] PALAMAND, S. R. and ALDENHOFF, J. M. (1973). *J. Agric. Food Chem.*, **21**, 535.
[203] GREENHOFF, K. and WHEELER, R. E. (1981). *J. Inst. Brewing*, **87**, 35.
[204] LANCE, D. G., BARRETT, P. A., KAVANAGH, T. E. and CLARKE, B. J. (1981). *J. Inst. Brewing*, **87**, 19.
[205] POLLOCK, J. R. A. (1981). *J. Inst. Brewing*, **87**, 16; 356.
[206] PEPPARD, T. L. and HALSEY, S. A. (1981). *J. Inst. Brewing*, **87**, 85.
[207] Ministry of Agriculture, Fisheries and Food – Food Additives and Contaminants Committee (1979). *Interim Report on the Review of the Colouring Matter in Food Regulations 1973*. FAC/REP/29. HMSO, London, pp. 61; 188.
[208] DELCOUR, J. A., VERHULST, L. L., GEYS, R., DELIEVER, H. and DONDEYNE, P. (1981). *J. Inst. Brewing*, **87**, 391.
[209] SLACK, P. T. and WAINWRIGHT, T. (1981). *J. Inst. Brewing*, **87**, 259.
[210] WAINWRIGHT, T. (1981). *J. Inst. Brewing*, **87**, 264.

Chapter 23

BEER FLAVOUR AND BEER QUALITY

The final arbiter of beer quality is the palate of the consumer and this can show wide variation between individuals, between geographical areas, and even from one time to another. Quality is defined as 'degree of excellence, relative nature, or kind, or character' and accordingly the brewer refers to the many varieties of ale, beer, stout, and lager which he brews to satisfy the varied demands as different qualities. When the customer has chosen the quality he wishes to drink he demands that his beverage shall have the 'degree of excellence' which he expects and that this shall not change from day to day. Much of the brewers' art is therefore concerned with quality control, with producing a constant product from variable raw materials by a biological process.

The enjoyment of a glass of beer may be received by many senses; the sight may be attracted first by, for example, the clarity of a pale ale or the rich creamy head of a stout. As the glass is raised to the lips the aroma of the beverage, possibly the bouquet of the essential oil of hops may excite the nostrils. Then, as the liquid flows over the taste buds in the back of the mouth and further volatile products diffuse into the back of the nose, the flavour of the beverage is perceived. Finally the beer enters the body where the alcohol is rapidly absorbed into the bloodstream and exerts its well-known physiological and psychological effects. Other beer constituents such as the simple sugars will also be rapidly absorbed into the bloodstream, but the dextrins will be hydrolysed before absorption. The alcohol and carbohydrates together are largely responsible for the nutritive value of beer. In addition, beer is a rich source of the B-group vitamins.

Alternatively we may define the characters which make up beer quality as:

1. Flavour – taste and aroma
2. Alcoholic content – food value
3. Colour
4. Formation and Head retention
5. Clarity – absence of haze
6. Absence of gushing

It is difficult to set these properties in any order of priority. The customer will choose his drink on the basis of 1 and 2 but, if any of the physical properties, 3, 4, 5 and 6, are not satisfactory, he may reject it untasted. On the other hand a brew of the right strength with excellent physical properties will be unacceptable if it suffers from an off-flavour. Thus, before making any change in the process designed to improve one aspect of beer quality, the brewer must ascertain that none of the others are affected adversely. Chemical and physical methods of analysis can provide valuable information on most aspects of beer quality (2, 3, 4, 5 and 6), but they are still incapable of providing a complete flavour profile for beer and for this the brewer must rely on his own palate and that of a taste panel. Nevertheless great advances in the sensory evaluation of foods [1] have been made in the last decade.

23.1 *Flavour – taste and odour* [1–8]

Flavour has been described as a complex sensation comprising taste, odour, roughness or smoothness, hotness or coolness, pungency or blandness [2]. If we consider beer within this context taste and odour are undoubtedly the most important properties. Texture refers more to solid foodstuffs than liquids but is probably related to what is referred to as 'palate fullness' or 'body'. This ill-defined beer property is thought to be related to the concentration of macromolecules, principally β-glucans, proteins and melanoidins, in the beer. Viscosity measurements have been suggested as a method for assessing this property but little data are available for evaluation. The importance of the temperature at which the beer is served is recognized throughout the world although nations do not agree as to what is the optimum temperature. In general bottom-fermentation beers are drunk at lower temperatures (0–10°C; 32–50°F) than those produced by top fermentation (10–20°C; 50–68°F). Finally, with regard to the above definition, beers lack pungency and indeed, many can be regarded as bland. One other property of food and drink akin to flavour, and not mentioned in the above definition, is astringency – the production of dryness in the mouth. This property is shown by many compounds, in particular polyphenols such as anthocyanogens, melanoidins and the principal imino acid in beer, proline.

Taste has been defined as the product of the chemical sensory system of the oral cavity. Two types of chemicoreceptor are recognized: free nerve endings, which occur throughout the oral cavity, and taste buds. The free nerve endings possess no recognizable receptors and are responsible for the perception of pungency and astringency. Taste buds (Fig. 23.1) are neural complexes of 25–50 specialized cells which occur in localized areas of the oral cavity. On the tongue they occur on protuberances called papillae. Four types of papillae are distinguished, the filiform papillae have no taste buds and the foliate papillae, which occur in folds in the sides of the back of the tongue, are not well developed in man. More important are the 13–400 mushroom-like fungiform papillae concentrated at the tip and sides of the tongue and the 6–15 large (circum)vallate papillae at the back of the tongue (Fig. 23.1) (see references [1] and [8] for microphotographs). Papillae in different areas of the oral cavity are innervated by different ganglions (Fig. 23.2). The fungiform papillae and the anterior soft palate are innervated by the geniculate ganglion of the facial nerve. The taste buds on the foliate papillae, the circumvallate papillae, and posterior palate are innervated by the petrous ganglion of the glossopharyngeal nerve and those on the epiglottis, the larynx, and the upper oesophagus are innervated by the nodose ganglion of the vagus nerve. The free nerve endings are innervated by the trigeminal ganglion. Typically, a single geniculate ganglion can innervate the taste buds in up to 15 papillae.

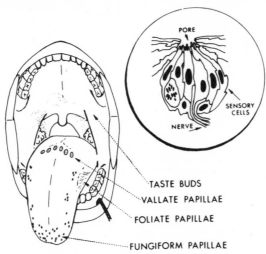

Fig. 23.1 Location of some oral chemosensory receptor systems. Taste buds (schematic, upper right) are found on specialized papillae on the tongue and scattered on the palate and posterior oral structures. Free nerve endings are found on all oral surfaces. (After Boudreau [7].)

Current knowledge of taste perception indicates that within the neuron, in each taste cell, the potassium ion concentration is higher within the cell than without, the converse being true with sodium ions so that a resting potential exists across the cell wall. It is thought that when a chemical stimulant arrives on the surface of a receptor it momentarily modifies the cell wall and allows K^+ ions to move out and Na^+ ions to move in, and the resultant depolarization is transmitted along the nerve. Once the neuron has fired, the membrane potential is re-established within about a millisecond and the process is repeated as long as there is sufficient stimulant. The frequency with which these impulses are sent to the brain, up to a maximum of 100–200/s, determines the intensity of the taste stimuli. Kinetic studies indicate that the stimulant is bound to the taste receptor by weak forces such as hydrogen bonding and that the impulse is not enzymatically controlled. Neurophysiological experiments with animals can measure the response of the taste neurons to various chemical stimuli [7] but such an approach is not possible in man where verbal descriptions of taste properties have to be analysed – a study called psychophysics.

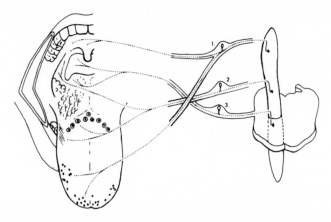

Fig. 23.2 Peripheral sensory ganglia that supply nerve endings to taste buds in the mammalian oral cavity: 1. geniculate ganglion, 2, petrous ganglion, 3. nodose ganglion. Trigeminal ganglion, which supplies free nerve endings to all oral surfaces, is not shown. (After Boudreau [7].)

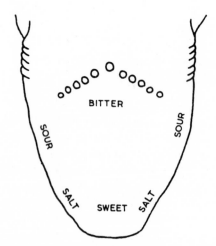

Fig. 23.3 Areas of the human tongue where the four tastes are most easily sensed. All four tastes are perceived but less readily over the central area.

TABLE 23.1

Partial summary of some human taste sensations

{After BOUDREAU [7]}

Sensation	Locus	Stimuli	Receptor	Ganglion
1. Salty	Ant. tongue, palate	NaCl, KCl	Taste buds	Geniculate
2. Sour	Ant. tongue, palate	Malic acid	Taste buds	Geniculate
3. Sweet$_1$	Ant. tongue, palate	L-Alanine, fructose	Taste buds	Geniculate
4. Bitter$_1$	Ant. tongue, palate	L-Tryptophan	Taste buds	Geniculate
5. Pleasant	Ant. tongue, palate	Lactones	Taste buds	Geniculate
6. Sweet$_2$	Post. tongue	Dihydrochalcone	Taste buds	Petrous
7. Bitter$_2$	Post. tongue	MgSO$_4$, phenolics	Taste buds	Petrous
8. Astringent	Oral cavity	Theaflavin	Free nerve	Trigeminal
9. Pungent	Oral cavity	Capsaicin	Free nerve	Trigeminal
10. Umami$_1$	Tongue	Monosodium glutamate	?	?
11. Umami$_2$	Post. mouth	IMP, GMP	?	?
12. Metallic	Tongue	Silver nitrate	Taste buds (?)	Petrous

Table 23.1 summarizes some human taste sensations. Although the four primary tastes salt, sour, sweet, and bitter can all be perceived by taste buds on the fungiform papillae, they are also perceived in other areas of the tongue (Fig. 23.3). Inspection of Fig. 23.3 shows that the bitter taste of beer can only be evaluated satisfactorily if the beer is swallowed and allowed to flow over the taste buds at the rear of the tongue. Surveying the sensations listed in Table 23.1, salty is produced by relatively high concentrations of inorganic ions in particular Na^+, K^+, and Li^+. The sour taste is evoked by various Bronsted acids. As may be expected from the anatomy, the sweet and bitter tastes are subdivided. $Sweet_1$ is perceived at the front of the tongue and is evoked by low concentrations of inorganic salts, sugars, and amino acids while $sweet_2$ is produced at the back of the mouth by, for example, dihydro-chalcones. Similarly, $bitter_1$ is evoked by hydrophobic amino acids and alkaloids at the front of the tongue while $bitter_2$ is produced by magnesium sulphate, phenolics, and presumably iso-α-acids at the rear of the tongue.

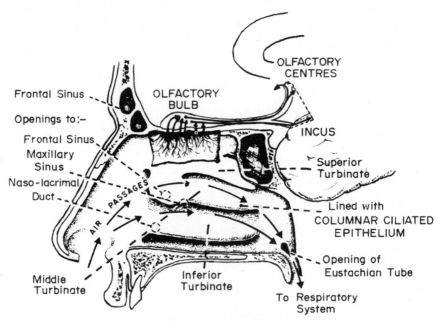

Fig. 23.4 Vertical section of the nasal region of the head.

Pleasant is associated with the small fibre geniculate ganglion system and is evoked by lactones and similar carbon–oxygen compounds. 'Umani' is a Japanese word used to describe the sensation elicited by the amino acid monosodium glutamate and the nucleotides sodium inosinate and sodium guanylate. The metallic sensation is produced by certain salts such as silver nitrate and by oct-1-en-3-one. Pungency and astringency have been mentioned earlier. Many other taste sensations can be distinguished but they are less well characterized and, in most cases contain a nasal component.

Odour is more complicated than taste [1, 5, 9]. Many different odours are perceived and distinguished by the olfactory epithelium in the upper respiratory passages (Fig. 23.4). In man it occupies 2–4 cm^2 and contains about 9 million neurons; it is more extensive in other animals. The axons from these cells, many of which cannot be seen with the light microscope, are grouped together in bundles and pass through the cribriform plate into the olfactory bulb, where they terminate in small bodies known as glomeruli. From the glomeruli, mitral cells pass directly into the olfactory lobe of the brain. No other stimuli are received by the brain in such a direct manner. With regard to perception of odour two stages are postulated [10]: In the first the volatile constituent is partitioned between air and the nasal mucous, essentially an aqueous medium, and in the second between the aqueous phase and the olfactory receptor site, which is assumed to be lipid. When a molecule has reached the receptor whether or not it will initiate a signal to the brain depends upon its size, shape, degree of ionization and charge pattern, etc.

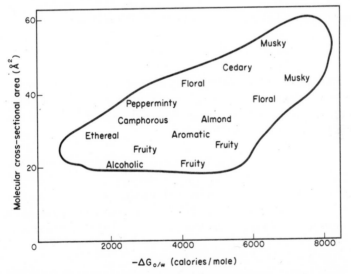

Fig. 23.5 Plot of molecular cross-sectional area versus the energy of desorption from a lipid–water interface into water. Certain regions on this graph are associated with certain odour types or qualities, these regions not being sharply defined but merging gradually into each other (1 Å = 10^{-10}m). (After Davies [14].)

Numerous attempts have been made to classify odours [11]; Amoore, for example, specifies seven primary odours – ethereal, camphoraceous, musky, floral, pepperminty, pungent, and putrid. Many theories have been proposed to correlate aroma and chemical structure [5]; in particular, Amoore [12] has postulated a stereochemical theory based on correlations between molecular cross-sectional areas (silhouettes) and different aromas. Wright [13], on the other hand, has correlated aromas with vibrations in the infrared spectra between 1000 and 80 cm^{-1}. This latter theory fails to explain the occurrence of enantiomers with different flavour characteristics but identical infrared spectra. When the molecular cross-sectional area is plotted against the free energy of desorption at the lipid–water interface particular types of odour are found in different areas of the plot (Fig. 23.5). This suggests that there are no primary odours but rather a continuous spectrum [14].

Taste and odour can be perceived separately but more often than not the two senses are integrated to produce the sensation of flavour. The measurement of taste, odour, or flavour intensity is the subject of at least two different approaches which use different mathematics [15]. Those working with strong flavours are concerned with suprathreshold effects and describe the perceived intensity R as a power factor n of the concentration S so that:

$$R = \text{constant} \times S^n$$

For example, with butanol in air with equation becomes:

$$R = 0.261 \times S^{0.66}$$

On the other hand, those working with more delicate flavours such as food, vegetables, whisky, wine, and beer, have assumed that the perceived intensity R is proportional to the concentration S and inversely proportional to the threshold concentration T so that:

$$R = (\text{constant}) \times S/T$$

The power factor n is assumed to be 1.00 and the constant is often omitted so that R is measured as S/T. This ratio has been given various names including 'odour units' (see p. 451) and 'flavour units' [15]. The power function n in the equation:

$$R = (S/T)^n$$

has been estimated for ethanol ($n = 1.54$), dimethyl sulphide ($n = 1.12$), diacetyl ($n = 0.89$), and isoamyl acetate ($n = 0.82$) [16]. Thus, except for ethanol, the error in assuming $n = 1.00$ is less than 12%.

At least four different types of threshold have been used and the use of the unqualified word is deprecated. They have been defined [17] as:

Stimulus threshold (absolute threshold, detection threshold). The lowest physical intensity at which a stimulus is perceptible.

Recognition threshold. The lowest physical intensity at which a stimulus is correctly identified.

Difference threshold (just noticeable difference). The smallest change in physical intensity of a stimulus which is perceptible.

Terminal threshold. The physical intensity of a stimulus above which changes are not perceptible.

Usually stimulus (detection) thresholds are lower than recognition thresholds but the literature does not always indicate which is being measured especially when the assessors know the identity of the test substance. When substances are added to beer we are concerned with difference thresholds but many of the methods used for estimation involve recognition of the old sample. In practice, with trained assessors the difference between difference and recognition thresholds is negligible [18]. Threshold values are subject to considerable biological variation and it is therefore desirable to include statistical limits in any estimation. Criteria which have been used in estimating thresholds [18] include:

1. That concentration that can just be perceived by 50% of the population.
2. The geometric mean of the individual thresholds (maximum likelihood threshold).
3. The lowest concentration that can be detected with a ** statistical significance ($P = 0.01$).
4. The concentration producing 50% correct choices (ASTM). Since in paired-sample tests 50% correct choices can occur by chance alone this may be amended to:
5. That concentration producing a frequency of 50% correct above chance.

Many factors influence the measurement of thresholds [1, 18]. For example, the influence of temperature on taste is not uniform and the buffering action of saliva (pH 7·0) may influence perception. The mode of presentation of the sample is also important; thus, the average sensitivity threshold for sodium chloride varied from 0·135% for three drops placed on the tongue to 0·047% for 10 ml swallowed and 0·016% when unlimited amounts of the salt solution and distilled water could be compared [19]. Similarly, repeated practice appears to lower the threshold at which tastes can be perceived. The following thresholds (percentages) were for the first and sixth determinations: sucrose, 0·753, 0·274; caffeine, 0·0272, 0·0078; citric acid, 0·0223, 0·00096; and sodium chloride, 0·123 and 0·047 [20]. There can be large differences in sensitivity from person to person. For the addition of dimethyl sulphide to beer, tasted by an international panel of 44 persons, 37 panelists (85%) had thresholds in the range 12–87 µg/l, but the remaining 7 panelists were much

less sensitive and had thresholds in the range 150–2000 µg/l [18]. Similar
results were obtained with diacetyl; with a panel of 16 assessors the geometric
mean threshold was 0·080 mg/l but one assessor had a threshold of 2·26
mg/l [16]. Thus, when measuring thresholds it is desirable to have a panel
of at least 25 persons and to calculate the individual thresholds so that
insensitive persons do not over-influence the group result [16, 18].

TABLE 23.2

Some taste thresholds [21]

	Median	
	N	%
Sour		
Hydrochloric acid	0·0009	0·0033
Acetic acid	0·0018	0·0108
Succinic acid	0·0032	0·0189
Tartaric acid	0·0012	0·00905
Citric acid	0·0023	0·0152
	M	%
Salt		
Sodium chloride (sensitivity)	0·01	0·058
Sodium chloride (recognition)	0·03	0·175
Potassium chloride	0·017	0·127
Lithium chloride	0·025	0·106
Calcium chloride	0·01	0·111
Magnesium chloride	0·015	0·143
	M	%
Sweet		
Sucrose (detection)	0·01	0·342
Sucrose (recognition)	0·017	0·582
Glucose	0·08	1·442
Saccharin sodium	0·000023	0·00047
	M	%
Bitter		
Quinine sulphate	0·000008	$5·98 \times 10^{-4}$
Quinine hydrochloride	0·00003	$1·08 \times 10^{-3}$
Caffeine	0·0007	$1·36 \times 10^{-2}$
Magnesium sulphate	0·0046	$5·54 \times 10^{-2}$
	M	%
Umani		
Monosodium glutamate	0·00075	0·0127
Disodium 5′-inosinate	0·00031	0·012
Disodium 5′-guanylate	0·000086	0·0035

Taste thresholds for representative compounds are collected in Table 23.2.
It should be noted that the concentration of the acids is expressed in normality
and percentage whereas other substances are expressed in molarity and

percentage. With mineral acids the sourness is proportional to the hydrogen ion concentration but this is not so with organic acids that are largely undissociated. At equimolecular concentration, hydrochloric acid tastes sourer than acetic acid, but at the same pH acetic acid tastes sourer than the mineral acid. Presumably, as the H^+ ions of the dissociated acetic acid react with the taste receptor, some of the undissociated acid ionizes to maintain the equilibrium. Sodium chloride has the characteristic salty taste above 0·05 M but weaker solutions taste sweet. Potassium chloride also tastes sweet in very dilute solutions and salty above 0·05 M but between 0·02 and 0·03 M only bitterness is perceived and this note persists at higher concentrations. In contrast, magnesium sulphate only tastes bitter (Table 23·2). Quinine is usually regarded as the standard bitter taste. Quinine tonic water contains 56 mg/l (0·5 grain/pint) of quinine sulphate together with sugar (45 g/l) and/or permitted artificial sweeteners. Caffeine is present in proprietary soft drinks such as Coca-Cola and Lucozade as well as tea and coffee.

The relative sweetness of a number of sugars and artificial sweeteners is given in Table 23.3. Somewhat lower thresholds than those given in Table 23.2 were obtained for sucrose (0·017 %), fructose (0·016 %), glucose (0·132 %), and lactose (0·0160 %) when expressed as the concentration at which 50 % of the responses correctly distinguished the sugar solution from a distilled water blank [23].

TABLE 23.3

Relative sweetness of sugars [22]

Lactose	39
Maltose	46
D-Xylose	67
α,β-D-Glucose	69
Glycerol	79
Invert sugar	95
Sucrose	100
Fructose	114
Calcium cyclamate	3 380
Saccharin	30 000

Reviewing the primary tastes in beer its sourness will be measured either as its pH (3·8–4·7) or as its titratable acidity. The level of acetic acid reported for normal beers (57–145 ppm) is below the taste threshold (400 ppm) and the same is true of lactic acid (Table 22.7). Infection of beer with microorganisms such as *Acetobacter* spp. and *Lactobacillus* spp. may reduce the pH and produce a sour taste. Thus with lambic and gueuze beer the pH may drop to pH 3·2. The level of acetic acid in these beers is 2·6–6·9 times the taste threshold and the level of lactic acid is 5·8–8·6 times its taste threshold [24].

Comparison of the level of inorganic constituents in beer (Table 22.2) with the thresholds quoted in Table 23.2, reveals that potassium and chloride ions predominate and that, as potassium chloride, the maximum level of these ions well exceed the taste threshold. The maximum level of sodium ions (0·01 M) just equals the taste threshold of sodium chloride. In none of the beers reported in Table 22.5 does the concentration of glucose or sucrose exceed the thresholds quoted in Table 23.2 but if the lower values given in the text [23] are considered it can be seen that in the primed beers (samples 2–4) and the lager (sample 11) the taste thresholds of both glucose and fructose are well exceeded. Similarly, the level of glucose in the ale (sample 10) and the lagers (13 and 14) is between 1 and 5 times the threshold. A comparable threshold for maltose is not available; that quoted (1·36%) well exceeds the concentration of maltose in the beers mentioned in Table 22.5 but, if the comparable threshold was similar to that given for lactose (0·16%), the level of maltose in beers no 1, 5, 6, 13, and 15 would exceed the threshold and so influence the taste. The taste threshold for isohumulone is reported to be 5·6 mg/l (1·5 × 10^{-5} M) and that of hulupone 7·7 mg/l (2·3 × 10^{-5} M) [25]. The levels of isohumulones (bitterness units) quoted in Tables 22.1 and 22.3 well exceed the taste threshold but the level of hulupones reported (1·1–4·3 ppm) does not exceed that threshold. By traditional scaling methods quinine hydrochloride was some six times more bitter than an iso-α-acid preparation which, in turn, was about ten times more bitter than caffeine [26]. The character of the bitterness of these compounds was also different. Iso-α-acids especially, and quinine to a minor extent, were perceived as a lingering bitterness at the back of the throat, while caffeine yielded a short-lived bitterness on the tongue. The levels of glutamic acid (Tables 14.5 and 22.12), 5′-inosine monophosphate and 5′-guanosine monophosphate (Table 22.13) are below the thresholds given in Table 23.2 but these compounds are reported to be flavour modifiers rather than primary flavours. Additions of 5′-guanosine monophosphate do modify beer flavour but the lowest level of addition of 5′-GMP required to alter beer flavour is greatly in excess of the amount naturally present in beer [27].

Despite their widespread use in the brewing literature the use of thresholds has been criticized [28]. 'Thresholds are but one point on a dynamic concentration continuum'. There is no evidence that the intensity/concentration curves for all substances are parallel differing only in the point where they cross the abscissa. Further, taste is not a single instantaneous sensation but has a temporal element. Tasters have been trained to record the intensity on a scale between 0 (none) and 100 (extreme) on a moving recorder chart whereby a time-intensity curve such as Fig. 23.6 is obtained [26–28]. Typically the sample was expectorated, or if beer swallowed, after ten seconds. As would be expected when a sucrose gelatine was expectorated the intensity of the sweet sensation immediately started to fall and declined to zero in about 10 s [26].

In contrast, when a sample of beer was swallowed the intensity of the bitterness continued to rise for a further 8 s before starting to fall (Fig. 23.6). The bitter sensation appears to persist longer (60–90 s) than the sweet sensation.

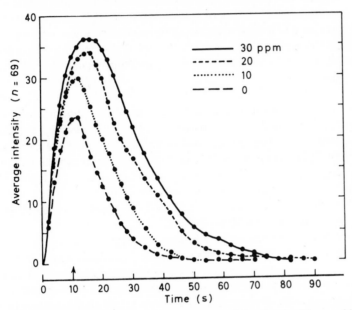

Fig. 23.6 Average time-intensity curves for bitterness of four levels of iso-α-acids in commercial lager. Samples were placed in the mouth at zero times and swallowed at 10 s. The judge continued to record intensity of bitterness until disappearance or for a maximum of 2 min. (After Lewis *et al.* [26].)

TABLE 23.4

Odour and taste thresholds of various compounds

	Odour threshold in water (ppb) [29]	Taste threshold in beer (ppb) [15]
Ethanol	100 000	14 000 000
Butyric acid	250	2 000
Nootkatone	170	—
Humulene	160	—
Butanal	70	1 000
Myrcene	15	—
n-Amyl acetate	5	5 000
Dimethyl sulphide	0·3	50
n-Decanal	0·1	6
Methyl mercaptan	0·02	2·0
β-Ionone	0·007	1·3
2-Methoxy-3-isobutylpyrazine	0·002	—

In general, the olfactory threshold of a compound is several orders lower than the taste threshold (Table 23.4). This may represent the probability of a compound taken into the mouth reaching the olfactory epithelium. In the ASBC triangular test (see later) the assessors are required to distinguish the similar beers first on the basis of odour. Similarly, with one brewery taste panel it was found that most members differentiated between two beers on the basis of aroma rather than taste 90–95% of the time [30]. The olfactory threshold (OT) can be calculated from the simplified equation:

$$\log (OT) = -\log K_{L/A} - 0.1A_0 + (22.13 \pm 0.5)$$

where $K_{L/A}$ is the absorption constant for molecules passing from air to the aqueous–lipid interface (usually between 6 and 8.5), and A_0 is the cross sectional area of the molecule (usually between 10–60 Å^2). Thus the olfactory threshold of a pure compound can be calculated to a first approximation from the partial pressure of the compound above an aqueous solution of the compound, its partition coefficient between water and light petroleum (substituting for the lipid membrane), and its cross-sectional area, which can be calculated from models [4].

These ideas have been developed further with regard to flavour the integral of taste and aroma. For a molecule to elicit a flavour it must reach and react with a specific receptor. To reach such a receptor the molecule will probably have to pass through a lipid membrane and its lipophilicity will govern this approach. Gardner [31] has shown highly significant correlations between taste thresholds and lipophilicity. Thus for homologous series of compounds (alcohols, esters, ketones, aldehydes, and acids) in beers:

$$\log(1/T) = a \log(P) + b$$

where T = threshold in mol/l and P = octanol/water partition coefficient representing lipophilicity. This relationship breaks down when P is greater than 3.0. Similarly, in many series of compounds with bitter tastes the bitterness increases with increasing lipophilicity [32]. When a molecule has reached a receptor whether or not it initiates a signal to the brain depends upon its size, shape, degree of ionization, and charge pattern etc. In recent years the size and shapes of molecules have been expressed in terms of molecular connectivity [33, 34] rather than the cross-sectional area. Again [31] significant correlations have been found between log 1/T and $^1\chi^V$, the first order valance connectivity index:

$$\log 1/T = a(^1\chi^V)^b$$

A compilation of threshold data has been published [35]. Threshold values, mainly for additions to Mexican and American beers [15], are included in the Tables of Chapter 22. Data for additions to Irish [36] and Norwegian [37, 38] beers are also available and much of the data have been collected [31]. Methods for measuring thresholds have been reviewed [16, 18]. Because of the wide range of thresholds observed, a factor of 2×10^{12}, it is necessary to purify each compound to constant flavour threshold to ensure that the observed flavour is not due to an impurity [15].

TABLE 23.5

Tentative scheme for role of constituents in determining the flavour of beer [15, 39]

1. *Primary flavour constituents* (above 2 FU[a])
   Ethanol
   Hop bitter compounds (e.g., isohumulone)
   Carbon dioxide

   Speciality beers
   Hop aroma compounds (e.g. humuladienone)
   Caramel flavoured compounds
   Several esters and alcohols (high-gravity beers)
   Short-chain acids

   Defective beers
   2-*trans*-nonenal (oxidized, stale)
   Diacetyl and 2,3-pentanedione (fermentation)
   Hydrogen sulphide, dimethyl sulphide and other
       compounds (fermentation)
   Acetic acid (fermentation)
   3-Methylbut-2-enylthiol (light-struck-hops)
   Others (microbial infection, etc.)

2. *Secondary flavour constituents* (0·5–2·0 FU)
   Volatiles
   Banana esters (e.g. isoamyl acetate)
   Apple esters (e.g. ethyl hexanoate)
   Fusel alcohols (e.g. isoamyl alcohol)
   C_6, C_8, C_{10} aliphatic acids
   Ethyl acetate
   Butyric and isovaleric acids
   Phenylacetic acid

   Non-volatiles
   Polyphenols
   Various acids, sugars, hop compounds

3. *Tertiary flavour constituents* (0·1–0·5 FU)
   2-Phenethyl acetate, *o*-aminoacetophenone
   Isovaleraldehyde, methional, acetoin
   4-Ethylguaiacol, *gamma*-valerolactone

4. *Background flavour constituents* (below 0·1 FU)
   Remaining flavour compounds

[a]Flavour Units (FU) = concentration/threshold.

On the basis of threshold values and flavour units (FU), Meilgaard in 1975 outlined the flavour chemistry of beer (Table 23.5). Removal of any of the primary flavour constituents would produce a decisive change in flavour.

Removal of any one of the secondary constituents would produce a small change in flavour. Together the secondary flavour constituents form the bulk of a beer's flavour. Any differences between one beer and another of the same type is mostly determined by variations within this class. Tertiary flavour constituents add subsidiary flavour notes. Removal of any one of this class produces no perceptible change in flavour. Similarly it is not possible to say whether the numerous compounds, which individually contribute less than 0·1 FU to the background flavour, are together of importance in beer flavour. Undoubtedly further work will modify this table. Indeed, considering the primary flavour constituents in speciality beers, more recent work has questioned the widespread influence of humuladienone but many of the oxygenated terpenes and sesquiterpenes listed in Table 13.6, such as linalool, humuleneol II, and humulene epoxide I, will significantly contribute to beer flavour. Threshold data for all of these compounds are not available. In contrast, very low thresholds have been found for several sulphur compounds recently characterized in hop oil (Table 13.7) but data on their level in beer are not yet available. Many heterocyclic compounds which will contribute caramel flavours to dark beers have now been characterized (Table 22.15; see also [40]). Consideration of the concentration and threshold data in Table 22.8 will demonstrate the alcohols, acids, and esters which will contribute over 2 FU to speciality beers and between 0·5 and 2·0 FU in regular beers. Octanoic acid (difference threshold, 4·5 mg/l), decanoic acid (1·5 mg/l), dodecanoic acid (0·5 mg/l), and to a lesser extent, hexanoic acid contribute to the *caprylic* flavour in beer [41]. The effect of the acids is additive and there is a linear relationship between the panel score for the *caprylic* flavour and the concentration of octanoic + decanoic acids [42]. Lager yeasts (*Saccharomyces uvarum*) produce larger amounts of these acids during fermentation than ale yeasts (*S. cerevisiae*). Thus the *caprylic* flavour was observed in most of the lagers and 25% of the ales examined [42].

The formation of off-flavours in beer has been reviewed [40]. Autoxidation of the lipids present in beer produces carbonyl compounds with very low taste thresholds. In particular, linoleic acid is oxidized to trihydroxyoctadecenoic acids (Table 22.7) which break down into 2-*trans*-nonenal. This aldehyde and related compounds impart a cardboard flavour to beer at very low concentrations. Other carbonyl are formed from the lipids in beer by irradiation with light including the C_9, C_{10}, and C_{11}-alka-2,4-dienals (thresholds 0·5, 0·3 and 0·01 ppb respectively) [40]. The level of diacetyl and pentane-2,3-dione in a range of commercial beers is given in Table 22.11. Quantities in excess of 0·15 ppm impart a buttery flavour more noticeable in lagers than in ales. Bacterial contamination and petite mutants of yeast result in high levels of diacetyl. The sulphur compounds characterized in beer are listed in Table 22.19 with some threshold data. Dimethyl sulphide is the major volatile sulphur compound in beer (Table 22.20) and high concentrations are a feature of lager flavour [43]. 3-Methylbut-2-enyl thiol (prenyl mercaptan) produces a 'sunstruck' flavour in lager beers at concentrations between 0·1 and 1·0 ppb. The threshold of the purified compound is 0·005 ppb in water and 0·05 ppb in beer [40]. Photolysis of iso-α-acids produces isoprenyl radicals which can either collapse to 2,7 dimethylocta-2,6-diene or react with cysteine to give 3-methylbut-2-enyl thiol. The high levels of acetic acid in lambic and gueuze beers was mentioned earlier. A beer with a phenolic off-flavour was shown to contain enhanced levels of 4-vinylphenol and 4-vinylguaiacol (threshold, 0·3 ppm). It was found that certain yeasts produce these compounds by de-carboxylation of p-coumaric and ferulic acids respectively but, in general brewing strains lack this facility. However, Bavarian 'Weizenbier' contains high levels of 4-vinylguaiacol (0·4–6·0 ppm) which imparts a spicy clove-like flavour to the beer [40]. Certain beers acquire a flavour described as catty or *Ribes* as a similar aroma is given off by the leaves and stems of flowering currants (*Ribes* spp). The development of this flavour is closely correlated with headspace air [44]. In beers bottled with high volumes of headspace air the flavour develops rapidly over 6 weeks but thereafter slowly declines. One substance responsible for the catty flavour is 4-mercaptopentan-2-one (threshold, 0·005 ppb in water, 0·05 ppb in beer). Beers with strong catty odours contained 1·5 ppb of the mercaptopentanone but there may be other beer constituents which contribute to this off-flavour [40]. Elsewhere (Table 23.7) 8-mercapto-p-menthan-3-one (p-menthane-8-thiol-3-one) has been proposed as the reference standard for the catty (*Ribes*) flavour.

23.2 *Sensory analysis of beer*

The brewer and his customer make a subjective assessment of beer flavour each time they taste but for a more objective appraisal it is usually desirable to submit the beer, with suitable controls, to a taste panel. Taste panels may be used to: (*i*) select qualified judges, (*ii*) correlate sensory with chemical and physical measurements, (*iii*) study processing effects, maintain quality, evaluate raw material selection, establish storage stability, and reduce costs, (*iv*) evaluate quality, and (*v*) determine consumer reaction [1]. The types of test used include: (*i*) difference tests, (*ii*) rank order, (*iii*) scoring tests, (*iv*) descriptive tests, (*v*) hedonic scaling, and (*vi*) acceptance and preference tests [1]. Difference tests are most commonly used in the brewing industry, the results of which are readily analysed by statistics. Several forms of difference test are used. The 'A-not-A' form of test is perhaps the simplest. Assessors are first familiarized with a standard A and then presented, in a random manner, either with A again or with the comparative sample B. In the paired-comparison test two samples are presented simultaneously (AA, AB, BA, or BB) and assessors report either 'there is a difference' or 'there is no difference'.

This test may also be used as a directed difference test when, having found a difference, the assessor is asked in which sample a particular flavour attribute is more prominent. Directed difference tests should only be used by trained and experienced tasters. The duo-trio test is a three-glass test in which the reference sample is specified and the assessor is required to say which of the others is the same as the reference. There is a 50% possibility that the correct choice is made by chance. In the triangular test the same beer is presented in two glasses and a different beer in the third. The assessor is asked to identify the odd sample with only a 33·3% possibility of the correct answer being obtained. However tasters may find difficulty in finding the odd beer from certain of the six possible arrangements (AAB, ABA, ABB, BAA, BAB, and BBA) when one of the samples has a lingering flavour or after-taste [27]. Again the assessor may be asked to specify the nature and the direction of the perceived difference. This additional information is only of value when the odd sample has been correctly identified.

INDIVIDUAL TWO-GLASS FLAVOUR TESTING FORM

Name of taster .... Date ....
Beers compared
 ....
Is there a flavour difference between the two? ....
Can you describe the difference? ....
Optional
Which beer do you prefer (if either)? ....

INDIVIDUAL THREE-GLASS FLAVOUR TESTING FORM

Name of taster .... Date ....
Beers compared ....
Which is the number of the different glass of beer? ....
Can you describe the difference? ....
Optional
Which beer do you prefer (if any)? ....

Fig. 23.7 Taste panel report forms Analytica-EBC [46].

The organization of tasting panels has been discussed [1, 45]. The EBC [46] gives details for two- and three-glass difference tests and the ASBC [47] for a three-glass triangular test. The panel should be housed comfortably in a room free from external disturbance or odour with smoking and talking prohibited.

TABLE 23.6
Significance levels of taste-test results [48]

Number of tasters	Two-sample test no. of concurring choices necessary to establish the significance of a result as indicated by			Triangular test — Difference test no. of correct answers necessary to establish the significance of a result as indicated by			Quality or preference test no. of concurring choices by tasters selecting correctly to establish the significance of a result as indicated by			Number of tasters
	*	**	***	*	**	***	*	**	***	
1	—	—	—	—	—	—	—	—	—	1
2	—	—	—	—	—	—	—	—	—	2
3	—	—	—	3	—	—	3	3	—	3
4	—	—	—	4	—	—	3	4	—	4
5	—	—	—	4	5	—	4	4	5	5
6	6	—	—	5	6	—	4	5	6	6
7	7	—	—	5	6	7	4	5	6	7
8	8	8	—	6	7	8	5	5	6	8
9	8	9	—	6	7	8	5	6	7	9
10	9	10	—	7	8	9	5	6	7	10
11	10	11	11	7	8	10	5	6	8	11
12	10	11	12	8	9	10	6	7	8	12
13	11	12	13	8	9	11	6	7	8	13
14	12	13	14	9	10	11	6	7	9	14
15	12	13	14	9	10	12	7	8	9	15
16	13	14	15	9	11	12	7	8	9	16
17	13	15	16	10	11	13	7	8	10	17
18	14	15	17	10	12	13	7	9	10	18
19	15	16	17	11	12	14	8	9	10	19
20	15	17	18	11	13	14	8	9	11	20
21	16	17	19	12	13	15	8	9	11	21
22	17	18	19	12	14	15	8	10	11	22
23	17	19	20	12	14	16	9	10	12	23
24	18	19	21	13	15	16	9	10	12	24
25	18	20	21	13	15	17	9	10	12	25
26	19	20	22	14	15	17	9	11	12	26
27	20	21	23	14	16	18	10	11	13	27
28	20	22	23	15	16	18	10	11	13	28
29	21	22	27	15	17	19	10	11	13	29
30	21	23	25	15	17	19	10	12	13	30
31	22	24	25	16	18	20	10	12	14	31
32	23	24	26	16	18	20	11	12	14	32
33	23	25	27	17	18	21	11	13	14	33
34	24	25	27	17	19	21	11	13	15	34
35	24	26	28	17	19	22	11	13	15	35
36	25	27	29	18	20	22	12	13	15	36
37	25	27	29	18	20	22	12	14	15	37
38	26	28	30	19	21	23	12	14	16	38
39	27	28	31	19	21	23	12	14	16	39
40	27	29	31	19	21	24	13	14	16	40
41	27	29	32	20	22	24	13†	14†	16†	41
42	28	30	32	20	22	25	13†	14	16†	42
43	28	30	33	21	23	25	13†	14	16	43
44	29	31	33	21	23	25	13	14	16	44
45	30	32	34	22	24	26	13	14	16	45
46	30	32	35	22	24	26	13	15	16	46
47	31	33	35	23	24	27	13	15	17	47
48	31	33	36	23	25	23	14	15	17	48
49	32	34	37	23	25	28	14	15	17	49
50	32	35	37	24	26	28	14	16	18	50
51	33	35	38	24	26	29	14	16	18	51
52	34	36	38	24	27	29	14	16	18	52
53	34	36	39	25	27	29	15	16	18	53
54	35	37	40	25	27	30	15	17	19	54
55	35	38	40	26	28	30	15	17	19	55
56	36	38	41	26	28	31	15	17	19	56
57	36	39	41	26	29	31	16	17	19	57
58	37	39	42	27	29	32	16	17	20	58
59	38	40	43	27	29	32	16	18	20	59
60	38	40	43	28	30	33	16	18	20	60
61	39	41	44	28	30	33	16	18	20	61
62	39	42	44	28	31	33	17	18	20	62
63	40	42	45	29	31	34	17	19	21	63
64	40	43	46	29	32	34	17	19	21	64
65	41	43	46	30	32	35	17	19	21	65
66	41	44	47	30	32	35	17	19	21	66
67	42	45	47	30	33	36	18	20	22	67

† Calculation by the χ^2 method gives a lower number, but adjustment has been made to conform with values obtained by binomial expansion. 1, 2 and 3 stars represent significance at the 5%, 1% and 0·1% levels respectively.

The beers presented to the panel should be at the same temperature, in the same condition (CO_2 content) and served without foam either in opaque glasses or in a darkened room to eliminate differences in colour or clarity. The EBC say the beers should have been stored overnight around 12°C (51·4°F) while the ASBC recommend a serving temperature between 5 and 17·5°C (40 and 60 °F). Each taster is provided with a form (Fig. 23.7) on which he must record his results immediately after tasting. No discussion of results is allowed until all the tasters have completed their report forms. The organizer must ensure that the beers are poured correctly into the glasses chosen by lot and that this order is immediately recorded on a summary sheet. Each taster's findings are also recorded on the summary sheet and the significance of the results evaluated by reference to Bengtsson's tables (Table 23.6). As chance plays a large part in the two-glass test it is particularly important to have a large tasting panel and for members to test again with the same beers on several successive days. With the three-glass test the EBC give no instructions other than those on the form (Fig. 23.7) but the ASBC say that the organizer should instruct the panel to:

1. Immediately compare the odours of the beers in the 3 glasses prior to and after each is swirled.
2. If an odour is detected, taste the one or 2 samples that appear to have the least intense aroma and then taste the remaining.
3. Decide which of the samples has an odour or flavour that is different from the other 2.
4. Fill in the form that is supplied and return it to the organizer.

Except for consumer reaction, when as many tasters as possible are desired, more consistent results are likely to be obtained from a panel consisting of trained judges than from untrained personnel. In choosing members for a flavour panel the EBC recommends the use of dilution, sweetness, and bitterness comparisons. In the first the beer is tasted against itself diluted by 10% with carbonated tap water. In the second the beer is tasted against a sample with 4 g/l sucrose added and in the last the beer is tasted against a sample with an additional 4 ppm of iso-α-acids added. Each of the tests is repeated on three successive days and tasters with low scores in all three series excluded. If a panel selected in this manner cannot distinguish between two beers significantly, it is most unlikely that the general public would detect any difference which is reassuring from a quality control viewpoint. However, if a difference is found it is desirable to be able to describe it as unambiguously as possible.

The most successful approach to the description of beer flavour to date is the application of the Arthur D. Little flavour profile method [49, 50]. In this method a panel of trained judges (16 were trained and 8 used in each panel) were asked to consider each flavour attribute listed on the format (Fig. 23.8) in turn and, if applicable, score the intensity of the aroma, flavour, and after-palate on a 5-point scale. (1 = slight; 2 = noticeable; 3 = marked; 4 = strong; 5 = extreme. A rating of 0 = absent was not used.) Four different formats were used in which the groups A, B, C, and D of Fig. 23.8 are arranged in a different order to minimize presentational bias to a single group of qualities. The position of the after-palate section was the same on all the forms.

Aroma		Flavour	Aroma		Flavour
	A Liveliness (CO_2 tingle) Sweet Sickly Toffee-like Fruity (citrus) Estery Fragrant Spicy Nutty Warming High-gravity fullness			**B** Diacetyl Earthy Musty Cabbagy, vegetable water Dimethyl sulphide Sulphury Cardboard Soapy, fatty Phenolic Yeasty Dough-like	
_____ _____ _____ _____ _____ _____ _____	**C** Smooth mouthfeel Viscous, thick Acidic (sharp) Sour Salty Metallic Mouth coating Astringent Drying Particulate (dusty)		_____ _____ _____	**D** Body (full) Watery (thin) Malty Worty Grainy Grassy Bitter Hoppy Catty Burnt Smoky	
		Afterpalate			
	Bitter Metallic Astringent Yeasty (yeast bite) Burnt			Sweet Toffee-like Sulphury Fruity Estery Hoppy	

Other comments: Try to relate these to terms already listed.

Fig. 23.8 Flavour profile format. (After Clapperton [49].)

After tasting, the organizer sums the scores for each attribute. For comparing beers the total scores are simplified to a five point scale and transferred to punch cards. Any quality recognized by 3 out of the 8 panelists is punched under aroma, flavour, and after-palate. The profiles produced by the panel, after training, were reproducible. Different beers gave different patterns but the same beer tasted on different days gave essentially the same pattern. The profiles thus provide a method for documenting information about beer flavour so that beers brewed today can be compared with those brewed in the past or the future. This information will only be of use outside the panel that generated it if there is a universally agreed terminology.

A joint working party of European and American specialists have now proposed a beer flavour terminology [51]. It is not regarded that any system of terminology is static but the industry is urged to use the terminology set out in Table 23.7 and comment on it. Each separately identifiable flavour character-istic has its own name and similar flavours are placed together in 14 classes. The terms used are compatible with the EBC Thesaurus and so the terminology should be capable of translation into other languages. Subjective or hedonic terms, which cannot be standardized have been excluded. As far as possible the meaning of each term is illustrated with readily available reference standards. Eleven standards have been adopted to date and proposed standards are given in parentheses. The concentrations used are three times the difference threshold in light lager beer and thus should be detected by 9 out of 10 persons. The class names and first tier descriptors are common terms familiar to most people. The second tier terms should allow for the naming of each separately identifiable flavour note in beer by specially trained panels. The system is illustrated by the flavour wheel (Fig. 23.9) which shows the relationship of the various terms and is presented as a memory aid. It is not intended that each taste panel should be presented with all of these terms. In any given brewery some may never be encountered. For the daily testing of a brewery's beer 10–20 terms is probably optimal but if, for example, the panel was trying to characterize a sulphury off-flavour, all of the terms in class 7 could be used. It is hoped that the approved terms, rather than any synonyms, will be used in official reports and scientific communications.

The terms used to describe ale flavours have been examined by multi-dimensional scaling – a technique of grouping like characters together and arranging these groups relative to each other by their degree of 'similarity' [52]. Such correlations cannot be perfect and deviations from the model are expressed as 'stress'. Thus the seven after-flavour terms (*sweet, toffee-like, caprylic, burnt, bitter, astringent* and *mouthcoating*) can be represented in a two-dimensional model with only 0·3% of stress. In contrast for odour and flavour terms a three-dimensional model is required and the stress value is approximately 13%. These terms fall roughly on the surface of a sphere so that those which are close together in the model (Fig. 23.10) have a close flavour relationship, e.g. *sour* and *acidic*, whereas widely different or opposite

TABLE 23.7

Recommended descriptors of beer flavour [51]

Class term	First tier	Second tier	Relevance	Comments, synonyms, definitions	Reference standard
Class 1 – Aromatic, Fragrant, Fruity, Floral					
0110 Alcoholic			OTW	The general effect of ethanol and higher alcohols.	Ethanol, 50 g/l
	0111	Spicy	OTW	Allspice, nutmeg, peppery, eugenol. See also 1003 Vanilla.	Eugenol, 120 µg/l
	0112	Vinous	OTW	Bouquet, fusely, wine-like.	(White wine)
0120 Solvent-like			OT	Like chemical solvents.	
	0121	Plastics	OT	Plasticizers.	
	0122	Can-liner	OT	Lacquer-like.	
	0123	Acetone	OT		(Acetone)
0130 Estery			OT	Like aliphatic esters.	
	0131	Isoamyl acetate	OT	Banana, peardrop.	(Isoamyl acetate)
	0132	Ethyl hexanoate	OT	Apple-like with note of aniseed. See also 0142 Apple.	(Ethyl hexanoate)
	0133	Ethyl acetate	OT	Light fruity, solvent-like. See also 0120 Solvent-like	(Ethyl acetate)
0140 Fruity			OT	Of specific fruits or mixtures of fruits.	
	0141	Citrus	OT	Citral, grapefruit, lemony, orange-rind.	
	0142	Apple	OT		
	0143	Banana	OT		
	0144	Blackcurrant	OT	Blackcurrant fruit. For blackcurrant leaves use 0810 Catty.	
	0145	Melony	OT		
	0146	Pear	OT		
	0147	Raspberry	OT		
	0148	Strawberry	OT		
0150 Acetaldehyde			OT	Green apples, raw appleskin, bruised apples.	(Acetaldehyde)
0160 Floral			OT	Like flowers, fragrant.	
	0161	2-Phenylethanol	OT	Rose-like.	(2-Phenylethanol)
	0162	Geraniol	OT	Rose-like, different from 0161. Taster should compare the pure chemicals.	(Geraniol)
	0163	Perfumy	OT	Scented.	(6-Nonenal, *cis* or *trans*)

TABLE 23.7 (continued)

Class term	First tier	Second tier	Relevance	Comments, synonyms, definitions	Reference standard
	0170 Hoppy		OT	Fresh hop aroma. Use with other terms to describe stale hop aroma. Does not include hop bitterness (see 1200 Bitter).	
		0171 Kettle-hop	OT	Flavour imparted by aroma hops boiled in the kettle.	
		0172 Dry-hop	OT	Flavour imparted by dry hops added in tank or cask.	
		0173 Hop oil	OT	Flavour imparted by addition of distilled hop oil.	
Class 2 – Resinous, Nutty, Green, Grassy					
	0210 Resinous		OT	Fresh sawdust, resin, cedarwood, pinewood, sprucy, terpenoid.	
		0211 Woody	OT	Seasoned wood (uncut).	
	0220 Nutty		OT	As in brazil-nut, hazelnut, sherry-like.	
		0221 Walnut	OT	Fresh (not rancid) walnut.	
		0222 Coconut	OT		
		0223 Beany	OT	Bean soup.	
		0224 Almond	OT	Marzipan.	(2,4,7-Decatrienal) (Benzaldehyde)
	0230 Grassy		OT	Green, crushed green leaves, leafy, alfalfa.	
		0231 Freshly-cut grass	OT		(cis-3-Hexenol)
		0232 Straw-like	OT	Hay-like.	
Class 3 – Cereal					
	0310 Grainy		OT	Raw grain flavour.	
		0311 Husky	OT	Husk-like, chaff, 'Glattwasser'.	
		0312 Corn grits	OT	Maize grits, adjuncty.	
		0313 Mealy	OT	Like flour.	
	0320 Malty		OT		
	0330 Worty		OT	Fresh wort aroma. Use with other terms to describe infected wort, e.g. 0731 Parsnip.	

TABLE 23.7 (continued)

Class 4 – Caramelized, Roasted

0410 Caramel		OT	Burnt sugar, toffee-like.
	0411 Molasses	OT	Black treacle, treacly.
	0412 Licorice	OT	
0420 Burnt		OTM	Scorched aroma, dry mouthfeel and sharp acrid taste.
	0421 Bread-crust	OTM	Charred toast.
	0422 Roast-barley	OTM	Chocolate malt.
	0423 Smoky	OT	

Class 5 – Phenolic

0500 Phenolic		OT	
	0501 Tarry	OT	Pitch, faulty pitching of containers.
	0502 Bakelite	OT	
	0503 Carbolic	OT	Phenol.
	0504 Chlorophenol	OT	Trichlorophenol (TCP), hospital-like.
	0505 Iodoform	OT	Iodophors, hospital-like, pharmaceutical.

Class 6 – Soapy, Fatty, Diacetyl, Oily, Rancid

0610 Fatty acid		OT	Soapy, fatty, goaty, tallowy.
	0611 Caprylic	OT	Dry, stale cheese, ⎫
	0612 Cheesy	OT	old hops. ⎬ Hydrolytic rancidity
	0613 Isovaleric	OT	⎭ (Octanoic acid).
	0614 Butyric	OT	Rancid butter. (Isovaleric acid)
0620 Diacetyl		OT	Butterscotch, buttermilk.
0630 Rancid		OTM	Oxidative rancidity ⎫ Butyric acid, 3 mg/l
	0631 Rancid oil	OTM	⎬ Diacetyl, 0·2 – 0·4 mg/l
0640 Oily		OTM	As in refined vegetable oil.
	0641 Vegetable oil	OTM	
	0642 Mineral oil	OTM	Gasoline (petrol), kerosene (paraffin), machine oil.

TABLE 23.7 (continued)

Class 7 – Sulphury

0700 Sulphury		
0710 Sulphitic	OT	Sulphur dioxide, striking-match, choking, sulphurous-SO₂. (KMS)
	OT	Rotten egg, sulphury-reduced, sulphurous-RSH.
0720 Sulphidic	OT	Rotten egg. (H₂S)
0721 H₂S	OT	Lower mercaptans, drains, stench. (Ethyl mercaptan)
0722 Mercaptan	OT	
0723 Garlic	OT	
0724 Lightstruck	OT	Skunky, sunstruck.
0725 Autolysed	OT	Rotting yeast (see also 0740 Yeasty).
0726 Burnt rubber	OT	Higher mercaptans.
0727 Shrimp-like	OT	Water in which shrimp have been cooked.
0730 Cooked vegetable	OT	Mainly dialkyl sulphides, sulphurous-RSR'.
0731 Parsnip/celery	OT	An effect of wort infection.
0732 DMS	OT	(Dimethyl sulphide) DMS, 100 μg/l
0733 Cooked cabbage	OT	Overcooked green vegetables.
0734 Cooked sweet corn	OT	Cooked maize, canned sweet corn.
0735 Cooked tomato	OT	Tomato juice (processed), tomato ketchup.
0736 Cooked onion	OT	
0740 Yeasty	OT	Fresh yeast, flavour of heated thiamine (see also 0725 Autolysed).
0741 Meaty	OT	Brothy, cooked meat, meat extract, peptone, yeast broth.

Class 8 – Oxidized, Stale, Musty

0800 Stale		
0810 Catty	OTM	Old beer, overaged, overpasteurized. (Heat with air)
0820 Papery	OT	Blackcurrant leaves, ribes, tomato plants, oxidized beer. (p-Menthane-8-thiol-3-one)
	OT	An initial stage of staling, bready (stale bread-crumb), cardboard, old beer, oxidized. 5-Methylfurfural, 25 mg/l

TABLE 23.7 (continued)

Class term	First tier	Second tier	Relevance	Comments, synonyms, definitions	Reference standard
		0830 Leathery	OTM	A later stage of staling, then often used in conjunction with 0211 Woody.	
	0840 Moldy				
		0841 Earthy	OT	Cellar-like, leaf-mold, woodsy.	
			OT	Actinomycetes, damp soil, freshly dug soil, diatomaceous earth.	(Geosmin)
		0842 Musty	OT	Fusty.	
Class 9 – Sour, acidic					
0900 Acidic					
	0910 Acetic		OT	Pungent aroma, sharpness of taste, mineral acid. Vinegar.	(Acetic acid)
	0920 Sour		OT	Lactic, sour milk. Use with 0141 for citrus-sour.	
Class 10 – Sweet					
1000 Sweet			OT	Can occur as an effect of beer staling, e.g. the odour of stale beer in a glass, oxidized (stale) honey.	Sucrose, 7·5 g/l
	1001 Honey		OT	May be qualified by sub-classes of 0140 Fruity.	
	1002 Jam-like		OT		
	1003 Vanilla		OT	Custard powder, vanillin.	(Vanillin)
	1004 Primings		OT		
	1005 Syrupy		OTM	Clear (golden) syrup.	
	1006 Oversweet		OT	Sickly sweet, cloying.	
Class 11 – Salty					
1100 Salty			T		Sodium chloride, 1·8 g/l
Class 12 – Bitter					
1200 Bitter			TAf		(Isohumulone)

TABLE 23.7 (*continued*)

Class 13 – Mouthfeel

1310 Alkaline	TMAf	Flavour imparted by accidental admixture of alkaline detergent.	(Sodium bicarbonate)
1320 Mouthcoating	MAf	Creamy, 'onctueux', (Fr.).	
1330 Metallic	OTMAf	Iron, rusty water, coins, tinny, inky.	(Ferrous ammonium sulphate)
1340 Astringent	MAf	Mouth puckering, puckery, tannin-like, tart	Quercitrin, 240 mg/l[*]
1341 Drying	MAf	Unsweet.	
1350 Powdery	OTM	O – Dusty cushion, irritating (with 0310 Grainy) mill-room smell. TM – Chalky, particulate, scratchy, silicate-like, siliceous.	
1360 Carbonation	M	CO_2 content.	
1361 Flat	M	Undercarbonated.	60% of normal CO_2 content for the product
1362 Gassy	M	Overcarbonated.	140% of normal CO_2 content for the product
1370 Warming	WMAf	See also 0110 Alcoholic and 0111. Spicy.	

Class 14 – Fullness

1410 Body	OTM	Fullness of flavour and mouthfeel.
1411 Watery	TM	Thin, seemingly diluted.
1412 Characterless	OTM	Bland, empty, flavourless.
1413 Satiating	OTM	Extra-full, filling.
1414 Thick	TM	Viscous, 'epais' (Fr.).

* Quercitrin is both astringent and bitter.

Particular Relevance: O = Odour; T = Taste; M = Mouthfeel; W = Warming; Af = After-flavour.

characteristics such as *sweet* and *bitter* or *body* (full) and *watery* (thin) are further apart or at opposite points on the surface. The flavours associated with strong ales are seen on the left hand side of the diagram (Fig. 23.10) while many of those on the right hand side are associated with oxidative deterioration or staling of beer. Terms in the central section of the diagram, including *diacetyl*, *caprylic*, *worty*, *grainy*, *lively*, *bitter*, *burnt* and *nutty* may be regarded as belonging to an intermediate category of flavours that are pleasant to some and unpleasant to others at their normal levels of perceived intensity in commercial beers. High levels of hop bitter substances, particularly in beers that are fermented to dryness, can impart astringency as well as bitterness to the flavour. Accordingly these two terms come close together on the model.

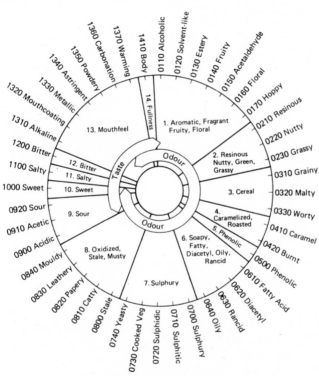

Fig. 23.9 Flavour wheel. (After Meilgaard *et al.* [51].)

Having agreed the terminology some of the results of profile analysis may be discussed. In comparing triangular (difference) and profile sensory analysis, some beers could be distinguished by profile analysis when a significant difference was not found in a triangular test [27]. In the triangular test a person has the additional mental task of maintaining a memory standard of the beer or beers he has just tasted. Thus, the order of presentation may affect the result. The profile test is psychologically simpler in that the taster is only concerned with describing the flavour of the immediate beer in question. Panel scores for the various attributes may be summed or analysed using the t-statistic and treating the data as a number of separate paired comparisons.

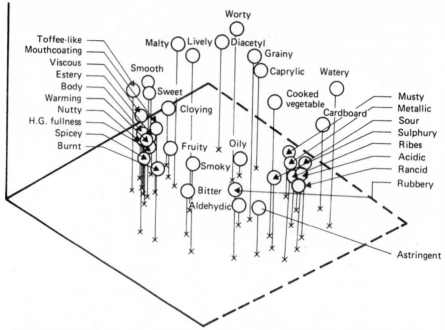

Fig. 23.10 Flavour terms by multi-dimensional scaling. (After Brown and Clapperton [52].)

More complex correlations can be obtained by use of the computer. For example, national and regional differences in lager beers were examined by discriminant (cluster) analysis [53]. In this technique each beer is represented as a point in multi-dimensional space, the coordinates of which are determined either by the individual flavour characteristics, determined by profile analysis, or by physicochemical parameters, determined by analysis. Only 27 of the terms on the profile format (Fig. 23.8) gave significant scores with lagers. The pattern of points in 27-dimensional space is simplified by the computer programme to produce eigen vectors (mathematical devices to convert a pattern of points in multi-dimensional space into an equivalent pattern of points in a smaller number of dimensions). This has the advantage of bringing things down to a level non-mathematicians can visualize, but it has the disadvantage that the axes only represent mathematical abstractions and not brewing parameters. Thus, the two-dimensional pattern of North American, Continental European, and British lagers gave three discrete tight clusters of points. When only the 12 highest scoring sensory characteristics were used the beers still fell into three groups but the clusters were more diffuse (Fig. 23.11). This result can be interpreted in terms of the perceived differences in bitterness, *dimethyl sulphide* (DMS) flavour, and palate fullness (OG). Of the flavour terms scored: (*i*) *dimethyl sulphide* and *cabbagy-vegetable water* both relate to the DMS factor; (*ii*) *body, warming* and *high gravity fullness,* and *viscous* relate to differences in original gravity; (*iii*) *bitter, drying* and possibly *smooth* (mouthfeel) relate to differences in bitterness [54].

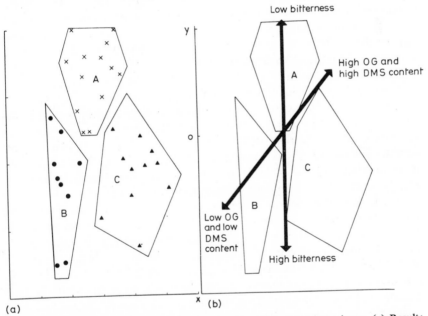

Fig. 23.11 Discriminant analysis of sensory data on thirty three lager beers. (a) Result; (b) Interpretation of result. Code: A = North American beers, B = British beers, C = Continental European beers. (After Brown and Clapperton [54].)

In a further trial 46 ales (OG 1030–1050) from 5 brewing companies were examined by sensory profile analysis and by instrumental analysis [54]. The most important variables in the discriminant analysis were: (*i*) iso-amyl alcohol content (instrumental), (*ii*) *caprylic* flavour (sensory), (*iii*) sodium content (instrumental), (*iv*) *meaty* aroma (sensory), (*v*) ethyl acetate content (instrumental), (vi) bitter after-flavour (sensory), (vii) dextrin content (instrumental), (viii) smoky flavour (sensory), and (ix) DMS content (instrumental). On the basis of these parameters 87% of the ales were correctly assigned to their brewing company. Similarly, the ales could be assigned to their gravity band either instrumentally on the basis of alcohol or dextrin content or by sensory analysis using 13 parameters. The sensory parameters, in order of importance, were: (i) body, (ii) aldehyde (odour), (iii) high-gravity fullness, (iv) viscous (thick), (v) estery, (vi) meaty (odour), (vii) cooked vegetable (odour), (viii) rubbery, (ix) caprylic, (x) DMS (odour), (xi) fruity, (xii) cloying, and (xiii) sour [54]. Another cluster analysis was carried out using both sensory terms and physicochemical parameters and the results are given in Table 23.8 [50]. The numbers refer to the order of formation of the clusters, i.e. the lower the number the better the correlation. Clusters which only contained sensory terms have been omitted. The first two clusters isolate terms that relate to esters, alcohols and original gravity. Although there is a curious reversal of ester and alcohol contents and the corresponding flavour effect between cluster 1 and 2, estery (odour) is grouped, as expected, with ethyl and isoamyl acetate content in cluster 4. Apart from cluster 16 the clusters indicate causative relationships between the physicochemical parameters and the corresponding sensory terms [50].

Principal component analysis is another statistical technique that has been applied to the results of profile analysis [55]. Ales and lagers were examined and two-dimensional plots of the results using the first two principal components as axes showed resolution of the ales from the lagers and the close proximity of the majority of duplicate samples. Profile analysis has also been used to differentiate various brands of whisky [56]. Throughout the work on profile analysis hedonic expressions have been strictly excluded but other workers [57] have used principal component analysis to classify Continental European beers correctly as good, average or poor on the basis of nine physicochemical parameters: colloidal stability (7 days at 40°C/1 day at 0°C), cold sensitivity (24 hours at 0°C), brightness at 12°C, six months test, the content of β-phenylethanol, ethyl caprylate, isoamyl acetate, and isobutanol and foam stability.

Another approach has been limited to the correlation of the headspace volatiles with flavour characteristics [30, 58]. Of the substances distinguished on the gas chromatograms the levels of the isoamyl alcohols, ethyl acetate, isoamyl acetate, and isobutanol have been shown to be important in the discriminant analyses discussed above. β-Phenylethanol and ethyl caprylate are not sufficiently volatile to be included in headspace analyses [39]. In this method [30, 58] the peak areas on the chromatograms were expressed as the percentage of the total peak area (excluding ethanol and the internal standard xylene). A chronologically updated data base was used to calculate the standard deviation for each peak and a two-tailed t-test was performed on mean values from duplicate determinations on the two beers. On the basis of the gas chromatography the results of the triangular tasting test were predicted as follows:

TABLE 23.8
Results of cluster analysis of sensory and physicochemical data on beer
{After CLAPPERTON [50]}

Odour terms		Physicochemical parameters	Flavour terms	
		Original gravity Isoamyl alcohol 2-Methylbutanol Total carbohydrate Dextrins	Body Estery Fruity Viscous	1
		Potassium		
4	Estery	Propanol Ethyl acetate Isoamyl acetate	Mouth coating Warming Spicy *Watery	2
		Phosphate		
		Total fatty acids Octanoic acid Decanoic acid	Caprylic	4
		Present gravity	Sweet Cloying Toffee-like *Astringent	5
		Bitterness	Bitter	9
		Sulphur	Metallic	17
12	Ribes	Air content		
16	Hoppy	Dodecanoic acid Tetradecanoic acid		

* Negatively correlated with other terms and parameters in the same cluster.

1. If none of the peaks are significantly different between samples at 0·005 risk, one predicts that the tasting panel results will be insignificant at 0·05 risk.
2. If one or more peaks is significantly different between samples at 0·001 risk, one predicts that panel results will be significant at a risk of 0·05 or less.

3. If one or more peaks is significantly different between samples at 0·005 risk but insignificant at 0·001 risk, no prediction is made and the sample number increased.

The taste panel found 200 significant results out of the 234 predicted and 70 insignificant results out of the 76 predicted and it was suggested tasting could be reduced by eliminating samples that were similar by headspace analysis. However it was acknowledged differences due to sulphur compounds, staling or certain hop compounds may go undetected. Nevertheless, the statistical method predicted and the taste panel found significant differences between the beers produced at three branch plants. When examined by step-wise discriminant analysis the beers from the three branch plants were well distributed into clusters. After process changes at plant 'Q' the beers were found to lie very close to those from plant 'P' in the discriminant analysis and the taste panel could not distinguish between them [30].

23.3 *Flavour stability*

Beer flavour is not static but in a continual state of change. The point when maturation ends and deterioration begins is undoubtedly different for different beers and probably different for different consumers. The off-flavour in one beer may be an essential character of another. Since the brewer can now largely control biological instability and non-biological haze, it is probably flavour instability that will determine the shelf life of his product [59]. Some of the changes in beer flavour that occur during ageing are illustrated in Fig. 23.12. The chemical changes that occur during staling have been reviewed [59] and many of the compounds responsible for off-flavours [40] have been mentioned in Chapters 22 and 23. Most of the chemical changes during storage involve oxidation and will be accelerated if the beer is allowed any contact with oxygen after it leaves the fermentation vessel The development of the *Ribes* or catty taint in bottled beer is strongly correlated with the amount of air in the headspace [44]. Roughly 1 ml of air in a 300 ml bottle will give an oxygen content of 1 ppm which is probably sufficient to oxidize all the reductones present in a light lager beer. The dissolved oxygen in beer rapidly disappears usually without the immediate formation of an off-flavour. But the damage may have been done as beer contains compounds, such as melanoidins and reductones, which act as oxygen carriers and can produce off-flavours at a later date. Antioxidants such as sulphur dioxide or ascorbic acid are sometimes added to beer but can cause other problems. In the presence of iron ascorbic acid becomes a potent oxygen carrier. The Indicator Time Test (ITT) [60], which measures the decolourization of 2,6-dichloroindophenol, gives an indication of the oxidation-reduction or redox level of a beer.

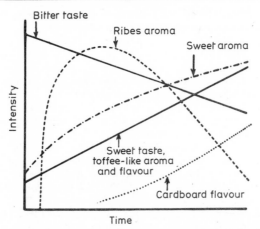

Fig. 23.12 Diagrammatic representation of sensory changes in beer flavour during ageing. (After Whitear *et al.* [59].)

Profile analysis is a convenient method for observing the changes in beer flavour during ageing [61]. It was found that different beers age in different ways and at different rates. In general the rate of change in flavour is inversely proportional to the original gravity (or alcohol content) and the content of coloured malt in the grist (or the level of reducing substances as judged by the ITT). Thus strong stouts are the most flavour stable and low gravity lagers the least stable. Stouts tend to develop *stale, cheesy* characteristics whereas light lagers develop mostly *sweet, papery/cardboard* and *metallic* notes. Ales become distinctly sweet with *molasses-type* cloying characters. At the same time as these aged characters develop, positive characters, such as *alcoholic, floral, malty, caramel* and *body*, decline. It is important when changing raw materials or making process changes to determine the effect on flavour stability as well as the flavour of the fresh beer. An example is given of a strong ale brewed with an experimental malt which, at packaging, had a flavour comparable with the control. However, after storage, the beer from the experimental malt developed much harsher flavours than the control. Other experiments showed that the development of aged flavours in beers stabilized either with polyvinylpyrrolidone or silica hydrogel was significantly different, but contrary to earlier work, no improvement in flavour stability resulted from high gravity brewing.

REFERENCES

[1] AMERINE, M. A., PANGBORN, R. M. and ROESSLER, E. B. (1965). *Principles of Sensory Evaluation of Food*, Academic Press, New York.

[2] MONCREIFF, R. W. (1967). *The Chemical Senses*, 3rd edn., Leonard Hill, London.

[3] GOULD, R. F. (ed.) (1966). *Flavour Chemistry*, Advances in Chemistry Series No. 56, American Chemical Society, Washington DC.

[4] HORNSTEIN, I. and TERANISHI, R. (April 3, 1967). *Chem. Eng. News* (15) 93.

[5] OHLOFF, G. and THOMAS, A. F. (1971). *Gustation and Olfaction*, Academic Press, New York.

[6] BOUDREAU, J. C. (ed.) (1979). *Food Taste Chemistry*, ACS Symposium Series 115, American Chemical Society, Washington DC

[7] BOUDREAU, J. C., ORAVEC, J., HOANG, N. K. and WHITE, T. D. (1979). In *Food Taste Chemistry* (ed. BOUDREAU, J. C.), ACS Symposium, Series 115, American Chemical Society, Washington DC, p. 1.

[8] BISHOP, L. R. (1971). *J. Inst. Brewing*, 77, 389.

[9] STODDART, D. M. (1980). *Olfaction in Mammals*. Symposium of the Zoological Society of London, No. 45, Academic Press, London.

[10] DAVIES, J. T. and TAYLOR, F. H. (1957). *Proc. 2nd. Cong. Surf. Act.*, Butterworths, London, 4, 329

[11] HARPER, R., BATE-SMITH, E. C. and LAND, D. G. (1968). *Odour Description and Odour Classification*, J. and A. Churchill, London.

[12] AMOORE, J. E. (1970). *Molecular Basis of Odour*, Charles C. Thomas, Springfield, Illinois.

[13] WRIGHT, R. H. (1964). *The Science of Smell*, George Allen and Unwin, London.

[14] DAVIES, J. T. (1965). *J. Theoret. Biol.*, 8, 1.

[15] MEILGAARD, M. C. (1975). *Tech. Quart. Master Brewers Assoc. Americas*, 12, 107; 151.

[16] MEILGAARD, M. C. and REID, D. S. in LAND, D. G. and NURSTEN, H. E. (eds.) (1979). *Progress in Flavour Research*, Applied Science Publishers, London, p. 67.

[17] British Standards Institution (1975). British Standard 5098.

[18] BROWN, D. G. W., CLAPPERTON, J. F., MEILGAARD, M. C. and MOLL, M. (1978). *J. Am. Soc. Brew. Chem.*, 36, 73.

[19] RICHTER, C. P. and MACLEAN, A. (1939). *Am. J. Physiol.*, 126, 1.

[20] PANGBORN, R. M. (1959). *Am. J. Clin. Nutrition*, 7, 280.

[21] PFAFFMANN, C. (1959). *Handbook of Physiology*, Vol. 1, American Physiological Society, p. 507.

[22] NIEMAN, C. (1960). quoted in *Principles of Sensory Evaluation of Food* (AMERINE, M. A., PANGBORN, R. M. and ROESSLER, E. B., 1965), Academic Press, New York, p. 95.

[23] PANGBORN, R. M. (1963). *J. Food Sci.*, 28, 726.

[24] VAN OEVELEN, D., DE L'ESCAILLE, F. and VERACHTERT, H. (1976). *J. Inst. Brewing*, 82, 322.

[25] GIENAPP, E. and SCHRÖDER, K. L. (1975). *Die Nahrung*, 19, 697.

[26] LEWIS, M. J., PANGBORN, R. M. and FUJII-YAMASHITA, J. (1980). *Proc. 16th Conv. Australian and New Zealand Section of the Institute of Brewing*, p. 165.

[27] CLAPPERTON, J. F. (1974). *J. Inst. Brewing*, 80, 164.

[28] PANGBORN, R. M. in KOIVISTOINEN, P. and HYVÖNEN, L. (1980). *Carbohydrate Sweeteners in Foods and Nutrition*, Academic Press, p. 87.

[29] GUADAGNI, D. G. (1970) quoted by TERANISHI, R. in *Gustation and Olfaction* (eds. OHLOFF, G. and THOMAS, A. F. (1971), Academic Press, New York, p. 170.

[30] HOFF, J. T., CHICOYE, E., HERWIG, W. C. and HELBERT, J. R. in CHARA-LAMBOUS, G. (ed.) (1978). *Analysis of Foods and Beverages Headspace Techniques*, Academic Press, New York, p. 187.

[31] GARDNER, R. J. (1979). *Tech. Quart. Master Brewers Assoc. Americas*, **16**, 106; 148; 204.

[32] GARDNER, R. J. (1978). *J. Pharm. Pharmacol.*, **30**, 531

[33] KIER, L. B., HALL, L. H., MURRAY, W. J. and RANDIC, M. J. (1975). *J. Pharm. Sci.*, **64**, 1971.

[34] KIER, L. B. and HALL, L. H. (1976). *Molecular Connectivity in Chemistry and Drug Research*, Academic Press, New York.

[35] FAZZALARI, F. A. (1978). *Compilation of Odour and Taste Threshold Values Data*, ASTM Data Series DS 48A. American Society for Testing and Materials, Philadelphia.

[36] HARRISON, G. A. F. (1970). *J. Inst. Brewing*, **76**, 486.

[37] ENGAN, S. (1972). *J. Inst. Brewing*, **78**, 33.

[38] ENGAN, S. (1974). *J. Inst. Brewing*, **80**, 162.

[39] LINDSAY, R. C. in SCANLAN, R. A. (ed.) (1977). *Flavour Quality: Objective Measurement*, American Chemical Society, Washington DC, p. 89; *Brewers Digest*, Dec. 1977, p. 44.

[40] TRESSL, R., BAHRI, D. and KOSSA, M. in CHARALAMBOUS, G. (ed.) (1980). *The Analysis and Control of Less Desirable Flavours in Foods and Beverages*, Academic Press, New York, p. 293.

[41] CLAPPERTON, J. F. (1978). *J. Inst. Brewing*, **84**, 107.

[42] CLAPPERTON, J. F. and BROWN, D. L. W. (1978). *J. Inst. Brewing*, **84**, 90.

[43] ANDERSON, R. J., CLAPPERTON, J. F., CRABB, D. and HUDSON, J. R. (1975). *J. Inst. Brewing*, **81**, 208.

[44] CLAPPERTON, J. F. (1976). *J. Inst. Brewing*, **82**, 175.

[45] HUDSON, J. R. (1960). *Development of Brewing Analysis, A Historical Review*, The Institute of Brewing, London.

[46] European Brewery Convention (1975). *Analytica-EBC*, 3rd edn., Schweizer Brauerei-Rundschau, Zurich.

[47] American Society of Brewing Chemists (1976). *Methods of Analysis*, 7th edn., American Society of Brewing Chemists, St. Paul, Minnesota.

[48] BENGTSSON, K. (1953). *Wallerstein Labs. Commun.*, **16**, 231.

[49] CLAPPERTON, J. F. (1973). *J. Inst. Brewing*, **79**, 495.

[50] CLAPPERTON, J. F. in LAND, D. G. and NURSTEN, H. E. (1979). *Progress in Flavour Research*, Applied Science Publishers, London, p. 1.

[51] MEILGAARD, M. C., DALGLIESH, C. E. and CLAPPERTON, J. F. (1979). *J. Inst. Brewing*, **85**, 38; *J. Am. Soc. Brew. Chem.*, **37**, 47; *Bios*, (Nancy), **10** (2), 23.

[52] BROWN, D. G. W. and CLAPPERTON, J. F. (1978). *J. Inst. Brewing*, **84**, 324.

[53] BROWN, D. G. W., CLAPPERTON, J. F. and DALGLIESH, C. E. (1974) *Proc. Annu. Meet. Am. Soc. Brew. Chem.*, p. 1.

[54] BROWN, D. G. W and CLAPPERTON, J. F. (1978). *J. Inst. Brewing*, **84**, 318.

[55] CLAPPERTON, J. F. and PIGGOTT, J. R. (1979). *J. Inst. Brewing*, **85**, 271.

[56] PIGGOTT, J. R. and JARDINE, S. P. (1979). *J. Inst. Brewing*, **85**, 82.

[57] MOLL, M., VINH, T. and FLAYEUX, R. in CHARALAMBOUS, G. and INGLETT, G. E. (eds.) (1978). *Flavours of Foods and Beverages – Chemistry and Technology*, Academic Press, New York, p. 329

[58] HOFF, J. T. and HERWIG, W. C. (1976). *J. Am. Soc. Brew. Chem.* **34**, 1.
[59] DALGLIESH, C. E. (1977). *Proc. Eur. Brewery Conv. Congr. Amsterdam*, p. 623.
[60] GRAY, P. P. and STONE, I. (1939). *J. Inst. Brewing*, **45**, 253.
[61] WHITEAR, A. L., CARR, B. L., CRABB, D. and JACQUES, D. (1979). *Proc. Eur. Brewery Conv. Congr., Berlin*, p. 13.

Appendix

UNITS OF MEASUREMENT

Two new systems of measurements have been introduced into Britain in the last ten years. Industry and commerce have seen the introduction of metrication to come into line with other European countries. Scientific and teaching establishments have adopted a related but not identical system called Système Internationale (SI for short) illustrated in Tables A.1 and A.2. Both have their place in Brewing Science as have the old systems based on the pound and the foot. Especial difficulties arise because the traditional US measures do not always correspond with the British. For instance the US gallon of water weighs 8 lb, and the constituent eight pints one pound each. The British imperial measure, revised in Queen Anne's reign, 'metricated' the gallon of water so that it weighed 10 lb, each pint weighing 1·25 lb. Measurements of volume such as the bushel or the barrel vary from one region to another. In this book, the barrel will be that used in England, namely 36 gallons. Filled with water this would weigh 360 lb. For rough calculation, it is convenient that the US beer barrel is rather similar to the hectolitre, exceeding it by about 17%. The use of degrees Fahrenheit is rapidly being replaced in the UK by °C (metric) or K (SI) but not in the USA for practical brewing (Table A.3).

With respect to units specifically used in brewing, certain metric units have been selected which are not in the SI, such as litres, hectolitres, metric tonnes and bars, because of their convenience. Other measurements used in brewing are becoming or have become obsolete, for instance Quarters as applied to barley (448 lb) or malt (336 lb). Methods of analysis have changed over the years so that comparisons are difficult. Elsewhere there may be no direct equivalence; a good example is measurement of extract as defined by the Institute of Brewing versus that given by the European Brewery Convention. Set out in Table A.4 are definitions of several SI and metric units plus conversions of non-metric units that are relevant to brewing. Table A.5 gives details of the various systems of measuring specific gravity and extract, while Table A.6 gives equivalents of hot water extracts of malts in the old and new nomenclature.

TABLE A.1

SI derived units

Physical quantity	Name	Symbol	Definition
Energy	joule	J	$kg\ m^2\ s^{-2}$
Force	newton	N	$kg\ m\ s^{-2} = J\ m^{-1}$
Power	watt	W	$kg\ m^2\ s^{-3} = J\ s^{-1}$
Electrical charge	coulomb	C	$A\ s$
Electrical potential difference	volt	V	$kg\ m^2\ s^{-3}\ A^{-1} = J\ A^{-1}\ s^{-1}$
Electrical resistance	ohm	Ω	$kg\ m^2\ s^{-3}\ A^{-2} = V\ A^{-1}$
Inductance	henry	H	$kg\ m^2\ s^{-2}\ A^{-1} = V\ A^{-1}\ s$
Luminous flux	lumen	lm	$cd\ sr$
Illumination	lux	lx	$cd\ sr\ m^{-2}$
Frequency	hertz	Hz	s^{-1}

where (1) m is the metre (2) kg is the kilogram
(3) s is the second (4) A is the ampere
(5) cd is the candela (luminous intensity) (6) sr is the steradian (solid angle)
other basic units are: (7) kelvin (K)—thermodynamic temperature and temperature interval
(8) mole (mol) molecular (or atomic) weight in $kg\ m^{-3}$

TABLE A.2

Prefixes for SI units

Fraction	Prefix	Symbol
10^{-12}	pico	p
10^{-9}	nano	n
10^{-6}	micro	μ
10^{-3}	milli	m
10^{-2}	centi	c
10^{-1}	deci	d
10^{1}	deka	da
10^{2}	hecto	h
10^{3}	kilo	k
10^{6}	mega	M
10^{9}	giga	G

TABLE A.3

Comparison of thermometers

Showing the relative indications of the
Fahrenheit, Centigrade and Réaumur thermometer scales

	Boiling point	Freezing point
Fahrenheit	212°	32°
Centigrade	100°	0°
Reaumur	80°	0°

Conversion of thermometer degrees

°C to °R, multiply by 4 and divide by 5. °C to °F, multiply by 9, divide by 5, then add 32. °R to °C, multiply by 5 and divide by 4. °R to °F, multiply by 9, divide by 4, then add 32. °F to °R, first subtract 32, then multiply by 4, and divide by 9. °F to °C, first subtract 32, then multiply by 5, and divide by 9.

F	C	R	F	C	R
230	**110**	**88**	120·2	49	39·2
221	**105**	**84**	118·4	48	38·4
212	**100**	**80**	116·6	47	37·6
210·2	99	79·2	114·8	46	36·8
208·4	98	78·4	**113**	**45**	**36**
206·6	97	77·6	111·2	44	35·2
204·8	96	76·8	109·4	43	34·4
203	**95**	**76**	107·6	42	33·6
201·2	94	75·2	105·8	41	32·8
199·4	93	74·4	**104**	**40**	**32**
197·6	92	73·6	102·2	39	31·2
195·8	91	72·8	100·4	38	30·4
194	**90**	**72**	98·6	37	29·6
192·2	89	71·2	96·8	36	28·8
190·4	88	70·4	**95**	**35**	**28**
188·6	87	69·6	93·2	34	27·2
186·8	86	68·8	91·4	33	26·4
185	**85**	**68**	89·6	32	25·6
183·2	84	67·2	87·8	31	24·8
181·4	83	66·4	**86**	**30**	**24**
179·6	82	65·6	84·2	29	23·2
177·8	81	64·8	82·4	28	22·4
176	**80**	**64**	80·6	27	21·6
174·2	79	63·2	78·8	26	20·8
172·4	78	62·4	**77**	**25**	**20**
170·6	77	61·6	75·2	24	19·2
168·8	76	60·8	73·4	23	18·4
167	**75**	**60**	71·6	22	17·6
165·2	74	59·2	69·8	21	16·8
163·4	73	58·4	**68**	**20**	**16**
161·6	72	57·6	66·2	19	15·2
159·8	71	56·8	64·4	18	14·4
158	**70**	**56**	62·6	17	13·6
156·2	69	55·2	60·8	16	12·8
154·4	68	54·4	**59**	**15**	**12**
152·6	67	53·6	57·2	14	11·2
150·8	66	52·8	55·4	13	10·4
149	**65**	**52**	53·6	12	9·6
147·2	64	51·2	51·8	11	8·8
145·4	63	50·4	**50**	**10**	**8**
143·6	62	49·6	48·2	9	7·2
141·8	61	48·8	46·4	8	6·4
140	**60**	**48**	44·6	7	5·6
138·2	59	47·2	42·8	6	4·8
136·4	58	46·4	**41**	**5**	**4**
134·6	57	45·6	39·2	4	3·2
132·8	56	44·8	37·4	3	2·4
131	**55**	**44**	35·6	2	1·6
129·2	54	43·2	33·8	1	0·8
127·4	53	42·4	**32**	**0**	**0**
125·6	52	41·6	30·2	−1	−0·8
123·8	51	40·8	**23**	**−5**	**−4**
122	**50**	**40**	**14**	**−10**	**−8**

TABLE A.4

Conversions

METRIC SYSTEM

m = 1·0936 yard = 3·2808 ft; cm = 0·3937 in;
hectare = 2·471 acre; m² = 10·764 ft²; cm² = 0·1550 in²;
m³ = 1000 dm³ (or litre) = 33·315 ft³ = 61024 in³;
hl = 100 dm³ (or litre) = 21·998 gal (British) = 26·418 gal (US) = 0·6111 barrel (British)
  = 0·8387 barrel (US) = 0·8522 *beer* barrel (US);
litre = 35·196 fl. oz (British) = 33·815 fl. oz (US);
tonne = 1000 kg = short ton = 0·9842 long ton = 2204·6 lb = 10 doppelzentner = 20
  zentner; zenter = 50 kg = 0·984 cwt = 110·231 lb;
g = 0·03527 oz = 15·432 grain.

BRITISH MEASURES

yard = 3 ft = 36 in = 0·9144 m;
in = 2.540 cm = 1000 thou (thousandth of an inch);
thou = 25·4 micron or micrometre;
acre = 4840 yd² = 0·4047 hectare;
yd² = 0·8361 m²; ft² = 9·290 dm²; in² = 6·452 cm²;
yd³ = 0·7646 m³; ft³ = 28·317 dm³; in ³ = 16·387 cm³;
ton (long) = 20 cwt = 2240 lb = 1016 kg;
lb = 16 oz = 256 dram = 7000 grains = 0·45359 kg;
oz = 28·35 g; grain = 64·80 mg;
gal = 160 fl. oz = 8 pints = 1·201 gal (US) = 4·546 litre = 0·1605 ft.³;
pint = 0·5682 litre; fl. oz = 28·412 ml;
butt = 2 hogshead = 3 barrel = 108 gal = 4·9096 hl;
brl = 2 kilderkin = 4 firkin = 36 gal = 1·6365 hl = 1·4 brl beer (US).

US MEASURES

beer brl = 31 gal (US) = 25·81 gal (British) = 1·1734 hl = 0·717 brl British;
standard brl = 31·5 gal (US) = 26·23 gal (British) = 1·1924 hl = 0·729 brl British;
gal = 8 pint = 128 fl. oz = 3·7853 litre = 0·8327 gal British = 231·0 in³.

BARLEY AND MALT MEASURES

Britain and South Africa:	Barley bushel = 56 lb = 25·401 kg; Barley quarter = 448 lb = 203·209 kg; Malt bushel = 42 lb = 19·051 kg; Malt quarter = 336 lb = 152·407 kg;
Australia and New Zealand:	Barley bushel = 50 lb; Malt bushel = 40 lb;
US and Canada:	Barley bushel = 48 lb; Malt bushel = 34 lb;

USEFUL DATA

1 kcal = 4·186 kJ = 3·968 BTU = 1·1628 Wh = 3088 ft lb;
  BTU = 1·055 kJ = 0·252 kcal = 0·2931 Wh = 778·2 ft lb;
  Wh = 3·6 kJ = 0·860 kcal = 3·412 BTU = 2655 ft lb;
  therm = 105·506 MJ = 29·307 kWh;
standard ton refrigeration per 24 hr = 12000 BTU/hr = 3024 kcal/hr;
atm = bar = 14·70 lb/in² = 750.1 mm Hg = 10^5 Nm⁻²;
lb in⁻² = 6894·76 Nm⁻² = 0.06895 bar = 703 kg m⁻² = 27·7 inches water;
lb/gal (British) = 99·76 g/l; lb/gal (US) = 119·8 g/l;
lb/brl (British) = 3.336 g/l; lb/brl (US) = 3·865 g/l;
grain/gal (British) = 14·25 mg/l; grain/gal (US) = 17·12 mg/l;
CO_2 in beer: g/100 ml = 5·06 vol/vol beer;
  vol/vol beer = 0·198 g/100 ml.

TABLE A.5
Specific gravity and extract table

The following table is based on those compiled by Dr Plato for the German Imperial Commission (*Normal-Eichungskommission*) and refers to apparent specific gravities, as determined in the usual manner by weighing in a specific gravity bottle in air or by means of a saccharometer. Cane sugar % wt/vol and % wt/wt represent grams per 100 ml and grams per 100 grams of solution respectively. The percentages by weight in column 6, corresponding with the specific gravities at 60°F given in column 1, were computed by interpolation from Plato's table for true specific gravities at 15°/15°C and 16°/15°C corrected to 60°/60°F and then brought to 60°/60° in air by adding $(SG - 1) \times 0.00121$. The cane sugar weight percentages were converted to volume percentages and the solution divisors calculated. The column headed Plato gives the specific gravities in air at 20°/20°C related to the cane sugar weight percentages and, with the latter, corresponds with the Plato Table commonly used in breweries and laboratories where 20°C is the standard temperature. The column headed Balling similarly gives the specific gravities at 17·5°/17·5°C from the Balling Table corresponding with the same sugar percentages. These specific gravities cannot accurately correspond with those at 60°/60°F and 20°/20°C on account of the errors in Balling's Table. The following densities were used in the calculations:

$$
\begin{array}{ll}
\text{Water at } 15°/4°C & 0.999126 \\
60°F/4°C & 0.999035 \\
20°/4°C & 0.998234
\end{array}
$$

SPECIFIC GRAVITY CONVERSION TABLE
FOR CANE SUGAR SOLUTIONS

SG 60°F	Brewers' pounds	British units Cane sugar % wt/vol	Solution divisor	Plato SG 20°C	Cane sugar % wt/wt Degrees Brix.	Balling SG 17·5°C	Baumé Modulus 145
1002·5	0·9	0·643	3·888	1·00250	0·641	1·00256	0·36
1005·0	1·8	1·287	3·885	1·00499	1·281	1·00513	0·72
1007·5	2·7	1·932	3·882	1·00748	1·918	1·00767	1·08
1010·0	3·6	2·578	3·879	1·00998	2·552	1·01021	1·43
1012·5	4·5	3·225	3·876	1·01247	3·185	1·01274	1·78
1015·0	5·4	3·871	3·875	1·01496	3·814	1·01528	2·14
1017·5	6·3	4·517	3·874	1·01745	4·439	1·01776	2·48
1020·0	7·2	5·164	3·873	1·01993	5·063	1·02025	2·83
1022·5	8·1	5·810	3·872	1·02242	5·682	1·02273	3·17
1025·0	9·0	6·458	3·871	1·02490	6·300	1·02523	3·52
1027·5	9·9	7·107	3·869	1·02740	6·917	1·02776	3·86
1030·0	10·8	7·755	3·868	1·02989	7·529	1·03027	4·20
1032·5	11·7	8·405	3·867	1·03238	8·140	1·03277	4·54
1035·0	12·6	9·054	3·866	1·03486	8·748	1·03527	4·88
1037·5	13·5	9·703	3·865	1·03736	9·352	1·03775	5·22
1040·0	14·4	10·354	3·863	1·03985	9·956	1·04024	5·55
1042·5	15·3	11·003	3·862	1·04234	10·554	1·04273	5·88
1045·0	16·2	11·652	3·862	1·04481	11·150	1·04523	6·21
1047·5	17·1	12·303	3·861	1·04731	11·745	1·04773	6·54
1050·0	18·0	12·953	3·860	1·04979	12·336	1·05022	6·87
1052·5	18·9	13·604	3·859	1·05227	12·925	1·05269	7·20
1055·0	19·8	14·255	3·858	1·05476	13·512	1·05515	7·52

SG 60°F	Brewers' pounds	British units Cane sugar % wt/vol	Solution divisor	Plato SG 20°C	Cane sugar % wt/wt Degrees Brix.	Balling SG 17·5°C	Baumé Modulus 145
1057·5	20·7	14·907	3·857	1·05726	14·097	1·05760	7·84
1060·0	21·6	15·560	3·856	1·05975	14·679	1·06005	8·16
1062·5	22·5	16·213	3·855	1·06224	15·259	1·06252	8·48
1065·0	23·4	16·866	3·854	1·06472	15·837	1·06500	8·80
1067·5	24·3	17·519	3·853	1·06720	16·411	1·06747	9·12
1070·0	25·2	18·173	3·852	1·06970	16·984	1·06995	9·44
1072·5	26·1	18·827	3·851	1·07218	17·554	1·07244	9·75
1075·0	27·0	19·482	3·850	1·07467	18·122	1·07494	10·06
1077·5	27·9	20·135	3·849	1·07717	18·687	1·07743	10·37
1080·0	28·8	20·791	3·848	1·07965	19·251	1·07990	10·69
1082·5	29·7	21·446	3·847	1·08213	19·812	1·08237	11·00
1085·0	30·6	22·101	3·846	1·08462	20·370	1·08486	11·30
1087·5	31·5	22·758	3·845	1·08712	20·927	1·08737	11·61
1090·0	32·4	23·414	3·844	1·08960	21·481	1·08986	11·91
1092·5	33·3	24·071	3·843	1·09209	22·033	1·09235	12·21
1095·0	34·2	24·726	3·842	1·09457	22·581	1·09481	12·51
1097·5	35·1	25·384	3·841	1·09707	23·129	1·09730	12·81
1100·0	36·0	26·041	3·840	1·09956	23·674	1·09980	13.11
1102·5	36·9	26·700	3·839	1·10204	24·218	1·10230	13·41
1105·0	37·8	27·360	3·838	1·10454	24·760	1·10480	13·71
1107·5	38·7	28·019	3·837	1·10703	25·299	1·10730	14·00
1110·0	39·6	28·679	3·836	1·10952	25·837	1·10983	14·30
1112·5	40·5	29·339	3·834	1·11200	26·372	1·11235	14·59
1115·0	41·4	30·000	3·833	1·11450	26·906	1·11486	14·88
1117·5	42·3	30·660	3·832	1·11698	27·436	1·11735	15·17
1120·0	43·2	31·321	3·831	1·11947	27·965	1·11984	15·46
1122·5	44·1	31·981	3·830	1·12195	28·491	1·12231	15·74
1125·0	45·0	32·643	3·829	1·12445	29·016	1·12478	16 03
1127·5	45·9	33·305	3·828	1·12694	29·539	1·12729	16·31
1130·0	46·8	33·970	3·827	1·12944	30·062	1·12980	16·60
1132·5	47·7	34·632	3·826	1·13191	30·580	1·13228	16·88
1135·0	48·6	35·295	3·825	1·13441	31·097	1·13477	17·16
1137·5	49·5	35·958	3·824	1·13689	31·611	1·13723	17·44
1140·0	50·4	36·621	3·823	1·13938	32·124	1·13971	17·72
1142·5	51·3	37·285	3·822	1·14186	32·635	1·14221	18·00
1145·0	52·2	37·951	3·821	1·14435	33·145	1·14473	18·27
1147·5	53·1	38·617	3·820	1·14685	33·653	1·14727	18·55
1150·0	54·0	39·284	3·818	1·14934	34·160	1·14980	18·82

TABLE A.6

Equivalence between Institute of Brewing (UK) units of hot water extract

Litre °/Kg (20°C) against lb/Qr. (15·5°C; 60°F) in the body of the table. Calculated from
the Institute of Brewing Recommended methods of Analysis, (1977), on the basis that for
litre °/kg (20°C) the equivalent values in lb/Qr. will be 0·5 greater than those for litre °/kg
(15·5°C). Example: 251 litre °/kg (20°C) is equivalent to 84·1 lb/Qr. (15·5°C), 251 litre °/kg
(15·5°C) is equivalent to 83·6 lb/Qr. (15·5°C).

	240	250	260	270	280	290	300	310	320	330
0	80·2	83·7	87·2	90·8	94·2	97·8	101·3	104·8	108·3	111·9
1	80·5	84·1	87·5	91·1	94·6	98·1	101·7	105·2	108·6	112·2
2	80·8	84·4	87·9	91·4	94·9	98·5	102·0	105·5	109·0	112·6
3	81·2	84·8	88·3	91·8	95·3	98·8	102·4	105·9	109·3	112·9
4	81·5	85·1	88·6	92·1	95·7	99·2	102·7	106·2	109·7	113·2
5	81·9	85·5	89·0	92·5	96·0	99·5	103·1	106·6	110·1	113·6
6	82·3	85·8	89·4	92·8	96·4	99·9	103·4	106·9	110·4	113·9
7	82·7	86·1	89·7	93·2	96·8	100·2	103·8	107·3	110·8	114·3
8	83·0	86·5	90·1	93·5	97·1	100·6	104·1	107·6	111·2	114·6
9	83·4	86·8	90·4	93·9	97·5	100·9	104·5	107·9	111·5	115·0

INDEX